WORTH THE WAIT African American voters wait outside the Haywood County court house in Tennessee to cast their ballots after passage of the 1965 Voting Rights Act.

MyPoliSciLab Video Series

◉ **Watch** on **MyPoliSciLab**

The Big Picture Author Edward S. Greenberg illustrates how almost every social, economic, and technological development affects people and how the resolution of problems related to these changes eventually bubbles up through the political system.

The Basics What function does government serve? In this video, you will analyze this question and explore the core values that shape our political system and how the growing diversity of our population is changing—and reaffirming—the definition of what it means to be American.

Who are Americans?

In Context Where did the basic principles of American government come from? Boston University political scientist Neta C. Crawford uncovers the Greek, Roman, and Iroquois roots of our political system. She also traces the expansion of the concept of accountability since the birth of the nation.

Think Like a Political Scientist Find out how and why research on American politics has shifted. Boston University political scientist Neta C. Crawford discusses how scholars who once focused on voters and institutions are now looking at deliberation as the primary indicator of the health of a democratic system.

In the Real World What is the government's function in everyday life? Real people share their opinions on how involved the federal government should be in education by evaluating the effectiveness of the No Child Left Behind Act, which encourages standardized testing.

So What? Most people reading this book are part of the least politically involved age group in the country. Author Edward S. Greenberg invites students to make sense of the political processes and national debates that shape their lives every day.

primarily of African American college students, SNCC worked to increase black voter registration, to challenge exclusionary rules like the poll tax and the literacy test, and to enter African American candidates in local elections. Its first step was to create "freedom schools" in some of the most segregated counties in Mississippi, Alabama, and Georgia to teach black citizens about their rights under the law. Needless to say, SNCC volunteers attracted the malevolent attention of police, local officials, and vigilantes.

The first of the freedom schools was founded in McComb, Mississippi, by a remarkable young man named Robert Parris Moses. Despite repeated threats to his life and more than a few physical attacks, Moses traveled the back roads of Amite and Walthall Counties, meeting with small groups of black farmers and encouraging them to attend the freedom school. At the school, he showed them not only how to fill out the registration forms, but also how to read and interpret the constitution of Mississippi for the "literacy test" required to register to vote. Once people in the school gathered the courage to journey to the county seat to try to register, Moses accompanied them to lend support and encouragement.

Moses paid a price. Over a period of a few months in 1963, he was arrested several times for purported traffic violations; attacked on the main street of Liberty, Mississippi, by the county sheriff's cousin and beaten with the butt end of a knife; assaulted by a mob behind the McComb County courthouse; hit by police while standing in line at the voting registrar's office with one of his students; and jailed for not paying fines connected with his participation in civil rights demonstrations.

Despite the efforts of Moses and other SNCC volunteers, African American registration barely increased in Mississippi in the early 1960s. Black Americans there and in other states of the Deep South would have to await the passage of the 1965 Voting Rights Act, which provided powerful federal government protections for all American citizens wishing to exercise their right to vote.[3] The Voter Education Project was a key building block of a powerful civil rights movement (see Chapters 8 and 16) that would eventually force federal action in the 1960s to support the citizenship rights of African Americans in the South. Robert Moses and many other African Americans were willing to risk all they had, including their lives, to gain full and equal citizenship in the United States. They surely would have been gratified by the election of African American Barack Obama in 2008 as the nation's 44th president.

The struggle for democracy is happening in many countries today, where people fight against all odds for the right to govern themselves and control their own destinies. The many brave people who toppled dictators during the Arab Spring uprisings in 2011 attest to this fact. Americans are participants in this drama, not only because American political ideas and institutions have often provided inspiration for democratic movements in other countries, but also because the struggle for democracy continues in our own society. Although honored and celebrated, democracy remains an unfinished project in the United States. The continuing struggle to expand and perfect democracy is a major feature of American history and a defining characteristic of our politics today. It is a central theme of this book.

Democracy

1.1 Explain the meaning of democracy and its use as a standard to evaluate American government and politics

Why should there not be a patient confidence in the ultimate justice of the people? Is there any better, or equal, hope in the world?

—ABRAHAM LINCOLN, FIRST INAUGURAL ADDRESS

With the exception of anarchists who believe that people can live in harmony without any form of authority, it is generally recognized that when people live together in groups and communities, an entity of some sort is needed to provide law and order; to protect against external aggressors; and to provide essential public goods such as roads, waste disposal, education, and clean water. It is safe to say that most people do not want to live in places where there is no government to speak of at all, as in Somalia, or where there is a failed state, as in Haiti. If government is both necessary and inevitable, certain questions become unavoidable: Who is to govern? How are those who govern to be encouraged to serve the best interests of society? How can governments be induced to make policies and laws that citizens consider legitimate and worth obeying? How can citizens ensure that those who govern both carry out laws and policies the people want and do so effectively? In short, what is the best form of government? For most Americans the answer is clear: democracy.

Democracy's central idea is that ordinary people want to rule themselves and are capable of doing so.[4] This idea has proved enormously popular, not only with Americans, but with people all over the world.[5] To be sure, some people would give top priority to other things besides self-government as a requirement for the good society, including such things as safety and security or the need to have religious law and values determine what government does. Nevertheless, the appealing notion that ordinary people can and should rule themselves has spread to all corners of the globe, and the number of people living in democratic societies has increased significantly over the past two decades.[6]

It is no wonder that a form of government based on the notion that people are capable of ruling themselves enjoys widespread popularity, especially compared with government by the few (e.g., the Communist Party rule in China and Cuba) or by a single person (e.g., the dictatorship of Kim Jong-un in North Korea). There are reasons for its appeal. Some political thinkers think that democracy is the form of government that best protects human rights because it is the only one based on a recognition of the intrinsic worth and equality of human beings. Others believe that democracy is the form of government most likely to produce rational policies because it can count on the pooled knowledge and expertise of a society's entire population: a political version, if you will, of the wisdom of crowds, something like the Wiki phenomenon.[7] Still others claim that democracies are more stable and long-lasting because their leaders, elected by and answerable to voters, enjoy a strong sense of legitimacy among citizens. Many others suggest that democracy is the form of government most conducive to economic growth and material well-being, a claim with some scholarly support. (The relative economic growth in the years ahead of India, a democracy, and China, a party-state, will be a good, real-world test of this proposition.) Others, finally, believe that democracy is the form of government under which human beings, because they are free, are best able to develop their natural capacities and talents.[8] There are many compelling reasons, then, why democracy has been preferred by so many people.

Americans have supported the idea of self-government and have helped make the nation more democratic over the course of our history.[9] Nevertheless, democracy remains an aspiration rather than a finished product. Our goal in this book is to help you think carefully about the quality and progress of democracy in the United States. We want to help you reach your own independent judgments about the degree to which politics and government in the United States make our country more or less democratic. We want to help you draw your own conclusions about which political practices and institutions in the United States encourage and sustain popular self-rule and which ones discourage and undermine it. To do this, we must be clear about the meaning of democracy.

☐ Democratic Origins

Many of our ideas about democracy originated with the ancient Greeks. The Greek roots of the word *democracy* are *demos*, meaning "the people," and *kratein*, meaning "to rule." Philosophers and rulers were not friendly to the idea that the *many* can and should rule themselves. Most believed that governing was a difficult art, requiring the greatest sophistication, intelligence, character, and training—certainly not the province of ordinary people. Aristotle expressed this view in his classic work *Politics*, where he observed that democracy "is a government in the hands of men of low birth, no property, and vulgar employments."

Instead, they preferred rule by a select *few* (such as an aristocracy, in which a hereditary nobility rules, or a clerical establishment as in Iran today, where religious leaders rule) or by an enlightened *one*, somewhat akin to the philosopher king

How Do You Measure Freedom?

Two common measures of freedom are the right to free speech and the right to privacy. History has shown us that defense of these rights becomes even more important in the face of a foreign threat. Below, we look at data that shows how committed Americans are to two ideals of freedom.

Free Speech Strengthens in the United States

Between 1980 and 2010, more Americans support free speech for more groups. The exceptions are for racists and radical Muslims.

Homosexual
66% in 1980
85% in 2010

Atheist
66% in 1980
76% in 2010

Militarist
57% in 1980
68% in 2010

Communist
55% in 1980
64% in 2010

Racist
62% in 1980
57% in 2010

Radical Muslim Cleric
not asked
41% in 2010

Right to Privacy Weakens in the United States

If the government suspects that a terrorist act is about to happen, do you think the authorities should have the right to ...

... detain people for as long as they want without putting them on trial?
55% YES
43.5% NO

... tap people's telephone conversations?
55.9% YES
43.9% NO

... stop and search people in the street at random?
41.3% YES
58.1% NO

SOURCE: Data from General Social Survey, 1980, 2006, and 2010

Investigate Further

Concept How does support for free speech and individual privacy measure freedom? Protecting free speech ensures that all ideas can be expressed and debated, even if they are unpopular. Likewise, protecting the privacy rights of everyone, even those who appear to be threatening, ensures that government

Connection How has Americans' support for free speech changed between 1980 and 2010? Overall, Americans are more tolerant of speech from "controversial" groups. More Americans support free speech for people who were previously marginalized, particularly atheists and homosexuals. Fewer are willing to tolerate racist speech

Cause How did the threat of terrorism change freedom in America? Most Americans will still not tolerate random public frisks of people who might not be suspects. But after 9/11, Americans don't support speech by radical Muslim clerics and they are willing to detain potential terrorists indefinitely and wire tap

democracy

A system of government in which the people rule; rule by the many.

oligarchy

Rule by the few, where a minority holds power over a majority, as in an aristocracy or a clerical establishment.

monarchy

Rule by the one, such as where power rests in the hands of a king or queen.

direct democracy

A form of political decision making in which policies are decided by the people themselves, rather than by their representatives, acting either in small face-to-face assemblies or through the electoral process as in initiatives and referenda in the American states.

described by Plato in his *Republic*, or a hereditary monarch as in England in the time of Elizabeth I. **Democracy**, then, is "rule by the people" or, to put it as the Greeks did, self-government by the many, as opposed to **oligarchy** (rule by the *few*) or **monarchy** (rule by the *one*). The idea that ordinary people might rule themselves represents an important departure from most historical beliefs.[10] In practice, throughout human history, most governments have been quite undemocratic.

Inherent in the idea of self-rule by ordinary people is an understanding that government must serve *all* its people and that ultimately none but the people themselves can be relied on to know, and hence to act in accordance with, their own values and interests.[11]

Interestingly, democracy in the sense described here is more a set of utopian ideas than a description of real societies. Athens of the fifth century BCE is usually cited as the purest form of democracy that ever existed. There, all public policies were decided upon in periodic assemblies of Athenian citizens, though women, slaves, and immigrants were excluded from participation.[12] Nevertheless, the existence of a society in Athens where "a substantial number of free, adult males were entitled as citizens to participate freely in government"[13] proved to be a powerful example of what was possible for those who believed that rule by the people was the best form of government. A handful of other cases of popular rule kept the democratic idea alive across the centuries. Beginning in the fifth century BCE, for example, India enjoyed long periods marked by spirited and broadly inclusive public debate and discourse on public issues. In the Roman Republic, male citizens elected the consuls, the chief magistrates of the powerful city-state. Also, during the Middle Ages in Europe, some cities were governed directly by the people (at least by men who owned property) rather than by nobles, church, or crown. During the Renaissance, periods of popular control of government (again, limited to male property holders) occurred in the city-states of Venice, Florence, and Milan.

☐ Direct Versus Representative Democracy

To the ancient Greeks, democracy meant rule by the common people exercised *directly* in open assemblies. They believed that democracy implied face-to-face deliberation and decision making about the public business. **Direct democracy** requires, however,

RULE BY THE FEW

President Mahmoud Ahmadinejab is the president of Iran despite the fact that his election in 2009 was widely regarded as fraudulent. However, real power in the country is exercised by an unelected clergy and the Revolutionary Guard. Here, the president receives a certificate of appreciation from Supreme Leader Ayatollah Ali Khamenei. Is a system that is responsive to the many in theory but run in reality by the few likely to retain its legitimacy over the long term? How might the people of Iran move their system to one where the majority rules rather than the few?

representative democracy
Indirect democracy, in which the people rule through elected representatives.

1.1

1.2

1.3

RULE BY THE MANY

In small towns throughout New England, local policies and budgets are decided upon at regular town meetings, in which the entire town population is invited to participate. What are some advantages to such a system? What might be the drawbacks? What other kinds of forums might there be where direct democracy is possible?

that all citizens be able to meet together regularly to debate and decide the issues of the day. Such a thing was possible in fifth century BCE Athens, which was small enough to allow all male citizens to gather in one place. In Athens, moreover, male citizens had time to meet and to deliberate because women provided household labor and slaves accounted for most production.

Because direct, participatory democracy is possible only in small communities where citizens with abundant leisure time can meet on a face-to-face basis, it is an unworkable arrangement for a large and widely dispersed society such as the United States.[14] Democracy in large societies must take the representative form, since millions of citizens cannot meet in open assembly. By **representative democracy** we mean a system in which the people select others, called *representatives*, to act on their behalf.

Although representative (or indirect) democracy seems to be the only form of democracy possible in large-scale societies, some political commentators argue that the participatory aspects of direct democracy are worth preserving as an ideal and that certain domains of everyday life—workplaces and schools, for instance— could be enriched by more direct democratic practices.[15] It is worth pointing out, moreover, that direct democracy can and does flourish in some local communities today. In many New England towns, for example, citizens make decisions directly at town meetings. At the state level, the initiative process allows voters in many states to bypass the legislature to make policies or amend state constitutions. Some observers believe that the Internet is empowering people to become more directly engaged and influential in the political process and that this process will accelerate in the future.[16] Increasingly, the Internet, mobile devices, and social media sites enable people to more easily gather information, deliberate with other citizens about important issues, organize political meetings and demonstrations, and directly communicate their interests and demands to political leaders at all levels of government.[17] These new forms of communication and mobilization were especially evident in the so-called Arab Spring in 2011 when popular uprisings drove autocratic leaders from power in several countries and forced leaders in others to pay attention to popular demands.

popular sovereignty

The basic principle of democracy that the people are the ultimate source of government authority and of the policies that government leaders make.

☐ Benchmarks of Representative Democracy

In large societies such as our own, then, democracy means rule by the people, exercised indirectly through representatives elected by the people. Still, this definition is not sufficiently precise to use as a standard by which to evaluate the American political system. It does not tell us what features indirect representative systems must have to ensure that those who govern do so on behalf of and in the interest of the people. You will see that this involves more than the existence of elections.[18] To help further clarify the definition of democracy, we add three additional benchmarks drawn from both the scholarly literature and popular understandings of democracy. These benchmarks are *popular sovereignty*, *political equality*, and *political liberty*, with the latter two being necessary for the first (that is to say, for popular sovereignty to work political equality and political liberty must exist). A society in which all three flourish, we argue, is a healthy representative democracy. A society in which any of the three is absent or impaired falls short of the representative democratic ideal. Let us see what each of them means.

POPULAR SOVEREIGNTY **Popular sovereignty** means that people are the ultimate source of government authority and that what the government does is determined by what the people want. If ultimate authority resides not in the hands of the *many* but in the hands of the *few* (as in an aristocratic order), or of the *one* (whether a benevolent sovereign or a ruthless dictator), democracy does not exist. Nor does it exist if government consistently fails to follow the preferences and serve the interests of the people.

How can we recognize popular sovereignty when we see it? The following seven conditions are especially important.

Government Leaders are Selected in Competitive Elections The existence of a close match between what the people want and what government does, however, does not necessarily prove that the people are sovereign. In a dictatorship, for example, the will of the people can be consciously shaped to correspond to the wishes of the leadership. For the direction of influence to flow from the people to the leadership, some mechanism must exist for forcing leaders to be responsive to the people's wishes and to be responsible to them for their actions. The best mechanism ever invented to achieve these goals is the contested election in which both existing and aspiring government leaders must periodically face the people for judgment. (See the "Mapping American Politics" feature on competition in U.S. presidential elections.)

Elections are Free and Fair If elections are to be useful as a way to keep government leaders responsive and responsible, they must be conducted in a fashion that is free and fair. By free, we mean that there is no coercion of voters or election officials and that virtually all citizens are able to run for office and vote in elections. By fair, we mean, among other things, that election rules do not favor some over others and that ballots are accurately counted.

People Participate in the Political Process Although government leaders may be elected in a balloting process that is free and fair, such a process is useful in conveying the will of the people and keeping leaders responsive and responsible only if the people participate. If elections and other forms of political participation only attract a minority of the eligible population, they cannot serve as a way to understand what the broad public wants or as an instrument forcing leaders to pay attention to it. Widespread participation in politics—including voting in elections, contacting public officials, working with others to bring matters to public attention, joining associations that work to shape government actions, and more—is necessary to ensure not only that responsive representatives will be chosen, but that they will also have continuous incentives to pay attention to the people. Because widespread participation is so central to popular sovereignty, we can say that the less political participation there is in a society, the weaker the democracy.

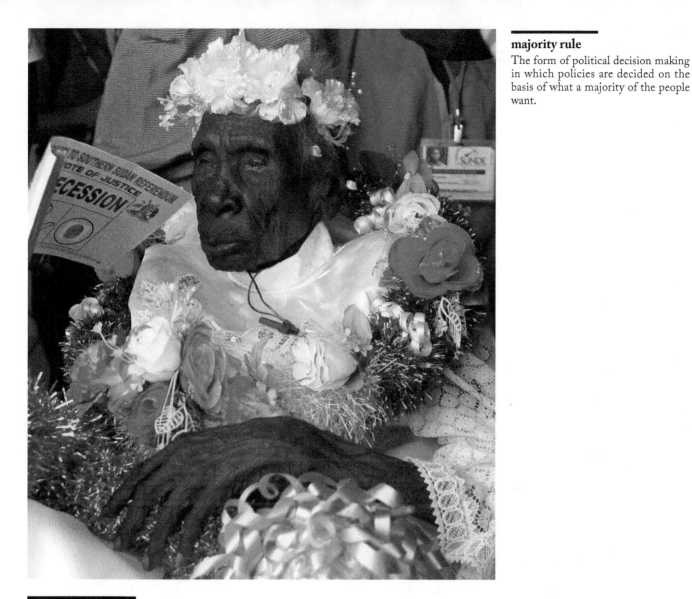

VOTING AT LONG LAST

Here the woman believed to be the oldest voter in the first democratic election in South Sudan rests after casting her vote for independence in the city of Juba in 2011. Is voting a sufficient condition for the existence of democracy or must other conditions exist to ensure that political leaders act as representatives of the people?

High-Quality Information is Available If people are to form authentic and rational attitudes about public policies and political leaders, they must have access to accurate political information, insightful interpretations, and vigorous debate. These are the responsibility of government officials, opposition parties, opinion leaders, and the news media. If false or biased information is provided, if policies are not challenged and debated, or if misleading interpretations of the political world (or none at all) are offered, the people cannot form opinions in accordance with their values and interests, and popular sovereignty cannot be said to exist.

The Majority Rules How can the opinions and preferences of many individual citizens be combined into a single binding decision? Because unanimity is unlikely—so the insistence that new policies should require unanimous agreement for them to be adopted would simply enshrine the status quo—reaching a decision requires a decision rule of some sort. If the actions of government are to respond to all citizens, each citizen being counted equally, the only decision rule that makes sense is **majority rule**, which means that the government adopts the policy that the *most* people want.[19] The only alternative to majority rule is minority rule, which would unacceptably elevate the preferences and the interests of the *few* over the *many*.

Mapping American Politics

All the States Are Purple

Introduction

Voting in elections in which people can choose among competing candidates and political parties is one of the hallmarks of democratic political systems. As we suggest in this chapter, democracy requires other things, such as political equality, civil liberties, and a free press, but competitive elections are essential. For the most part, at all levels of government in the United States, the most important public offices are filled by election, including that of the president. Both the map and the cartogram show the results from the 2008 presidential election won by Democrat Barack Obama over Republican John McCain, focusing on turnout and competition between the candidates.

Different Maps; Different Stories

The standard geographic map of the United States on this page shows states won by John McCain (in red) and Barack Obama (in blue). Election maps like this are widely distributed in newspapers, magazines, and on television. However, they are misleading in a very fundamental way because they emphasize geographical space over people and overplay the partisan divisions in the country. They take no account of the relative populations of the states and exaggerate the political importance of large, underpopulated spaces. This map suggests a country that is mostly red, or Republican, yet we know that the Democratic candidate won a relatively decisive victory. So, is there a better way to visualize who voted and for whom in 2008?

The second map on this page is called a cartogram. We will be using cartograms throughout this book to learn more about American politics. A cartogram is a way to visually present information that is organized on a geographical basis, with each unit (in this case, state) sized in proportion to the data being reported (in this case, number of voters). So rather than thinking of the cartogram as a "map," think of it as a figure displaying some aspect of American politics in a geographical fashion. Sometimes a cartogram shows geographical units in relation to one another in direct proportion to some simple measure, such as population size. Sometimes a cartogram shows geographical units drawn to reflect some measure on a per capita basis (such as the distribution of homeland security defense dollars to states divided by population size, which we use in Chapter 17). Sometimes a cartogram shows geographical units expanded or diminished from their "normal" geographical scale using mathematical transformations that enable the viewer to easily compare units (such as states and countries) while preserving the rough outlines of the normal shapes of these units. In each "Mapping American Politics" feature in this book, we will specify clearly what sort of cartogram we are using.

The cartogram here uses a simple and direct proportion; each state is sized according to the number of votes cast in the 2008 presidential election. By adjusting the size of the states to reflect the number of citizens who voted for president in 2008, this cartogram shows clearly that California, Florida, New York, Texas, and Ohio have

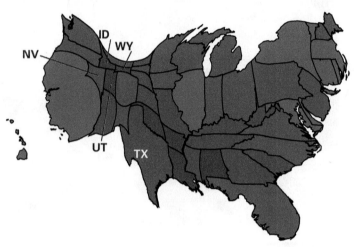

Standard U.S. Map, Blue for Obama States, Red for McCain States

Size of States Adjusted to Reflect Voter Turnout; Each State Is a Mixture of Red and Blue, Reflecting the Percentage of Obama and McCain Voters

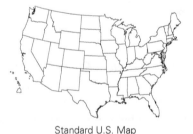

Standard U.S. Map

lots of voters and Idaho, Wyoming, Montana, Nebraska, and Maine have relatively few.

Color is often used to convey additional information in cartograms, as we do here. The proportions of blue (for Democratic voters) and red (for Republican voters) in each state reflect the proportions of Democratic and Republican voters in that state. The result is a map with various shades of purple, because all states contain a mix of Democratic and Republican voters. The closer a state comes to the blue end of the spectrum, the more Democratic voters it has relative to Republicans; the closer a state comes to the red end of the spectrum, the

(Continued)

more Republicans it has relative to Democrats. There are no pure red or blue states, no pure Republican or Democratic states. Even states that are deep purple (more blue), such as California, have many Republican voters, while states that are more red, such as Utah and Wyoming, have many Democratic voters.

What Do You Think?

- How does the cartogram convey more information than the conventional map about competition in the 2008 election and where the most voters are located? Do you see anything interesting in either the map or the cartogram that we have not mentioned here? How about your own state? What, if anything, about its portrayal in the cartogram surprises you?

SOURCE: http://clerk.house.gov/members/electionInfo/2008/Table.htm. Details about methods for producing such cartograms can be found in the pioneering publication by Michael T. Gastner and Mark E. J. Newman, " Diffusion-Based Method for Producing Density-Equalizing Maps," *Proceedings of the National Academy of Sciences* 101 (May 18, 2004), pp. 7499–7504.

Government Policies Reflect the Wishes of the People   The most obvious sign of popular sovereignty is the existence of a close correspondence between what government does and what the people want it to do. It is hard to imagine a situation in which the people rule but government officials continuously make policies contrary to the expressed wishes of the majority of the people; sovereign people would most likely react by removing such officials from power.

But does the democratic ideal require that government officials always do exactly what the people want, right away, responding to every whim and passing fancy of the public? This question has troubled many democratic theorists, and most have answered that democracy is best served when representatives and other public officials respond to the people after the people have had the opportunity to deliberate among themselves about the issues.[20] We might, then, want to speak of democracy as a system in which government policies conform to what the people want over some period of time.

Government Policies are Effective   Finally, for the people to rule, it is not sufficient that government policies are put into place that reflect what the people want it to do. Additionally, these policies must be carried out as intended and must effectively address the problems or concerns that led to the formation of these policies in the first place. Without this seventh and last condition for popular sovereignty, the people might end up with policies in place that reflect their wishes in name only. Government policies must be turned into government actions that work. Thus for example, if the government, in response to popular pressures, institutes a program to provide student loans for higher education, that program must be designed and carried out in such a way that funds for the program get to the intended beneficiaries—they are not wasted or diverted to financial institutions—and access to higher education is expanded. Anything less, and the people cannot be said to fully rule.

POLITICAL EQUALITY   The second benchmark of representative democracy and a necessary condition for popular sovereignty to exist is **political equality**, the idea that each person, being of equal intrinsic value as other human beings, carries the same weight in voting and other political decision making.[21] Imagine, if you will, a society in which one person could cast 100 votes in an election, another person 50 votes, and still another 25 votes, while many unlucky folks had only 1 vote each—or none at all. Democracy is a way of making decisions in which each person has one, and only one, voice.

Most people know this intuitively. Our sense of what is proper is offended, for instance, when some class of people is denied the right to vote in a society that boasts the outer trappings of democracy. The denial of citizenship rights to African Americans in the South before the passage of the 1965 Voting Rights Act is such an example. We count it as a victory for democracy when previously excluded groups win the right to vote.

Political equality also involves what the Fourteenth Amendment to the Constitution calls "equal protection," meaning that everyone in a democracy is treated the same

political equality
The principle that each person carries equal weight in the conduct of the public business.

civil rights
Guarantees by government of equal citizenship to all social groups.

political liberty
The principle that citizens in a democracy are protected from government interference in the exercise of a range of basic freedoms, such as the freedoms of speech, association, and conscience.

social contract
The idea that government is the result of an agreement among people to form one, and that people have the right to create an entirely new government if the terms of the contract have been violated by the existing one.

by government. Government programs, for example, cannot favor one group over another or deny benefits or protections to identifiable groups in the population, such as racial and religious minorities. Nor should people be treated better or worse than others by law enforcement agencies and the courts. Taken together, political equality and equal treatment are sometimes called **civil rights**, a subject we will address in more detail in Chapter 16.

But does political equality require that people be equal in ways that go beyond having a voice in decision making and treatment by government? In particular, does democracy require that inequalities in the distribution of income and wealth not be too extreme? While many do not think this to be the case, thinkers as diverse as Aristotle, Rousseau, and Jefferson thought so, believing that great inequalities in economic circumstances are almost always translated into political inequality.[22] Political scientist Robert Dahl describes the problem in the following way:

> If citizens are unequal in economic resources, so are they likely to be unequal in political resources; and political equality will be impossible to achieve. In the extreme case, a minority of rich will possess so much greater political resources than other citizens that they will control the state, dominate the majority of citizens, and empty the democratic process of all content.[23]

In later chapters, we will see that income and wealth are distributed in a highly unequal way in the United States, that the scale of this inequality has become dramatically more pronounced over the past two decades,[24] and that this inequality is sometimes translated into great inequalities among people and groups in the political arena. We will see for example, how powerful groups representing the most privileged sectors of American society shape not only elections and legislation more than other Americans. We will see how government agencies and leaders administer laws and regulations. In such circumstances, the political equality benchmark is in danger of being violated.

POLITICAL LIBERTY A third benchmark of democracy in representative systems, and a necessary condition for popular sovereignty to exist, is **political liberty**. Political liberty refers to basic freedoms essential to the formation and expression of majority opinion and its translation into public policies. These essential liberties include the freedoms of speech, of conscience and religion, of the press, and of assembly and association embodied in the First Amendment to the U.S. Constitution. Philosopher John Locke thought that individual rights and liberties were so fundamental to the good society that their preservation was the central responsibility of any legitimate government and that their protection was the very reason people agreed to enter into a **social contract** to form government in the first place.

Without these First Amendment freedoms, as well as those freedoms involving protections against arbitrary arrest and imprisonment, the other fundamental principles of democracy could not exist. Popular sovereignty cannot be guaranteed if people are prevented from participating in politics or if opposition to the government is crushed by the authorities. Popular sovereignty cannot prevail if the voice of the people is silenced and if citizens are not free to argue and debate, based on their own ideas, values, and personal beliefs, and to form and express their political opinions.[25] Political equality is violated if some people can speak out but others cannot.

For most people today, democracy and liberty are inseparable. The concept of *self-government* implies not only the right to vote and to run for public office, but also the right to speak one's mind; to petition the government; and to join with others in political parties, interest groups, or social movements.

Over the years, a number of political philosophers and practitioners have viewed liberty as *threatened* by democracy rather than as essential to it. We will have more to say about this subject in the next section as we consider several possible objections to democracy. But it is our position that self-government and political liberty are inseparable, in the sense that the former is impossible without the latter.[26] It follows that a majority cannot deprive an individual or a minority group of its political liberty without violating democracy itself.

☐ Objections to Liberal Democracy

What we have been describing—a system of representative government characterized by popular sovereignty, political equality, and liberty—commonly is called
liberal democracy. Not everyone is convinced that liberal democracy is the best form
of government. Following are the main criticisms that have been leveled against liberal
democracy as we have defined it.

"MAJORITY TYRANNY" THREATENS LIBERTY James Madison and the other Founders of the American republic feared that majority rule was bound to undermine freedom and threaten the rights of the individual. They created a constitutional system (as
you will see in Chapter 2) that was designed to protect certain liberties against the unwelcome intrusions of the majority. The fears of the Founders were not without basis.
What they called the "popular passions" have sometimes stifled the freedoms of groups
and individuals who have dared to be different. In the 1950s, for example, many people
in the movie industry, publishing, and education lost their jobs because of the anti-
communist hysteria whipped up by Senator Joseph McCarthy and others.[27] For a time
after the 9/11 attacks on the United States, Muslims in the United States became targets of popular hostility (see Chapter 15). As well, Mexican American immigrants have
become the object of popular disapproval in many places in the United States recently,
blamed for taking jobs from others in the midst of a period of high unemployment.

Although there have been instances during our history of **majority tyranny**, in
which the majority violated the citizenship rights of a minority—the chapter-opening
story is a good example—there is no evidence that the *many* consistently threaten liberty more than the *few* or the *one*. To put it another way, the majority does not seem

FEAR CAN UNDERMINE DEMOCRACY

Political hysteria has periodically blemished the record of American democracy. Fear of domestic communism,
and anarchism, captured in this editorial cartoon, was particularly potent in the twentieth century and led
to the suppression of political groups by federal and state authorities acting, in their view, in the name of a
majority of Americans. Why was such hysteria able to take hold in the United States? How likely is it that
political hysteria will emerge today in the United States given the current economic troubles?

to be a special or unique threat to liberty. Violations of freedom seem as likely to come from powerful individuals and groups or from government officials responding to vocal and narrow interests as from the majority of the people.

Liberty is essential to self-government, and threats to liberty, whatever their origin, must be guarded against by all who value democracy. But we must firmly reject the view that majority rule inevitably or uniquely threatens liberty. Majority rule is unthinkable, in fact, without the existence of basic political liberties.[28]

THE PEOPLE ARE IRRATIONAL AND INCOMPETENT Political scientists have spent decades studying the attitudes and behaviors of citizens in the United States, and some of the findings are not encouraging. For the most part, the evidence shows that individual Americans do not care a great deal about politics and are rather poorly informed, unstable in their views, and not much interested in participating in the political process.[29] These findings have led some observers to assert that citizens are ill-equipped for the responsibility of self-governance and that public opinion (the will of the majority) should not be the ultimate determinant of what government does.

This is a serious charge and bears a great deal of attention, something we shall address in various places in this book. In Chapter 5, for example, we will see that much of the evidence about individual opinions often has been misinterpreted and that the American public is more informed, sophisticated, and stable in its views than it is generally given credit for, though there remains considerable room for improvement on this front.

MAJORITARIAN DEMOCRACY THREATENS MINORITIES We have suggested that when rendering a decision in a democracy, the majority must prevail. In most cases, the minority on the losing side of an issue need not worry unduly about its well-being, because many of its members are likely to be on the winning side in future decisions about other matters. Thus, people on the losing side of one issue, such as welfare reform, may be part of the majority and winning side on another issue, such as how much to spend on education. What prevents majority tyranny over a minority in most policy decisions in a democracy is that the composition of the majority and the minority is always shifting, depending on the issue.

However, what happens in cases that involve race, ethnicity, religion, or sexual orientation, for example, where minority status is fixed? Does the majority pose a threat to such minorities? Many people worry about that possibility.[30] The worry is that unbridled majority rule leaves no room for the claims of minorities. This worry has some historical foundations, because majorities have trampled on minority rights with alarming frequency. Majorities long held, for example, that Native Americans and African Americans were inferior to whites and undeserving of full citizenship. Irish, Eastern European, Asian, and Latin American immigrants to our shores, among others, have been subjected to periods of intolerance on the part of the majority, as have Catholics and Jews. Gays and lesbians have been discriminated against in housing and jobs and have sometimes been violently victimized.

As Robert Dahl points out, however, there is no evidence to support the belief that the rights of minorities are better protected under alternative forms of political government, whether rule by the *few* (note the persecution of the Christian minority in China by the Communist ruling party) or by the *one* (note the persecution of Shia Muslims under the rule of Saddem Hussein in Iraq), and that given the other benefits of majority rule democracy, it is to be preferred.[31]

In any case, democracy, as we have defined it, requires the protection of crucial minority rights. Recall that majority rule is only one of the defining conditions of popular sovereignty and that popular sovereignty is only one of the three basic benchmarks of democracy, the others being political equality and political liberty. The position of minorities is protected in a fully developed liberal democracy, in our view, by the requirements of equal citizenship (the right to vote, to hold public office, to be protected against violence, and to enjoy the equal protection of the law) and access to the full range of civil liberties (speech, press, conscience, and association). To the

How Democratic Are We?

After this discussion, it should be easy to see how and why the democratic ideal can be used as a measuring rod with which to evaluate American politics. We have learned that the fundamental attributes of a liberal representative democracy are popular sovereignty, political equality, and political liberty. Each suggests a set of questions that will be raised throughout this book to encourage critical thinking about American political life.

■ *Questions about popular sovereignty.* Do citizens participate in politics? Can citizens be involved when they choose to be, and are political leaders responsive? Do political linkage institutions, such as political parties, elections, interest groups, and social movements, effectively transmit what citizens want to political leaders? What is the quality of the public deliberation on the major public policy issues of the day? Do the news media and political leaders provide accurate and complete information? Does government do what citizens want it to do? Does government effectively carry out the policies they have instituted in response to what the people want?

■ *Questions about political equality.* Do some individuals and groups have persistent and substantial advantages over other individuals and groups in the political process? Or is the political game open to all equally? Do government decisions and policies benefit some individuals and groups more than others?

■ *Questions about political liberty.* Are citizens' rights and liberties universally available, protected, and used? Are people free to vote? Can they speak openly and form groups freely to petition their government? Do public authorities, private groups, or the majority threaten liberty or the rights of minorities?

These questions will help us assess where we are and where we are going as a democracy. They will help us go past superficial evaluations based on the existence or nonexistence of this institution or that institution—for example, an elected legislature—and allow us to raise questions about the quality of democracy in the United States and its prospects. Popular sovereignty, political equality, and political liberty are benchmarks to help us in this evaluation. None are attainable, of course, in perfect form. They are, rather, ideals to which our nation can aspire and standards against which we can measure everyday reality.

extent that a majority violates the citizenship rights and liberties of minorities, society falls short of the democratic ideal.

A Framework for Understanding How American Politics Works

Outline a systematic framework for thinking about how government and politics work

I n addition to helping you answer questions about the quality of democracy in the United States, our goal in this textbook is to help you understand how American government and politics work. To help you, we describe in this section a simple way to organize information and to think about how our political system works.

❋ Explore on MyPoliSciLab
Simulation
You Are a Candidate for Congress

☐ Organizing the Main Factors of Political Life

If we are to understand why things happen in government and politics—for example, the passage of the 1965 Voting Rights Act that Robert Moses and his SNCC colleagues did so much to bring about—we must begin with what biologists call *taxonomy*: placing things in their proper categories. We believe that each and every actor, institution, and process that influences what our politics are like and what our national government does can be placed into four main categories: structure, political linkage, government, and government action.

Jim Crow
Popular term for the system of legally sanctioned racial segregation that existed in the American South until the middle of the twentieth century.

- *Structure.* Structural factors are enduring features of American life that play key roles in determining what issues become important in politics and government, how political power is distributed in the population, and what attitudes and beliefs guide the behavior of citizens and public officials. This category includes the economy and society, the constitutional rules, the political culture, and the international system: the most fundamental and enduring factors that influence government and politics. They form the foundation upon which all else is built. They are the most enduring parts of the American system, the slowest to change.[32]

- *Political linkage.* Political linkage factors are all of those political actors, institutions, and processes that transmit the wants and demands of people and groups in our society to government officials and that together help shape what government officials do and what policies they adopt. These include public opinion, political parties, interest groups, the news media, and elections. While not a formal part of government, they directly influence what sorts of people are chosen to be government officials and what these officials do once they are in office.

- *Government.* Government factors include all public officials and institutions that have formal, legal responsibilities for making public policy for the United States. These include Congress, the president and the executive branch, the federal bureaucracy, and the federal courts, including the Supreme Court.

- *Government action.* This is about what government does. This category includes the wide range of actions carried out by government: making laws, issuing rules and regulations, waging war and providing national defense, settling civil disputes, providing order, and more.

☐ Connecting the Main Factors of Political Life

To understand passage of the landmark legislation, we might begin with *government*, focusing our attention on Congress and its members; President Lyndon Johnson (who was the most vigorous proponent of the voting rights legislation) and his advisers; and the Supreme Court, which was becoming increasingly supportive of civil rights claims in the mid-1960s.

Knowing these things, however, would not tell us all that we needed to know. To understand why Congress, the president, and the Court behaved as they did in 1965, we would want to pay attention to the pressures brought to bear on them by *political linkage* actors and institutions: public opinion (increasingly supportive of civil rights), the growing electoral power of African Americans in the states outside the South, and most important, the moral power of the civil rights movement inspired by people like Robert Moses and Martin Luther King.

Even knowing these things, however, would not tell us all that we needed to know about why the 1965 Voting Rights Act happened. Our inquiry would have to go deeper to include *structural* factors: economic, cultural, and social change; constitutional rules; and the international position of the United States. For example, economic changes in the nation over the course of many decades triggered a "great migration" of African Americans from the rural South to the urban North. Over the long run, this population shift to states with large blocs of Electoral College votes, critical to the election of presidents, increased the political power of African Americans. Cultural change increased the number of Americans bothered by the second-class citizenship of African Americans, even as combat service in World War II and the Korean War led many black Americans to insist on full citizenship rights. Finally, the Cold War struggle of the United States against the Soviet Union played an important role. Many American leaders, recognizing the contradiction between asking for the support of people of color in Third World countries in the struggle against communism while treating African Americans in the United States as second-class citizens, sought an end to the system of official segregation in the South (known as **Jim Crow**).[33]

We see, then, that a full explanation of why the 1965 Voting Rights Act happened (government action) requires that we take into account how governmental, political linkage, and structural factors interact with one another to bring about significant change in American politics.

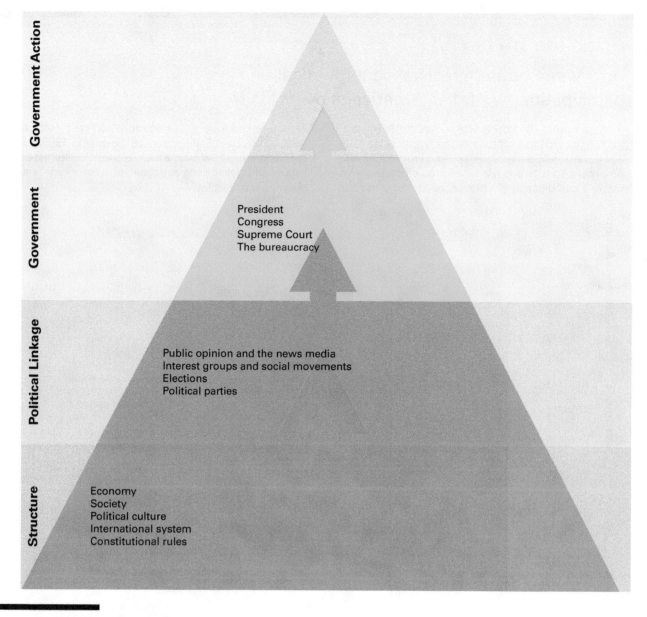

FIGURE 1.1 THE ANALYTICAL FRAMEWORK

Various actors, institutions, and processes interact to influence what government does in the United States. Structural factors such as the economy, the political culture, the international system, and constitutional rules play a strong role in political events. They may influence the government directly, or, as is more often the case, through political linkages such as elections, parties, and interest groups. In a democratic society, the policies created by the government should reflect these influences.

☐ Understanding American Politics Holistically

This way of looking at things—that what government does can only be understood by considering structural, political linkage, and governmental factors—will be used throughout this book and will help bring order to the information presented. We will suggest throughout this book that action by public officials is the product not simply of their personal dessires (although these are important), but also of the influences and pressures brought to bear by other governmental institutions and by individuals, groups, and classes at work in the political linkage sphere. Political linkage institutions and processes, in turn, can often be understood only when we see how they are shaped by the larger structural context, including such things as the national and global economies and the political culture. This way of understanding how American government and politics work is illustrated in the "Using the Framework" feature on page 20. This feature appears in each chapter to explore why particular government actions happen.

You should also keep in mind that, as in all complex systems, feedback also occurs. That is to say, influences sometimes flow in the opposite direction, from government to political linkage actors and institutions to structural factors. For example, federal tax laws

Using the FRAMEWORK

How was Southern resistance to political participation by African Americans overcome?

Background: The Voting Rights Act of 1965 transformed the politics of the American South. Under federal government protection, the Act permitted African Americans to vote and run for elected office in states where a combination of violence, economic pressure, and state and local government rules made political participation difficult if not impossible prior to 1965. We can understand how such a momentous transformation happened by examining structural, political linkage, and governmental factors.

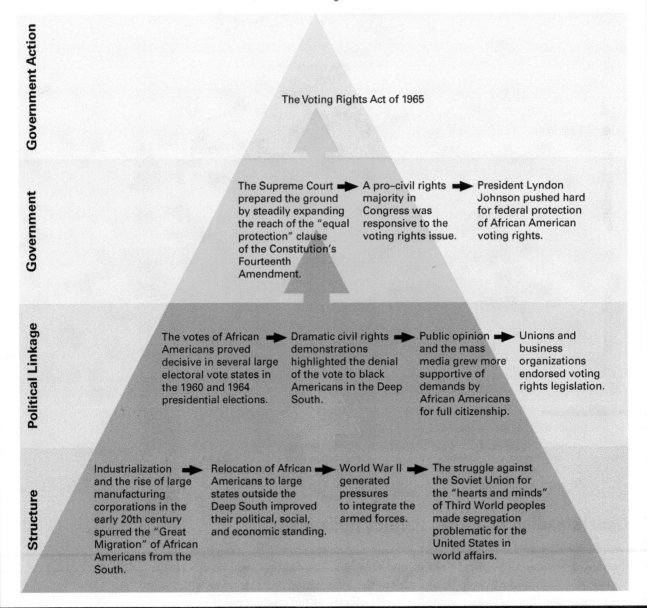

Government Action

The Voting Rights Act of 1965

Government

The Supreme Court prepared the ground by steadily expanding the reach of the "equal protection" clause of the Constitution's Fourteenth Amendment. ➡ A pro–civil rights majority in Congress was responsive to the voting rights issue. ➡ President Lyndon Johnson pushed hard for federal protection of African American voting rights.

Political Linkage

The votes of African Americans proved decisive in several large electoral vote states in the 1960 and 1964 presidential elections. ➡ Dramatic civil rights demonstrations highlighted the denial of the vote to black Americans in the Deep South. ➡ Public opinion and the mass media grew more supportive of demands by African Americans for full citizenship. ➡ Unions and business organizations endorsed voting rights legislation.

Structure

Industrialization and the rise of large manufacturing corporations in the early 20th century spurred the "Great Migration" of African Americans from the South. ➡ Relocation of African Americans to large states outside the Deep South improved their political, social, and economic standing. ➡ World War II generated pressures to integrate the armed forces. ➡ The struggle against the Soviet Union for the "hearts and minds" of Third World peoples made segregation problematic for the United States in world affairs.

influence the distribution of income and wealth in society, government regulations affect the operations of corporations, and decisions by the courts may determine what interest groups and political parties are able to do. We will want to pay attention, then, to these sorts of influences in our effort to understand how the American political system works.

You need not worry about remembering exactly which actors and influences belong to which of the four categories. That will become obvious because the chapters of the book are organized into sections corresponding to them. Nor do you need to worry about exactly how the people and institutions in the different levels interact with one another. This will become clear as materials are presented and learned and as you become more familiar with the American political process.

Does Government Work?

1.3   Think about ways to analyze the question: "Does government work?"

1.1

1.2

1.3

We bring the democracy standard and the analytical framework together by asking throughout this book about the extent to which government policies reflect the wishes of the people and the degree to which government programs reflecting these wishes are carried out efficiently and effectively. We will want to know, for example, what conditions and developments at the structural level in the analytical model give rise to problems and issues that the American people want addressed. We will want to know the degree to which people can transmit their concerns and wishes to government leaders, and how responsive these leaders are to popular pressures as compared to pressures brought by powerful private interests. As well, we will want to examine how the various branches and levels of government work together in fashioning and carrying out policies the people say they want. Do they cooperate most of the time, for example, or are they at loggerheads and unable to fashion appropriate policies? When government settles on a policy and government officials try to put a policy into practice, is government always handicapped in its efforts either because of obstacles created by political opponents and special interests, or because, as some believe, government is inherently inefficient and ineffective compared to the private sector?

We will address these complex issues at various places in this book, particularly in the feature "Can Government Do Anything Well?" In this feature, we will highlight some important areas of federal government activity that seem to have functioned well over the years, and we will examine claims that the private sector would have done and can do a better job, providing supporting evidence for both positions. We then ask you to weigh the claims and propose what you believe might be the optimal division of labor between the public and private sectors in fulfilling the wishes and needs of the American people regarding a particular area of activity, whether it be interstate highways or overseeing the safety of the food supply. In providing this feature, we hope we can help bridge the deep divide that separates those who believe that "government is always the solution" and those who believe that "government is always the problem."

The debate between pro–free market/anti–big government advocates and regulated markets/pro–big government advocates is an old one in American politics. At various times, one side has controlled the debate and held sway over government policymaking. During the Great Depression, for example, Franklin Roosevelt's New Deal mostly prevailed, with government doing more than most Americans had ever imagined, mostly at the urging of the American people and many business and cultural leaders. Beginning with Ronald Reagan's administration in the early 1980s, however, anti–big government proponents and political actors have steadily gained ground.

Ronald Reagan?

We are now deeply into a mostly anti-government moment in American history. The conservative and Tea Party-dominated Republican Party national and state-level landslide election victories in 2010 were an indicator of this trend. So too was the focus of Congress and President Obama in 2011 and 2012 on the problem of budget deficits (which involves deep cuts in government programs) rather than on the problem of stimulating job growth (which often requires new government spending) during the most serious economic crisis since the Great Depression in the 1930s. (The budget deficit debate tends to focus on cutting back government; the stimulating jobs debate tends to center on new or expanded government programs.) To be sure, many liberals also have been unhappy with government recently as shown by the rapid spread across the nation of the "Occupy Wall Street" movement, whose participants wanted government to do more to rein in the financial industry, create jobs, and make incomes more equal. It is of enduring interest and importance whether anti-government or pro-government advocates and political leaders in the coming years gain the upper hand in response to our present economic difficulties or whether some mixed system of public sector and private sector partnership gains traction. This enduring debate on the role of government will be highlighted throughout this textbook.

Review the Chapter

 Listen to **Chapter 1** on **MyPoliSciLab**

Democracy

 1.1 Explain the meaning of democracy and its use as a standard to evaluate American government and politics, p. 5

Democracy is a system of rule by the people, rooted in three fundamental principles: popular sovereinty (meaning that the people ultimately rule), political equality (meaning that each person has an equal say in determining what government does), and political liberty (meaning that the people are protected from government interference in exercising their rights).

Ensuring that all three aspects of democracy are available and practiced has played an important role in American history, and remains an important theme in our country—as well as many other parts of the world—today.

The United States is a liberal representative democracy—meaning that the people do not rule directly but through elected representatives, and have broad civil and political rights, but the majority does not always get its way.

Because democracy holds a very special place in Americans' constellation of values and is particularly relevant to judging political processes, it is the standard used throughout this text to evaluate the quality of our politics and government.

A Framework for Understanding How American Politics Works

1.2 Outline a systematic framework for thinking about how government and politics work, p. 17

The organizing framework presented in this chapter visualizes the world of American politics as a set of interrelated *actors* and *influences*—institutions, groups, and individuals—that operate in three interconnected realms: the *structural*, *political linkage*, and *governmental* sectors. This way of looking at American political life as an ordered, interconnected whole will be used throughout the remainder of the book.

Does Government Work?

1.3 Think about ways to analyze the question: "Does government work?", p. 21

People often forget how effective many government programs have been.

We are now in a period of deep distrust of government and what it does.

Learn the Terms

 Study and **Review** the **Flashcards**

democracy, p. 8
oligarchy, p. 8
monarchy, p. 8
direct democracy, p. 8
representative democracy, p. 9

popular sovereignty, p. 10
majority rule, p. 11
political equality, p. 13
civil rights, p. 14
political liberty, p. 14

social contract, p. 14
liberal democracy, p. 15
majority tyranny, p. 15
Jim Crow, p. 18

Test Yourself

 Study and **Review** the **Practice Tests**

Answer key begins on page T-1.

 1.1 Explain the meaning of democracy and its use as a standard to evaluate American government and politics.

1. Which of the following is the essence of democracy?
   a. Economic well-being
   b. Self-government
   c. Promotion of moral values
   d. Protection of human rights
   e. Creation of rational public policies

1.2 Outline a systematic framework for thinking about how government and politics work.

2. These factors involve all of the political actors, institutions, and processes that transmit the wants and demands of people and groups in our society to government officials.
   a. Political linkage factors
   b. Public opinion factors
   c. Structural factors
   d. Fundamental factors
   e. Government action factors

1.3 Think about ways to analyze the question: "Does government work?"

3. Beginning with this president's administration, anti–big government proponents and political actors have steadily gained ground.
   a. George Washington
   b. Ronald Reagan
   c. Richard Nixon
   d. Franklin Roosevelt
   e. Bill Clinton

Explore Further

INTERNET SOURCES

Think Progress Blog thinkprogress.org/ A blog written by liberals.

The Foundry blog.heritage.org/ A blog written by conservatives.

Top 100 Political Blogs **technorati.com/blogs/directory/politics/** A list of the most popular political blogs.

CNN Politics (Political Blog) politicalticker.blogs.cnn.com/ Political blog by CNN analysts.

New York Times, Politics Navigator **www.nytimes.com/library/politics/polpoints.html** Internet portal that contains information on a variety of political topics.

International Political Science Association, Top 300 Political Science Websites **ipsaportal.unina.it** A portal to a broad array of web sites on political systems around the world and scholarly research about them.

SUGGESTIONS FOR FURTHER READING

Bartels, Larry M. *Unequal Democracy: The Political Economy of the New Gilded Age. New York and Princeton*, NJ: The Russell Sage Foundation and Princeton University Press, 2008.

An examination of rising income inequality and how it undermines several of the basic foundational requirements of political democracy.

Dahl, Robert A. *Democracy and Its Critics.* New Haven, CT: Yale University Press, 1989.

A sweeping defense of democracy against its critics by one of the most brilliant political theorists of our time.

Dahl, Robert A. *On Democracy.* New Haven, CT: Yale University Press, 1998.

A brief yet surprisingly thorough examination of classical and contemporary democracy, real and theoretical.

Putnam, Robert D. *Making Democracy Work: Civic Traditions in Modern Italy.* Princeton, NJ: Princeton University Press, 1993.

A brilliant and controversial argument that the success of democratic government depends on the vitality of a participatory and tolerant civic culture.

Wolfe, Alan. *Does American Democracy Still Work?* New Haven, CT: Yale University Press, 2006.

A pessimistic reading of trends in American politics, society, and economy that are diminishing the quality of American democracy.

Zakaria, Fareed. *The Future of Freedom: Illiberal Democracy at Home and Abroad.* New York: Norton, 2004.

The author suggests that majority rule democracy can only happen and be sustained in societies where individual freedom and the rule of law already exist, suggesting that democracy is unlikely to take hold in places such as Russia and Iraq.

2

The Constitution

DETAINEES, CHECKED AND BALANCED

Senator John McCain (R–AZ)—who had spent five years as a prisoner of war in Vietnam—offered an amendment to the 2005 Defense Department Authorization bill banning cruel, inhuman, and degrading treatment of detainees. President Bush threatened to veto the bill if it contained the McCain "anti-torture" amendment, but the Senate and House voted overwhelmingly for it. In supporting the amendment, senators and representatives from both parties cited their concerns about prevailing policies, noting the free-fall in America's international reputation after revelations about harsh treatment of detainees at U.S. prisons at Guantanamo Bay (Cuba) and Abu Ghraib (Iraq) and their sense that many of our detainee policies were at odds with basic American values. Seeing the handwriting on the wall, the president signed the bill with the anti-torture amendment.[1]

End of the matter? According to most textbook expositions, a bill becomes law once it is passed by both houses of Congress and signed by the president.[2] All citizens and government officials are then obligated to abide by the law. Of course, in real life, the president and executive branch officials sometimes carry out the provisions of a law with less enthusiasm than Congress might like. In this case, President George W. Bush went much further, essentially nullifying his bill-signing by issuing a signing statement stating that "the executive branch shall construe [the law] in a manner consistent with the constitutional authority of the President . . . as Commander-in-Chief . . . [this] will assist in achieving the shared objective of the Congress and the President . . . of protecting the American people from further terrorist attacks."[3] The president was announcing that he would not feel obliged to follow the provisions of the new law when he and he alone, acting in his constitutional capacity as commander in chief, deemed it necessary for the protection of the American people.[4]

2.1	2.2	2.3	2.4	2.5	2.6
Assess the enduring legacies of the American Revolution and the Declaration of Independence, p. 28	Describe the governmental system established by our first constitution, p. 31	Analyze the developments that led to the Constitutional Convention, p. 32	Evaluate the framework for government that emerged from the Constitutional Convention, p. 36	Explain the difficulties of ratifying the Constitution, p. 49	Identify three processes by which the Constitution changes, p. 51

HARSH CONFINEMENT President George W. Bush was heavily criticized about the use of harsh interrogation techniques at Guantanamo Bay and other prison facilities housing terrorism suspects. While he signed a bill from Congress banning such techniques, he also issued a signing statement saying he would ignore the new law when it endangered national security. Here heavily guarded prisoners are escorted to their cells.

The Big Picture Author Edward S. Greenberg discusses how the Constitution provides the basic rules for how government operates in the United States and how the rules affect the degree to which the American people are able to govern themselves.

The Basics What is the purpose of a Constitution? In this video, you will discover the reasons why the framers wrote the Constitution and how the Constitution sets up checks and balances, the protection of liberties, and the framework we need for a functioning democracy.

How does the Constitution change?

In Context Why is it unusual that the United States Constitution has governed so long in its present form? Fordham University political scientist Costas Panagopolos explains why the Constitution is such a rarity and how it has succeeded in an evolving American society.

Think Like a Political Scientist How do the institutions created by the U.S. Constitution operate and how has their role changed over time? Fordham University political scientist Costas Panagopolos examines this and other emerging issues in the research and in the study of the Constitution.

In the Real World How well does the system of checks and balances in the United States work, and is it actually fair? Real people voice their opinions on whether or not they believe it is constitutional for Congress to check the power of the president—and vice versa.

So What? How hard is it to change the Constitution? While some features of the modern political process—such as political parties and lobbyists—developed without being mentioned in the Constitution, author Edward S. Greenberg explains how the constitution is structured to favor the status quo.

President George W. Bush was not the first president to issue signing statements setting out his thinking on the meaning of new statutes. But most presidents before him, starting with James Monroe, used the device sparingly and rarely used it to contravene the intent of Congress. President Bush, on the other hand, issued more than 1,200 of them during his eight years in office—far more than all presidents had issued collectively during the entire course of American history. A fair proportion of them fell into the category of "will not" or "cannot" carry out the law because of intrusions on the president's constitutional prerogatives and powers as commander in chief or as head of the executive branch.

During the 2008 election campaign, Barack Obama promised to end this practice if elected. On March 9, 2009, he issued an executive order that all executive branch officials must consult with the attorney general before following any of the signing statements issued by President Bush, suggesting that most of them would no longer be operative. Interestingly, however, President Obama also said that signing statements were legitimate if used properly and that he reserved the right to issue them when he deemed it to be appropriate, though he promised he would act with "caution and restraint."[5] He mostly was true to his word, issuing only 18 through the end of 2011, and only a few said or implied that he "would not" or "could not" carry out the law as Congress intended. One of these, in which he rejected a proviso in a statute limiting the president's ability to hire advisors, he deemed contrary to his constitutional powers, brought abundant criticism, but he was undeterred.[6] Apparently, President Obama was unwilling to reject entirely an important tool of presidential power that had evolved over the years.

In the Constitution, the framers designed a framework for a government of separated powers and checks and balances. By that we mean that the framers divided executive, legislative, and judicial powers and placed them into separate branches of the national government. While the framers situated a set of unique powers within each, they also gave each branch an important role in the affairs of the other branches in a bid at preventing any one of them from becoming too powerful. Giving legislative power to Congress but giving the president a central role in the legislative process, including the president's role in signing bills into law and having the ability to veto congressional enactments, is an example of this constitutional design. As you might suspect, a system of separation of powers and checks and balances is rife with potential conflict between the branches. It has been so since the beginning of the Republic. It is exactly the sort of thing the framers had in mind. This chapter is about the constitutional design of the American government, why the framers fashioned the sort of constitution they did, how the Constitution shapes political life and government actions in the United States, and how the meaning of the Constitution has changed over the years.

proviso—
a condition attached to an agreement

Thinking Critically About This Chapter

This chapter is about the founding of the United States (see Figure 2.1) and the formulation of the constitutional rules that structure American politics to this day.

Using the Framework

You will see in this chapter how structural factors such as the American political culture, economic developments, and the composition of the Constitutional Convention shaped the substance of our Constitution. You will also see how the Constitution itself is an important structural factor that helps us understand how American government and politics work today.

Using the Democracy Standard

Using the conception of democracy you learned about in Chapter 1, you will be able to see how and why the framers were uneasy about democracy and created a republican form of government that, although based on popular consent, placed a number of roadblocks in the path of popular rule.

The American Revolution and the Declaration of Independence

2.1 Assess the enduring legacies of the American Revolution and the Declaration of Independence

Initially, the American Revolution (1775–1783) was waged more to preserve an existing way of life than to create something new. By and large, American colonists in the 1760s and 1770s were proud to be affiliated with Great Britain and satisfied with the general prosperity that came with participation in the British commercial empire.[7] When the revolution broke out, the colonists at first wanted only to preserve their traditional rights as British subjects. These traditional rights of life, liberty, and property seemed to be threatened by British policies on trade and taxation. Rather than allowing the American colonists to trade freely with whomever they pleased and to produce whatever goods they wanted, for instance, England was restricting the colonists' freedom to do either in order to protect its own manufacturers. To pay for the military protection of the colonies against raids by Native Americans and their French allies, England imposed taxes on a number of items, including sugar, tea, and stamps (required for legal documents, pamphlets, and newspapers). The imposition of these taxes without the consent of the colonists seemed an act of tyranny to many English subjects in America.

Although the initial aims of the Revolution were quite modest, the American Revolution, like most revolutions, did not stay on the track planned by its leaders. Although it was sparked by a concern for liberty—understood as the preservation of traditional rights against the intrusions of a distant government—it also stimulated the development of sentiments for popular sovereignty and political equality. As these sentiments grew, so did the likelihood that the American colonies would split from their British parent and form a system of government more to the liking of the colonists.

When the Second Continental Congress began its session on May 10, 1775—the First had met only briefly in 1774 to formulate a list of grievances to submit to the British Parliament—the delegates did not have independence in mind, even though armed conflict with Britain had already begun with the battles of Lexington and Concord. Pushed by the logic of armed conflict, an unyielding British government, and Thomas Paine's incendiary call for American independence in his wildly popular pamphlet *Common Sense*, however, the delegates concluded by the spring of 1776 that separation and independence were inescapable.[8] In early June, the Continental Congress appointed a special committee, composed of Thomas Jefferson, John Adams, and Benjamin Franklin, to draft a declaration of independence. The document, mostly Jefferson's handiwork, was adopted unanimously by the Second Continental Congress on July 4, 1776.

☐ Key Ideas in the Declaration of Independence

The ideas in the Declaration of Independence are so familiar that we may easily miss their revolutionary importance. In the late eighteenth century, most societies in the world were ruled by kings with authority purportedly derived from God, subject to little or no control by their subjects. Closely following John Locke's ideas in *The Second Treatise on Government*, Jefferson's argument that legitimate government can be established only by the people, is created to protect inalienable rights, and can govern only with their consent, seemed outrageous at the time. However, these ideas sparked a responsive chord in people everywhere when they were first presented, and they remain extremely popular all over the world today. The argument as presented in the Declaration of Independence goes as follows:

- Human beings possess rights that cannot be legitimately given away or taken from them. *"We hold these truths to be self-evident, that all men are created equal, that*

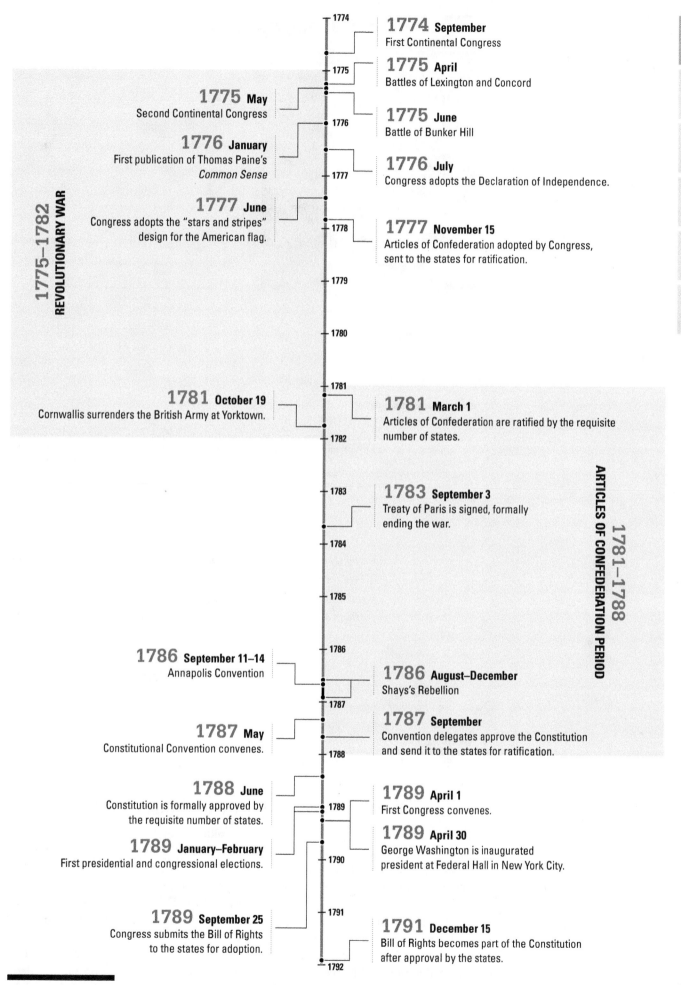

1774 1774 September
First Continental Congress

1775 April
Battles of Lexington and Concord

1775 May
Second Continental Congress

1775 June
Battle of Bunker Hill

1776 January
First publication of Thomas Paine's
Common Sense

1776 July
Congress adopts the Declaration of Independence.

1777 June
Congress adopts the "stars and stripes"
design for the American flag.

1777 November 15
Articles of Confederation adopted by Congress,
sent to the states for ratification.

1775–1782
REVOLUTIONARY WAR

1781 October 19
Cornwallis surrenders the British Army at Yorktown.

1781 March 1
Articles of Confederation are ratified by the requisite
number of states.

1783 September 3
Treaty of Paris is signed, formally
ending the war.

1786 September 11–14
Annapolis Convention

1786 August–December
Shays's Rebellion

1787 May
Constitutional Convention convenes.

1787 September
Convention delegates approve the Constitution
and send it to the states for ratification.

1788 June
Constitution is formally approved by
the requisite number of states.

1789 April 1
First Congress convenes.

1789 January–February
First presidential and congressional elections.

1789 April 30
George Washington is inaugurated
president at Federal Hall in New York City.

1789 September 25
Congress submits the Bill of Rights
to the states for adoption.

1791 December 15
Bill of Rights becomes part of the Constitution
after approval by the states.

1781–1788
ARTICLES OF CONFEDERATION PERIOD

FIGURE 2.1 TIMELINE OF THE FOUNDING OF THE UNITED STATES, 1774–1791

2.1

2.2

2.3

2.4

2.5

2.6

social contract

A philosophical device, used by Enlightenment thinkers such as Locke, Rousseau, and Harrington, to suggest that governments are only legitimate if they are created by a voluntary compact among the people.

COMMON SENSE;

ADDRESSED TO THE

INHABITANTS

OF

AMERICA,

On the following interesting

SUBJECTS.

I. Of the Origin and Design of Government in general, with concise Remarks on the English Constitution.

II. Of Monarchy and Hereditary Succession.

III. Thoughts on the present State of American Affairs.

IV. Of the present Ability of America, with some miscellaneous Reflections.

Man knows no Master save creating HEAVEN,
Or those whom choice and common good ordain.

THOMSON.

PHILADELPHIA;
Printed, and Sold, by R. BELL, in Third-Street.

MDCCLXXVI.

THOMAS PAINE ESQ.
Late Secretary for Foreign Affairs to the American Congress.
Author of
The Rights of Man, Common Sense, &c.

CLARION CALL FOR INDEPENDENCE

American leaders were reluctant at first to declare independence from Great Britain. One of the things that helped change their minds was Thomas Paine's wildly popular—it is said that a higher proportion of Americans read it than any other political tract in U.S. history—and incendiary pamphlet *Common Sense,* which mercilessly mocked the institution of monarchy and helped undermine the legitimacy of British rule. What are some modern-day examples of Paine's pamphlet? Are influential bloggers or tweeters good examples?

they are endowed by their Creator with certain unalienable Rights, that among these are Life, Liberty, and the Pursuit of Happiness."

- People create government to protect these rights. *"That to secure these rights, Governments are instituted among Men, deriving their just powers from the consent of the governed."*

- If government fails to protect people's rights or itself becomes a threat to them, people can withdraw their consent from that government and form a new one, that is, void the existing **social contract** and agree to a new one. *"That whenever any Form of Government becomes destructive of these ends, it is the Right of the People to alter or to abolish it, and to institute new Government, laying its foundation on such principles, and organizing its powers in such form, as to them shall seem most likely to effect their Safety and Happiness."*

☐ Important Omissions in the Declaration

The Declaration of Independence carefully avoided several controversial subjects, including what to do about slavery. Jefferson's initial draft denounced the Crown for violating human rights by "captivating and carrying Africans into slavery," but this was considered too controversial and was dropped from subsequent versions. The contradiction between the institution of slavery and the Declaration's sweeping claims for self-government, "unalienable" individual rights, and equality ("all men are created equal") was obvious to many observers at the time and is glaringly apparent to us today. The Declaration was also silent about the political status of women and the inalienable rights of Native Americans (referred to in the Declaration as "merciless Indian savages") and African Americans, even those who were not slaves. Indeed, it is safe to assume that neither Jefferson, the main author of the Declaration, nor the other signers of the document had women, Native Americans, free blacks, or slaves in mind when they were fomenting revolution and calling for a different kind of political society. Interestingly, free blacks and women would go on to play important roles in waging the Revolutionary War against Britain.[9]

The Articles of Confederation: The First Constitution

Describe the governmental system established by our first constitution

T
he leaders of the American Revolution almost certainly did not envision the creation of a single, unified nation. At most, they had in mind a loose **confederation** among the states. This should not be surprising. Most Americans in the late eighteenth century believed that a government based on popular consent and committed to the protection of individual rights was possible only in small, homogeneous republics, where government was close to the people and where fundamental conflicts of interest among the people did not exist. Given the great geographic expanse of the colonies, as well as their varied ways of life and economic interests, the formation of a single unified republic seemed unworkable.

☐ Provisions of the Articles

Our first written **constitution**—a document specifying the basic organization, powers, and limits of government—passed by the Second Continental Congress in the midst of the Revolutionary War in 1777 (although it was not ratified by the requisite number of states until 1781), created a nation that was hardly a nation at all. The **Articles of Confederation** created in law what had existed in practice from the time of the Declaration of Independence: a loose confederation of independent states with little power in the central government, much like the United Nations today. Under the Articles, most important decisions were made in state legislatures.

The Articles provided for a central government of sorts, but it had few responsibilities and virtually no power. It could make war or peace, but it had no power to levy taxes (even customs duties) to pursue either goal. It could not regulate commerce among the states, nor could it deny the states the right to collect customs duties. It had no independent chief executive to ensure that the laws passed by Congress would be enforced, nor had it a national court system to settle disputes between the states. There were no means to provide a sound national money system. The rule requiring that all national laws be approved by 9 of the 13 states, with each state having one vote in Congress, made lawmaking almost impossible. And, defects in the new constitution were difficult to remedy because amending the Articles required the unanimous approval of the states.

☐ Shortcomings of the Articles

The Articles of Confederation did what most of its authors intended: to preserve the power, independence, and sovereignty of the states and ensure that the central government would not encroach on the liberty of the people. Unfortunately, there were also many problems that the confederation was ill-equipped to handle.

Most important, the new central government could not finance its activities. The government was forced to rely on each state's willingness to pay its annual tax assessment. Few states were eager to cooperate. As a result, the bonds and notes of the confederate government became almost worthless, dramatically undermining the creditworthiness of the new country.

confederation
A loose association of states or territorial units without any or much power in a central authority.

constitution
The basic framework of law for a nation that prescribes how government is to be organized, how decisions are to be made, and what powers and responsibilities government shall have.

Articles of Confederation
The first constitution of the United States, adopted during the last stages of the Revolutionary War, created a system of government with most power lodged in the states and little in the central government.

2.1
2.2
2.3
2.4
2.5
2.6

CLASHES ON THE FRONTIER

As settlers moved west, they inevitably came into conflict with Native Americans already living there. Many of the settlers were angry and distressed when the national government under the Articles of Confederation proved unable to protect them against the people being displaced. This painting shows a battle waged between settlers and Native Americans on the Kentucky frontier in 1785. What weakness of the Articles led to such problems?

The central government was also unable to defend American interests in foreign affairs. Without a chief executive or a standing army, and with the states holding a veto power over actions of the central government, the confederation lacked the capacity to reach binding agreements with other nations or to deal with a wide range of foreign policy problems. These included the continuing presence of British troops in western lands ceded to the new nation by Britain at the end of the Revolutionary War, violent clashes with Native Americans on the western frontier, and piracy on the high seas.

The government was also unable to prevent the outbreak of commercial warfare between the states. As virtually independent nations with the power to levy customs duties, many states became intense commercial rivals of their neighbors and sought to gain every possible advantage against the products of other states. New York and New Jersey, for instance, imposed high tariffs on goods that crossed their borders from other states. This situation was an obstacle to the expansion of commercial activities and economic growth.

Factors Leading to the Constitutional Convention

2.3   Analyze the developments that led to the Constitutional Convention

Historians now generally agree that the failings of the Articles of Confederation led most of the leading citizens of the confederation to believe that a new constitution was desperately needed for the fledgling nation. What is left out of many accounts of the convening of the Constitutional Convention in Philadelphia, however, is the story of the growing concern among many of the most influential men in the confederation that the passions for democracy and equality among the common people set loose by the American Revolution were getting out of hand. During the American Revolution, appeals to the people for the defense of freedom and for the spread of the blessings of liberty were often translated by the people to mean their right to better access to the means of government and to the means of livelihood.[10] The common people were convinced that success would bring substantial improvements in their lives.[11]

The Eighteenth-Century Republican Beliefs of the Founders

This fever for popular participation and greater equality is not what most of the leaders of the American Revolution had in mind.[12] The Founders were believers in a theory of government known as **republicanism** (please note that we are not referring here to the Republican Party or its members and supporters).[13] Like all republicans of the eighteenth century, the framers were seeking a form of government that would not only be based on the consent of the governed but would prevent **tyranny**, whether tyranny came from the misrule of a single person (a king or military dictator, let us say), a small group of elites (an aristocracy, a clerical theocracy, or moneyed merchant class), or even the majority of the population. The solution to the problem of tyranny for eighteenth-century republican thinkers was threefold: to elect government leaders, limit the power of government, and place roadblocks in the path of the majority. The election of representatives to lead the government, in their view, would keep potentially tyrannical kings and aristocratic factions from power while ensuring popular consent. Limiting the power of government, both by stating what government could and could not do in a written constitution and by fragmenting governmental power, would prevent tyranny no matter who eventually won control, including the majority of the people. The influence of the majority could be limited by making only a portion of government subject to election by the people.

Although eighteenth-century republicans believed in representative government— a government whose political leaders are elected by the people—they were not sympathetic to what we might today call popular democracy. For the most part, they thought that public affairs ought to be left to men from the "better" parts of society. The conduct of the public business was, in their view, the province of individuals with wisdom and experience, capacities associated mainly with people of social standing, substantial financial resources, and high levels of education. They expected that voters would be interested in having such people in office and would cast their ballots consistent with this view. Eighteenth-century republicans believed that once in office, elected representatives should not be overly responsive to public opinion; representatives were to exercise independent judgment about how best to serve the public interest, taking into account the needs and interests of society rather than the moods and opinions of the people. They believed that such a deliberative approach would not only protect liberty but result in better government decisions and policies.[14]

Why the Founders Were Worried

Eighteenth-century republicans, then, did not believe that the people could or should rule directly. While they favored a system that allowed the common people to play a larger role in public life than existed in other political systems of the day, the role of the people was to be a far more limited one than we find acceptable today. They worried that too much participation by the people could only have a bad outcome. As James Madison put it in *The Federalist Papers*, "[Democracies] have ever been spectacles of turbulence and contention; have ever been found incompatible with personal security or the rights of property; and have in general been as short in their lives as they have been violent in their deaths."[15] (See Table 2.1 on the differences between democracy and eighteenth-century republicanism.)

AN EXCESS OF DEMOCRACY IN THE STATES Worries that untamed democracy was on the rise were not unfounded.[16] In the mid-1780s, popular assemblies (called conventions) were created in several states to keep tabs on state legislatures and to issue instructions to legislatures concerning what bills to pass. Both conventions and instructions struck directly at the heart of the republican conception of the legislature as a deliberative body made up of representatives shielded from popular opinion.[17]

republicanism
A political doctrine advocating limited government based on popular consent, protected against majority tyranny.

tyranny
The abuse of the inalienable rights of citizens by government.

2.1

2.2

2.3

2.4

2.5

2.6

unicameral
A legislative body with a single chamber.

stay acts
Laws forbidding farm foreclosures for nonpayment of debts.

TABLE 2.1 COMPARING EIGHTEENTH-CENTURY REPUBLICANISM AND THE DEMOCRATIC IDEAL

18th-Century Republicanism	The Democratic Ideal
Government is based on popular consent.	Government is based on popular consent.
Rule by the people is indirect, through multiple layers of representatives.	Rule by the people may be direct or indirect through representatives.
The term *people* is narrowly defined (by education, property holding, and social standing).	The term *people* is broadly defined.
Office holding is confined to a narrow and privileged stratum of the population.	Broad eligibility for office holding.
Elected representatives act as "trustees" (act on their own to discover the public good).	Elected representatives act as "delegates" (act as instructed by the people; accurately reflect their wishes).
Barriers to majority rule exist.	Majority rule prevails.
Government is strictly limited in what it can do.	Government does what a majority of the people want it to do.
Government safeguards rights and liberties, with a special emphasis on property rights.	Government safeguards rights and liberties, with no special emphasis on property rights.

The constitution of the state of Pennsylvania was also an affront to republican principles. Benjamin Rush, a signatory to the Declaration of Independence, described it as "too much upon the democratic order."[18] This constitution replaced the property qualification to vote with a very small tax (thus allowing many more people to vote), created a **unicameral** (single-house) legislative body whose members were to be elected in annual elections, mandated that legislative deliberations be open to the public, and required that proposed legislation be widely publicized and voted on only after a general election had been held (making the canvassing of public opinion easier).

To many advocates of popular democracy, including Tom Paine, the Pennsylvania constitution was the most perfect instrument of popular sovereignty. To others, like James Madison, the Pennsylvania case was a perfect example of popular tyranny exercised through the legislative branch of government.[19]

THE THREAT TO PROPERTY RIGHTS IN THE STATES One of the freedoms that eighteenth-century republicans wanted to protect against the intrusions of a tyrannical government was the right of the people to acquire and enjoy private property. Developments toward the end of the 1770s and the beginning of the 1780s seemed to put this freedom in jeopardy. For one thing, the popular culture was growing increasingly hostile to privilege of any kind, whether of social standing, education, or wealth. Writers derided aristocratic airs; expressed their preference for unlettered, plain-speaking leaders; and pointed out how wealth undermined equal rights.[20] Legislatures were increasingly inclined, moreover, to pass laws protecting debtors. For example, Rhode Island and North Carolina issued cheap paper money, which note holders were forced to accept in payment of debts. Other states passed **stay acts**, which forbade farm foreclosures for nonpayment of debts. Popular opinion, while strongly in favor of property rights (after all, most of the debtors in question were owners of small farms), also sympathized with farmers, who were hard-pressed to pay their debts with increasingly tight money, and believed—with some reason—that many creditors had accumulated notes speculatively or unfairly and were not entitled to full repayment.

What pushed American notables over the edge was the threat of insurrection represented by what came to be called Shays' Rebellion. Named after its leader Daniel Shays, the rebellion occurred in western Massachusetts in 1786 when armed men took over court houses in order to prevent judges from ordering the seizure of farms for nonpayment of state taxes and the incarceration of their owners in debtors prison. The crisis in western Massachusetts was the result of a near "perfect storm" of developments: plummeting prices for crops, a dramatic increase in state taxes to pay off

2.1

2.2

2.3

2.4

2.5

2.6

SHAYS' REBELLION

Shays' Rebellion aimed at easing financial pressures on debt-ridden small farmers by closing state courts to prevent foreclosure hearings from taking place. Here, Daniel Shays encourages his fellow citizens to close the courts. Why did the rebellion push American leaders to propose a constitutional convention? Are big changes in forms of government always triggered by some form of social protest?

Revolutionary War debts, and Governor James Bowdoin's insistence that note-holders be paid in full by the state (mostly financial speculators who had bought up the state debt for pennies on the dollar). Unlike most other states in similar circumstances, Massachusetts did not take action to help its debt-ridden farmers. While other states, for example, passed legislation postponing tax and mortgage payments, it instead raised taxes and insisted upon full and timely payment with forfeiture of farms and jail the penalties for noncompliance. Although the state succeeded in putting down the rebellion and reopening the courts, it required the dispatch of the state militia, two pitched battles, and arrests of most of the leaders of the insurrection.

Most of the new nation's leading citizens were alarmed by the apparent inability of state governments to maintain public order under the Articles of Confederation.[21] Shays's Rebellion realized the worst fears of national leaders about the dangers of ineffective state governments and popular democracy spinning out of control, unchecked by a strong national government. As George Washington said, "If government cannot check these disorders, what security has a man?"[22] It was in this climate of crisis in 1786 that 12 delegates from five states meeting in Annapolis issued a call to the other states and Congress to convene a constitutional convention of all the states to correct the flaws in our first constitution. Rather than amend the Articles of Confederation, however, the delegates who gathered at the subsequent convention in Philadelphia in the summer of 1787 did a very surprising thing; they wrote an entirely new constitution.

The Constitutional Convention

2.4 Evaluate the framework for government that emerged from the Constitutional Convention

Most of America's economic, social, and political leaders were convinced by 1787 that the new nation and the experiment in self-government were in great peril. These concerns helped convince leaders in the states to select 73 delegates to attend the Constitutional Convention in Philadelphia (only 55 actually showed up for its deliberations). The goal was to create a new government capable of providing both energy and stability.

The convention officially convened in Philadelphia on May 25, 1787, with George Washington presiding. It met in secret for a period of almost four months. By the end of their deliberations, the delegates had hammered out a constitutional framework that has served as one of the structural foundations of American government and politics to the present day.

☐ Who Were the Framers?

The delegates were not common folk. There were no common laborers, skilled craftspeople, small farmers, women, or racial minorities in attendance. Most delegates were wealthy men: holders of government bonds, real estate investors, successful merchants, bankers, lawyers, and owners of large plantations worked by slaves. They were, for the most part, far better educated than the average American and solidly steeped in the classics. The journal of the convention debates kept by James Madison of Virginia shows that the delegates were conversant with the great works of Western philosophy and political science; with great facility and frequency, they quoted Aristotle, Plato, Locke, Montesquieu, and scores of other thinkers. Finally, they were a group with broad experience in American politics—most had served in their state legislatures—and many were veterans of the Revolutionary War.[23]

Judgments about the framers, their intentions, and what they produced vary widely. Historian Melvin Urofsky wrote that "few gatherings in the history of this or any other country could boast such a concentration of talent."[24] Supreme Court Justice Thurgood Marshall, the first African American member of the Court, on the other hand, once claimed that the Constitution was "defective from the start" because the convention at which it was written did not include women or blacks.[25]

The most influential criticism of the framers and what they created was mounted in 1913 by the Progressive historian Charles Beard in his book *An Economic Interpretation of the Constitution*.[26] Beard boldly claimed that the framers were engaged in a conspiracy to protect their immediate and personal economic interests. Those who controlled the convention and the ratification process after the convention, he suggested, were owners of government bonds and notes who were interested in a government that could pay its debts, merchants interested in protections of commerce, and land speculators interested in the protection of property rights.

Beard has had legions of defenders and detractors.[27] Historians today generally agree that Beard overemphasized the degree to which the framers were driven by the immediate need to "line their own pockets," failed to give credit to their more noble motivations, and even got many of his facts wrong. So a simple self-interest analysis is not supportable. But Beard was probably on the mark when he suggested that broad economic and social-class motives were at work in shaping the actions of the framers. This is not to suggest that they were not concerned about the national interest, economic stability, or the preservation of liberty. It does suggest, however, that the ways in which they understood these concepts were fully compatible with their own positions of economic and social eminence. It is fair to say that the Constitutional Convention was the work of American notables who were authentically worried about the instability and economic chaos of the confederation as well as the rise of a democratic and equalitarian culture among the common people.[28]

That being said, we must also acknowledge that the framers were launched on a novel and exciting adventure, trying to create a form of government that existed nowhere else during the late eighteenth century. The success of their efforts was not

How Long Did It Take to Ratify the Constitution?

Americans today overwhelmingly support the principles of the Constitution, but after the Framers adjourned on September 17, 1787, three years passed before all thirteen states approved the document. The ensuing ratification debate was an inherently political game of multiple moves, in which the Constitution was kept alive by relatively narrow majorities, particularly in two strategically located states.

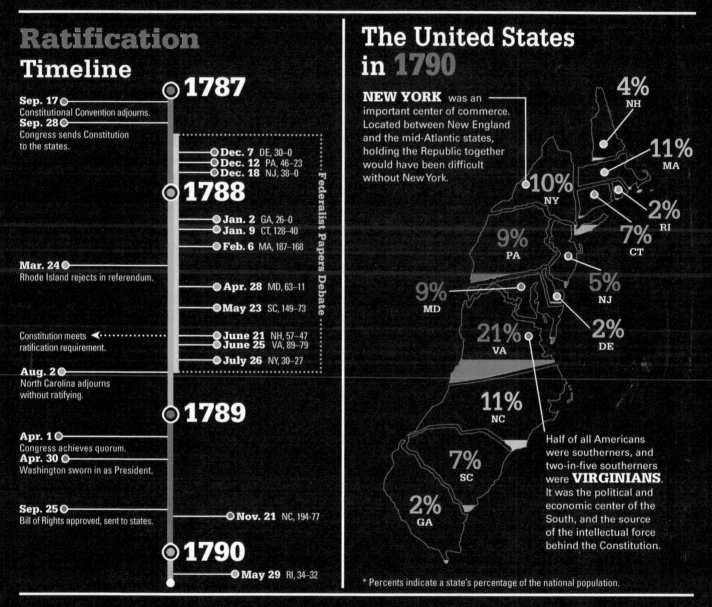

Ratification Timeline

1787

Sep. 17
Constitutional Convention adjourns.
Sep. 28
Congress sends Constitution to the states.

Dec. 7 DE, 30–0
Dec. 12 PA, 46–23
Dec. 18 NJ, 38–0

1788

Jan. 2 GA, 26–0
Jan. 9 CT, 128–40
Feb. 6 MA, 187–168

Mar. 24
Rhode Island rejects in referendum.

Apr. 28 MD, 63–11

May 23 SC, 149–73

Constitution meets ◄··········· ratification requirement.

June 21 NH, 57–47
June 25 VA, 89–79
July 26 NY, 30–27

Aug. 2
North Carolina adjourns without ratifying.

Federalist Papers Debate

1789

Apr. 1
Congress achieves quorum.
Apr. 30
Washington sworn in as President.

Sep. 25
Bill of Rights approved, sent to states.

Nov. 21 NC, 194-77

1790

May 29 RI, 34–32

The United States in 1790

NEW YORK was an important center of commerce. Located between New England and the mid-Atlantic states, holding the Republic together would have been difficult without New York.

4% NH

11% MA

10% NY

2% RI

7% CT

9% PA

9% MD

5% NJ

21% VA

2% DE

11% NC

7% SC

2% GA

Half of all Americans were southerners, and two-in-five southerners were **VIRGINIANS**. It was the political and economic center of the South, and the source of the intellectual force behind the Constitution.

* Percents indicate a state's percentage of the national population.

Investigate Further

Concept Why did it take three years to ratify the Constitution? The first states to ratify the Constitution did so with a strong majority of support for the document. But as those states signed on, opposition in remaining states grew, and the ratification debate intensified.

Connection Which states were most closely divided on ratification? The debate intensified in two strategic states: New York and Virginia. Ratification in those two holdout states was necessary in order to lend legitimacy to the new government.

Cause What were the issues of the debate? Written in support of the new government, *The Federalist Papers* addressed New Yorkers' concerns about federal power. For Virginians, the sticking point was a Bill of Rights, which James Madison promised to introduce in the new Congress.

Virginia Plan

Proposal by the large states at the Constitutional Convention to create a strong central government with power in the government apportioned to the states on the basis of population.

New Jersey Plan

Proposal of the smaller states at the Constitutional Convention to create a government with slightly more power in a central government than under the Articles, with the states equally represented in a unicameral national legislature.

Connecticut Compromise

Also called the *Great Compromise*; the compromise between the New Jersey and Virginia plans formulated by the Connecticut delegates at the Constitutional Convention; called for a lower legislative house based on population size and an upper house based on equal representation of the states.

guaranteed. They were, in effect, sailing in uncharted waters, guided by their reading of history and of the republican philosophers, their understanding of the nature of the unwritten English constitution, and their experience with colonial governments before the Revolution and state governments after the Revolution.

☐ Consensus and Conflict at the Convention

The delegates to the convention were of one mind on many fundamental points. Most importantly, they agreed that the Articles of Confederation had to be scrapped and replaced with a new constitution.

Most of the delegates also agreed about the need for a substantially strengthened national government to protect American interests in the world, provide for social order, and regulate interstate commerce. Such a government would diminish the power and sovereignty of the states. Supporters of the idea of a strong, centralized national government, such as Alexander Hamilton, had long argued this position. By the time of the convention, even such traditional opponents of centralized governmental power as James Madison had changed their minds. As Madison put it, some way must be found "which will at once support a due supremacy of the national authority, and leave in force the local authorities so far as they can be subordinately useful."[29]

But the delegates also believed that a strong national government was potentially tyrannical and should not be allowed to fall into the hands of any particular interest or set of interests, particularly the majority of the people, referred to by Madison as the "majority faction." The delegates' most important task became that of finding a formula for creating a republican government based on popular consent but a government not unduly swayed by public opinion and popular democracy. As Benjamin Franklin put it, "We have been guarding against an evil that old states are most liable to, excess of power in the rulers, but our present danger seems to be a defect of obedience in the subjects."[30]

THE GREAT COMPROMISE By far the most intense disagreements at the convention concerned the issue of representation in Congress, especially whether large or small states would wield the most power in the legislative branch. The **Virginia Plan**, drafted by James Madison, proposed the creation of a strong central government dominated by a powerful bicameral Congress controlled by the most populous states: Virginia, Massachusetts, and Pennsylvania. The Virginians proposed that seats in the national legislature be apportioned to the states on the basis of population size and that the legislature be vested with the power to appoint executive and judiciary branches and to veto state laws. The smaller states countered with a set of proposals drafted by William Paterson of New Jersey (thereafter known as the **New Jersey Plan**), whose central feature was a unicameral national legislature whose seats were apportioned equally among the states with representatives selected by state legislatures. The New Jersey Plan envisioned a slightly more powerful national government than the one that existed under the Articles of Confederation, but one that was to be organized on representational lines not unlike those in the Articles, in which each of the states remained sovereign and equal. The Virginia Plan, by contrast, with its strong national government run by a popularly elected legislature, represented a fundamentally different kind of national union, one in which national sovereignty was superior to state sovereignty.[31]

Debate over this issue was so intense that no decision could be reached on the floor of the convention. As a way out of this impasse, the convention appointed a committee to hammer out a compromise. The so-called Committee of Eleven met over the Fourth of July holiday while the convention was adjourned. It presented its report, sometimes called the Great Compromise and sometimes the **Connecticut Compromise** (because it was drafted by Roger Sherman of that state), on July 5, 1787. Its key feature was a bicameral (two-house) national legislature in which each state's representation in the House of Representatives was to be based on population (thus favoring the large states), while representation in the Senate was to be equal for each of the states (thus favoring the small states). The compromise, adopted on July 16, broke the deadlock at the convention and allowed the delegates to turn their attention to other matters.[32] (See the "Mapping American Politics" feature for more on the enduring effects of the compromise.)

Mapping American Politics

Equal and Unequal Representation in the House and Senate

Introduction

One of the fundamental decisions made by the framers at the Constitutional Convention in Philadelphia in 1787 was to create a two-chamber legislative branch with each branch based on a different principle of representation. Each state's representation in the House of Representatives is based on its relative population size, with the proviso that no state shall have fewer than one representative. Representation in the House, because it very nearly mirrors the distribution of the American population among the states, then, can fairly be called democratic, based on the principle of one person, one vote. The Senate, on the other hand, is based on equal representation of the states—each state has two senators regardless of its population size—giving disproportionate political power to low-population states. We can see this by comparing the two cartograms.

in the Senate, combined with vast population differences among the states, however, leads to serious representational distortions from a democratic theory point of view. In 2010, for example, over 37 million people lived in California while about 560,000 people lived in Wyoming—yet each state had two senators. Thus, each California senator represented over 18.5 million people, while each Wyoming senator represented about 280,000. In terms of representation, each person in Wyoming, then, had 66 times the power in the Senate in 2010 as each person in California. The cartogram on the right reflects the representational power of the people in each state in the Senate, measured as the number of senators—always two—divided by state population size. The most populous states, such as California, New York, Texas, and Florida, almost disappear, while less populous states, such as Wyoming, Montana, Delaware, and the two Dakotas, loom large.

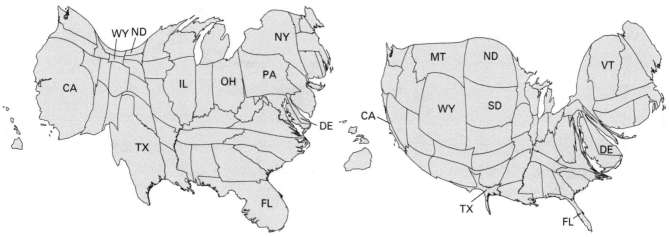

States in Proportion to Number of U.S. Representatives

States in Proportion to Number of Residents per Senator

Different Maps; Different Stories

The cartogram on the left shows states drawn in proportion to the number of representatives each has in the House of Representatives. Because representation in the House is based roughly on population size, the largest numbers of representatives come from more populous states, such as California, Texas, Florida, Ohio, Illinois, New York, and Pennsylvania, as one would expect in a democratic system. Equal representation of each state

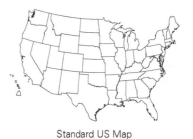

Standard US Map

What Do You Think?

- For the most part, the framers of the Constitution were eighteenth-century republicans, distrustful of popular democracy. They created the Senate not only as a tactical maneuver to gain ratification of the Constitution by nine states, but to make the legislative branch more deliberative and less prone to follow the ebbs and flows of public opinion. Was it a wise decision by the framers to give equal representation to the states in the Senate? How might Congress make different kinds of policies if the Senate were organized to more closely reflect the size of state populations?

SOURCES: www.house.gov; www.census.gov/population/www/censusdata/apportionment.html; and www.senate.gov.

2.1

2.2

2.3

2.4

2.5

2.6

SLAVERY Despite great distaste for the institution of slavery among many delegates—it is said that Benjamin Franklin wanted to insert a provision in the Constitution condemning slavery and the slave trade but was talked out of it for fear of splintering the convention[33]—slavery was ultimately condoned in the Constitution, although only indirectly; the word *slavery*, in fact, does not appear in the Constitution at all. But even without using the term, the legal standing of slaves is affirmed in three places. First, the delegates agreed, after much heated debate, to count three-fifths of a state's slave population (referred to as "three-fifths of all other Persons") in the calculation of how many representatives a state was entitled to in the House

Using the FRAMEWORK

Why was slavery allowed in the Constitution of 1787?

Background: Slavery was allowed in the Constitution until passage, after the Civil War, of the Thirteenth Amendment, which ended involuntary servitude in the United States. Although the words "slave" or "involuntary servitude" never appear in the document, slavery is given constitutional standing in the original document in Article I, Section 2, paragraph 3; Article I, Section 9; and Article IV, Section 2, paragraph 3. For Americans today, it seems almost inconceivable that such a thing could have happened. Taking a broader and more historical view makes the story clearer, though hardly more acceptable.

Government Action

The framers allowed the institution of slavery to continue in Article I, Section 2; Article I, Section 9; and Article IV, Section 2 of the Constitution.

Government

Slaveholders and merchants involved in the slave trade were well represented among the convention delegates.

 Many other delegates, although personally opposed to slavery as an institution, feared that the introduction of a provision to end slavery would cause those states with high numbers of slaves to leave the convention and doom the effort to create a United States of America.

Political Linkage

Slaves and free blacks played no significant political role in America during the Articles of Confederation period. Their concerns about slavery had no political weight.

Few private organizations— interest groups, churches, or newspapers—were actively pressing for an end to slavery at the time of the Constitutional Convention.

Structure

For the most part, individuals of European descent in America during the time of the constitutional convention did not believe that people of African descent were equal to whites in any respect, nor did they believe they were beings who possessed basic human rights.

The slave trade was a profitable business.

of Representatives (Article I, Section 2, paragraph 3). Much harm was done by this; counting noncitizen slaves for purposes of representation in the House increased the power of the slave states in Congress as well as the number of their electoral votes in presidential elections. This imbalance would continue until 1865, when the Civil War and the Thirteenth Amendment, ratified after the war, ended slavery in the United States. Second, it forbade enactments against the slave trade until the year 1808 (Article I, Section 9). Third, it required nonslave states to return runaway slaves to their owners in slave states (Article IV, Section 2, paragraph 3).

Many Americans today are bothered by the fact that a significant number of the delegates to a convention whose goal was to build a nontyrannical republic were themselves slaveholders (although a few, including George Washington, had provisions in their wills freeing their slaves upon their death). To understand more fully why the delegates did not abolish slavery, see the "Using the Framework" feature.

It would take a terrible civil war to abolish slavery in the United States. At the convention, Virginia delegate George Mason had a foreboding of such an outcome when he observed about slavery that "providence punishes national sins by national calamities."[34]

THE PRESIDENCY The Virginia Plan called for a single executive, while the New Jersey Plan called for a multiperson executive. In the spirit of cooperation that pervaded the convention after the Great Compromise, the delegates quickly settled on the idea of a single executive. They could not agree, however, on how this executive should be selected. Both sides rejected direct election of the chief executive by the prople, of course, because this would be "too much upon the democratic order," but they locked horns over the Virginia Plan's method of selection: by the vote of state legislatures. The compromise that was eventually struck involved a provision for an **Electoral College** that would select the president. In the Electoral College, each state would have a total of votes equal to its total number of representatives and senators in

Electoral College

Elected representatives of the states chosen during the November presidential election, a majority of whose votes cast at a later date formally elect the president of the United States. The number of electors in each state is equal to the total number of its senators and representatives. In all but two states, the candidate who wins a plurality of the popular vote wins all of a state's electoral votes.

THE FRAMERS RETAIN SLAVERY

One of the great shortcomings of the framers was their inability or unwillingness to abolish slavery in the Constitution. Here, slaves pick cotton under the watchful eye of an overseer. What were some of the consequences for the nation of the framers allowing slavery in our new nation?

Congress. Selection of electors was left to state legislatures. (Electoral College votes are determined today by popular vote in each state.) Elected members of the Electoral College would then cast their votes for president. Should the Electoral College fail to give a majority to any person, which most framers assumed would usually happen, the House of Representatives would choose the president, with each state having one vote (Article II, Section 1, paragraphs 2 and 3). See the "By the Numbers" feature below in this chapter to better understand how the Electoral College and majoritarian democracy are sometimes at odds.

By the Numbers

Did George W. Bush really win the 2000 presidential vote in Florida?

George W. Bush was officially certified the winner of the presidential contest in Florida on December 12, 2000—35 days after the November election—thereby winning all of Florida's 25 electoral votes. This pushed Bush's national electoral vote total to 271, a bare majority but enough to win the White House.

Interestingly, however, a comprehensive review of Florida ballots has come up with several other possible outcomes to the Florida popular vote, depending on different ways the ballots might have been counted. In one of these scenarios, Gore would have won the Florida popular vote, added its electoral votes to his total in the nation, and been declared the winner of the presidential election.

Why It Matters

Elections must be fair if they are to play the role assigned to them in democratic theory. Part of a fair election is an accurate count of votes cast. Without an accurate count, voter wishes will not be conveyed to public officials, and the legitimacy of elected officials is at risk, making governance more difficult.

Behind the Vote Count Numbers

A consortium of eight leading news organizations—including *The Wall Street Journal*, *The New York Times*, *The Washington Post*, the Associated Press, and CNN—sponsored a 10-month study by the widely respected National Opinion Research Center at the University of Chicago. Center researchers examined every uncounted "under-vote" ballot (where no vote for president was recorded by the voting machine), with an eye toward determining each voter's intent. Only ballots that showed evidence of clear voter intention were included in the consortium's recount. These included punch card ballots with "hanging" and "pregnant" chads which the machines failed to record and optical scan ballots where voters indicated their vote with a check mark or an "X" rather than filling in the bubble as instructed.

Calculating the Winner's Margin of Victory

The official tally concluded that Bush won by 537 votes. However, Center investigators found that different counting methods would have yielded the results shown on page 43. There are some incredible ironies in these numbers.

- **Scenario 1** Had the Gore team gotten everything it asked for from election officials and the courts, Al Gore still would have lost to George W. Bush.

- **Scenario 2** The U.S. Supreme Court did not steal the election, as many Gore supporters claimed, for had it allowed the Florida Supreme Court's solution to stand, Bush would have won anyway.

- **Scenario 3** A majority of Florida voters went to the polls on November 8 to cast a vote for Al Gore for president. The method proposed by the U.S. Supreme Court shows this; recounting all "under-count" disputed ballots on a statewide basis using consistent standards yields a Gore victory. The upshot: Gore was badly advised by his team of lawyers, who insisted on recounts in only certain counties that were deemed favorable to him.

Because of the enormous boost in George W. Bush's popularity following the terrorist attack on the United States and the widely supported attack on the Taliban regime in Afghanistan that followed, most Americans ignored the consortium's findings when they were published after 9/11. Most seemed perfectly content to have Bush as president, no matter what had happened in Florida.

Criticisms of the Florida "Recount"

Some have argued that the consortium's recount was flawed in two major ways:

- First, it did not include "over-votes" in its estimates—those ballots where the same name was entered more than once—which were also ruled invalid by election officials in Florida. For the most part, these involved ballots where voters wrote in the same name as the candidate they had punched or marked, presumably to make clear to election officials who they had voted for. A substantial majority of over-vote ballots had selected Gore.

- Second, there is the issue of absentee ballots from overseas armed forces personnel. Had they been counted in the same way other ballots were counted—that is, not counting ballots kicked out because of "under-vote" or "over-vote"

(Continued)

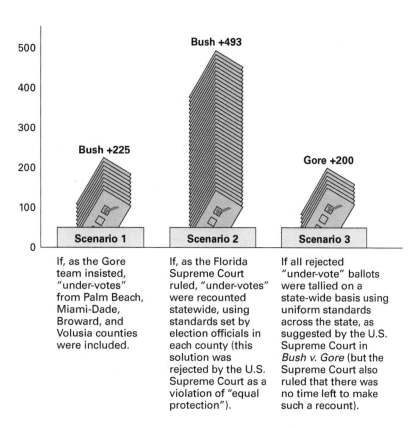

Bush +493

Bush +225

Gore +200

Scenario 1	Scenario 2	Scenario 3
If, as the Gore team insisted, "under-votes" from Palm Beach, Miami-Dade, Broward, and Volusia counties were included.	If, as the Florida Supreme Court ruled, "under-votes" were recounted statewide, using standards set by election officials in each county (this solution was rejected by the U.S. Supreme Court as a violation of "equal protection").	If all rejected "under-vote" ballots were tallied on a state-wide basis using uniform standards across the state, as suggested by the U.S. Supreme Court in *Bush v. Gore* (but the Supreme Court also ruled that there was no time left to make such a recount).

problems—Bush would have lost hundreds of votes to Gore and probably lost Florida and the White House.

What to Watch For

When counting votes, as in all other counts, the rules matter. This is why the lawyers from the Gore and Bush teams fought so ferociously following the Florida election about how to do the recount. Whenever you run across a statistic that involves counting, in one form or another, you might want to look further into what counting rules were used.

What Do You Think?

Can you think of any other way to decide the winner of an election when the race ends up in a dead heat? Some countries use a "runoff" system in which the two top people run against each other to determine who has won a majority of popular votes before a winner is declared. In the 2000 presidential elections, this would have meant a runoff election between Gore and Bush, without Ralph Nader on the ballot, most of whose votes would probably have gone to Gore in the second round. How might a runoff have changed the face of the election?

☐ What the Framers Created

The Constitution of the United States (which is reprinted in its entirety in the Appendix) deserves a careful reading. Each word or phrase tells something important about how American government works. If you keep in mind how the document is organized, it will help you understand the structure of the Constitution, locate specific provisions, and understand what kind of government the framers created. (A brief outline of provisions is provided in Table 2.2.) Let us examine the fundamental design for government laid out in the Constitution.

A REPUBLICAN FORM OF GOVERNMENT Recall that eighteenth-century republican doctrine advocated a form of government that, while based on popular consent and some popular participation, places obstacles in the path of majoritarian democracy and limits the purposes and powers of the government in order to prevent tyranny.

Elections and Representation Republican government is based on the principle of representation, meaning that public policies are made not by the people directly but by the people's elected representatives acting in their stead. Under the rules created by

43

TABLE 2.2 READING THE CONSTITUTION

Article	What It's About	What It Does
Preamble	States the purpose of the Constitution	Declares that "we the people" (not just the separate states) establish the Constitution.
Article I	The Legislative Branch	Provides for a House of Representatives, elected by the people and apportioned according to population. Provides for a Senate, with equal representation for each state. Discusses various rules and procedures, including the presidential veto. Enumerates specific powers of the Congress, concluding with the necessary and proper clause. Limits Congress's powers. Limits the powers of the states.
Article II	The Executive Branch	Vests executive power in a single president of the United States. Describes the Electoral College scheme for electing presidents indirectly (changed, in effect, by the development of a party system). Describes the qualification, removal, compensation, and oath of office for the presidency. Describes presidential powers and duties. Provides for impeachment.
Article III	The Judicial Branch	Vests judicial power in a Supreme Court, letting Congress establish other courts if desired. Provides for a limited original jurisdiction and (subject to congressional regulation) for broader appellate jurisdiction (i.e., jurisdiction to review lower court decisions). Specifies a right to jury trials. Defines treason, ruling out certain punishments for it.
Article IV	Interstate and Federal Relations	Requires that full faith and credit be given other states. Requires that fugitives (slaves) be delivered up to the authorities. Provides for the admission of new states and the regulation of new territories. Guarantees a republican form of government to the states.
Article V	Amending the Constitution	Provides two ways of proposing amendments to the Constitution and two ways of ratifying them. Forbids amendments changing equal state suffrage in the Senate or (before 1808) prohibiting the slave trade or changing the apportionment of taxes.
Article VI	Miscellaneous	Assumes the debts of the Confederation. Makes the Constitution, laws, and treaties of the United States the supreme law of the land. Requires an oath by U.S. and state officials.
Article VII	Ratification of the Constitution	Provides that the Constitution will be established when ratified by nine state conventions.

federal

Describing a system in which significant governmental powers are divided between a central government and smaller territorial units, such as states.

supremacy clause

The provision in Article VI of the Constitution which states that the Constitution and the laws and treaties of the United States are the supreme law of the land, taking precedence over state laws and constitutions.

the Constitution, the president and members of Congress are elected by the people, although in the case of the presidency and the Senate, to be sure, they are elected only indirectly (through the Electoral College and the state legislatures, respectively). The upshot, then, is that government policies at the national level are mostly made by either directly or indirectly elected officials. (The Seventeenth Amendment, ratified in 1913, transferred election of senators from legislatures to the people.) This filters the voices of the people by encouraging the election to office of those "whose enlightened views and virtuous sentiments render them superior to local prejudices and to schemes of injustice."[35] This guarantees a degree of popular consent and some protection against the possibilities of tyrannical government arising from misrule by the *one* or by the *few*, given the electoral power of the *many*, but the many are still several steps removed from direct influence over officials.

Federalism The Articles of Confederation envisioned a nation structured as a loose union of politically independent states with little power in the hands of the central government. The Constitution fashioned a **federal** system in which some powers are left to the states, some powers are shared by the states and the central government, and some powers are granted to the central government alone.

The powers in the Constitution tilt toward the center, however.[36] This recasting of the union from a loose confederation to a more centralized federal system is boldly stated in Article VI, Section 2, commonly called the **supremacy clause**:

> This Constitution and the Laws of the United States which shall be made in Pursuance thereof; and all Treaties made, or which shall be made, under the Authority of the United States, shall be the supreme Law of the Land; and the Judges in every State shall be bound thereby, any Thing in the Constitution or Laws of any State to the Contrary notwithstanding.

The tilt toward national power is also enhanced by assigning important powers and responsibilities to the national government: to regulate commerce, to provide a uniform currency, to provide uniform laws on bankruptcy, to raise and support an army and a navy, to declare war, to collect taxes and customs duties, to provide for the common defense of the United States, and more. (See Article I, Section 8.) Especially important for later constitutional history is the last of the clauses in Section 8, which states that Congress has the power to "make all laws which shall be necessary and proper" to carry out its specific powers and responsibilities. We shall see later how this **elastic clause** became one of the foundations for the growth of the federal government in the twentieth century.

The Constitution left it up to each of the states, however, to determine qualifications for voting within their borders. This left rules in place in all the states that denied the right to vote to women, slaves, and Native Americans; it left rules untouched in many states that denied the vote to free blacks and to white males without property. Most states removed property qualifications by the 1830s, establishing universal white male suffrage in the United States. It would take many years and constitutional amendments to remove state restrictions on the voting rights of women and racial minorities, however.

Limited Government The basic purpose of the U.S. Constitution, like any written constitution, is to define the purposes and powers of the government. Such a definition of purposes and powers automatically places a boundary between what is permissible and what is impermissible. By listing the specific powers (as in Article I, Section 8) of the national government and specifically denying others to the national government (as in Article I, Section 9, and in the first 10 amendments to the Constitution, known as the **Bill of Rights**), the Constitution limited what government may legitimately do.

Checks on Majority Rule Afraid of unbridled democracy, the framers created a constitution by which the people rule only indirectly, barriers are placed in the path of majorities, and deliberation is prized over conformity to majority opinion. As political philosopher Robert Dahl puts it, "To achieve their goal of preserving a set of inalienable rights superior to the majority principle . . . the framers deliberately created a framework of government that was carefully designed to impede and even prevent the operation of majority rule."[37] Let us see what the framers did to try to dilute the power of the majority in the national government.

Of the three branches of government, they made only a part of one of them subject to election by the direct vote of the people: the House of Representatives (Article I, Section 2, paragraph 1). They left the election of the president to an electoral college whose members were selected by state legislatures and not by the direct vote of the people. They gave the responsibility of electing senators to state legislatures (since changed by the Seventeenth Amendment). They placed selection of federal judges in the hands of the president and the Senate. They arranged, as well, that representatives, senators, and presidents would serve for different terms (two years for representatives, four years for presidents, and six years for senators), and be beholden to different constituencies. These non-congruencies in terms of office, constituencies, and methods for selecting members of each of the branches were intended to ensure that popular majorities, at least in the short run, would be unlikely to overwhelm those who govern. Finally, the framers rejected the advice of radical democrats, such as Thomas Paine, Samuel Adams, and Thomas Jefferson, to allow the Constitution to be easily amended. Instead, they created an amending process that is exceedingly cumbersome and difficult (see Figure 2.2).

Thus, the framers designed a system in which majority opinion, although given some play (more than anywhere in the world at the time),[38] was largely deflected and slowed, allowing somewhat insulated political leaders to deliberate at their pleasure.

elastic clause
Article I, Section 8 of the Constitution, also called the *necessary and proper clause*; gives Congress the authority to make whatever laws are necessary and proper to carry out its enumerated responsibilities.

Bill of Rights
The first 10 amendments to the U.S. Constitution, concerned with the protection of basic liberties.

VENERATING THE CONSTITUTION
Americans generally believe that the Constitution fashioned by the framers in Philadelphia in 1788 is one of the main reasons the American system of government has proved to be so enduring. Here, young people look at the original document at the National Archives. What reasons might there be for our system enduring, other than the Constitution?

separation of powers
The distribution of government legislative, executive, and judicial powers to separate branches of government.

checks and balances
The constitutional principle that each of the separate branches of government has the power to hinder the unilateral actions of the other branches as a way to restrain an overreaching government and prevent tyranny.

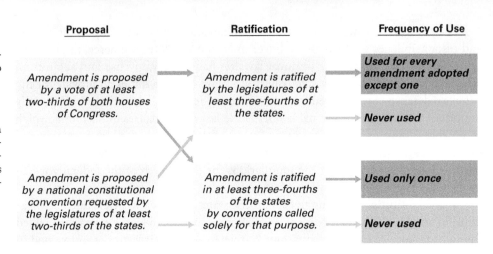

	Proposal	Ratification	Frequency of Use

FIGURE 2.2 AMENDING THE CONSTITUTION

With two ways of proposing a constitutional amendment and two ways of ratifying one, there are four routes to changing the Constitution. In all but one case (the Twenty-First Amendment, which repealed Prohibition), constitutional amendments have been proposed by Congress and then ratified by the state legislatures.

Separation of Powers; Checks and Balances During the American Revolution, American leaders worried mainly about the misrule of executives (kings and governors) and judges. As an antidote, they substituted legislative supremacy in state constitutions and in the Articles of Confederation, thinking that placing power in an elected representative body would make government effective and nontyrannical. The men who drafted the Constitution, however, though still leery of executive and judicial power, were more concerned by 1787 about the danger of legislative tyranny. To deal with this problem, the framers turned to the ancient notion of balanced government, popularized by the French philosopher Montesquieu. The central idea of balanced government is that concentrated power of any kind is dangerous and that the way to prevent tyranny is first to fragment governmental power into its constituent parts—executive, legislative, and judicial—then place each into a separate and independent branch. In the U.S. Constitution, Article I (on the legislative power), Article II (on the executive power), and Article III (on the judicial power) designate separate spheres of responsibility and enumerate specific powers for each branch. We call this the **separation of powers**.

To further ensure that power would not be exercised tyrannically, the framers arranged for the legislative, executive, and judicial powers to check one another in such a way that "ambition . . . be made to counteract ambition."[39] They did this by ensuring that no branch of the national government would be able to act entirely on its own without the cooperation of the others. To put it another way, each branch has ways of blocking the actions of the others. For example, Congress is given the chief lawmaking power under the Constitution, but a bill cannot become law if a president exercises his veto, unless Congress manages to override it with a two-thirds majority in both the House and Senate. The Supreme Court, moreover, has the power (although it is not specifically mentioned) to reject a law formulated by Congress and signed by the president if it is contrary to the Constitution. What is at work here was described nicely by Thomas Jefferson: "The powers of government should be so divided and balanced among several bodies of magistracy, as that no one could transcend their legal limits, without being effectually checked and constrained by the others."[40] We call the provisions that accomplish this objective **checks and balances**. Figure 2.3 shows in detail how each separate branch of the federal government can be checked by the other two. In this constitutional scheme, each branch has power, but none is able to exercise all of its powers on its own, without some concurrence and cooperation from the other branches.

FIGURE 2.3 SEPARATION OF POWERS AND CHECKS AND BALANCES

The framers of the Constitution believed that tyranny might be avoided if the powers of government were fragmented into its executive, legislative, and judicial components and if each component were made the responsibility of a separate branch of government. To further protect against tyranny, they created mechanisms by which the actions of any single branch could be blocked by either or both of the other branches.

THE FOUNDATIONS FOR A NATIONAL FREE ENTERPRISE ECONOMY The framers believed that the right to accumulate, use, and transfer private property was one of the fundamental and inalienable rights that governments were instituted to defend, so they looked for ways to protect it. They also believed that the obstacles to trade allowed under the Articles of Confederation were threatening to block the emergence of a vibrant national economy in which most of them were involved.

Property rights are protected in several places in the Constitution. Article I, Section 10, forbids the states to impair the obligation of contracts, to coin money, or to make anything but gold and silver coin a tender in payment of debts. In other words, the states could no longer help debtors by printing inflated money, forgiving debts, or otherwise infringing on the property of creditors, as had happened in such places as Rhode Island and North Carolina under the Articles of Confederation. Article IV, Section 1, further guarantees contracts by establishing that the states must give "full faith and credit" to the public acts, records, and judicial proceedings of every other state, which means that one could no longer escape legal and financial obligations in one state by moving to another. In addition, the Constitution guaranteed that the U.S. government would pay all debts contracted under the Articles of Confederation (Article VI, Section 1). Article IV, Section 2, paragraph 3, even protected private property in slaves by requiring states to deliver escaped slaves back to their owners.

Besides protecting private property, the framers took additional steps to encourage the emergence of a national **free enterprise** economy. Article I, Section 8, grants Congress the power to regulate interstate commerce (thus ending the chaos of individual states' regulations), to coin money and regulate its value (thus establishing a uniform national currency), to establish uniform laws of bankruptcy, and to protect the financial fruits of invention by establishing patent and copyright

Can Government Do Anything Well?

Encouraging American Economic Development

The American economy, measured by GDP, is the largest in the world in total size and among the largest in terms of GDP per person. This remains the case even after the financial collapse of 2008 and the deep recession associated with it (the worst since the Great Depression in the 1930s). Over the long haul, and despite many recessions and a few depressions along the way, the American economy has grown at a consistently steady pace over the course of its history. For example, economic historians reckon that between 1820 and 1952, the average American grew eight times richer. Between 1945 and 2007, during the post–World War II boom, the average American became three times richer. Is this story of historic economic growth one that can be explained entirely by the efforts of private individuals—investors, entrepreneurs, and consumers—and private business firms seeking profits in a free market? Or, did government play a significant role as well?

Support for the claim that government has been a key player in the story of American economic growth:

Providing the foundations of a market economy:

- Anarchy is not conducive to a thriving, growing economy over the long run. Government provides "law and order," protecting property against both local thieves and foreign invaders.

- Government provides legal and statutory protections and helpful tools that allow business to operate in a safe and reasonably predictable environment. Contracts are enforced in courts, for example, and invention and innovation are encouraged by a system of copyright and patent law.

- The federal government also has been and remains responsible for providing a common currency for the nation, easing market transactions for consumers, investors, and firms.

Instituting policies to stimulate growth:

- High tariff barriers in the nineteenth century protected infant American industries from foreign competition.

- The federal government helped open the West to development when it passed the Homestead Act granting tracts of public land to those who would farm them.

- The government stimulated the growth of railroads by giving vast tracts of land to railroad companies for rights-of-way and town sites along railroad lines.

- Major procurements of goods and weaponry during our several wars poured substantial monies into private firms, fueling their expansion and encouraging technological innovation.

- In the post–World War II period, the federal government invested heavily in higher education and basic scientific research. This better-educated workforce and an array of new technologies flowing from publicly funded research and development, according to most economists, helped fuel the great economic boom of the second half of the twentieth century.

Rejection of the claim that government has been a key player in the story of American economic growth:

A too active government hurts the economy, invites tyranny, and has unintended consequences (the view from the Right):

- Beyond providing law and order, a rule-of-law regime, a common currency, and protection against invasion, government action can only interfere in the processes by which the free market makes society richer and intrude upon the freedoms of the people.

- Heavy taxes to support an active government take away the hard-earned gains of the most successful members of society, taking their private property, as it were, and discouraging others who might create and grow businesses.

- Real economic growth comes not from distant lawmakers and bureaucrats in Washington but from the private sector, where innovation and investment happen.

- When government tries to help, it often makes things worse. Lawmakers' and regulators' interest in getting disadvantaged people into their own homes, it has been argued, forced lenders to give loans to people who couldn't afford them.

Government policies to enhance economic growth have usually served the interests of the wealthy and large business firms (the view from the Left):

- Tax breaks, subsidies, and loan guarantees have increased income and wealth inequality in the United States.

- The deregulation of the financial industry since the 1980s favored large investment banks and hedge funds to the disadvantage of middle class Americans.

2.1
2.2
2.3
2.4
2.5
2.6

(Continued)

laws. At the same time, Article I, Sections 9 and 10, broke down barriers to trade by forbidding the states from imposing taxes or duties on other states' exports, entering into foreign treaties, coining money, or laying any imposts or duties on imports or exports.

It took a little while for a national free enterprise system to emerge and flower in the United States because of the existence of an entirely different sort of economy in the slave South. Although free enterprise was thriving in the northern and western states by the 1820s, it took the destruction of slavery during and after the Civil War to create a free enterprise economy for the country as a whole. (See "Can Government Do Anything Well?" for a discussion of government's role in economic growth and development.)

The Struggle to Ratify the Constitution

2.5 Explain the difficulties of ratifying the Constitution

Congress had instructed the delegates to the convention to propose changes to the Articles of Confederation. Under the provisions of the Articles of Confederation, such alterations would have required the unanimous consent of the 13 states. To follow such a course would have meant instant rejection of the new constitution, because Rhode Island, never friendly to the deliberations in Philadelphia, surely would have voted against it, and one or two additional states may well have joined Rhode Island. Acting boldly, the framers decided that ratification would be based on guidelines specified in Article VII of the unratified document they had just written, namely, approval by nine states meeting in special constitutional conventions. Congress agreed to this procedure, voting on September 28, 1787, to transmit the Constitution to the states for their consideration.

The battle over ratification was heated, and the outcome was far from certain. That the Constitution eventually carried the day may be partly attributed to the fact that the **Federalists** (those who supported the Constitution) did a better job of making their case than the **Anti-Federalists** (those who opposed the Constitution). Their intellectual advantages were nowhere more obvious than in the 85 articles written in defense of the Constitution for New York newspapers, under the name "Publius," by Alexander Hamilton (who wrote the most), James Madison, and John Jay (who wrote only three). Collected later and published as *The Federalist Papers* (which Thomas Jefferson judged to be "the best commentary on the principles of government which ever was written"[41]), these articles strongly influenced the debate over ratification and remain the most impressive commentaries ever written about the U.S. Constitution.

Anti-Federalist opposition to the Constitution was based on fear of centralized power and concern about the absence of a bill of rights.[42] Although the Federalists firmly believed that a bill of rights was unnecessary because of the protection of rights in the state constitutions and the many safeguards against tyranny in the federal Constitution, they promised to add one during the first session of Congress. Without this promise, ratification would probably not have happened. The Federalists kept their word. The 1st Congress passed a bill of rights in the form of 10 amendments to the Constitution (see Table 2.3), and the amendments were eventually ratified by the required number of states by 1791.

Ratification of the Constitution was a close call. Most of the small states quickly approved, attracted by the formula of equal representation in the Senate. Federalists organized a victory in Pennsylvania before the Anti–Federalists realized what had happened. After that, ratification became a struggle. Rhode Island voted no. North Carolina abstained because of the absence of a bill of rights and did not vote its approval until 1790. In the largest and most important states, the vote was exceedingly close. Massachusetts approved by a vote of 187–168; Virginia, by 89–79; and New York, by 30–27. The struggle was especially intense in Virginia, where prominent, articulate, and influential men were involved on both sides. The Federalists could call on George Washington, James Madison, John Marshall, and Edmund Randolph. The Anti-Federalists countered with George Mason, Richard Henry Lee, and Patrick Henry. Patrick Henry was particularly passionate, saying that the Constitution "squints towards monarchy." Although New Hampshire technically put the Constitution over the top, being the ninth state to vote approval, the proponents did not rest easily until Virginia and New York approved it.

TABLE 2.3 THE BILL OF RIGHTS

Amendment I	Freedom of religion, speech, press, and assembly
Amendment II	The right to bear arms
Amendment III	Prohibition against quartering of troops in private homes
Amendment IV	Prohibition against unreasonable searches and seizures
Amendment V	Rights guaranteed to the accused: requirement for grand jury indictment; protections against double jeopardy and self-incrimination; guarantee of due process
Amendment VI	Right to a speedy and public trial before an impartial jury, to cross-examine witnesses, and to have counsel
Amendment VII	Right to a trial by jury in civil suits
Amendment VIII	Prohibition against excessive bail and fines and against cruel and unusual punishment
Amendment IX	Traditional rights not listed in the Constitution are retained by the people
Amendment X	Powers not denied to them by the Constitution or given solely to the national government are retained by the states or the people

Note: See the Appendix for the full text.

The Changing Constitution, Democracy, and American Politics

The Constitution is the basic rule book for the game of American politics. Constitutional rules apportion power and responsibility among governmental branches, define the fundamental nature of the relationships among governmental institutions, specify how individuals are to be selected for office, and tell how the rules themselves may be changed. Every aspiring politician who wants to attain office, every citizen who wants to influence what government does, and every group that wants to advance its interests in the political arena must know the rules and how to use them to their best advantage. Because the Constitution has this character, we understand it to be a fundamental *structural* factor influencing all of American political life.

Like all rules, however, constitutional rules can and do change over time, which is why we sometimes speak of the "living Constitution." Constitutional changes come about in three specific ways: formal amendment, judicial interpretation, and political practices.

The Constitution may be formally amended by use of the procedures outlined in Article V of the Constitution (again, refer to Figure 2.2). This method has resulted in the addition of 27 amendments since the founding, the first 10 of which (the Bill of Rights) were added within three years of ratification. That only 17 have been added in the roughly 220 years since suggests that this method of changing the Constitution is extremely difficult. Over the years, proponents of constitutional amendments that would guarantee equal rights for women, ban same-sex marriages, and ban the burning of the American flag have learned how difficult it is to formally amend the Constitution; none of these amendments were added, despite public opinion polls reporting majorities in favor of them. Nevertheless, several formal amendments have played an important role in expanding democracy in the United States by ending slavery; extending voting rights to African Americans, women, and young people ages 18–20; and making the selection of senators the business of voters, not state legislatures.

The Constitution is also changed by decisions and interpretations of the U.S. Supreme Court found in the written opinions of the justices. In *Marbury v. Madison* (1803), the Court claimed the power of **judicial review**—the right to declare the actions of the other branches of government null and void if they are contrary to the Constitution—even though such a power is not specifically mentioned in the Constitution (see Chapter 14 for a full discussion of judicial review). In *Griswold v. Connecticut* (1965), and later in *Roe v. Wade* (1973), actually, to take two more examples, the Court supported a claim for the existence of a fundamental right to privacy even though such a right is not explicitly mentioned in the Constitution. Many conservatives believe that such actions by the Supreme Court are illegitimate because they go beyond the original intentions of the framers, or cannot be justified in the written provisions of the Constitution. Many others disagree, believing that the Court has and must interpret the Constitution in light of changing circumstances that the framers could not have envisioned.

The meaning of the Constitution also changes through changing political practices, which end up serving as precedents for political actors. Political parties, party primaries, and presidential nominating conventions are not mentioned in the Constitution, for example, but it would be hard to think about American politics today without them. It is also fair to say that the framers would not recognize the modern presidency, which is now a far more important office than they envisioned, a change that has been brought about largely by the political and military involvement of the United States in world affairs, tied to vigorous assertion of the office's diplomatic and

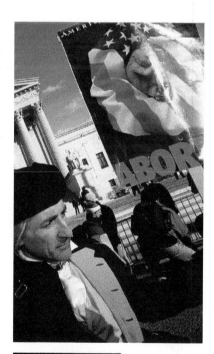

VOICING CONCERNS AT THE COURT

The Constitution has evolved over the years in three ways: through the amendment process, through evolving political practices, and through the Supreme Court's changing interpretation of the Constitution's meaning. Here antiabortion protesters demonstrate in front of the Supreme Court building on the anniversary of the Court's *Roe v. Wade* decision to demand a reversal of that landmark decision. How does the Constitution protect both the Supreme Court's decision and these people's public protest of it? How likely is it that the present Supreme Court will listen to these and other voices and overturn *Roe*?

2.1

2.2

2.3

2.4

2.5

2.6

signing statement
A document sometimes issued by the president in connection with the signing of a bill from Congress that sets out the president's understanding of the new law and how executive branch officials should carry it out.

commander-in-chief powers by many presidents, and the widespread demand that the president do something during economic crises. The Constitution does not specify, for example, that the Treasury secretary, acting for the president, can force the merger of failing financial firms as was done in the last months of the George W. Bush presidency in the depths of the recession. Nor would they have predicted the increasing use of **signing statements** (see the chapter-opening story) by which a president can alter the meaning of a bill even while signing it into law.

Throughout this book you will see many examples of these three forms of constitutional change that have shaped our current understanding of the meaning of the Constitution and its many provisions. You also will learn that the third factor, changing political practices—itself a product of social and cultural change and pressure from the American people—is at least as important as amendments and judicial rulings in adjusting the Constitution to its times.[43]

Using the DEMOCRACY STANDARD

How democratic is the Constitution?

Scarred by the failings of the Articles of Confederation, the framers endeavored to create a republic that would offer representative democracy without the threat of majority tyranny. Consequently, they wrote a number of provisions into the Constitution to control the purported excesses of democracy. These include the separation of powers into executive, legislative, and judicial branches; checks and balances to prevent any of the branches from governing on its own; federalism to fragment government powers between a national government and the states; an appointed federal judiciary with life tenure charged with, among other things, protecting private property; selection of the president by the Electoral College; election of members of the Senate by state legislatures; and a process for changing the Constitution that makes it exceedingly easy for small numbers of people in Congress and a very few states to block amendments favored by a majority of Americans.

Although the framers had every intention of creating a republic and holding democracy in check, the tide of democracy has gradually transformed the original constitutional design. For example, the Seventeenth Amendment created a Senate whose members are directly elected by the people. The Supreme Court, moreover, has extended civil rights protections to racial and ethnic minorities. And, the presidency has become both more powerful and more attentive to majority opinion. By formal amendment, through judicial interpretations, and through changing political practices, government has been fashioned into a more responsive set of institutions that, eventually, must heed the voice of the people.

Yet it can be argued that, despite these changes, the American system of government remains essentially "republican" in nature, with the majority finding it very difficult to prevail. Provisions of the Constitution, designed to keep the majority in check, effectively provide minorities with disproportionate power in government. For example, four times in our history, presidents have taken office after an election without having won a majority of the popular vote (John Quincy Adams, 1825; Rutherford B. Hayes, 1877; Benjamin Harrison, 1889; George W. Bush, 2001). And while the Seventeenth Amendment did make the election of senators more democratic, the Senate itself—which provides equal representation to all states regardless of population—remains skewed toward smaller states, thus serving as a major barrier in the translation of what the American people want into what government does.[44] Moreover, as we will see in later chapters, the ability of private and privileged groups to use the many blocking points provided by the Constitution has grown, often frustrating majority interests and demands.

Review the Chapter

 Listen to **Chapter 2** on **MyPoliSciLab**

The American Revolution and the Declaration of Independence

2.1 Assess the enduring legacies of the American Revolution and the Declaration of Independence, p. 28

The Revolutionary War and the Declaration of Independence helped establish the ideas of self-government and inalienable individual rights as the core of the American political ideology.

The Articles of Confederation: The First Constitution

2.2 Describe the governmental system established by our first constitution, p. 31

The first constitution joining the American states was the Articles of Confederation. Under its terms, the states were organized into a loose confederation in which the states retained full sovereignty and the central government had little power.

Factors Leading to the Constitutional Convention

2.3 Analyze the developments that led to the Constitutional Convention, p. 32

Defects in the Articles of Confederation, along with fears that democratic and egalitarian tendencies were beginning to spin out of control, prompted American leaders to gather in Philadelphia to amend the Articles. The delegates chose instead to formulate an entirely new constitution.

The Constitutional Convention

2.4 Evaluate the framework for government that emerged from the Constitutional Convention, p. 36

The framers created a constitutional framework for republican government including representative elections, separation of powers, checks and balances, and federalism.

The Connecticut Compromise settled the tensions between large and small states by giving states equal representation in the Senate and representation based on population in the House of Representatives.

The framers legitimated slavery.

The framers created the legal foundations for a thriving commercial republic.

The Struggle to Ratify the Constitution

2.5 Explain the difficulties of ratifying the Constitution, p. 49

The Constitution was ratified in an extremely close vote of the states after a hard-fought struggle between the Federalists, who wanted a more centralized republicanism, and the Anti-Federalists, who wanted small-scale republicanism.

The promise by the Federalists to introduce amendments specifying the rights of Americans in the 1st Congress helped swing the vote in favor of ratification in a number of key states.

Despite its "close shave," the Constitution became very popular among the American people within only a few years of the ratification fight.

The Changing Constitution, Democracy, and American Politics

2.6 Identify three processes by which the Constitution changes, p. 51

The Constitution changes by three processes: amendments to the document, judicial interpretations of the meaning of constitutional provisions, and the everyday political practices of Americans and their elected leaders.

Because the American people continue to struggle for democracy, the Constitution has become far more democratic over the years than was originally intended by the framers.

Learn the Terms

 Study and **Review** the **Flashcards**

Test Yourself

✓ **Study** and **Review** the **Practice Tests**

Answer key begins on page T-1.

2.1 Assess the enduring legacies of the American Revolution and the Declaration of Independence

1. At the time of the American Revolution, this concept was understood as the preservation of traditional rights against the intrusion of a distant government.

   a. Democracy
   b. Popular sovereignty
   c. Political equality
   d. Liberty
   e. Justice

2.2 Describe the governmental system established by our first constitution

2. According to the Articles of Confederation, all national laws had to be approved by:

   a. 6 of the 13 states
   b. 7 of the 13 states
   c. 8 of the 13 states
   d. 9 of the 13 states
   e. 10 of the 13 states

2.3 Analyze the developments that led to the Constitutional Convention

3. Some states passed these types of acts, which forbade farm foreclosures for nonpayment of debts.

   a. Farm acts
   b. Agriculture acts
   c. Revolutionary acts
   d. Stay acts
   e. Debt acts

4. Shays's Rebellion took place in reaction to:

   a. Increased taxes to pay off war debts
   b. Increased taxes and the imprisonment of debtors
   c. Dropping prices for crops, increase in taxes, and an insistence that note holders be paid in full by the state
   d. An increase in taxes, and an insistence that note holders be paid in full by the state
   e. Dropping prices for crops and increased taxes

2.4 Evaluate the framework for government that emerged from the Constitutional Convention

5. This plan proposed the creation of a strong central government dominated by a powerful bicameral congress that would be controlled by the most populous states.

   a. New Jersey Plan
   b. Massachusetts Plan
   c. Virginia Plan
   d. Pennsylvania Plan
   e. Maryland Plan

2.5 Explain the difficulties of ratifying the Constitution

6. Those who supported the Constitution were known as:

   a. Federalists
   b. Anti-Federalists
   c. Supremacists
   d. Compromisers
   e. Revolutionists

2.6 Identify three processes by which the Constitution changes

7. How many amendments are in the Bill of Rights?

   a. 5
   b. 10
   c. 12
   d. 15
   e. 20

54

Explore Further

INTERNET SOURCES

The Library of Congress and The Articles of Confederation **www.loc.gov/rr/program/bib/ourdocs/articles.html**. An overview of the Articles of Confederation with numerous links to other sources involving the writing and development of the articles.

The Avalon Project: Notes on the Debates at the Federal Convention **avalon.law.yale.edu**. As complete a compilation as exists on Madison's notes and the less complete but important notes of other participants.

Best of History Websites **besthistorysites.net/index.php/american-history/1700/constitution**. A comprehensive collection of links to websites about early American history.

Biographical Sketches of the Delegates to the Constitutional Convention **www.archives.gov/exhibits/charters/constitution_founding_fathers.html**. Profiles of the delegates to the Constitutional Convention.

Political Science Resources: Political Thought **www.politicalresources.net**. A vast collection of documents on democracy, liberty, and constitutionalism around the world.

SUGGESTIONS FOR FURTHER READING

Ellis, Joseph J. *Founding Brothers: The Revolutionary Generation.* New York: Alfred Knopf, 2001.

An entertaining and accessible look at the intertwined lives of the men who wrote the Declaration of Independence, fought the Revolutionary War, fashioned the Constitution, and launched the new American government.

Levinson, Sanford. *Our Undemocratic Constitution: Where the Constitution Goes Wrong.* New York: Oxford University Press, 2006.

An argument by a leading constitutional scholar that the framers did their job of protecting against majority rule so well that it severely cripples American democracy today.

Rossiter, Clinton, ed. *The Federalist Papers.* New York: New American Library, 1961.

Classic commentaries on the Constitution and its key provisions, written by Alexander Hamilton, John Jay, and James Madison.

Storing, Herbert J. *What the Anti-Federalists Were For.* Chicago: University of Chicago Press, 1981.

The most complete collection available on the published views of the Anti-Federalists. Includes convincing commentary by Storing.

Sunstein, Cass R. *A Constitution of Many Minds: Why the Founding Document Doesn't Mean What It Meant Before.* Princeton, NJ: Princeton University Press, 2009.

An analysis of why the meaning of the Constitution has changed over the course of American history and will do so in the future.

Wood, Gordon S. *The Creation of the American Republic.* New York: W. W. Norton, 1972.

The most exhaustive and respected source on America's changing ideas during the period 1776–1787, or from the start of the American Revolution to the writing of the Constitution.

Wood, Gordon S. *The Radicalism of the American Revolution.* New York: Alfred Knopf, 1992.

Examines and rejects the argument that the American Revolution was merely a political and not a social and economic revolution.

3

Federalism: States and Nation

THE AFFORDABLE CARE ACT'S PYRRHIC VICTORY?

he Supreme Court's ruling in 2012 to uphold the constitutionality of the Affordable Care Act of 2010 surprised nearly everyone. While President Barack Obama, Democrats and liberals hoped for the best, contingency plans were in place to make the Court's rejection of the Obama administration's most defining piece of legislation a center-piece of the 2012 presidential election campaign. Conservative legal scholars and Republican leaders and activists for the most part were confident that the Court's five-member conservative majority would side with the twenty-six Republican state attorneys-general who had filed suit against the Act who had claimed that it unconstitutionally expanded the power of the federal government over the states and the people, particularly with regard to its mandate that everyone secure health insurance on pain of a financial penalty for those who did not. For the most part, liberals and Democrats rejoiced on hearing news of the ruling; conservatives and Republicans seemed both surprised and angry, with the conservative talk shows and blogs filled with attacks on Chief Justice John Roberts for abandoning the cause. Things may not be as they first appeared on first viewing, however. The seeming endorsement by the Court of a massive increase in the federal government's role and power in the American federal system may turn out in the long run to diminish the federal government's continued growth relative to the states. There are a number of reasons why this may be so. They are related to the interpretation of two constitutional provisions that Congress and presidents have used to expand the national government, the commerce clause and the spending power. Both took a hit in the Court's ruling in *National Federation of Independent Business v. Sebelius* (2012).[1]

3.1	3.2	3.3	3.4	3.5
Define federalism and explain why we have it, p. 60	Establish the basis for federalism in the Constitution, p. 62	Trace the evolution of American federalism, p. 66	Analyze how federal grants structure national and state government relations, p. 78	Evaluate the arguments for and against federalism, p. 83

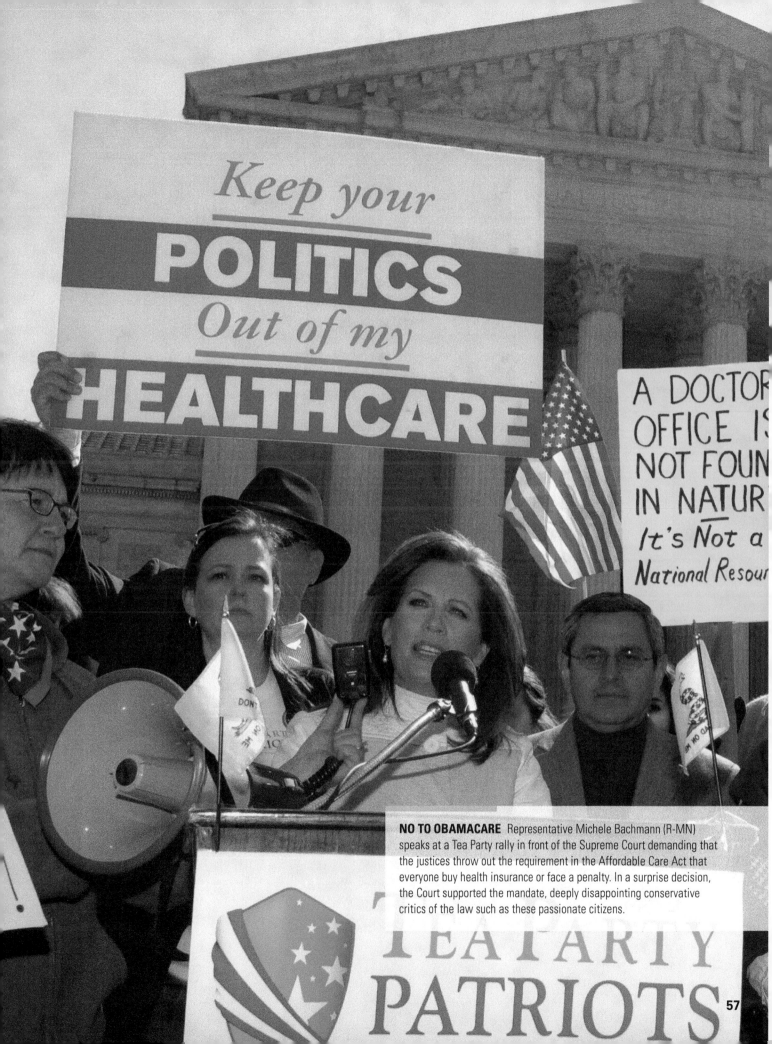

NO TO OBAMACARE Representative Michele Bachmann (R-MN) speaks at a Tea Party rally in front of the Supreme Court demanding that the justices throw out the requirement in the Affordable Care Act that everyone buy health insurance or face a penalty. In a surprise decision, the Court supported the mandate, deeply disappointing conservative critics of the law such as these passionate citizens.

MyPoliSciLab Video Series

◉ **Watch** on **MyPoliSciLab**

The Big Picture How did the national government become so much more powerful than state governments? Author Edward S. Greenberg traces the change to the Constitution itself and to a number of economic, social, and international developments.

The Basics Are you a states-right advocate? This video will help you understand how powers and responsibilities are divided between the national and state governments. You'll also discover how the powers of the national government have expanded and consider whether this is in the best interests of the people.

Should the national government have so much power?

In Context What is the primary mechanism for federalism in the United States? In this video, Barnard College political scientist Scott L. Minkoff explains how the national government tries to force state governments to adopt its policies and how state governments respond.

Think Like a Political Scientist Find answers to the most current questions that scholars of federalism are raising in the areas of welfare reform and state rights. Barnard College political scientist Scott L. Minkoff explores the challenges faced by state-rights advocates once they are elected to Congress.

In the Real World Should the federal government be allowed to mandate health care reform or should that power belong to the states? Hear supporters and detractors of Obamacare explain their opinions, and learn about the recent Supreme Court decision that handed this power to the federal government.

So What? Should the national government be involved in student loan programs? What about disaster aid? Author Edward S. Greenberg defines federalism and encourages students to decide if they believe in a strong central government or in stronger state governments.

President Obama and Democratic leaders in Congress based their health care reform legislation on the commerce clause—which gives Congress the power to regulate interstate commerce and of which Chief Justice John Marshall write in an 1824 opinion that "Congress may exercise [it] to its utmost extent"—a reliable foundation for most of the major legislative landmarks of Franklin Roosevelt's New Deal during the 1930s and Lyndon Johnson's Great Society during the 1960s. New Deal efforts to boost agricultural prices during the Great Depression by limiting the acreage that could be planted with particular crops that would eventually be directly or indirectly put into interstate commerce, for example, was upheld by the Court as were similar programs legislated in the years since. To take another example, the "public accommodations" section of the 1964 Civil Rights Act barred denial of service to people on the basis of race in hotels and restaurants because such businesses use products in their establishments that are invariably purchased across state lines (bed linens, towels, soap, napkins, vegetables, salt and pepper, dishes and glasses, and the like). In *NFIB*, however, Justice Roberts joined his four conservative colleagues in firmly rejecting this justification of the Affordable Care Act saying that, while Congress may regulate existing commerce, it cannot force people into commerce by requiring them to buy health insurance. Roberts wrote that "the commerce clause is not a general license to regulate an individual from cradle to grave." The Affordable Care Act can only be justified, he wrote, under Congress's power to tax, with the penalty tied to non-purchase of health insurance under the Act nothing more or less than a tax, and a modest one at that.

Though the Court upheld the Act, then, it struck a blow at one of the foundation stones of federal government power, and probably portends future limitations on Washington. Liberal Harvard University professor Laurence Tribe said of this, "There may be a dark gray lining: it is the Court's narrowing of the federal commerce power....the narrowing might be the longest-lasting doctrinal legacy of the ruling." Libertarian attorney David Rivkin celebrated despite approval of the Act, saying that the Court's interpretation of the commerce clause is the "ultimate silver lining....it reaffirms with enormous vigor the fundamental limits to the government's power. The administration sailed under the flag of the commerce clause and it was decisively rebuked. No one will try to do this type of mandate again...We won on the principle."

In another section of the ruling, Roberts and the Court's other conservatives (Alito, Kennedy, Scalia, and Thomas) said that the Affordable Care Act's expansion of the Medicaid program to cover more uninsured Americans was unconstitutional because it represented a coercive use of the Congress's spending power (the Constitution includes the proviso that Congress can lay and collect taxes and spend such revenues to "provide for the common Defence and general Welfare of the United States"). Though the Act provided that the federal government would pay 100 percent of the cost of the expansion of Medicaid for the first two years and 90 percent thereafter, it also imposed a cut-off of all federal Medicaid monies (not simply the new, expanded Medicaid) to states that refused to participate. The Court said Congress had gone too far. This represents the very first time since the New Deal that the Supreme Court has struck down Congress's spending power for use as an inducement for the states to participate in a federal program and may have the a profound impact over the long run. For example, the federal government places many conditions on the grants it gives to the states as a way to meet national objectives on such things as environmental protection, non-discrimination against racial and ethnic minorities, and highway safety standards.

The commerce clause has been used to justify many things that most Americans now take for granted, such as protection of wetlands against destructive development, regulation of the safety of the food supply, and protection of women, the disabled, and ethnic and racial minorities against discrimination. The spending power has been used to justify programs that are now familiar and widely accepted including giving girls an equal opportunity to participate in sports in colleges and universities and providing health care and food assistance for poor families. With the Robert's Court now firmly committed to a more restricted view of Congress's powers under the commerce clause and the spending power, it is likely that many cases will be brought to the courts by Republicans, conservatives, and business groups questioning the constitutionality of a broad range of federal programs. In *National Federation of Independent Business v. Sebelius*, advocates of an activist national government may have won the battle but may yet lose the war.

federalism

A system in which governmental powers are divided between a central government and smaller units, such as states.

confederation

A loose association of states or territorial divisions in which very little power or no power at all is lodged in a central government.

unitary system

A system in which a central government has complete power over its constituent units or states.

Thinking Critically About This Chapter

This complex mixture of state and national government authority and responsibilities highlighted in the chapter-opening story is an important characteristic of American federalism today and in the past.

Using the Framework

In this chapter, you will learn how and why federalism is one of the most important structural factors that affect American politics and government and shape public policy. You will learn how federalism influences our entire system, from the kinds of political parties we have and the workings of Congress to how domestic programs are affected. You will also learn how federalism itself has changed over time.

Using the Democracy Standard

Using the evaluative tools you learned in Chapter 1, you will be able to judge for yourself whether federalism enriches or diminishes democracy in the United States.

Federalism as a System of Government

3.1 Define federalism and explain why we have it

The United States is full of governments. We have not only a federal government in Washington, D.C., but also governments in each of the 50 states and in each of thousands of smaller governmental units, such as counties (about 3,000 of them), cities, towns and townships, school districts, and special districts that deal with such matters as parks and sanitation.

All these governments are organized and related to one another in a particular way. The small governments—those of counties, cities, towns, and special districts—are legal creations of state governments. They can be created, changed, or abolished by state legislatures or by state constitutional revisions, at the convenience of the states or its voters. But state governments themselves have much more weight and permanence because of their prominent place in the Constitution. Together with the central government in Washington, D.C., they form what is known as a federal system. The federal system is part of the basic structure of U.S. government, deeply rooted in our Constitution and history. It is one of the most important features of American politics, since it affects practically everything.

☐ The Nature of Federalism

Federalism is a system under which significant government powers are divided between the central government and smaller units, such as states or provinces. Neither one completely controls the other; each has some room for independent action. A federal system can be contrasted with two other types of government: a confederation and a unitary government. In a **confederation**, the constituent states get together for certain common purposes but retain ultimate individual authority and can veto major central governmental actions. The United Nations and the American government under the Articles of Confederation are examples. In a **unitary system**, the central government has all the power and can change its constituent units or tell them what to do. China, Japan, Turkey, Iran, and France have this kind of government, as do a substantial majority of nations around the world. These three different types of governmental systems are contrasted in Figure 3.1.

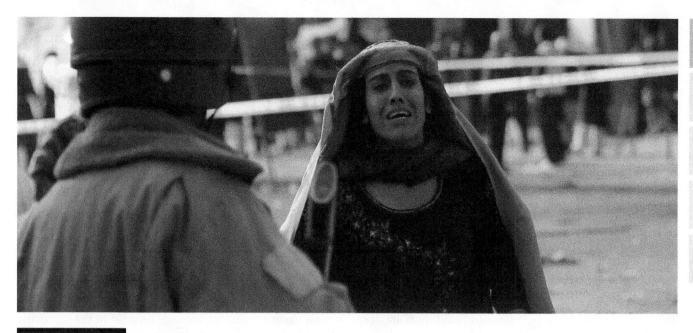

SECTARIAN VIOLENCE IN AFGHANISTAN

Deep divisions among Pashtuns, Tajiks, Uzbeks, Hazaris, and Turkmen, as well as religious differences between Shi'ite and Sunni Muslims, mean that the new government in Afghanistan will probably take the form of a federation after the dust settles there. This women mourns in the aftermath of the bombing of a Shi-ite mosque by a Pashtun Sunni group in 2011. Were there deep ethnic and religious divisions among America's framers? If so, how did it affect their design of federalism?

Comparing American Federalism

Some of the elements of federalism go back in history at least as far as the Union of Utrecht in the Netherlands in 1579, but federalism as it exists today is largely an American invention[2], although it has come to take on a variety of forms internationally. Including the United States, only 18 nations, accounting for more than one-third of the world's population and 40 percent of its land area, are however, federal in nature.[3]

HISTORICAL ORIGINS OF AMERICAN FEDERALISM American federalism emerged from the way in which the states declared independence from Britain—becoming, in

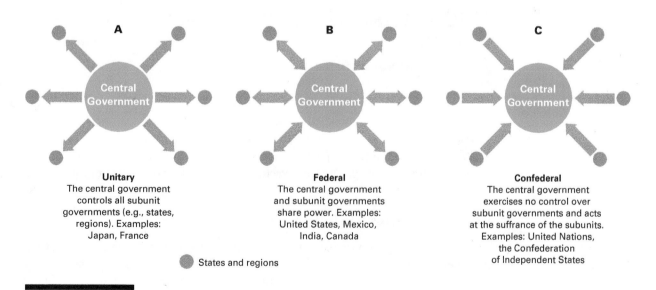

A

Unitary
The central government controls all subunit governments (e.g., states, regions). Examples: Japan, France

B

Federal
The central government and subunit governments share power. Examples: United States, Mexico, India, Canada

C

Confederal
The central government exercises no control over subunit governments and acts at the suffrance of the subunits. Examples: United Nations, the Confederation of Independent States

States and regions

FIGURE 3.1 TYPES OF POLITICAL SYSTEMS

A majority of countries have unitary systems (A), in which the central government controls the state and local governments, which in turn exert power over citizens. The United States, however, has a federal system (B), in which the central government has power on some issues, the states have power on other issues, and the central and state governments share power on yet others. In a confederation (C), the central institutions have only a loose coordinating role, with real governing power residing in the constituent states or units.

effect, separate countries—and then joined to form a confederation, and then a single nation, as discussed in Chapter 2. Recall that the framers of the Constitution turned to federalism as a middle-ground solution between a confederation form of government—which was deemed a failed model based on the experience under the Articles of Confederation—and a unitary form of government—which a majority of states, jealous of their independence and prerogatives, found unacceptable. Conveniently, federalism also was a form of government that was consistent with the eighteenth-century republicanism of the framers to the extent that it further fragments government power. But we can gain further insight into *why* the United States adopted and has continued as a federal system if we look at what other countries with similar systems have in common.

ROLE OF SIZE AND DIVERSITY Federalism tends to be found in nations that are large in a territorial sense and in which the various geographical regions are fairly distinctive from one another in terms of religion, ethnicity, language, and forms of economic activity. In Canada, for example, the farmers of the central plains are not much like the fishers of Nova Scotia, and the French-speaking (and primarily Catholic) residents of Quebec differ markedly from the mostly English-speaking Protestants of the rest of the country. In Spain there are deep divisions along ethnic and language lines (as in the distinctive Basque and Catalán regions).[4] Other important federal systems include such large and richly diverse countries as India, Pakistan, Russia, and Brazil. In all these countries, federalism gives diverse and geographically concentrated groups the degree of local autonomy they seem to want, with no need to submit in all matters to a unified central government.

The United States, too, is large and diverse. From the early days of the republic, the slave-holding and agriculture-oriented South was quite distinct from the mercantile Northeast, and some important differences persist today. Illinois is not Louisiana; the farmers of Iowa differ from defense and electronics workers in California. States today also vary in their approaches to public policy, their racial and ethnic composition, and their political cultures.[5] In *The Federalist Papers*, the Founders argued that this size and diversity made federalism especially appropriate for the new United States.

While the American system of federalism was truly exceptional at the founding, other large and important countries have adopted federalism in the years since, especially since the end of World War II. To this extent, the United States is no longer the single exception or one among a handful of exceptions to the unitary nature of the majority of the world's governments.

Federalism in the Constitution

3.2 Establish the basis for federalism in the Constitution

ederalism is embodied in the U.S. Constitution in two main ways: (1) power is expressly given to the states, as well as to the national government, and (2) the states have important roles in shaping and choosing officials for the national government itself, and in amending the Constitution.

☐ Independent State Powers

Although the Constitution makes the central government supreme in certain matters, it also makes clear that state governments have independent powers. The **supremacy clause** in Article VI states that the Constitution, laws, and treaties of the United States shall be the "supreme law of the land," but Article I, Section 8, enumerates what kinds of laws Congress has the power to pass, and the **Tenth Amendment** declares that the powers not delegated to the central government by the Constitution or prohibited by the Constitution to the states are "*reserved to the states* [emphasis added] respectively, or to the people." This provision is known as the **reservation clause**.

In other words, the U.S. Constitution specifically lists what the national government can do. Its powers include authority to levy taxes, regulate interstate commerce, establish post offices, and declare war, plus make laws "necessary and proper" for carrying out those powers. The Constitution then provides that all other legitimate government functions may be performed by the states, except for a few things, such as coining money or conducting foreign policy, that are forbidden by Article I, Section 10. This leaves a great deal in the hands of state governments, including licensing lawyers, doctors, and dentists; regulating businesses within their boundaries; chartering banks and corporations; providing a system of family law; providing a system of public education; and assuming the responsibility for building roads and highways, licensing drivers, and registering cars. Under terms of the reservation clause, states exercise what are called their police powers to protect the health, safety, and general well-being of people living in their states. The police powers have allowed states to make decisions independent of the federal government and other states on matters such as stem-cell research, minimum gas mileage standards for cars, the death penalty, emissions of greenhouse gases, and the regulation of abortion services.[6] The reservation clause is unique to the United States and shows how important states are in American federalism. Other federal systems, such as Canada's and Germany's, reserve to the national government all functions not explicitly given to the states.

Lest this sound too clear-cut, there also are broad areas of overlapping or shared powers—called **concurrent powers**; both levels of government, for example, can and do levy taxes, borrow money for public purposes, and spend money for the protection and well-being of their populations (e.g., public health programs and product safety regulation). With both independent national and state powers and responsibilities, as well as concurrent or overlapping powers and responsibilities, the Constitution is not crystal clear about the exact shape of federalism, leaving ample room for the meaning of federalism to change with the times, the preferences of the American people, and the calculations of political leaders. Figure 3.2 shows how powers and responsibilities are distributed.

concurrent powers
Powers under the Constitution that are shared by the federal government and the states.

☐ The States' Roles in the National Government

Moreover, the Constitution's provisions about the formation of the national government recognize a special position for the states. The Constitution declares in Article VII that it was "done in Convention by the unanimous consent of the *states* present"

Federal Powers
- Coin money (and by extension, manage the currency and money supply)
- Conduct foreign relations
- Raise an army and navy
- Declare and conduct war (and by extension, provide national defense)
- Establish a federal court system to supplement the Supreme Court
- Regulate interstate commerce
- Establish a postal system
- Establish a system of patents and copyrights
- Make laws that are necessary and proper to carry out the foregoing powers

Concurrent Powers
- Tax
- Borrow money
- Establish courts
- Provide public safety
- Make and enforce laws
- Charter banks and corporations
- Spend money for the general welfare
- Take private property for public purposes, paying just compensation in return

State Powers
- Conduct elections
- Ratify amendments to the U.S. Constitution
- Provide public education
- Charter banks
- License professions
- Establish a system of family law
- Take measures for public health, safety, and morals
- Exercise powers that the Constitution does not specifically prohibit from the states, nor delegate to the national government
- Establish local governments
- Regulate commerce within the states

FIGURE 3.2 HOW RESPONSIBILITIES ARE DISTRIBUTED IN THE FEDERAL SYSTEM

horizontal federalism

Term used to refer to relationships among the states.

BUT LET ME TELL YOU, MR PRESIDENT

State governors and presidents have not always seen eye-to-eye on the issues but the level of conflict among Republican state leaders and Democratic president Barack Obama reached fever pitch during the national debate over health care reform and immigration in 2011 and 2012. Here Arizona governor Jan Brewer tells the president why her state passed harsh anti-immigration measures designed to purge her state of illegals. The Supreme Court later over-turned most of the state measure as an unconstitutional state intrusion on federal authority.

(emphasis added) and provides that the Constitution would go into effect, not when a majority of all Americans voted for it, but when the conventions of nine *states* ratified it. Article V provides that the Constitution can be amended only when conventions in or the legislatures of three-quarters of the states ratify an amendment. Article IV, Section 3, makes clear that no states can be combined or divided into new states without the consent of the state legislatures concerned. Thus, the state governments have charge of ratifying and amending the Constitution, and the states control their own boundaries.

The Constitution also provides special roles for the states in the selection of national government officials. The states decide who can vote for members of the U.S. House of Representatives (Article I, Section 2) and draw the boundaries of House districts. Each state is given two senators (Article V) who were, until 1913, to be chosen by the state legislatures rather than by the voters (Article I, Section 3; altered by the Seventeenth Amendment). And the states play a key part in the complicated Electoral College system of choosing a president in which each state has votes equal to the number of its senators and representatives combined, with the president elected by a majority of electoral votes, not a majority of popular votes (Article II, Section 1).

☐ Relations Among the States

The Constitution also regulates relations among the states (these state-to-state relations are sometimes called **horizontal federalism**). Article IV of the Constitution is particularly important in this regard (see Table 3.1). For example, each state is required to give "full faith and credit" to the public acts, records, and judicial proceedings of every other state. This means that private contractual or financial agreements among people or companies

TABLE 3.1 CONSTITUTIONAL UNDERPINNINGS OF FEDERALISM

Provisions	Where to Find Them in the Constitution	What It Means
Supremacy of the national government in its own sphere	Supremacy clause: Article VI	The supremacy clause establishes that federal laws and the Constitution take precedence over state laws and constitutions.
Limitations on national government powers and reservation of powers to the states	Enumerated national powers: Article I, Section 8	The powers of the federal government are laid out specifically in the Constitution, as are strict limitations on the power of the federal government. Powers not specifically spelled out are reserved to the states or to the people.
	Limits on national powers: Article I, Section 9; Article IV, Section 3; Eleventh Amendment	
	Bill of Rights: First through Tenth Amendments	
	Reservation clause: Tenth Amendment	
Limitations on state powers	Original restrictions: Article I, Section 10	The Constitution places strict limitations on the power of the states in particular areas of activity.
	Civil War Amendments: Thirteenth through Fifteenth Amendments	Compels the states to uphold the civil liberties and civil rights of people living within their borders.
State role in national government	Ratification of Constitution: Article VII	The states' role in national affairs is clearly laid out. Rules for voting and electing representatives, senators, and the president are defined so that state governments play a part.
	Amendment of Constitution: Article V	
	Election of representatives: Article I, Section 2 and Section 4	
	Two senators from each state: Article I, Section 3	
	No deprivation of state suffrage in Senate: Article V	
	Choice of senators: Article I, Section 3 (however, see Seventeenth Amendment)	
	Election of president: Article II, Section 1 (however, see Twelfth Amendment)	
Regulation of relations among states	Full faith and credit: Article IV, Section 1	Constitutional rules ensure that the states must respect each other's legal actions and judgments.
	Privileges and immunities: Article IV, Section 2	Citizens from other states have same rights and privileges as a state's own citizens.

in one state are valid in all the other states and that civil judgments by the courts of one state must be recognized by the others. Because of this constitutional provision, people in one state cannot evade financial obligations—for example, credit card or department store debts and alimony or child-support payments—by moving to another state.

Many people who oppose same-sex marriage are afraid that the "full faith and credit" provision may be a way for this institution to become legal nationwide. Same-sex marriage is now legal in states: New York, Vermont, New Hampshire, Massachusetts, Connecticut, Washington, Maine, Maryland, and Iowa. When people of the same sex are married in these states, do they remain legally married when they move elsewhere? Are they eligible for federal benefits that go to married heterosexual couples? Worried about the possibility that such things might happen, Congress passed the Defense of Marriage Act (DOMA) in 1996 denying federal benefits (such as Medicaid and Medicare) to spouses in same-sex marriages and allowing states to decide whether or not to recognize the legal status of same-sex couples married in other states when such couples come within their boundaries. As of 2011, 41 have decided against same-sex marriage, either by statute or state constitutional amendment.[7] Opponents wonder whether the Supreme Court might yet decide that such statutes and amendments are unconstitutional based on "full faith and credit"; that states without same-sex marriage would be obligated to recognize marriages from other states. So far, the Court has not rendered such a decision and is unlikely to do so given its conservative leanings and its propensity to allow Congress broad latitude in regulating interstate relations. (Nor is the Court likely to rule same-sex marriage a fundamental right based on the "equal protection" clause of the Fourteenth Amendment [see Chapter 16].)

interstate compacts
Agreements among states to cooperate on solving mutual problems; requires approval by Congress.

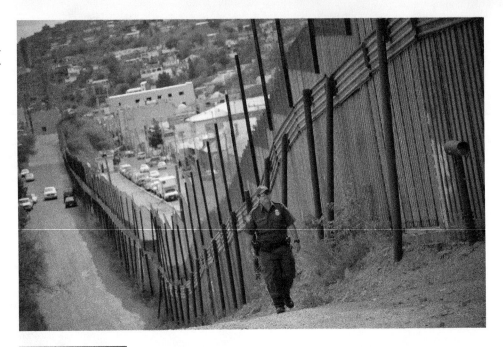

BORDER FENCE
How to control illegal immigration across the U.S.–Mexican border, and what to do about those who make it across, have become contentious issues between several border states and the federal government. Why might this be an issue where some state majorities conflict with the wishes of the national majority?

Article IV also specifies that the citizens of each state are entitled to all the "privileges and immunities" of the citizens in the several states. That means that whatever citizenship rights a person has in one state apply in the other states as well. For example, because of this provision, out-of-state residents have the same access to state courts as in-state residents, as well as an equal right to own property and to be protected by the police. However, the Supreme Court has never clearly defined the meaning of "privileges and immunities," nor have they been entirely consistent in applying them in practice. The Court has allowed states to charge students different tuition rates in their public universities, for example, depending on their in-state or out-of-state status (see the "Using the Framework" feature later in this chapter).

Agreements among a group of states to solve mutual problems, called **interstate compacts**, require the consent of Congress. The framers inserted this provision (Article I, Section 10) into the Constitution as a way to prevent the emergence of coalitions of states that might threaten federal authority or the union itself. Interstate compacts in force today cover a wide range of cooperative state activities. For example, New York and New Jersey created and Congress approved a compact to create the Port Authority of New York & New Jersey. Other compacts among states include agreements to cooperate on matters such as pollution control, crime prevention, transportation, and disaster planning.

The Evolution of American Federalism

3.3 Trace the evolution of American federalism

Explore on MyPoliSciLab
Simulation
You Are a Federal Judge

I t took a long time after the adoption of the Constitution for the present federal system to emerge. There were (and continue to be) ebbs and flows in the nature of the relationship between the states and national government and in the relative power of the states and the federal government as they interacted with one another.[8] Eventually, however, the national government gained ground.[9] There are many reasons for this:

- Economic crises and problems generated pressures on the government in Washington to do something to help fix the national economy. The Great Depression in the 1930s is the primary example, but even today, we expect the president, Congress, and the Federal Reserve to competently manage national economic affairs, something the states cannot do for themselves. Most Americans wanted the government in Washington to do something to get us out of the Great Recession and jobless recovery of 2008–2012, though many did not like what was done in the end (bailing out banks without limiting executive pay and bonuses, for example, or the big deficits that resulted from new government programs and declining tax revenues).

- War and the preparation for war are also important spurs to national-level actions, rather than state-level ones, because only the government in Washington can raise an army and a navy, generate sufficient revenues to pay for military campaigns, and coordinate the productive resources of the nation to make sustained war possible. It is no accident, then, that each of our major wars has served to enhance the power of government in Washington.

- Finally, a number of problems emerged over the course of our history that most political leaders and the public believed could be solved most effectively by the national government rather than by 50 separate state governments: air and water pollution; unsafe food, drugs, and consumer products; the denial of civil rights for racial minorities; anticompetitive practices by some large corporations; poverty; and more.

The Perpetual Debate About the Nature of American Federalism

From the very beginnings of our nation, two political philosophies have contended with one another over the nature of American federalism and the role to be played by the central government. These are generally referred to as the **nationalist position** and the states' rights position.

THE NATIONALIST POSITION Nationalists believe that the Constitution was formed by a compact among the people to create a single national community, pointing to the powerful phrase that opens the preamble: "We the People of the United States" (not "We the States"). Nationalists also point to the clear expression in the preamble of the purposes for which "we the people" formed a new government, namely to "create a more perfect union . . . and to promote the General Welfare." Also important in the nationalist brief are provisions in the Constitution that point toward a strong central government with expansive responsibilities, including the "commerce clause," the "supremacy clause," and the "elastic" or **"necessary and proper" clause**. Not surprisingly, proponents of the nationalist position such as Alexander Hamilton, Chief Justice John Marshall, Abraham Lincoln, Woodrow Wilson, and the two Roosevelts (Theodore and Franklin) advocated an active national government with the capacity and the will to tackle whatever problems might emerge to threaten the peace and prosperity of the United States or the general welfare of its people. Liberal Democrats, including Barack Obama, are the main proponents of this position today, believing that civil rights and environmental protection, for example, are safer in the hands of the federal government than the state governments.

THE STATES' RIGHTS POSITION Proponents of the states' rights position argue that the Constitution was created as a compact among the states and that the framers meant for the states to be coequal with the national government. They base their argument on a number of things. They note, for instance, that the Constitution was written by representatives of the states; that it was ratified by the states and not by a vote of the public; and that the process for amending the Constitution requires the affirmative votes of three-fourths of the states, not three-fourths of the people. They

nationalist position
The view of American federalism that holds that the Constitution created a system in which the national government is supreme, relative to the states, and that it granted that government a broad range of powers and responsibilities.

necessary and proper clause
Article I, Section 8, of the Constitution, also known as the *elastic clause*; gives Congress the authority to make whatever laws are necessary and proper to carry out its enumerated powers and the responsibilities mentioned in the Constitution's preamble.

3.1

3.2

3.3

3.4

3.5

states' rights position
The view of American federalism that holds that the Constitution created a system of dual sovereignty in which the national government and the state governments are sovereign in their own spheres.

dual federalism
An interpretation of federalism in which the states and the national government have separate jurisdictions and responsibilities.

nullification
An attempt by states to declare national laws or actions null and void.

also point to the Tenth Amendment's "reservation" clause, which says, as we pointed out earlier, that powers not given to the national government nor denied to the states reside in the states and the people.

Not surprisingly, proponents of the **states' rights position** have argued that the Constitution created a form of government in which the national government is strictly limited in size and responsibility and in which states retain broad autonomy in the conduct of their own affairs. Popular among states' rights proponents is the concept of **dual federalism**, which suggests that, much like in a layer cake, there are distinct, nonoverlapping areas of responsibility for the national government and the state governments and that each level of government is sovereign in its own sphere. Thomas Jefferson, John C. Calhoun, the New England and Southern secessionists, the Southern resistors to the civil rights revolution, and many contemporary conservative Republican Tea Party activists are associated with this view of federalism.

We shall see in the pages ahead that the nationalist view has prevailed over the long haul of American history. (See Figure 3.3 for an overview of this history.) However, the states' rights view has always been and remains today a vital position from which to oppose too much power and responsibility in the government in Washington. After the Affordable Care Act was passed in 2010, for example, several states passed laws proclaiming that the mandatory health insurance provisions of the national law did not hold within their boundaries, and 26 state attorneys general took the issue to the federal courts. As we saw in the chapter-opening story, the Supreme Court ruled against the states regarding the mandate.

☐ Federalism Before the Civil War

In the late 1790s, during the administration of John Adams, Thomas Jefferson's Democratic Republicans deeply resented the Alien and Sedition Acts, which the Federalists used to punish political dissent by followers of Jefferson. In response, Jefferson and Madison secretly authored the Virginia and Kentucky Resolutions, which declared that the states did not have to obey unconstitutional national laws and left it to the states to decide what was unconstitutional. In this case, the Democratic Republicans, representing the more agricultural South, were advocating states' rights and the principle of dual federalism against a national government run by the more merchant-oriented Federalists of the Northeast. About a decade later, however, the merchants of New England used the Southerners' own arguments to oppose President Madison's War of 1812 against Britain, which they felt interfered with their trade. Neither of these efforts at **nullification** prevailed.

One crucial question about federalism in the early years of the United States concerned who, if anyone, would enforce the supremacy clause. Who would make sure that the U.S. laws and Constitution were actually the "supreme law of the land," controlling state laws? The answer turned out to be the U.S. Supreme Court, but this answer emerged only gradually and haltingly as the Court established its power within the federal system. Only after the strong-willed and subtle John Marshall became chief justice and, in 1803, established the Supreme Court's authority to declare national laws unconstitutional (called judicial review; discussed in detail in Chapter 14) did the Supreme Court turn to the question of national power relative to the states. In *Fletcher v. Peck* (1810), it established the power of judicial review over the states, holding a state law unconstitutional under the U.S. Constitution.[10] Chief Justice Marshall cleverly avoided explicit discussion of the Court's power of judicial review over state laws. He simply took it for granted and used it.

The Supreme Court also provided crucial legal justification for the expansion of federal government power in the historic case of *McCulloch v. Maryland* (1819), which affirmed the supremacy clause and declared that Congress had broad powers under the "necessary and proper" clause. The case involved action by the state of Maryland to impose a tax on the Bank of the United States. The state of Maryland argued

1788
Constitution replaces
Articles of Confederation

1803
Marbury v. Madison

1810
Fletcher v. Peck

1819
McCulloch v. Maryland

1824
Gibbons v. Ogden

1860–1865
Civil War

1865–1870
Adoption of Thirteenth,
Fourteenth, and Fifteenth
amendments to Constitution

1870–1914
**INDUSTRIAL REVOLUTION, RISE OF
MODERN CORPORATION AND
URBAN WORKING CLASS**

1903–1916
Progressive reform movement
and legislation

1917–1918
U.S. participation in World War I

1925
Gitlow v. New York

1941–1945
U.S. participation in World War II

1929–1941
The Great Depression
(New Deal begins in 1993)

1954–1965
Civil Rights revolution

1954
Brown v. Board of Education

**1945–1989
COLD WAR AGAINST
SOVIET UNION**

1965–1968
LBJ's "Great Society"

1964
Wesberry v. Sanders

1965
Griswold v. Connecticut

1970s
Environmental and consumer
protection legislation

1980–1988
Reagan presidency

2004–2007
State push-back on "No Child Left
Behind" and stem-cell research

2001
"No Child Left Behind" Act passed,
war on terror begins following 9/11

2009 February
Obama economic stimulus package

2008 February
Bush economic stimulus package

2010 March
Affordable Care Act

2012
SCT decisions on immigration and health care

FIGURE 3.3 TIMELINE: LANDMARKS IN THE HISTORY OF U.S. FEDERALISM*

*The items on this timeline are discussed in this chapter and in Chapters 13–16.

preemption
Exclusion of the states from actions that might interfere with federal authority or statutes.

that the creation of the bank had been unconstitutional, exceeding the powers of Congress, and that, in any case, states could tax whatever they wanted within their own borders.

But Chief Justice Marshall upheld the constitutionality of the bank's creation and its immunity from taxation and, in the process, made a major statement justifying extensive national authority.[11] In his opinion for the Court, Marshall declared that the Constitution emanated from the sovereign people who had made their national government supreme to all rivals within the sphere of its powers, and those powers must be construed generously if they were to be sufficient for the "various crises" of the age to come. Congress, declared Marshall, had the power to incorporate the bank under the clause of Article I, Section 8, authorizing Congress to make all laws "necessary and proper" for carrying into execution its named powers. Moreover, Maryland's tax was invalid because "the power to tax involves the power to destroy," which would defeat the national government's supremacy. Justice Marshall's broad reading of the *necessary and proper* clause laid the foundation for an expansion of what the national government could do in the years ahead. He made it clear that states would not be allowed to interfere.

In several later cases, the Supreme Court also ruled that provisions of the U.S. Constitution excluded the states from acting in certain areas where they might interfere with federal statutes or authority. According to this doctrine known as **preemption**, which remains in place today,[12] states cannot act in certain matters when the national government has authority. The Supreme Court's rejection in 2012 of much of Arizona's immigration law was based on this doctrine.

☐ The Civil War and the Expansion of National Power

The Civil War profoundly affected the relationship between the states and the national government. First, the unconditional Southern surrender decisively established that

OUR BLOODY CIVIL WAR

One important principle of American federalism was settled by the Civil War: the nation is indissoluble; no state or group of states can decide on its own to withdraw from it. Establishing that principle required a bloody contest of arms. Here, Union soldiers rest in camp after an engagement with Confederate troops. Why was this outcome so crucial to the survival of the country?

the Union was indissoluble; states could not withdraw or secede. Hardly any American now questions the permanence of the Union.

Second, passage of what has become known as the **Civil War Amendments** resulted in constitutional changes that subordinated the states to certain new national standards, enforced by the central government. For example, the Thirteenth Amendment abolished slavery, and the Fifteenth gave former male slaves and their descendants a constitutional right to vote. (This right was enforced by the national government for a short time after the Civil War; it was then widely ignored until passage of the 1965 Voting Rights Act.)

Most importantly, the Fourteenth Amendment (1868) included broad language limiting state power in a number of areas: it declared that no state shall "deprive any person of life, liberty, or property, without due process of law, nor deny to any person within its jurisdiction the equal protection of the laws." The **due process clause** eventually became the vehicle by which the Supreme Court ruled that many civil liberties in the Bill of Rights, which originally protected people only against the national government, also provided protections against the states (see Chapter 15). And the **equal protection clause** eventually became the foundation for protecting the rights of African Americans, women, and other categories of people against discrimination by state or local governments (see Chapter 16).

Civil War Amendments
The Thirteenth, Fourteenth, and Fifteenth Amendments to the Constitution, adopted immediately after the Civil War, each of which represented the imposition of a national claim over that of the states.

due process clause
The section of the Fourteenth Amendment that prohibits states from depriving anyone of life, liberty, or property "without due process of law," a guarantee against arbitrary government action.

equal protection clause
The section of the Fourteenth Amendment that provides for equal treatment by government of people residing within the United States and each of its states.

☐ Expanded National Activity Since the Civil War

Since the Civil War, and especially during the twentieth century, the activities of the national government expanded greatly, so that they now touch on almost every aspect of daily life and are thoroughly entangled with state government activities.

THE LATE NINETEENTH CENTURY TO WORLD WAR I During the late nineteenth century, the national government was increasingly active in administering western lands, subsidizing economic development (granting railroads enormous tracts of land along their transcontinental lines, for example), helping farmers, and beginning to regulate business, particularly through the Interstate Commerce Act of 1887 and the Sherman Antitrust Act of 1890. Woodrow Wilson's New Freedom domestic legislation—including the Federal Reserve Act of 1913 and the Federal Trade Commission Act of 1914—spurred even greater national government involvement in social and economic issues, as did the great economic and military effort of World War I. During that war, for example, the War Industries Board engaged in a form of economic planning whose orders and regulations covered a substantial number of the nation's manufacturing firms.

THE NEW DEAL AND WORLD WAR II Still more important, however, was Franklin Roosevelt's New Deal of the 1930s. In response to the Great Depression, the New Deal created many new national regulatory agencies to supervise various aspects of business, including communications (the Federal Communications Commission, or FCC), airlines (the Civil Aeronautics Board, or CAB), financial markets (the Securities and Exchange Commission, or SEC), utilities (the Federal Power Commission, or FPC), and labor–management relations (the National Labor Relations Board, or NLRB). The New Deal also brought national government spending to such areas as welfare and relief, which had previously been reserved almost entirely to the states, and established the Social Security old-age pension system.

World War II involved a total economic and military mobilization to fight Germany and Japan. Not surprisingly, directing that mobilization, as well as collecting taxes to support it, planning for production of war materials, and bringing on board the employees to accomplish all of this, was centered in Washington, D.C., not in the states.

devolution

The delegation of power over and responsibilities for federal programs to state and/or local governments.

THE POST-WAR PERIOD TO THE 1990s Ever since World War II, the federal government has spent nearly twice as much per year as all of the states and localities put together. Much of the money has gone in direct payments to individuals (including, most especially, Social Security benefits) and for national defense, particularly during the height of the Cold War with the Soviet Union, and during the Vietnam War.

Two other trends in the last third of the twentieth century enhanced the role of the national government relative to the states. The first was the civil rights revolution (discussed in Chapters 8 and 16), and the second was the regulatory revolution, especially regulation related to environmental and consumer protection (discussed in Chapter 17). With respect to these, national standards, often fashioned by bureaucrats under broad legislative mandates and watched over by federal courts, were imposed on both states and localities. The civil rights revolution also had a great deal to do with the creation of Lyndon Johnson's Great Society program designed both to alleviate poverty and politically empower the poor and racial minorities. The Great Society not only increased the level of domestic spending but also increased the federal role in the political lives of states and localities.

THE SUPREME COURT'S LONG-TERM SUPPORT FOR THE NATIONALIST POSITION For several decades, beginning in the late nineteenth century, the U.S. Supreme Court resisted the growth in the federal government's power to regulate business. In 1895, for example, it said that the Sherman Antitrust Act could not forbid monopolies in manufacturing, since manufacturing affected interstate commerce only "indirectly." In 1918, the Court struck down as unconstitutional a national law regulating child labor. During the 1930s, the Supreme Court declared unconstitutional such important New Deal measures as the National Recovery Act and the Agricultural Adjustment Act.[13]

After 1937, perhaps chastened by President Roosevelt's attempt to enlarge the Supreme Court and appoint more friendly justices, the Court became a centralizing force, immediately upholding essential elements of the New Deal, including the Social Security Act and the National Labor Relations Act. In 1942 in *Wickard v. Filburn*, the Court said that Congress has very broad powers under the commerce clause to regulate economic activities even if such activities are only indirectly related to interstate commerce. Since that time, and until the Rehnquist Court began to rethink federalism questions in the 1990s, the Court upheld virtually every piece of national legislation that came before it, even when this legislation preempted or limited powers of the states.

An important example is the Civil Rights Act of 1964, which rests on a very broad *Wickard*-based reading of the commerce clause. In the 1964 act, the national government asserted a power to forbid discrimination at lunch counters and other public accommodations on the grounds that they are engaged in interstate commerce; restaurants serve food imported from out of state, for instance, while hotels buy bedding, towels, flooring, and bathroom fixtures from companies in a variety of states. State economies are so closely tied to each other that by this standard, practically every economic transaction everywhere affects interstate commerce and is therefore subject to national legislative power. Another example of the powerful impetus towards national supremacy by way of the commerce clause (and federal grants) is the interstate highway system, which we discuss in the "Can Government Do Anything Well?" feature.

DEVOLUTION During the 1980s and 1990s, **devolution**—the idea that some of the powers and responsibilities of the national government ought to be distributed back to the states—became popular. President Ronald Reagan made this one of the hallmarks of his administration, as did George H.W. Bush, who followed him in office. President Bill Clinton, a former governor of the state of Arkansas, was also an enthusiastic devotee of devolution, freely granting waivers from federal regulations to the states for

Can Government Do Anything Well?

The Interstate Highway System

The federal interstate highway system is so much a part of our lives and has been for so many years that it is hard to imagine a time in America when long-distance car and truck travel was by two-lane roads, rife with dangerous crossroads, innumerable access points to main highways from businesses, schools, and homes, and numerous traffic lights and stop signs in the more populated areas. Car travel and commercial truck transportation was slow and fairly dangerous compared to what was to come. Legislation for a new system of federal multilane, limited-access highways was proposed by Republican president Dwight Eisenhower and passed by Congress in 1956. The planned construction was completed in the early 1980s, but more highway miles have been added each year since then. Today its total length is almost 47,000 miles and it carries about one-fourth of all traffic in the United States though it comprises less than one percent of our highways. The system is funded by a tax of 18.4 cents per gallon on gasoline—unchanged since 1993—and most of its outlays today are for maintenance and repair.

Support for the claim that government should be responsible for providing and maintaining national infrastructure, such as interstate highways:
Conservative commentator George Will likes the interstates, calling them "the most successful public works programs in the history of the world." A little over the top, perhaps, but there is no denying the fact that the system helped push economic growth in the United States and bound us together as a nation.

The most important argument in favor of the federal government's role is that its actions have provided essential infrastructure that no other entity could plan, fund, and complete.

■ Most products that are used in the United States today get to their destinations by truck. Products come from factories and businesses here in the United States and from producers abroad, trucked to customers from container ports on the east, south, or west coasts, or across the Canadian and Mexican borders. The backbone of this truck-based distribution system is the interstate highway system. Without it, our economy would be less robust and efficient, and our everyday travel on roads shared with trucks would be less safe.

■ Left to itself, the private market has not and cannot provide this public good. We have seen no cases where private firms have built extensive and safe highways on a broad geographic scale that are not associated with the particular activity of their own businesses, say roads to bring out cut timber from forest plots or ores from mining sites. The reason is fairly obvious: though the economy and society as a whole benefit from the existence of such a road system, no single firm or set of firms has an economic interest in making an investment on this scale that might take decades to complete and to see economic payoffs. Nor could private firms secure the financing for such a project.

Rejection of the claim that government should be responsible for providing and maintaining national infrastructure, such as interstate highways:

■ There is, of course, the familiar argument that government cannot do anything well and that matters of economic and social development should best be left to the private sector. As Charles Murray has so directly put it in his book *What It Means to Be a Libertarian* (p. 147): "The reality of daily life is that, by and large, the things the government does tend to be ugly, rude, slovenly—and not to work."

■ Cato and the American Enterprise Institute, market-oriented think tanks, on the other hand, accept that the national government did the country a great service in creating the interstate highway system but that it is now so big and so complex that the system cannot be run effectively and efficiently, nor properly maintained and improved, by the federal government. Thinkers there favor either total private ownership or public–private partnerships, with revenues generated by tolls.

■ Critics from all political persuasions lament the fact that the system is showing signs of wear and tear; construction and maintenance are not keeping up with deteriorating roads and bridges. Conservatives believe it is because highway money has been diverted to non-highway purposes such as bike paths, mass transit, and historic preservation. Liberals believe the problem is not enough money in the highway trust fund and that the federal tax on gasoline is not high enough, falling orders of magnitude short of those in other rich democracies.

WHAT DO YOU THINK?

What do you think about the past, present, and future role of the government in the interstate highway system? Which of the following positions is closest to your own?

- The government should never undertake such large infrastructure projects.
- Building the interstate highway system represents one of the most successful government programs in the history of the United States and demonstrates the capacity of the public sector to engage in other large-scale projects in the future.
- The interstate highway system represents a government project that was successful in the past, but current infrastructure challenges cannot be handled by the government alone and will need private attention moving forward.

How would you defend this position to a fellow student? What would be your main line of argument? What evidence do you believe best supports your position? For help in developing your argument, please refer to the sources listed in the "Can Government Do Anything Well" feature in Chapter 2 on p. 48.

Additional sources for this feature: "Interstate Facts," The Federal Highway Administration (www.fhwa.dot.gov).

experimenting with new forms of welfare, boasting of cuts in federal government employment, and touting the benefits of state government. And the Republican majority in the 104th Congress, working with President Clinton (but few from his party), passed legislation restricting "unfunded mandates" (about which we will have more to say later) and transferring welfare responsibility to the states. The public seemed to be on board at the time. Polls showed, for example, that a substantial majority of Americans believed that state governments were more effective and more trustworthy than the government in Washington and more likely to be responsive to the people. And Americans said that they wanted state governments to do more and the federal government to do less.[14]

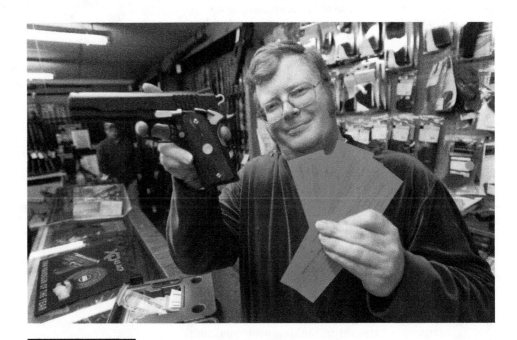

GUNS FOR SALE

Many states and localities have tried to ban the importation of guns into their jurisdictions. Here, a gun dealer in Virginia in 2007 offers "Bloomberg gun give-away" tickets in honor of New York City Mayor Michael Bloomberg, who filed a federal lawsuit to keep out of his city guns bought in places with weak gun-control laws, such as Virginia. The efforts of Mayor Bloomberg and others taking such actions were undermined in 2008 and again in 2010 when the Supreme Court ruled that gun ownership is an individual right under terms of the Second and Fourteenth Amendments. Why is the right to bear arms such an important issue to many Americans?

For a time during the height of devolution's popularity, the Rehnquist Court supported increasing the power of the states and decreasing that of the national government. It overruled a number of federal actions and laws on the grounds that Congress had exceeded its constitutional powers, reversing more than half a century of decisions favoring an increased federal government role. In 1995, for example, the Court overturned federal legislation banning guns from the area around schools and legislation requiring background checks for gun buyers, arguing that both represented too broad a use of the commerce power in the Constitution. The Court used similar language in 2000 when it invalidated part of the Violence Against Women Act and in 2001 when it did the same to the Americans with Disabilities Act.

In the last years of Rehnquist's leadership, however, the Court retreated a bit from this states' rights position, supporting federal law over that of the states on issues ranging from the use of medical marijuana to the juvenile death penalty, affirmative action, and gay rights. In each of these areas, several states wanted to go in more liberal directions than the rest of the country—making medical marijuana available, for example, or using affirmative action to create diversity in government hiring and contracting—but the Court affirmed the more restrictive federal statutes.

NATIONAL POWER REASSERTED Talk of devolution ended with the Democratic Clinton presidency. Republican George W. Bush, who followed Clinton in the Oval Office, signaled during the 2000 presidential campaign that he was willing to use the federal government to serve conservative ends. He termed his position "compassionate conservatism," suggesting that he would use the power of his office to try to, among other things, end abortion and protect the family, enhance educational performance, and do more to move people from welfare to jobs. While preserving his traditional Republican conservative credentials on a number of fronts—cutting taxes, for example, and pushing for looser environmental regulations on businesses—on gaining the presidency Bush gave a big boost to the power, cost, and scope of the federal government.[15] Most important was his sponsorship of the No Child Left Behind educational reform, which imposed testing mandates on the states, and a prescription drug benefit under Medicare, which substantially increased the cost of the program. Mandatory Medicaid spending by the states also expanded rapidly during the Bush presidency.

The terrorist attacks of September 11, 2001, the subsequent global "war on terrorism" (the president's phrase), and the wars in Iraq and Afghanistan further focused the nation's attention on national leaders in Washington, D.C. As in all wartime situations during our country's history, war and the mobilization for war require centralized coordination and planning. This tendency toward nationalism during war has been further exaggerated by the perceived need for enhancing homeland security, with the national government in Washington playing a larger role in areas such as law enforcement, intelligence gathering, bank oversight (to track terrorist money), public health (to protect against possible bioterrorism), and more. Many of these activities continued during Barack Obama's time in the White House.

Perhaps inevitably, the flow of power to Washington during the Bush years triggered a reaction among the public and leaders in the states, disturbed by the increasing budget demands, regulatory burdens, and loss of state control tied to programs: the No Child Left Behind Act; the Real ID Act, aimed at standardizing driver's license issuance among the states; and changes in states' ability to write work rules in TANF (welfare program for the poor, discussed in Chapter 18). Combined with a sense among many at the state level that important national problems were being ignored and mishandled and the collapse in public support for President Bush and his policies after 2004, the ground was set for a rather extraordinary revitalization of state innovations.[16] Between 2004 and 2008, several states passed laws allowing, and sometimes subsidizing, stem-cell research. Others passed minimum wage legislation, while others legislated gas mileage requirements for cars and trucks. Many legislated incentives for companies and consumers to use energy more efficiently and find alternative fuel sources. California even passed legislation to reduce overall greenhouse gas emissions.

Mapping American Politics

Federal Dollars: Which States Win and Which Ones Lose?

Our system of federalism involves a complex set of relationships between the federal government and the states. These relationships are spelled out in the text of the Constitution; decisions of the Supreme Court, interpreting the meaning of constitutional provisions concerning federalism; and bills passed by Congress and signed by the president, creating federal programs and imposing taxes and regulations. One aspect of federalism that often draws attention is the flow of money between the federal government and the states. The flow goes in two directions. Money flows from people and firms in the states to the federal government in the form of taxes (income, corporate, excise, and payroll). Money flows from the federal government to people and firms in the states in the form of grants-in-aid, block grants, and expenditures for specific programs (such as payments to defense contractors) and projects (such as payments for highways and bridges). Given the nature of the political process and differences in the needs and resources of people and firms in the states, some states will inevitably come out ahead in this process, getting more money from Washington than they pay in taxes, and some will come out behind, paying more than they receive.

Note how New York, Illinois, Texas, and California fare; each is dramatically diminished. They receive back from the federal government only a portion of what they pay in taxes.

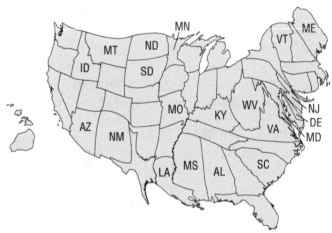

State Sizes Adjusted to Reflect Ratio of Federal Taxes Paid and Federal Monies Received per Capita

The Story in the Cartogram

The cartogram shows winners and losers in the federalism money story. The size of each state has been adjusted using a mathematical formula derived by Gastner and Newman that takes into account a simple ratio: federal funds received by each state on a per capita basis divided by taxes paid by each state on a per capita basis. If a state received and paid the same amount, the ratio would be 1, meaning that its size in the cartogram would not change from its normal size. States that receive more from Washington than they pay in taxes have ratios higher than 1 and are expanded proportionally in size in the cartogram. States that receive less than they pay have ratios less than 1 and are reduced.

It is readily apparent that a number of states are winners, namely, those in the southeast and the middle south, with Connecticut thrown in (their ratios are above 1, thus expanding its size in the cartogram), while a handful of large states are the biggest losers.

What Do You Think?

Why do monies flow between Washington and the states as they currently do? What would be the consequences if all states had similar money flow profiles? Do monies flow to where they are needed? Why do you think some states stand out from others on this issue? Where does your own state fit in the overall picture?

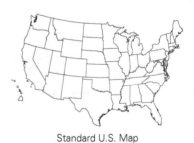

Standard U.S. Map

SOURCES: IRS Data Book for FY 2008 (Table 5); *Statistical Abstract of the United States, 2010* (Table 467); Michael T. Gastner and Mark E.J. Newman, "Diffusion-Based Method for Producing Density-Equalizing Maps," *Proceedings of the National Academy of Sciences 101* (May 18, 2004), pp. 7499–7504.

The economic crisis that began in 2008, sometimes called the Great Recession (much like the Great Depression), generated an expanded role for the national government relative to the states in economic affairs. In the last months of the Bush presidency, Congress passed a $700 billion rescue package for financial institutions that gave the Treasury secretary broad powers to rescue and reorganize banks and investment firms even as the Federal Reserve (the Fed), under the leadership of Ben Bernanke, undertook its own rescue and reorganization efforts. These mandates greatly expanded the role of the federal government in managing the economy. When he became president, Barack Obama not only continued to support the efforts of the Treasury and the Fed to bolster the national economy, but insisted on the sale of Chrysler and the managed bankruptcy of General Motors as conditions of a rescue package. Within 30 days of his inauguration as president, moreover, Congress passed his $787 billion stimulus bill that did a great deal to backstop the states, almost all of whom were in deep budgetary crises. The stimulus package was a combination of tax cuts and new expenditures in programs that, among other things, extended unemployment benefits, funded new research and development in alternative energy sources, put monies into school construction and keeping teachers on the job, massively increased spending on infrastructure projects (i.e., roads, bridges, canals, and the like), and helped the states pay for some of their rising Medicaid outlays.

Perhaps most consequentially, in a long-term sense, President Obama and the Democratic Congress passed a health care bill that will transform America's health care system and a financial regulation bill they hope will prevent the type of financial collapse that happened in 2008 and brought on the Great Recession.[17] President Obama also proposed a major effort to make the nation less dependent on fossil fuels, hoping that the tragic Gulf oil spill and the environmental disaster that followed would convince Americans that the time was ripe for such a change. Republicans and coal-state Democrats stopped the climate bill in the Senate, however, in July 2010.

RECENT PUSHBACK As suggested earlier in this chapter, there has been a great deal of pushback at this increase in national government power relative to the states, suggesting that the states remain significant actors in the American system. Several states, primarily Republican in their voting habits, for example, have passed laws opposing the health care initiative, and also have challenged its constitutionality in Court. Republican Florida governor Rick Scott refused federal health care monies he believed might be associated with the health reform law in 2011, and Scott again and Republican Wisconsin governor Scott Walker turned down federal monies for high-speed rail projects that obligated their states to make future outlays to maintain the new rail systems. The anti-tax, anti–big government Tea Party movement has become a major force in deciding who GOP nominees are in local, state, and national contests, and has influenced Republicans in Congress to act as a united front against virtually every important proposal offered by President Obama. The Tea Party also helped change the agenda in Washington from stimulus and job creation efforts after Obama was elected in 2008, to doing something about the deficit problem following the dramatic victory of the Republicans in the 2010 national elections. The Supreme Court joined in with decisions in 2011 that affirmed state sovereignty in several areas, basing its decisions on the Tenth Amendment, thereby echoing many of the federalism rulings of the Rehnquist Court.[18] In 2012, the Supreme Court, while approving most of the Affordable Care Act, signalled that it wanted to rein-in federal government powers on a broader front, saying that Congress long had been giving too broad a reading of its powers under the commerce and spending clauses. (see the chapter-opening story).

CHANGING AMERICAN FEDERALISM Today's federalism is very different from what it was in the 1790s or early 1800s.[19] One major difference is that the national government is dominant in many policy areas; it calls many shots for the states. Another difference is that state and national government powers and activities have become deeply intertwined and entangled. The old, simple metaphor for federalism was a "layer cake": a system of dual federalism in which state and national powers were neatly divided into separate layers, with each level of government going its own way, unencumbered by the

cooperative federalism

Federalism in which the powers and responsibilities of the states and the national government are intertwined and in which they work together to solve common problems; said to have characterized the 1960s and 1970s.

fiscal federalism

That aspect of federalism having to do with federal grants to the states.

grants-in-aid

Funds from the national government to state and local governments to help pay for programs created by the national government.

categorical grants

Federal aid to states and localities clearly specifying what the money can be used for.

other. If we stay with bakery images, a much more accurate metaphor for today's federalism is a "marble cake," in which elements of national and state influence swirl around each other, without very clear boundaries.[20] The "marble cake" itself has taken on several forms. During the 1960s and 1970s, for example, the federal and state governments seemed to many to be working smoothly together to solve problems, leading scholars and politicians to use the term **cooperative federalism** to characterize the period. Today, no one talks any longer of cooperative federalism, although no single term has replaced it.

Whether cooperative or not, our federal system today is a marble cake in which the federal government and state governments are densely intertwined. Much of this intertwining is a product of the financial links among the national and state governments, which we address in the next section, as well as in the "Mapping American Politics" feature.

Fiscal Federalism

3.4   Analyze how federal grants structure national and state government relations

O ne of the most important elements of modern American federalism is **fiscal federalism**—the transfer of money from the national government to state and local governments. These **grants-in-aid** have been used to increase national government influence over what the states and localities do. The grants have grown from small beginnings to form a substantial part of state government budgets. In the following sections, you will learn how and why this trend began, what kinds of grants have and are being made, and how they affect national–state relationships.

☐ Origin and Growth of Grants

National government grants to the states began at least as early as the 1787 Northwest Ordinance. The U.S. government granted land for government buildings, schools, and colleges in the Northwest Territory and imposed various regulations, such as forbidding slavery there. During the early nineteenth century, the federal government provided some land grants to the states for roads, canals, and railroads, as well as a little cash for militias; after 1862, it helped establish agricultural colleges. Some small cash-grant programs were begun around 1900 for agriculture, vocational education, and highways.[21]

However, it was during the 1950s, 1960s, and 1970s, under both Republican and Democratic administrations, that federal grants to the states really took off. Such programs as President Dwight Eisenhower's interstate highway system and President Lyndon Johnson's Great Society poured money into the states.[22] After a pause during the Reagan presidency, grants began to increase again in the 1990s (see Figure 3.4). Federal grants to the states increased because presidents and Congress sought to deal with many nationwide problems—especially transportation, education, HIV/AIDS, poverty, crime, and air and water pollution—by setting policy at the national level and providing money from national tax revenues, while having state and local officials carry out the policies. The big jump in grant totals in 2010 and 2011 were tied to various efforts by the federal government to stimulate the economy during the Great Recession, including assistance to states for Medicaid, unemployment insurance, education, and infrastructure.[23]

☐ Types of Grants

Over the years, many of the new programs were established through **categorical grants**, which give the states money but clearly specify the category of activity for which the money has to be spent and often define rather precisely how the program should work. For example, Lyndon Johnson's antipoverty initiatives—in the

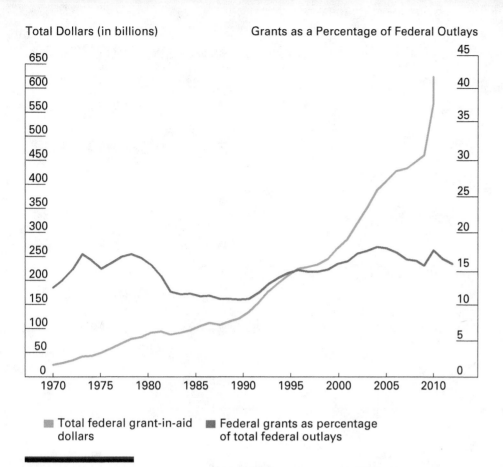

Total Dollars (in billions)   Grants as a Percentage of Federal Outlays

Legend:
Total federal grant-in-aid dollars   Federal grants as percentage of total federal outlays

FIGURE 3.4 THE GROWTH IN FEDERAL GRANTS-IN-AID TO STATES AND LOCALITIES

Federal grants-in-aid to state and local governments have grown steadily since 1970, the only exception being during the first half of the 1980s during the Reagan presidency. A big jump occurred in 2010 and 2011 as federal assistance to the states increased to address problems caused by the financial collapse and economic recession.

Source: Statistical Abstract of the United States, 2010, and the Federal Budget, Fiscal Year 2013, "special topics," table 18.2.

areas of housing, job training, medical assistance, and more—funneled substantial federal money to states and localities, but attached strict rules on how the money could be used.

Responding to complaints from the states and seeking to reduce federal government power to better fit their ideas about the proper role of government, Republican presidents Nixon and Ford succeeded in convincing Congress to loosen centralized rules and oversight, first instituting **block grants** (which give money for more general purposes, such as secondary education, and with fewer rules than categorical grant programs), then, for a short time, **general revenue sharing**, which distributed money to the states with no federal controls at all. President Nixon spoke of a "New Federalism" and pushed to increase these kinds of grants with few strings attached. General revenue sharing ended in 1987 when even proponents of a smaller federal government realized that giving money to the states with "no strings attached" meant that elected officials in the federal government were losing influence over policies in which they wanted to have a say.

Categorical and block grants often provide federal money under an automatic formula related to the statistical characteristics of each state or locality (thus the term "formula grant"), such as the number of needy residents, the total size of the population, or the average income level. Disputes frequently arise when these formulas benefit one state or region rather than another. Because statistical counts by the census affect how much money the states and localities get, census counts themselves have become the subject of political conflict.

☐ Debates About Federal Money and Control

Most contemporary conflicts about federalism concern not just money but also control.

Which States Win and Lose the Federal Aid Game?

Explore on MyPoliSciLab

The national government collects taxes from everyone, but it doesn't always spend money in the state where it gets it. Instead, the federal government transfers wealth from state to state. Recipient states pay less in federal taxes than they receive, while donor states pay more in taxes than they receive back. In 2007, there were 19 donor states and 31 recipient states. The political explanation for who were donor and recipient states is surprising.

Who pays?
DELAWARE, MINNESOTA, NEW JERSEY, and CONNECTICUT all paid at least $6,000 more in federal taxes per person than they received in federal aid. 15 other states were net donors.

Net Donor: Over $5,000 Per Person	Connecticut $6,241	New Jersey $6,644	Minnesota $7,431	Delaware $12,285
Net Donor: Between $1 and $5,000 per person	Ohio $49	North Carolina $1,108	Massachusetts $2,133	Rhode Island $2,732
	Georgia $434	California $1,466	Colorado $2,176	Illinois $3,640
	Washington $773	Nevada $1,616	Nebraska $2,850	New York $4,502
	Wisconsin $1,000	Arkansas $1,723	Texas $2,243	

Who receives?
ALASKA took in twice the federal money in 2007 that it paid in taxes. 31 states are recipient states. Of the top six recipient states, four are southern.

Net Recipient: Over $5,000 Per Person	Alaska -$7,448	New Mexico -$7,143	Mississippi -$6,765	Virginia -$6,239	West Virginia -$5,820	Alabama -$5,130
Net Recipient: Between $1 and $5,000 per person	Hawaii -$4983	South Carolina -$3,756	Arizona -$1,976	Utah -$792	Pennsylvania -$385	
	North Dakota -$4,856	Kentucky -$3,012	Idaho -$1,281	Indiana -$723	Oklahoma -$376	
	South Dakota -$4,414	Maryland -$3,010	Wyoming -$1,205	Tennessee -$603	New Hampshire -$349	
	Maine -$4,221	Vermont -$2,854	Missouri -$1,190	Florida -$581	Michigan -$171	
	Montana -$4,149	Louisiana -$2,180	Iowa -$1,075	Oregon -$474	Kansas -$154	

SOURCE: Data from United States Internal Revenue Service; *Statistical Abstract of the United States 2012;* and *U.S. Census of Population and Housing, 2010.*

Who are the Recipient States?

Recipient states by party

- 18 out of 23 Republican-voting states (78%) are recipient states compared to 8 out of the 19 Democratic-voting states (42%).

Recipient states by poverty level

- 9 of 13 states with high poverty levels are recipient states (69%), while only 9 of 17 states with low poverty levels are recipient states (53%).

Investigate Further

Concept How do we determine donor and recipient states? Per person, we subtract the federal aid dollars sent to a state from the federal tax dollars paid in a state. If the result is positive, a state is a donor state, otherwise it's a recipient state.

Connection What relationship exists between politics and whether a state is a recipient or donor? Recipient states are most often Republican in national politics, while donor states tend to be more Democratic in national politics.

Cause Is there a policy explanation for which states are recipient states? The federal government fights poverty by moving money around the country. Recipient states usually have higher poverty levels and lower average incomes. Therefore, they tend to pay less federal tax than they receive per person.

CONDITIONS ON AID As we have seen, categorical grant-in-aid programs require that the states spend federal money only in certain restricted ways. Even block grants—such as grants that support social welfare for the poor—have conditions attached, thus the term **conditional grants**. In theory, these conditions are "voluntary" because the states can refuse to accept the aid. But in practice, there is no clear line between incentives and coercion. Because the states cannot generally afford to give up federal money, they normally must accept the conditions attached to it.

Some of the most important provisions of the 1964 Civil Rights Act, for example, are those that declare that no federal aid of any kind can be used in ways that discriminate against people on grounds of race, gender, religion, or national origin. Thus, the enormous program of national aid for elementary and secondary education, which began in 1965, became a powerful lever for forcing schools to desegregate. To take another example, the federal government in 1984 used federal highway money to encourage states to adopt a minimum drinking age of 21. As we saw in the chapter opening story on the ruling on the Affordable Care Act, the Court now seems inclined to entertain challenges to grant programs to the states that are unduly coercive.

MANDATES The national government often imposes a **mandate**, or demand, that the states carry out certain policies even when little or no national government aid is offered. (An "unfunded" mandate involves no aid at all or less aid than compliance will cost.) Mandates have been especially important in the areas of civil rights and the environment. Most civil rights policies flow from the equal protection clause of the Fourteenth Amendment to the U.S. Constitution or from national legislation that imposes uniform national standards. Most environmental regulations also come from the national government, since problems of dirty air, polluted water, and acid rain spill across state boundaries. Many civil rights and environmental regulations, therefore, are enforced by the federal courts.

Federal courts have, for example, mandated expensive reforms of overcrowded state prisons. National legislation and regulations have required state governments to provide costly special facilities for the disabled, to set up environmental protection agencies, and to limit the kinds and amounts of pollutants that can be discharged. The states often complain bitterly about federal mandates that require state spending without providing the money.

conditional grants
Federal grants with provisions requiring that state and local governments follow certain policies in order to obtain funds.

mandate
A formal order from the national government that the states carry out certain policies.

SPEWING POLLUTION

Industrial pollution, such as these untreated emissions from this coal-burning power plant in Tennessee, often affects people of more than one state and requires the participation of the national government to clean up the mess and prevent recurrences. What role should the federal government take in environmental issues within states whose effects spill over into other states?

Using the FRAMEWORK

I thought that attending a public university would save a lot of money, but it hasn't because I have to pay out-of-state tuition. Why do I have to pay so much money?

Background: All over the United States, students who choose to attend out-of-state public universities pay much higher tuition than state residents. For example, at the University of Colorado, Boulder, tuition in 2011–2012 for in-state students was $9,152; out-of-state students paid $29,480. Some educational reformers have suggested that the system be reformed so that students might attend public universities wherever they choose without financial penalty. They have suggested that over the long haul and on average, such a reform would not have much impact on state budgets because students would randomly distribute themselves across state borders. Such proposals have never gotten very far. Taking a broad view of how structural, political linkage, and governmental factors affect this issue will help explain the situation.

Government Action

The Supreme Court rules that different tuition rates for in-state and out-of-state residents do not violate the "privileges and immunities" section of Article IV, Section 2, of the Constitution.

State legislatures decline to pass uniform tuition legislation.

Government

Elected leaders know that voters want access to low-cost higher education for state residents. ➡ Elected leaders are not subject to political pressures to change tuition policy. ➡ Elected leaders are concerned with short-term budget issues; high out-of-state tuition allows them to raise part of the higher education budget.

Political Linkage

Voters in each state insist on access for their children and the children of their neighbors to low-cost public higher education. ➡ There is little political pressure on elected leaders within the states to lower or eliminate out-of-state tuition, whether from
– Public opinion and voters,
– Parties,
– The mass media,
– Interest groups,
– Social movements. ➡ Out-of-state students rarely vote in the states where they go to school; politicians have no incentive to think seriously about their tuition concerns.

Structure

The states are mainly responsible for education in our federal system; standardizing national tuition rates would require agreements among all the states, or federal legislation preempting the states.

Cutting back on these "unfunded mandates" was one of the main promises in the Republicans' 1994 Contract with America.[24] The congressional Republicans delivered on their promise early in 1995 with a bill that had bipartisan support in Congress and that President Clinton signed into law. Because it did not apply to past mandates, however, and did not ban unfunded mandates but only regulated them (e.g., requiring cost–benefit analyses), unfunded mandates have continued to proliferate, as has the debate about their use. The main complaints coming from governors today concern the substantial costs imposed on the states by the No Child Left Behind testing program and by the rising costs to the states of required Medicaid support for certain categories of people. Pressures on state budgets became especially pronounced during the Great Recession when revenues from sales and other taxes plummeted because of the national economic downturn. Hard-fought budget agreements between Congress and President Obama in 2011 to address the problem of federal government deficits cut federal spending across a wide range of programs—including money to keep teachers and first-responders from being laid off and help with Medicaid—and plunged most states even further into the red. Many responded by making deep cuts in education, social programs for the poor, and programs for maintaining and improving infrastructure (roads, bridges, and dams, for example), and several tried to tame public employee unions or rescind the collective bargaining rights of state workers (see Governor Walker in Wisconsin).

PREEMPTION The doctrine of preemption, based on the supremacy clause in the Constitution and supported by a series of Supreme Court decisions, says that federal treaties, statutes, and rules must prevail over state statutes and rules when the two are in conflict. Recently, for example, several states attempted to tax Internet purchases by people residing in their jurisdictions, but Congress has forbidden them to do so. Research suggests that the number of preemption statutes passed by Congress has increased substantially over the past three decades and has been unaffected by which political party is in control.[25]

U.S. Federalism: Pro and Con

3.5 Evaluate the arguments for and against federalism

ver the years, from the framing of the U.S. Constitution to the present day, people have offered a number of strong arguments for and against federalism, in contrast to a more unitary system. Let us consider some of these arguments.

PRO: DIVERSITY OF NEEDS The oldest and most important argument in favor of decentralized government is that in a large and diverse country, needs and wants and conditions differ from one place to another. Why not let different states enact different policies to meet their own needs? California, New York, and New Jersey, for example, all densely populated, have tougher fuel mileage standards in place than those set by the federal government. (See the "Using the Framework" feature on tuition for out-of-state students.) The border state of Arizona, feeling overwhelmed by illegal immigrants, passed a law in 2010 allowing police to stop and interrogate people they think may be in the country illegally. A federal judge threw out most provisions of the law soon after, a decision that was upheld by the Ninth Circuit Court of Appeals. The Supreme Court ruled in 2012 that the state had gone too far in usurping the powers of the federal government on issues of immigration.

CON: THE IMPORTANCE OF NATIONAL STANDARDS However, the needs or desires that different states pursue may not be worthy ones. Political scientist William Riker has pointed out that, in the past, one of the main effects of federalism was to let white majorities in the Southern states enslave and then discriminate against black people, without interference from the North.[26] Perhaps it is better, in some cases, to insist on national standards that apply everywhere.

PRO: CLOSENESS TO THE PEOPLE It is sometimes claimed that state governments are closer to the ordinary citizens, who have a better chance to know their officials, to be aware of what they are doing, to contact them, and to hold them responsible for what they do.

CON: LOW VISIBILITY AND LACK OF POPULAR CONTROL However, others respond that geographic closeness may not be the real issue. More Americans are better informed about the federal government than they are about state governments, and more people participate in national than in state elections. When more people know what the government is doing and more people vote, they are better able to insist that the government do what they want. For that reason, responsiveness to ordinary citizens may actually be greater in national government.

PRO: INNOVATION AND EXPERIMENTATION When the states have independent power, they can try out new ideas. Individual states can be "laboratories." If the experiments work, other states or the nation as a whole can adopt their ideas, as has happened on such issues as allowing women and 18-year-olds to vote, fighting air pollution, reforming welfare, and dealing with water pollution. Massachusetts passed a law in 2006 mandating health insurance coverage for every person in the state. Also in 2006, California passed a law committing itself to reducing greenhouse gas emissions to 1990 levels by 2020.

Likewise, when the national government is controlled by one political party, federalism allows the states with majorities favoring a different party to compensate by enacting different policies. This aspect of diversity in policymaking is related to the Founders' contention that tyranny is less likely when government's power is dispersed. Multiple governments reduce the risks of bad policy or the blockage of the popular will; if things go wrong at one governmental level, they may go right at another.

CON: SPILLOVER EFFECTS AND COMPETITION Diversity and experimentation in policies, however, may not always be good. Divergent regulations can cause bad effects that spill over from one state to another. When factories in the Midwest spew out oxides of nitrogen and sulfur that fall as acid rain in the Northeast, the northeastern states acting on their own can do nothing about it. Only nationwide rules can solve such problems. Similarly, it is very difficult for cities or local communities in the states to do much about poverty or other social problems. If a city raises taxes to pay for social programs, businesses and the wealthy may move out of town, and the poor may move in, impoverishing the city.[27]

WHAT SORT OF FEDERALISM? As the pros and cons indicate, a lot is at stake in determining the nature of federalism. It is not likely, however, that Americans will ever have a chance to vote yes or no on the federal system as a whole or to choose a unitary government instead. What we can decide is exactly *what sort* of federalism we will have—how much power will go to the states and how much will remain with the federal government. Indeed, we may want a fluid system in which the balance of power varies from one kind of policy to another. Over the long term of American history, of course, the nationalist position on federalism has generally prevailed over the states' rights position, but the states remain important, and there are many reasons to expect that the American people will continue to want the states to play an important role in fashioning policies that affect them.

It is important to keep in mind that arguments about federalism do not concern just abstract theories; they affect who wins and who loses valuable benefits. People's opinions about federalism often depend on their interests, their ideologies, and the kinds of things they want government to do.

Using the DEMOCRACY STANDARD

American Federalism: How Democratic?

Federalism is one of the foundation stones of the Constitution of the United States. Along with the separation of powers and checks and balances, its purpose, from the framers' point of view, was to make it impossible for any person or group (and, most especially, the majority faction) to monopolize the power of government and use it for tyrannical purposes. By fragmenting government power among a national government and 50 state governments and by giving each of the states some say on what the national government does, federalism makes it difficult for any faction, minority or majority, to dominate government. On balance, federalism has served the intentions of the framers by toning down the influence of majoritarian democracy in determining what the national government does, even while maintaining the principle of popular consent.

Federalism successfully constrains democracy in at least five ways:

1. It adds complexity to policymaking and makes it difficult for citizens to know which elected leaders to hold responsible for government actions.

2. Many policy areas, including education and voting eligibility, are mainly the responsibility of the states, where policymakers are insulated from national majorities, although not from majorities in their own states.

3. Small-population states play a decisive role in the constitutional amending process, where each state counts equally, regardless of the size of its population.

4. Small and large states have equal representation in the Senate, meaning that senators representing a minority of the population can block actions favored by senators representing the majority.

5. State politics are much less visible to the public; citizens are much less informed about what goes on in state governments where many important policies are made, and thus, popular participation tends to be lower.

All of this makes state-level politics especially vulnerable to the influence of special interests and those with substantial political resources. Because the well-organized and the affluent have extra influence, political equality and popular sovereignty have pretty tough challenges in many of the states.

In the end, the story of federalism is not entirely about the persistence of the framer's initial eighteenth-century republican constitutional design. The democratic aspirations of the American people have also shaped federalism and turned it into something that might not be entirely familiar to the framers. We noted in this chapter how the nature of federalism has changed over the course of American history, with the national government assuming an ever-larger role relative to the states. Much of this, we have suggested, has been brought about by the wishes of the American people as expressed in elections, public opinion polls, and social movements. Repeatedly, Americans have said they want a national government capable of addressing a broad range of problems, including economic difficulties (such as depressions, recessions, and inflation); persistent poverty; environmental degradation; unsafe food, drugs, and other consumer products; racial and ethnic discrimination; and foreign threats to the United States. Over the years, public officials and candidates have responded to these popular aspirations, altering federalism in the process.

Review the Chapter

 Listen to **Chapter 3** on **MyPoliSciLab**

Federalism as a System of Government

3.1 Define federalism and explain why we have it, p. 60

Federalism is a system under which political powers are divided and shared between the state and federal governments, and is a key structural aspect of American politics.

Federalism in the United States was the product of both important compromises made at the Constitutional Convention and eighteenth-century republican doctrines about the nature of good government.

Federalism in the Constitution

3.2 Establish the basis for federalism in the Constitution, p. 62

There is no section of the Constitution where federalism is described in its entirety. Rather, federalism is construction from scattered clauses throughout the document that describe what the federal government may do and not do, how relations among the states are structured, the role of the states in amending the Constitution and electing the president, and how the states are represented in the national government.

The U.S. Constitution specifies the powers of the national government and reserves all others (except a few that are specifically forbidden) to the states. Overlapping, or concurrent, powers fall within the powers of both the national government and the states.

The Evolution of American Federalism

3.3 Trace the evolution of American federalism, p. 66

The story of American federalism is the story of the increasing power of the federal government relative to the states.

The trend toward national power is lodged in the "supremacy" and "elastic" clauses in the Constitution and propelled by war and national security demands, economic troubles and crises, and a range of problems that no state could handle alone.

Fiscal Federalism

3.4 Analyze how federal grants structure national and state government relations, p. 78

Contemporary federalism involves complex "marble cake" relations among the national and state governments, in which federal grants-in-aid play an important part. Except for the Reagan years, grant totals have grown steadily; they took a big jump upward as the country battled the Great Recession and jobless recovery in the 2008–2012 period, then leveled out after the anti-tax, anti-government, deficit-reducing agenda came to dominate Washington politics.

The national government also influences or controls many state policies through mandates and through conditions placed on aid.

U.S. Federalism: Pro and Con

3.5 Evaluate the arguments for and against federalism, p. 83

Arguments in favor of federalism have to do with diversity of needs, closeness to the people, experimentation, and innovation.

Arguments against federalism involve national standards, popular control, and needs for uniformity.

Learn the Terms

 Study and **Review** the **Flashcards**

federalism, p. 60
confederation, p. 60
unitary system, p. 60
supremacy clause, p. 62
Tenth Amendment, p. 62
reservation clause, p. 62
concurrent powers, p. 63
horizontal federalism, p. 64
interstate compacts, p. 66

nationalist position, p. 67
necessary and proper clause, p. 67
states' rights position, p. 68
dual federalism, p. 68
nullification, p. 68
preemption, p. 70
Civil War Amendments, p. 71
due process clause, p. 71
equal protection clause, p. 71

devolution, p. 72
cooperative federalism, p. 78
fiscal federalism, p. 78
grants-in-aid, p. 78
categorical grants, p. 78
block grants, p. 79
general revenue sharing, p. 79
conditional grants, p. 81
mandate, p. 81

Answer key begins on page T-1.

3.1 Define federalism and explain why we have it

1. What is federalism?

   a. A system of government where the states are sovereign and have authority over the central government.
   b. A system of government where the central government has complete power and can tell lower levels of government what to do.
   c. A system of government where local representatives are elected directly by the voters. These representatives then select the members of the central government.
   d. A system of government where the representatives of the central government are elected directly by the voters. These representatives then select the members of the local government.
   e. A system of government where power is divided between the central government and smaller units, such as states.

2. Why did the authors of the U.S. Constitution create a federal system of government?

   a. Federalism is best suited for small, homogenous countries such as the United States was at its founding.
   b. The U.S. Constitution was modeled after European countries, most of which used a federal system.
   c. Federalism had worked well under the Articles of Confederation, and the framers wanted to build on this success.
   d. Federalism was a reasonable compromise between a confederation and a unitary system.
   e. The system would help ensure a concentration of powers between the federal government and the state governments.

3.2 Establish the basis for federalism in the Constitution

3. The reservation clause in Article IV states that the constitution, laws, and treaties of the United States shall be the "supreme law of the land."
   True/False

4. This amendment says that those powers not given to the federal government and not prohibited are reserved for the states and the people.

   a. Sixth Amendment
   b. Tenth Amendment
   c. Second Amendment
   d. Eighth Amendment
   e. Fourth Amendment

3.3 Trace the evolution of American federalism

5. Who enforced the supremacy clause?

   a. Thomas Jefferson
   b. John Adams
   c. The Supreme Court
   d. James Madison
   e. Congress

6. This eventually became the vehicle by which the Supreme Court ruled that many civil liberties in the Bill of Rights also provided protections against the states.

   a. Due process
   b. Equal protection
   c. Civil War Amendments
   d. Preemption
   e. Nullification

3.4 Analyze how federal grants structure national and state government relations

7. One of the most important elements of modern American federalism is fiscal federalism.
   True/False

8. These types of grants give money for more general purposes such as secondary education.

   a. General grants
   b. Sharing grants
   c. Categorical grants
   d. Block grants
   e. Growth grants

3.5 Evaluate the arguments for and against federalism

9. One of the main effects of federalism allowed slavery in the South.
   True/False

10. The purpose of federalism, from the framers' point of view, was to make it impossible for:

   a. One group or person to monopolize power and use it for tyrannical purposes
   b. The government to fall
   c. One party to be in complete control of the United States
   d. Democracy to turn into communism
   e. States to be in control of the government

Explore Further

INTERNET SOURCES

History of Federalism **plato.stanford.edu/entries/federalism/**
A comprehensive study of the history of federalism in the west.

Federalism: National vs. State Government **usgovinfo.about.com/od/rightsandfreedoms/a/federalism.htm**
A site explaining the powers of national and state governments with links to articles on the federalist papers.

Block Grants **www.urban.org/publications/310991.html**
A historical overview of block grants.

National Conference of State Legislatures **www.ncsl.org**
Information about state governments and federal relations, including the distribution of federal revenues and expenditures in the states. Links to the "Mandate Monitor" and the "Preemption Monitor."

State Constitutions **www.findlaw.com/**
A site where the constitutions of all the states may be found.

Stateline **www.stateline.org**
A comprehensive, nonpartisan look at politics and policies in the American states.

SUGGESTIONS FOR FURTHER READING

Brinkley, Douglas G. *The Great Deluge: Hurricane Katrina, New Orleans, and the Mississippi Gulf Coast.* New York: Harper Collins, 2006.
Much more than a blow-by-blow telling of the Hurricane Katrina story, this text provides a detailed description of how the complex interactions of local, state, and federal politics and policies over the years contributed to the disaster.

Derthick, Martha. *Keeping the Compound Republic: Essays in American Federalism.* Washington, D.C.: Brookings, 2001.
An examination of the enduring features of federalism, as well as its most important changes, in light of the framers' original design, in Madison's words, of a compound republic.

Hero, Rodney E. *Faces of Inequality: Social Diversity in American Politics.* New York: Oxford University Press, 1998.
An impressive argument with strong empirical evidence that the racial and ethnic composition of states matters for patterns of state politics.

Nagel, Robert. *The Implosion of American Federalism.* New York: Oxford University Press, 2002.
Argues that American federalism has largely disappeared as power in the United States has flowed steadily to Washington, D.C.

Peterson, Paul E. *The Price of Federalism.* Washington, D.C.: Brookings Institution, 1995.
Describes modern federalism and argues that the national government is best at redistributive programs, while the states and localities are best at economic development.

Riker, William H. *The Development of American Federalism.* Boston: Kluwer Academic, 1987.
An influential discussion of what American federalism is and how it came about.

6

The News Media

BIG STORIES WITHOUT LEGS

I t had all the makings of a major news story that would rock Washington and trigger a major rethinking of war policies in Iraq.[1] All the pieces appeared to be in place. In an article published on April 30, 2005, the prestigious British newspaper, *The Times* of London, reported the minutes of a secret meeting between Prime Minister Tony Blair and his top military and intelligence officials that featured a report by a British intelligence operative that Washington officials had "cooked the books" to justify the invasion of Iraq in spring 2003. The operative had been at several prewar meetings with White House and Pentagon officials where it was evident, he claimed, that the decision for war already had been made and that intelligence information about Saddam Hussein's purported "weapons of mass destruction" program and ties to the 9/11 terrorists was being organized and interpreted to build a case for going to war. In his words, the "facts were being fixed around the policy."[2]

As news stories go, the seeming blockbuster turned out to be a dud. The story failed to merit a lead on any of the network newscasts. While the story of the so-called Downing Street memo appeared on the front page of the *Washington Post*, it was there for only a single day. Other newspapers relegated it to the inside pages. For the most part, the story was ". . . treated as old news or a British politics story" rather than a story about Americans being misled into war by the Bush administration, something that might call into question the entire enterprise.[3] The liberal blogosphere jumped on the issue, but the story failed to stir more mainstream media attention or action from congressional Democrats, who were in the minority in both the House and Senate and unsure about what position to take on the war in the upcoming 2006 elections. When Representative John Conyers (D–MI) sought to bring attention to the misuse of intelligence information to encourage the Iraq war by holding an "informational hearing" (being

6.1	**6.2**	**6.3**	**6.4**
Evaluate the various roles of the news media in a democracy, p. 166	Assess the respective roles of traditional and other news media today, p. 167	Analyze how the news is gathered and disseminated and evaluate the outcomes of this process, p. 174	Identify the ways in which the news media affect public opinion and policymaking, p. 188

WEAPONS OF MASS DESTRUCTION The Bush administration sold the American people on the invasion of Iraq in 2003 on the grounds that Saddam Hussein had developed nuclear and biological weapons that threatened the region and the world. We learned later from British government sources that the intelligence was "cooked" to support the invasion—there were no such military capabilities—but the new information failed to become important news in America's media. Was this an unusual occurrence or all too common regarding important public affairs? If the latter, what does this mean for creating an informed public in a democracy?

MyPoliSciLab Video Series

 Watch on MyPoliSc

The Big Picture Should we even pay attention to "old media" like The New York Times or The Washington Post? Author Edward S. Greenberg gives two reasons why these forms of journalism remain relevant in the age of tweets and blog posts.

The Basics How do the media help support our democratic institutions? In this video, you will find out how a free press functions not just as a source of knowledge, but also as a public forum and a government watchdog. You'll also analyze how private ownership and partisanship impact the ability of the media to do its job.

Why is the freedom of the press so important in our democracy?

In Context Trace the evolution of media outlets from newspapers to the new media that exists today. In this video, University of Oklahoma political scientist Tyler Johnson examines the history of media outlets and the effect of both traditional and new media on the political information and messages that reach the public.

Think Like a Political Scientist How does the media shape public opinion? In this video, University of Oklahoma political scientist Tyler Johnson discusses how media framing works and what market factors are influencing this process.

In the Real World What is the ideal relationship between the government and the media? Real people consider whether leaks of confidential government information to the press is good for democracy or whether leaks give the government too much control over the stories being told in the newspapers.

So What? Should the news be entertaining? Author Edward S. Greenberg discusses what kinds of stories appear on television—and why they are not always the most important ones—and he provides some rationale for why the in the minority, the Democrat Conyers could not schedule an official set of hearings), the *Washington Post* treated it as a joke; the headline read "Democrats Play House to Rally Against the War" and opened with the line, "In the Capitol basement yesterday, long suffering House Democrats took a trip to the land of make-believe."[4]

Similarly, in an article published in early 2006—roughly three years after the invasion of Iraq—the *New York Times* reported a British press story, based on a memo written by a Blair aide who had attended a prewar January 2003 meeting of Prime Minister Tony Blair and President George W. Bush at the White House, where the president had made it clear to the British leader that he was determined to go to war even without evidence that Iraq was building weapons of mass destruction or had links to Al Qaeda. (At the same time, the president was making numerous statements that he had not made up his mind about an invasion and was making every effort to solve the issue diplomatically in cooperation with the United Nations and close allies.) While the revelation elicited a few comments from Democratic leaders and some blog activity, it didn't get a mention on CBS, NBC, or Fox News, and no follow-up stories appeared in the *Los Angeles Times*, the *Wall Street Journal*, the *Washington Post*, or *USA Today*. At around the same time this story about the Bush–Blair meeting came and went with hardly a murmur, a feeding frenzy was swirling around an unfortunate incident in which Vice President Richard Cheney accidentally shot a long-time friend in the face while hunting. For four or five days after the accidental shooting, every type of news media outlet—including the network and cable news networks, news magazines, local and national newspapers, news websites, and blogs—ran full coverage on the story, examining every nuance and speculating about why it happened, why an official press release about it was delayed for a few hours, and what it might all mean. Late-night comedy hosts had a field day with the story for months.

Many critics claim the news media are biased and cannot be relied upon to tell an objective story. Other critics claim that the mainstream news media in particular are becoming irrelevant in the face of the Internet, with its multiple information and opinion sources. We suggest that the principal problems of the news media concern their underreporting of stories that might help American citizens better understand events and trends that are affecting their lives, including those involving government and political leaders, and overattention to stories that involve sensation, entertainment, or scandals. This chapter is about the news media and why certain things become news we pay attention to while other things, many of them very important to public conversations about government policies and the direction of the country, do not.

Thinking Critically About This Chapter

In this chapter, we turn our attention to the diverse news media in the United States to learn how they are organized, how they work, and what effects they have on the quality of our political life.

Using the Framework

In this chapter, you will learn about the role the news media play in influencing significant actors in the political system, including citizens and elected leaders. You also will learn how the news media can shape what government does. And you will learn how the news media are influenced by changes in technology and business organization.

Using the Democracy Standard

Using the tools already presented, you will be able to evaluate the degree to which the news media advance democracy in the United States or retard it. You will be able to judge whether the media promote popular sovereignty, political equality, and liberty. Finally, you will see how certain changes in the media may be cause for concern in terms of the health of democracy.

watchdog
The role of the media in scrutinizing the actions of government officials.

6.1

6.2

6.3

6.4

Roles of the News Media in Democracy

6.1   Evaluate the various roles of the news media in a democracy

T he central idea of democracy is that ordinary citizens should control what their government does. However, citizens cannot hope to control officials, choose candidates wisely, speak intelligently with others about public affairs, or even make up their minds about which policies they favor unless they have good information about politics and policies. Most of that information must come through the news media, whether newspapers, radio, television, or, increasingly, the Internet. How well democracy works, then, depends partly on how good a job the news media are doing. The news media, ideally, should fulfill several roles in this democracy.

☐ Watchdog Over Government

One role of the news media in a democracy is that of **watchdog** over government. The Founders, although not entirely enamored of democracy, as we have seen, nevertheless fully subscribed to the idea that a free press was essential for keeping an eye on government and checking its excesses. This is why protection of press freedom figured so prominently in the First Amendment. This role for the press is essential to the practice of democracy as well. The idea is that the press should dig up facts and warn the public when officials are doing something wrong. Citizens can hold officials accountable for setting things right only if they know about errors and wrongdoing.

The First Amendment to the Constitution ("Congress shall make no law . . . abridging the freedom . . . of the press") helps ensure that the news media will be able to expose officials' misbehavior without fear of censorship or prosecution. This is a treasured American right that is not available in many other countries. Under dictatorships and other authoritarian regimes, the news media are usually tightly controlled, with government censorship of the press and intimidation of journalists all too common.[5] Even in a democratic country such as Great Britain, strict secrecy laws limit what the press can say about certain government activities. In many countries, including France, Israel, and Sweden, the government owns and operates major television channels and sometimes pressures news executives to tone down their criticism of political leaders, though citizens in these countries have access to alternative channels by satellite and on the Internet.

As you will see, even without formal censorship or government ownership of the media, various factors, including the way in which the news media are organized as privately owned, profit-seeking enterprises, and their routines of news gathering, may limit how willing or able the news media are to be critical of government policies. In addition, the media may be too quick to blow scandals out of proportion and to destroy political leaders' careers.[6]

☐ Clarifying Electoral Choices

A second role of the news media in a democracy is to make clear what electoral choices the public has: what the political parties stand for and how the candidates shape up in terms of personal character, knowledge, experience, and positions on the issues. Without such information, it is difficult for voters to make intelligent choices. Unfortunately, the news media tend to pay attention more to the "horse race" (who is ahead? who is behind?) aspect of campaigns, or go overboard digging up dirt and reporting negative material, rather than covering the policy positions of the candidates.

☐ Providing Policy Information

A third role of the news media is to present a diverse, full, and enlightening set of facts and ideas about public policy. Citizens need to know about emerging problems that will need attention and how well current policies are working, as well as the pros and

DARNED REPORTERS

Richard Nixon resigned his presidency in August, 1974 rather than face a trial in the Senate following his impeachment in the House after investigative reporters Bob Woodward and Carl Bernstein of The Washington Post uncovered evidence of the president's close involvement in illegal spying on political opponents and in efforts to cover-up these activities from law enforcement authorities in what has come to be called the Watergate Affair. Here he leaves Washington after his resignation. Do you believe the news media played an important role in enhancing American democracy in this case or did reporters like Woodward and Bernstein go too far?

cons of alternative policies that might be tried. In a democracy, government should respond to public opinion, but that opinion should be reasonably well informed. You will see later in this chapter why many observers worry that the news media do not provide quality information and analyses on a consistent basis.

Mainstream and Nonmainstream News Media

6.2 Assess the respective roles of traditional and other news media today

T he Pew Research Center's Project for Excellence in Journalism (www .journalism.org) claims that the coming of the digital age in the news media represents "an epochal transformation, as momentous probably as the invention of the telegraph or television."[7] This new digital age in news is described as one in which there is virtually unlimited access to information, news, and analysis, untold opportunities for ordinary people to express their views on public issues, and a decline in the presence and importance of the mainstream or traditional media.[8] Despite the unmistakable and dramatic growth of alternative news and information sources and outlets for people to express themselves and to report what is going on around them (at a political demonstration such as Occupy Wall Street, for example), however, we suggest that the mainstream media and traditional forms of reporting remain at the center of the news operations that most affect American politics and government.

☐ Alternatives to the Mainstream

The most important development in the collection, organization, and distribution of information of all kinds is, of course, the Internet, allowing instant access to a vast treasure trove

BLOGGING THE REPUBLICAN NATIONAL CONVENTION

Alternative media are becoming increasingly mainstream. Both the Republican and Democratic conventions in 2008 allocated space not only to the mainstream media but to bloggers as well. These bloggers are sharing ideas and interpretations on proceedings at the GOP convention that nominated John McCain and Sarah Palin for the national ticket. How did this development happen, and to what extent does it enhance the quality of political information that is available to the public?

of digitalized information in every field of human knowledge. (See Figure 6.1 for a timeline on the development of the Internet.) The growth in the reach, capabilities, and use of the Internet, through broadband connections in homes, schools, libraries, and the workplace, and increasingly over wireless networks to handheld devices such as e-readers, smart phones, tablets, and other smart devices, has been stunning. By the end of 2011, according to the Pew Research Center, 62 percent of Americans reported having a broadband connection in their home, for example.[9] (While this may seem like a big number, it puts us only in seventh place among nations, down from fourth place in 2000; other countries are growing their broadband penetration much faster than the United States, especially South Korea and Sweden, where over 90 percent are connected.)[10] Fully 78 percent of Americans claim to have used the Internet in 2011, however.[11] Moreover, the ownership of handheld devices with access to the Internet—iPhones, iPod Touch, Kindle readers, BlackBerrys, Android-enabled phones, tablet computers such as the iPad with Wi-Fi and/or 3G connections, and more—is rapidly rising here and abroad, though the exact numbers are hard to pin down.

To be sure, most people use the Internet for such nonpolitical activities as sending and receiving e-mail, sharing photos and videos, sending tweets about their lives, arranging travel and vacations, participating in online auctions, shopping for products, playing interactive games, following their friends and relations on Facebook, and more. But many millions use it for explicitly political purposes, to both inform and express themselves. Here are a few examples:

- People visit political party and candidate websites, as well as interest and advocacy group websites, to get information, make contributions, learn how to organize, and leave comments. They also visit fact-check sites to test the claims of government officials, candidates, and parties.

- People visit government websites to access a vast trove of information ranging from statistics on demographic change and performance of the economy to the details of the U.S. budget and bills being considered by Congress. Over 100 million people have done so.[12]

- People read commentaries on thousands of political blogs, or follow politically oriented people via Twitter and Facebook, and respond with their own commentary. Or they can easily set up their own blogs, Twitter accounts, or Facebook pages to convey their political commentaries.

1965

1969
Defense Department launches Internet (ARPANET)

1970

1972
E-mail introduced

1975

1980

1982
Word *Internet* first used

1984
Domain name system established (.org; .com; .edu)

1985

1989
Creation of hypertext, graphical interface system, basis for the World Wide Web

1995
Dial-up Internet service introduced

1990

1996
Internet traffic in United States hits 45 million daily hits

1999
Napster invented; file-sharing begins on widespread basis

2000
Internet "bubble" bursts; many Internet-based companies fail

1995

2004
Howard Dean uses Internet for campaign organizing and fundraising, political blogs begin to proliferate

2003
Spam reaches 50 percent of all e-mail traffic

2000

2006
92 million websites

2005
Blogs reach 53.4 million worldwide; YouTube.com launched

2007
Google surpasses Microsoft as most valuable global brand

2005

2008
Microsoft makes hostile takeover bid for Yahoo to try to catch Google

2009
2 billion iPhone apps downloaded

2010
Facebook users number 500 million worldwide

2010

2011
100 million active Twitter users worldwide; WikiLeaks leaks secret U.S. government diplomatic files; Twitter and Facebook important tools in organizing the Arab Spring

2012
Facebook users worldwide reaches 800 million

FIGURE 6.1 TIMELINE: THE INTERNET

Sources: Infoplease, www.infoplease.com; "The New News Landscape: Rise of the Internet" (Washington, D.C.: Pew Research Center, March 1 , 2010).

6.1
6.2
6.3
6.4

podcasts
Digital audio and video files made readily available to interested people via computers and portable devices.

- People visit specialized political news websites, some with their own reporters like Politico.com or the Huffington Post, for breaking news and background information on what is going on in Washington or state capitals.

- Millions of people go to the websites of traditional news organizations such as CNN, the *New York Times*, and the *Wall Street Journal* for their news. They also go to news aggregator sites such as Instapaper, Yahoo! News, and Google News.

- People use the Internet to access public affairs information from online university and public libraries, as well as from online encyclopedia-type sites such as Wikipedia.

- People watch newscasts, political commentators, and breaking or audience-generated news on video sites like YouTube.

- People increasingly use social-networking sites like Twitter and Facebook to inform others about breaking stories—demonstrations in Cairo, for example, or a sighting of financial swindler Bernie Madoff walking near his condo in Manhattan—to pass on bits and pieces of news stories from other sources. They also sometimes use social-networking sites to organize demonstrations, as Tea Party activists did several times in their effort to stop health care reform and the Occupy movement did to protest economic inequality and the lack of jobs.

- People use various devices to listen to political **podcasts**, though most listeners, to be sure, are more interested in music and entertainment podcasts.

The Internet has gained in leaps and strides in making and consuming campaign news. During the 2009–2010 election cycle, about one-third of Americans reported that they depended on the Internet as their main source for news about the campaigns, candidates, and issues, about one-third more than during the 2008 campaign cycle, and better than two and one-half times more than in 2004.[13]

At the same time that Internet use has expanded at an exponential rate, there has been a decline in the audience for the most traditional news outlet: newspapers (see

MADOFF SIGHTING

Cell and smart phones with cameras and links to social media sites make it easier for people to gather for celebrity sightings, follow the mistakes and misdeeds of public figures, and organize demonstrations. Here people swarm financial swindler Bernie Madoff on the sidewalk near his New York residence before his conviction. In what ways have such new technologies refashioned how Americans are engaged in political life?

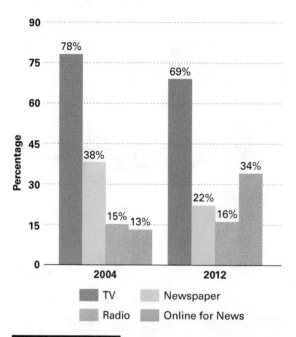

FIGURE 6.2 WHERE PEOPLE GET THEIR NEWS

In recent years, people have turned increasingly to the Internet as a source of news, while decreasing somewhat their reliance on television, newspapers, and radio. Although the Internet still trails television as people's main source of news, it is closing the gap.

Source: Pew Research Center.

wire services
Organizations such as the Associated Press and Reuters that gather and disseminate news to other news organizations.

Figure 6.2). People consistently report that television is their main source of news over newspapers and news magazines, with the Internet closing fast. The collapse in circulation for metropolitan newspapers has been stunning. In 2009, for example, the *Los Angeles Times* lost 11 percent of its readers, the *Boston Globe* lost 18 percent, and the *San Francisco Chronicle* bled 26 percent. The average daily circulation of almost 400 newspapers across the country fell by almost 11 percent between 2005 and 2009.[14] Young people have almost entirely given up on newspaper reading; one survey reports that only 16 percent of 18- to 30-year-olds said they read a newspaper every day.[15] By early 2012, only 11 percent of this group said that newspapers were an important source of news for them. (More than a third of 18- to 24-year-olds reported they got no news at all on the previous day, from whatever source, new media or old.)[16] Network news programs on ABC, CBS, and NBC have now fallen behind cable TV as important sources of campaign and political news, headed by Fox News, CNN, and MSNBC. Though network and cable news networks have changed positions, television remains the favorite source of political news for Americans.[17] A substantial fraction of younger news consumers report that they also rely on satirical television shows like *The Daily Show* or *The Colbert Report* on Comedy Central for their news.

☐ The Continuing Importance of the Mainstream

Despite these developments, the mainstream news media retain their central role in the gathering and reporting of serious political and governmental news. The mainstream or traditional news media are the collection of nationally prominent newspapers (such as the *Wall Street Journal*, the *New York Times*, and the *Washington Post*), national news magazines (such as *Time* and *Newsweek*), TV network news organizations, local newspapers, and local TV news operations that gather, analyze, and report politically important events, developments, and trends, usually with the help of **wire services** such as the Associated Press (AP) and Reuters, the resources of newspaper chains, and syndication services, but sometimes on their own.[18] Research by media scholars shows that the mainstream news organizations, taken as a whole, remain the most important set of institutions for setting the agenda of American politics and shaping how we interpret what is going on in politics and government.

NEWS WITH LAUGHS

Increasingly, young people report that their most trusted news sources are to be found on Comedy Central on shows like *The Daily Show* and *The Colbert Report*, rather than from the major network or cable news offerings. Here the two shows' stars, Jon Stewart and Stephen Colbert, exhort crowds at their semi-mock Rally to Restore Sanity in Washington in 2010.

There are a number of reasons the mainstream or traditional news organizations remain central to political news. For one thing, much of the rich and diverse information on the Internet, whether in the form of advocacy organization websites, political blogs, citizen journalism, or academic and government reports, only reach small and fragmented audiences and usually have an impact only when and to the extent they can attract the attention of the mainstream news media. Bloggers' unearthing of news anchor Dan Rather's sloppy reporting on President George W. Bush's National Guard service during the Vietnam War, for example, only mattered once the story began to run in the nation's leading newspapers and on network and cable news networks. Tens of thousands of bloggers voice their views every day, to take another example, but few gain an audience. One scholar, using a vast database to chronicle the number of daily hits on blogger sites, has determined that only 10 to 20 of them have a readership of any size. Of the 5,000 most-visited political blog sites, for example, the top 5 of them accounted for 28 percent of all blog visits, while the top 10 accounted for almost half. Also, fully half of the top 10 bloggers are or were at one time professional journalists.[19]

It turns out, moreover, that with the exception of the Huffington Post, the most visited hard-news sites are those that are run by traditional media organizations. Among the most popular are those of CBS News, ABC News, the *New York Times*, the *Washington Post*, CNN, Fox News, and MSNBC. The most visited site, the Huffington Post, is a mix of its own original journalism, posts by its regular contributors, and news aggregated from the traditional media.[20]

Much more telling, most political and public policy-related news on the Internet at news aggregator sites such as Yahoo! News and Google News is simply content collected from the mainstream wire services and major newspaper and network news organizations. The same is true for the matters that most political bloggers talk about, and the bits of news that get passed around on social-networking sites: they come mainly from material that has been collected by reporters in the traditional news sector. The grist for commentary at the most popular political sites, including the liberal *Huffington Post* and the conservative *Free Republic* and Townhall.com, comes mainly from traditional news organizations. Much of the airtime on cable news networks such as Fox News, moreover, is devoted to reporting or commenting on material gathered from the major wire services such as the AP or Reuters or prestigious newspapers. And it is to the mainstream media that eager politicians and government officials generally look for clues about what the public and other leaders want and where they try to gain attention for their own views and achievements.

What seems on the surface, then, to be a fantastic expansion in the amount of political news in reality is an expansion in the number of ways in which the news is distributed. It is the same news being passed around and around on the Internet. An exponential growth in commentary on that news is not the same thing as an expansion in the size or quality of the core of political news.[21] As far as scholars have been able to tell, the new digital age news operations have done very little by way of original, in-depth stories.[22] To be sure, this may change before too long. Some mainstream media organizations have been quite aggressive in using citizen reporters to gather and submit news stories—see CNN's iReport website—while new types of social media sites have found ways for people to arrange Facebook posts and tweets, often of a political nature, into chronological narratives to be reposted to social media sites. Mainstream media also use the new media as sources for constructing their own news stories, as when in 2010 the *New York Times* reported about and released much of the raw diplomatic cables gathered by WikiLeaks under the leadership of its founder, Julian Assange.

So, while the news media have changed greatly over our history and continue to change ever more rapidly, and while people can get their news and commentary from many different places ranging from the Internet to cable television, talk radio, and television satire and comedy programs, mainstream news organizations remain the most important set of institutions in the American political news system, even if they are fighting for their lives in an economic sense. It is the reason we mostly focus on the mainstream news media in this chapter, asking how well they play the role assigned to them by democratic theorists.

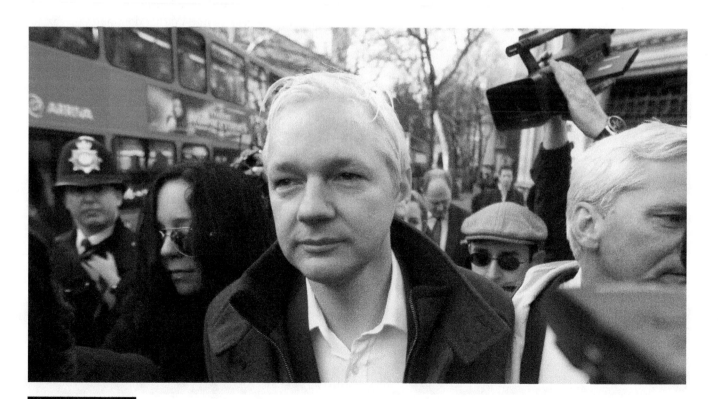

WIKILEAKS FOUNDER IN TROUBLE

WikiLeaks a web-based virtual organization, says it is committed to ending secrecy in government. To that end, it released a massive library of raw American diplomatic cables that came into its possession, causing great embarrassment to American officials and officials in many other countries. Here WikiLeaks founder Julian Assange leaves a hearing before the High Court in Great Britain in 2011. He was fighting his extradition to Sweden, where he faced sexual assault charges. His followers claim these charges were fabricated by government leaders concerned about the spread of the WikiLeaks phenomenon. To what extent should there be secrecy in government? Does a democracy require complete openness?

How the Mainstream News Media Work

6.3	Analyze how the news is gathered and disseminated and evaluate the outcome of this process

Explore on MyPoliSciLab
Simulation
You Are a Newspaper Editor

Whether citizens get from the news media the kinds of information they need for democracy to work properly depends on how the media are organized and function. In the remainder of this chapter, we focus on news media organizations and journalists with an eye toward better understanding the influences that affect the content of their news product and how the news shapes politics and government in the United States.

☐ Organization of the News Media

News media in the United States are almost entirely privately owned businesses. Most are either very large businesses in their own right or, more typically, part of very large corporate empires.

CORPORATE OWNERSHIP Some television stations and newspapers—especially the smaller ones—are still owned locally by families or by groups of investors, although they account for a rapidly declining share of the total. Most of the biggest stations and newspapers, however, as well as the television and cable networks, are owned by large media corporations, some of which, in turn, are subsidiaries of enormous conglomerates.

Each media sector is dominated by a few firms.[23] Gannett dominates the newspaper business, a media sector that has fallen on hard times because of declining readership, especially among young adults, and shrinking ad revenues as classified advertising migrates to online sites such as Craigslist. Time Warner dominates magazine

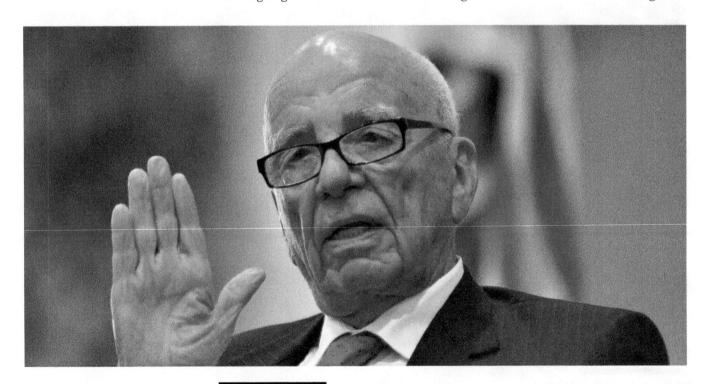

I WANT MORE

Rupert Murdoch has created a global entertainment and news operation that gives him influence with the public, opinion leaders, and government officials in a wide range of countries. Though revelations about reporters from several of his publications in Britain illegally tapping into cell phones damaged his reputation, his company, News Corp., continues to be among the biggest players in the world and in the United States. Does this development of giant media empires diminish the number of viewpoints citizens get to consider, or is there sufficient alternative information from other outlets such as the Internet?

publishing. Comcast, Disney, CBS, News Corp., and Time Warner dominate network and cable television. Clear Channel, while suffering major setbacks, still owns about 600 stations across the country and dominates radio with 16.7 million listeners. And six firms (Paramount, Warner Brothers, Columbia, Disney, Universal, and 20th Century Fox) receive most of the gross box office revenues from movies.[24]

Mergers across media lines have accelerated in recent years, leaving a handful of giant conglomerates. Disney, for example, owns not only its theme parks, movie production and distribution operations, and sports teams, but the ABC television network, local TV and radio stations in the nation's largest cities, cable television operations, and book publishers. Rupert Murdoch's News Corp. owns local TV stations in many of the nation's largest cities, cable and satellite operations (including Fox News and DirecTV), the 20th Century Fox film company, the *New York Post* and major newspapers in Great Britain and Australia, a stable of magazines and journals, HarperCollins and Harper-Morrow book companies, and radio and TV operations in Europe and Asia. In 2007, he acquired one of the most influential news organizations in the world, the *Wall Street Journal*. (Journalists at the paper were dismayed, perhaps because Murdoch says he "finds long stories about complicated subjects to be rather trying").[25]

So, behind the apparent proliferation of news sources—new magazines, online news and opinion operations, cable television news and commentary, handheld devices with links to the Web, and the like—is substantial concentration of ownership and dense interconnections among the vast cornucopia of news and entertainment outlets. Some have used the term **media monopoly** to suggest how serious the situation is, though most scholars are loath to go that far, believing that much competition remains among the giant firms.[26]

Scholars disagree about the effects of corporate ownership and increased media concentration. A few see efficiency gains and an increase in the output and availability of information. But some critics maintain that the concentrated corporate control of our media adds dangerously to the already strong business presence in American politics. Those who use the term *media monopoly* worry that media corporations are so large, powerful, and interconnected that alternative voices to the economically and politically powerful cannot have their views aired. Still others are concerned that the concentration of media ownership may lead to less diversity of news and opinion or a preference for entertainment values trumping news values as powerful profit-seeking enterprises focus on the bottom line. Still others worry that news organizations may pull their punches when reporting about the activities of their corporate parents or partners. Will ABC News go easy on problems at Disney, for example, which owns ABC?

UNIFORMITY AND DIVERSITY Whoever owns them, most newspapers and television stations depend largely on the same sources for news. Political scientist Lance Bennett points out that while there is a growing diversity of news outlets in the United States—more specialized magazines, television channels, and newspaper home pages on the Web—news sources are contracting. That is to say, much of what comes to us over a multitude of media avenues originates in fewer and fewer centralized sources.[27] Local radio stations increasingly buy headlines for their brief on-the-hour updates from a handful of headline service providers. Television news increasingly buys raw video footage, for in-house editing and scripting, from a handful of providers, including Independent Television News (ITN), rather than having their own reporters and film crews on the ground. The AP supplies most of the main national and international news stories for newspapers and local news (although Reuters is increasingly important)—even those that are rewritten to carry a local reporter's byline. Most of what appears on network and cable television news, too, is inspired by the AP wire, although they often take their lead on the major stories of the day from the major national newspapers such as the *New York Times*, the *Wall Street Journal*, and the *Washington Post*.[28] National and local television news organizations depend on centralized news and video suppliers, with fewer of them using their own reporters. This is why viewers are likely to see the same news (and sports) footage on different stations as they switch channels, although each station adds its own "voiceover" from a reporter or news anchor. In most cases, the person doing the voiceover has no direct relationship to the story. (For more on the state of local news, see the "By the Numbers" feature.)

media monopoly
Term used to suggest that media corporations are so large, powerful, and interconnected that the less economically and politically powerful cannot have their views aired.

6.1

6.2

6.3

6.4

Where Do You Get Your Political News?

Politically-interested people get their news from four news outlets—television, the Internet, print, and radio. Among these media sources, no single one dominates the others, but partisan trends do exist. Republicans more often go to Fox News, while more Democrats go to NPR's "All Things Considered".

Americans Go To These News Sources

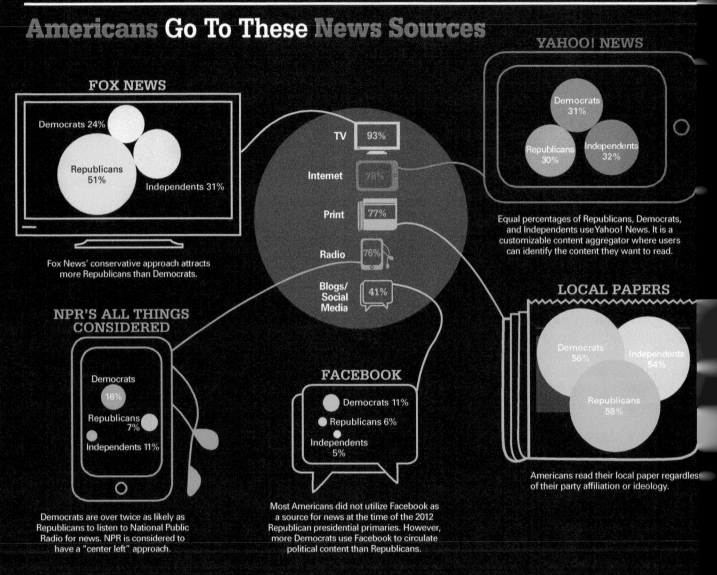

FOX NEWS

Democrats 24%
Republicans 51%
Independents 31%

Fox News' conservative approach attracts more Republicans than Democrats.

YAHOO! NEWS

Democrats 31%
Republicans 30%
Independents 32%

Equal percentages of Republicans, Democrats, and Independents use Yahoo! News. It is a customizable content aggregator where users can identify the content they want to read.

TV 93%
Internet 78%
Print 77%
Radio 76%
Blogs/Social Media 41%

NPR'S ALL THINGS CONSIDERED

Democrats 16%
Republicans 7%
Independents 11%

Democrats are over twice as likely as Republicans to listen to National Public Radio for news. NPR is considered to have a "center left" approach.

FACEBOOK

Democrats 11%
Republicans 6%
Independents 5%

Most Americans did not utilize Facebook as a source for news at the time of the 2012 Republican presidential primaries. However, more Democrats use Facebook to circulate political content than Republicans.

LOCAL PAPERS

Democrats 56%
Independents 54%
Republicans 58%

Americans read their local paper regardless of their party affiliation or ideology.

SOURCE: Data from American National Election Survey, "Evaluations of Government and Society Study," Release Wave 4, February 2012.

Investigate Further

Concept Where are people getting their political news? Politically-interested Americans go to several types of outlets for political news. Television is still the most popular news source, but the Internet, print, and radio hold substantial ground. Despite widespread popularity among youth, social media—like Facebook—is not a dominant source for political news.

Connection How is politics related to media choices? In general, Americans tend to seek information that reinforces their politics. The rise of cable television and Internet sources compartmentalized information. People can't read or watch all the news, so they choose a few "comfortable" content providers who reinforce their opinions and beliefs.

Cause Do the major parties exhibit particular media consumption habits? Both parties have certain news sources that they favor over others. For example, Republicans rely more on Fox News while Democrats tend toward NPR's "All Things Considered". However, party crossover in media use does exist, particularly for Internet and social media sources.

By the Numbers

How much serious crime is there in the United States?

"If it bleeds, it leads" seems to be the mantra of television news. Indeed, we are in danger in this country of being overwhelmed by news stories about crime, and the problem seems to be getting worse. While coverage of public affairs and foreign affairs has been falling, news coverage of crime has flourished, especially on local news telecasts.

Why It Matters

If television news broadcasts are accurately portraying real trends in crime, then they are doing a public service. If portrayals are inaccurate, then the public is being misled. This is problematic because public and official perceptions about the scale of particular social problems affect politics and government deeply. For example,

- When pressed by the public to address a perceived problem, government officials respond by redirecting resources at the problem and make budget and personnel decisions in light of it. If the problem is a false one, then government attention and resources get used ineffectively.

- Candidates campaign on issues that are most salient to the public. When the public misperceives the scale of a problem, it makes electoral choices based on irrelevant grounds.

- The more threatening the public finds a particular problem, the more it pushes aside other public priorities, such as education and health care.

The Story Behind the Crime Numbers

How accurately are the news media portraying the true state of affairs? To put it bluntly, not very well. Crime in general, and violent crime in particular, declined substantially during the 1990s, at precisely the same time that concerns about crime were at the forefront of media, popular attention, and political saliency. How do we know this to be the case?

The two most widely used measures of the incidence of crime in the United States are the Uniform Crime Report (UCR) of the FBI and the National Crime Victimization Survey (NCVS) of the Department of Justice. Each counts the incidence of crime in a different way. The UCR is based on reports from law enforcement agencies and is meant to help state and local police departments track their own performance and plan their budgets. The NCVS is based on a survey of victims of crime and is used to assess how crime is experienced by Americans and how it affects them and their families.

Calculating the Crime Rate

The FBI's UCR, based on reports submitted voluntarily by state and local law enforcement agencies, counts the annual incidence of "violent crimes" (murder, forcible rape, robbery, and aggravated assault), "property crimes" (burglary, larceny-theft, motor vehicle theft, and arson), and "serious crimes" (all of the above). However, here is what is most important about the FBI's methodology: *it only counts crimes that come to the attention of police.*

The Justice Department's NCVS is based on an annual survey of roughly 50,000 randomly selected U.S. households. One person over the age of 18 in each household is interviewed about any crimes that may have been committed against any member of the household during the previous year. The result is annual crime *victimization* information for more than 100,000 people, a very large number for a national survey. Because the NCVS includes crimes experienced by people that are never reported to the authorities, it tends to show higher rates of serious crime than the UCR.

SERIOUS VIOLENT CRIMES

Source: Crime Victimization 2011 and Uniform Crime Reports, Bureau of Justice Statistics, 2011.

Criticisms of Crime Rate Calculations

The experts generally prefer the NCVS numbers to those of the UCR for understanding the dimensions of the crime problem. The principal problems with the UCR concern the accuracy of recording and reporting crime. For example,

■ Many serious crimes, especially rape, go unreported to police. The fact that the UCR came closer to the NCVS numbers starting in the 1990s may mean that more crimes are being reported than in the past.

■ Ideas about what constitutes a serious crime may change as social mores change. Domestic violence was treated in the past by police as a family matter; now it tends to get recorded and reported by police.

■ A small number of law enforcement agencies do not participate in the UCR reporting system or do not treat it with the seriousness that the FBI hopes for.

What to Watch for

Each way of measuring crime is valid and has its purposes. Although the UCR measure has some problems, it does a fairly good job of telling us what is going on year to year with respect to police encounters with crime. This, in turn, is useful to national, state, and local governments in deciding on budget and staffing issues for law enforcement. The NCVS does a very good job of telling us what is going on year to year with respect to overall victimization trends, and gives us a handle on the size of the underlying crime problem. The lesson here is to use the statistic that conforms most closely to the purposes of your inquiry.

What Do You Think?

How do television news programs underplay or overplay the incidence of violent crime? Monitor local and national news for the next week or so and try to keep a running count of stories about crime. How does your count match what the UCR and NCVS numbers are telling us about crime?

---

infotainment

The merging of hard news and entertainment in news presentations.

PROFIT MOTIVES Media companies, like other companies, are in business to make a profit. This is entirely appropriate in general terms but has some important and unfortunate consequences for how media companies create and disseminate the news. For many newspapers and television news organizations, this often means closing down foreign bureaus and cutting the number of reporters focused on government affairs in Washington or the economy and financial system. For many traditional news organizations, there are market pressures to alter their news coverage to appeal to audiences who are more interested in entertainment than public affairs and want their news short, snappy, and sensational. This sort of **infotainment** is increasingly offered on network and cable television news and in *USA Today*. If consumers of the news do not want long and detailed investigative reports, and given that such stories are very expensive to do because of the cost of having many seasoned reporters on the payroll—according to one seasoned newsman, "a skilled investigative reporter can cost a news organization more than $250,000 a year in salary and expenses for only a handful of stories"[29]—then news media companies may be tempted to shift to infotainment or to use generic news created by others. These trends toward infotainment and generic news are especially well developed in evening local news broadcasts, where coverage of politics, government, and policies that affect the public have been "crowded out by coverage of crime, sports, weather, lifestyles, and other audience-grabbing topics."[30]

☐ Political Newsmaking

The kind of news that the media present is affected by the organization and technology of news gathering and news production. Much depends on where reporters are, what sources they talk to, and what sorts of video is available.

THE LIMITED GEOGRAPHY OF POLITICAL NEWS Serious national news comes from surprisingly few places. For the most part, the news comes from Washington, D.C., the seat of the federal government, and New York City, the center of publishing and finance in the United States. This is where most news media companies locate their reporters, though a few other areas get coverage as well. We show how the news is geographically concentrated in the "Mapping American Politics" feature.

Mapping American Politics

The Limited Geography of National News

Introduction

Most national political reporters are located in and file their stories from two main locations: Washington, D.C., site of the federal government and most of the nation's most influential think tanks and interest group organizations, and New York City, the center of most media operations and key national and global financial institutions. For national news involving more than politics and governmental affairs or closely related economic issues, reporters tend to file stories from a broader range of geographical locations, although not equally from all areas around the United States. This is hardly surprising: maintaining reporters is expensive, so news organizations concentrate their news gathering where they will get the most bang for the buck—where the most important news occurs.

Mapping the News

The cartogram depicts the states and the District of Columbia resized from normal in proportion to the number of headlines in wire service stories originating from these locations in recent years. If news stories had originated in various states in proportion to their populations, the states' size would correspond to the relative sizes of their populations. In this cartogram, however, New York City, New York State, New Jersey, and California stand out as sites that generate a disproportionate share of news stories, as do Georgia, Florida, and, given its tiny geographic area (less than 10 miles square), Washington, D.C. New York City, its metropolitan area (which includes parts of New York State, New Jersey, and Connecticut),

and Washington, D.C. generate so much news for the reasons cited earlier. Georgia's relatively large size may be due to the fact that both CNN and the federal government's Centers for Disease Control and Prevention are based there. Florida is in the news often because of tight and controversial political contests as well as more than its share of hurricanes. California generates many stories from the entertainment industry, much of which is centered there, as well as from Silicon Valley, the heart of the nation's high-tech industry. Some states virtually disappear, with very few news stories originating in the Mountain West, Southwest, Great Plains, and Midwest (other than Illinois), or the New England states of New Hampshire, Vermont, and Maine. News stories from Texas are less than one might expect, given the importance of the state in American politics, energy production, music, and the high-tech industry in Austin.

What Do You Think?

Why might one argue that it is reasonable that news stories are concentrated in America's centers of governance, communications, finance, and entertainment? Can you think of some way that news might be gathered to avoid such concentrations? Some people say that the news media are out of touch with the American people. What is the basis of this argument? Does the pattern in the cartogram showing the origins of news stories help explain the situation?

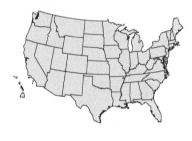

Headline News: Size of States in Proportion to Number of Headlines

MAP NOTE: Alaska is not shown (although information about Alaska is included in calculations where relevant), and Hawaii is moved closer to the mainland.

SOURCE: Data from Michael Gastner and described in M. T. Gastner and M. E. J. Newman, "Diffusion-Based Method for Producing Density-Equalizing Maps," *Proceedings of the National Academy of Sciences* 101 (May 18, 2004), pp. 7499–7504. Wire service news headlines from 1994 to 1998.

beat
The assigned location where a reporter regularly gathers news stories.

The major television networks and most newspapers cannot afford to station many reporters outside Washington, D.C. or New York.[31] The networks usually add just Chicago, Los Angeles, Miami, and Houston or Dallas. When stories break in San Francisco or Seattle, news organizations can rush reporters to the area or turn to part-time "stringers" to do the reporting. Some significant stories from outside the main media centers simply do not make it into the national news. News-only channels, such as CNN, CNBC, and Fox News, have a big advantage on fast-breaking news, which they are ready to cover (through their own reporters or the purchase of local footage) and broadcast immediately on their continuous newscasts.

While some newspapers have strong regional bureaus, the majority print mostly wire service reports of news from elsewhere around the country. The television networks' assignment editors also rely on the wire services to decide what stories to cover.

Because so much expensive, high-tech equipment is involved, and because a considerable amount of editing is required to turn raw video into coherent stories, most television news coverage is assigned to predictable events—news conferences and the like—long before they happen, usually in one of the cities with a permanent television crew. For such spontaneous news as riots, accidents, and natural disasters, special video camera crews can be rushed to the location, but they usually arrive after the main events occur and have to rely on "reaction" interviews or aftermath stories. This is not always true; occasionally television news organizations find themselves in the middle of an unfolding series of events and can convey its texture, explore its human meaning, and speculate about its political implications in particularly meaningful ways. This was certainly true of television coverage of the Hurricane Katrina disaster and its immediate aftermath in 2005.

DEPENDENCE ON OFFICIAL SOURCES Most political news is based on what public officials say. This fact has important consequences for how well the media serve democracy.

Beats and Routines A newspaper or television reporter's work is usually organized around a particular **beat**, which he or she checks every day for news stories. Most political beats center on some official government institution that regularly produces news, such as a local police station or city council, the White House, Congress, the Pentagon, an American embassy abroad, or a country's foreign ministry.

In fact, many news reports are created or originated by officials, not by reporters. Investigative reporting of the sort that Carl Bernstein and Robert Woodward did to uncover the Watergate scandal, which led to the impeachment and resignation of President Richard Nixon in 1974, is rare because it is so time-consuming and expensive. Most reporters get most of their stories quickly and efficiently from press conferences and the press releases that officials write, along with comments solicited from other officials. One pioneering study by Leon Sigal found that government officials, domestic or foreign, were the sources of nearly three-quarters of all news in the *New York Times* and the *Washington Post*. Moreover, the vast majority, 70 to 90 percent of all news stories, were drawn from situations over which the newsmakers had substantial control: press conferences (24.5 percent), interviews (24.7 percent), press releases (17.5 percent), and official proceedings (13 percent).[32] Recent research suggests that the situation described by Sigal remains relatively unchanged.[33]

Beats and news-gathering routines encourage a situation of mutual dependence by reporters (and their news organizations) and government officials. Reporters want stories; they have to cultivate access to people who can provide stories with quotes or anonymous leaks. Officials want favorable publicity and to avoid or counteract unfavorable publicity. Thus, a comfortable relationship tends to develop. Even when reporters put on a show of aggressive questioning at White House press conferences, they usually work hard to stay on good terms with officials and to avoid fundamental challenges of the officials' positions. Cozy relationships between the Washington press corps and top government officials are further encouraged by the fact that the participants know each other so well, often living in the same neighborhoods, attending the same social gatherings, and sending their children to the same private schools.[34]

While often decried by officials hurt by a damaging revelation, the **leak** is an important part of news gathering that is useful both to journalists and officials, and so is a part of the normal currency of journalist–official working relationships. Indeed, Woodward and Bernstein's Watergate story got its start with leaks from the anonymous "Deep Throat," revealed in 2005 to be Mark Felt, deputy director of the FBI during the Nixon administration. Most commonly, leaking is a way for officials to float policy ideas, get themselves noticed and credited with good deeds, undercut rivals in other government agencies, or report real or imagined wrongdoing. Because the practice is so common and useful, it is likely to remain central to how news is made.

Government News Management The news media's heavy reliance on official sources means that government officials are sometimes able to control what journalists report and how they report it.[35] This is commonly referred to as **spin**. Every president and high-ranking official wants to help reporters spin a story in a way that is most useful or favorable to the office holder. The Reagan administration was particularly successful at picking a "story of the day" and having many officials feed that story to reporters, with a unified interpretation.[36] The Clinton administration tried to do the same but was not disciplined enough to make it work. President George W. Bush's administration pushed the news management envelope the farthest, eventually acknowledging that it had paid three journalists to write favorable stories, encouraged executive agencies to create news videos for media outlets without revealing the source of the videos, and allowed a political operative to be planted among the accredited White House press corps to ask questions at presidential news conferences.[37] President Obama's team ran an impressive news management operation using many of the same Internet-based tools honed during his nomination and election campaigns to get his administration's story out, partially bypassing the traditional news media. But he also generated a great deal of criticism when his press aides announced in 2009 that the president and his administration would have nothing more to do with Fox News because the network, in their view, failed to separate its news reporting and editorial (strongly conservative) functions. Obama did this after Fox News allowed on-screen personalities like Glenn Beck and Sean Hannity to help mobilize the Tea Party movement to hold rallies across the country to protest the health reform bill, then sent its news cameras and correspondents to give the gatherings extensive coverage.

leak
Inside or secret information given to a journalist or media outlet by a government official.

news management
The attempt by those in political power to put the presentation of news about them and their policies in a favorable light.

spin
The attempt by public officials to have a story reported in terms that favor them and their policies; see news management.

NEWS FROM THE FIELD
Increasingly, news from the battlefield is reaching the public from soldiers blogging about their experiences and observations. Tight control of the news by officials has become more difficult because of this. To what extent does this help or hinder the public's understanding of our engagement in armed conflict abroad?

6.1

6.2

6.3

6.4

newsworthy
Worth printing or broadcasting as news, according to editors' judgments.

Managing images in press reports is also important. Every administration in the modern era has tried to manage public perceptions by staging events that convey strong symbolic messages. For example, George W. Bush announced that the invasion of Iraq had been successfully concluded not in a press release but from the deck of the aircraft carrier *USS Lincoln* on May 2, 2003, in front of a massive sign "Mission Accomplished," after landing in a jet on its runway. Barack Obama told Americans about his new strategy in Afghanistan not from his desk in the Oval Office but in a televised address in front of the cadets at West Point.

Of course, news management doesn't always work as planned. When the war in Iraq took a bad turn, Bush's "Mission Accomplished" came to seem false and hollow to many Americans, and the president's popularity took a dramatic plunge. With fewer American casualties in Afghanistan—by 2012, most of the fighting there was being done by Special Forces units and drone aircraft—President Obama was more insulated from the effects of bad war news.

Military Actions Dependence on official sources is especially evident in military actions abroad. Because it is wary of the release of information that might help an adversary or undermine public support for U.S. actions—as happened during the Vietnam conflict—the Defense Department tries to restrict access of reporters to military personnel and the battlefield and provide carefully screened information for use by the news media. Information management was especially evident during the 1991 Gulf War to expel Saddam Hussein from Kuwait, with its carefully stage-managed news briefings at U.S. military headquarters in Saudi Arabia featuring video of "smart" weapons, Defense Department organization of press pools to cover parts of the war, and tight restrictions on reporters' access to the battlefields in Kuwait and Iraq.

During the rapid advance to Baghdad to topple Hussein's regime in 2003, the Defense Department encouraged coverage of combat by journalists embedded in combat units, although administration officials continued to exercise control over information about the big picture during the initial stages of the war. In the end, however, the administration was unable to control news about military and civilian casualties during the long occupation, the difficulties of helping to create a new constitution and government for that country, and the abuse of Iraqi prisoners at Abu Ghraib and other prisons. There were simply too many journalists and news organizations from around the world reporting on events there—and too many American soldiers and Iraqi civilians posting what they were seeing and experiencing to blogs—for the administration and military officials to be able to control the news.

NEWSWORTHINESS Decisions about what kinds of news to print or televise depend largely on professional judgments about what is **newsworthy**. Exactly what makes a story newsworthy is difficult to spell out, but experienced editors make quick and confident judgments of what their audiences (and their employers) want. If they were consistently wrong, they would probably not remain in their jobs for very long.

In practice, newsworthiness seems to depend on such factors as novelty (man bites dog, not dog bites man), drama and human interest, relevance to the lives of Americans, high stakes (physical violence or conflict), and celebrity. Some trivial topics are judged newsworthy, such as the recurring troubles of movie actress Lindsay Lohan. As the term *news story* implies, news works best when it can be framed as a familiar kind of narrative: an exposé of greed, sex, or corruption; conflict between politicians; or a foreign affairs crisis. On television, of course, dramatic or startling film footage helps make a story gripping. Important stories without visuals are often pushed aside for less important stories for which visuals exist.

This can often lead to missing very big stories in the making. For example, though experts had been worried for many years about the safety of New Orleans, and had been publishing their research results in specialized journals for some time, the news media did not pay much attention until the levees broke when Hurricane Katrina struck in 2005. To take another example, no reporters were at an important 2004 meeting of the Securities and Exchange Commission when the SEC decided to relax capital requirements—how much money firms had to have on hand to deal with crises—for big financial firms.[38] This decision played an important role in the collapse of the financial system in the late summer and early fall of 2008.

objective journalism
News reported with no evaluative language and with opinions quoted or attributed to a specific source.

TEMPLATES On many important stories, a subtle "governing template" may prevail—a sense among both reporters and editors that news stories must take a generally agreed-upon slant to be taken seriously and to make it into the news broadcast or the newspaper. This is not because of censorship but because of the development of a general agreement among news reporters and editors that the public already knows what the big story looks like on a range of issues—filling in the details is what is important. Take reporting from China as an example. For many years, editors only wanted to hear about economic prosperity, emerging democratic freedoms, and happy peasants liberated from the economic and personal straightjacket of the Maoist collective farm system. After the pro-democracy demonstrations in Tiananmen Square were brutally repressed by the People's Liberation Army, however, reporters say that it became almost impossible to write anything positive about China, because the prevailing template about China had changed.[39] Now that China has become a very important trading partner, stories about the Chinese economic miracle have proliferated (as well as some worrying about China as a potential economic, diplomatic, and military rival and as a source of tainted goods). Coverage of the Beijing Olympics became almost euphoric, despite ill-treatment of dissidents during the Games.

EPISODIC FOREIGN COVERAGE Very few newspapers other than the *New York Times* can afford to station reporters abroad. Even the *Times* and the networks and wire services cannot regularly cover most nations of the world. They keep reporters in the countries of greatest interest to Americans—those that have big effects on American interests or enjoy close economic or cultural ties with the United States, such as Great Britain, Germany, Japan, Israel, Russia, and China—and they have regional bureaus in Africa and Latin America. In many countries, however, they depend on "stringers" (local journalists who file occasional reports). During major crises or big events, the media send in temporary news teams, such as the armies of reporters that swarmed to Bosnia and Kosovo during the conflicts with the Serbs. The result is that most media devote the majority of their attention to limited areas of the world, dropping in only occasionally on others.

Foreign news, therefore, tends to be episodic. An unfamiliar part of the world, such as the Darfur region of the Sudan, suddenly jumps into the headlines with a spectacular story of ethnic cleansing, or elsewhere a coup, an invasion, or a famine comes as a surprise to most Americans because they have not been prepared by background reports. (Journalism.org, the website of the Columbia Journalism Review, reports that only 0.2 percent of news coverage in the United States in 2011 was about Sub-Sahara Africa.)[40] For a few days or weeks, the story dominates the news, with intensive coverage through pictures, interviews, and commentaries. Then, if nothing new and exciting happens, the story grows stale and disappears from the media. Most viewers are left with little more understanding of the country than they began with. Thus, they find it difficult to form judgments about U.S. foreign policy.[41]

INTERPRETING Political news may not make much sense without an interpretation of what it means. Under the informal rules of **objective journalism**, taught in university journalism schools and practiced by the nation's leading newspapers and network news programs, however, explicit interpretations by journalists are avoided, except for commentary or editorials that are labeled as such (some cable news operations, however, and without apology, freely mix commentary and news). Thus, even if a reporter knows that an official is lying, he or she cannot say so directly but must find someone else who will say so for the record.[42] Staged events—such as a president holding a "town meeting" using carefully selected and screened audience members—are rarely identified by reporters as staged events. In news stories, most interpretations are left implicit (so that they are hard to detect and argue with) or are given by so-called

pundits
Somewhat derisive term for print, broadcast, and radio commentators on the political news.

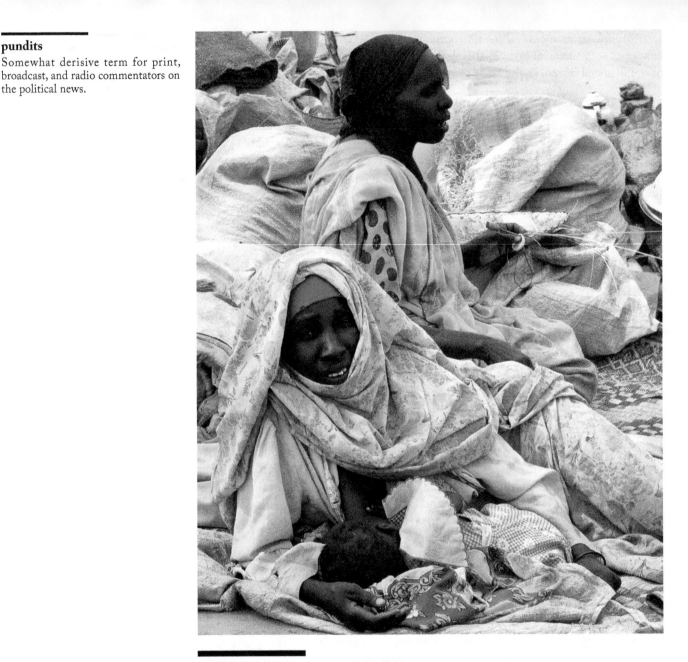

WAITING FOR HELP

These women refugees from the genocidal conflict in the Darfur region of Sudan wait for their daily food ration in the El Fasher camp. The conflict in this region displaced almost 2 million people, with most living in dreadful conditions. News coverage of Darfur and the state of its people is spotty, however, gaining attention for a time when a celebrity or prominent politician visits a refugee camp, or when a demonstration takes place in a major city in Europe or the United States, then fading into the background. Why isn't media coverage of these kinds of international issues more consistent?

experts who are interviewed for comments. Often, particular experts are selected by print, broadcast, and telecast journalists because the position the experts will take is entirely predictable.

Experts are selected partly for reasons of convenience and audience appeal: scholars and commentators who live close to New York City or Washington, D.C., who like to speak in public, who look good on camera, and who are skillful in coming up with colorful quotations on a variety of subjects, are contacted again and again. They often show up on television to comment on the news of the day, even on issues that are far from the area of their special expertise. In many cases, these **pundits** are simply well-known for being on television often and are not experts on any subject at all. The experts and commentators featured in the media are often ex-officials. Their views are usually in harmony with the political currents of the day; that is, they tend to reflect a fairly narrow spectrum of opinion close to that of the party in power in Washington, D.C., or to the prevailing "conventional wisdom" inside the Beltway.

☐ Is the News Biased?

Few topics arouse more disagreement than the question of whether the mass media in the United States have a liberal or conservative **bias**—or any bias at all. Many liberal critics believe the news media favor Republicans and the business establishment,[43] while many conservative critics believe the news media are unfair to Republicans and favor liberal social causes.[44] A big majority of Americans (67 percent in 2012) supported the proposition that the news media are biased; only 31 percent thought the news was unbiased or not too biased.[45] Much, of course, is in the eye of the beholder; experimental research shows that strong Democrats and strong Republicans, reading the exact same news accounts, believe the stories are biased against their favored positions and candidates.[46]

LIBERAL REPORTERS Surveys of reporters' and journalists' opinions suggest that these individuals tend to be somewhat more liberal than the average American on certain matters, including the environment and such social issues as civil rights and liberties, affirmative action, abortion, and women's rights.[47] This is especially true of those employed by certain elite media organizations, including the *New York Times,* the *Washington Post,* and PBS. It is likely that reporters' liberalism has been reflected in the treatment of issues such as global warming, same-sex marriage, and abortion. In recent years, to be sure, more conservative reporters and newscasters have gained prominence, especially on cable news telecasts; Bill O'Reilly, Sean Hannity, and Glenn Beck at Fox News are some examples (Beck is no longer at Fox).

There is, however, little or no systematic evidence that reporters' personal values regularly affect what appears in the mainstream news media.[48] Journalists' commitment to the idea of objectivity helps them resist temptation, as do critical scrutiny and rewriting by editors. In any case, the liberalism of journalists may be offset by their need to rely on official sources, their reliance on experts who are either former officials or associated with centrist or conservative think tanks, and the need to get their stories past editors who are accountable to mostly conservative owners and publishers. So for every set of stories considered biased by conservatives. For example, reporting on the abuse of prisoners at Guantanamo Bay—there is a matching set of stories considered biased by liberals—for example, not carefully examining the Bush administration's claims about weapons of mass destruction in Iraq before we invaded.

NOT-SO-LIBERAL OWNERS AND CORPORATIONS The owners and top managers of most news media organizations tend to be conservative and Republican. This

bias

Deviation from ideal standards such as representativeness or objectivity.

STUNNED BY KATRINA

Many conservative commentators charged that the news media focused on poor African Americans in New Orleans as the main victims of Hurricane Katrina when, in fact, the range of victims was much more diverse and living across a broader swath of Gulf Coast states. Is this a fair assessment of the media coverage?

is hardly surprising. The shareholders and executives of multi-billion-dollar corporations are not very interested in undermining the free enterprise system, for example, or, for that matter, increasing their own taxes, raising labor costs, or losing income from offended advertisers. These owners and managers ultimately decide which reporters, newscasters, and editors to hire or fire, promote or discourage. Journalists who want to get ahead, therefore, may have to come to terms with the policies of the people who own and run media businesses.[49]

BIASES THAT MATTER The question of political bias in the mainstream news media—whether in a liberal or conservative sense, or in a Democratic or Republican sense—is not so easily answered. Both reporters and news media owners considered as individuals have such biases, but it is difficult to see that these views consistently move news reports in one direction or another. Other biases perhaps matter more. One such bias is reporters' dependence on official sources, a matter examined in a previous section. Another is the bias or set of biases generated by the marketplace. News media organizations are themselves business enterprises or part of larger corporate entities and are in business to make a profit for themselves or their corporate parents. This leads many of them to engage in certain practices in news gathering and presentation that may be harmful to their central role in a democratic society. We examine these practices in much of the remainder of this chapter.

☐ Prevailing Themes in Political News

Even if we cannot be sure whether or how the news media are biased, it is easy to identify certain tendencies in news coverage, certain beliefs that are assumed, and certain values and points of view that are emphasized.

NATIONALISM Although perhaps not terribly surprising, most news about foreign affairs takes a definitely pro-American, patriotic point of view, usually putting the United States in a favorable light and its opponents in an unfavorable light. This tendency is especially pronounced in news about military conflicts involving U.S. troops, as in Iraq and Afghanistan, but it can be found as well in a wide range of foreign affairs news reports, including those concerning conflicts with other governments on trade, arms control, immigration, and intellectual property rights (patents and copyrights).

News organizations also focus on subjects that interest and concern ordinary Americans, regardless of their importance in the larger picture. For example, in the early 1990s, they exhaustively covered a U.S. pilot, Scott O'Grady, who had been shot down over Bosnia. But much less attention was paid to the slaughter of millions of people during the same time in Indonesia, Nigeria, East Timor, Cambodia, and Rwanda.

This nationalistic perspective, together with heavy reliance on U.S. government news sources, means that coverage of foreign news generally harmonizes well with official U.S. foreign policy. Thus, the media tend to go along with the U.S. government in assuming the best about our close allies and the worst about official "enemies." When the United States was assisting Iraq in its war against Iran during the 1980s, for example, Saddam Hussein was depicted in a positive light; during the 1991 Gulf War and the Iraq War that started 12 years later, media characterizations of him turned dramatically negative.

In foreign policy crisis situations, the reliance on official news sources means that the media sometimes propagate government statements that are false or misleading, as in the announcement of unprovoked attacks on U.S. destroyers in the Gulf of Tonkin at the beginning of the Vietnam War. Secret information can also be controlled by the government. And political leaders know that the news media will be cautious in its criticism when troops are deployed and put in harm's way.

It is important to point out that when the use of American armed forces abroad drags on beyond expectations and goals are not met (as in the conflicts in Vietnam and Iraq), the news media can and do become exceedingly negative in their coverage. This may simply reflect the mood change among nonadministration leaders and the public, or it might be a reaction among journalists and news organizations to their initial uncritical coverage of administration policies.

APPROVAL OF THE AMERICAN ECONOMIC SYSTEM Another tendency of the news media is to run stories generally approving of the basics of the American free enterprise system—free markets, strong property rights, and minimal government—and critical of systems that take a different approach. European social democracies with comprehensive social welfare programs, for example, rarely win praise and are often chided for their economic inefficiencies. Countries such as France, Italy, and Germany are commonly criticized for labor policies that make it difficult to fire employees and downsize companies, again on economic efficiency grounds. Meanwhile, countries whose economic policies mirror those of the U.S. economy, such as Poland and Chile, win praise. To be sure, individual U.S. companies (e.g., Lehman Brothers, AIG, and Goldman Sachs) and particular industries (e.g., the sub-prime mortgage sector) are criticized for errors and misdeeds, but the basics of the economic system itself are rarely challenged. When an economic disaster like the Great Recession happens, news consumers and news organizations are eager to focus on "who is to blame" rather than on issues like the instability that may be inherent in market-driven financial systems.[50]

NEGATIVITY AND SCANDAL One sign that the news media are neither Republican nor Democratic, conservative nor liberal in their sympathies is the relish they take in covering and magnifying scandals involving political leaders and candidates of all stripes. Although the catalyst for these stories may be leaks from inside the government; negative ads aired by rival candidates, political parties, or advocacy groups; or postings to partisan and ideological blogs, they often are picked up by major news media outlets and developed further, occasionally with great gusto.[51] These stories are especially compelling to the news media when even the appearance of wrongdoing in the personal lives of prominent people creates dramatic human interest stories. Sex scandals dogged Bill Clinton for most of his presidency and contributed to his eventual impeachment. Sex or financial scandals also claimed, among others, Senator Gary Hart (D–CO), former House Speakers Jim Wright (D–TX), Newt Gingrich (R–GA), Mark Foley (R–FL), Larry Craig (R–ID), and South Carolina Governor Mark Sanford, whose staff in 2009 reported him hiking the Appalachian Trail while he was in Argentina visiting his mistress.

INFOTAINMENT The prominent place of scandal in the news media is but one example of a larger and troubling trend: the massive invasion of entertainment values into political reporting and news presentation. As little as 15 to 20 years ago, news was monopolized by the three major television networks and the big-city daily newspapers, and the audiences for the news were fairly stable. In the intervening years, we have seen the media revolutionized by the growth of cable television and the Internet and the multiplication of news outlets. In this new world, the networks and the big-city dailies have lost audience, leaving the fragments of the old and new media to fight for audience share. The best way to do this, media executives have discovered, is to make the news more entertaining, for the worst sin of this brave new media world is to be boring.[52] All too often, "more entertaining" means that sensation and scandal replace consideration of domestic politics, public policies, and international affairs. In June 2007, for example, Paris Hilton's incarceration was the fifth most frequent story in the news; on February 8 and 9 of the same year, Anna Nicole Smith's death took up 60 percent of the time of the morning news shows.[53] In 2009, Michael Jackson accounted for 60 percent of television news shows during the two days following his death, far more coverage than the mass antigovernment demonstrations in Iran.[54] More entertaining also means short and snappy coverage rather than longer, more analytical coverage; dramatic visuals push aside stories that cannot be easily visualized; and stories that feature angry conflict displace stories in which political leaders are trying to make workable compromises.[55]

The current culture wars between liberals and conservatives over the various legacies of the 1960s involving issues such as abortion, affirmative action, religious values, teaching evolution in schools, same-sex marriage, and more are perfect grist for the infotainment

6.1

6.2

6.3

6.4

agenda setting
Influencing people's opinions about what is important.

mill.[56] Thus, a current staple of cable and broadcast television public affairs programming is the gathering of pundits from both sides of the cultural and political divide angrily shouting at one another for 30 or 60 minutes. And, because bringing together shouting pundits is far cheaper than sending reporters into the field to gather hard news, this form of news coverage is becoming more and more common, especially in the world of cable TV. It is highly unlikely that this emergent journalism of assertion and attack improves public understanding of the candidates, political leaders, or public policies.

Conflict and contest are also evident in coverage of campaigns, where the media concentrate on the "horse-race" aspects of election contests, focusing almost exclusively on who is winning and who is losing the race and what strategies candidates are using to gain ground or to maintain their lead. When candidates sometimes make a stab at talking seriously about issues, the media almost always treat such talk as a mere stratagem of the long campaign. The perpetual struggle between Congress and the president, built into our constitutional system, is also perfect for the infotainment news industry, especially if the struggle can be personalized, as it was in 2011 when President Obama was doing battle with House Speaker John Boehner and House majority leader Eric Cantor over raising the debt ceiling.

LIMITED, FRAGMENTED, AND INCOHERENT POLITICAL INFORMATION Most communications scholars agree that the media coverage of political news has certain distinctive features that result from characteristics of the mass media themselves, including the prevailing technology and organization of news gathering, corporate ownership, and the profit-making drive to appeal to mass audiences. These characteristics of the media mean that news, especially on television, tends to be episodic and fragmented rather than sustained, analytical, or dispassionate. Information comes in bits and pieces, out of context, and without historical background. Its effect is to entertain more than to inform. This may or may not be what people want—some scholars suggest that the people, in fact, do not want hard news at all; others suggest that they want a strong dose of entertainment and diversion with their news[57]—but it is what they get.

Having said that, it is important to point out that the news media often do deep and thorough investigative reporting that matters. The *Wall Street Journal*, *New York Times*, and *Bloomberg/Businessweek*, for example, each did in-depth stories in late 2009 and early 2010 on lobbying and big campaign contributions by large financial firms who tried, with some success, to turn back regulatory reforms in Congress not to their liking. But the pressure to stick to infotainment is relentless, and all news organizations feel it in one way or another—even the best of them.

Effects of the News Media on Politics

6.4 Identify the ways in which the news media affect public opinion and policymaking

The old idea among social scientists that the news media have only "minimal effects" on politics is now discredited. The contents of the news media do make a difference; they affect public opinion and policymaking in a number of ways, including setting the agenda for public debate and framing how issues are understood.[58]

☐ Agenda Setting

Several studies have demonstrated the effect known as **agenda setting**. The topics that get the most coverage in the news media at any point in time are the same ones that most people tell pollsters are the most important problems facing the country. This correlation does not result just from the news media's reporting what people are most interested in; it is a real effect of what appears in the news. In controlled experiments, people who are shown doctored television news broadcasts emphasizing a particular problem (e.g., national defense) mention that problem as being important more often than people who have seen broadcasts that have not been tampered with.[59] Another line of research has shown that news media polling often is used as the basis for reporting about what the American people want regarding a certain policy (say, intervening in a civil war in Liberia) when few Americans know or care about the subject matter of the opinion survey. The polling story, if it is picked up by other news media outlets, bloggers, and pundits, however, then becomes part of the general news landscape and sparks interest among much of the public about that subject. It becomes part of the public agenda.[60]

Of course, media managers do not arbitrarily decide what news to emphasize; their decisions reflect what is happening in the world and what American audiences care about. If there is a war or an economic depression, the media report it. But some research has indicated that what the media cover sometimes diverges from actual trends in problems. Publicity about crime, for example, may reflect editors' fears or a few dramatic incidents rather than a rising crime rate. When the two diverge, it seems to be the media's emphasis rather than real trends that affects public opinion.[61]

When the media decide to highlight a human rights tragedy in "real time," such as "ethnic cleansing" in Kosovo, public officials often feel compelled to act, as Bill Clinton did when he was president. (This is sometimes called the CNN effect.) When the media ignore equally troubling human tragedies, such as the genocide in Darfur, public officials can attend to other matters. One scholarly study shows that in the foreign policy area, media choices about coverage shape what presidents pay attention to.[62] But influences go in both directions. News media scholar Lance Bennett suggests that journalists and the news organizations they work for are very attuned to the relative power balance in Washington between Democrats and Republicans, and between liberals and conservatives, and focus on matters that are of most concern to those in power at any particular time. Thus, Social Security reform becomes an important issue in the press when important political actors want to talk about it. The same is true for other issues, whether it's taxes or nuclear threats from countries such as Iran and North Korea.[63]

☐ Framing and Effects on Policy Preferences

Experiments also indicate that the media's **framing**, or interpretation of stories, affects how people think about political problems and how they assign blame.[64] Several commentators noticed during the Katrina disaster in New Orleans, for example, that TV news stories featuring whites talked of "foraging for food and supplies," while those featuring blacks talked of looting. There are reasons to believe that public impressions of what was going on in the city were affected by this coverage. To take another example, whether citizens ascribe poverty to the laziness of the poor or to the nature of the economy, for example, depends partly on whether the news media run stories about poor individuals (implying that they are responsible for their own plight) or stories about overall economic trends such as economic recessions and unemployment.[65] (See the "Using the Framework" feature for another example.)

What appears in the news media affects people's policy preferences as well. One study found, for example, that the public is more likely to favor government programs to help African Americans when the news media frame racial problems in terms of failures of society to live up to the tradition of equality in the United States. The public is less supportive of these programs when the news media frame the origins of racial problems in terms of individual failures to be self-reliant and responsible.[66] Another study found that changes in the percentages of the public that favored various policies could be predicted rather accurately by what sorts of

framing
Providing a context for interpretation.

THE TELEVISED WAR

The Vietnam War was the first American war fully covered by television. Footage of American deaths and casualties, as well as visual reminders of the terrible consequences of the conflict on the Vietnamese civilian population, helped turn public opinion in the United States against the war. This still from television footage of children napalmed by an accidental American attack on a village of Trang Bang in 1972 is a particularly powerful example of the war coming home to American living rooms. How do the media continue to influence American public opinion about our role in foreign conflicts?

stories appeared on network television news shows between one opinion survey and the next. News from experts, commentators, and popular presidents had especially strong effects.[67]

☐ Fueling Cynicism

Americans are quite cynical about the political parties, politicians, and most incumbent political leaders. To some extent, this has been true since the founding of the nation. Nevertheless, scholars and political commentators have noted a considerable increase in negative feelings about the political system over the past two decades or so. Many students of the media believe that news media coverage of American politics has a great deal to do with this attitude change.[68] As the adversarial-attack journalism style and infotainment have taken over political reporting, serious consideration of the issues, careful examination of policy alternatives, and dispassionate examination of the actions of government institutions have taken a back seat to a steady diet of charges about personal misbehavior and political conflict. When President George H. W. Bush joined a world leader at a press conference in 1992 to describe the nature of the agreement they had reached, reporters asked him instead about rumors of an extramarital affair a few years earlier. With the message being delivered by the mass media that political issues are really about special-interest maneuvering, that political leaders and aspiring political leaders never say what they mean or mean what they say, that all of them have something in their personal lives they want to hide, and that even the most admired of the lot have feet of clay, is it any wonder that the American people are becoming increasingly disenchanted with the whole business?

News reports feed a constant stream of messages about the failure of government: programs that don't work, "bridges to nowhere," wasteful spending, lazy and incompetent public employees, looming government deficits, and people receiving benefits they don't deserve. Though not entirely absent, stories about government working in a way that enhances the well-being of Americans are less common, probably because such stories are not terribly dramatic. Mail gets delivered every day into the remotest

Using the FRAMEWORK

Why talk of deficits filled the air rather than talk of jobs

Background: The battle between Democrats and Republicans, and President Barack Obama and the Republican-controlled House of Representatives over increasing the national government's debt ceiling—how much the government could borrow—was dominated by talk of decreasing the size of the annual federal deficit, with the threat of a government shutdown and default on U.S. debts looming. While this was going on in the summer of 2011, the United States was in the midst of its longest period of economic stagnation since the Great Depression, characterized by tepid GDP growth, an unemployment rate of over 9 percent (the underemployment rate was near 17 percent), and long-term unemployment at its highest level since the end of World War II. When asked what their most important concerns were, every major poll showed that Americans listed jobs first, with deficit reduction down the list at eighth or ninth position. This disconnect between what was happening in Washington and what the American people wanted had many causes, but one was surely the news media's tendency to emphasize issues of greatest concern to our leading political actors. We see here how structural, political, and governmental factors combine to create this outcome.

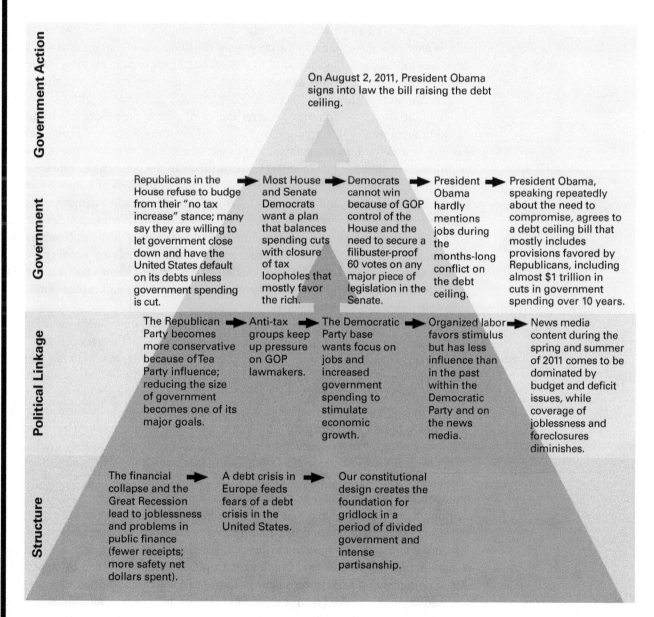

Government Action

On August 2, 2011, President Obama signs into law the bill raising the debt ceiling.

Government

Republicans in the House refuse to budge from their "no tax increase" stance; many say they are willing to let government close down and have the United States default on its debts unless government spending is cut. ➡ Most House and Senate Democrats want a plan that balances spending cuts with closure of tax loopholes that mostly favor the rich. ➡ Democrats cannot win because of GOP control of the House and the need to secure a filibuster-proof 60 votes on any major piece of legislation in the Senate. ➡ President Obama hardly mentions jobs during the months-long conflict on the debt ceiling. ➡ President Obama, speaking repeatedly about the need to compromise, agrees to a debt ceiling bill that mostly includes provisions favored by Republicans, including almost $1 trillion in cuts in government spending over 10 years.

Political Linkage

The Republican Party becomes more conservative because of Tea Party influence; reducing the size of government becomes one of its major goals. ➡ Anti-tax groups keep up pressure on GOP lawmakers. ➡ The Democratic Party base wants focus on jobs and increased government spending to stimulate economic growth. ➡ Organized labor favors stimulus but has less influence than in the past within the Democratic Party and on the news media. ➡ News media content during the spring and summer of 2011 comes to be dominated by budget and deficit issues, while coverage of joblessness and foreclosures diminishes.

Structure

The financial collapse and the Great Recession lead to joblessness and problems in public finance (fewer receipts; more safety net dollars spent). ➡ A debt crisis in Europe feeds fears of a debt crisis in the United States. ➡ Our constitutional design creates the foundation for gridlock in a period of divided government and intense partisanship.

regions of the country, for example, while cars and trucks make heavy use of the interstate highway system. The Center for Disease Control keeps on constant alert for dangerous pathogens, even as park rangers keep watch on our national parks.

Using the DEMOCRACY STANDARD

Do the news media help or hinder democracy?

The framers favored a form of government based on the consent of the governed, but one in which most of the governed played only a limited and indirect role in political life. They believed that government was best run by talented, educated, and broad-minded individuals who attained office through indirect elections based on a limited franchise, and who governed at several removes from the people. According to such an understanding of the ideal form of government, there was no pressing need for news media to educate the general public and prepare it for active participation in politics. For the framers, the purpose of the news media—newspapers, in their day—was to serve as a mechanism allowing economic, social, and political leaders to communicate with each other and to help them deliberate on the issues of the day.

For democratic theorists, the people play a more central role in governance and the news media play an accordingly larger role in preparing the people to participate. As we pointed out earlier, accurate, probing, and vigorous news media are essential building blocks for democratic life to the extent that the broad general public cannot be rationally engaged in public affairs without them. In this respect, the spread of the news media in the United States, and the penetration of millions of homes by newspapers, radio, television, and the Internet, has undoubtedly enriched democracy. It has made it much easier for ordinary citizens to form policy preferences, to judge the actions of government, and to decide whom they want to govern them. News media thus tend to broaden the scope of conflict and contribute to political equality. When citizens as well as political leaders and special-interest groups know what is going on, they can have a voice in politics. Moreover, interactive media and media-published polls help politicians hear that voice.

Scholars and media critics who want the news media to be highly informative, analytical, and issue oriented, however, are often appalled by the personalized, episodic, dramatic, and fragmented character of most news stories, which do not provide sustained and coherent explanations of what is going on. Still other critics worry that constant media exposés of alleged official wrongdoing or government inefficiency, and the mocking tone aimed at virtually all political leaders by journalists and talk-radio hosts, have fueled the growing political cynicism of the public. To the extent that this is true, the news media are not serving democracy as well as they might.

It is undeniably the case that the news media have not performed their civic responsibilities very well. They do tend to trivialize, focus on scandal and entertainment, and offer fragmented and out-of-context political and governmental information. However, things may not be quite as bad as they appear. For one thing, for those who are truly interested in public affairs, there is now more readily accessible information than at any time in our history. For those willing to search for it, there is now little information that is relevant to public affairs that can be kept hidden, ranging from official government statistics to academic and other expert studies. Additionally, the American people have demonstrated an admirable ability on many occasions to sift the wheat from the chaff, to glean the information they need from the background noise, as it were.[69] On balance, then, the news media have probably helped advance the cause of democracy in the United States and helped transform the American republic into the American democratic republic. There is no doubt, however, that the news media could also do a considerably better job than they do at the present time.

Review the Chapter

 Listen to **Chapter 6** on **MyPoliSciLab**

Roles of the News Media in Democracy

6.1 Evaluate the various roles of the news media in a democracy, p. 166

One role for the news media in a democracy is to serve as a watchdog over government, uncovering government corruption and keeping government officials accountable to the public.

Other important roles are to help citizens evaluate candidates for public office and to think about what kinds of government policies might best serve the public interest.

Mainstream and Nonmainstream News Media

6.2 Assess the respective roles of traditional and other news media today, p. 167

Traditional news media such as newspapers and television still gather and report the most news, even as more people get their information from the Internet.

Internet news is rarely based on independent reporting. Most is from the traditional media, either taken directly, rewritten, or commented upon.

Television is still the most trusted source of news.

How the Mainstream News Media Work

6.3 Analyze how the news is gathered and disseminated and evaluate the outcome of this process, p. 174

The shape of the news media in the United States has been determined largely by structural factors: technological developments; the growth of the American population and economy; and the development of a privately owned, corporation-dominated media industry.

New Internet-based media have not replaced traditional reporting and news organizations. For the most part, these new media use materials gathered by old media.

News gathering is limited by logistics. Most news gathering is organized around New York City, Washington, D.C., and a handful of major cities in the United States and abroad. Most foreign countries are ignored unless there are crises or other big stories to communicate.

Effects of the News Media on Politics

6.4 Identify the ways in which the news media affect public opinion and policymaking, p. 188

News media stories have substantial effects on the public's perceptions of problems, its interpretations of events, its evaluations of political candidates, and its policy preferences.

The news media affects the public not only by providing information but also by agenda setting and framing.

Learn the Terms

 Study and **Review** the **Flashcards**

watchdog, p. 166
podcasts, p. 170
wire services, p. 171
media monopoly, p. 175
infotainment, p. 178

beat, p. 180
leak, p. 181
news management, p. 181
spin, p. 181
newsworthy, p. 182

objective journalism, p. 183
pundits, p. 184
bias, p. 185
agenda setting, p. 188
framing, p. 189

Test Yourself

Study and **Review** the **Practice Tests**

Answer key begins on page T-1.

6.1 Evaluate the various roles of the news media in a democracy

1. The three roles of the news media in democracy are:

   a. Be a watchdog over the government, present electoral choices, and expose scandals.
   b. Present electoral choices, expose scandals, and cover breaking news stories.
   c. Be a watchdog over the government, present breaking news stories, and provide information about public policy.
   d. Be a watchdog over the government, present electoral choices, and provide information about public policy.
   e. Expose scandals, cover breaking news stores, and protect the reputation of high-ranking government officials.

6.2 Assess the respective roles of traditional and other news media today

2. The preferred source for political news for Americans is:

   a. Printed newspapers
   b. Online newspapers
   c. Campaign websites
   d. Facebook
   e. Television

6.3 Analyze how the news is gathered and disseminated and evaluate the outcome of this process

3. This is a common way for officials to float policy ideas, get noticed, undercut rivals, and report real or imagined wrongdoing.

   a. Floating information
   b. Spinning information
   c. Leaking information
   d. News management
   e. Tipping information

6.4 Identify the ways in which the news media affect public opinion and policymaking

4. Many students of media believe that news media coverage of American politics has a lot to do with this growing feeling in the American people:

   a. Cynicism
   b. Happiness
   c. Anger
   d. Disappointment
   e. Security

Explore Further

INTERNET SOURCES

The Pew Project for Excellence in Journalism **www .stateofthenewsmedia.org**
Annual scholarly review of the state of the news media, with attention to new developments.

The Berkman Center for Internet & Society **cyber.law.harvard.edu**
A research and information center at the Harvard Law School that follows the development of the Internet and its impact on law and society.

The Columbia Journalism Review **www.cjr.org/**
The website of the leading scholarly monitor of journalism and journalists; loaded with useful information about all aspects of newsmaking and dissemination.

The Pew Research Center for the People and the Press **www .people-press.org**
The most complete public opinion surveys on citizen evaluations of the quality of media coverage of public affairs.

Wired Magazine Online **www.wired.com**
Attempts to report on what is at the cutting edge in terms of technology, computing, and the Internet with some coverage of their economic, social, and political impacts.

News Bias Explored: The Art of Reading the News **www.umich .edu/~newsbias/links.html**
A comprehensive collection of links to objective sources discussing omission and bias in news reporting.

The New York Times **www.nytimes.com**
The home page for *The New York Times*.

The Huffington Post **www.huffingtonpost.com**
The home page for *The Huffington Post*.

SUGGESTIONS FOR FURTHER READING

Alterman, Eric. *What Liberal Media? The Truth About Bias and the News.* New York: Basic Books, 2003.
An impassioned yet well-documented answer to the charge that the news media are biased against conservatives.

Bennett, W. Lance. *News: Politics of Illusion*, 9th ed. New York: Longman, 2011.
A critique of the news as trivial and uninformative.

Bennett, W. Lance, Regina G. Lawrence, and Steven Livingston. *When the Press Fails: Political Power and the News from Iraq to Katrina.* Chicago: University of Chicago Press, 2007.
A devastating critique of the news media limited by the pressures of the marketplace and the balance of political power in Washington.

Goldberg, Bernard. *Bias: A CBS Insider Exposes How the Media Distort the News.* New York: Harper Paperbacks, 2003.

A conservative critique of CBS News in particular and the mainstream news media in general.

Hindman, Matthew. *The Myth of Digital Democracy.* Princeton, NJ: Princeton University Press, 2009.

Based on compelling empirical evidence, the author shows that many of the inequalities that characterize American society and politics are recreated on the Internet.

Graber, Doris. *Mass Media and American Politics,* 8th ed. Washington, D.C.: CQ Press, 2010.

A comprehensive examination of the news media's effect on American politics.

Shapiro, Robert Y. and Lawrence R. Jacobs, eds. *The Oxford Handbook of American Public Opinion and the Media.* Oxford: Oxford University Press, 2011.

A comprehensive collection of articles by leading scholars on the organization, operations, and impact of the news media, both old and new.

7

Interest Groups and Business Corporations

DISASTER IN THE GULF

I   n the Gulf of Mexico on April 20, 2010, just before midnight the Deepwater
Horizon drilling rig was ripped apart by a series of spectacular explosions that
killed 11 oil rig workers and unleashed an oil spill of near-historic proportions.[1]
The Deepwater Horizon, owned by the Transocean Corporation and leased to
oil giant BP, was finishing the final phases of drilling a well more than a mile
beneath the platform when disaster struck. The temporary cement cap that topped off the well
failed, releasing a potent and out-of-control flow of a natural gas and crude oil mixture to the platform where a spark set off the explosion. The shattered pipe in the middle of the drill hole poured
natural gas and crude oil into the Gulf at the rate of 35,000 to 60,000 barrels a day, defying initial
efforts to cut off the flow at the pipe. Efforts to funnel the crude oil to storage and transport ves-
sels on the surface in the months after the blowout, even as relief wells were being drilled, did
some good, but massive amounts of natural gas and crude oil continued to escape for months.
The spill fouled the beaches and marshlands of Gulf Coast states and formed deep, underwater

7.1	7.2	7.3	7.4	7.5	7.6
Compare and contrast theories about the role of interest groups in a democracy, p. 201	Distinguish the two kinds of interests at work in American politics, p. 203	Explain why interest groups have proliferated, p. 208	Distinguish the methods through which interest groups try to shape government policy, p. 211	Determine the biases in the interest group system, p. 218	Assess the steps that have been taken to control factions, p. 226

DISASTER IN THE GULF Risky behavior by drilling companies, pressure from the parent oil company BP, and lax government regulatory oversight, all contributed to the Deepwater Horizon disaster in the Gulf of Mexico in 2010. By all accounts, it represents the most serious environmental disaster in American history, with its effects still being felt in the Gulf region. What can and should be done to prevent similar such disasters in the future?

MyPoliSciLab Video Series

The Big Picture Why does a hedge fund manager making $8 billion pay 15% of that in taxes, while someone else making $200,000 pays 30%? Edward S. Greenberg illustrates how much power interest groups have over the government and its policies if they have sufficient time, resources, and access.

The Basics What are interest groups and what role do they play in our democracy? Listen to real people tackle these and other questions. Learn what types of interest groups exist in our country, what tactics they use to achieve their goals, and why interest groups matter.

In Context Examine the emergence of interest groups in American politics. In this video, Boston College political scientist Kay Schlozman traces the roots of interest group involvement in American politics and why they are an important part of the political process today.

Think Like a Political Scientist Do interest groups have an impact on policy? Boston College political scientist Kay Schlozman explains why this is not an easy question to answer. She also discusses how scholars determine which groups are represented and which groups are not.

In the Real World Is pizza a vegetable? This video illustrates the difference between elitist and populist theories of interest groups by examining real people's reactions to the recent debate over whether school cafeterias should count pizza sauce as a full serving of vegetables.

So What? Interest groups are another way for people to have their voices heard but some groups have more influence in government than others. Author Edward S. Greenberg considers how interest groups are unequal, and he offers some tips on methods you can use to make your voice heard.

natural gas and oil plumes, whose long-term environmental effects are unknowable at this time. Needless to say, the Gulf Coast fishing and shrimping industries suffered serious losses, with many customers turning to foreign sources of supply.

How did it happen? We know that BP, putting cost-saving before safety, insisted that the platform operator, Transocean, take a number of operational steps that were quite risky and ill-advised. These included using too few "centralizers" to stabilize the cement that held the drilling pipe in place in the ocean floor, skipping critical inspections and tests of emergency cut-off mechanisms, using one rather than the industry-standard two pipe "pinchers" (called "blind shear rams") to cut off oil flow in the main pipe in the event of a blowout, and using pipes of lower quality than BP's own experts advised. Though Transocean engineers and many workers aboard the Deepwater rig apparently expressed concerns about these decisions, operations never slowed as BP executives pushed everyone to finish on time and under budget so it could temporarily cap the well and move on to other drilling opportunities.

Though BP was at fault in this case, it emerged in congressional testimony during early summer 2010 that other oil company operators doing deep well drilling in the Gulf and other places in the world had no better solutions to a blowout at these depths than BP did. Oil and drilling company executives testified that, at a minimum, more onsite testing of critical blowout preventers should be done in light of the Deepwater Horizon event, but they were somewhat at a loss for words when congressional committee members produced a report from the industry itself pointing out that most companies cut corners in their testing programs given the costs involved: about $700 a minute to suspend operations while testing.

We have a rough idea, then, of why the Deepwater Horizon happened from a technical point of view. But other factors involving the oil industry's political influence are also important in this story. There is, first, the absence of a national energy policy that might encourage the development and use of renewable energy. Without this, for now and the foreseeable future, Americans must depend on fossil fuels, especially coal, natural gas, and oil, to provide the power they need to run a modern, industrial society. Inevitably, as easily recoverable oil reserves are depleted, and as global climate change concerns put a damper on a greater reliance on coal, oil companies are forced to look in less hospitable places for oil, including the deep ocean floor. But the absence of a national energy policy is itself the result of the long-term oil industry influence in American politics; the industry has been among the very largest contributors to the campaigns of presidential, congressional, and state-level candidates and among the industries that spend the most on direct lobbying to keep oil at the center of our energy economy.

The oil industry also has been a central player in the four-decade-long effort to deregulate the American economy, that is, leave more and more decisions to private firms operating in the marketplace, largely freed from federal and state government oversight. Business leaders, the economics profession, conservative think tanks, and Republican and centrist Democrats came to believe that government is generally bad for economic efficiency and growth and ought to exit the game, as it were.[2] The oil industry contribution to the deregulation movement has been multifaceted, including campaign contributions and lobbying, but also the generous funding of anti–big government think tanks that have churned out reports on the evils of regulation for many years. Deregulation has had some good outcomes, to be sure, as in restraining air travel and freight shipping costs, but bad ones in a wide range of areas, including the collapse of the financial system as the most obvious recent case. But the deregulation spirit has infused the oil industry as well, with fewer personnel in agencies that are responsible for oversight and less willingness on the part of mid-level government bureaucrats, given the political environment, to ask too much of industry operators. One of the things congressional testimony revealed in summer 2010 was how few rules the Minerals Management Service (MMS) issued regarding deep ocean drilling and how often they failed to enforce the few rules that were in place.

Finally, there is what political scientists call "agency capture," in which a regulatory agency, designed to regulate an industry in the public interest, comes to act as a partner instead. This happens for a number of reasons, including possible future employment in the regulated industry for the regulator, dependence on the industry for the technical information that the agency needs to issue regulations and monitor performance, and long-term relationships among regulators and firms that encourage commonality in points of view. Sometimes, there is even gift-giving from the wealthy industry to those who work in the regulatory agency.

Each of these elements of "capture" can be seen in the MMS oil and drilling industry relationship. Congressional hearings and an Interior Department inspector general's report in 2010 revealed, for example, that companies paid for meals and hotel stays, elaborate vacations, and tickets to premium athletic events for agency employees and that several inspectors had examined operations at companies where they hoped to work. The hearings and report also uncovered the cozy relationship that developed between oil rig inspectors and drilling companies. For example, many instances were uncovered in which industry officials were allowed to fill out MMS inspection report forms in pencil, with the inspectors going over the pencil traces later in pen. Equally important, the MMS was entirely dependent on the technical information provided by regulated companies, having neither the personnel nor agency resources to develop information or independent testing equipment and instruments "in-house." During the Coast Guard inquiry on the failure of the various safety devices to work at the Deepwater Horizon platform, Captain Hung Nguyen was astonished when he received a simple "yes" answer from the MMS's regional supervisor for field operations to the following question: "So my understanding is that [the shear ram tool] is designed to industry standard, manufactured by industry, installed by industry, with no government witnessing oversight of the construction or the installation. Is that correct?"

Much of what the federal government does in the United States is influenced by what the general public wants it to do. Elected and other public officials, you have seen, pay attention to things such as public opinion polls and news media characterizations of popular preferences. You will see in later chapters in this book, moreover, that, political leaders must be responsive to the electorate if they want to gain and retain their elected offices. But it is also the case that a wide array of private interest and advocacy groups, with business leading the way, also play an enormously important, although less visible, role in determining what government does and influencing who wins and who loses from public policies.

Thinking Critically About This Chapter

This chapter is about the important role interest groups play in American government and politics, how they go about achieving their ends, and what effects they have in determining government policies in the United States.

Using the Framework

You will see in this chapter how interest groups, in combination with other political linkage institutions, help convey the wishes and interests of people and groups to government decision makers. You will also learn how the kind of interest group system we have in the United States is, in large part, a product of structural factors, including our constitutional rules, political culture, social organization, and economy.

Using the Democracy Standard

Interest groups have long held an ambiguous place in American politics. To some, interest groups are "special" interests that act without regard to the public interest and are the instruments of the most privileged parts of American society. To others, interest groups are simply another way by which people and groups in a democratic society get their voices heard by government leaders. Using the democracy standard, you will be able to evaluate these two positions.

Interest Groups in a Democratic Society: Contrasting Views

Compare and contrast theories about the role of interest groups in a democracy

interest groups
A private organization or voluntary association that seeks to influence public policy as a way to protect or advance its interests.

factions
Madison's term for groups or parties that try to advance their own interests at the expense of the public good.

Interest groups are private organizations and voluntary associations that seek to advance their interests by trying to influence what government does. They are not officially a part of government. Nor are they political parties that try to place candidates carrying the party banner into government offices, though, as shown later in this chapter, interest groups play an important role in U.S. elections. Interest groups are formed by people or firms that share an interest or cause they are trying to protect or advance with the help of government.[3] The interests and causes they press on government range from narrowly targeted material benefits (e.g., passage of a favorable tax break or the issuance of a helpful regulation) to more broadly targeted outcomes for society at large (e.g., new rules on auto emissions or abortion availability). To do this, interest groups try to influence the behavior of public officials, such as presidents, members of Congress, bureaucrats, and judges. The framers knew that interest groups were inevitable and appropriate in a free society but were potentially harmful as well, so they paid special attention to them in the design of the Constitution.

☐ The Evils of Faction

The danger to good government and the public interest from interest groups is a familiar theme in American politics. They are usually regarded as narrowly self-interested, out for themselves, and without regard for the public good.

This theme is prominent in *The Federalist* No. 10 (see the Appendix), in which James Madison defined **factions** (his term for interest groups and narrow political parties) in the following manner: "A number of citizens, whether amounting to a majority

BOSSES OF THE SENATE

In the late nineteenth century, most Americans thought of the Senate as the captive of large corporate trusts and other special-interest groups, as depicted in this popular cartoon, "Bosses of the Senate." How has the public's view changed, if at all? Is there any basis for believing that the situation today is substantially different from that of the late nineteenth century?

7.1
7.2
7.3
7.4
7.5
7.6

pluralism
The political science position that American democracy is best understood in terms of the interaction, conflict, and bargaining of groups.

or a minority of the whole, who are united and actuated by some common impulse of passion, or of interest, adverse to the rights of other citizens or to the permanent and aggregate interests of the community."[4] The "evils of faction" theme recurs throughout our history, from the writings of the "muckrakers" at the turn of the twentieth century to news accounts and commentary on the misdeeds of the leaders of the financial industry in the 2008 financial collapse.

☐ Interest Group Democracy: The Pluralist Argument

According to many political scientists, however, interest groups do not hurt democracy and the public interest but are an important instrument in attaining both. This way of looking at American democracy is called **pluralism** and takes the following form (also see Figure 7.1):[5]

- Free elections, while essential to a democracy, do not adequately communicate the specific wants and interests of the people to political leaders on a continuous basis. These are more accurately, consistently, and frequently conveyed to political leaders by the many groups and organizations to which people belong.

- Interest groups are easy to create; people in the United States are free to join or to organize groups that reflect their interests.

- Because of federalism, checks and balances, and the separation of powers, government power in the United States is broadly dispersed, leaving governmental institutions remarkably porous and open to the entreaties of the many and diverse groups that exist in society.

- Because of the ease of group formation and the accessibility of government, all legitimate interests in society can have their views taken into account by some public official. Farmers and business owners can get heard; so too can consumers and workers. Because of this, the system is highly democratic.

Pluralists see interest groups, then, not as a problem but as an additional tool of democratic representation, similar to other democratic instruments such as public opinion and elections. We shall explore the degree to which this position is valid in this and other chapters.

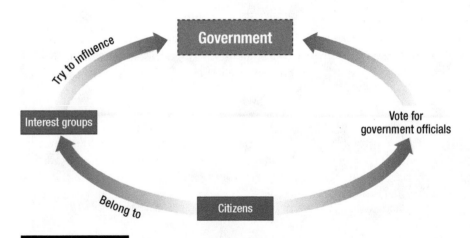

FIGURE 7.1 THE PLURALIST VIEW OF AMERICAN POLITICS

In the pluralist understanding of the way American democracy works, citizens have more than one way to influence government leaders. In addition to voting, citizens also have the opportunity to participate in organizations that convey member views to public officials. Because of weak political parties, federalism, checks and balances, and the separation of powers, access to public officials is relatively easy.

The Universe of Interest Groups

hat kinds of interests find a voice in American politics? A useful place to start is with political scientist E.E. Schattschneider's distinction between "private" and "public" interests. Although the boundaries between the two are sometimes fuzzy, the distinction remains important. **Private interests** are organizations and associations that try to gain protections or material advantages from government for their own members rather than for society at large.[6] For the most part, these represent economic interests of one kind or another. **Public interests** are organizations and associations that try to gain protections or benefits for people beyond their own members, often for society at large. Some are motivated by an ideology or by the desire to advance a general cause—animal rights, let us say, or environmental protection—or by the commitment to some public policy—gun control or an end to abortion. Some represent the nonprofit sector, and some even represent government entities, such as state and local governments.

Private and public interest groups come in a wide range of forms. Some, including the AARP, are large membership organizations with sizable Washington and regional offices. Some large membership organizations have passionately committed members active in their affairs—such as the National Rifle Association—while others have relatively passive members who join for the benefits the organization provides—such as the American Automobile Association with its well-known trip assistance and car buying service. Other groups are trade associations whose members are business firms. Still others are rather small organizations without members; are run by professionals and sustained by foundations and wealthy donors; and have sizable mailing, Internet, and telephone lists for soliciting contributions—the Children's Defense Fund and the National Taxpayers Union come to mind. We examine these in more detail below (see also Table 7.1).

☐ Private Interest Groups

Many different kinds of private interest groups are active in American politics.

BUSINESS Because of the vast resources at the disposal of businesses and because of their strategic role in the health of local, state, and national economies, groups and associations representing businesses wield enormous power in Washington. Large corporations such as Boeing, Microsoft, and Google are able to mount their own **lobbying** efforts and often join with others in influential associations, such as the Business Roundtable. Medium-sized businesses are well represented by organizations such as the National Association of Manufacturers and the U.S. Chamber of Commerce. Even small businesses have proved to be quite influential when joined in associations such as the National Federation of Independent Business, which helped stop the Clinton health plan in 1994. Agriculture and agribusinesses (fertilizer, seed, machinery, biotechnology, and food-processing companies) have more than held their own over the years through organizations such as the American Farm Bureau Federation and the Farm Machinery Manufacturer's Association and through scores of commodity groups, including the American Dairy Association and the National Association of Wheat Growers.

THE PROFESSIONS Several associations represent the interests of professionals, such as doctors, lawyers, dentists, and accountants. Because of the prominent social position of professionals in local communities and their ability to make substantial campaign contributions, such associations are very influential in the policymaking process on matters related to their professional expertise and concerns. The American Medical

private interests
An interest group that seeks to protect or advance the material interests of its members.

public interests
An interest group that works to gain protections or benefits for society at large.

lobbying
Effort by an interest or advocacy group to influence the behavior of a public official.

TABLE 7.1 THE DIVERSE WORLD OF INTEREST ASSOCIATIONS

Interest	Interest Subtypes	Association Examples
Private Interests (focus on protections and gains for their members)		
Business	Corporations that lobby on their own behalf	Google Boeing
	Trade associations	Chemical Manufacturers Association
		Health Insurance Association of America
	Peak business organizations	Business Roundtable
		Federation of Small Businesses
Professions	Doctors	American Medical Association
	Dentists	American Dental Association
	Accountants	National Society of Accountants
	Lawyers	American Bar Association
Labor	Union	International Association of Machinists
	Union federation	AFL-CIO
Public Interests (focus on protections and gains for a broader public or society in general)		
Ideological and cause	Environment	Environmental Defense
	Pro-choice	National Abortion Rights Action League
	Pro-life	National Right to Life Committee
	Anti-tax	Americans for Tax Reform
	Civil rights	National Association for the Advancement of Colored People
		Human Rights Campaign
Nonprofit sector	Medical	American Hospital Association
	Charitable	American Red Cross
Governmental entities	State	National Conference of State Legislatures
	Local	National Association of Counties

Association (AMA) and the American Dental Association (ADA), for instance, lobbied strongly against the Clinton health care proposal and helped kill it in the 103rd Congress. (These associations changed their tune in 2009, however, when they backed Barack Obama's health care reform overhaul, perhaps because the new law promised to bring about 32 million more insured people into the existing system.) The Trial Lawyers Association has long been a major financial contributor to the Democratic Party and active in blocking legislation to limit the size of personal injury jury awards.

LABOR Although labor unions are sometimes involved in what might be called public interest activities (such as supporting civil rights legislation), their main role in the United States has been to protect the jobs of their members and to secure maximum wages and benefits for them. Unlike labor unions in many parts of the world, which are as much political and ideological organizations as economic, American labor unions have traditionally focused on so-called bread-and-butter issues. As an important part of the New Deal coalition that dominated American politics well into the late 1960s, labor unions were influential at the federal level during the years when the Democratic Party controlled Congress and often won the presidency.

Although organized labor is still a force to be reckoned with in electoral politics—they played a big role in fund-raising and mobilizing voters for Barack

7.1
7.2
7.3
7.4
7.5
7.6

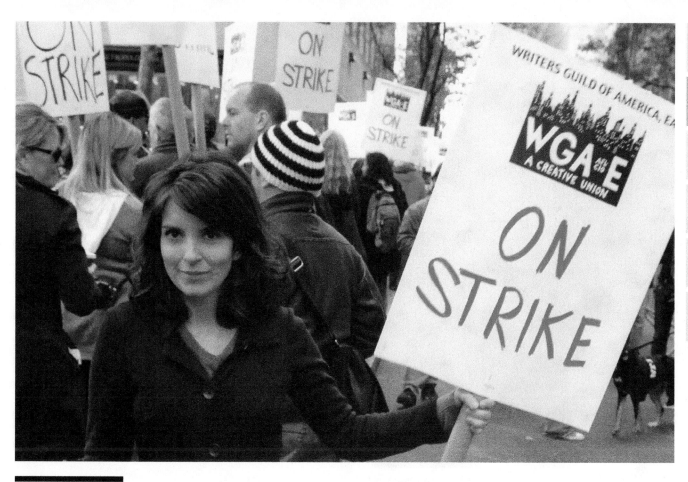

TINA FEY ON THE PICKET LINE AT NBC HEADQUARTERS

A long strike in 2007 by television and film writers to gain concessions from the networks and film studios on use of writers' materials on the Internet was succussful, party because of the strong support it received from leading actors and performers, including Tina Fey (herself a writer and a member of the Writers Guild of America). Despite success such as this one, union membership has been steadily declining in the United States. What accounts for declining union membership?

Obama and the Democrats in the 2008 and 2010 presidential and congressional races—most observers believe that the political power of labor unions has eroded in dramatic ways over the past several decades.[7] Organized labor's main long-range problem in American politics and its declining power relative to business in the workplace is its small membership base; in 2010, only 11.9 percent of American wage and salary workers—and only 6.9 percent of private sector workers—were members of labor unions compared with 35 percent in 1954.[8] The long but steady decline in union membership in the private sector is explained by a number of things. First, there has been a dramatic decline in the proportion of American workers in manufacturing, the economic sector in which unions have traditionally been the strongest. Fewer manufacturing workers are needed now than in the past because of outsourcing, gains in productivity (more can be manufactured with fewer workers), and pressures on companies to cut operating costs in a hyper-competitive global economy.[9] Second, business firms have become much less willing to tolerate unions and have become much more sophisticated at efforts to decertify unions and undermine union organization drives.[10] The long-term decline of private sector labor unions was vividly on display in the successful campaign by business groups and associations to pass a so-called "right to work" law in Indiana, long an important manufacturing state with strong labor unions. Republican governor Mitch Daniels signed the bill into law in February 2012 allowing employees in union plants free choice on whether to join the union or pay dues to support it. "Right to work" laws have long been considered anathema to organized labor but, despite strenuous efforts, labor was unable to prevent Indiana

RECALL GOVERNOR WALKER

Here teachers and other public sector workers and sympathizers take over the Wisconsin Capital Rotunda in 2011 to protest Governor Scott Walker's plan to end collective bargaining rights for state government employees. Walker was successful in passing the new law and survived a state-wide effort to recall him from office in 2012.

from becoming the first state from the old manufacturing heartland of the country to pass such legislation.

The overall decline in labor union membership would have been more precipitous had it not been for the substantial levels of unionization among public sector workers such as teachers, firefighters, police, and civil servants in local and state governments, 36 percent of whom belong to unions. Today there are more public sector workers than private sector workers in labor unions in the United States; public sector union members numbered 7.6 million in 2010 compared to 7.1 million employees from the private sector in unions. Though stable for several decades now, union density in the public sector may well decline by an-as-yet undetermined amount if Republican-controlled state governments manage to take away collective bargaining rights from government workers as they have vowed to do. As of this writing, the Wisconsin collective bargaining rollback has succeeded, while the Ohio law was overturned by state voters in 2011, with labor unions playing a key roll in voter mobilization.

The changing fortunes of private sector organized labor can be seen, first, in the passage of a minimum wage law during the Great Depression as unions flexed their growing organizational muscle; second, in the steady rise in the minimum wage during the height of union political power in the three decades following the end of World War II; and third, in the erosion of the purchasing power of the minimum wage as union membership and political influence began to wane after that, continuing to the present day. We examine the pros and cons of the minimum wage in the "Can Government Do Anything Well?" feature.

Can Government Do Anything Well?

The Federal Minimum Wage

The minimum wage and 40-hour workweek were first introduced in 1938 by Congress in the Fair Labor Standards Act. FDR claimed the law was "the most far-sighted program for the benefit of workers ever adopted," arguing that fair wages ensure a "minimum standard of living necessary for health, efficiency and general well-being." The FLSA established minimum wage, overtime pay, recordkeeping, and youth employment standards affecting employees in the private sector and in governments at all levels. Covered workers today are entitled to a minimum wage of not less than $7.25 per hour, and overtime pay of at least 150 percent of the regular rate of pay.

The U.S. Chamber of Commerce, one of the largest and most influential interest groups in the United States with over 3 million business and organizational members, has been a staunch foe of the minimum wage. Their opposition over the years, and their role in campaign finance, is one of the reasons that members of Congress have been reluctant to increase the minimum wage to keep up with the cost of living. When adjusting for inflation, the minimum wage was almost $2/hour higher in the 1960s and 1970s than it is today.

The value of the minimum wage peaked in 1968, a product of Lyndon Johnson's Great Society, the high water mark of postwar Democratic Party liberalism and the political influence within the Democratic Party of organized labor. The decline of organized labor, the main interest group in favor of a generous minimum wage, is another reason why the minimum wage has not kept pace.

Support for the claim that government should specify a minimum wage:

- The minimum wage guarantees a basic, if low, income safety net for Americans who are working; it keeps more people from becoming poor when the gap between rich and poor is widening.

- The minimum wage helps the economy by increasing overall purchasing power; it allows low-income working Americans to be able to buy more products and services from private firms than they might otherwise be able to do.

- Major academic studies do not support the claims below that the minimum wage significantly and adversely affects overall employment levels or increases inflation.

Rejection of the claim that government should specify a minimum wage:

- Wage determination should always be left to the free market; it is the most efficient and fairest way to determine wages.

- Because employers cannot pay less than the minimum wage, it makes them less able and likely to hire teens and the unskilled with spotty work histories; unemployment among these groups, particularly African Americans, remains higher than it might be.

- Unemployment is increased when the minimum wage goes up because it becomes more expensive for businesses to keep workers.

- Because minimum wage laws mean employers must pay higher wages than given by market forces, prices for consumers must be higher to cover the additional costs.

WHAT DO YOU THINK?

What do you think about the past, present, and future role of the government in legislating a minimum wage?

- Increases to the minimum wage (specifically over the past decade) have increased the standard of living for the lowest socioeconomic classes and have not increased unemployment in the United States.
- Increases to the minimum wage (specifically over the past decade) have contributed to modest increases in the standard of living for the lowest socioeconomic classes, but have also contributed to increasing unemployment in the United States.
- Increases to the minimum wage (specifically over the past decade) have not increased the standard of living for the lowest socioeconomic classes and have contributed significantly to increased unemployment in the United States.

How would you defend this position to a fellow student? What would be your main line of argument? What evidence do you believe best supports your position?

Additional sources for this feature: The Living Wage Calculator at www.livingwage.geog.psu.edu/states/25, the Chamber of Commerce website at www.uschamber.com, and the Wage and Hour Division of the U.S. Department of Labor at www.dol.gov/whd/flsa.

7.1
7.2
7.3
7.4
7.5
7.6

7.1

7.2

7.3

7.4

7.5

7.6

advocacy group
An interest group organized to support a cause or ideology.

lobbyists
A person who attempts to influence the behavior of public officials on behalf of an interest group.

▢ Public Interest Groups

Public interest groups or associations try to get government to act in ways that will serve interests that are broader and more encompassing than the direct economic or occupational interests of their own members. Such groups claim to be committed to protecting and advancing the public interest, at least as they see it.[11]

One type of public interest group is the **advocacy group**. People active in advocacy groups tend to be motivated by ideological concerns or a belief in some cause. Such advocacy groups have always been around, but a great upsurge in their number and influence has taken place since the late 1960s.[12] Many were spawned by social movements. In the wake of the civil rights and women's movements, it is hardly surprising that a number of associations have been formed to advance the interests of particular racial, ethnic, and gender groups in American society. The National Organization for Women advocates policies in Washington that advance the position of women in American society. For example, the League of Latin American Citizens has been concerned, among other things, with national and state policies that affect migrants from Mexico and other Latin American countries. Similarly, the NAACP and the Urban League are advocates for the interests of African Americans. The environmental movement created organizations such as the Environmental Defense Fund, the Nature Conservancy, Clean Water Action, and the Natural Resources Defense Council, to take another example. The evangelical Christian upsurge led to the creation of such organizations as the Moral Majority, the Christian Coalition, the National Right to Life Committee, Focus on the Family, and the Family Research Council. The gay and lesbian movement eventually led to the creation of organizations such as the Gay and Lesbian Alliance Against Defamation (GLAAD). Some have been around for many years, such as the American Civil Liberties Union, committed to the protection of First Amendment freedoms, and the Children's Defense Fund, an advocate for poor children.

Most advocacy groups retain a professional, paid administrative staff and are supported by generous large donors (often foundations), membership dues, and/or donations generated by direct mail campaigns. While some depend on and encourage grassroots volunteers and some hold annual membership meetings through which members play some role in making association policies, most advocacy associations are organizations without active membership involvement (other than check writing) and are run by lobbying and public education professionals.[13]

Two other types of public interest groups play a role in American politics, although usually a quieter one. First, associations representing government entities at the state and local levels of our federal system attempt to influence policies made by lawmakers and bureaucrats in Washington. The National Association of Counties is one example, as is the National Governors Association. Second, nonprofit organizations and associations try to influence policies that advance their missions to serve the public interests. Examples include the American Red Cross and the National Council of Nonprofit Associations.

Why There Are So Many Interest Groups

7.3 Explain why interest groups have proliferated

Nobody knows exactly how many interest groups exist in the United States, but there is wide agreement that the number began to mushroom in the late 1960s and grew steadily thereafter. We can see this increase along several dimensions. The number of groups listed in the *Encyclopedia of Associations*, for example, has increased from about 10,000 in 1968 to about 22,000 today. Moreover, the number of paid **lobbyists**, that is, people who work for interest groups in Washington and try to affect government policies on their behalf, today totals about 35,000, double what it was then, and that number does not include thousands of others who work for law firms whose main business is lobbying. One estimate is that about 260,000 people in Washington and its surrounding areas work in the lobbying sector.[14] (Even more work in public relations, accounting, and technology firms linked to the lobbying sector.) These associations and other lobbyists spent around $3.5 billion on lobbying efforts in Washington in 2010, double the total in 2000.[15] Because lobbying Congress is only a part of what interest groups do, as you will see in the next section, these statistics show only the tip of a very large iceberg.

There are a number of reasons so many interest groups exist in the United States.

□ The Constitution

The constitutional rules of the political game in the United States encourage the formation of interest groups. The First Amendment to the Constitution, for instance, guarantees citizens the right to speak freely, to assemble, and to petition the government, all of which are essential to citizens' ability to form organizations to advance their interests before government. Moreover, the government is organized in such a way that officials are relatively accessible to interest groups. Because of federalism, checks and balances, and the separation of powers, there is no dominant center of decision making, as there is in unitary states such as Great Britain and France. In unitary states, most important policy decisions are made in parliamentary bodies. In the United States, important decisions are made by many officials, on many matters, in many jurisdictions. Consequently, there are many more places where interest group pressure can be effective; there are more access points to public officials.

□ Diverse Interests

Being a very diverse society, there are simply myriad interests in the United States. Racial, religious, ethnic, and occupational diversity is pronounced. Also varied are the views about abortion, property rights, prayer in the schools, and environmental protection. Our economy is also strikingly complex and multifaceted, and becoming more so. In a free society, these diverse interests usually take organizational forms. Thus, the computer revolution spawned computer chip manufacturers, software companies, software engineers, computer magazines and blogs, Internet services, technical information providers, computer component jobbers, Web designers, social media sites, and countless others. Each has particular interests to defend or advance before government, and each has formed an association to try to do so.[16] Thus, software engineers have an association to look after their interests, as do software and hardware companies, Internet access providers, digital content providers, industry writers, and so on. After it went public in 2004, Google opened its own Washington office to ensure that its interests were protected before Congress and important regulatory agencies against competing interests such as Microsoft and wireless phone carriers such as AT&T, Verizon, and Sprint.[17] Facebook opened a Washington D.C. office in 2010 and ramped it up very quickly.

□ A More Active Government

Government does far more today than it did during the early years of the Republic. As government takes on more responsibilities, it quite naturally comes to have a greater effect on virtually all aspects of economic, social, and personal life. People, groups, and organizations are increasingly affected by the actions of government, so the decisions made by presidents, members of Congress, bureaucrats who write regulations, and judges are increasingly important. It would be surprising indeed if in response, people, groups, and organizations did not try harder to influence the public officials' decisions that affect them.[18] During the long, drawn-out deliberations in Congress in 2009 and 2010 that resulted in new rules for banks and the financial industry, bank and financial industry lobbyists flooded Capitol Hill to make sure that the most onerous provisions—for example, a limit on the size of banks so they would not be "too big to fail"—did not make it into the final bill.

Some part of the growth in lobbying by business firms and industry and trade groups may be tied to the emergence of hyper-competition in the global economy, where even giant enterprises like Microsoft must fight to protect their positions not only against competitors but against threatening actions by one or more government agencies. The Seattle-based company has been fighting antitrust actions initiated by the U.S. Justice Department and the European Union Commission for many years and has dramatically enhanced its lobbying presence in Washington (and Brussels) and increased its campaign contributions.[19]

Some groups form around government programs in order to take advantage of existing government programs and initiatives. The creation of the Department of Homeland Security (DHS), with its large budget for new homeland defense technologies, stimulated the formation of new companies to serve this market, as well as new trade associations—including the Homeland Security Industries Association—to represent them. Rising interest in alternative energy and its prominent place in President Obama's stimulus package, which became law in 2009, led to an explosion of lobbying for attractive tax breaks and government spending in the bill by firms and associations—including the American Wind Energy Association and Hawkeye Renewables—in the corn and ethanol, wind and solar, geothermal, and biomass industries, among others.

☐ Disturbances

The existence of diverse interests, the rules of the game, and the importance of government decisions and policies enable and encourage the formation of interest groups, but formation seems to happen only when interests are threatened,

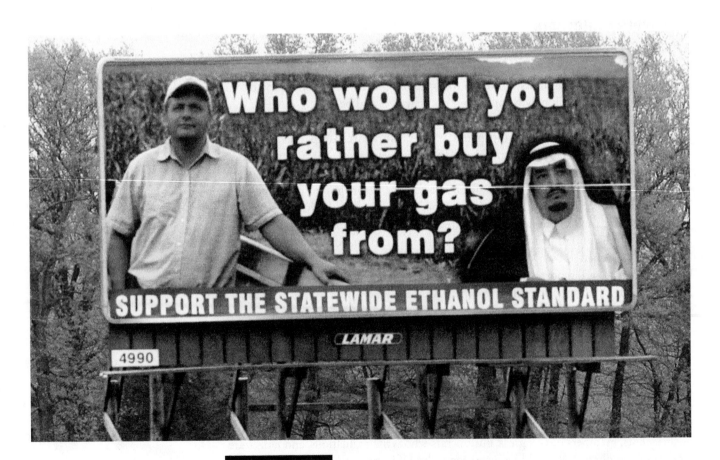

LOBBYING FOR ETHANOL

Corn farmers and organizations that represent them have been very successful in convincing Americans and their elected officials to pass laws requiring that ethanol from corn be added to gasoline and to keep out—mainly by the imposition of high tariffs—more efficiently produced ethanol from other countries, especially Brazil, which uses sugar cane and switchgrass. Billboards along major highways such as this one near Boone, Missouri, have been very effective tools of public persuasion in this campaign by corn and domestic ethanol producers, but they deploy many other tools as well. What are some other powerful lobbying tools?

usually by some change in the social and economic environment or in government policy. This is known as the **disturbance theory** of interest group formation.[20] To take one example, Focus on the Family, a conservative religious advocacy group, was formed when many evangelical Christians began to feel threatened by what they considered to be a rise in family breakdown, an increase in the number of abortions, the sexual revolution, and the growing visibility of gays and lesbians in American life.

What Interest Groups Do

7.4 Distinguish the methods through which interest groups try to shape government policy

Interest groups, whether public or private in nature, are in the business of conveying the policy views of individuals and groups to public officials. There are two basic types of interest group activity: the inside game and the outside game.[21] The inside game—the older and more familiar of the two—involves direct, personal contact between interest group representatives and government officials. Some political scientists believe this inside game of influencing the actions of those who make and carry out government policy in Washington—representatives and senators, judges, and regulators—is the thing that big interest groups and business corporations care about the most in politics and where they put most of their political resources. As they put it, "For powerful groups the center of action is in Washington, not the swing states."[22] The outside game involves interest group mobilization of public opinion, voters, and important contributors in order to bring indirect pressure to bear on elected officials. Increasingly today, the most powerful interest groups use both inside and outside methods to influence what policies government makes and carries out.

☐ The Inside Game

When lobbying and lobbyists are in the news, the news generally is not good. In early 2006, "super-lobbyist" Jack Abramoff pled guilty to three felony counts for fraud, tax evasion, and conspiracy to bribe public officials; he was then convicted and sentenced to 10 years in prison. Prosecutors had amassed evidence that he had funneled millions on behalf of his clients to a long list of representatives and senators, mostly on the Republican side of the aisle, for campaign war chests and elaborate gifts, including vacations. During the 2008 presidential campaign, Republican candidate John McCain made the very common practice of **earmarking**—setting aside money in appropriations bills for pet projects for constituents and private interests, usually at the behest of an army of lobbyists[23]—an important theme. Tea Party Caucus Republicans in Congress in 2011 made the elimination of earmarks an important element in their effort to reduce government deficits. President Obama also supported elimination of earmarks.

The inside game of lobbying—so named because of the practice of interest group representatives talking to legislators in the lobbies outside House and Senate committee rooms—does not customarily involve bribing legislators, however. Rather, it is more the politics of insiders and the "good ole' boy" network (although, increasingly, women are also part of the network). It is the politics of one-on-one persuasion, in which the skilled lobbyist tries to get a decision-maker to understand and sympathize with the interest group's point of view or to see that what the interest group wants is good for the politician's constituents. Access is critical if one is to be successful at this game.

Many of the most successful lobbyists are recruited from the ranks of retired members of the House and Senate, congressional staff, and high levels of the bureaucracy. Almost 30 percent of outgoing lawmakers, for example, are hired by lobbying

disturbance theory
A theory positing that interest groups originate with changes in the economic, social, or political environment that threaten the well-being of some segment of the population.

earmarking
Practice of appropriating money for specific pet projects of members of Congress, usually done at the behest of lobbyists, and added to bills at the last minute with little opportunity for deliberation.

firms or hang out their own lobbying shingle.[24] Former Democratic Senate leader Tom Daschle consults for the United Health Group, an association of health insurance giants deeply involved in the formulation of the health care reform bill, as does Steve Elmendorf, former chief of staff to Democratic House leader Dick Gephardt.[25] Between 1998 and 2009, 39 people associated with Senator Ted Kennedy (D–MA) became high-profile lobbyists, as did 32 people associated with Max Baucus (D–MT), 29 with Mitch McConnell (R–KY), and 21 with Nancy Pelosi (D–CA). The promise of lucrative employment based on their skills—and especially on their many contacts—is what keeps so many of them around Washington after they leave office or quit federal employment.

The inside game seems to work best when the issues are narrow and technical, do not command much media attention or public passion, and do not stir up counteractivity by other interest groups.[26] This is not to say that interest groups play a role only on unimportant matters. Great benefit can come to an interest group or a large corporation from a small change in a single provision of the Tax Code or in a slight change in the wording of a regulation on carbon emissions or what percentage of deposits banks must keep in reserve. Enron was very successful at getting Congress to remove federal oversight on many of its energy-trading and acquisitions activities. These stayed well out of public view until they came to light after Enron's spectacular collapse in 2001.

Lobbyists from citizens groups also play the inside game, often with great skill and effect. Many environmental regulations have been strengthened because of the efforts of skilled lobbyists from the Sierra Club, for example. But it is inescapably the case that lobbyists representing business and the wealthy are far more numerous and deployed on a wider range of issues than those of any other interest, as we will show later in the chapter.

Political scientist E.E. Schattschneider has pointed out that the inside game—traditional lobbying—is pretty much outside the view of the public.[27] That is to say, the day-to-day details of this form of lobbying are not the stuff of the evening news, nor the fodder of open political campaigns or conflict; such lobbying largely takes place behind closed doors.

LOBBYING CONGRESS In Congress, lobbyists are trying to accomplish two essential tasks for those who hire them: First, have bills and provisions in bills which they favor passed. Second, stop bills and provisions of bills they do not like from seeing the light of day. The essence of this inside game in Congress is the cultivation of personal relationships with people who matter—Senate and House leaders, other influential and well-placed legislators, chairpersons of important committees or subcommittees, a broad swath of rank-and-file members, and key staff members.[28] Because much of the action in Congress takes place in the committees and because senators and representatives are busy with a wide range of responsibilities, cultivating relationships with important legislative and committee staff members is especially important for successful lobbyists. As one lobbyist put it, "If you have a staff member on your side, it might be a hell of a lot better than talking to the member [of Congress]."[29]

Lobbyists are also expected to make substantial contributions to the campaign war chests of representatives and senators and to persuade their clients to do the same.[30] One influential lobbyist is reported to have said recently that "about one-third of my day is spent raising money from my clients to give to people I lobby."[31]

LOBBYING THE EXECUTIVE BRANCH After bills become law, they must be carried out or implemented. This is done by the executive branch. In this process of implementation, career civil servants, political appointees in top executive branch bureaus and departments, and regulators have a great deal of discretionary authority in deciding how to transform the wishes of the president and Congress into action on the ground. This happens because Congress and the president usually legislate broad policies, leaving it to executive branch bureaus and agencies to promulgate procedures,

Can Interest Groups Buy Public Policy?

Interest groups such as banks and labor unions participate in activities that influence legislation their members care about, such as tax policy or social benefits. During the election season, interest groups team up with political action committees (PACs) to finance different campaigns. Directing contributions to the party in power, and specifically to committee members who write legislation, is a common practice in American politics. Both labor unions and banks donate similar amounts of money to candidates, but they have different contribution strategies.

Banks and Labor Unions Have Similar Campaign Funding

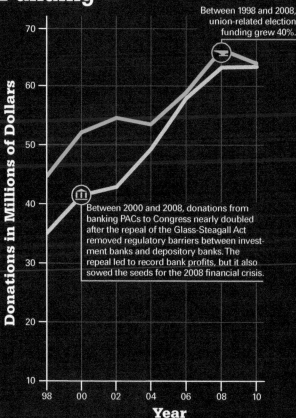

Between 1998 and 2008, union-related election funding grew 40%.

Between 2000 and 2008, donations from banking PACs to Congress nearly doubled after the repeal of the Glass-Steagall Act removed regulatory barriers between investment banks and depository banks. The repeal led to record bank profits, but it also sowed the seeds for the 2008 financial crisis.

Labor donations to all candidates
Banking donations to all candidates

SOURCE: Data from the Federal Election Commission, www.fec.gov.

Banks and Labor Unions Have Different Party Priorities

Labor PACs consistently give less than 20% of their money to Republicans no matter which party is in power.

Banking PACs mainly give to Republicans, except in 2008 and 2010 when they split their money between Republicans and Democrats.

% of Labor PAC Money to Republicans
% of Banking PAC Money to Republicans

*As of reporting period ending October 1, 2012.

Investigate Further

Concept Are banks or labor unions giving more money to politicians through their PACs? They are giving roughly similar amounts of money. In fact, labor PACs donate more money than banking PACs.

Connection How are labor unions' donation strategies different from those of banks? Labor PACs consistently give the majority of their PAC money to Democrats even when Republicans control Congress. Banking PACs give more strategically. During most years, they focus their money on Republicans, but when Democrats are in power they split their donations between both parties.

Cause How do interest groups buy policy? Interest groups use PACs and campaign financing to reinforce political friendships with legislators. Labor PACs use their donations to support Democrats who share their ideological values, while banking PACs change their donation strategy depending on which party is in power.

213

7.1
7.2
7.3
7.4
7.5
7.6

rules, and regulations to fill in the details of how laws will actually work in practice and how the mandates of regulatory agencies will be accomplished. So, for example, while Congress appropriates monies for the Army Corps of Engineers, it is, for the most part, decision-makers in the Corps who decide which specific levee and river dredging projects will be funded. Lobbyists for big contractors and for state and local governments try to make sure they have a regular presence with the Corps's top officials and staffers.

Because of the technical complexity of many of the issues that come before them, regulatory agencies such as the SEC (Securities and Exchange Commission), the EPA (the Environmental Protection Agency), and the FCC (the Federal Communications Commission) have been granted broad leeway in promulgating rules designed to meet the goals the president and Congress have set for them. The rules they issue have the force of law, moreover, unless these rules are subsequently overturned by Congress (which is very hard for Congress to do) or the courts. Congress rarely passes legislation involving details of television and radio broadcasting, for example, leaving regulatory decisions to the Federal Communications Commission. Because of this, the National Association of Broadcasters focuses its time and energies on the FCC, trying to establish stable and friendly relationships with them. The payoffs can be quite high for lobbying executive branch agencies like the FCC. In 2003, for example, large media company and news organization leaders and lobbyists met with the top staff of the FCC in a successful effort to get the agency to loosen rules on ownership so that big companies could grow even bigger.

The key to success in lobbying the executive branch is similar to that in lobbying Congress: personal contact and cooperative long-term relationships that a civil servant, a department or bureau leader, or a regulator finds useful.[32] Interest group representatives can convey technical information, for example, provide the results of their research, help a public official deflect criticism, and show that what the group wants is compatible with good public policy and the political needs of the official.

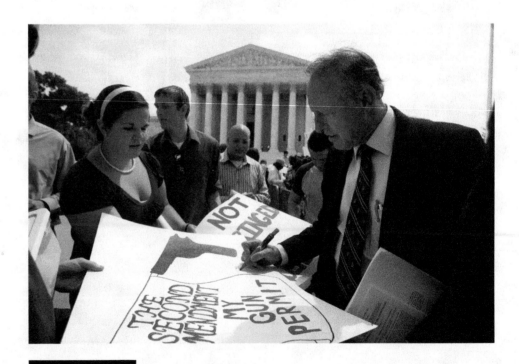

CELEBRATING A HISTORIC COURT DECISION

Dick Heller—here signing his autograph on the placards of gun rights advocates in front of the Supreme Court in June 2008—won his suit against the city government of Washington, D.C., in a case that established a constitutional right to own a firearm. The legal and financial resources that made his suit possible were provided by the NRA and other organizations against gun control. Why are gun lobbies such a powerful force in American politics?

LOBBYING THE COURTS Interest groups sometimes lobby the courts, although not in the same way as they lobby the other two branches. A group may find that neither Congress nor the White House is favorably disposed to its interests and will bring a test case to the courts. Realizing that the improvement of the lot of African Americans was very low on the agenda of presidents and members of Congress during the 1940s and 1950s, for example, the NAACP turned to the courts for satisfaction. The effort eventually paid off in 1954 in the landmark *Brown v. Board of Education* decision.

Interest groups sometimes lobby the courts by filing **amicus curiae** ("friends of the court") briefs in cases involving other parties. In this kind of brief, a person or an organization that is not a party in the suit may file an argument in support of one side or the other in the hope of swaying the views of the judge or judges. Major controversies before the Supreme Court on such issues as abortion, free speech, or civil rights attract scores of *amicus curiae* briefs. Nineteen *amicus* briefs were filed by supporters and opponents of gun control, for example, in the recently decided case, *District of Columbia v. Heller* (2008), in which the Court ruled that Americans have an individual right under the Constitution to own a gun.

Interest groups also get involved in the appointment of federal judges. Particularly controversial appointments, such as the Supreme Court nominations of Robert Bork (whom many women's and civil rights interests considered too conservative) in 1987, Clarence Thomas (who was opposed by liberal and women's groups) in 1992, and Samuel Alito in 2005 (Democrats and liberals considered him much too conservative on a wide range of issues), drew interest group attention and strenuous efforts for and against the nominees. Though they ultimately failed, conservative groups mobilized in 2009 to block the appointment of Sonia Sotomayor to the Court.

☐ The Outside Game

The outside game is being played when an interest group tries to mobilize local constituencies and shape public opinion to support the group's goals and to bring that pressure to bear on elected officials. Defenders of the status quo can mostly depend on the inside game; those who are trying to change existing policies or create new legislation are more likely to use the outside game.[33] By all indications, the outside game—sometimes called **grassroots lobbying**—has been growing steadily in importance in recent years.[34] This may be a good development for democracy, and here is why. Although groups involved in the outside game often try to hide their true identities—Americans for Fair Drug Prices, for example, may well be funded by the pharmaceutical industry—and while some groups involved in the outside game have more resources than others, it is still the case that this form of politics has the effect of expanding and heightening political conflict. This brings issues out into the open and subjects them to public scrutiny—what Schattschneider has called the "socialization of conflict."[35]

MOBILIZING MEMBERSHIP Those interest groups with a large membership base try to persuade their members to send letters and to make telephone calls to senators and representatives when an important issue is before Congress. They sound the alarm, using direct mail and, increasingly, e-mail. They define the threat to members; suggest a way to respond to the threat; and supply the addresses, phone numbers, and e-mail addresses of the people to contact in Washington. Members are grouped by congressional district and state and are given the addresses of their own representatives or senators. The National Rifle Association (NRA) is particularly effective in mobilizing its considerable membership whenever the threat of federal gun control rears its head. Environmental organizations such as Friends of the Earth sound the alarm to people on their mailing list whenever Congress threatens to loosen environmental protections.

amicus curiae
Latin for "friend of the court"; a legal brief in which individuals not party to a suit may have their views heard in court.

grassroots lobbying
The effort by interest groups to mobilize local constituencies, shape public opinion to support the group's goals, and bring that pressure to bear on elected officials.

7.1

7.2

7.3

7.4

7.5

7.6

ORGANIZING THE DISTRICT Members of Congress are especially attuned to the individuals and groups in their states or districts who can affect their reelection prospects. The smart interest group, therefore, not only will convince its own members in the state and district to put pressure on the senator or congressional representative, but will also make every effort to be in touch with the most important campaign contributors and opinion leaders there.

SHAPING PUBLIC OPINION "Educating" the public on issues that are important to the interest group is one of the central features of new-style lobbying. The idea is to shape opinion in such a way that government officials will be favorably disposed to the views of the interest group. These attempts to shape public and elite opinion come in many forms. One strategy is to produce and distribute research reports that bolster the group's position. Citizen groups such as Environmental Defense and the Food Research and Action Center have been very adept and effective in this area.[36]

Another strategy is media advertising. Sometimes this takes the form of pressing a position on a particular issue, such as the Teamsters Union raising the alarm about open borders with Mexico, focusing on the purported unsafe nature of Mexican trucks roaming American highways. Sometimes it is "image" advertising, in which some company or industry portrays its positive contribution to American life.[37] Thus, large oil companies often feature their regard for the environment in their advertising, showing romantic forest scenes or a pristine beach, with nary a pipeline, a tanker, or a refinery in sight.

In the effort to shape public opinion, the well-heeled interest group will also prepare materials that will be of use to radio and television broadcasters and to newspaper and magazine editors. Many produce opinion pieces, magazine articles, television spots and radio "sound bites," and even television documentaries. Others stage events to be covered as news. The environmentalist group Greenpeace puts the news media on full alert, for example, when it tries to disrupt a whaling operation.

Finally, interest groups, using the latest computer technology, identify target groups to receive information on particular issues. Groups pushing for cuts in the capital gains tax rate, for instance, direct their mail and telephone banks to holders of the American Express card or to addresses in ZIP code areas identified as upper-income neighborhoods. They are increasingly using the Internet, as well, in the effort to mobilize the public on issues of concern to them. For example, most have their own websites and publish position papers and other materials there. Many arrange postings to friendly blogs in hopes of further disseminating their message. Some will use their websites and e-mail to organize e-mails to lawmakers from their constituents.[38] Many interest and advocacy groups have made big commitments recently to the use of social media such as Facebook and Twitter to spread their message.

GETTING INVOLVED IN CAMPAIGNS AND ELECTIONS Interest groups try to increase their influence by getting involved in political campaigns.[39] Many interest groups, for example, issue a report card indicating the degree to which members of the House and Senate supported the interest group's position on a selection of key votes. The report card ratings are distributed to the members of the interest group and other interested parties in the hope that the ratings will influence their voting behavior. We show how groups do this in the "By the Numbers" feature.

Interest groups also encourage their members to get involved in the electoral campaigns of candidates who are favorable to their interests. Groups often assist campaigns in more tangible ways—allowing the use of their telephone banks; mail, telephone, and e-mail lists; fax and photocopy machines; computers; and the like. Some interest groups help with fund-raising events or ask members to make financial contributions to candidates.

Interest groups also endorse particular candidates for public office. The strategy may backfire and is somewhat risky, for to endorse a losing candidate is to risk losing access to the winner. Nevertheless, it is fairly common now for labor unions,

7.1
7.2
7.3
7.4
7.5
7.6

By the Numbers

Is there a reliable way to evaluate the performance of your representative in Congress?

Imagine you are at the end of the semester and four different teachers give you a grade in your introductory political science course. One looks at your performance and gives you a grade of 100 percent. Your day is made! Teacher number 2 gives you an 83. OK, you might say, "I can live with that." Teachers 3 and 4 slam you with a 20 and a 10. Ouch! How to make sense of all of this? Why is it that two teachers love you and two hate you? Surely they must be biased in some way.

This is exactly what happens to members of Congress when they are graded on their performance by interest groups. Unlike you, the confused student in the preceding example, congressional representatives expect the wide disparity in the grades they receive, understand what is going on, and are even proud of most of their grades, whether high or low. Note the wildly contrasting grades for Republican Senator Jim DeMint of South Carolina and Democratic Senator Barbara Boxer of California given by four organizations: the Americans for Democratic Action (ADA), the American Conservative Union (ACU), the League of Conservation Voters (LCV), and the National Taxpayers Union (NTU).

Why It Matters

Having a consistent and reliable way to grade each member of Congress can help voters make more rational electoral choices. Without such grades, each citizen would have to investigate the record of his or her member of Congress, rely on news reports, or depend on information provided by the member.

Behind the Numbers

How are members of Congress graded? The answer is pretty straightforward. Each interest group in this example is strongly ideological or committed to a certain set of concerns, and each grades members of Congress in terms of these standards. The ADA is very strongly liberal—interested in civil liberties, civil rights, and economic and social justice; while the ACU is strongly conservative—in favor of capitalism, traditional moral values, and a strong national defense. The LCV supports legislation to protect the environment, while the NTU wants lower taxes, less wasteful government spending, and a balanced budget. So, members of Congress who vote to increase spending on child welfare programs, let us say, are likely to get high grades from the ADA, but low grades from the ACU and the NTU. Members who vote to open the Alaska National Wildlife Reserve for oil exploration would surely receive a low grade from the folks at LCV.

Calculating Interest Group Scores

Although each group uses a slightly different method to do its grading, at base, each approaches grading in pretty much the same way. For each interest group, its professional staff, sometimes in conjunction with outside experts, selects a set of key votes on which to assess members of Congress. The particular votes selected by each group will differ—a group interested solely in civil rights issues will not, for example, use a vote on the defense budget for its scorecard—but each identifies a set of votes it considers to be a good indicator of ideological or policy loyalty. On each vote, members of Congress are scored "with the group" or "against the group." The numbers are added up, then transformed to percentage terms, with 100 being the highest score and 0 the lowest.

What to Watch for

Oddly enough, although not terribly sophisticated in either conceptual or computational terms, these are numbers you can trust. You can, as they say, "Take them to

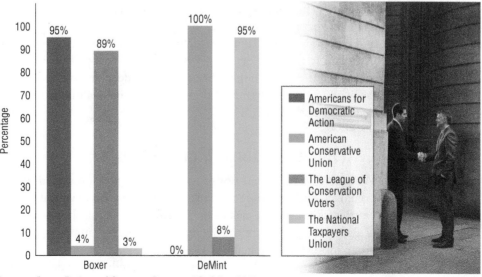

Interest Group Ratings of Senators Boxer and DeMint, 2010
Source: Project Vote Smart

7.1
7.2
7.3
7.4
7.5
7.6

(Continued)

the bank." Why? Because each interest group is clear about what it stands for, and each makes it clear that it is judging members of Congress from a particular perspective. When you are considering whether to vote for or against an incumbent member of Congress, a good method would be to check member scores from organizations whose ideology and/or policy views you support.

What Do You Think?

How does your representative in Congress score with those groups whose values and policy positions come closest to your own? You can investigate this at the Project Vote Smart website at www.votesmart.org, where you can find how your representative is evaluated by different interest groups.

environmental organizations, religious groups, and liberal and conservative ideological groups to make such endorsements.

Interest groups are also an increasingly important part of campaign fund-raising. The rise of so-called super PACs is especially noteworthy, injecting the super-rich individuals and companies directly into the middle of electoral campaigns. This topic will be explored briefly in the next section.

Interest Groups, Corporations, and Inequality in American Politics

7.5 Determine the biases in the interest group system

Explore on MyPoliSciLab
Simulation
You Are a Lobbyist

Overall, between the inside game and the outside game, interest groups have a diverse set of tools for influencing elected officials, bureaucrats in the executive branch, judges, and the public. And the number of groups capable of deploying these tools is large and growing every year. On the surface, it might look like the proliferation of interest groups has enhanced the democratic flavor of our country, allowing more and more Americans to have their interests represented. But not all scholars and students of politics agree that this is so.

Political scientist E.E. Schattschneider once observed that the flaw in the pluralist (or interest group) heaven is "that the heavenly chorus sings with a strong upper class accent." We would amend this, based on our reading of the evidence, in the following way: the flaw in the pluralist heaven is "that the heavenly chorus sings with a strong upper class and *corporate* accent." We show a schematic of how this works in shaping what government does in Figure 7.2. If this observation about an "upper class and corporate accent" is accurate, then political equality is undermined by the interest group system, and democracy is less fully developed than it might be, even taking into account the new importance of the outside game (which, as we have said, tends to "socialize conflict"). In this section, we look at inequalities in the interest group system and evaluate their effects.

☐ Representational Inequalities

We would suggest that power in the interest group system over time goes to the organized and to those among the organized who have the most resources and the best access to decision makers in government. We start by noting that not all segments of American society are equally represented in the interest group system. The interest group inside lobbying game in Washington, D.C., is dominated in sheer numbers and weight of activity, by business corporations, industry trade associations, and associations of the professions, although liberal and conservative advocacy groups lobby as well.[40] Organized labor, we have seen, although still a powerful player in Washington,

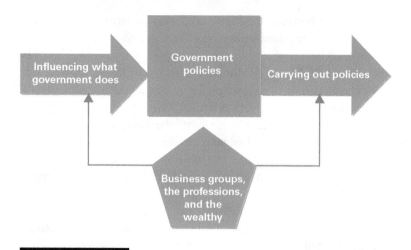

FIGURE 7.2 THESE INTERESTS EXERCISE THE MOST INFLUENCE AT EACH STAGE OF THE POLICY-MAKING PROCESS?

7.1
7.2
7.3
7.4
7.5
7.6

has lost much of its lobbying clout in recent years, mainly because of declining membership. Passage in 2005 of several pro-business bills that it strongly opposed—namely, bills making it more difficult to declare bankruptcy and to bring class-action lawsuits in state courts—showcases labor's declining fortunes. For their part, the vast majority of advocacy groups, even those that perceive themselves as liberal and lean toward the Democrats, attract members and contributors who have much higher incomes, more elite occupations, and more education than the general public. Not surprisingly, given those whom these advocacy groups represent, they tend to focus less on issues of poverty, jobs, and income inequality, the traditional purview of labor unions, let us say, and more on "quality of life" issues such as environmental protection, consumer protection, globalization, women's rights, racial and ethnic civil rights, gay and lesbian rights, and civil liberties.[41]

☐ Resource Inequalities

Business corporations and financial institutions, corporate and financial institution executives and top managers, heads of private equity and hedge funds, and professionals are the most economically well-off parts of American society. As firms, they are the most important actors; as individuals, they account for a disproportionately large share of income and wealth in the United States. It is hardly surprising that interest groups representing them can afford to spend far more than other groups to hire professional lobbying firms, form their own Washington liaison office, place advertising in the media, conduct targeted mailings on issues, mobilize their members to contact government officials, and pursue all of the other activities of old- and new-style lobbying. Lobbying in Washington is heavily dominated by lobbyists and lobbying firms that represent business.[42] Registered lobbyists for the various drug companies, for example, typically total more than the combined membership of the House and Senate;[43] in 2011 there were 1,497 registered lobbyists for the pharmaceutical industry, according to the Center for Public Integrity. (You can learn more about the influence of the drug industry, as well as the insurance industry, in the "Using the Framework" feature on passage of the Medicare drug prescription program.)

To take another important example, business lobbyists flooded Capitol Hill during the long and drawn-out deliberations on a bill to regulate the financial industry in the wake of the collapse of the financial sector in 2008 and the Great Recession that followed. Despite anger at Wall Street, the bill that passed in 2010 did not include a number of provisions that some analysts say are essential to prevent another financial collapse but were opposed by financial industry lobbyists: a cap on the size of

7.1

7.2

7.3

7.4

7.5

7.6

political action committees (PACs)
An entity created by an interest group whose purpose is to collect money and make contributions to candidates in federal elections.

institutions so that they cannot become "too big to fail," a tax on large bonuses, oversight of derivatives markets, and a required separation of trading and commercial banking.[44] (One of the leading advocates of letting the banking industry regulate itself is Jamie Dimon, the chairman and CEO of JPMorgan Chase. Under his watch, the bank lost $2 billion of their depositors money on a single day in May, 2012, after it placed a risky and failed debt in the unregulated derivatives market.) The lopsided lobbying situation in Washington is shown in Table 7.2 which reports the amount of money spent by different sectors of American society on lobbying activities. It is worth noting that nonbusiness groups and associations—listed in the table as other, ideological/single-issue, city/county, and organized labor—spent only a small fraction of what was spent by business in 2009.

Corporate, trade, and professional associations also are important in campaign finance, with an especially prominent role played by **political action committees (PACs)**, which are entities created by interest groups—whether business firms, unions, membership organizations, or liberal or conservative advocacy groups—to collect money and make contributions to candidates in federal elections (i.e., to candidates for the presidency, the House of Representatives, and the Senate). Corporate, trade, and professional PACs lead other groups in both sheer numbers and levels of spending, although labor unions give a great deal, and large and committed advocacy organizations such as the NRA are also important. During the 2009–2010 election cycle, for example, political action committees representing business and the professions accounted for more than 70.4 percent of the $473 million spent by all PACs on candidates for federal office, while labor unions accounted for only about 14.6 percent.[45] PACs representing the least-privileged sectors of American society are notable for their absence. As former Senator (R–KS) and presidential candidate Bob Dole once put it, "There aren't any poor PACs or food stamp PACs or nutrition PACs or Medicaid PACs."[46]

Perhaps more important than regular PACs, in the long run, may be parallel campaign advertising organizations funded by corporations and unions. This is the result of the Supreme Court's ruling in *Citizens United v. The Federal Election Commission* (2009) that the provisions of the McCain–Feingold law prohibiting corporations, unions and advocacy organizations from spending whatever and whenever they would like on electioneering for and against candidates was an unconstitutional violation of free speech. While this likely will increase union advocacy group spending in elections, most seasoned observers believe the big winners will be large corporations, given the big financial advantages corporations have over unions and other groups, and their keen interest in electing people who will be sympathetic to business interests.[47] (The biggest contributors during the 2012 elections, however, were rich individuals advocating through SuperPACs and 501 organizations).

TABLE 7.2 MAJOR SPENDING ON FEDERAL LOBBYING IN 2011, BY INDUSTRY SECTOR

Sector	Total
Health	$376,208,233
Miscellaneous business	354,208,233
Finance, insurance, and real estate	352,144,294
Energy and natural resources	289,481,814
Communications/electronics	290,691,276
Transportation	178,061,934
Other	174,076,331
Ideological/single-issue	100,733,128
Agribusiness	92,768,164
Defense	98,949,480
Construction	38,025,693
Labor	37,152,473
Lawyers and lobbyists	5,160,306

Source: Center for Responsive Politics, 2012.

The *Citizens United* decision turned heavily on the doctrine that corporations are "persons" with the same rights and privileges as any natural person residing in the United States, including free speech. Several scholars have pointed out that this doctrine has been pushed for a very long time in the courts by legal firms representing corporations in a broad set of cases. It need hardly be pointed out that the decades-long effort required a staying power based on access to substantial financial resources not available to most individuals, advocacy groups, or labor unions. Interestingly, corporations have managed to avoid criminal prosecution even when they have broken the law because criminal punishment is relevant only to "natural" persons. This is why most of the key players that brought about the financial collapse in 2008 have not gone to jail.[48]

☐ Access Inequality

Inequalities of representation and resources are further exaggerated by vast inequalities in access to government decision makers. Powerful interest organizations and lobbying firms that primarily represent business, professionals, and the wealthy have the resources to employ many former regulators and staff from independent regulatory agencies, former members of Congress and congressional staff, and top employees of other federal executive departments, including many from the Department of Defense and the Internal Revenue Service. They are hired partly for their technical expertise but also for the access they can provide to those with whom they formerly worked. *Bloomberg/Businessweek* reported, for example, that firms hired 60 former staffers from Congress in 2011 to work solely on convincing Congress to repeat a tax holiday on "repatriated earnings" (earnings brought back to the United States by global firms, normally taxed at the rate of 35 percent) that dropped the tax rate to 5.25 percent in 2004, saving firms $312 billion.[49]

Access inequality may also be seen in the ability of some groups to play a central role in the formation and implementation of government policies based on the membership of these groups in informal networks within the government itself. These networks are of two kinds. The first, **iron triangles** or **sub-governments**, customarily include a private interest group (usually a corporation or business trade association), an agency in the executive branch, and a committee or subcommittees in Congress, which act together to advance and protect certain government programs that work to the mutual benefit of their members. Most scholars believe that iron triangles have become less important in American government.[50] The second, called **issue networks**, are understood to be more open and inclusive than iron triangles. They are said to be coalitions that form around different policy areas that include a range of public and private interest groups and policy experts as well as business representatives, bureaucrats, and legislators. Iron triangles suggest a closed system in which a small group of actors controls a policy area. Issue networks suggest a more fluid situation with more actors and visibility, where control of policymaking is less predictable.

Be that as it may, corporations, trade associations, and associations of professionals not only play a prominent role in issue networks, but also participate in those iron triangles that are still around.[51] These are especially prominent in shaping and carrying out public policies in the areas of agriculture, defense procurement, public lands, highway construction, and water. Large-scale water projects—dams, irrigation, and levees, for example—are supported by farm, real estate developer, construction, and barge-shipping interest groups; members of key Senate and House committees responsible for these projects, who can claim credit for bringing jobs and federal money to their constituencies; and the Army Corps of Engineers, whose budget and responsibilities grow apace as it builds the projects. Another iron triangle is shown in Figure 7.3.

☐ The Privileged Position of Business Corporations

Economist and political scientist Charles Lindblom has argued that corporations wield such disproportionate power in American politics that they undermine democracy. He closes his classic 1977 book *Politics and Markets* with this observation:

iron triangles
An enduring alliance of common interest among an interest group, a congressional committee, and a bureaucratic agency.

sub-governments
Another name for an iron triangle.

issue networks
Broad coalitions of public and private interest groups, policy experts, and public officials that form around particular policy issues; said to be more visible to the public and more inclusive.

7.1
7.2
7.3
7.4
7.5
7.6

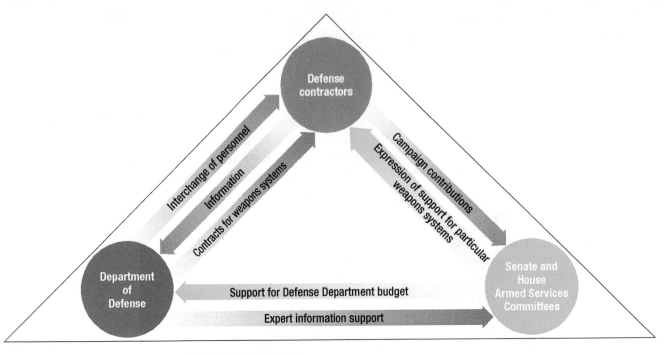

FIGURE 7.3 IRON TRIANGLE

In an iron triangle, an alliance based on common interests is formed among a powerful corporation or interest group, an agency of the executive branch, and congressional committees or subcommittees. In this example from the defense industry, an alliance is formed among parties that share an interest in the existence and expansion of defense industry contracts. Most scholars think iron triangles are less common today than in the past, though they are alive and well in a number of policy areas, including the one illustrated here.

"The large private corporation fits oddly into democratic theory. Indeed, it does not fit."[52] Twenty years later, political scientist Neil Mitchell concluded his book *The Conspicuous Corporation*, which reported the results of careful empirical testing of Lindblom's ideas, with the conclusion that "business interests (in the United States) are not routinely countervailed in the policy process. Their political resources and incentives to participate are usually greater than other interests."[53] Let's see why these scholars reached their somber conclusion about business corporations in American politics.

We have already learned about many of the advantages that corporations and business trade associations representing groups of corporations enjoy over others in the political process. The largest corporations are far ahead of their competitors in the number of lobbyists they employ, the level of resources they can and do use for political purposes, their ability to shape public perceptions and opinions through such instruments as issue advertising and subsidization of business-oriented think tanks like the American Enterprise Institute, and the ease of access they often have to government officials.

An additional source of big business power is the high regard in which business is held in American society and the central and honored place of business values in our culture. Faith in free enterprise gives special advantages to the central institution of free enterprise, the corporation. Any political leader contemplating hostile action against corporations must contend with business's special place of honor in the United States. To be sure, scandals involving large business enterprises such as Enron, Goldman Sachs, and BP can tarnish big business now and then, but in the long run, as President Coolidge once famously said, "The business of America is business."

Business corporations are also unusually influential because the health of the American economy—and thus the standard of living of the people—is tied closely to the economic well-being of large corporations. It is widely and not entirely unreasonably believed that what is good for business is good for America. Because of their vital role in the economy, government officials tend to interpret business corporations

7.1
7.2
7.3
7.4
7.5
7.6

Using the FRAMEWORK

How did the long-awaited prescription drug benefit get added to Medicare in 2003, and why were drug and insurance companies so happy about it?

Background: Democratic presidents and members of Congress had tried—but failed—for more than 20 years to add a prescription drug benefit to the Medicare program. Stealing the Democrat's thunder, President George W. Bush, with his Republican Party in control of both the House and Senate, was able in 2003 to deliver on his campaign promise to the elderly for a prescription drug subsidy. Most of the elderly are now paying considerably less than they would have without the new program. But others gained as well: drug companies won provisions forbidding the importation of cheaper drugs from abroad, and the

negotiation of lower prices for drugs by the government; insurance companies were granted subsidies for providing drug benefit policies; and doctors won a provision in the bill loosening some of the restrictions on fees they receive under Medicare. Passage of the prescription drug benefit may even have paved the way for passage of Barack Obama's health reform bill in 2010 as provider resistance to reform began to weaken. So how did the 2003 drug benefit bill happen? Looking at how structural, political linkage, and governmental factors affected the political process will help us explain the outcome.

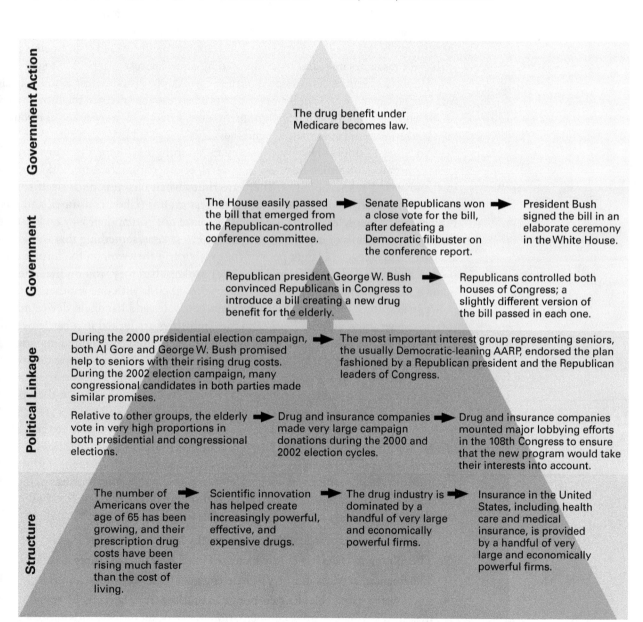

Government Action

The drug benefit under Medicare becomes law.

Government

The House easily passed the bill that emerged from the Republican-controlled conference committee. ➡ Senate Republicans won a close vote for the bill, after defeating a Democratic filibuster on the conference report. ➡ President Bush signed the bill in an elaborate ceremony in the White House.

Republican president George W. Bush convinced Republicans in Congress to introduce a bill creating a new drug benefit for the elderly. ➡ Republicans controlled both houses of Congress; a slightly different version of the bill passed in each one.

Political Linkage

During the 2000 presidential election campaign, both Al Gore and George W. Bush promised help to seniors with their rising drug costs. During the 2002 election campaign, many congressional candidates in both parties made similar promises. ➡ The most important interest group representing seniors, the usually Democratic-leaning AARP, endorsed the plan fashioned by a Republican president and the Republican leaders of Congress.

Relative to other groups, the elderly vote in very high proportions in both presidential and congressional elections. ➡ Drug and insurance companies made very large campaign donations during the 2000 and 2002 election cycles. ➡ Drug and insurance companies mounted major lobbying efforts in the 108th Congress to ensure that the new program would take their interests into account.

Structure

The number of Americans over the age of 65 has been growing, and their prescription drug costs have been rising much faster than the cost of living. ➡ Scientific innovation has helped create increasingly powerful, effective, and expensive drugs. ➡ The drug industry is dominated by a handful of very large and economically powerful firms. ➡ Insurance in the United States, including health care and medical insurance, is provided by a handful of very large and economically powerful firms.

not as "special interests" but as the voice of the national interest and to listen more attentively to their demands than they do to those of other sectors of American society. Some companies are so important for the overall operation of the American and global economies that they are considered "too big to fail"—think AIG, Citigroup, Bank of America, and General Motors, among others in 2008 and 2009—and were bailed out even when their downfall was from self-inflicted wounds. In this sense, corporations enjoy an especially privileged position in American politics. (See the "Mapping American Politics" feature for an example of how the power of large auto and oil companies has had important negative impacts on the environment.)

Corporations are also powerful because their mobility is an important counterweight to any government effort (local, state, or national) to raise taxes or impose regulations that business deems especially onerous. Increasingly, large corporations are able to design, produce, and market their goods and services all over the world; they are not irrevocably tied to a single location. If government threatens their interests, large corporations can credibly counter with a threat to move all or part of their operations elsewhere. In this new global economic environment, political leaders are increasingly of a mind to maintain a friendly and supportive business climate.

Large corporations do not, of course, run the show entirely. Although they have the most resources, for instance, these resources do not translate automatically into real political influence. One interest group may have enormous resource advantages over other interest groups, for instance, but may use its resources ineffectively. Or an interest group with great resources may find itself opposed by other interest groups that together are able to mobilize impressive resources of their own. A powerful interest group may also find that an elected politician is not cooperative because the voters in the district are of a different mind from the interest group. So even with this immense set of resources, business power is not automatically and inevitably translated into political power.[54]

Nor does business always get its way in Washington. There are many issues of great importance on which business in general, or one corporation in particular, loses in the give-and-take of politics. There are times when business finds itself squared off against powerful coalitions of other interest groups (labor, consumer, and environmentalist groups, let us say). Corporations have not gotten their way on loosening immigration controls or expanding the pool of H1-B visas, something that would have allowed them access to a larger pool of cheap labor had they won on the former, and a pool of highly skilled scientific and technical workers, had they won on the latter. On many occasions, corporations also find themselves at odds with one another on public policy issues. Thus, Internet service providers, computer and handheld device makers, software developers, and the music and film industries are locked in a battle over the ease of file-sharing and royalty compensation for distributed copyrighted material.

Corporations are most powerful when they can build alliances among themselves. Most of the time, corporations are in competition with one another; they do not form a unified political bloc capable of moving government to action on their behalf. On those occasions when corporations feel that their collective interests are at stake, however—as on taxes, for example, or executive compensation—they are capable of coming together to form powerful and virtually unbeatable political coalitions.[55] Large corporations and the wealthy—the vast majority of the top 1 percent derive their wealth from their positions as corporate executives, hedge fund managers, and the leaders of financial firms, so corporations and the wealthy can be understood as one and the same—recently have won some notable long-term victories.[56]

1. The long-term tax rates of the super-wealthy have declined (see Figure 7.4).
2. The minimum wage has hardly increased at all over the past three decades.
3. The financial services industry was deregulated (with disastrous results in 2008).
4. Laws were passed shielding corporate executives from lawsuits by stockholders, thereby allowing executive compensation to skyrocket in the 1990s and 2000s.
5. IRS audits of top income earners decreased during the past three decades even as audits of the working poor recently increased (those who use the Earned Income Tax Credit).

Mapping American Politics

7.1
7.2
7.3
7.4
7.5
7.6

Fueling the American Driving Habit

Introduction

The United States uses enormous amounts of fuel to power its economy and enhance the quality of life of its citizens, with a great deal of it taking the form of gasoline for cars and trucks. Indeed, all rich countries use enormous amounts of fuel; it is essential for powering industrialization, people's homes and apartments, and modern transportation and shipping systems, including cars, trucks, trains, and planes. Recently, rapidly industrializing and modernizing countries such as India and China have joined the ranks of the high–fuel-consuming countries. With the many benefits that come with high fuel consumption, however, come some problems as well. There is, most importantly perhaps, the massive amount of carbon that is released into the atmosphere when fuels are burned, contributing to the problem of global climate change. There is also the problem of dependency on foreign oil that worries many Americans. There is reason to worry. About two-thirds of all the fuel consumed in the United States is in the form of gasoline for cars and trucks. This requires massive imports of crude oil to be refined in the United States as well as rising imports of gasoline because refining capacity here has not kept up with demand.

Mapping Fuel Usage

This cartogram shows the proportion of the world's fuel used by each country. Fuel includes oil, coal, nuclear, and wood. For the entire world in 2004, the fuel equivalent of about 11.6 trillion kilograms of oil was consumed. Examining the cartogram, it is evident that the United States accounts for an enormous proportion of the world's fuel consumption, with two-thirds of its annual fuel consumption in the form of gasoline for cars and

trucks, as pointed out earlier. While European countries taken together account for a large proportion of the world's fuel consumption, Europe uses only about one-half as much gasoline per person to fuel vehicles as the United States.

There are many reasons Americans use so much vehicle-related gasoline, including the vast size of the country, space for cities to expand into suburban-dominated metropolitan areas, excellent road systems, and low investment in mass transportation. But also important is the low gas mileage efficiency of cars and trucks, much of this the product of the lobbying activities of oil companies and automobile manufacturers to block higher CAFE (corporate average fuel economy) requirements. Although rising gasoline prices and troubles in oil-producing nations and regions such as Nigeria, Venezuela, and the Persian Gulf finally compelled lawmakers to increase CAFE requirements for cars and trucks in 2007, which the EPA increased even more in 2009 and 2011 under directives from President Obama, the tougher standards were a long time coming because of the resistance of these industries—and will take some time to go into effect. Automakers must boost the average for their cars and small trucks (including SUVs) to 54.5 mpg by 2025.

What Do You Think?

How concerned are you about global climate change and America's dependence on imports of foreign oil? Is there a way to use less fuel in general and gasoline in particular without undermining the American standard of living and the well-being of its people? Does solving these problems require curtailing the lobbying power of the energy and automobile industries, or would this be an unacceptable limitation of free speech and the right to petition the government?

Fuel Use

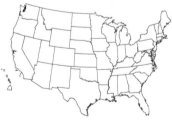

Standard US Map

source: © Copyright 2006 SASA Group (University of Sheffield) and Mark Newman (University of Michigan). (www.worldmapper.org).

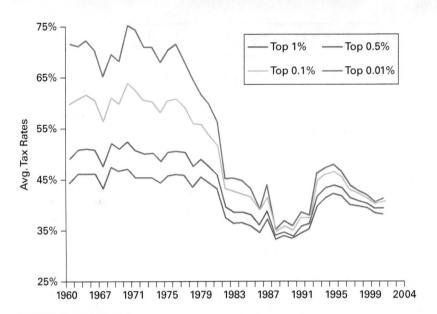

FIGURE 7.4 TAX RATES FOR THE WEALTHIEST AMERICANS

Tax rates for the wealthiest Americans, particularly the super-wealthy, have dropped dramatically over the past three and a half decades. The drops occurred not only when Republicans were in control in Washington, but during the Democratic Carter administration, and during periods when Democrats controlled Congress and Republicans held the presidency. This suggests that the political influence of these Americans has been fairly constant no matter which party was heading the government.

Source: Internal Revenue Service

6. The National Labor Relations Board became less willing during the 1980s, 1990s, and 2000s to penalize corporations for illegal anti-union activities.

7. Congress has refused to confirm the appointments of top officials to new financial industry regulatory agencies that business does not approve of.

These "wins" on important government policies that advance their interests are the best evidence available confirming political scientist David Vogel's observation that "when business is both mobilized and unified, its political power can be formidable."[57] Though interest group specialists in political science have not been able to empirically demonstrate links between things like money spent in lobbying or campaign contributions and specific votes in Congress,[58] we believe that an analysis of who wins and who loses from government policies is the best tool for understanding who exercises influence and power in Washington.

In our view, the best way to think about corporations in American politics is to see their power waxing and waning within their overall privileged position. Corporate power may be greater at certain times and weaker at other times, but it is always in a game in which, most of the time, corporations enjoy advantages over other groups in society. If corporations feel that their collective interests are at stake—as when labor unions are particularly aggressive or when government's regulatory burden is perceived to be too heavy—and they are able to present a united front, they are simply unbeatable. This cannot be said about any other sector of American society.[59]

Curing the Mischief of Factions

7.6   Assess the steps that have been taken to control factions

mericans have worried about the "mischief of factions" ever since James Madison wrote about them in *The Federalist* No. 10 (see the Appendix). Over the years, various things have been tried to control the purported negative effects of these special interests.[60] Disclosure has been the principal tool of regulation. In 1946, Congress imposed a requirement (in the Federal Regulation of Lobbying Act) that all lobbyists working in Congress be registered. The Lobby Disclosure Act of 1995 requires a wider range of political actors to register as lobbyists and makes them report every six months on which policies they are trying to influence and how much they are spending to do it.

Reformers have also tried to regulate some of the most troublesome abuses of the politics of factions. Sections of the Ethics in Government Act (1978) aim at the so-called **revolving door** in which former government officials become lobbyists for interests with whom they formerly dealt in their official capacity. A 1995 measure specifies that former U.S. trade representatives and their deputies are banned for life from lobbying for foreign interests. The 2007 measure increases the one-year waiting period in the 1995 measure to two years and adds representatives and senators to those who must wait.

Reformers have also tried to control the effects of interest group money in politics. The McCain–Feingold bill, passed in 2002, was designed to limit the use of soft money, but it left a huge loophole for nonprofit, advocacy 527 organizations—so named because of their location in the Tax Code—to use unlimited amounts of money to support or oppose candidates and issues, the only restrictions being a ban on radio and television advertising for a period before elections. It also increased the amount people could give to PACs. Another measure passed in 2007 requires congressional leaders to identify all earmarks in appropriations bills and post them to the Internet at least 48 hours before their consideration by the full House and Senate, along with information about their sponsors and intended purposes. The same measures require lobbyists to certify that no one in their firm or organization has provided gifts to members of Congress or their staffs and post this to a site on the Internet. Moreover, the measures require lobbyists to file and also post to the Internet quarterly reports on their lobbying activities in Congress.

The 2007 lobbying reform measure was passed in the wake of the corruption conviction of super-lobbyist Jack Abramoff, revelations of widespread influence peddling by lobbyists who formerly worked in Congress or the executive branch agencies, and the explosion of special interest earmarks in appropriations bills. Most keen Washington observers remain unconvinced that the new rules will diminish in a major way the influence of privileged interest groups in shaping what government does. Like water seeking its own level, it may be that powerful and wealthy interests will find a way to have their needs and wishes attended to in one way or another.

revolving door

The common practice in which former government officials become lobbyists for interests with whom they formerly dealt in their official capacity.

Using the DEMOCRACY STANDARD

Do interest groups help or hinder American democracy?

There is no doubt that the interest group system plays an important role in shaping what government does in the United States; elected officials pay lots of attention to them, for all the reasons explored in this chapter. Whether the interest group system advances or retards democracy, however, can only be determined by knowing which sectors of the American population are represented by interest groups, and how well interest groups represent the people they claim to be representing. There is considerable disagreement regarding the role that interest groups play in American politics and governance.

There are many who believe that the interest group system enhances democracy because it gives individuals and groups in American society another tool to keep elected and appointed officials responsive and responsible to their needs, wants, and interests. Political parties are important for making popular sovereignty work, to be sure, but being broad and inclusive umbrella organizations, they often ignore the interests of particular groups. And, although elections are essential for keeping public officials on their toes, they happen only every two to four years. Proponents of this pluralist view argue that the day-to-day work of popular sovereignty is done

7.1

7.2

7.3

7.4

7.5

7.6

by interest groups. Additionally, pluralists point to the rise of advocacy groups—supported by thousands of ordinary people with ordinary incomes—as an indication that the interest group system is being leveled, with a wider range of groups representing a broad swath of the population now playing a key role in the political game.

Having said that, there is more than ample evidence that narrow, special, and privileged interests dominate the interest group world and play the biggest role in determining what government does in the United States. The powerful interest groups that play the largest role in shaping public policies in the United States represent, by and large, wealthier and better-educated Americans, corporations, and other business interests and professionals, such as doctors and lawyers. In this view, the proliferation of interest groups, mostly in the form of associations and firms that represent business, has made American politics less and less democratic. This inequality of access and influence violates the democratic principle of political equality, with less influence in the hands of ordinary Americans. Thus, some argue, the present interest group system poses a real threat to democratic ideals.

Review the Chapter

Interest Groups in a Democratic Society: Contrasting Views

7.1 Compare and contrast theories about the role of interest groups in a democracy, p. 201

Americans have long denigrated special interests as contrary to the public good. Many political scientists, however, see interest groups as an important addition to the representation process in a democracy, enhancing the contact of citizens with government officials in the periods between elections.

The Universe of Interest Groups

7.2 Distinguish the two kinds of interests at work in American politics, p. 203

Private interests are organizations and associations that try to gain protections or material advantages from government for their own members rather than for society at large. For the most part, these represent economic interests of one kind or another.

Public interests are organizations and associations that try to gain protections or benefits for people beyond their own members, often for society at large. Public interests are motivated by ideological or issue concerns.

Why There Are So Many Interest Groups

7.3 Explain why interest groups have proliferated, p. 208

There has been a significant expansion in the number of public interest or citizen groups since 1968.

The United States provides a rich environment for interest groups because of our constitutional system, our political culture, and the broad responsibilities of our government.

Interests tend to proliferate in a complex and changing society, which creates a diversity of interests.

Government does more than it did in the past and affects the interests of various people, groups, and firms who organize to exert influence over laws and regulations.

What Interest Groups Do

7.4 Distinguish the methods through which interest groups try to shape government policy, p. 211

One way that interest groups attempt to influence the shape of public policy is the inside game: interest group representatives are in direct contact with government officials and try to build influence on the basis of personal relationships.

The outside game is being played when an interest group tries to mobilize local constituencies and shape public opinion to support the group's goals and to bring that pressure to bear on elected officials.

Interest Groups, Corporations, and Inequality in American Politics

7.5 Determine the biases in the interest group system, p. 218

Some groups, especially corporations, trade associations, high-income professionals, and the wealthy, have more resources to put into lobbying officials and better access to them than other groups.

The business corporation enjoys what has been called a "privileged position" in American society that substantially enhances its influence on government policies.

Business corporations and the wealthy made big gains in a number of important areas of government policy during the past two decades, particularly on policies related to taxes, financial deregulation, and executive compensation.

Curing the Mischief of Factions

7.6 Assess the steps that have been taken to control factions, p. 226

Lobbying reform has focused on requiring interest and advocacy groups to report on their lobbying activities, trying to control the revolving door, and limiting what private and public interest groups are allowed to spend in elections.

Learn the Terms

interest groups, p. 201
factions, p. 201
pluralism, p. 202
private interests, p. 203
public interests, p. 203
lobbying, p. 203

advocacy group, p. 208
lobbyists, p. 208
disturbance theory, p. 211
earmarking, p. 211
amicus curiae, p. 215
grassroots lobbying, p. 215

political action
    committees (PACs), p. 220
iron triangles, p. 221
sub-governments, p. 221
issue networks, p. 221
revolving door, p. 227

Test Yourself

Answer key begins on page T-1.

7.1 Compare and contrast theories about the role of interest groups in a democracy

1. Government power in the United States is broadly dispersed, leaving governmental institutions porous and open to the entreaties of diverse groups that exist in society. This can be attributed to

   a. Federalism and checks and balances
   b. The separation of powers
   c. Federalism, checks and balances, and the separation of powers
   d. Interest groups
   e. Factions

7.2 Distinguish the two kinds of interests at work in American politics

2. The main role of labor unions in the United States has been to

   a. Support public interest groups
   b. Support political parties and protect the jobs of their members
   c. Protect the jobs of their members
   d. Secure maximum wages for their members
   e. Protect the jobs and secure maximum wages and benefits for their members

7.3 Explain why interest groups have proliferated

3. According to the disturbance theory, interest group formation often seems to happen when:

   a. Interests are threatened
   b. Congress passes a law
   c. The government acquires too much power
   d. New interest groups are formed
   e. There is an increase in lobbying

7.4 Distinguish the methods through which interest groups try to shape government policy

4. This describes a legal brief in which individuals not involved in a suit may have their views heard in court:

   a. Grassroots lobbying
   b. *Amicus curiae*
   c. Lobbying Congress
   d. Earmarking
   e. Disturbance theory

7.5 Determine the biases in the interest group system

5. Coalitions that which form around different policy areas that include public and private interest groups and policy experts are called

   a. Iron triangles
   b. Sub-triangles
   c. Informal networks
   d. Issue networks
   e. Sub-governments

7.6 Assess the steps that have been taken to control factions

6. This bill, passed in 2002, was designed to limit the effect of interest group money in politics.

   a. Revolving door
   b. McCain–Feingold
   c. Ethics in government
   d. Federal regulation of lobbying
   e. Lobby disclosure

Explore Further

INTERNET SOURCES

Center for Responsive Politics **www.opensecrets.org/**

Follow the money trail—who gets it? who contributes?—in American politics.

National Taxpayers Union **www.ntu.org**

Conservative group that advocates for lower taxes.

National Organization for Women **www.now.org**

The women's organization that has long been a "player" in Washington politics.

National Rifle Association **www.nra.org**

Home page of one of America's most politically successful interest groups.

Project VoteSmart **www.votesmart.org**

Information on interest group campaign contributions to and ratings for all members of Congress.

U.S. Chamber of Commerce **www.uschamber.org**

The leading peak association lobbying for business.

Student Environmental Action Coalition **www.seac.org**

A grassroots coalition of student environmental groups.

Townhall **www.townhall.com**

A portal to scores of conservative organizations and citizen groups.

Yahoo/Organizations and Interest Groups **www.yahoo.com/ Government/Politics/**

Direct links to the home pages of scores of public and private interest groups as well as to Washington lobbying firms.

U.S. Public Interest Research Group **www.uspirg.org**

A site dedicated to information on public interest research groups.

ALL (American League of Lobbyists) **www.alldc.org**

The American League of Lobbyists is a site dedicated to educating others about the profession of lobbying.

Lobbyists.info **www.lobbyists.info**

A database of lobbyists, lobbying firms, and organizations.

SUGGESTIONS FOR FURTHER READING

Ainsworth, Scott H. *Analyzing Interest Groups: Group Influence on People and Policies.* New York: W. W. Norton, 2002.

Shows how economic forms of reasoning can be used to better understand how interest groups work and what effect they have on politics and government.

Andres, Gary J. *Lobbying Reconsidered: Under the Influence.* New York: Pearson Longman, 2009.

A fascinating tour of the world of lobbying by an author who not only knows the scholarly literature on the subject, but also has years of experience as a lobbyist.

Berry, Jeffrey M., and Clyde Wilcox. *The Interest Group Society,* 5th ed. New York: Pearson Longman, 2009.

A leading textbook on interest groups, filled with up-to-date insights from scholars and political journalists.

Dahl, Robert A. *A Preface to Democratic Theory.* Chicago: University of Chicago Press, 1956.

The leading theoretical statement of the pluralist position and the democratic role of interest groups.

Davidson, Roger H., Walter J. Oleszek, and Frances E. Lee. *Congress and Its Members,* 13th ed. Washington, D.C.: CQ Press, 2012.

A comprehensive book on Congress that carefully examines the role of organized interests in the legislative process.

Hacker, Jacob S., and Paul Pierson. *Winner-Take-All Politics: How Washington Made the Rich Richer—and Turned Its Back on the Middle Class.* New York: Simon and Schuster, 2010.

Shows how interest groups representing business and the wealthy have dominated public policymaking in Washington and made the distribution of income and wealth much more unequal.

Skocpol, Theda. *Diminished Democracy: From Membership to Management in American Civil Life.* Norman, OK: University of Oklahoma Press, 2003.

An analysis of the decline of mass membership associations and how it hurts American civic life and the middle class.

Smith, Mark A. *American Business and Political Power: Public Opinion, Elections, and Democracy.* Chicago: University of Chicago Press, 2000.

An argument, counter to that of Lindblom, that business corporations are not as powerful in American politics as often perceived.

8

Social Movements

WOMEN WIN THE RIGHT TO VOTE

The struggle for women's suffrage (i.e., the right to vote) was long and difficult. The main instrument for winning the struggle to amend the Constitution to admit women to full citizenship was a powerful social movement that dared to challenge the status quo, used unconventional tactics to gain attention and sympathy, and demanded bravery and commitment from many women.[1] One of these women was Angelina Grimké.

Abolitionist Angelina Grimké addressed the Massachusetts legislature in February 1838, presenting a petition against slavery from an estimated 20,000 women of the state. In doing so, she became the first woman to speak before an American legislative body. Because women at this time were legally subordinate to men and shut out of civic life—the life of home and church were considered their proper domains—Grimké felt it necessary to defend women's involvement in the abolitionist movement to end slavery. She said the following to the legislators:

> Are we aliens because we are women? Are we bereft of citizenship because we are mothers, wives and daughters of a mighty people? Have women no country—no interests staked in public weal—no partnership in a nation's guilt and shame? . . . I hold, Mr. Chairman, that American women have to do this subject [the abolition of slavery], not only because it is moral and religious, but because it is political, inasmuch as we are citizens of the Republic and as such our honor, happiness and well-being are bound up in its politics, government and laws.

Although this bold claim of citizenship for women did not fall on receptive ears—Grimké was derided as ridiculous and blasphemous by press and pulpit—it helped inspire other women who had entered political life by way of the abolitionist movement to press for women's rights as well. Meeting at Seneca Falls, New York, in 1848, a group of women issued a declaration written by

8.1	**8.2**	**8.3**	**8.4**	**8.5**	**8.6**
Define social movements and who they represent, p. 236	Illustrate how important social movements have shaped American society, p. 238	Evaluate how social movements make U.S. politics more democratic, p. 246	Identify factors that give rise to social movements, p. 249	Evaluate tactics used by social movements to influence what government does, p. 253	Determine what makes a social movement successful, p. 255

DEMANDING THE RIGHT TO VOTE Here a member of a women's suffrage organization speaks on a street corner in New York demanding that women be granted the right to vote in the United States. Women's struggle to gain the vote blew hot and cold for over 130 years, but persistence paid off at last in 1920 when the Nineteenth Amendment was adopted. How might one explain why such a basic democratic right was so long in coming?

The Big Picture Why do some social movements work while others don't? Using the civil rights movement as an example, author Edward S. Greenberg lists the three things that affect how politically influential a movement will be.

The Basics Can social movements arise at any time? Or does there have to be pre-existing factors, and if so, what are these factors? This video grapples with these questions and reveals what answers scholars have uncovered.

What elements give rise to social movements?

In Context What is the relationship between social movements, civil society, and government? In this video, University of Colorado at Boulder political scientist Anne N. Costain discusses Alexis de Tocqueville's study of civic life in nineteenth century America and connects his work to social movements today.

Think Like a Political Scientist What is the main obstacle that researchers face when trying to determine whether political engagement in the United States has increased or decreased? In this video, University of Colorado at Boulder political scientist Anne N. Costain analyzes the possible denotations of political engagement and why it is such a hard concept to measure.

In the Real World Civil disobedience is a controversial form of political engagement. In this segment, we'll hear what real Americans think about breaking the law to make a political statement, and whether they feel that the Occupy movement was justified in using the tactics that it did to get its point across.

So What? Learn how social movements break through the government gridlock. Author Edward S. Greenberg explains why social movements focus on disrupting the patterns of everyday life, and he discusses the movements that successfully changed how the government works.

Elizabeth Cady Stanton stating that "all men and women are created equal, endowed with the same inalienable rights." The declaration, much like the Declaration of Independence on which it was modeled, then presented a long list of violations of rights.

The Seneca Falls Declaration remains one of the most eloquent statements of women's equality ever written, but it failed to have an immediate effect because most politically active women (and men) in the abolitionist movement believed that their first order of business was to end slavery. Women's rights would have to wait.

After the Civil War destroyed the slave system, women's rights leaders such as Stanton, Susan B. Anthony, and Lucy Stone pressed for equal citizenship rights for all, white or black, male or female. They were bitterly disappointed when the Fourteenth Amendment, ratified after the war, declared full citizenship rights for all males born or naturalized in the United States, including those who had been slaves, but failed to include women. Women's rights activists realized that they would have to fight for rights on their own, with their own organizations.

Women's rights organizations were formed soon after the Civil War. For more than two decades, though, the National Woman Suffrage Association (NWSA) and the American Woman Suffrage Association (AWSA) feuded over how to pressure male politicians. Susan B. Anthony (with the NWSA) and Lucy Stone (with the AWSA) were divided by temperament and ideology. Anthony favored pressing for a broad range of rights and organized dramatic actions to expose men's hypocrisy. At an 1876 centennial celebration of the United States in Philadelphia, Anthony and several other women marched onto the platform, where the emperor of Brazil and other dignitaries sat, and read the declaration aloud. Stone favored gaining the vote as the primary objective of the rights movement and used quieter methods of persuasion, such as petitions.

In 1890, the two main organizations joined to form the National American Woman Suffrage Association (NAWSA). They dropped such controversial NWSA demands as divorce reform and legalized prostitution in favor of one order of business: women's suffrage. The movement was now focused, united, and growing more powerful every year.

In 1912, the NAWSA organized a march to support a constitutional amendment for suffrage. More than 5,000 women paraded through the streets of Washington before Woodrow Wilson's inauguration. The police offered the marchers no protection from antagonistic spectators who pelted the marchers with rotten fruit and vegetables and an occasional rock, despite the legal parade permit they had obtained. This lack of protection outraged the public and attracted media attention to the suffrage movement.

Almost immediately after the United States entered World War I in April 1917, with the express purpose of "making the world safe for democracy," women began to picket the White House, demanding that full democracy be instituted in America. One demonstrator's sign quoted directly from President Wilson's war message, "We shall fight for the right of those who submit to authority to have a voice in their own government," and asked why women were excluded from American democracy. As the picketing at the White House picked up in numbers and in intensity, the police began arresting large groups of women. Other women took their place. The cycle continued until local jails were filled to capacity. When suffragists began a hunger strike in jail, authorities responded with forced feedings and isolation cells. By November, public outrage forced local authorities to relent and free the women. By this time, public opinion had shifted in favor of women's right to vote.

In the years surrounding U.S. entry into the war, other women's groups worked state by state, senator by senator, pressuring male politicians to support women's suffrage. After two prominent senators from New England were defeated in 1918 primarily because of the efforts of suffragists and prohibitionists, the political clout of the women's groups became apparent to most elected officials. In June 1919, Congress passed the Nineteenth Amendment, and the necessary 36 states ratified it the following year. By uniting around a common cause, women's organizations gained the right to vote for all women.

Although few social movements have been as effective as the women's suffrage movement in reaching their primary goal, other social movements have also played an important role in American political life. This chapter is about what social movements are, how and why they form, what tactics they use, and how they affect American political life and what government does.

social movement

A loosely organized group that uses unconventional and often disruptive tactics to have their grievances heard by the public, the news media, and government leaders.

Thinking Critically About This Chapter

This chapter is about the important role of social movements in American government and politics.

Using the Framework

You will see in this chapter how social movements are a response to structural changes in the economy, culture, and society and how they affect other political linkage actors and institutions—parties, interest groups, and public opinion, for example—and government. You will learn, most importantly, under what conditions social movements most effectively shape the behavior of elected leaders and the content of government policies.

Using the Democracy Standard

At first glance, because social movements are most often the political instrument of numerical minorities, it may seem that they have little to do with democracy, which is rooted in majority rule. You will see in this chapter, however, that social movements play an especially important role in our democracy, principally by broadening public debate on important issues and bringing outsiders and nonparticipants into the political arena.

What Are Social Movements?

8.1 Define social movements and who they represent

Social movements are loosely organized collections of ordinary people, working outside normal political channels, to get their voices heard by the public at large, the news media and leaders of major institutions, and government officials, in order to promote, resist, or undo some social change. They are different than interest groups, which are longer lasting and more organized, with permanent employees and budgets, for example, and more committed to conventional and nondisruptive methods such as lobbying and issue advertising. They are different than political parties, whose main purpose is to win elective offices for candidates who campaign under the party banner and to control government and what it does across a broad range of policies. Social movements are more ephemeral in nature, coming and going as people feel they are needed, sometimes leaving their mark on public policies, sometimes not. What sets social movements apart from parties and interest groups is their focus on broad, society-wide issues and their tendency to act outside the normal channels of government and politics, using unconventional and often disruptive tactics.[2] Some scholars call social movement politics "contentious politics."[3] When suffragists disrupted meetings, went on hunger strikes, and marched to demand the right to vote, they were engaged in contentious politics. The most important such social movement in recent times is the civil rights movement, which pressed demands for equal treatment for African Americans on the American public and elected officials, primarily during the 1960s.

This general definition of social movements requires further elaboration if we are to understand their role in American politics.[4] Here we highlight some important things to know about them:

- *Social movements are the political instrument of political outsiders.* Social movements often help people who are outside the political mainstream gain a hearing from the public and from political decision makers. The women's suffrage movement forced the issue of votes for women onto the public agenda. The civil rights movement did the same for the issue of equal citizenship for African Americans. Gays and lesbians forced the country to pay attention to issues that had long been left "in the closet." Insiders don't need social movements; they can rely instead on interest groups, political action committees (PACs), lobbyists, campaign contributions, and the like to make their voices heard.

Christian conservatives, now a political force to reckon with, with many well-established interest groups, such as the Family Research Council and the remarkable influence within the Republican Party, were at one time largely ignored by the cultural and political establishment. Their grassroots movement to resist the general **secularization** of American life and to promote their vision of religious values in American life was built at first around local churches and Bible reading groups and often took the form of protests, whether at abortion clinics or at government locations where some religious symbol (like a manger scene at Christmas-time) was ordered removed by the courts because it violated the principle of separation of church and state.

- *Social movements are generally mass grassroots phenomena.* Because outsiders and excluded groups often lack the financial and political resources of insiders, they must take advantage of what they have: numbers, energy, and commitment. They depend on the participation of large numbers of ordinary people to act in ways that will move the general public and persuade public officials to address issues of concern to those in the movement.

- *Social movements are populated by individuals with a shared sense of grievance.* People would not take on the considerable risks involved in joining others in a social movement unless they felt a strong, shared sense of grievance against the status quo and a desire to bring about social change. Social movements tend to form when a significant number of people come to define their own troubles and problems, not in personal terms, but in more general social terms (the belief that there is a common cause for all of their troubles) and when they believe that the government can be moved to take action on their behalf. Because this is a rare combination, social movements are very difficult to organize and sustain.

- *Social movements often use unconventional and disruptive tactics.* Officials and citizens almost always complain that social movements are ill-mannered and disruptive. For social movements, that is precisely the point. Unconventional and disruptive tactics help gain attention for movement grievances. While successful movements are ones that eventually bring many other Americans and public officials over to their side, it is usually the case that other Americans and public officials are not paying attention to the issues that are of greatest concern to movement participants, so something dramatic needs to be done to change the situation.

- *Social movements often turn into interest groups.* Although particular social movements eventually fade from the political scene, for reasons we explore later, the more successful ones create organizations that carry on their work over a longer period of time. Thus, the women's movement spawned the National Organization for Women, while the environmental movement created organizations such as Environmental Defense Fund and the Nature Conservancy. The movement of Christian evangelicals spurred the creation of groups such as the Family Research Council and the National Right to Life Committee.

secularization
The spread of nonreligious values and outlooks.

8.1

8.2

8.3

8.4

8.5

8.6

8.1

8.2

8.3

8.4

8.5

8.6

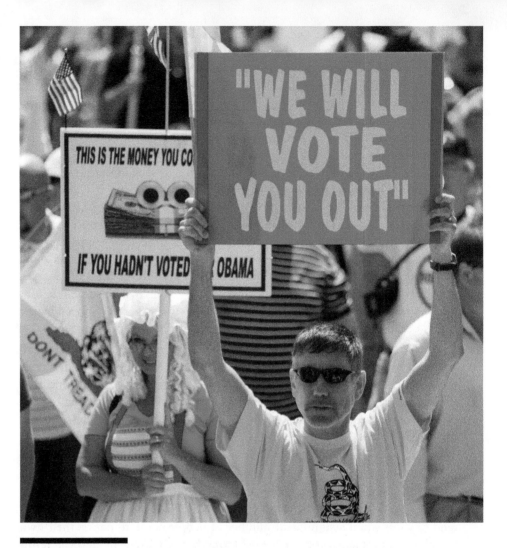

TEA'D OFF

The Tea Party movement, deeply opposed to President Obama and his agenda for an energetic government to solve the economic crisis and longer-term problems like health care, became a force to be reckoned within American politics only months after the president's inauguration. These people gathered in Freedom Plaza in Washington, D.C., in April 2009 to express their anger at passage of the economic "stimulus package."

Major Social Movements in the United States

Illustrate how important social movements have shaped American society

Many social movements have left their mark on American political life and have shaped what government does in the United States. Here we describe some of the most important.

□ The Abolitionists

This movement's objective was to end slavery in the United States. The movement was most active in the northern states in the three decades before the outbreak of the Civil War. Their harsh condemnation of the slave system helped heighten the tensions between the North and the South, eventually bringing on the war that ended slavery. Their tactics included antislavery demonstrations and resistance (sometimes violent) to enforcement of the Fugitive Slave Act, which required all states to identify, capture, and return runaway slaves to their owners.

8.1
8.2
8.3
8.4
8.5
8.6

☐ The Populists

The Populist movement was made up of disaffected farmers of the American South and West in the 1880s and 1890s who were angry with business practices and developments in the American economy that were adversely affecting them. Their main grievance was the concentration of economic power in the banking and railroad industries, both of which favored (with loans on better terms, cheaper shipping rates, and the like) their larger customers. The aim of the movement was to force public ownership or regulation of banks, grain storage companies, and the railroads. Small demonstrations at banks and at foreclosed farms were part of their repertoire, but they used the vote as well. For a short time, they were quite successful, winning control of several state legislatures, sending members to Congress, helping to nominate William Jennings Bryan as the Democratic candidate for president in 1896, and forcing the federal regulation of corporations (e.g., in the Interstate Commerce Commission Act).

☐ Women's Suffrage

This movement, active in the late nineteenth and early twentieth centuries, aimed to win women the right to vote. As we saw in the chapter-opening story, the movement won its objective when the Nineteenth Amendment to the Constitution was ratified in 1920. We also saw that the tactics of the movement were deliberately disruptive and unsettling to many.

☐ The Labor Movement

The labor movement represented efforts by working people over the years to protect jobs, ensure decent wages and benefits, and guarantee safe workplaces. The periods of greatest militancy—when working people took to the streets and the factory floors to demand recognition of their unions—were in the 1880s, the 1890s, and the 1930s. (Their militancy during the Great Depression, joined with that of other groups pressing for a more activist government committed to social justice, led to the passage of the Social Security Act, which we examine in the "Can Government Do Anything Well?" feature.) The labor movement eventually forced the federal government to recognize the right of working people to form labor unions to represent them in negotiations with management. However, labor unions, the fruit of this successful movement, have been steadily losing members, especially in the private sector.

☐ The Civil Rights Movement

The civil rights movement began in the mid-1950s, reached the peak of its activity in the mid-1960s, and gradually lost steam after that (see Figure 8.1). The movement, which was committed to nonviolent civil disobedience as one of its main tactics, remains one of the most influential on record, having pressed successfully for the end of formal segregation in the South and discriminatory practices across the nation. The main weapons of the movement were nonviolent civil disobedience and mass demonstrations. The outbreak of violence in urban centers after the assassination of Martin Luther King, Jr. in 1968 and the rise in prominence at the same time of black power advocates like Stokely Carmichael and Malcolm X,[5] who rejected nonviolence as a basic principle, marked for many people the end of the movement.

☐ Contemporary Antiwar Movements

Antiwar movements have accompanied virtually every war the United States has waged. The most important ones that have affected American politics in contemporary times were associated with military conflicts in Southeast Asia and the Middle East. The *anti–Vietnam War* movement was active in the United States in the late 1960s and early 1970s. Its aim was to end the war in Vietnam. It used a wide variety of tactics in this effort, from mass demonstrations to voting registration and nonviolent civil disobedience. Fringe elements even turned to violence, exemplified by the Days

Can Government Do Anything Well?

Old-age pensions in Social Security

Social Security was passed in 1936 as part of Franklin Roosevelt's New Deal program to fight the Great Depression. In the beginning it provided very modest provisions for a limited number of working Americans once they reached the age of 65. It was the product not only of the liberal political thinking of the day, but of mass movements rocking the country demanding greater economic justice and security across the board in the United States. The Communist and Socialist parties had made significant gains in American politics since the beginning of the Depression, while radical populist politicians demanding "soak the rich" and poor relief programs such as the radio priest Father Coughlin and Louisiana governor Huey Long had gained enormous followings. Labor unions were on the rise, demanding not only better wages and working conditions but a better deal for other ordinary Americans. Most importantly, the Townsend Movement, which advocated that everyone over 65 be given a $200 per month benefit (so long as all the money was spent by the recipient), was gaining adherents by the millions as established by signed petitions that poured into the White House and Congress. Franklin Roosevelt, his labor secretary Francis Perkins, and members of Congress felt that something had to be done. Some have suggested, to be sure, that Roosevelt and other Social Security advocates used the popular pressures created by these movements to achieve something they had wanted to do all along.

Since its original passage, the average Social Security monthly payment gradually has grown larger and a higher proportion of Americans are now covered. This has happened because the program has become incredibly popular, and elected leaders, recognizing the voting power of those near or over 65, lean much more strongly toward increasing the size and reach of benefits and try to avoid any cutbacks in benefits. It is telling that there have been signs at antigovernment Tea Party rallies saying, "Keep government out of my Social Security." Today, the average benefit is $1,193 a month, and 87 percent of those over 65 years of age receive Social Security benefits. Two-thirds of all recipients receive 50 percent or more of their total income from their Social Security checks.

Support for the claim that government should provide at least the current levels of income support for the elderly:

- Social Security is the nation's most important antipoverty program; poverty among the elderly, once the highest among population age groups, is now the lowest.
- Social Security pensions, though not overly generous, allow most of our elderly to live with dignity, especially when paired with Medicare.
- The purported Social Security financing crisis is easily fixed by raising the retirement age or raising the payroll tax or raising the ceiling on income subject to payroll taxes (benefit payments could be cut theoretically, but this is politically unpalatable).
- Privatizing Social Security would subject all retirees to the vagaries of the market, leaving many in dire straits, if things go badly on Wall Street, just when they need it most.

Rejection of the claim that government should provide at least the current levels of income support for the elderly:

- The current system is expensive and inefficient. Part of the problem could be solved by partially privatizing the system, allowing working Americans to put all or part of the payroll tax into 401(k)-style private accounts.
- The long-term budget crisis of the country cannot be seriously addressed without making substantial cuts in entitlement programs, among which Social Security and Medicare are the largest.
- As the American population ages there will be more older Americans receiving Social Security benefits every year and fewer younger working Americans paying payroll taxes, so the fiscal crisis of the system is bound to get worse unless major steps are taken to cut the program or raise the retirement age. Increasing taxes is off the table because of the depressing impacts such taxes would have on the overall economy.

WHAT DO YOU THINK?

What do you think about the past, present, and future role of the government in providing old-age pensions under Social Security?

- Government was right to establish Social Security and now needs to make it more generous.
- Government was right to establish Social Security and, because it is working well, should leave it unchanged.
- Government was right to establish Social Security but now needs to cut it back.
- Government should not have created Social Security in the first place. At most, it should have used tax incentives to encourage people to establish private accounts.

How would you defend this position to a fellow student? What would be your main line of argument? What evidence do you believe best supports your position?

Additional sources for this feature: David Kennedy, *Freedom from Fear: The American People in Depression and War* (Oxford, UK: Oxford University Press, 1999); and the Social Security Administration at www.ssa.gov.

1954 May
In *Brown v. Board of Education,* "separate but equal" in education declared unconstitutional

1955 December
Montgomery bus boycott begins

1957 September
Federal troops enforce court-ordered integration of Little Rock, Arkansas, schools

1957 February
Southern Christian Leadership Conference formed to encourage nonviolent civil disobedience

1960 February
College students sit in at segregated lunch counter in Greensboro, North Carolina

1960 April
Student Nonviolent Coordinating Committee (SNCC) founded to fight segregation and register black voters

1961 May
"Freedom riders" begin to ride interstate buses in South to press for integration of public transportation

1962 October
James Meredith integrates University of Mississippi; federal troops quell violence

1961–1964
NONVIOLENT DEMONSTRATIONS FOR INTEGRATION THROUGHOUT SOUTH AND BORDER STATES

1963 April
Martin Luther King, Jr. writes "Letter from Birmingham Jail" to explain nonviolent civil disobedience

1963 Summer
Freedom summer launched to register black voters in most segregated counties in South; four civil rights workers murdered

1963 August
About 500,000 join "March on Washington" to demand passage of civil rights bill

1964 July
Civil Rights Act ends segregation in public accommodations

1965 March
Voting rights march in Selma, Alabama, met with police violence; spurs passage of Voting Rights Act

1965 October
Black Panther Party founded, rejects nonviolence

1966 April
Stokely Carmichael calls for "black power"

1968 April
Martin Luther King, Jr. assassinated; riots break out across U.S.

FIGURE 8.1 TIMELINE: THE NONVIOLENT CIVIL RIGHTS MOVEMENT

8.1
8.2
8.3
8.4
8.5
8.6

NON-VIOLENT PROTEST SPARKS A MOVEMENT

When African American college students sat at the whites-only lunch counter of a Woolworth's department store in Greensboro, North Carolina in 1957 to protest the company's segregationist policies, often braving assaults by angry counter-demonstrators like this one spraying insect repellant, it inspired college students across the nation to conduct sit-ins in their own communities.

Equal Rights Amendment (ERA)

Proposed amendment to the U.S. Constitution stating that equality of rights shall not be abridged or denied on account of a person's gender; it failed to win the approval of the necessary number of states.

of Rage vandalism along Chicago's Gold Coast mounted by a wing of Students for a Democratic Society and the bombing of a research lab at the University of Wisconsin in which a graduate student was killed.

An *anti–Iraq War* movement quickly formed in the months leading up to the U.S. invasion of Iraq in 2003. The movement's most dramatic political act was the organization of massive demonstrations across the world on February 15, 2003. In the United States, demonstrations took place in 150 cities; in New York, the crowd converging on the U.N. headquarters building filled a space 20 blocks long, along First and Second Avenues (huge demonstrations occurred around the world as the "Mapping American Politics" feature shows).[6] The massive demonstrations did not convince President Bush to put off the Iraq invasion, however. The movement lost support after the invasion of Iraq in April 2003, as patriotic feelings rose as troops went into battle, but the subsequent insurgency, and the high cost to the United States of the insurgency in lives and money, rekindled the movement in late 2005. Changing public opinion on the war, some of it attributable to the antiwar demonstrations, perhaps, helped set the stage for the Republicans' big losses in the 2006 congressional elections.

☐ The Women's Movement

This movement has been important in American life since the late 1960s. Its aim has been to win civil rights protections for women and to broaden the participation of women in all aspects of American society, economy, and politics. Although it did not win one of its main objectives—passage of the **Equal Rights Amendment (ERA)** to the U.S. Constitution that guaranteed equal treatment for men and women by all levels of government—the broad advance of women on virtually all fronts in the United States attests to its overall effectiveness. The movement has been sufficiently successful, in fact, that it helped trigger a counter-movement among religious conservatives of all denominations worried about purported threats to traditional family values.

Mapping American Politics

Worldwide Demonstrations Against the Invasion of Iraq

Introduction

The buildup to the invasion of Iraq was a long time coming. President Bush named Iraq one of the three members of his "axis-of-evil" countries in his State of the Union address in January 2002 because of their purported weapons of mass destruction (WMD) programs. U.S. diplomats urged the U.N. Security Council to pass a resolution pushing for renewed inspections of possible violations of international restrictions on chemical, biological, and nuclear weapons programs in Iraq. U.N. inspectors found very little and reported skepticism that such programs still existed. The administration kept up the pressure, gaining congressional approval in October 2002 for the use of force against Iraq if there was evidence of WMD programs and the United Nations failed to act. Other Security Council members were not convinced by Secretary of State Colin Powell's presentation of evidence for WMDs in early 2003, causing the United States to withdraw its resolution for the use of force in early March 2003. The United States then pulled together a group of 18 countries that President Bush called the "coalition of the willing" that agreed to use force if necessary and warned U.N. weapons inspectors to leave Iraq. The invasion of Iraq began on March 20, 2003.

Mapping World Demonstrations

Rough estimates are that about 16 million people worldwide gathered over the weekend of February 13–15, 2003, to protest against the coming invasion of Iraq. Researchers at Worldmapper found evidence of protest demonstrations in 96 of the world's mapped countries and territories. The cartogram map, showing the proportion of the world total accounted for by each country, reveals that the largest demonstrations took place in Europe, especially in Italy, Spain, and the United Kingdom, and also in the United States. The demonstrations in Rome drew 3 million; the ones in London, about 1.4 million. New York saw about 125,000 protestors, while the march in San Francisco drew about 65,000. It is worth noting, however, as you look at this map, that estimates of the size of demonstrations are just that—estimates—though whenever possible, the researchers depended on more than a single source, leaning toward academic, press, and official estimates rather than those of the demonstration organizers. (See the "By the Numbers" feature in this chapter on how to count crowds.)

What Do You Think?

Why might the president and his advisers make decisions or policies with which large portions of the domestic and foreign publics disagree? Given what occurred in Iraq after the invasion in March 2003, how could American officials have better taken into account what protesters around the world and in the United States were saying? Even if you believe that presidents must be free to act as they choose, within the constitutional boundaries of their office, how should global and American public opinion factor into their policymaking, if at all?

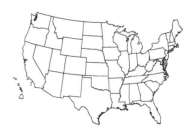
Standard US Map

Worldwide Demonstrations Against the Invasion of Iraq

Source: © 2006 SASI Group (University of Sheffield) and Mark Newman (University of Michigan).

☐ The Environmental Movement

The environmental movement has been active in the United States since the early 1970s. Its aim has been to encourage government regulation of damaging environmental practices and to raise the environmental sympathies of the public. While the vitality of the movement has waxed and waned over the years, the public's strong support for environmental regulation suggests that it has been unusually successful. Although disruptive and even violent tactics have sometimes been used, the movement has depended more on legal challenges to business practices and the creation of organizations to lobby in Washington. Rising concerns among many Americans about fuel shortages, high gasoline prices, and global climate change have revitalized the movement and enhanced its influence.

☐ The Gay and Lesbian Movements

These movements began in earnest in the late 1960s. Their aim was to gain the same civil rights protections under the law enjoyed by African Americans and other minority groups and to gain respect from the public. Ranging from patient lobbying and voting to mass demonstrations and deliberately shocking actions by groups such as ACT-UP, the movement's efforts have been only partially successful. They also have sparked strong counterattacks by groups such as the Christian Coalition and Focus on the Family that are opposed to their objectives.

☐ Religious Conservatives

Religious conservative movements have occurred at several different moments in American history and have been very influential. These movements have brought together strongly religious people trying to infuse American society and public policies with their values. The contemporary movement of religious conservatives falls within this tradition and has become very important in American politics, especially on the issues of abortion, school prayer, educational curriculum, and same-sex marriage. The *pro-life (anti-abortion)* movement is part of this larger religious conservative movement. Its main objective is to end the legal availability of abortion in the United States.

☐ The Antiglobalization Movement

An emergent antiglobalization movement announced itself to the public with demonstrations in Seattle in late 1999 targeted at the World Trade Organization (WTO), whose trade ministers were meeting in the city to fashion an agreement to further open national borders to trade and foreign investment.[7] The demonstrations were mostly peaceful, but some demonstrators turned violent. This movement is extremely diverse and includes people who are worried about the effects of globalization on the environment, income inequality in the United States and Third World countries, food safety, labor rights, sweat shops, unfair trade, and national sovereignty. The movement remains intermittently active, with protesters showing up at large WTO gatherings, as well as those put on by the World Bank, the International Monetary Fund, the World Economic Forum (which meets annually in Davos, Switzerland), and meetings of the leaders of the major industrial democracies, such as the G8.

☐ Undocumented Immigrants Movement

A series of massive demonstrations in the spring of 2006 in cities across the nation signaled the rise in the United States of a movement of and for illegal immigrants. Although the goals of movement leaders, activists, and joiners were quite diverse, they were joined by a wish to give legal status to those presently living and working in the United States illegally, to allow more legal immigration from Mexico, and to increase Americans' understanding of the positive role played by immigrants—legal and illegal—in the American economy. Demonstration participants included not only legal immigrants, American citizens of Mexican descent, and sympathizers from many

8.1

8.2

8.3

8.4

8.5

8.6

other ethnic and racial groups but, remarkably, tens of thousands of undocumented people subject to deportation if they came to the attention of the authorities.[8] This and subsequent demonstrations failed to convince Republicans in Congress in 2007 to support an immigration bill favored by President Bush that included a path toward citizenship for people living in the United States illegally. It also helped galvanize groups of Americans opposed to illegal immigration.

☐ Tea Party Movement

This movement exploded onto the American political scene on tax deadline day (April 15) 2009, with demonstrations in scores of locations around the country denouncing bank bailouts, the Democrats' health care reform effort, rising government deficits, taxes and regulations, illegal immigration, and, for many among the participants, the legality of the Obama presidency. Urged on by conservative talk radio hosts and the intense coverage of their activities by Fox News, and funded by the Koch brothers' oil fortune, the Tea Party staged a series of demonstrations across the country and mobilized in August 2009 to flood and take over health care town hall meetings held by Democratic members of Congress. The movement seems to represent a modern-day angry populism directed against an activist federal government that, in the view of movement activists and followers, has been taking too many taxes from hard-working people and saddling the country with huge debts, all for programs that support the undeserving poor (people unwilling to work), and those who are in the country illegally. (See Figure 8.2 for how Tea Party sympathizers differ from other Americans and other Republicans.)

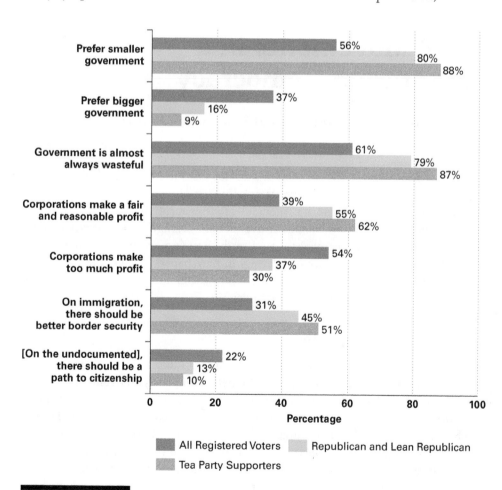

FIGURE 8.2

Polls show that while Tea Party identifiers are overwhelmingly Republican, they are from the most conservative wing of the party, with stronger antigovernment and anti-immigration views than mainstream Republicans. Their views diverge even farther from those of all registered voters.

Source: Scott Clement and John Green, "The Tea Party, Religion, and Social Issues," (Washington, D.C.: Pew Forum on Religion and Public Life, February 23, 2011).

☐ The Occupy Wall Street Movement

This movement, organized almost wholly through the new social media, came dramatically to public attention in September 2011 when protestors took over Zuccotti Park in the Wall Street section of New York. The number of occupiers quickly increased in New York, then Occupy sites rapidly spread to many cities and communities across the country. Though the message of the movement was somewhat garbled because of the many diverse groups it attracted, its most common underlying theme was the purported unfairness of the American economy and the failure of government to do anything about it: diminished job prospects, stagnant or declining living standards, rising income and wealth inequality, and bailouts and bonuses for corporations and their top executives. The movement coined the phrase, "We are the 99 percent," as a way of calling attention to their contention that most of the gains of economic growth over the past two decades had gone to the top 1 percent. Some labor unions joined the protests in New York and Oakland, among other places, and many celebrities voiced support and made contributions. Because the movement believed in actual "occupation," setting up tents, feeding stations, first-aid centers, and the like in the places they took over, police eventually moved in to clear away the demonstrators, with officials citing safety concerns as their motivations. In New York, closing down the Occupy site was relatively peaceful; in Oakland and Berkeley it proved to be more violent. Though it is too early to assess how long the movement will hold together or what its impact may eventually prove to be, a Pew poll in October 2011 showed that 39 percent of Americans said they agreed with the movement's goals, more than said they supported the Tea Party's (32 percent).[9]

Social Movements in a Majoritarian Democracy

8.3 Evaluate how social movements make U.S. politics more democratic

A t first glance, social movements do not seem to fit very well in a democracy. First, social movements usually start out with only a small minority of people, whereas democracy requires majority rule. Second, social movements often use disruptive tactics—though rarely overtly violent ones—when it seems that many channels already exist (e.g., voting, petitioning and writing to policymakers, and writing letters to newspapers) for people to express their grievances. In this section, we talk about how social movements can (and often do) help make American politics more democratic.

☐ Encouraging Participation

Social movements may increase the level of popular involvement and interest in politics. In one sense, this is true simply by definition: social movements are the instruments of outsiders. Thus, the women's suffrage movement showed many middle-class women that their activities need not be confined exclusively to home, family, church, and charity work and encouraged them to venture into political life by gathering petitions or joining demonstrations demanding the vote for women. The civil rights movement in the 1960s encouraged southern African Americans, who had long been barred from the political life of their communities, to become active in their own emancipation. The religious fundamentalist movement spurred the involvement of previously politically apathetic evangelicals. The pro-immigration movement may yet spur increased political participation by Hispanic citizens.

How Are People Involved in Politics?

There are a lot of ways to participate in politics. According to the 2008 American National Election Study, most Americans have attended a city council meeting, participated in a school board meeting, or signed a paper petition. But many have not protested, given money to political organizations, or distributed political information. How people engage in politics—and how often—is in part a function of efficacy, or whether or not individuals believe they have a say in government.

Political **Activity**

Signed a paper petition	56%
Attended a city council or school board meeting	55%
Gave money to a social/political organization	42%
Attended meeting on a political or social issue	34%
Distributed social/political group information	21%
Joined a protest rally or march	19%

Do You **Have a Say** in Government?

I HAVE A SAY

67% 69% 50% 44% 24% 24%

Of individuals who believe they have a say in government, over two-thirds attend government meetings and sign petitions. Half also give money to political and social organizations. They are personally and financially active in politics.

I DON'T HAVE A SAY

51% 46% 33% 24% 17% 17%

Less than 20% of individuals who do NOT believe they have a say in government take part in protests or disseminate information. They are generally less active than people who think they have a say.

SOURCE: Data from The American National Election Study, 2008 Time Series Study, post-election interview responses only.

Investigate Further

Concept   What are the most frequent forms of participation? Americans most frequently participate by attending local government meetings and signing paper petitions. Attending protests and rallies and distributing political information are less common.

Connection   How are city council and school board meetings different from protests and petitions? Council and board meetings can make policy for government. Protests and petitions are ways of communicating information about issues to people with authority to make policy.

Cause   How is participation related to efficacy? Those who believe they don't have a say in government are generally less active, while those who do think they have a say are more likely to engage in all forms of political activity. Regardless of their perceived influence, people are more likely to engage

scope of conflict

Refers to the number of groups involved in a political conflict; a narrow scope of conflict involves a small number of groups, and a wide scope of conflict involves many.

mass mobilization

The process of involving large numbers of people in a social movement.

The Great Depression

The period of economic crisis in the United States that lasted from the stock market crash of 1929 to America's entry into World War II.

Social movements also encourage popular participation by dramatizing and bringing to public attention a range of issues that have been ignored or have been dealt with behind closed doors. The reason is that their contentious actions make these movements' members highly visible. They offer irresistible fare for the television camera. This ability to make politics more visible—called broadening the **scope of conflict** by political scientist E.E. Schattschneider[10]—makes politics the province of the many rather than the few.

☐ Overcoming Political Inequality

Social movements also sometimes allow individuals and groups without substantial resources to enter the game of politics. Many social movements are made up of people who do not have access to the money, time, contacts, or organizational resources that fuel normal politics.[11] The ability of those without resources to disrupt the status quo by mobilizing thousands to take to the streets to voice their demands—what sociologists call **mass mobilization**—is a powerful political tool for people on the outside looking in. In the right circumstances, the disruptive politics of social groups can become as politically useful as other resources such as money and votes. Seemingly politically powerless women were able to mobilize to win the vote in the early part of the twentieth century; seemingly politically powerless African Americans in the Deep South were able to secure full citizenship rights in the 1960s.

☐ Creating New Majorities

Over time, social movements may also help create new majorities in society. Social movements are the province of numerical minorities in most cases, and in a majoritarian democracy, minorities should have their way only if they can convince enough of their fellow citizens that what they want is reasonable. Before the 1930s, for instance, only a minority of Americans may have been convinced that labor unions were a good idea. The **Great Depression** and a vigorous, militant labor movement changed the opinion climate in the nation and created the basis for federal laws protecting the right of working people to form labor unions. Such issues as gender-based job discrimination and pay inequity, to take another example, were not important to the general public until they were brought center stage by the women's movement.

☐ Overcoming Constitutional Limitations on Change

Sometimes it takes the energy and disruption of a social movement to overcome the antimajoritarian aspects of our constitutional system and get anything done at all.[12] As political scientist Theodore Lowi describes the issue:

> Our political system is almost perfectly designed to maintain an existing state of affairs. Our system is so designed that only a determined and undoubted majority could make it move. This is why our history is replete with social movements. It takes that kind of energy to get anything like a majority . . . Change comes neither from the genius of the system nor from the liberality or wisdom of its supporters and of the organized groups. It comes from new groups or nascent groups—social movements—when the situation is most dramatic.[13]

It is important to note that many of the social reforms of which most Americans are most proud—women's right to vote, equal citizenship rights for African Americans, Social Security, collective bargaining, and environmental protection—have been less the result of "normal" politics than of social movements started by determined and often disruptive minorities.[14]

Factors That Encourage the Creation of Social Movements

 certain combination of factors seems necessary for a social movement to develop.[15] We review the most important ones here.

☐ Real or Perceived Distress

People who are safe, prosperous, respected, and contented generally have no need of social movements. By contrast, those whose lives are difficult and unsafe, whose way of life or values are threatened, or whose way of life is disrespected often find social movements an attractive means of calling attention to their plight and of pressing for changes in the status quo.[16]

Social distress caused by economic, social, and technological change helped create the conditions for the rise of most of the major social movements in American history. For example, the Populist movement occurred after western and southern farmers suffered great economic reverses during the latter part of the nineteenth century. The labor movement during the 1930s was spurred by the Great Depression—the virtual collapse of the industrial sector of the American economy, historically unprecedented levels of unemployment, and widespread destitution. The rise of the Christian conservative movement seems to be associated with the perception among conservatives that religious and family values had been declining in American life. For many women, distress caused by discriminatory hiring, blocked career advancement—in the form of the "glass ceiling" and the "mommy track"—and unequal pay at a time when they were entering the job market in increasing numbers during the 1960s and 1970s made participation in the women's movement attractive.[17] Discrimination, police harassment, and violence directed against them spurred gays and lesbians to turn to "contentious politics."[18] The AIDS epidemic added to their sense of distress and stimulated further political participation.[19] The rise of the Minute Men volunteers to help control the border with Mexico and legislation in several border states to deny certain benefits to illegal immigrants helped spur the mass demonstrations in 2006 and 2007 in favor of both legal and illegal immigrants. The Great Recession and the slow job recovery that followed sowed the seeds for the Occupy Wall Street movement.

Ironically, perhaps, as is evident from the previous paragraph, the rise of one social movement demanding a change in how its people are regarded and treated often triggers the rise of a counter-movement among people who come to feel distressed in turn. Thus, the women's and gay and lesbian movements were powerful stimulants for the rise of the Christian conservative movement, whose people worried that traditional family values were under assault.

☐ Availability of Resources for Mobilization

Social strain and distress are almost always present in society. But social movements occur, it seems, only when aggrieved people have the resources sufficient to organize those who are suffering strain and distress. A pool of potential leaders and a set of institutions that can provide infrastructure and money are particularly helpful. The grievances expressed by the labor movement had existed for a long time in the United States, but it was not until a few unions developed—generating talented leaders like John L. Lewis and Walter Reuther, a very active labor press, and widespread media attention—that the movement began to take off. Martin Luther King, Jr. and the nonviolent civil rights movement found traction in the 1960s partly because network news telecasts had just

consciousness-raising groups
Meetings of small groups of women designed to raise awareness of discrimination against women and to encourage involvement in movement activities.

increased from 15 minutes to half an hour and civil rights demonstrations and marches, and the sometimes violent response to them, provided dramatic footage to fill out the news programs. The women's movement's assets included a sizable population of educated and skilled women, a lively women's press, and a broad network of meetings to talk about common problems[20] (generally called **consciousness-raising groups**). The Christian conservative movement could build on a base of skilled clergy (for instance, Jerry Falwell and Pat Robertson), an expanding evangelical church membership, religious television and radio networks, and highly developed fund-raising technologies. The antiglobalization and anti–Iraq War movements, highly decentralized and organizationally amorphous, skillfully used social networking sites and cell phone messaging to spread information, raise money, and organize demonstrations here and abroad.[21] Spanish-language radio stations played a big role in mobilizing people to join pro-immigrant marches and rallies in spring 2006.

☐ A Supportive Environment

The rise of social movements requires more than the existence of resources for mobilization among aggrieved groups. The times must also be right, in the sense that a degree of support and tolerance must exist for the movement among the public and society's leaders.[22] The civil rights movement took place when overt racism among the public was declining (even in the then-segregated South) and national leaders were worried about the bad effects of segregation in the South on American foreign policy. Christian conservatives mobilized in an environment in which many other Americans were also worried about changes in social values and practices and when the Republican Party was looking for a way to detach traditional Democratic voters from their party. The labor movement's upsurge during the 1930s coincided with the electoral needs of the Democratic Party.[23] The women's movement surged at a time when public opinion was becoming much more favorable toward women's equality.[24] In 1972, for example, two out of three Americans reported to pollsters that they supported the proposal for an Equal Rights Amendment; the same proportion said they believed that the issues raised by the women's movement were important.[25] Gays and lesbians have benefited from the more tolerant attitudes toward alternative lifestyles, including homosexuality, that have developed in the United States since the late 1960s. Asked whether school boards should have the right to fire teachers who are homosexuals, only 28 percent of Americans agreed with the statement in 2009, compared with 51 percent as recently as 1987.[26] The Occupy movement almost surely reflected a widespread sentiment that there is too much inequality in the country and that government mostly helps the wealthy (54 percent of Americans agreed).[27]

Especially important for a social movement is acceptance among elites that the concerns and demands of a social movement are worth supporting. A group of corporate leaders in the 1930s, for example, believed that labor peace was crucial for ending the Great Depression and making long-term economic stability possible, and openly supported labor union efforts to organize industries and enter into labor-management contracts.[28] As noted earlier, in the 1950s and 1960s, American political leaders—concerned that widespread reports of violence and discrimination against African Americans were undermining U.S. credibility in the struggle against the Soviet Union for the loyalties of people of color in Asia, Africa, and Latin America—were ready for fundamental changes in race relations in the South and supported the civil rights movement. Leaders of the film, music, and television industries, whether for reasons of belief or economic gain, have increased the visibility of gay and lesbian performers and themes in their offerings.

☐ A Sense of Efficacy Among Participants

Some scholars believe that to develop an effective social movement, people who are on the outside looking in must come to believe that their actions can make a difference, that other citizens and political leaders will listen and respond to their grievances.[29] Political scientists call this "I can make a difference" attitude a sense of **political efficacy**.

Without a sense of efficacy, grievances might explode into brief demonstrations or riots, but they would not support a long-term effort requiring time, commitment, and risk.

It may well be that the highly decentralized and fragmented nature of our political system helps sustain a sense of efficacy, because movements often find places in the system where they will be heard by officials. Christian conservatives have had little effect on school curricula in unitary political systems like that of Great Britain, for instance, where educational policy is made centrally, so few try to do anything about it. In the United States, however, they know they can gain the ear of local school boards and state officials in parts of the country in which conservative religious belief is strong. For their part, gays and lesbians have been able to convince public officials and local voters to pass antidiscrimination ordinances in accepting communities—such as San Francisco, California, and Boulder, Colorado—and to win cases in several state courts.

Some scholars have suggested that a strong sense of common identity among protest groups contributes to efficacy. Knowing that one is not alone, that others see the world in common ways and have common concerns, is often the basis for people's willingness to commit the time and energy and to take the risks that social movements require. (Large demonstrations often help in this development; how the size of demonstrations is calculated is shown in the "By the Numbers" feature.) Growing gay and lesbian identity seems to be an important component of the rising political self-confidence of this movement.[30] The same can be said for Christian conservatives and Tea Party activists.

political efficacy
The sense that an individual can affect what government does.

By the Numbers

Just how many people were at that demonstration?

Calculating the size of demonstrations has always depended on estimates, although, as we will see, some estimates are more reliable than others. It was once standard practice for people to make educated guesses, with demonstration organizers always guessing on the very high side and officials in charge of controlling the crowd or sometimes unfriendly to the message of the demonstrators guessing on the very low side. For example, the organizers of the March 2003 antiwar rally in Washington, D.C., variously claimed, depending on which one was being quoted, a crowd of between 200,000 and 600,000, while D.C. police said it was more like 60,000. The same mismatch happened in 1996 when Louis Farrakhan claimed a crowd between 1.5 and 2 million at his Million Man March, a bit higher, to say the least, than the National Park Service's estimate of 400,000. Farrakhan threatened to sue over the disparity, arguing that the Park Service was out to discredit him and his movement.

Why It Matters
Whether it makes sense or not, demonstration organizers, sympathetic supporters, and critics of any particular protest demonstration often use the size of the crowd to convey the reach and strength of a movement and make it the foundation for why the public and elected officials should pay attention to it or not. Organizers want a big number; critics want a small number. Journalists often simply average the high and low estimates and report that as the actual number. The rest of us would probably like a reliable number. But how to do that without lining everyone up and counting them or having them go through a turnstile on their way to a demonstration?

Calculating Crowd Sizes
A fairly reliable method has emerged based on advances in aerial photography and digitalized remote sensing. What is now done regularly by news organizations and many governments is to take an aerial photograph, divide the area the crowd occupies into grids, then determine the density of each area, namely, how many people are in the bounded area of the grid. Researchers do not take the time, of course, to count each person in each grid, but divide the grids into a range of density types—from very tightly packed to very thinly packed—count the actual number in a sample grid of each type, then multiply by the number of grids of each. As an example, say that one type of 10' × 10' grid packs in 25 people, another 10' × 10' type packs in 20 people, and yet another has only 10 people wandering around the space. If there are 100 grids of the first type (let's call it "very dense"), 100 grids of the second type (let's call it "dense"), and 100 grids of the third type (let's call it "not very dense"), then the total crowd is 5,500 based on the formula: (25 × 100) + (20 × 100) + (10 × 100). This is not a very big crowd, of course, not likely to make an impression, but you get the idea.

What to Watch for
What to mainly watch out for and avoid are crowd estimates based on guesswork methods from "interested" parties, that is, from those who have an "axe to grind." Numbers from demonstration organizers should simply not be believed because they have an interest in reporting as high a number as they can. Numbers from critics of a demonstration—say, spokespersons from

251

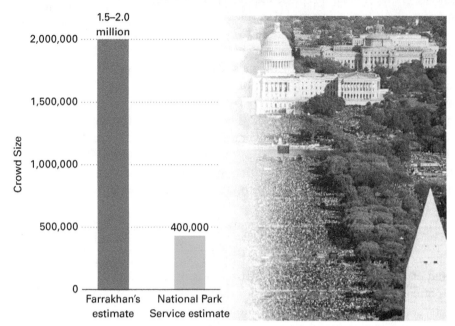

Variations in Crowd Size Estimates at the Million Man March

pro-life organizations estimating the size of a pro-choice rally—should be dismissed out of hand. Rely instead on reports from disinterested parties such as mainstream news organizations or academics, if possible, who use one form or another of counting using aerial photography. But note as well, even here, that the photograph/grid method is an estimate (just how dense is that grid, one might ask?), though it comes closer than any other method available for producing a hard and accurate number.

What Do You Think?

Do you think that the size of a demonstration or a series of demonstrations is a good indicator of the strength of a movement? If not, why not? Should movements that are able to mount large demonstrations, like the Tea Party did on April 15, 2009 (tax deadline day), in Washington and in many other cities across the nation, have more attention paid to them by the public and elected officials than movements that can't do so? Why? Can you think of mass demonstrations that have had a big impact on what government does? Or, on the other hand, can you think of mass demonstrations that have had no impact at all?

Sources: Farouk El-baz, "Remote Sensing, Controversy, and the Million Man March," Earth *Observation Magazine* (February 1996), accessed at www.eomonline.com/Common/Archives/1996feb; J. Patrick Coolican, "Crowd Count Adds Up to Infinite Interpretation," *Seattle Times* (February 17, 2003), p. 1; "Using Aerial Photography to Estimate the Size of Sunday's Peace March in San Francisco," *The San Francisco Chronicle* (February 21, 2003).

☐ A Spark to Set Off the Flames

Social movements require, as we have seen, a set of grievances among a group of people, the resources to form and sustain organization, a supportive environment, and a sense of political efficacy among the potential participants in the movement. But they also seem to require something to set off the mix, some dramatic precipitating event (or series of events), sometimes called a *catalyst*, to set them in motion. Passage of the Fourteenth Amendment, protecting the citizenship rights of males, galvanized the early women's suffrage movement, as we saw in the chapter-opening story. The gay and lesbian movement seems to have been sparked by the 1969 "Stonewall rebellion"—three days of rioting set off by police harassment of the patrons of a popular gay bar in New York City's Greenwich Village. An important catalyst for the civil rights movement was Rosa Parks's simple refusal to give up her seat on a Montgomery, Alabama, bus in 1957. Sending her to jail spurred the Montgomery bus boycott and associated demonstrations, led by a young minister named Martin Luther King, Jr. In 2006, Latinos were moved to action when the House passed a bill sponsored by James Sensenbrenner (R–WI) making illegal immigrants felons, subjecting long-time undocumented immigrants to deportation, and beefing up control of the U.S.–Mexican border.

Tactics of Social Movements

Because they often represent people and groups that lack political power, social movements tend to use unconventional tactics to make themselves heard. Such tactics depend on the dramatic gesture and are often disruptive.[31] As you saw in the chapter-opening story, the women's suffrage movement used mass demonstrations and hunger strikes to great effect. The labor movement invented **sit-down strikes** and plant takeovers as its most effective weapons in the 1930s. Pro-life activists added to the protest repertoire clinic blockades and the harassment of clinic patients, doctors, and employees. The Occupy Wall Street movement learned to take over and prevent any other activities from happening in publicly prominent urban spaces such as parks, squares, and in front of government buildings and banks.

The most effective tool of the civil rights movement was nonviolent **civil disobedience**, a conscious refusal to obey a law that a group considers unfair, unjust, or unconstitutional, courting arrest by the authorities and assault from others, without offering resistance, as a way to highlight injustice and gain broader public sympathy. Dr. Martin Luther King, Jr. was the strongest advocate for and popularizer of this strategy, having borrowed it from Mahatma Gandhi, who used it as part of the campaign that ended British colonial rule in India after the Second World War.[32] A particularly dramatic and effective use of this tactic took place in Greensboro, North Carolina. Four black students from North Carolina Agricultural and Technical State University sat down at a "whites only" lunch counter in a Woolworth's store on February 1, 1960, and politely asked to be served. When requested to leave, they refused. They stayed put and remained calm even as a mob of young white men screamed at them, squirted them with ketchup and mustard, and threatened to lynch them. Each day, more students from the college joined them. By the end of the week, more than 1,000 black students had joined the sit-in to demand an end to segregation. These actions ignited the South. Within two months, similar sit-ins had taken place in nearly 60 cities

Explore on
MyPoliSciLab
Simulation
You Are a Social Movement Leader

sit-down strike
A form of labor action in which workers stop production but do not leave their job site.

civil disobedience
Intentionally breaking a law and accepting the consequences as a way to publicize the unjustness of the law.

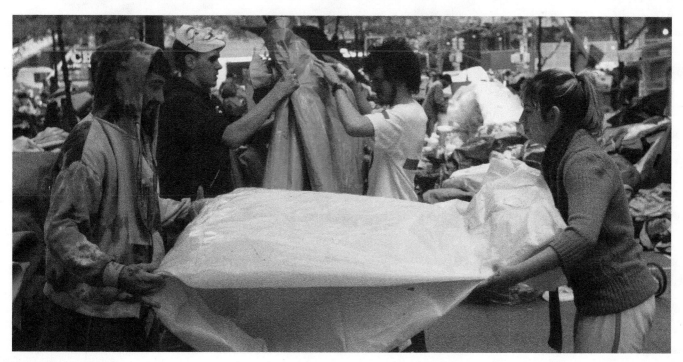

PROTEST COMMUNITY

The Occupy Wall Street movement was formed not only to protest rising income inequality and the dim job prospects for young people but to highlight the possibilities for forming a sense of community amidst a competitive, individualistic-oriented society. Here protesters work together to clean up their camp site in New York's Zuccotti Park in 2011.

across nine states; almost 4,000 young people, including a number of white college students from outside the South, had tasted a night in jail for their actions. Their bravery galvanized blacks across the nation and generated sympathy among many whites. The student sit-in movement also spawned a new and more impatient civil rights organization, the Student Non-Violent Coordinating Committee (SNCC).

For his part, Dr. King led a massive nonviolent civil disobedience campaign in Birmingham, Alabama, in 1963, demanding that the city abide by the Supreme Court's decision in *Brown v. Board of Education* (1954) to end the segregation of schools in addition to the more broadly based **integration** of public services, especially public transportation. Nonviolent demonstrators, many of them schoolchildren, were assaulted by snarling police dogs, electric cattle prods, and high-pressure fire hoses that sent demonstrators sprawling. Police Commissioner Eugene "Bull" Connor filled his jails to overflowing with hundreds of young marchers, who resisted only passively, alternately praying and singing civil rights songs, including "We Shall Overcome." The quiet bravery of the demonstrators and the palpable sense among public officials and private sector leaders in the nation that matters were quickly spinning out of control convinced President John Kennedy on June 11, 1963, to introduce his historic civil rights bill for congressional consideration.

This is not to say that unconventional and disruptive tactics always work, something addressed in more detail in the next section. No matter how peaceful, some fail to strike a chord with the public or elites. And, there are times when fringe elements within movements do things that are so disruptive or violent that the movement itself is discredited. In the late 1960s, urban riots and the rise of African American leaders and groups committed to black power undermined the broad popularity of the civil rights movement. The antiglobalization movement has been similarly undermined by its anarchist wing, which, committed to violence against property and confrontations with police, usually draws the most attention from the television cameras at antiglobalization gatherings, whether in Seattle or Davos.

COURAGE UNDER FIRE

Under the leadership of Chief of Public Safety "Bull" Connor, peaceful civil rights demonstrators protesting segregation in Birmingham, Alabama were met with fire hoses, police billy clubs, snarling police dogs, and jail in 1963. The national and international outcry over the treatment of peaceful protestors contributed to passage of the 1964 Civil Rights Act ending most forms *de jure* segregation in the United States.

Why Some Social Movements Succeed and Others Do Not

8.1
8.2
8.3
8.4
8.5
8.6

8.6 Determine what makes a social movement successful

ocial movements have had a significant effect on American politics and on what government does. Not all social movements are equally successful; here is why: [33]

- *The proximity of the movement's goals to American values.* Movements that ask for fuller participation in things that other Americans consider right and proper—such as voting and holding office or opportunities for economic advancement—are more likely to strike a responsive chord than movements that, let us say, demand a redistribution of income from the rich to the poor.
- *The movement's capacity to win public attention and support.* Potential movements that fail to gain public attention, either because the news media do not pay much attention, or because there is little sympathy for the cause the movement espouses, never get very far. Things become even more problematic when a social movement stimulates the formation of a counter–social movement.
- *The movement's ability to affect the political fortunes of elected leaders.* Politicians tend to pay attention to movements that can affect their electoral fortunes one way or another. If support for the aims of a movement will add to their vote totals among movement members and a broader sympathetic public, politicians likely will be more inclined to help. If opposition to the movement is a better electoral strategy for politicians, they are likely to act as roadblocks to the movement.

We can see how these factors play out in the life-histories of the social movements that have made their mark or tried with varying degrees of success to make their mark in American political life.

Low-Impact Social Movements

The poor people's movement, which tried to convince Americans to enact policies that would end poverty in the United States, failed to make much of a mark in the late 1960s. This social movement was never able to mobilize a large group of activists, had little support among the general public because of its fairly radical proposals for income redistribution, and was unable to disrupt everyday life significantly or to affect the electoral prospects of politicians.

The women's movement, while successful in a number of areas, was unable to win passage of a proposed Equal Rights Amendment to the Constitution banning discrimination on the grounds of gender. The ERA failed to receive the approval of the necessary three-fourths of the states by the amendment's 1979 deadline, mainly because the effort to ratify this new amendment stirred up a counter-movement among religious conservatives in every religious denomination. [34]

Repressed Social Movements

Social movements committed to a radical change in the society and the economy tend to threaten widely shared values and the interests of powerful individuals, groups, [35] and institutions. [36] As a result, they rarely gain widespread popular support and almost always arouse the hostility of political leaders. Such movements very often face repression of one kind or another. [37] In the late nineteenth and early twentieth centuries, for instance, the labor movement was hindered by court injunctions forbidding strikes and boycotts, laws against the formation of labor unions, violence by employer-hired armed gangs, and strikebreaking by the National Guard and the U.S. armed forces. In 1877, 60,000 National Guardsmen were mobilized in 10 states to break the first national railroad strike. The strike against Carnegie Steel in 1892 in Homestead, Pennsylvania, brought the mobilization of 10,000 militiamen, the arrest of 16 strike leaders on conspiracy charges, and the indictment of 27 labor leaders for treason.

☐ Partially Successful Social Movements

Some social movements have enough power and public support to generate a favorable response from public officials but not enough to force them to go very far. In these situations, government may respond in a partial or halfhearted way. President Franklin D. Roosevelt responded to the social movements pressing for strong antipoverty measures during the Great Depression by proposing the passage of the Social Security Act, which fell far short of movement expectations.[38] The pro-life movement discovered that President Reagan was willing to use movement rhetoric to appoint sympathetic judges but was unwilling to submit anti-abortion legislation to Congress. Christian conservatives enjoyed some legislative successes during the height of their power in the 1990s and were important voices in the nominations of John Roberts and Samuel Alito to the Supreme Court by President Bush in 2005, but they failed to achieve some of their primary objectives: enact a law to ban late-term (in their words, "partial birth") abortions, pass a constitutional amendment banning same-sex marriages, and remove Bill Clinton from the presidency by impeachment and trial. Gays and lesbians enjoyed some important successes, but encountered setbacks as well. The Tea Party eventually gained important influence within the Republican Party. Their increased numbers in Congress after the 2010 election forced a deficit reduction plan fashioned by the Republican House leadership and President Obama in summer 2011 after Tea Party sympathizers held up a bill to raise the national debt limit, bringing the country to the edge of the first-ever default on its debts.

☐ Successful Social Movements

Social movements that have many supporters, win wide public sympathy, do not challenge the basics of the economic and social orders, and wield some clout in the electoral arena are likely to achieve a substantial number of their goals. The women's suffrage movement, described in the chapter-opening story, is one of the best examples. The civil rights movement is another, yielding, after years of struggle, the Civil Rights Act of 1964, which banned segregation in places of public accommodations such as hotels and restaurants, and the Voting Rights Act of 1965, which put the might of the federal government behind efforts to allow African Americans to vote and hold elected office. These enactments helped sound the death knell of the "separate but equal" doctrine enunciated in the infamous *Plessy* decision (1896), and engineered the collapse of legal segregation in the South.

The Voting Rights Act was particularly important in transforming the politics of the South. Black registration and voting turnout increased dramatically all over the region during the late 1960s and the 1970s. Elected black officials filled legislative seats, city council seats, the mayors' offices in large and small cities, and sheriffs' offices. Between 1960 and 2001—the last year for which this statistic is available—the number of elected black officials in the United States increased from a mere 40 to more than 9,000.[39] Also, white politicians, tacking with the new winds of change, began to court the black vote in the years after passage of the Voting Rights Act. George Wallace, who first became famous by "standing in the schoolhouse door" to prevent the integration of the University of Alabama and who once kicked off a political campaign with the slogan, "Segregation Now, Segregation Tomorrow, Segregation Forever," actively pursued the black vote in his last run for public office.

To be sure, being successful in achieving specific policy goals may not in the end make matters better for a group across the board. Though the civil rights movement achieved its legislative goals—passage of the Civil Rights Act in 1964 guaranteeing equal treatment in public accommodations and the 1965 Voting Rights Act protecting African Americans' right to vote—the social and economic condition of African Americans today lags behind that of other Americans. This is true with respect to educational attainment, income and wealth, and life expectancy, for example.[40]

Movements can be successful even if no new laws are passed. Other measures of success include increased respect for members of the movement, changes in

Using the FRAMEWORK
Why did Barack Obama and Congress overturn Bill Clinton's policy of "don't ask, don't tell"?

Background: A 1982 Defense Department policy directive stated that homosexuality was "incompatible with military service." The directive simply stated what had been common practice for many years before: gays and lesbians could not serve, and unit commanders made active efforts to discover and root out homosexuals from the ranks of the military. After his election in 1992, helped in part by his promise to end this discrimination, Bill Clinton instituted a policy that came to be called "don't ask, don't tell, don't pursue" (DADT). This policy of "turning a blind eye," yet allowing dismissal of gay and lesbian military personnel once discovered, proved deeply troubling to the gay and lesbian community. This community strongly backed Barack Obama after he promised to end "don't ask, don't tell" and push legislation allowing gays and lesbians to openly serve in the military. Congress passed a bill to that effect in December 2010, right before a new Republican majority came to power in the House, and the president signed it in a White House ceremony. The new law went into effect on December 20, 2011, after the president, the secretary of defense, and the chairman of the Joint Chiefs certified that the new law would not adversely affect readiness, unit cohesion, or recruiting. How did all of this happen? We can only understand by taking a broad look at how structural, political linkage, and governmental factors affected passage of new legislation.

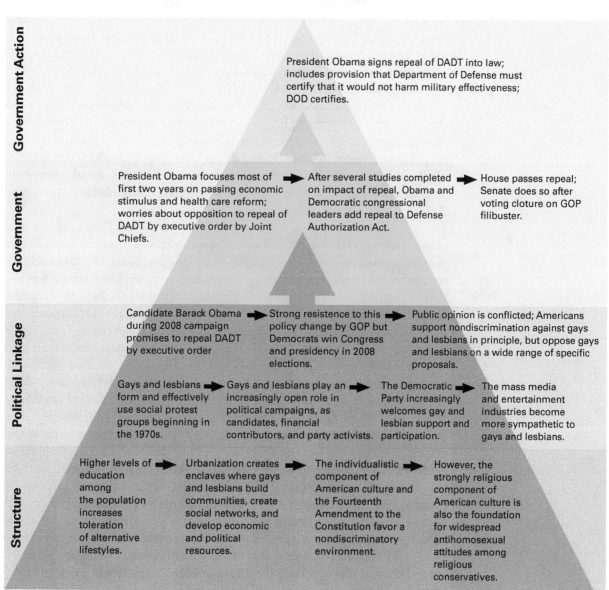

Government Action

President Obama signs repeal of DADT into law; includes provision that Department of Defense must certify that it would not harm military effectiveness; DOD certifies.

Government

President Obama focuses most of first two years on passing economic stimulus and health care reform; worries about opposition to repeal of DADT by executive order by Joint Chiefs. ➡ After several studies completed on impact of repeal, Obama and Democratic congressional leaders add repeal to Defense Authorization Act. ➡ House passes repeal; Senate does so after voting cloture on GOP filibuster.

Political Linkage

Candidate Barack Obama during 2008 campaign promises to repeal DADT by executive order ➡ Strong resistence to this policy change by GOP but Democrats win Congress and presidency in 2008 elections. ➡ Public opinion is conflicted; Americans support nondiscrimination against gays and lesbians in principle, but oppose gays and lesbians on a wide range of specific proposals.

Gays and lesbians form and effectively use social protest groups beginning in the 1970s. ➡ Gays and lesbians play an increasingly open role in political campaigns, as candidates, financial contributors, and party activists. ➡ The Democratic Party increasingly welcomes gay and lesbian support and participation. ➡ The mass media and entertainment industries become more sympathetic to gays and lesbians.

Structure

Higher levels of education among the population increases toleration of alternative lifestyles. ➡ Urbanization creates enclaves where gays and lesbians build communities, create social networks, and develop economic and political resources. ➡ The individualistic component of American culture and the Fourteenth Amendment to the Constitution favor a nondiscriminatory environment. ➡ However, the strongly religious component of American culture is also the foundation for widespread antihomosexual attitudes among religious conservatives.

8.1

8.2

8.3

8.4

8.5

8.6

fundamental underlying values in society, and increased representation of the group in decision-making bodies. The women's movement has had this kind of success. Although the Equal Rights Amendment (the movement's main goal) failed, women's issues came to the forefront during these years, and, to a very substantial degree, the demands of the movement for equal treatment and respect made great headway in many areas of American life.[41] Issues such as pay equity, family leave, sexual harassment, and attention to women's health problems in medical research are now a part of the American political agenda. Women have made important gains economically and are becoming more numerous in the professions, corporate managerial offices (although only 15 percent of corporate board members in the United States were female in 2011)[42], and political office. In 2008, Hillary Clinton came close to winning the Democratic presidential nomination, and Sarah Palin gained the GOP's vice presidential nomination.

Using the DEMOCRACY STANDARD

Do social movements make us more or less democratic?

The story of American democracy has been shaped by social movements—from the first stirrings of rebellion in the British colonies to the emancipation of African American slaves to the granting of the right to vote to women. But in a nation that is supposed to be governed by majority rule, expressed primarily through elections, are social movements that empower minorities truly democratic? Just what role do social movements play in a democracy?

In a perfect democratic society, of course, social movements would be unnecessary: change would happen through political linkages like elections and public opinion and through party and interest group activity. Indeed, a democracy that depended entirely on social movements to bring needed change would not be working very effectively at all. But in an imperfect and incomplete democracy like ours, social movements play a valuable and important role, creating an additional linkage between portions of the American public and their government.

Social movements affect our democracy in several ways. First of all, social movements represent a way—a difficult way, to be sure—by which political outsiders and the politically powerless can become players in the political game. Our constitutional system favors the status quo—federalism, separation of powers, and checks and balances make it extremely difficult to institute fundamentally new policies or to change existing social and economic conditions. The primacy of the status quo is further enhanced by the political power of economically and socially privileged groups and individuals who generally resist changes that might undermine their positions. Movements present a way for outsider groups and individuals to gain a hearing for their grievances, work to win over a majority of their fellow citizens, and persuade elected leaders to take action. Equal citizenship for women and for African Americans, for example, would not have happened at all, or would have been much longer in coming, if not for the existence of social movements demanding change. Thus, social movements are valuable tools for ensuring that popular sovereignty, political equality, and political liberty—the key ingredients in a democracy as we have defined it—are more fully realized.

To be sure, in some cases, at least theoretically, social movements can pose a threat to democracy. Small minorities who force elected officials to respond to their demands because of the tangible threat of social disruption might occasionally get their way, even though the majority does not favor such action. Some social movements, moreover, might push policies that run counter to democratic ideals of popular sovereignty, political equality, and political liberty, making them dangerous for democracy if they take hold. Anti-immigrant movements during several periods in the nineteenth century, for example, tried to deny citizenship rights to various groups, including people from China and Southern and Eastern Europe. But these threats to the fundamentals of democracy emanating from social movements seem minor compared to the persistent citizen inequalities that arise from other quarters, including the interest group system described in the previous chapter.

Review the Chapter

What Are Social Movements?

8.1 Define social movements and who they represent, p. 236

Social movements emphasize rather dramatically the point that the struggle for democracy is a recurring feature of our political life.

Social movements are mainly the instruments of political outsiders with grievances who want to gain a hearing in American politics.

Major Social Movements in the United States

8.2 Illustrate how important social movements have shaped American society, p. 238

Social movements, by using disruptive tactics and broadening the scope of conflict, can contribute to democracy by increasing the visibility of important issues, encouraging wider participation in public affairs, often creating new majorities, and sometimes providing the energy to overcome the many antimajoritarian features of our constitutional system.

Social Movements in a Majoritarian Democracy

8.3 Evaluate how social movements make U.S. politics more democratic, p. 246

Social movements often produce changes in government policies.

Social movements try to bring about social change through collective action.

Movements can also serve as a tension-release mechanism for aggrieved groups even when major policy shifts do not happen.

Social movements have had an important effect on our political life and in determining what our government does. Some of our most important legislative landmarks can be attributed to them.

Social movements do not always get what they want. They seem to be most successful when their goals are consistent with the central values of the society, have wide popular support, and fit the needs of political leaders.

Factors that Encourage the Creation of Social Movements

8.4 Identify factors that give rise to social movements, p. 249

Social distress caused by economic, social, and technological change often creates the conditions for the rise of social movements in the United States.

Social distress that encourages the formation of social movements comes from change that proves difficult and unsafe for people, threatens their way of life or basic values, and lessens the respect they feel from others.

Social movements can be a means for calling attention to their plight and pressing for changes in the status quo.

Tactics of Social Movements

8.5 Evaluate tactics used by social movements to influence what government does, p. 253

Social movements use unconventional and often disruptive tactics to attract attention to their cause.

Social movements tend to be most successful when the political environment is supportive, in the sense that at least portions of the general population and some public officials are sympathetic to the movements' goals.

Movement ideas often are taken up by one of the major political parties as it seeks to add voters.

To the degree that parties attract new voters and change the views of some of their traditional voters because of social movement activities, elected officials are more likely to be receptive to responding to grievances.

Social movements sometimes spark counter–social movements, which, if strong enough, can make government leaders reluctant to address grievances.

Why Some Social Movements Succeed and Others Do Not

8.6 Determine what makes a social movement successful, p. 255

Social movements that have many supporters, win wide public sympathy, do not challenge the basics of the economic and social orders, and wield some clout in the electoral arena are most likely to achieve their goals.

Learn the Terms

✓ **Study** and **Review** the **Flashcards**

Test Yourself

✓ **Study** and **Review** the **Practice Tests**

Answer key begins on page T-1.

8.1 Define social movements and who they represent

1. Which statement about social movements is NOT true:

   a. Social movements are the political instrument of political outsiders.
   b. Social movements are generally mass grassroots phenomena.
   c. Social movements use unconventional and disruptive tactics.
   d. Social movements are often easily organized and sustained.
   e. Social movements often turn into interest groups.

8.2 Illustrate how important social movements have shaped American society

2. One antiwar movement that most affected American politics had to do with this war:

   a. World War I
   b. World War II
   c. Vietnam War
   d. Persian Gulf War
   e. Afghanistan War

8.3 Evaluate how social movements make U.S. politics more democratic

3. Over time, social movements may also help create
   a. More social reforms
   b. Social equality in society
   c. New majorities in society
   d. More labor unions
   e. New minorities in society

8.4 Identify factors that give rise to social movements

4. In addition to the existence of resources for mobilization, the rise of social movements requires two things:

   a. Acceptance of the movement among elites, and financial resources
   b. The right timing, and acceptance of the movement among elites
   c. Financial resources, and the right timing
   d. More than 1,000 people, and the right timing
   e. More than 1,000 people, and a strong leader

8.5 Evaluate tactics used by social movements to influence what government does

5. The antiglobalization movement has been undermined by

   a. Media coverage
   b. Peaceful sit-ins
   c. Civil disobedience
   d. Nonviolent protests
   e. Violent protests

8.6 Determine what makes a social movement successful

6. Between 1960 and 2001, the number of elected black officials in the United States increased from.

   a. 5 to 50,000
   b. 20 to 100
   c. 40 to 9,000
   d. 50 to 65
   e. 100 to 400

Explore Further

INTERNET SOURCES

Center for the Study of Social Movements, Notre Dame University **nd.edu/~cssm/**
A leading academic research center that disseminates the research of its own distinguished faculty and provides information about current social movements.

Family Research Council **www.frc.org**
Information, news, and links from one of the nation's most influential Christian conservative organizations.

The Gay and Lesbian Alliance Against Defamation **www.glaad.org**
News, issues, and links related to the gay and lesbian movement.

Pew Hispanic Center **pewhispanic.org**
A rich site for data on Hispanic immigration to the United States and public opinion polling information on immigration topics.

The Smithsonian Exhibits: Disability Rights **americanhistory .si.edu/disabilityrights/welcome.html**
A Smithsonian online exhibit featuring the history of the disability rights movement.

The Tea Party Movement **www.teapartypatriots.org**
The official website of the Tea Party movement.

The Civil Rights Movement **faculty.smu.edu/dsimon/Change-Civ%20Rts.html**
A timeline of the civil rights movement, along with links to important documents and speeches made between 1954 and 1963.

Yahoo! Society and Culture **www.yahoo.com/Society_and_ Culture/Issues_and_Causes/**
A gateway with links to a multitude of social movements, issues, and groups.

SUGGESTIONS FOR FURTHER READING

Branch, Taylor. *Parting the Waters: America in the King Years, 1954– 1963*. New York: Simon & Schuster, 1988.

A detailed and compelling description of the civil rights movement, with a particular focus on Martin Luther King, Jr.; winner of the National Book Award and the Pulitzer Prize.

Chafe, William H. *The Unfinished Journey: America Since World War II*. New York: Oxford University Press, 2006.

A justly celebrated history of America since 1945, with a particular focus on the civil rights and women's movements.

Dudziak, Mary L. *Cold War Civil Rights*. Princeton, NJ: Princeton University Press, 2002.

A compelling history of how the Cold War struggle with the Soviet Union provided a supportive environment for the civil rights movement.

Horton, Carol A. *Race and the Making of American Liberalism*. New York: Oxford University Press, 2005.

Suggests that American liberalism has been useful in ending discrimination and expanding diversity, but much less useful in diminishing dramatic racial inequalities in status, power, and wealth.

McAdam, Doug, Sidney Tarrow, and Charles Tilly. *Dynamics of Contention*. Cambridge, UK: Cambridge University Press, 2001.

A book that attempts to bridge the gap between the leading but competing theories of social movements by the field's three leading scholars.

Opp, Karl-Dieter. *Theories of Political Protest and Social Movements*. New York: Routledge, 2009.

A comprehensive examination of the scholarly debates surrounding our understanding of social movements and the role they play not only in the United States but in other countries as well.

Rosen, Ruth. *The World Split Open: How the Modern Women's Movement Changed America*. New York: Penguin, 2006.

A history of the modern women's movement, filled with detailed accounts of its origins, operations, and impacts.

9

Political Parties

PARTISAN DEBT CEILING STRUGGLE PUSHES AMERICA TO THE BRINK

C ongress annually passes tax and appropriations bills, which become law once signed by the president. Ever since the end of the Clinton administration in 2000, Congress has decided every year, regardless of which party was in control of the House and Senate, to spend more than it takes in, creating annual deficits and a consequent growth in the national debt. To cover the deficit, we borrow from others, including individuals and financial institutions here and abroad, and from other nations, in the form of U.S. Treasury bills, notes, and bonds. Every year, as well, Congress routinely passes legislation to increase the debt ceiling beyond which borrowing is not allowed to go.

All of this changed in 2011 after 87 new Republican Tea Party–affiliated or supported members were elected in the 2010 elections, having promised to slash federal government spending no matter what the consequences. The instrument House leaders chose to fulfill this pledge was the bill to increase the debt ceiling to $14.3 trillion, usually a routine matter. The GOP and Tea Party position was that the budget could only be fixed by massive cuts and that tax increases of any kind, including closing so-called loopholes, were off the table. Tea Party Republicans vowed to win on this issue even if it meant not reaching an agreement and defaulting on debts owed to American and foreign bondholders, including the Chinese and Japanese governments who fund much of our debt.

Treasury Secretary Tim Geithner announced that his department would be forced, in the absence of a debt ceiling bill, to stop paying what the country owes on August 2, 2011; we would, that is, default on our loans. In the view of most economists and financial experts, default

9.1	9.2	9.3
Evaluate the importance of political parties in democracies, p. 267	Distinguish American political parties from parties in other democracies, p. 268	Compare and contrast today's Republican and Democratic parties, p. 276

TO THE BRINK WHILE AMERICANS SUFFER The bitter partisan deadlock over a bill to raise the debt limit in 2011 almost caused the country to default on its national debt. The drama surrounding this and other budget issues kept the Congress from addressing important problems like high unemployment. Here job candidates drop off their resumes at a job fair in Illinois.

Watch on MyPoliSci

The Big Picture While political parties are key to almost any democracy, America is the only one that has maintained a two-party system for over a century. Author Edward S. Greenberg looks at why our parties are different from those in other developed democracies.

The Basics Why do we have political parties in America? In this video, you will learn about the rise of political parties in the United States, the reasons why the two-party system continues to dominate American politics, and how the major parties differ from one another.

Why do we have only two major parties in the United States?

In Context Trace the development of political parties in the United States from the time of the ratification of the Constitution. Oklahoma State University political scientist Jeanette M. Mendez explains why political parties emerged and what role they play in our democratic system.

Think Like a Political Scientist How can we tell that Americans are increasingly polarized and what are the implications of this trend? In this video, Oklahoma State University political scientist Jeanette M. Mendez reveals how scholars measure party polarization at the elite and mass level and who is behind this phenomenon.

In the Real World Why do Americans only have two party choices—Democrats and Republicans? Real people evaluate the effectiveness of the "winner takes all" electoral system in the United States, and they weigh in on whether third parties—such as the Libertarians and the Green Party—should have more representation in national elections.

So What? Democrats and Republicans today are deeply divided. Author Edward S. Greenberg explains that while partisan politics is nothing new in American history, partisanship is so pronounced now that it makes governing in would have been catastrophic for the United States—a steep decline in stocks and the value of the dollar and a substantial increase in the costs of borrowing on business loans, mortgages, car loans, and student loans would follow—with a new recession highly likely. Rating agencies warned they would down-grade America's AAA rating if serious steps were not taken to both fix long-term budget problems and end the uncertainty caused by the partisan warfare over the debt ceiling bill with the promise of more partisan brinksman-ship to come in the future on all budget issues.

All seemed lost on July 13 when talks between President Obama and Republican con-gressional leaders broke down in bitter acrimony. Things turned darker still on July 21 when Republican House Speaker John Boehner was forced to pull a bill he had painstakingly put together because his party whips told him there were not enough Republican votes to pass the bill, with hardly any of the Tea Party-87 on board. On the Senate side, Democrats were balking at the size of cuts in government discretionary spending, without any contri-bution to deficit reduction by taxes on the wealthy.

Pushed by the business community, foreign governments, and growing unease among the public, the president and congressional leaders finally agreed on a bill just two days before the August 2 deadline and only hours before Asian markets were to open with the likely prospect of American stocks and the dollar getting hammered. Though the bill passed in the nick of time, and promised the deepest spending cuts in our peacetime history, America's credit rating still took a hit because of worries about the dysfunctional qualities of our governing process. Moody's, worried about how this situation might impact the abil-ity of the United States to address its budget problems over the long haul, downgraded America's credit rating from AAA to AA+ the very next day after the debt ceiling bill was passed. The *Economist* blamed this downgrade and another by Standard and Poor's on the growing dysfunction of American politics:

> As it revoked America's triple-A credit rating on August 5th, Standard & Poor's explained that the gulf between the political parties was becoming unbridgeable, and that policymaking was becoming unpredictable.[1]

The debt ceiling bill left much of the hard work of balancing the budget to a super com-mittee of the House and Senate that was required to issue its legislative recommenda-tions by the end of November 2011. To spur the committee to action, the debt ceiling bill contained a deadly trigger: automatic and deep cuts in domestic and defense pro-grams at the start of 2013 if an agreement was not reached. The super committee negotiations broke down in partisan acrimony a week or so before the deadline and disbanded.[2]

This story illustrates big changes in our party system. American political parties often are described as "big tent" parties, comprised of broad and diverse coalitions of groups and viewpoints. This was generally true for most of our history. But starting in the 1980s, things began to change. Since then, the Democratic Party has become slightly more ec-onomically and socially liberal while the Republican Party has become much more eco-nomically and socially conservative. The number of moderate Democrats in Congress has declined, though they remain significant—senators Ben Nelson (NE) and Max Baucus (MT), for example, were key architects of the health care reform bill. Moderates have almost dis-appeared from the Republican Party in Congress, however. Increasingly, Republicans in the House and Senate vote on important bills as relatively homogeneous blocs. The Obama stimulus bill in 2009, for example, drew no Republican votes in the House and only three in the Senate. The health care reform bill drew only a single Republican vote in the House of Representatives and none in the Senate.

Democrats and Republicans in Washington and across the country have become en-gaged in increasingly bitter disputes over many issues, including the wars in Iraq and Af-ghanistan, abortion, same-sex marriage, global warming, Social Security reform, judicial appointments, spending and taxes, disaster and homeland security preparedness, and changes in bankruptcy and tort law. Incivility has become the order of the day when party leaders and elected officials deal with one another. Opponents in Congress are accused of being scoundrels, liars, or cowards. Conference committees to iron out differences between Senate and House versions of important bills freeze out members of the minority partisan

A committed supporter of a political party; also, seeing issues from the point of view of a single party.

party. Presidents are accused by their **partisan** opponents of plotting to undermine civil liberties, squash religious freedom, enrich their friends, or turn the country toward socialism. In this environment, it is hardly surprising that cooperation across party lines is increasingly rare, not only in Congress but in state legislatures and city councils as well. And those who try to do so are, more often than not, vilified by their co-partisans.

Partisanship seems likely to rise even more in the near future. Moderate Democratic Senator Ben Nelson and moderate Republican Senator Olympia Snowe, perhaps growing tired of it all or fearing defeat in the next round of elections, announced in 2011 that they would not seek reelection. Moderate Republican and long-serving Senator Richard Lugar of Indiana lost to a Tea Party-backed candidate in the state party primary in 2012 whose main campaign theme was that Lugar cooperated too often with his Democratic colleagues.

American politics is no stranger to partisanship; to one extent or another, Democratic and Republican leaders and activists have always been in the business of making the other party look bad. It's good politics. However, things seem to be getting worse, at least according to most veteran observers of American politics.[3]

What accounts for the intense partisanship of American politics today? Scholars and journalists have lots of ideas on this. Many point to the explosion in the number and influence of liberal and conservative advocacy groups, and their blogosphere cousins, who demand unity on bedrock issues such as abortion, taxes, and global warming. Others point to the decline in the number of competitive districts in House races, meaning that most representatives can win and retain their seats without regard to voters in the other party. Others suggest that our presidential primary system forces candidates for party presidential nominations to play to the most ideologically extreme elements within each of the parties. Still others suggest that the very closeness of presidential and congressional elections in the late 1990s and much of the 2000s convinced party strategists that the best way to win elections was to mobilize the party base and get them to the polls. And what better way to do this than to get partisans angry at the other party and worried about what it would do if it were to win?

Political parties are an important part of democratic political systems. How well they function and fulfill their responsibilities has a lot to do with determining the health and vitality of democratic polities. We examine political parties in this chapter and ask whether heightened levels of interparty conflict make our system more or less responsive to the people and our government more or less able to fashion coherent and workable public policies. We will suggest that while "partisanship" can play an important role in enhancing democracy in the abstract, it often leads to gridlock in our constitutional system of separated powers where divided government is common.

Thinking Critically About This Chapter

This chapter is about American political parties, how they evolved, what they do, and how their actions affect the quality of democracy in the United States.

Using the Framework

You will see in this chapter how parties work as political linkage institutions connecting the public with government leaders and institutions. You will see, as well, how structural changes in the American economy and society have affected how our political parties function.

Using the Democracy Standard

You will see in this chapter that political parties, at least in theory, are one of the most important instruments for making popular sovereignty and majority rule a reality in a representative democracy, particularly in a system of checks and balances and separated powers such as our own. Evaluating how well our parties carry out these democratic responsibilities is one of the main themes of this chapter.

The Role of Political Parties in a Democracy

political party
An organization that tries to win control of government by electing people to office who carry the party label.

party platform
A party's statement of its positions on the issues of the day passed at the quadrennial national convention.

❉ Explore on MyPoliSciLab
Simulation
You Are a Voter

 lthough the framers worried about the possible pernicious effects of factions, a category that included interest groups and political parties in today's terminology, and designed a constitution to address these effects, most political thinkers today believe that political parties are essential to democracy. They agree with E.E. Schattschneider that "political parties created democracy and . . . modern democracy is unthinkable save in terms of the parties."[4] So, what are political parties and why are they essential to the practice of democracy?

A "**political party** is a group organized to nominate candidates, to try to win political power through elections, and to promote ideas about public policies."[5] In representative democracies, parties are the principal organizations that recruit candidates for public office, run their candidates against the candidates of other political parties in competitive elections, and try to organize and coordinate the activities of government officials under party banners and programs. In going about the business of electing people to office and running government, political parties make it possible for the people to rule,[6] for parties can only gain power and govern with the approval of the majority. Majority rule is one of the things that makes popular sovereignty possible. As Schattschneider once put it: "The parties are the special form of political organization adapted to the mobilization of majorities. How else can the majority get organized? If democracy means anything at all it means that the majority has the right to organize for the purpose of taking over the government."[7]

In theory, political parties can do a number of things to make popular sovereignty and political equality possible:[8]

- *Keep elected officials responsive.* Competitive party elections help voters choose between alternative policy directions for the future. They also allow voters to make a judgment about the past performance of a governing party and decide whether to allow that party to continue in office. And, a party can adjust its **party platform**—the party's statement of its position on the issues—to reflect the preferences of the public as a way to win elections.

- *Stimulate political interest.* When they are working properly, moreover, political parties stimulate interest in politics and public affairs and increase participation. They do this as a natural by-product of their effort to win or retain power in government; they mobilize voters, bring issues to public attention, and educate on the issues that are of interest to the party.[9] Party competition, by "expanding the scope of conflict," attracts attention and gets people involved.[10]

- *Ensure accountability.* Parties can help make office holders more accountable. When things go wrong or promises are not kept, it is important in a democracy for citizens to know who is responsible. Where there are many offices and branches of government, however, it is hard to pinpoint responsibility. Political parties can simplify this difficult task by allowing for collective responsibility. Citizens can pass judgment on the governing ability of a party as a whole and decide whether to retain the incumbent party or to throw it out of office in favor of the other party.

- *Help people make sense of complexity in politics.* Party labels and party positions on the issues help many people make sense of the political world. Few people have the time or resources to learn about and reach decisions on every candidate on the ballot or the issues before the public at any period in time. Party labels and policy positions can act as useful shortcuts or cues enabling people to cut through the complexities and reach decisions that are consistent with their own values and interests.[11]

two-party system
A political system in which two parties vie on relatively equal terms to win national elections and in which each party governs at one time or another.

multiparty system
A political system in which three or more viable parties compete to lead the government; because a majority winner is not always possible, multiparty systems often have coalition governments where governing power is shared among two or more parties.

- *Make government work.* In a system like ours of separation of powers and checks and balances, designed to make it difficult for government to act decisively, political parties can encourage cooperation across the branches of government among public officials who are members of the same party. Thus, some of the constitutionally induced tension between a president and Congress may diminish when they are members of the same political party.

Political parties, then, can be tools of popular sovereignty. Whether our own political parties fulfill these responsibilities to democracy is the question we explore in the remainder of this chapter. We will see that our political parties fulfill many of the democracy-supporting roles listed above. But we also will see that rising cohesion within our political parties and intensified and increasingly bitter competition between them is making it more difficult when there is divided government to achieve the kinds of cooperation needed to allow our political system to address the most important problems facing the nation today. We saw some of this in our opening story.

The American Two-Party System

9.2 Distinguish American political parties from parties in other democracies

The United States comes closer to having a "pure" **two-party system** than any other nation in the world. Most Western democracies have **multiparty systems**. In the United States, however, two parties have dominated the political scene since 1836, and the Democrats and the Republicans have controlled the presidency and Congress since 1860. As eminent political party scholar Marjorie Randon Hershey shows in Table 9.1, there have only been five major parties in the history of the United States, that is, parties that have led at least one of the branches of the national government at one time or another. Minor or third parties have rarely polled a significant percentage of the popular vote in either presidential or congressional

TABLE 9.1 MAJOR POLITICAL PARTIES IN AMERICAN HISTORY

1. **The Federalist Party, 1788–1816.** The champion of the new Constitution and strong national government, it was the first American political institution to resemble a political party, although it was not a full-fledged party. Its strength was rooted in the Northeast and the Atlantic Seaboard, where it attracted the support of shopkeepers, manufacturers, financiers, landowners, and other established families of wealth and status. Limited by its narrow electoral base, it soon fell before the success of the Democratic-Republicans.

2. **The Democratic-Republican Party, 1800–1832.** Many of its leaders had been strong proponents of the Constitution but opposed the extreme nationalism of the Federalists. This was a party of the small farmers, workers, and less privileged citizens, plus southern planters, who preferred the authority of the state governments and opposed centralizing power in the national government. Like its leader, Thomas Jefferson, it shared many of the ideals of the French Revolution, especially the extension of the right to vote and the notion of direct popular self-government.

3. **The Democratic Party, 1832–Present.** Growing out of the Jacksonian wing of the Democratic-Republicans, it was the first really broad-based, popular party in the United States. On behalf of a coalition of less-privileged voters it opposed such business-friendly policies as national banking and high tariffs. It also welcomed the new immigrants (and sought their votes) and opposed nativist (anti-immigrant) sentiment.

4. **The Whig Party, 1834–1856.** This party, too, had roots in the old Democratic-Republican Party, but in the Clay–Adams faction and in opposition to the Jacksonians. Its greatest leaders, Henry Clay and Daniel Webster, stood for legislative supremacy and protested the strong presidency of Andrew Jackson. For its short life, the Whig Party was an unstable coalition of many interests, among them nativism, property, and business and commerce.

5. **The Republican Party, 1854–Present.** Born as the Civil War approached, this was the party of northern opposition to slavery and its spread to the new territories. Therefore it was also the party of the Union, the North, Lincoln, the freeing of slaves, victory in the Civil War, and the imposition of Reconstruction on the South. From the Whigs it also inherited a concern for business and industrial expansion.

Source: Hershey, Marjorie R. PARTY POLITICS IN AMERICA, 14th Ed., c 2011, p. 15. Reprinted and Electronically reproduced by permission of Pearson Education, Inc., Upper Saddle River, New Jersey.

Which Party Governs Better?

When asked which party governs better, Americans are guided by partisanship—Democrats and Republicans each think government runs better when their party is in charge. Even so, general dissatisfaction with both major parties is substantial, and many Americans believe that a third party option is needed in the United States.

Your Level of Trust Depends on Your Party

Does the United States Need a Third Party?

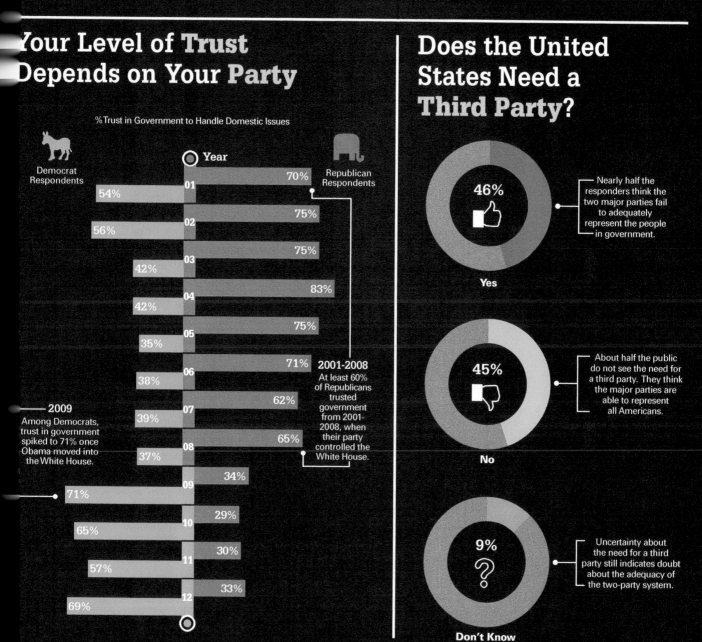

% Trust in Government to Handle Domestic Issues

Democrat Respondents

Republican Respondents

Year

Year	Democrat	Republican
01	54%	70%
02	56%	75%
03	42%	75%
04	42%	83%
05	35%	75%
06	38%	71%
07	39%	62%
08	37%	65%
09	71%	34%
10	65%	29%
11	57%	30%
12	69%	33%

2009
Among Democrats, trust in government spiked to 71% once Obama moved into the White House.

2001-2008
At least 60% of Republicans trusted government from 2001-2008, when their party controlled the White House.

46% Yes — Nearly half the responders think the two major parties fail to adequately represent the people in government.

45% No — About half the public do not see the need for a third party. They think the major parties are able to represent all Americans.

9% Don't Know — Uncertainty about the need for a third party still indicates doubt about the adequacy of the two-party system.

SOURCE: Data from Gallup.

Investigate Further

Concept How do we measure which party governs better? Survey research allows us to track public opinion on party performance on certain issues. Historically, when it comes to trusting government, partisans trust their party to govern, but not the other. Partisanship is the lens through which voters evaluate and determine trust of parties and government.

Connection Which party do Americans think governs better? Voters think *their* party governs better. Democrats think we are governed better when Democrats rule. Republicans think the same when Republicans rule. The parties represent different governing philosophies, so each party has a different definition of what it means to "govern better."

Cause When do third parties become viable? Third parties become viable when major parties fail on divisive issues that matter to the public, like the economy or racial issues. Third parties emerge to address those issues and often capture a lot of support. However, the third party is usually absorbed by a major party that co-opts their issues and supporters.

proportional representation
The awarding of legislative seats to political parties to reflect the proportion of the popular vote each party receives.

elections (more will be said later about third parties), although they are sometimes successful at the state and local levels. Jesse Ventura, for example, a former professional wrestler, was elected governor of Minnesota in 1998 as the nominee of the Reform Party.

☐ Why a Two-Party System?

Why are we so different from other countries? Why do we have only two major parties? There are several reasons.

ELECTORAL RULES The kinds of rules that organize elections help determine what kind of party system exists.[12] Which rules are chosen, then, have important consequences for a nation's politics.

Proportional Representation Most other democratic nations use some form of **proportional representation** (PR) to elect their representatives. In PR systems, each party is represented in the legislature in rough proportion to the percentage of the popular vote it receives in an election. In a perfect PR system, a party winning 40 percent of the vote would get 40 seats in a 100-seat legislative body, a party winning 22 percent of the vote would get 22 seats, and so on. In such a system, even very small parties would have a reason to maintain their separate identities because no matter how narrow their appeal, they would win seats as long as they could win a proportion of the popular vote. Voters with strong views on an issue or with strong ideological outlooks could vote for a party that closely represented their views. A vote for a small party would not be wasted, because it would ultimately be translated into legislative seats and, perhaps, a place in the governing coalition.

Israel and the Netherlands come closest to having pure PR systems, organized on a national basis; most Western European nations depart in various ways from the pure form. Most, for instance, vote for slates of party candidates within multimember electoral districts, apportioning seats in each district according to each party's percentage of the vote. In Germany, seats in the Bundestag (the lower house of the national parliament) are filled by a combination of elections from single-member districts and a party's share of the nationwide vote. Most democracies that use proportional representation also have a minimum threshold (often 5 percent) below which no seats are awarded to a party. Ten parties ran in the Norwegian elections in 2009, for example, with five of them passing the minimum threshold to win parliamentary seats.

Winner-Take-All, Plurality Election, Single-Member Districts Elections in the United States are organized on a winner-take-all, single-member-district basis. Each electoral district in the United States—whether it is an urban ward, a county, a congressional district, or a state—elects only one person to a given office and does so on the basis of whoever wins the *most* votes (not necessarily a majority). This is why our way of electing leaders is sometimes called a "first past the post" system, analogous to a horse race. This arrangement creates a powerful incentive for parties to coalesce and for voters to concentrate their attention on two big parties. The two-party outcome of plurality elections in single-member-district voting systems is often called Duverger's Law after the French political scientist who first discovered and systematically examined the relationship.[13] Here is how it works.

From the vantage point of party organizations, this type of election discourages minor-party efforts because failure to come in first in the voting leaves a party with no representation at all. Leaders of such parties are tempted to merge with a major party. Also, a disaffected faction within a party is unlikely to strike out on its own because the probability of gaining political office is very low. Thus, Tea Party candidates in 2010 ran as Republicans.

From the voter's point of view, a single-member, winner-take-all election means that a vote for a minor party is wasted. People who vote for a minor party may feel good, but most voters have few illusions that such votes will translate into representation and so are not inclined to cast them.

IT'S ALL ABOUT THE ELECTORAL COLLEGE

The winner of the presidential election is the candidate who receives a majority of Electoral College votes, not the candidate who wins the most popular votes. Here two workers fill in the winner of each state on a U.S. map drawn on the ice rink at Rockefeller Center in New York as 2008 election night results are tallied. Why is the Electoral College method preferable to a majority popular vote? Or is it?

Note that the most important office in American government, the presidency, is elected in what is, in effect, a single-district (the nation), winner-take-all election. The candidate who wins a majority of the nation's votes in the Electoral College wins the presidency. A party cannot win a share of the presidency; it is all or nothing. In parliamentary systems, the executive power is lodged in a cabinet, however, where several parties may be represented.

RESTRICTIONS ON MINOR PARTIES Once a party system is in place, the dominant parties often establish rules that make it difficult for other parties to get on the ballot.[14] A number of formidable legal obstacles stand in the way of third parties and independent candidates in the United States. While many of these restrictions have been eased because of successful court challenges by recent minor-party and independent presidential candidates such as Ross Perot, the path to the ballot remains tortuous in many states, where a considerable number of signatures are required to get on the ballot. Moreover, the requirements for ballot access are different in every state. While the two main parties, with party organizations in place in each of the states and well-heeled national party committees, are able to navigate this legal patchwork, new and small parties find it quite difficult.

The federal government's partial funding of presidential campaigns has made the situation of third parties even more difficult. Major-party candidates automatically qualify for federal funding once they are nominated. Minor-party candidates must attract a minimum of 5 percent of the votes cast in the general election to be eligible for public funding, and they are not reimbursed until after the election. In recent decades, only the Reform Party among the legion of minor parties has managed to cross the threshold to qualify for federal funding. Because the Green Party's candidate, Ralph Nader, won only 2.7 percent of the national vote in the 2000 election, it was not eligible for federal funding for the 2004 election, something that hobbled its candidate.

realignment

The process by which one party supplants another as the dominant party in a two-party political system.

David Cobb, the Green Party's presidential candidate in 2004, hardly registered at the polls, winning about 0.1 percent of the vote.

The Role of Minor Parties in the Two-Party System

Minor parties have played a less important role in the United States than in virtually any other democratic nation, and have become even less important.[15] In our entire history, only a single minor party (the Republicans) has managed to replace one of the major parties. Only six (not including the Republicans) have been able to win even 10 percent of the popular vote in a presidential election, and only seven have managed to win a single state in a presidential election.

Minor parties have come in a number of forms:

- *Protest parties* sometimes arise as part of a social movement. The Populist Party, for instance, grew out of the western and southern farm protest movements in the late nineteenth century. The Green Party was an offshoot of the environmental and antiglobalization movements.

- *Ideological parties* are organized around coherent sets of ideas. The several Socialist parties have been of this sort, as has the Libertarian Party. The Green Party ran in the 2000 elections on an anticorporate, antiglobalization platform.

- *Single-issue parties* are barely distinguishable from advocacy groups. What makes them different is their decision to run candidates for office. The Prohibition Party and the Free-Soil Party fall into this category, as did Perot's "balanced budget" Reform Party in 1996.

- *Splinter parties* form when a faction in one of the two major parties bolts to run its own candidate or candidates. An example is the Bull Moose Progressive Party of Teddy Roosevelt, formed after Roosevelt split with Republican Party regulars in 1912.

Minor parties do a number of things in American politics. Sometimes they articulate new ideas that are eventually taken over by one or both major parties. Ross Perot's popular crusade for a balanced budget during his 1992 campaign helped nudge the major parties toward a budget agreement that, for a while, eliminated annual deficits in the federal budget. The success of the Tea Party in primaries and local elections leading up to 2010—the Tea Party was less a third party than a large faction within the Republican Party[16]—pushed the already strongly conservative Republican Party establishment in an even more conservative direction after 2010. One result was even less cooperation with President Obama and congressional Democrats in 2011 and 2012 than before.

It is also the case that third parties can sometimes change the outcome of presidential contests by changing the outcome of the electoral vote contest in the various states: in 1992, a substantial portion of the Perot vote was comprised of people who otherwise would have voted Republican, allowing Bill Clinton to win enough states to beat George H. W. Bush; in 2000, a substantial portion of the Nader vote in Florida was composed of people who otherwise would have voted Democratic, allowing George W. Bush to win Florida's electoral votes and the presidency over Al Gore.

Shifts in the American Two-Party System

While the United States has had a two-party system for most of its history, it is important to point out that the system has not been static. Scholars have identified a number of party eras in the United States, each different in one or more important ways from the others. Some scholars have developed a fairly elaborate theory of party **realignment** in which a party dominates American politics for periods lasting between 30 and 40 years, then gives way to the other major party during a short realigning period as voting coalitions in the country change around.[17] There are good reasons to be skeptical of a theory of realignment that posits decades of stability interspersed by sudden changes; recent history, for example, shows an entirely different pattern of change.[18] Nevertheless, there seem to have been identifiable party eras over the course of our history. We show seven such periods in American history in Figure 9.1, though we only examine the last three in this book.

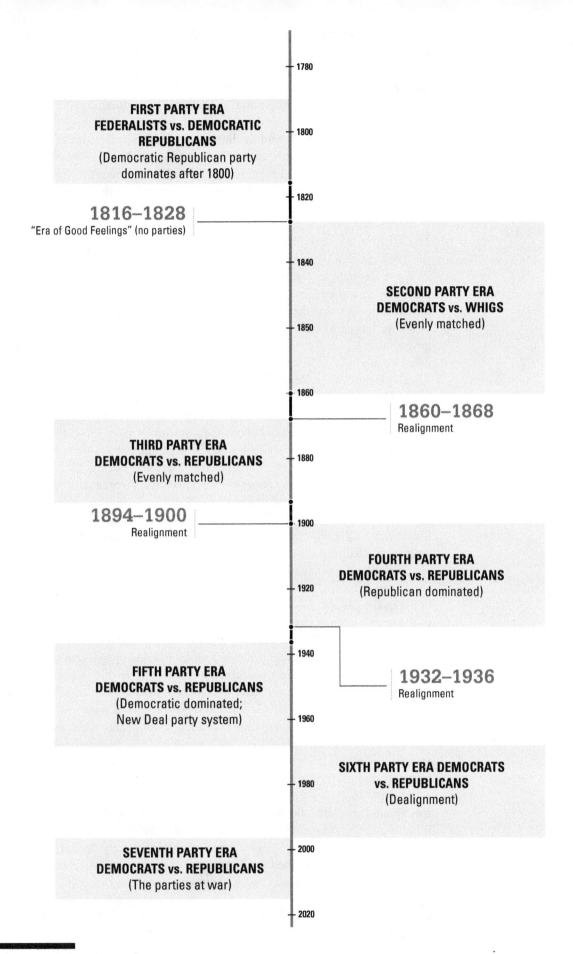

FIGURE 9.1 TIMELINE: PARTY ERAS IN THE UNITED STATES

American politics has been characterized by a series of relatively stable political party eras punctuated by periods of transition—some sudden, others much more drawn out—from one party era to another.

9.1

New Deal

The programs of the administration of President Franklin D. Roosevelt.

9.2

New Deal coalition

The informal electoral alliance of working-class ethnic groups, Catholics, Jews, urban dwellers, racial minorities, and the South that was the basis of the Democratic party dominance of American politics from the New Deal to the early 1970s.

9.3

divided government

Control of the executive and legislative branches by different political parties.

dealignment

A gradual reduction in the dominance of one political party without another party supplanting it.

THE NEW DEAL PARTY ERA The Great Depression, the **New Deal**, and the leadership of President Franklin D. Roosevelt ushered in a long period of Democratic Party dominance. From 1932 through 1964, the Democrats won seven of nine presidential elections, controlled the Senate and the House of Representatives for all but four years, and prevailed in a substantial majority of governorships and state legislatures across the nation. Democratic dominance was built on an alliance of workers, Catholics, Jews, unionists, small- and medium-sized farmers, urban dwellers, white ethnics, southerners, and blacks that came to be known as the **New Deal coalition**. The New Deal coalition supported an expansion of federal government powers and responsibilities, particularly in the areas of old-age assistance, aid for the poor, encouragement of unionization, subsidies for agriculture, and regulation of business.

THE DEALIGNMENT ERA The New Deal coalition began to slowly disintegrate in the 1968 election (won by Republican Richard Nixon) and finally collapsed in 1980 with the Republican capture of the presidency and the Senate.[19] The change in the party system was triggered by three major developments. First, strong support by the Democratic Party for the civil rights revolution—which brought new antidiscrimination laws, busing to achieve school integration, and, eventually, minority set-asides for government jobs and contracts and affirmative action programs in higher education—caused many white southerners and blue-collar workers to switch their loyalties from the Democrats to the Republicans, even while African Americans became more loyal to the Democrats.[20] Second, the tendency of the Democrats to openly welcome feminists, gay men, and lesbians and support their bid for equal rights, as well as the growing identification of Democrats with the doctrine of strict separation of church and state, caused religious conservatives to abandon the party. Third, perceived Democratic Party opposition to the Vietnam War, especially during the Nixon years (1969 through 1973), caused many Americans who favored a strong national defense and an aggressive foreign policy to drift away as well.

After 1980, the pace of Democratic decline began to pick up, with Democrats losing their big advantage in control of governorships and state legislatures, as well as in party identification among the electorate (see Figure 9.5 toward the end of this chapter). They also began to lose control in Congress, first in the Senate and then the House after the 1994 elections. The period was characterized by growing parity between the parties and the existence of **divided government**—one party in control of the presidency and the other with a majority in at least the House or Senate (sometimes both). Divided government was also typical in the states, where Democrats and Republicans divided the governor's office and one or two chambers of state legislatures. Because each party contained a small wing within it open to cooperation with the other party—conservative Democrats, mainly from the South, and liberal Republicans, mainly from the Atlantic and New England states—a certain degree of bipartisanship was possible, especially on foreign and defense policies.[21]

The transition from the New Deal party era to the dealignment era was not the same as the classic party realignments of 1896 and 1932 in which a party era dominated by one party was replaced in rather short order by an era dominated by the other party. In this case, while the dominant Democratic Party lost its overall lead, the Republican Party did not emerge as the unchallenged, across-the-board leader in politics and governance. Nor did very many additional Americans call themselves Republicans. This form of change in which a dominant party declines without another taking its place often is called **dealignment**,[22] though not all American politics scholars think this concept explains much about why party eras come and go.[23]

THE PARTIES AT WAR ERA We have taken the liberty of proposing in this book the emergence of a seventh party era in the mid-1990s that we call the "parties at war" era. The exact date it started is hard to pin down. But two developments are particularly important. First, there was the historic victory for Republicans in the congressional elections of 1994 in which they gained control of both houses of Congress for the first time since 1946, with much of the credit going to a unified conservative surge led

FDR ADDS TO HIS COALITION

The wealthy and patrician Franklin D. Roosevelt attracted a wide range of common people to his Democratic Party, including industrial workers, poor farmers, and farm laborers. Here he talks with Georgia farmers during his campaign for the presidency in 1932. How did a man of wealth and privilege become so popular among America's working class?

by Republican House leader Newt Gingrich (R–GA) and supported by an array of conservative think tanks, media, and advocacy groups. Second, there was the successful effort by House Republicans to impeach Democratic president Bill Clinton in 1998 and a close vote along party lines in the Senate in early 1999 that fell just short of removing him from office—despite Democratic gains in the 1998 congressional elections and large majorities among the public saying they opposed these actions.

By the time of the historic and disputed 2000 Bush–Gore presidential election, the new era was solidly in place. National elections from then on would be fought by two well-funded and ideologically unified parties. The central electoral strategy of the parties increasingly focused on using emotional appeals to turn out one's own party base voters on Election Day as the first priority, gaining just enough independents to tip the balance. Adding to the partisan warfare was the fact that election outcomes (with the exception of 2006) in state and national races became extremely close, with Democratic and Republican votes on a national basis closely divided, and control of the House, the Senate, and the presidency seemingly hanging in the balance at every election.[24] In the governing process, bipartisanship largely absented the scene, as we showed in the chapter-opening story; consultations across the aisles in Congress and between the president and Congress during periods of divided government became rare. Compromise with the other party came to be seen as traitorous, so wedded were the parties to core policy positions. Underlying it all has been a fundamental settling in of a new electoral geography defined by the shift of the South to the Republicans and the Northeast and coastal West to the Democrats (see the "Mapping American Politics" feature on this shift).

Interestingly, the party polarization may be more an elite affair than a reflection of polarization of views in the mass electorate, according to one leading scholar. That is to say, while party office holders, activists, and advocacy groups associated with each party have become more internally unified and partisan, the public at large remains fairly moderate or middle-of-the-road on most issues that deeply divide the parties from one another.[25] Be that as it may, elections and governing are now characterized by partisan warfare at nearly every turn.

PARTISANSHIP AT THE BOILING POINT

Republican members of Congress show their displeasure with President Barack Obama during his State of the Union address to the nation in January 2010. Representative Joe Wilson of South Carolina, in the center of the photo, shocked much of the country when he shouted out "you lie" during one part of the speech, demonstrating the poisonous level of party division that has long prevailed in Washington. Does this heightened partisanship serve some useful purpose in our system of government or does it make successful self-government less likely.

The Democratic and Republican Parties Today

9.3 Compare and contrast today's Republican and Democratic parties

hough our two major parties, the Republican Party and the Democratic Party, remain more decentralized and free-wheeling than parties in other rich democracies, each has become much more organized and ideologically cohesive than has traditionally been the case in American politics.

☐ The Parties as Organizations

The Republican and Democratic parties are not organizations in the usual sense of the term, but rather loose collections of local and state parties, campaign committees, candidates and office holders, and associated interest and advocacy groups that get together every four years to nominate a presidential candidate. Unlike a corporation, a bureaucratic agency, a military organization, or even a political party in most other countries, the official leaders of the major American parties cannot issue orders that get passed down a chain of command. Even popular, charismatic, and skillful presidents, including George Washington, Abraham Lincoln, Woodrow Wilson, Franklin Roosevelt, Harry Truman, John Kennedy, and Ronald Reagan, have had nearly as much trouble controlling the many diverse and independent groups and individuals within their own parties as they have had dealing with the opposition. George W. Bush discovered this in his second term when a significant number of Republican members of the House and Senate, loyal followers throughout his first term, abandoned him on his plans for a pathway to citizenship for many undocumented immigrants.

PARTY MEMBERSHIP The ill-defined nature of Republican and Democratic party membership is another indicator of how different American political parties are from political parties in other countries, as well as from private organizations. What does it mean, in fact, to be a Republican or a Democrat in the United States? Americans do not join parties in the sense of paying dues and receiving a membership card. To Americans, being a member of a party may mean voting most of the time for the candidate of a party or choosing to become a candidate of one of them. Or it may mean voting in a party primary. Or it may mean contributing money to, or otherwise helping in, a local, state, or national campaign of one of the party candidates. Or it may just mean generally preferring one party over another most of the time. These are loose criteria for membership, to say the least—looser than for virtually any other organization that might be imagined.

However, membership in the sense of feeling closer to and identifying with one party or another—what political scientists call **party identification**—has proved to be a very powerful thing indeed. A majority of Americans say they identify with or lean towards one of the two major parties. Party identification is important on a number of accounts. Most importantly, what party one identifies with and how strongly one holds that identification shapes how a person feels about a wide range of public issues, how likely that person is to vote, and which candidates the person votes for. (Party identification is addressed in greater depth later in this chapter.)

Among party identifiers one can identify groups of people who are especially strong supporters of the party and its candidates at all levels. Each party has a set of core supporters—often called the party base[26]—upon which it can count for votes, campaign contributions, and activists to advance the fortunes of the parties and their candidates for elected office.[27] The strongest Republican supporters may be found among whites (particularly in the South and Rocky Mountain West), conservative Christians and the most religiously committed (those who express a belief in God and say they regularly attend religious services) among all denominations, businesspeople (whether small business owners or top executives in large corporations), economic

party identification
The sense of belonging to one or another political party.

YET ANOTHER CONSERVATIVE ALTERNATIVE
Many conservatives were disappointed during the Republican presidential nomination contest that Mitt Romney remained the front-runner from the first. They supported a series of conservative alternatives, including Michelle Bachmann, Herman Cain, Newt Gingrich, and, finally Rick Santorum (shown here), before rallying behind Romney when none proved successful.

Mapping American Politics

The Shifting Geography of the Parties

Introduction

The centers of strength of each of the major political parties changed during the last half century. In 1960 the Democrats tended to dominate in the southern states and in the industrial states of the Middle Atlantic and upper Midwest, while Republicans were particularly strong in parts of New England, the Great Plains, the Mountain West, and the Pacific Coast. Until 2004, the Plains and Mountain West states (other than Colorado) had become more reliably Republican, and the South moved solidly into the Republican column. At the same time, the Pacific Coast and New England became more reliably Democratic. In the 2008 election, Barack Obama's big victory can be attributed to his success in former Republican or battleground states, including Colorado, New Mexico, Iowa, Indiana, Ohio, Virginia, North Carolina, and Florida.

Because of population shifts, moreover, the distribution of electoral votes has shifted among the states over time, changing the calculations of those who plan and wage presidential campaigns.

Mapping Party Electoral Votes

The states in the three cartograms are sized in proportion to their electoral votes in presidential elections and colored by whether they cast their electoral votes for Democrats (blue) or Republicans (red) in 1960, 2004, and 2008. Because each state's electoral votes are the total of their representatives and senators in Congress, they are roughly proportional to the size of their populations. We can see at least three important things in the cartograms. First, between 1960 and 2006, electoral votes of the Middle Atlantic states, New England, and the upper

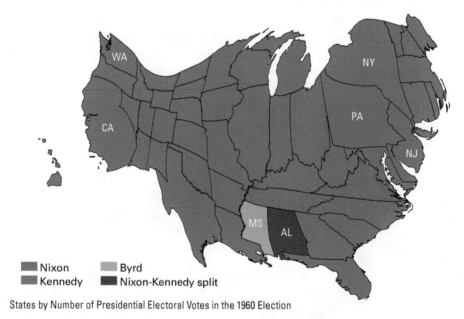

Nixon · Byrd · Kennedy · Nixon-Kennedy split

States by Number of Presidential Electoral Votes in the 1960 Election

Source: Election data are from historical tables, U.S. Bureau of the Census, Statistical Abstract of the United States, 2010.

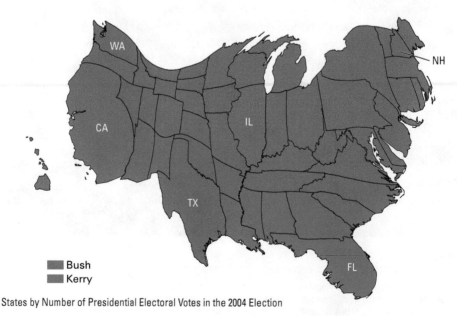

Bush · Kerry

States by Number of Presidential Electoral Votes in the 2004 Election

Source: Election data are from historical tables, U.S. Bureau of the Census, Statistical Abstract of the United States, 2010.

(*Continued*)

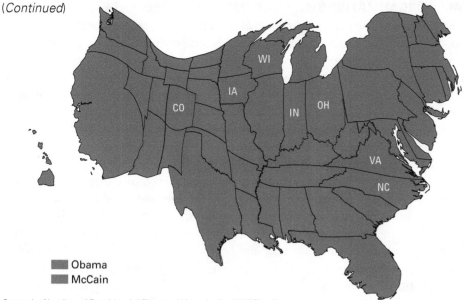

■ Obama
■ McCain

States by Number of Presidential Electoral Votes in the 2008 Election

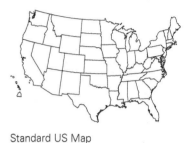

Standard US Map

Source: Election data are from historical tables, U.S. Bureau of the Census, *Statistical Abstract of the United States*, 2010.

Midwest decreased while they increased in California, the Southwest, and the South, reflecting the shift in the populations of the states over this time period. Second, the states that came together to elect Democrats John F. Kennedy in 1960 and Barack Obama in 2008 were quite different, although there is some overlap. These changes have changed the strategies of the parties. The Democrats today could pretty much count on winning California, Washington, Illinois, the New England states, New York, and New Jersey; Republicans can count on the South outside of Florida and the Southwest, Mountain West, and Plains states. The remaining states—often called battleground states—are where presidential campaigns recently have been waged and where presidential elections are now won and lost.

What Do You Think?

Why does it make sense to elect presidents by electoral votes rather than direct popular vote when so many states are safe for one party or the other? Some critics argue that having so many noncompetitive states in the Electoral College, with the bulk of the electioneering going on in the handful of states where the outcome is in doubt, deprives the majority of Americans of being fully engaged in the process of electing the president. How would you support this argument? How would you dispute it?

MAP NOTE: In 1960, Mississippi electoral votes were cast for Harry Byrd, an independent candidate. Alabama split its 11 electoral votes: 6 for Kennedy and 5 for Nixon.

SOURCE: Election data are from historical tables, U.S. Bureau of the Census, *Statistical Abstract of the United States*, 2010.

and social conservatives, people in rural areas, and those with the highest incomes. The strongest Democratic supporters may be found among African Americans, Jews, non-Cuban Hispanics, people who are secular in belief, people with postgraduate degrees, union households, economic and social liberals, people living on the West Coast and the Northeast, and lower-income people. Democrats find strong support, as well, among teachers and other government employees at the local, state, and national levels, and people living in university towns and science and technology research centers such as the Silicon Valley (stretching from San Jose to San Francisco), Austin, Seattle, Boulder, the Research Triangle area in North Carolina, and the Route 128 economic corridor around Boston and Cambridge.[28]

Increasingly in recent years, Republicans and Democrats have tried to win elections by first mobilizing these core supporters—in a process often called "rallying the base"—by focusing on issues and symbolic gestures that will bring them to the polls, then trying to win a majority among those voters not automatically predisposed to one party or the other (Catholics are a good example of such a swing vote, as are self-identified independents). In a situation where Republican and Democratic core supporters are about equal in strength, winning even a small majority among these less partisan groups while mobilizing one's own partisans is the key to winning elections. Issue and ideological appeals are important in these efforts.

PARTY ORGANIZATIONS AS CANDIDATE-CENTERED Unlike a traditional organization and unlike political parties in other democracies, the various elements of the Democratic and Republican parties are relatively independent from one another and act in concert not on the basis of orders, but on the basis of shared interests, sentiment, ideology, fund-raising, and the desire to win elections,[29] which can be quite powerful coordinators of party activities, to be sure. (See Figure 9.2 for a graphical representation of these ideas.) Most important, perhaps, the official party organizations do not control the nomination of candidates running under the party label—their most vital political role—or the flow of money that funds electoral campaigns or the behavior of their office holders once elected. This was apparent in 2010 and 2012 when Tea Party candidates enjoyed great success in wresting the Republican nominations for congressional and gubernatorial seats away from candidates favored by party leaders. In the past, party candidates were usually nominated in district, state, and national conventions, where party regulars played a major role. They are now almost exclusively nominated in primaries or grassroots caucuses in the states, where the party organizations help but do not run the show. Nomination comes to those who are best able to raise money, gain access to the media, form their own campaign organizations, and win the support of powerful interest and advocacy groups (such as the National Rifle Association in the GOP and the National Education Association in the Democratic Party). To a very large extent, Democratic and Republican party organizations are there to help candidates in these efforts, not order them about.[30] They have become, in effect, campaign machines in the service of candidates running for elected office.[31] It is because of this that many commentators have come to describe American political parties as being "candidate-centered."[32] Party presidential nominees who go on to win the office in the November elections often reward supporters and contributors by appointing them to positions in the executive branch. (Sometimes these appointees are not up to the task; see the "Can Government Do Anything Well?" feature.)

THE PARTY CONVENTIONS The national party conventions are the governing bodies of the parties. Convention delegates meet every four years not only to nominate presidential and vice presidential candidates but also to write a party platform and revise party rules.

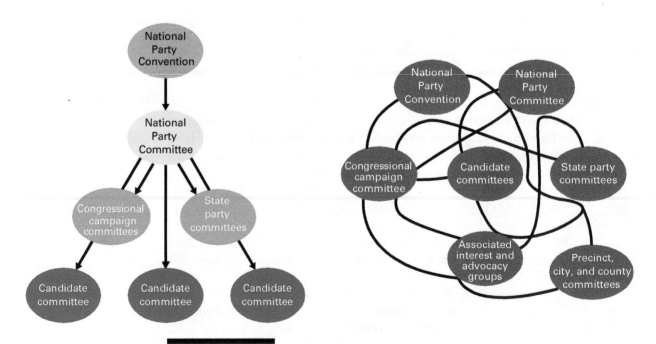

FIGURE 9.2 POLITICAL PARTY ORGANIZATION IN THE UNITED STATES

The graphic on the left shows a hypothetical organizational chart of the Republican and Democratic parties as if they were structured hierarchically like many other organizations you are familiar with. It would be a mistake, however, to think of our national parties this way. The drawing on the right, which depicts our national parties as network or web-like organizations, where there is neither central authority nor a chain of command, is closer to reality. The ties between elements of the parties include money, ideology, sentiment, and common interests.

Can Government Do Anything Well?

FEMA and disaster relief

Democrats and Republicans each have their favored agencies in the executive branch in which to hide party activists and financial contributors who want a position in the administration but bring with them few qualifications. They tend to be agencies for which the party in power has little respect or regard. For the Democrats, the Commerce Department has traditionally been that place. For Republican president George W. Bush, the Federal Emergency Management Agency, which merged into the Department of Homeland Security in 2003, was one of the favored destinations. To head that agency, he placed Michael Brown, a lawyer from Enid, Oklahoma, and the commissioner of the International Arabian Horse Association, who had had no emergency management or relief experience other than a stint in the White House on a committee planning assistance to New York City following the 9/11 attacks. This ill prepared him for handling coordination of the relief and recovery effort following Hurricane Katrina that devastated New Orleans and a long stretch of the Gulf Coast in Louisiana and Mississippi.

FEMA was created in 1979 and is responsible for coordinating relief efforts with state and local first responders and authorities and for mobilizing and delivering resources that are beyond what is available on the ground in the immediate aftermath of a disaster. FEMA has had a checkered history. It failed miserably, by all accounts, in responding to the Loma Prieta, California, earthquake in 1989 (one California member of Congress concluded that FEMA "could screw up a two-car parade"), Hurricane Hugo in Puerto Rico that same year, and Hurricane Andrew in Florida in 1992 (failed to appear for three days, late with supplies and field hospitals, botched coordination of relief efforts, and more). With 10 times the number of political appointees as the average federal agency, FEMA was headed by political contributors and activists, not emergency relief specialists. After Congress threatened to eliminate FEMA and gave it a clearer mission and set of guidelines, the newly elected president Bill Clinton, a believer in an activist government run by highly qualified people, cleaned house and filled top positions with experienced disaster relief people from other federal agencies and from several states. The transformation was almost immediate, with the agency receiving high marks for its responses in 1993 to a series of floods in the Midwest and the Oklahoma City bombing. The agency performed well for the remainder of the 1990s. After the 2000 election, however, FEMA again became a place to put people who had supported a party that believed a strong federal government was not such a good thing.

Support for the claim that government can and should play a significant role in disaster relief through FEMA:

- FEMA performance during the presidency of Bill Clinton suggests that committed and talented leadership of the agency can make it a valuable participant in the emergency response to human-made and natural disasters.

- FEMA can only do its job, however, if properly funded and its mission redirected to immediate relief only, leaving long-term recovery to other federal agencies and state and local authorities.

- The agency needs to be led by people who are professionally trained in and have experience in emergency relief.

- Proper leadership of the agency, adequate resources, and clarity of mission are only possible if the president, Congress, and the people pay attention to it on a continuous basis rather than treat it as an afterthought until disaster strikes.

Rejection of the claim that government can and should play a significant role in disaster relief through FEMA:

- FEMA's long history of botched emergency responses shows that the federal government cannot do this job properly.

- Presidents are increasingly prone to issue FEMA emergency declarations, with President Obama on a near-record pace; this is done more for political reasons than for addressing real emergencies and strains FEMA capacities.

- Because disasters vary so much from community to community and because local authorities and citizens best know what needs to be done in particular places, emergency relief should be decentralized to states and localities; there is no need for federal government involvement except for topping up money and supplies as needed.

- Dependence on FEMA allows states and localities to skimp on their own emergency relief preparations; elimination of FEMA would force states and localities to build emergency preparation capabilities.

WHAT DO YOU THINK?

What do you think about the past, present, and future role of the federal government in disaster relief through agencies such as FEMA?

- The government should play a *big* role in the immediate response to disasters through agencies such as FEMA, but to function properly, these agencies need increased funding and adequate leadership.
- The government should play *some* role in the immediate response to disasters through agencies such as FEMA, mostly offering logistical support for state and local efforts and other aid as requested.
- There is no need for the federal government to play a role in disaster relief and recovery. This should be a state and local responsibility, possibly in partnership with the private sector.

How would you defend your position to a fellow student? What would be your main line of argument? What evidence do you believe best supports your position?

Additional sources for this feature: Daniel Franklin, "The FEMA Phoenix: Reform of the Federal Emergency Management Agency," *The Washington Monthly* (July/August, 1995), pp. 14–17; "Report on FEMA Performance During the Hurricane Katrina Disaster," (Washington, D.C.: Government Accounting Office, 2006).

Although the national convention is the formal governing body of each of the parties, it cannot dictate to party candidates or party organizations at other levels of jurisdiction. The presidential nominee need not adhere to either the letter or the spirit of the party platform, for instance, although most nominees stay fairly close to the platform most of the time (usually because the winning candidate's supporters control the platform-writing committee). State and local party organizations may nominate whomever they choose to run for public office and may or may not support key planks in the national party's platform.

NATIONAL PARTY COMMITTEES The Democratic and Republican national committees conduct the business of the parties during the four years between national conventions. The national committees are made up of elected committeemen and committee women from each of the states, a sizable staff, and a chairperson, but they rarely meet. The real business of the committee is run by the party chair, assisted by the committee staff. The chair exercises little power when a president from the party is in office, because the party chair is compelled to take direction from the White House. When the opposition controls the presidency, the party chair exercises more influence in party affairs, although the extent of that power is still not very great.

Although the national committees have little direct power, they have become increasingly important as campaign service organizations for party candidates running for national and state offices.[33] In addition to substantial financial contributions to candidate campaign organizations, they do a wide variety of things to help. Out of their Washington, D.C., in-house TV and radio studios come attack ads aimed at the other party and its candidates, tailored to the particular district or state in which the ads will be used. Other ads extol the sponsoring party and its achievements. Direct mail campaigns are mounted to disseminate information and party positions on the issues and to make appeals for campaign contributions, increasingly using sophisticated data-mining techniques to allow very narrow targeting of messages to different groups of people.[34] News releases are prepared for the media, as are campaign-oriented sound and video bites to be used as news clips on local radio and television. Each party also produces training courses for potential candidates, complete with "how-to" manuals and videos. Each has a website where people can access information about the party, get news about the nefarious behavior of the opposition, and make monetary contributions to the party and party candidates. And, they funnel campaign money to state and local party organizations, with the bulk going to states where competition between the parties is closest.[35]

To carry out these activities, both the Republican and Democratic national committees have steadily increased the number of employees in their national offices, especially in the areas of finance, advertising, information technology, campaign planning, and video specialist and support personnel, and they have expanded their budgets to carry out an ever-broader range of campaign activities for party candidates. Each of the national committees has become a highly professional campaign organization, filled with highly skilled people able to provide party candidates with what they need to wage first-rate electoral campaigns.

CONGRESSIONAL CAMPAIGN COMMITTEES Almost as old as the national party committees, but entirely independent of them, are the four congressional campaign committees—Republican and Democratic, for the House and for the Senate—that aid members of Congress in their campaigns for reelection. They help raise money, provide media services (e.g., making short videotapes of the members of Congress for local television news shows), conduct research, and do whatever else the party members in Congress deem appropriate. Increasingly, these committees have turned their attention to identifying and encouraging quality party candidates in districts and states where competition between the parties is close. Rahm Emanuel (D–IL), later President Obama's chief of staff, and currently mayor of Chicago, did this particularly well during the 2005–2006 elections cycle when he was head of the Democratic House Campaign Committee; many gave him the main credit for the Democrats' retaking the House in the 2006 elections.[36] These committees are controlled by the party members in Congress, not the party chair, the national committees, or even the president. Much as with the national committees, the congressional campaign committees have become highly professional and well funded.[37]

STATE PARTY ORGANIZATIONS As expected in a federal system, separate political party organizations exist in each of the states. Although tied together by bonds of ideology, sentiment, and campaign money and constrained in what they can do according to rules set by the national party committees and conventions—rules on how and when to choose delegates to the national convention, for example—the state party organizations are relatively independent of one another and of the national party.

ASSOCIATED INTEREST AND ADVOCACY GROUPS Although not technically part of the formal party organizations, some groups are so closely involved in the affairs of the parties that it is hard to draw a line between them and the political parties.[38] Some have even argued that networks of conservative organizations such as American Crossroads (founded by Karl Rove), the American Action Network, and Americans for Prosperity (backed by the energy billionaire Koch brothers) have taken over much of the role of the Republican National Committee with regard to fund-raising, campaign messaging, and recruiting new party candidates.[39] Organized labor has had a similar relationship with the Democratic Party since the Great Depression and the New Deal.

The main effect of the rise of advocacy groups in recent years has been to push the parties and their candidates into more ideological and partisan directions. MoveOn .org, for example, and liberal blogs such as the Daily Kos, and Demos, funded by George Soros, push Democrats to be more assertive in opposing Republicans, offering a more liberal policy agenda, and pushing the candidacy of people they favor. Republican advocacy groups, talk radio hosts such as Rush Limbaugh, and conservative blogs push the party and its candidates to oppose abortion and more open borders for immigrants and to favor tax cuts and fewer government regulations. We look at the issue of ideology in the parties in more detail in the next section.

☐ Party Ideologies

Ideology may be understood as a coherently organized set of beliefs about the fundamental nature of a good society and the role government ought to play in achieving it. Because the Republican and Democratic parties have traditionally organized themselves as fairly broad coalitions, seeking to attract as many voters as possible in order to prevail in winner-take-all, single-member-district elections, there always have been

liberal

The political position, combining both economic and social dimensions, that holds that the federal government has a substantial role to play in providing economic justice and opportunity, regulating business in the public interest, overcoming racial discrimination, protecting abortion rights, and ensuring the equal treatment of gays and lesbians.

conservative

The political position, combining both economic and social dimensions, that holds that the federal government ought to play a very small role in economic regulation, social welfare, and overcoming racial inequality, that abortion should be illegal, and that family values and law and order should guide public policies.

strong pressures on them to tone down matters of ideology.[40] However, each party also has a core of loyal supporters and party activists, such as delegates to the party convention and caucus attendees, contributors to election campaigns, and closely allied advocacy groups, who are more ideologically oriented than the general public (34 percent of whom call themselves independents).[41] Each party, moreover, has a stable core set of voters from groups concerned about particular issues and problems and committed to particular government policies. The result is a party system composed of parties with significant and growing ideological and policy unity within them and differences between them.[42] One veteran observer even claims that today, "Political leaders on both sides now feel a relentless pressure for party discipline and intellectual conformity more common in parliamentary systems than through most of American history,"[43] (see the "Using the Framework" feature to see how greater ideological cohesion and discipline have affected party behavior in Congress).

While Americans of all political stripes hold a range of core beliefs about free enterprise, individualism, the Constitution, and the Bill of Rights, the differences between Democrats and Republicans are becoming clearer every day. The Republican Party tends to endorse positions held by social and economic conservatives; for example, opposing abortion and same-sex marriage and regulating business, higher taxes, and generous social safety nets. The Democratic Party tends to endorse positions held by social and economic liberals; for example, supporting a strong government role in guiding the economy, protecting the environment, and providing civil rights protections for ethnic and racial minority groups and gays and lesbians. Ideological and policy differences between the Democrats and Republicans are becoming so marked, and the tendency of the Republicans to become a more internally cohesive conservative party is so pronounced, that a number of observers now talk about the "Europeanization" of the American party system.[44] Pressure from Tea Party activists on candidates for nominations in the Republican Party in 2010 and 2012 helped make the GOP even more conservative than it had been. For example, Senator Orrin Hatch (R-UT), perhaps sensing the same fate for himself as that which befell his long-time colleague and fellow conservative Robert Bennett who was defeated by a Tea Party-backed candidate in his bid for his party's senatorial nomination in Utah in 2010, began to vote even more consistently conservative in the Senate. In 2010 and 2011, Hatch average a score of 99.5 from the conservative advocacy group Club for Growth, well above his lifetime score of 78 awarded to him previously by that group. For his part, Mitt Romney, a fairly moderate Republican for most of his career, took on a much more conservative ideological hue in the course of gaining the GOP's presidential nomination in 2012, repudiating his previous positions on issues such as immigration, health insurance mandates, and affirmative action.

Let's see how ideological and policies differences manifest themselves in our political parties.

IDEOLOGY AND PARTY IN PUBLIC PERCEPTIONS For one thing, the Democratic and Republican parties differ in the electorate's perceptions of them; 79 percent of Americans, for example, report that they see the parties as different on a whole range of issues, up from 64 percent in 2004.[45] Most accurately see the Democrats as the more **liberal** party (in the sense of favoring an active federal government; helping citizens with jobs, education, and medical care; supporting a woman's right to choose; and protecting civil rights) and the Republicans as the more **conservative** party (opposing such government activism, supporting business, and opposing abortion and same-sex marriage) (See Figure 9.3).[46] Democrats, moreover, are much more likely to say they are liberals; Republicans are much more likely than others to say they are conservative.[47] Additionally, those Americans who classify themselves as liberals overwhelmingly support Democratic candidates; self-described conservatives overwhelmingly support Republicans. In 2008, for example, 90 percent of self-identified Republicans voted for John McCain for president, while 89 percent of Democrats voted for Barack Obama. This association of liberalism with the Democrats and conservatism with the Republicans is growing stronger all the time, with the gap in outlooks between the two parties growing ever larger.[48]

Using the FRAMEWORK

How did Republicans manage to pass so many laws with such small majorities after they came to power in 2001?

Background: In the 1990s, official Washington seemed to grind to a screeching halt. Divided government was the rule. Not only was major legislation tough to come by, but partisan warfare between a Republican-dominated Congress and a Democratic president (Clinton) led to a budget crisis that twice closed the federal government (except for essential services) and to the impeachment of Bill Clinton on a straight party-line vote in the House. After the disputed election of George W. Bush in 2000, however, new bills were passed with a fair degree of regularity despite very slim majorities for Republicans in Congress: three different tax cuts, No Child Left Behind, a new prescription drug benefit under Medicare, creation of the Department of Homeland Security, the USA Patriot Act, restrictions on class-action lawsuits, the Energy Policy Act of 2005, the Bankruptcy Act of 2005, and the Sarbanes-Oxley Act regulating corporate accounting practices. Taking a look at how structural, political linkage, and governmental factors affect policymaking in Washington will help explain the changed situation from 2001 through 2005.

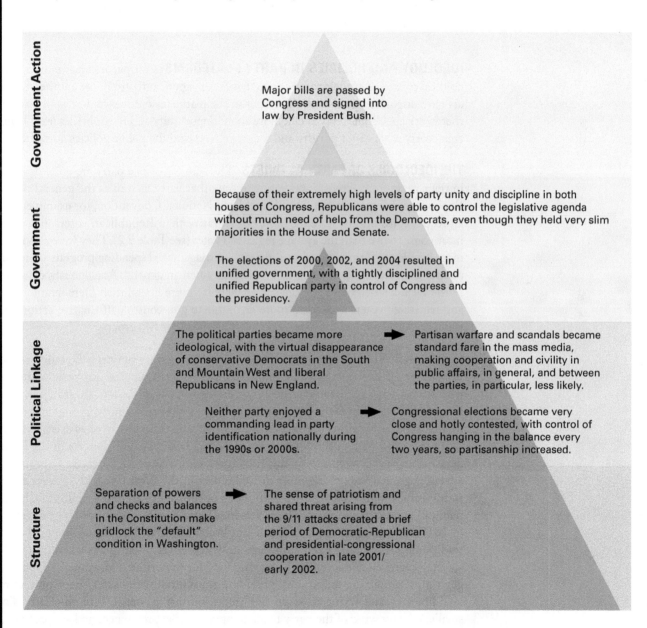

Government Action

Major bills are passed by Congress and signed into law by President Bush.

Government

Because of their extremely high levels of party unity and discipline in both houses of Congress, Republicans were able to control the legislative agenda without much need of help from the Democrats, even though they held very slim majorities in the House and Senate.

The elections of 2000, 2002, and 2004 resulted in unified government, with a tightly disciplined and unified Republican party in control of Congress and the presidency.

Political Linkage

The political parties became more ideological, with the virtual disappearance of conservative Democrats in the South and Mountain West and liberal Republicans in New England.

Partisan warfare and scandals became standard fare in the mass media, making cooperation and civility in public affairs, in general, and between the parties, in particular, less likely.

Neither party enjoyed a commanding lead in party identification nationally during the 1990s or 2000s.

Congressional elections became very close and hotly contested, with control of Congress hanging in the balance every two years, so partisanship increased.

Structure

Separation of powers and checks and balances in the Constitution make gridlock the "default" condition in Washington.

The sense of patriotism and shared threat arising from the 9/11 attacks created a brief period of Democratic-Republican and presidential-congressional cooperation in late 2001/ early 2002.

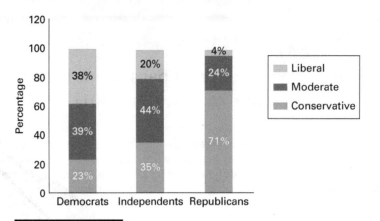

FIGURE 9.3 PARTY IDENTIFICATION AND IDEOLOGY, 2011

Party identification and political ideology go hand in hand, something that has not always been the case in the United States. In 2011, Democrats were overwhelmingly liberal. Among Republicans, only a tiny percentage of their identifiers called themselves liberal. Not surprisingly, perhaps, a majority of independents—the largest group among Americans—defined its ideology as moderate.

Source: The Gallup Poll, June 7, 2011.

IDEOLOGY AND POLICIES IN PARTY PLATFORMS Our parties also tend to write political platforms at their conventions that differ significantly from one another. Scholars have discovered persistent differences in the platforms of the two parties in terms of rhetoric (Republicans tend to talk more about opportunity and freedom), issues (Democrats worry more about poverty and social welfare), and the public policies advocated.[49]

THE IDEOLOGIES OF PARTY ACTIVISTS The activists of one party are quite different in their views from activists and voters in the other party, as well as the general public. Republican delegates to the 2012 Republican National Convention, for example, as in all recent conventions, were far more conservative than Republican voters and much more conservative than the average registered voter (see Table 9.2). They were also much more hostile to affirmative action, same-sex marriage, social spending programs, and gun control than Republican voters and registered voters in general. Analogously, delegates to the Democratic National Convention were far more liberal than Democratic voters and registered voters and much more favorable to gun control, affirmative action, gay rights, and a woman's right to an abortion than the other two groups.[50]

DIVISIONS WITHIN THE PARTIES While differences between Democrats and Republicans have become more pronounced, and while ideological and policy cohesion within the parties has been increasing, especially in the GOP, there are still important disagreements within each of the parties.[51] There is not perfect unity, as one might have found in the past within communist and socialist parties, let us say, or as exists today in Islamist parties, such as the Muslim Brotherhood in Egypt. The division in the Democratic Party is between a very liberal wing—found among Democratic activists and advocacy groups and among most office holders in the West Coast and northeastern states—and a more "centrist" wing—typified by moderates elected in traditionally Republican areas such as senators Ben Nelson (D–NE)—who announced his retirement in 2011—Max Baucus (D–MT), and Jim Webb (D–VA). The liberal wing supports traditional Democratic Party programs in which government plays a central role in societal improvement, leveling the playing field for minorities and women, supporting gay rights, protecting union jobs, providing substantial social safety nets, protecting civil liberties, and trying to avoid the use of military power in foreign affairs. The smaller centrist wing of the party tends to oppose racial preferences and support lower taxes, free trade, deregulation, a crackdown on crime, and a strong military supported by a large defense budget.

Fissures have existed for a long time in the Republican Party, with the fault lines most evident between economic and social conservatives, between, that is to say, those whose main priority is lower government spending, taxes, and regulations

TABLE 9.2 COMPARING DELEGATES TO THE 2008 NATIONAL PARTY CONVENTIONS WITH OTHER AMERICANS

	Delegates to Democratic National Convention	Democratic Voters	All Voters	Republican Voters	Delegates to Republican National Convention
Is it more important to provide **health care** coverage for all Americans or hold down taxes? (percent saying "health care")	94	90	67	40	7
Looking back, do you think the United States did the right thing in taking military action against **Iraq**, or should the U.S. have stayed out? (percent saying "right thing")	2	14	37	70	80
Should protecting the environment or developing new sources of **energy** be a higher priority for the government? (percent saying "environment")	25	30	21	9	3
Should **abortion** be generally available to those who want it, be available but under stricter limits than it is now, or should it not be permitted? (percent saying "should not be permitted")	3	16	24	37	43
Should **gay couples** be allowed to legally marry, be allowed to form civil unions but not legally marry, or should there be no legal recognition? (percent choosing "same-sex marriage")	55	49	34	11	6

Source: New York Times/CBS News poll, September 1, 2008.

pitted against those who most want to emphasize "family values" and religious belief. Among economic conservatives there is also evidence of a split between those who recognize that a long-term budget solution for the country must involve some revenue enhancements as well as cuts in government spending and those in the Tea Party wing who believe that cutting spending is paramount and that every weapon must be deployed to win that goal even if it means default on the public debt and a shutdown of the government.

Divisions are evident as well in the Democratic Party, particularly between the liberal base and the more moderate office holders. The liberal wing of the party, for example, was not happy with many actions and policies of President Obama that seemed to hug the middle of the public policy spectrum: continuing many Bush-era policies on bailouts and financial industry regulation; giving in to Republican congressional demands at almost every turn to cut government spending without much in the way of tax increases on top income groups in trade; failing to close the detainee facilities at Guantanamo Bay; and continuing the war in Iraq and escalating the one in Afghanistan.[52]

☐ The Parties in Government and in the Electorate

The Republican and Democratic parties exist not only as network-like organizations of candidates, activists, contributors, and interest and advocacy groups, but as a presence in government and in the electorate.

GOVERNMENT Fearful of the tyrannical possibilities of a vigorous government, the framers designed a system of government in which power is so fragmented and competitive that effectiveness is unlikely. One of the roles that political parties can play in a democracy such as ours is to overcome this deadlock by persuading officials of the same party in the different branches of government to cooperate with one another on the basis of party loyalty.[53] The constitutionally designed conflict between the

9.1

unified government
Control of the executive and legislative branches by the same political party.

9.2

gridlock
A situation in which things cannot get done in Washington, usually because of divided government.

9.3

president and Congress can be bridged, it has been argued, when there is **unified government**—when a single party controls both houses of Congress and the presidency—as the Democrats did during much of the 1960s and during Barack Obama's presidency in 2009 and 2010, and the Republicans did between 2001 and 2006 when George W. Bush was in office. When the parties are strong and unified, this bridging can occur even when a party controls the legislative branch with the tiniest of margins. (See "Using the Framework.") On the other hand, the existence of strong parties during periods of divided government, when Republicans and Democrats each control a branch of the federal government—as in 1995–2000 when Democrat Bill Clinton was president and the Republicans controlled both houses of Congress, and in 2011 and 2012 when Barack Obama was president and Republicans controlled the House—often leads to **gridlock**, when very little gets done.[54]

It matters a great deal whether Democrats or Republicans control the House, the Senate, and the presidency, because the two parties differ in what they do when they win control of government. Republican members of Congress tend to vote differently from Democrats; for example, the former are considerably more economically and socially conservative on domestic issues. This difference translates into public policy. Republicans and Democrats produce different policies on taxes, corporate regulation, abortion and stem cell research, and social welfare when they are in power.[55] It also matters whether a single party controls Congress and the presidency or whether control is divided between two parties not only for what bills become law but also for the composition of the federal judiciary and for what policies are implemented and what actions are taken by executive branch agencies. Consideration of the many complex issues associated with how political parties act in office and why it matters will be left to chapters later in this book that look in depth at the branches of the federal government.

THE ELECTORATE Parties are not only political organizations and sets of office holders in government, but also images in the minds of voters and potential voters—that is, mental cues that affect the behavior of the electorate. This aspect of the parties is called party identification. The distribution of party identification among the American people is important on a number of grounds. First, party identification helps determine people's political attitudes on a wide range of issues; for a majority of Americans, party identity is a stable and powerful shaper of one's overall political identity. People use the party label to help organize their thinking about politics: to guide them in voting, judging new policy proposals, and evaluating the government's performance.[56] Second, how the parties stand relative to one another in the affections of the American people has a lot to do with who wins elections and thereby determining which party controls the presidency, Congress, and, eventually, the federal courts. That distribution has changed over time and has affected what government does. (How party identification is measured by political scientists is shown in the "By the Numbers" feature.)

Beginning at the time of Roosevelt's highly popular New Deal in the 1930s and continuing to the late 1980s, the Democratic lead over Republicans among party identifiers was substantial, making them the majority party. At times their advantage was on the order of 35 percentage points. From the 1980s through the early 2000s, the Democrats gradually lost their big lead primarily because of the increasing number of Americans who say they are independent (see Figure 9.4). Since then, the Democratic identification lead over the Republicans has become much smaller. While the Democrats retain a small lead over Republicans, the parties are closer than they have been in a very long time among those Americans who identify with one or the other. Because they are so close, even very small swings from election to election in Democratic and Republican voting turnout and the parties' ability to attract independent "leaners" have had big effects on who wins and loses in presidential and congressional contests. Barack Obama's strong "get out the vote" effort among Democrats and independents helped him win big in the 2008 presidential election. Similar Republican efforts in 2010 led to huge GOP gains in Congress, governorships, and state legislative chambers across the country.

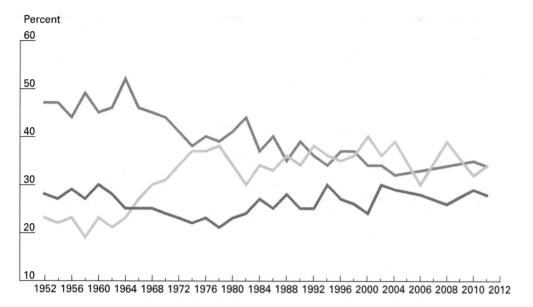

FIGURE 9.4 TRENDS IN PARTY IDENTIFICATION

The decades-long gap between the percentages of those who call themselves Democrats and those who call themselves Republicans has been getting smaller. This has happened because fewer Americans than in the 1950s were identifying as Democrats and more were identifying as independents. Interestingly, there has not been much change in the proportion of Americans who identify as Republicans over the years. If these trends continue, how might the landscape of American politics change?

Source: American National Election Studies (through 2008) and Pew Research Center (2010 and 2011).

While Democratic and Republican identifiers are moving farther apart on which policies they support, the distances are even greater between Democratic and Republican **active partisans**, those Republican and Democratic identifiers who not only vote but are engaged in other party, candidate, and party-support activities, such as making campaign contributions, attending candidate meetings, making phone calls for the parties and candidates, knocking on doors to get out the party vote, putting bumper stickers on their cars, and the like. Democratic active partisans are strongly liberal, with, for example, 78 percent supporting abortion, 70 percent supporting the use of diplomacy over force in international relations, and 70 percent favoring environmental protection over job protection. For their part, Republican active partisans are a near mirror image, reporting only 41 percent, 11 percent, and 24 percent approval, respectively, for these things.[57]

The proportion of people who say they are independents—including **leaners**, or those who say they are independents but lean fairly consistently to one party or another—has steadily increased, from the low 20s in the 1960s to the high 30s today (the remainder are respondents who choose "no preference" or "don't know"). Although some scholars maintain that these figures exaggerate the rise of independents because many leaners behave the same way as people who say they consider themselves Republicans or Democrats[58]—in 2009, 17 percent of independents said they leaned Democratic, while 12 percent leaned Republican[59]—there has clearly been a decline in the proportion of Americans who identify outright with either of the two major parties. Oddly, then, while a growing proportion of the American population is calling itself independent—though a large majority of Americans identify with one or the other of the two parties—views about public policies in the United States are becoming increasingly polarized along party lines, primarily because partisans vote more than independents and participate more in campaigns, electing more liberal Democrats and conservative Republicans and fewer moderates in either party. Independents tell journalists, pollsters, and scholars that they are fed up with the general nastiness in politics and government ineffectiveness that seems to be associated with the intensification of partisanship in the political life of the country.[60]

active partisans

People who identify with a party, vote in elections, and participate in additional party and party-candidate activities.

leaners

People who claim to be independents but consistently favor one party over another.

By the Numbers

Are you a Republican, a Democrat, or an independent?

One often hears people refer to themselves as a Republican or a Democrat or an independent. But what does that mean? Do people formally join a party organization? Do they fill out a paper or online form, pay annual membership dues, receive membership cards to slip into their wallets, and attend meetings with other members? Is it like joining, let us say, a labor union like the United Automobile Workers or the Screenwriters Guild? Is it like joining a service organization like the Rotary or a religious organization like the Knights of Columbus? Or is it like joining the Social Democratic Party in Germany, where people do, in fact, join the party organization? And where do independents go in the United States? Who do they join? These questions are, of course, rhetorical. To be a Republican or a Democrat or an independent for most people in the United States—except for people who are, let us say, employed by or do volunteer work for the Democratic or Republican National Committees—is really a matter of sentiment, about which party one identifies with most of the time.

Why It Matters

As you have learned in this chapter, one's party identification is very important in how one thinks about issues and decides who to vote for. Notice the directionality in this statement. There is growing evidence that people do not take on a party identification after assessing the issues and the candidates for elective office but the other way around: party identification does most of the shaping. Party identification matters not only because it influences the choices people make in politics but also because the distribution of party identifiers in the population is decisive in determining the outcome of elections and who controls the government. This is because party identifiers almost always vote for candidates with their preferred party's label. During times when Democratic identifiers enjoy strong pluralities—that is,

when there are substantially more Democratic identifiers than Republican ones or people who say they are independents—they dominate elective office. When self-declared independents lead the other categories and the proportions identifying with the two major parties are very close, elections are close and likely to go in unpredictable directions or switch from one election to the next given the "unanchored" status of independent voters.

Measuring Party Identification

Every major polling organization—whether commercial like Gallup, nonprofit like Pew, or academic/scholarly like the American National Election Study at the University of Michigan—asks people one form or another of the question: "Generally speaking, do you usually think of yourself as a Republican, Democrat, independent, or what?" (Pew); or "In politics, as of today, do you consider yourself a Republican, a Democrat, or an independent?" (Gallup). Typically, the polling organizations then ask people who have answered Republican or Democrat whether they consider themselves to be strong or weak Republicans and Democrats. Independents are asked if they generally lean toward one of the two major parties, or whether they tend to vote for candidates of one party or the other. These so-called leaners, according to some researchers, tend to vote for the candidates of a particular party almost as frequently as people who pick a party identification. Other researchers are not convinced.

What to Watch for

Pay attention in reports of whether Republicans or Democrats are in the lead in the country to how independents and leaners are counted. For example, in a report issued in 2011, Pew reported that Democrats were the biggest group at 47 percent, with Republicans a little ways back at 43 percent. In this report,

FIGURE 9.5 PARTY IDENTIFICATION IN THE UNITED STATES, 2011, BY THE PEW RESEARCH CENTER

Source: Pew Research Center

FIGURE 9.6 PARTY IDENTIFICATION IN THE UNITED STATES, 2011, BY THE GALLUP POLL

Source: Gallup Poll

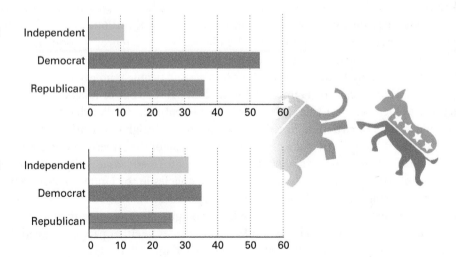

(Continued)

Pew put Democratic leaners into the Democratic camp and Republican leaners into the Republican side of the ledger, leaving only 10 percent as independents. The Gallup Poll, by contrast, in its 2011 report, put all independents together, whether pure or party leaners, so they come up with different numbers for Democrats and Republicans. They reported a bigger Democratic advantage over Republicans, with independents sharing the lead.

What Do You Think?

Do you identify with one party rather than the other? If so, are you a strong or weak partisan? Or do you consider yourself an independent? How do you think this identification affects how you think about the issues and who you vote for? What is your reaction to the fact that people so often respond to political developments in the context of the party they identify with? Why do people respond in this way?

SOURCE: L. Sandy Maisel, *American Political Parties and Elections* (New York: Oxford University Press, 2007).

Using the DEMOCRACY STANDARD

How do our major political parties affect democracy?

Democratic theorists, you will recall, believe that vigorous and healthy political parties are essential for democracy. They are essential because, in theory at least, they are among the principal political institutions that can make popular sovereignty and political equality a reality. They are able to do so—again, in theory—because they can help keep elected officials responsive and responsible to the broad public, stimulate interest and participation among ordinary Americans, include a broad range of groups from all economic and social levels of the population, simplify voter choices, and make government work for the people by overcoming the problems of democratic government created by the separation of powers and checks and balances. For all these reasons, of course, the framers looked askance at political parties and worried about their effects on republican government. They were not inclined to include all groups in the population in political life, they were certainly not interested in stimulating widespread interest and participation by ordinary Americans, and they most certainly were not in favor of an institution that might overcome the constraints on the national government they had created.

The framers might have rested a bit easier had they known that our political parties were never quite able to fulfill their democratic promise primarily because the constitutional system they created makes it hard for even unified parties, swept into power by electoral majorities, to get their way. In the Senate, for example, a unified minority party representing a minority of Americans (because each state gets two senators no matter the size of its population) can block important bills favored by the majority party. Still, our parties are the only mechanism we have for allowing voters to decide on a program for the government and to hold elected officials responsible in a collective sense, even if imperfectly. Interest groups and social movements are much too narrow in their outlooks and policy objectives, and voters have no control over what they do. Our parties are becoming better organized and more ideologically distinctive and clearer on the policy alternatives offered to the public, so voters increasingly know what they are getting when they put a party into office. However, the rise in the ideological coherence of the parties, potentially a boon to responsiveness and responsibility in government when a single party controls the presidency and Congress, adds to the possibilities of gridlock in periods of divided government, which are now quite common.

Review the Chapter

 Listen to **Chapter 9** on **MyPoliSciLab**

The Role of Political Parties in a Democracy

9.1 Evaluate the importance of political parties in democracies, p. 267

Theoretically, the electoral activities of political parties enable citizens to determine what the government does and to hold elected leaders accountable for achieving or failing to achieve what they promise.

Theoretically, some of the gridlock built into our constitutional system can be overcome when the same party controls more than one branch of government.

The American Two-Party System

9.2 Distinguish American political parties from parties in other democracies, p. 268

The American party system is unique among the Western democracies in that it is a relatively pure two-party system and has been so since the 1830s.

The American parties are candidate-centered, having very little power in their national party organizations to affect the behavior of individual candidates, office holders, or state and local party organizations.

American parties traditionally have been less unified internally and less ideologically coherent than parties in many other democracies, although partisanship between the parties and ideological coherence within the parties are becoming much more pronounced and politically important.

The Democratic and Republican Parties Today

9.3 Compare and contrast today's Republican and Democratic parties, p. 276

The Republican and Democratic parties differ from one another in the demographic groups that make up their electoral coalitions, the interest and advocacy groups that support them, and their stance on a wide range of public policies.

The parties are becoming more ideologically coherent; the GOP is increasingly conservative on social and economic issues while Democrats are increasingly liberal, though the Democrats have many more moderate supporters and elected officials than their Republican counterparts.

It matters a great deal which party is in power for the kinds of public policies that the federal government produces.

Learn the Terms

 Study and **Review** the **Flashcards**

partisan, p. 266
political party, p. 267
party platform, p. 267
two-party system, p. 268
multiparty system, p. 268
proportional representation, p. 270

realignment, p. 272
New Deal, p. 274
New Deal coalition, p. 274
divided government, p. 274
dealignment, p. 274
party identification, p. 277

liberal, p. 284
conservative, p. 284
unified government, p. 288
gridlock, p. 288
active partisan, p. 289
leaners, p. 289

Answer key begins on page T-1.

9.1 Evaluate the importance of political parties in democracies

1. Which factor listed below is NOT something political parties can do to make popular sovereignty and political equality possible:

   a. Keep elected officials responsible
   b. Discourage cooperation between parties
   c. Ensure accountability
   d. Stimulate political interest
   e. Help people make sense of politics

9.2 Distinguish American political parties from parties in other democracies

2. This slowly began to disintegrate in the 1968 election and finally collapsed in 1980 with the Republican capture of the presidency and the Senate.

   a. The New Deal Coalition
   b. The New Deal
   c. The Democratic Party
   d. The Independent Party
   e. The Reform Party

9.3 Compare and contrast today's Republican and Democratic parties

3. The Republican Party typically attracts supporters who fit into which of the following categories:

   a. People who have secular beliefs, union households, and those with lower incomes
   b. People who have secular beliefs, people with postgraduate degrees, and people in suburban areas
   c. White southerners, people with postgraduate degrees, and those with lower incomes
   d. Conservative Christians, people in rural areas, and those with the highest incomes
   e. Conservative Christians, people in suburban areas, and those with the highest incomes

Explore Further

INTERNET SOURCES

A Plain Blog About Politics **plainblogaboutpolitics.blogspot.com**
A blog on politics, but scholarly—active political scientists with links to other first-rate scholarly and journalist blogs of all persuasions.

Democratic National Committee **www.democrats.org**
Information about Democratic Party candidates, party history, convention and national committees, state parties, stands on the issues, affiliated groups, upcoming events, and more.

National Political Index **www.politicalindex.com**
Links to state and local parties and affiliated organizations and interest groups, as well as news and information about the parties.

Real Clear Politics **www.realclearpolitics.com**
News and commentary on American politics from a wide and diverse range of sources.

Project Vote Smart **www.votesmart.org**
A comprehensive collection of information on national and state party candidates and public officials, including biographies, voting records, and campaign finances.

Republican National Committee **www.rnc.org**
Information about Republican Party candidates, party history, convention and national committees, state parties, stands on the issues, affiliated groups, upcoming events, and more.

SUGGESTIONS FOR FURTHER READING

Black, Earl, and Merle Black. *Divided: The Ferocious Power Struggle in American Politics.* New York: Simon and Schuster, 2007.
The authors demonstrate the extent to which the regional bases of the two major parties have changed and why it happened.

Brownstein, Ronald. *The Second Civil War: How Extreme Partisanship Has Paralyzed Washington and Polarized America.* New York: Penguin Press, 2007.
A passionate chronicle of the growth of partisanship, the coarsening of public life, and our consequent inability, in the author's view, to tackle the nation's problems.

Gould, Lewis. *Grand Old Party: A History of the Republicans.* New York: Random House, 2003.
A comprehensive history of the Republican Party in the United States.

Hershey, Marjory. *Party Politics in America*, 14th ed. New York: Pearson Longman Publishers, 2011.
A leading textbook on political parties in the United States; comprehensive, detailed, yet engaging.

Maisel, L. Sandy. *American Political Parties and Elections: A Very Short Introduction.* New York: Oxford University Press, 2007.
The best short guide to American parties and elections.

Witcover, Jules. *Party of the People: A History of the Democrats.* New York: Random House, 2003.
A comprehensive history of the Democratic Party in the United States.

10

Voting, Campaigns, and Elections

BARACK OBAMA WINS A SECOND TERM

After an exhausting and expensive campaign, incumbent president Barack Obama scored a decisive electoral vote victory over Republican challenger Mitt Romney in the 2012 presidential election, winning by a margin of 332 to 206. The Obama-Biden ticket's victory in the national popular vote was narrower, though it prevailed over the Romney-Ryan ticket by almost 3 million votes, winning by a margin of 50 percent to 48. To forge this victory, Obama maintained the coalition that helped him win in 2008, and won virtually every battleground state that both campaigns had targeted.

President Obama's reelection victory was not a foregone conclusion. When Romney announced his candidacy in 2011, Obama seemed quite vulnerable. The United States was still mired in wars in Iraq and Afghanistan. The country's economy was in serious trouble—unemployment topped 9 percent, GDP growth was tepid, and the housing market remained in the doldrums. Additionally, the Gallup organization reported that fewer than 50 percent approved of the way President Obama was doing his job, and 74 percent thought the "country was on the wrong track." Romney's assumption was that focusing on the weak economy and the president's failure to improve it, would be sufficient to win the election. Adding to the Romney campaign's confidence was the belief that enthusiasm had waned for Obama among groups that had been central to his 2008 election winning coalition, and that turnout among these groups would be lower in 2012.

Republican operatives and the Romney campaign were wrong on almost all counts. Though it will take political scientists some period of time to more scientifically determine which factors played the key roles in Barack Obama's victory, a number of things seem fairly apparent at

10.1	10.2	10.3	10.4	10.5	10.6
Evaluate three models of how elections can lead to popular control, p. 298	Distinguish American elections from those in other countries, p. 301	Analyze the importance of political participation in elections, p. 304	Identify demographic factors that increase the likelihood of voting, p. 310	Outline the process of campaigns for the presidency and Congress, p. 315	Assess how presidential elections are decided, p. 328

CONTEMPLATING HIS SECOND TERM A solemn President Barack Obama waves to his enthusiastic supporters at McCormick Place in Chicago late on the evening of November 7 after his decisive electoral vote win over Republican Mitt Romney in the 2012 presidential election. His mood may have been tempered by the prospect of having to deal at the start of his second term with a Republican-dominated House of Representatives on a wide range of pressing issues.

MyPoliSciLab Video Series

The Big Picture America has a lower voting turnout than many other countries in the world. Author Edward S. Greenberg considers why this is, and argues that the various obstacles to voting contribute to one of the greatest inequalities in our democracy today.

The Basics Do you have trouble figuring out when all the elections are and who you should vote for? If you do, you are not alone. This video will help you understand why the United States has so many types of elections, what purposes they serve, and whether money and campaign staff is vital to campaign victories.

 Do you think money is important in elections?

In Context Discover how voter turnout has changed over the course of American history. Has enfranchising women, African Americans, or young people increased turnout? Columbia University political scientist Donald P. Green addresses these and other questions in this video.

Think Like a Political Scientist Why has the United States experienced a surge in voter turnout? Columbia University political scientist Donald P. Green analyzes voter turnout trends, and takes a look at how research conducted by political scientists on this subject has contributed to increased voter turnout.

In the Real World Not every citizen of the United States has a photo ID. Should everyone be required to have one when they vote? Real people discuss the issue of voter fraud, and whether it is a serious enough problem to warrant possibly disenfranchising a large segment of the population.

So What? How have elections changed in the United States over the last few years? Author Edward S. Greenberg lists some of the trends that students should look out for, including longer campaigns, increased concentration in America's "swing states," and unconventional forms of campaign financing.

this writing. First Barack Obama remained popular, even among those who did not think he was doing a good job on the economy. Moreover, though the Romney campaign believed that people would blame the president for the country's economic troubles, exit polls showed that Americans overwhelmingly blamed his predecessor George W. Bush. To make matters worse for Romney's prospects, the economy slowly improved in the months before the election, with evidence of private sector job growth, a fall in the unemployment rate below 8 percent, a boom in the auto sector and a surge in U.S. exports. The upshot was an increase in the president's job approval to about 50 percent in the weeks before the election, a rise in consumer confidence to a three-year high and a twenty point decrease in the percentage of Americans thinking that the country was on the wrong track.[1]

Many Republican observers were predicting a landslide Romney victory based on the assumption that the 2008 Obama coalition would not hold and that voting turnout among its various groups would be dramatically lower in 2012. The Republicans were wrong. The young, urban dwellers, racial and ethnic minorities, and women, especially unmarried women, voted in high numbers and cast their ballots for the Obama-Biden ticket. For example, 93 percent of African Americans voted for Obama, as did 55 percent of women, 71 percent of Asian Americans, 71 percent of Hispanics, 69 percent of people in big cities, 60 percent of 18-29 year olds, 55 percent of people with post-graduate degrees, and 92 percent of Democrats. A number of actions by Republican office-holders and candidates seems to have driven Hispanics and women towards the Democrats. Many Hispanics were troubled by harsh anti-immigration measures passed in states that often brought legal immigrants and citizens of Hispanic ancestry into unwelcome contact with authorities. Further, during the Republican presidential primaries, the main contenders vied with one another to be the toughest on illegal immigrants, with Romney promising laws of such vigor that such people would "self export." Many women (not all, to be sure) were troubled by strong anti-abortion rhetoric and were shocked by the remarks of two Republican senate candidates who talked of "legitimate rape" and pregnancy following a rape as part of God's plan. While Obama fared well among those groups that will soon be the demographic majority in population, Romney did best among 45 and older white men without a college degree, a substantial group still, but a population on the decline. In the many post-mortems after the election, leading conservatives expressed grave concern about these trends.

Another factor in the election, though it is difficult to measure empirically, was the "ground game," the ability of the campaign organizations to identify supporters and get them to cast their votes. Observers agreed that the Obama team was much better at this than the Romney team. The Obama ground game was especially effective in the battleground states.

Thinking Critically About This Chapter

The story of the 2012 presidential election focuses our attention on the issue of democratic control of the national government through the electoral process and on the degree to which the public participates in this key activity of the representative democratic process.

Using the Framework

You will see in this chapter that elections are affected by the different rates of participation of groups in American society and how structural factors such as constitutional rules, unequal access to resources, and cultural ideas help determine why some groups participate more than others. You will also learn how elections affect the behavior of public officials.

Using the Democracy Standard

We suggest in this chapter that elections are the lynchpin of any discussion about the democratic quality of any system of government because they are, in theory, what makes popular sovereignty possible. You will see in this chapter that while elections in the United States do much to make our system democratic, they fall short of their democratic promise.

| 10.1 |
| 10.2 |
| 10.3 |
| 10.4 |
| 10.5 |
| 10.6 |

responsible party
The notion that a political party will take clear and distinct stands on the issues and enact them as policy once elected to office.

prospective voting model
A theory of democratic elections in which voters decide what government will do in the near future by choosing one or another responsible party.

Elections and Democracy

lections are fundamental to democratic politics, the chief means by which citizens control what their government does. Many important struggles for democracy in the United States have involved conflicts over the right to vote. But can elections actually ensure that governments will do what their people want?

Democratic theorists have suggested several ways that elections in a two-party system like that found in the United States can bring about popular control of government. We will briefly discuss three of these ways, indicating how they might work in theory.[2] The remainder of this chapter is concerned with what actually happens in American national elections and with the question of whether these elections really bring about popular control of government.

☐ The Prospective (or Responsible Party) Voting Model

The idea of **responsible party** elections is based on the old commonsense notion that elections should present a "real choice": political parties should stand for different policies, the voters should choose between them, and the winning party should carry out its mandate. Political scientists call this the **prospective voting model**, meaning that voters are interested in and capable of deciding what government will do in the future.

THEORY   For this system to work perfectly, each of the two parties must be cohesive and unified; each must take clear policy positions that differ significantly from the other party's positions; citizens must accurately perceive these positions and vote on the basis of them; and the winning party, when it takes office, must do exactly what it said it would do. It is in this sense—that parties stand for something and have the wherewithal and willingness to follow through once in power—that the model also is called the responsible party model. If all these conditions are met, then the party with the more popular policy positions will win and enact its program. In such an electoral system, government will do what the majority of the voters want.[3]

POTENTIAL PROBLEMS   One potential problem of elections fought by responsible parties is that it might increase the frequency and intensity of political conflicts in the country. If each party in such a system stands for ideologies and policies different from the other party, feels duty-bound to put promises into effect on attaining power, and has the means to do so, there would be no need for the victorious party to reach compromises with the losing party, even if it won by a razor-thin margin. The party in power can make the policies it wants, disregarding the objections of the losing party. The high stakes involved in winning and losing elections in such a system would make campaigns and elections very heated.

Others have pointed out that while responsible parties might make choices at the ballot box easier for voters, in a system of separation of powers and federalism, it is likely to lead to gridlock—a situation in which government cannot function very well because the different branches of government are controlled by different parties that are not prone to compromise with one another. It is quite common, for example, for Congress to be controlled by one party and the presidency by another (something that cannot happen in a parliamentary system) and, if the parties controlling them disagree clearly and fundamentally, then it's hard to get things done.[4] This is what happened several times in the late 1990s when a Republican-controlled Congress and Democratic President Bill Clinton could not agree on the budget, forcing parts of the government to shut down. The frequency of these types of events is likely to increase if our parties become more responsible, as seems to be happening.[5] We saw this in 2011 in the partisan warfare over raising the debt ceiling and the near-default on its debts by the United States.

Another potential problem for the model is when the voters choose a party to solve one set of problems but the party, on assuming office, carries out policies that, while consistent with those of its most ardent ideological supporters, are not what the voters expected. An example might be what followed the 2010 state-level elections swept by the Republicans because of voters' concerns, according to polls, about the dreadful state of the economy. In control of state houses and governorships in many places, the GOP focused their legislative efforts on rolling back illegal immigration, abortions, and the power of public and private sector unions.

The Electoral Competition Voting Model

A very different, and less obvious, sort of democratic control can be found in what political scientists call the **electoral competition model** of democratic elections. In this sort of electoral model, unified parties compete for votes by taking the *most popular* positions they can. They do so by trying to take positions that will appeal to the voter at the exact midpoint of the political spectrum, the so-called **median voter**. Both parties are therefore likely to end up standing for the *same* policies: those favored by the most voters.

THEORY Scholars have proved mathematically that if citizens' preferences are organized along a single dimension (such as the liberal–conservative continuum shown in Figure 10.1), and if parties are simply vote-seeking entities—that is, they have no particular ideological preferences—both parties will take positions exactly at the *median* of public opinion, that is, at the point where exactly one-half the voters are more liberal and one-half are more conservative. If either party took a position even a bit away from the median, the other party could easily win more votes by taking a position closer to the median.[6]

If electoral competition drives parties together in this way, and if they keep their promises, then, in theory, it should not matter which party wins; the winner enacts the policies that the most voters want. Democracy is ensured by the hidden hand of competition, much as efficiency is ensured by competitive markets, according to standard economic theory.

POTENTIAL PROBLEMS Again, however, the conditions for this electoral model to work perfectly are not likely to be met in the real world. Electoral competition ensures democratic control only if the parties are unified and take stands on the issues for pure

electoral competition model
A form of election in which parties seeking votes move toward the median voter or the center of the political spectrum.

median voter
The voter at the exact middle of the political issue spectrum.

10.1
10.2
10.3
10.4
10.5
10.6

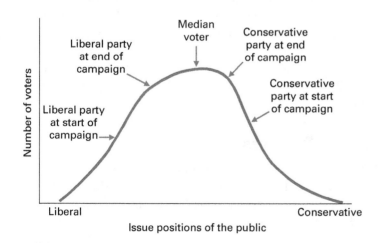

FIGURE 10.1 ELECTORAL COMPETITION MODEL
This model suggests that in the interest of winning the election, parties will move toward the median voter (where most votes are to be found) as the campaign progresses.

10.1

10.2

10.3

10.4

10.5

10.6

electoral reward and punishment
The tendency to vote for incumbents when times are good and against them when times are bad; same as retrospective voting.

retrospective voting
A form of election in which voters look back at the performance of a party in power and cast ballots on the basis of how well it did in office.

and direct vote-seeking reasons; it can break down if the parties are fragmented or ambiguous, if they care about policies for ideological reasons rather than for reasons of securing the most votes, or if they seek contributors' dollars rather than citizens' votes. Moreover, in this model, the voters must consider nothing but the policy stands of the parties (e.g., not being distracted by candidates' personalities or images) and must know exactly where the parties stand. And the parties have to keep their promises. There are reasons to doubt that any of these things will happen flawlessly.[7] Some political scientists are coming to believe, moreover, that it is not politicians and party officials who are in charge of what parties do—moving to where the median voter resides—but activists who care more about ideology and public policies than about winning the next election.[8] If this is true, then the entire basis of the median voter model is undermined.

Still, we will see that these conditions are close enough to the truth so that electoral competition does work, to a significant extent, in real elections. Indeed, electoral competition is probably one of the main ways that elected officials are influenced by public opinion.

The Retrospective (or Reward and Punishment) Voting Model

A third process by which elections might bring about democratic control of government is **electoral reward and punishment**, a form of election in which voters judge how well a group in power has governed and decide if they want this group to continue in office.

THEORY Here the idea is that the voters simply make **retrospective**, backward-looking judgments about how well incumbent officials have done in the past, rewarding success with reelection and punishing failure by throwing the incumbents out. The result, in theory, is that politicians who want to stay in office have strong incentives to bring about peace and prosperity and to solve problems that the American people want solved. Politicians' ambitions force them to anticipate what the public wants and to accomplish it.[9] The reward-and-punishment process of democratic control has the advantage of simplicity. It requires very little of voters: no elaborate policy preferences, no study of campaign platforms, just judgments of how well or how badly things have been going. Voters seem to have punished Republicans in 2008 in such a way, expressing their displeasure with George W. Bush over the wars in Iraq and Afghanistan and a collapsed economy.[10]

POTENTIAL PROBLEMS However, reward and punishment may be a rather blunt instrument. It gets rid of bad political leaders only after (not before) disasters happen, without guaranteeing that the next leaders will be any better. It relies on politicians *anticipating* the effects of future policies, which they cannot always do successfully. Moreover, the reward-and-punishment process focuses only on the most prominent issues and may leave room for unpopular policies on matters that are less visible. It may also encourage politicians to produce deceptively happy but temporary results that arrive just in time for Election Day and then fade away.

Imperfect Electoral Democracy

We will see that each of the three processes of democratic control we have discussed exists, to some extent, in American elections. On occasion, even, the three processes converge and help produce an election that is enormously consequential for the direction of the nation. The 1932 election was one of these occasions and is described in the "Using the Framework" feature.

But none of the three processes works well enough to guarantee perfectly democratic outcomes most of the time. In certain respects, they conflict: responsible parties and electoral competition, for example, tend to push in opposite directions. In other respects, all three processes require similar conditions that are not met in reality.

For example, none of the three can ensure government responsiveness to all citizens unless *all* citizens have the right to vote and exercise that right. Unfortunately, tens of millions of Americans cannot or do not go to the polls. Their voices are not heard; political equality is not achieved.

Another problem with our system of elections was brought to public attention by the chaos and uncertainty of the disputed 2000 presidential election in Florida: not all ballots cast by voters are actually counted. For a variety of reasons, ranging from lack of voter education to confusing ballot layouts and malfunctioning voting machines, a number of ballots in every election in the United States are disqualified and not included in the final vote tally. A study commissioned by Congress on the 2000 election estimated that from 4 to 6 million votes of the roughly 100 million cast nationally were not counted, with the votes of poor people and members of racial minorities three times more likely than those of other Americans to be uncounted in the 2000 election.[11]

provisional ballot
A vote that is cast but not counted until determination is made that the voter is properly registered.

The Unique Nature of American Elections

10.2 Distinguish American elections from those in other countries

American elections differ quite dramatically from those of most other democratic countries. The differences are the result of rules—mainly found in the Constitution but also in federal statutes and judicial decisions—that define offices and tell how elections are to be conducted. Here are the distinguishing features of elections in the United States:

ELECTIONS ARE NUMEROUS AND FREQUENT In some sense, we are "election happy" in the United States. We not only elect the president and members of Congress (senators and representatives), but also, being a federal system, we elect governors, state legislators, and (in most states) judges. In addition, state constitutions allow autonomy for counties, cities, and towns, and all of their top officials are elected by the people. All in all, we fill about 500,000 offices through elections.[12] We also elect school boards in most places, and the top positions in special districts (e.g., water or conservation districts). And then there are the many state and local ballot initiatives that add to the length and complexity of the ballot at election time. No other country holds so many elections, covering so many offices and public policy issues.

ELECTIONS ARE SEPARATE AND INDEPENDENT FROM ONE ANOTHER Not only do we have a multitude of elections, but the election to fill each particular office is separate and independent from the others. In parliamentary systems, one votes for a party, and the party that wins a majority gets to appoint a whole range of other officials. The majority party in the British parliament (the legislative branch), for example, chooses the prime minister and cabinet ministers (the executive branch), who run the government. The government, in turn, appoints officials to many posts that are filled by elections here. In the United States, the president and members of Congress are elected independently from one another, as are governors, state legislators, mayors of cities, city council members, and school boards.

INCONSISTENT ELECTION PROCEDURES AND VOTE-COUNTING With very few exceptions—such as the 1965 Voting Rights Act to protect the rights of African American voters and the 2002 law allowing the use of **provisional ballots** when voter registration issues arise on election day—the federal government plays no role in regulating and overseeing elections. This mainly is the role of states that, in most cases, further decentralize the process by lodging the management of elections in the hands of county officials.

Using the FRAMEWORK

Do elections matter? Has an election ever fundamentally changed the course of American government?

Background: Occasionally in American history, a national election is so consequential that it alters the overall direction of government policy and the role of government in the United States. The election of Franklin Delano Roosevelt and an overwhelmingly Democratic Congress in the 1932 elections was just such a moment. In the first 100 days of his administration, Roosevelt launched his New Deal, convincing Congress to pass bills to regulate the banking and securities industries, to bail out failing banks and protect the deposits of the public, to launch public works and relief efforts, and to provide price supports for farmers. This revolution in the role of the federal government was made possible by the 1932 elections, but to fully understand what happened, structural, political linkage, and governmental factors have to be taken into account.

Government Action

Major emergency and reform legislation is passed beginning in early 1933, launching the New Deal.

Government

Franklin Roosevelt interpreted the 1932 election as a mandate for immediate and far-reaching actions by the federal government to meet the crisis of the Great Depression. → Roosevelt mobilized business and labor leaders, as well as the public, behind his emergency program. → The Democratic-controlled Congress, aware of Roosevelt's enormous popularity, and concerned about the national crisis, passed all the president's emergency measures.

Political Linkage

Public opinion strongly supported a greater role for the federal government in fighting the depression. → Social disorder was widespread, leading to concerns that the country was near the point of collapse. → Social movements that demanded government action were growing and making their presence felt. → Democrats won big majorities in the House and the Senate in 1932. → Roosevelt won an overwhelming victory in the 1932 presidential election, tallying 472 electoral votes to Hoover's 59.

Structure

The 1932 election was held in the midst of the Great Depression, with unemployment reaching 33 percent, bank failures at an all-time high, and industrial and farm production at 50 percent of their levels in the mid-1920s. → The preamble to the Constitution says that the Constitution was intended to create a government that would "...insure Domestic tranquility...[and]...promote the general Welfare."

The result is wide variation across the country in voter registration rules, how absentee and early ballots are handled and counted, what types of election devices are used (paper ballots, either counted by hand or scanned, computerized touch screen systems, and more), when and how recounts are done, and how election disputes are resolved.[13]

ELECTED POSITIONS HAVE FIXED TERMS OF OFFICE The office of president of the United States is fixed at four years, representatives serve for two years, and senators for six. At the state level, terms of office for all important elected positions are fixed, whether for governors or legislators. The same holds true for county, city, and town elected offices. In parliamentary systems, the government can call an election at any time within a certain number of years (in Britain, it is five years), timing the election to maximize chances for reelection. One implication of fixed elections in the United States is that presidents cannot call for new elections in hopes of changing the party mix in Congress to their advantage. It also means that an unpopular president can stay in office until the next election, because there is no method to remove him other than by impeachment and trial. In parliamentary systems, elections customarily are held when the majority party or majority coalition in parliament loses support among its members, shown in a defeat on a major `bill proposed by the government (the prime minister and cabinet) or on a "vote of confidence" called by the opposition. Governments deemed not up to the task of rescuing their countries from impending financial collapse were replaced in both Greece and Italy during the European debt crisis in 2011, for example.

ELECTIONS ARE HELD ON A FIXED DATE In 1845, Congress determined that elections for president and members of Congress will occur on the Tuesday after the first Monday in November (the Constitution only requires that national elections be held on the same day throughout the country). States have generally followed suit for election of governors and members of the legislature. One implication, related to the fixed terms of offices just described, is that neither presidents nor governors can time elections to their political advantage as we have seen can happen in parliamentary systems. Another implication

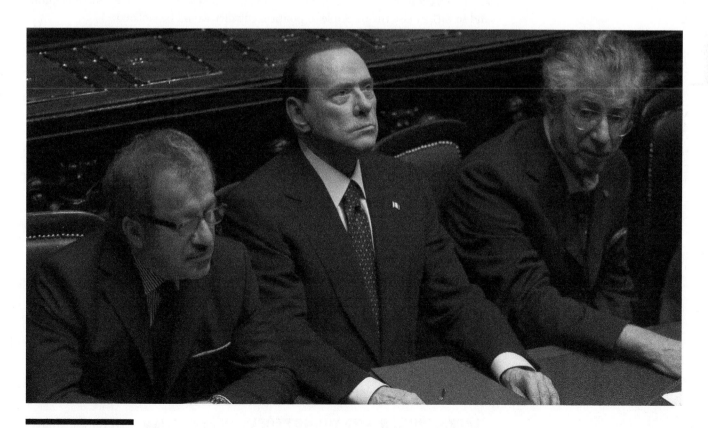

I'M NO LONGER PRIME MINISTER?

After Silvio Berlusconi's party lost a confidence vote in the Italian parliament in 2011, the president of the Republic called for new parliamentary elections. Parliamentary systems such as Italy's do not have fixed election dates or fixed terms of office for its members as we do in the United States.

franchise
The legal right to vote; see suffrage.

suffrage
The legal right to vote; see franchise.

is that Tuesday elections may cut down on participation. In other democracies, elections are held either on the weekend or on days that are declared a national holiday.

"FIRST-PAST-THE-POST" WINS Winners in most elections in the United States are those who win the most votes—not necessarily a majority—in a particular electoral district. This type of election is often called "first-past-the-post," as in a horse race where the winner is the first past the finish line. This includes congressional elections and presidential contests for electoral votes in each of the states. We do not have proportional representation in national-level races, nor do we have "run-off" elections between the top two vote-getters in presidential or congressional elections to ensure a majority victor. In 2004, as a matter of fact, George W. Bush became the first president since the election of his father in 1988 to win a majority of the national popular vote (all elected presidents come to office based on winning a majority in the electoral college), a feat repeated by Barack Obama in 2008. In France and Finland, by way of contrast, a second election is held if no candidate wins a majority in the first round of voting for the president. This type of election ensures that the person who is elected comes to office with majority support.

Voting in the United States

In this section, we turn our attention to political participation. For elections to be democratic—whether in the prospective, electoral competition, or retrospective voting models—participation in elections must not only be at high levels, but also must not vary substantially across social groups in the population (e.g., by race, gender, income, occupation, religion, ethnicity, region, and so on), or else the principle of political equality would be violated.

☐ Expansion of the Franchise

Until passage of the Fourteenth and Fifteenth Amendments after the Civil War, it was up to each state to determine who within its borders was eligible to vote. In the early years of the United States, many of the states limited the legal right to vote—called the **franchise**—quite severely. In fact, a majority of people could not vote at all. Slaves, Native Americans, and women were excluded altogether. In most states, white men without property or who had not paid some set level of taxes were not allowed to vote. In some states early on, white men with certain religious beliefs were excluded.

One of the most important developments in the political history of the United States, an essential part of the struggle for democracy, has been the expansion of the right to vote. The extension of the franchise has been a lengthy and uneven process, spanning 200 years.[14]

WHITE MALE SUFFRAGE The first barriers to fall were those concerning property and religion. So strong were the democratic currents during Thomas Jefferson's presidency (1801–1809) and in the years leading up to the election of Andrew Jackson in 1828 that by 1829, property, taxpaying, and religious requirements had been dropped in all states except North Carolina and Virginia. That left universal **suffrage**, or the ability to vote, firmly in place for most adult white males in the United States. Most of Europe, including Britain, did not achieve this degree of democracy until after World War I.

BLACKS, WOMEN, AND YOUNG PEOPLE Despite this head start for the United States compared with the rest of the world, the struggle to expand the suffrage to include African Americans, women, and young people proved difficult and painful. Ironically, universal white male suffrage was often accompanied by the withdrawal

AT THE POLLS

Early U.S. elections were poorly organized and hard to get to. In addition, only a small proportion of the population was eligible to vote. Here a group of white men, the only people with the right to vote in most places in the United States at the time, wait to vote in the presidential election of 1824 at a polling station near Boston. How did the voter profile of the time shape government policies?

of voting rights from black freedmen, even in states that did not permit slavery.[15] It took the bloody Civil War to free the slaves and the Fifteenth Amendment to the U.S. Constitution (1870) to extend the right to vote to all black males, both North and South. Even so, most blacks were effectively disfranchised in the South by the end of the nineteenth century and remained so until the 1960s civil rights movement and the Voting Rights Act of 1965.

Women won the right to vote in 1920 in all the states with the Nineteenth Amendment to the Constitution, after a long political battle. Residents of the District of Columbia were allowed to vote in presidential—but not congressional—elections after 1961, and 18- to 20-year-olds gained the franchise in 1971.

The result of these changes at the state and national levels was an enormous increase in the proportion of Americans who were legally eligible to vote: from about 23 percent of the adult population in 1788–1789 to nearly 98 percent by the beginning of the 1970s—practically all citizens above the age of 18, except people who have recently moved to another state, people in mental institutions, and incarcerated felons (and, in many states, former felons).

DIRECT PARTISAN ELECTIONS A related trend has involved the more direct election of government officials, replacing the old indirect methods that insulated officials from the public. At the same time, the development of a two-party system has clarified choices by focusing citizens' attention on just two alternatives for each office.

The election of the president, even with the existence of the **Electoral College**, has become more directly democratic. By the time of the Jefferson–Adams presidential campaign of 1800, which pitted the new Republican and Federalist parties against each other, most state legislatures had stopped picking the presidential electors themselves (as the Constitution permits). Instead, the legislatures allowed a popular vote for electors, most of whom were pledged to support the presidential candidate of one party or the other.

This is the same system we use today: in practically every state, there is a winner-take-all popular vote for a slate of electors—positions usually awarded by each of the political parties to loyal party workers and contributors—who are pledged to

305

10.1

10.2

10.3

10.4

10.5

10.6

party convention

A gathering of delegates who nominate a party's presidential candidate.

primary election

Statewide elections in which voters choose delegates to the national party conventions.

party caucuses

The process for selecting delegates to the national party conventions characterized by neighborhood and area-wide meetings of party supporters and activists.

turnout

The proportion of either eligible or all voting-age Americans who actually vote in a given election; the two ways of counting turnout yield different results.

a particular presidential candidate. In fact, only the name of the candidate and the party to whom the electors are pledged, not the names of the electors we are actually voting for, appear on the ballot. Thus, when the winning electors meet as the Electoral College in their respective states and cast ballots to elect the president, their actions are generally controlled by the popular vote that chose them. This system, odd and cumbersome as it is, almost always ensures that American citizens choose their president more or less directly. One recent exception is the 2000 election, when Democrat Al Gore won the popular vote by more than 500,000, but Republican George W. Bush captured a majority of the electoral votes after the Supreme Court ruled in Bush's favor on who should receive Florida's 25 electoral votes.

By 1840, the parties had started nominating presidential candidates in national **party conventions** instead of in congressional party caucuses. Later still, the parties began letting voters select many convention delegates directly in state **primary elections** instead of having party activists choose them in political party conventions in each of the states. Today, most delegates to the Republican and Democratic national conventions are selected in primary elections or in state **party caucuses** in which party supporters and activists hold neighborhood and area-wide meetings to select delegates. The important role of primaries and caucuses in nominating party candidates for elected office enhances democratic control of government, although we will see that each of them has antidemocratic features, too.

Until 1913, when the Seventeenth Amendment to the Constitution was ratified, U.S. senators were selected by state legislatures rather than directly by the people. Since then, all members of the Senate have been subject to direct choice by the voters.

Taken together, the expansion of the franchise and the development of direct, two-party elections have represented major successes in the struggle for democracy. But problems remain on the voting participation front.

☐ Low Voting Turnout

During the first 100 years or so of the United States's existence, not only did more and more people gain the right to vote, but also higher and higher proportions of voters actually turned out on Election Day and voted. Because of data inaccuracies and voter fraud, it is difficult to determine voter **turnout** accurately in early American elections. But the percentage of American voters appears to have increased rapidly, from roughly 11 percent of eligible voters in 1788–1789, to about 31 percent in 1800 (when Thomas Jefferson was first elected), and to about 57 percent in 1828 (Andrew Jackson's first victory). By 1840, the figure had reached 80 percent, and it stayed at about that level until 1896.[16]

The disturbing fact is that today, despite higher turnout in recent presidential elections, proportionally fewer people vote than during most of the nineteenth century. Since 1912, only about 50 to 65 percent of Americans have voted in presidential elections (see Figure 10.2) and still fewer in other elections: 40 to 50 percent in off-year (non-presidential-year) congressional elections and as few as 10 to 20 percent in primaries and minor local elections, although the exact number depends on how turnout is measured (see the "By the Numbers" feature). In addition, turnout in presidential elections remains well below turnout in other democratic countries; in Western Europe, turnout rates regularly top 75 percent. When only 60 percent of Israeli's voting-age population voted in that nation's 2006 Israeli parliamentary elections, it generated a flurry of news and academic commentary about what might be amiss with Israel's democracy.[17]

Why do so few Americans vote compared to people in other democracies? Scholars have identified several possible factors.[18]

BARRIERS TO VOTING In the United States, only citizens who take the initiative to register in advance are permitted to vote in an election. Most commonly, the registration period is ten to thirty days before an election (nine states allow same-day registration)[19]. Many people do not make the extra effort to register, or circumstances make it difficult.

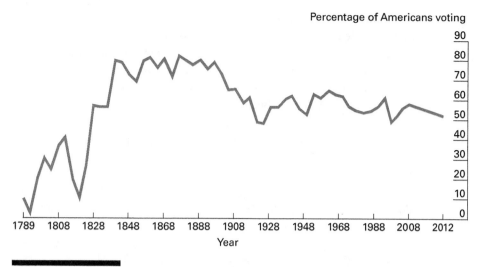

Percentage of Americans voting

FIGURE 10.2 THE RISE AND FALL OF TURNOUT IN PRESIDENTIAL ELECTIONS, 1789–2012

Turnout in presidential elections rose sharply during the nineteenth century—except during the "era of good feelings" when there was no party competition and little interest in politics among the public—but declined in the twentieth century. In 2004, turnout increased dramatically, but only to a level typical of the 1950s and 1960s.

Note: From 1920, the Census Bureau has calculated voting turnout as the percentage of the voting-age population voting, not as a percentage of the total voting-eligible population.

Source: U.S. Bureau of the Census, 2009; post-election estimates the authors based on data collected by Michael McDonald, "United States Elections Project," George Washington University, November 7, 2012.

For example, people who move, either within a state or to another state, must find out where and when to register in their new location. Many procrastinate and do not register in time, lowering turnout, according to one study, by 9 percentage points.[20] In most European countries with high turnout rates, the government, rather than individual citizens, is responsible for deciding who is listed as eligible to vote and registers them automatically.

If one's goal is to increase voting turnout, then doing things to make registering easier seems sensible. That is because research has shown a strong relationship between being registered and voting. We know, for example, that voting turnout in the United States among those who have registered to vote has hovered at about 85 percent and that voting participation in the states that allow same-day registration has been significantly higher than in other states.[21] In Minnesota and Wisconsin in 2008, where same-day registration is in effect, turnout was 78 percent and 73 percent, respectively, similar to turnout in other rich democracies. These findings suggest that the registration requirement for voting is probably a significant barrier to participation, because participation rates go up when such barriers are lowered.

A number of reforms have been instituted to make registration and voting more convenient. The National Voter Registration Act came into force in 1996, requiring states to allow people to sign up to vote in a variety of places where they are in contact with state and local government, as in welfare offices and motor vehicle facilities (why it is almost always called the "Motor Voter" law). Interestingly, while registration rates went up after the law came into being, voting turnout did not increase at similar rates, surprising advocates of the law and many scholars.[22]

Other reforms designed to ease the voting act itself have been instituted at the state level. These include allowing an extended voting period—usually called early voting—which many states have instituted in recent elections; and expanding the use of mail balloting over a period of several weeks, which a growing number of states allow.

Several reform ideas have not gotten very far. One is to make Election Day a legal holiday when people could vote without missing work, as many European countries do. Some have even suggested that people be required to vote, as many countries do. Needless to say, we do not require people to vote in this country and it does not seem likely to happen here any time soon.

Though much has been done recently to make registration and voting easier, there is a countermovement tied directly to the "parties at war" narrative that seeks

referenda

Procedures available in some states by which state laws or constitutional amendments proposed by the legislature are submitted to the voters for approval or rejection.

initiatives

Procedures available in some states for citizens to put proposed laws and constitutional amendments on the ballot for voter approval or rejection.

to make registration and voting harder for many. It has been mostly Democrats who have sought an expanded electorate, believing, perhaps, that those least likely to vote under older arrangements—lower-income and less educated people, and racial and ethnic minorities—would more likely vote for them. Claiming they are interested in rooting out voter fraud in our present system, but also wishing perhaps to take away Democratic votes, Republicans have been pushing hard to more tightly regulate the voting process. In virtually every state where they ended up in control of state government in the wake of their 2010 electoral landslide victory, Republicans passed laws requiring government-issued photo IDs for voting, while many of them, including Ohio and Florida, cut back the length of early voting periods. Maine ended same-day registration. Alabama and Kansas now require proof of citizenship. Florida and Iowa no longer allow ex-felons (presumably, "ex" means they have served their sentences and paid their debts to society) to vote. It remains to be seen what the turnout effects of these changes will be, though no one doubts that it will keep many eligible citizens from voting, especially those most likely to cast their ballots for Democrats.[23]

TOO MUCH COMPLEXITY As we suggested earlier, when voters go to the polls in the United States, they must make voting choices for a multitude of federal, state, and local offices and often decide on constitutional and policy measures put on the ballot by state legislatures (called **referenda**) or the public (called **initiatives**), especially in states such as California and Colorado where these are common. Research demonstrates that many potential voters are simply overwhelmed by the complexity of the issues and the number of choices they must make in the voting booth; some choose to stay home.[24]

A DECLINE IN COMPETITIVE ELECTIONS It may seem exceedingly odd to suggest, given the rise of intense partisanship, an increase in the shrillness and incivility in recent election campaigns, and the frequency of close elections in recent electoral rounds for the presidency and control of Congress, that very few Americans experience competitive elections where they live.[25] In most recent congressional elections, for example, no more than 30 or so of the 435 seats in the House really have been up for grabs (in 2008, it rose to about 60; in 2010, it jumped to about 100[26]). The remainder have resided safely in the hands of incumbents who won with at least 55 percent of the vote. In presidential elections, most states find themselves solidly in the Democratic or Republican columns, and little campaigning takes place in them. California is safely Democratic in presidential elections, for example, so Republican presidential candidates don't spend much time or money there. Democratic candidates tend to skirt places that are reliably Republican, such as Utah, Wyoming, and Mississippi. In a recent presidential election (see the "Mapping American Politics" feature later in this chapter), 88 percent of media ad buys in the last month of the presidential campaign were concentrated in only 10 states. If competition drives up voter turnout, as political scientists suggest, then an important reason for low turnout in the United States may be that most Americans do not live in an environment where elections are strongly contested.

WEAK VOTER MOBILIZATION BY LOCAL PARTIES Low turnout may be tied to the failure of the political parties to rouse people broadly and get them to the polls to vote. The national parties mostly are in the business of getting their own supporters to the polls, to rally the base, as it were, not in the business of increasing the voter turnout in general as a sort of civic duty. The problem is that aiming at your own voters with highly partisan appeals delivered by mail, telephone, television, e-mail, and social media by highly professional but distant party organizations and advocacy groups does not increase turnout among the non-committed public and may even persuade many of them to stay home.[27] Old-style, door-to-door canvassing in neighborhoods, historically the province of local party organizations that now seem increasingly enfeebled, is more effective in raising turnout than modern methods but less commonly used than in the past. Both parties have renewed their efforts in this area,[28] however, with the

By the Numbers

Is voting turnout declining in the United States?

Commentators have been decrying the declining rate of voting in the United States for many years now. All sorts of explanations have been advanced to explain the decline; all sorts of remedies for the problem have been proposed. But what if the decline is less severe than generally believed?

Why It Matters

We have argued in this chapter that widespread participation in voting and other civic activities is one measure of the health of democracy in any society. If the way we measure participation is inaccurate, we cannot do a good job of assessing the quality of democracy in the United States, or identify what problems and shortcomings in our political system need to be addressed to make it more democratic.

Behind the Traditional Voting Turnout Measure

Voter turnout in American elections *normally* is determined by a very simple calculation: the number of people who vote in a national election divided by the number of people in the United States who are of voting age, that is, 18 years of age and older. The denominator for this equation—voting-age population, or VAP—is provided by the Census Bureau. But there is a problem: the denominator may be misleading, because it includes millions of people who are not eligible to vote at all—residents who are not citizens, felons (some states), people with past felonies (some states), and the mentally incompetent. If we calculated voting turnout as the number of voters divided by the number of people in the United States who *actually* are eligible to vote—the voting-eligible population, or VEP—turnout would always be higher than is now reported because the denominator would be smaller.

Calculating a VEP-based Measure of Turnout

Two political scientists, Michael McDonald and Samuel Popkin, have done us the great service of transforming the Census Bureau's VAP number to a VEP number for every national election from 1948 to 2012, pulling out noncitizens and ineligible felons and former felons in states where they cannot vote. Using the voting-eligible population rather than the resident population over the age of 18 as the denominator in the voting turnout equation, McDonald and Popkin's figures show the following:

- Voting turnout is actually four or five percentage points higher in recent elections than usually reported.
- Voting turnout declined between 1960 and 1972 regardless of which method was used. However, voting turnout appears to have declined further after 1972 only when using the traditional VAP method; the VEP method shows declines only in 1996 and 2012.
- Voting turnout jumped substantially in 2004 and 2008 for the hotly contested races between John Kerry and George W. Bush, and Barack Obama and John McCain, whether using the VEP numbers or the VAP numbers. Turnout dropped in 2012 for the Obama-Romney contest, however.

The main reason voting turnout has declined in recent elections using the traditional VAP method is that the number of people who are residents of the United States but who are not eligible to vote in American elections has increased at every election, mostly due to the number of noncitizens living here.

Criticism of the VEP-based Measure of Turnout

Some critics suggest that the old way of calculating voting turnout serves a very useful purpose, namely, pointing out how far short we fall in our claim to being a democratic society. The low turnout number reported by VAP, it is argued, helps focus attention on the

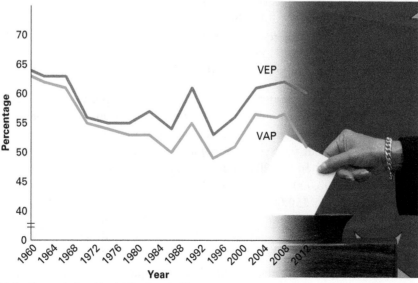

Voting Turnout in Presidential Elections by Year

Sources: Michael P. McDonald and Samuel L. Popkin, "The Myth of the Vanishing Voter," The American Political Science Review, 95, no. 4 (December 2001), pp. 963–974; authors' estimates based on preliminary data from Michael McDonald, United States Elections Project, George Mason University.

issue of nonvoting in the United States and encourages efforts to reform voting rules to increase turnout. Even using the VEP-based measure, American voting turnout remains the lowest among the rich democracies of the world.

What to Watch for

When you come across voter turnout numbers, pay attention to whether the figure has been calculated based on the voting-age population or on the voting-eligible population. The latter will always be higher than the former. It is important to be aware that both methods of calculating turnout make sense in their own way; each has a slightly different story to tell.

What Do You Think?

How could the United States increase the rate of voting turnout, which, regardless of the calculation method, is low in comparison to other democratic countries? Should we have compulsory voting in the United States like several other democratic countries? What are the pros and cons of making noncitizens—who pay taxes and are subject to U.S. laws—eligible to vote? How about former felons who have paid their debt to society?

Obama campaign in 2008 particularly effective in increasing voter turnout by knocking on the doors of potential voters.

OTHER POSSIBILITIES Political scientists, journalists, and political practitioners have suggested a number of other possible reasons for low turnout. For example, it may be that the increase in negative advertising, the increasing partisanship, and the growing incivility of American politics overall are adding to peoples' cynicism about the political system and politicians, causing Americans to turn away in disgust or despair. There has been some speculation that the time available to Americans for political participation has declined either because of longer working hours for many or because of the availability of other diversions, most especially television and the Internet. Unfortunately, scholars still are tussling with these issues; there is much disagreement among them about whether and the extent to which these factors affect voting turnout.[29]

Who Votes?

10.4 Identify demographic factors that increase the likelihood of voting

Explore on MyPoliSciLab
Simulation
You Are a Voting Registration Volunteer

Voting in the United States varies a great deal according to people's income, education, age, and ethnicity. This means that some kinds of people have more representation and influence with elected officials than others, and, other things being equal, they are more likely to have their preferences and interests reflected in what government does.

☐ Income and Education

For the most part, politically active people tend to be those with higher-than-average incomes and more formal education.[30] These people also are more likely to vote, even in off-year elections when there is not a presidential contest, when voting turnout for the entire population is about half of that during presidential election years. In the 2010 midterm elections, about 59 percent of those with incomes of $100,000 or above said they had voted, but only 43 percent of those with incomes under $50,000 said they had done so (see Figure 10.3). About 63 percent of those earning postgraduate degrees reported that they had voted, but only 35 percent of high school graduates and 21 percent of those who had not graduated from high school had done so. Some statistical analyses have indicated that the most important factor determining whether people vote is their level of formal education. When other factors are controlled—including race, income, and gender—college-educated people are much more likely to tell interviewers that they have voted than are the less educated. There are several possible reasons: people with more education learn more

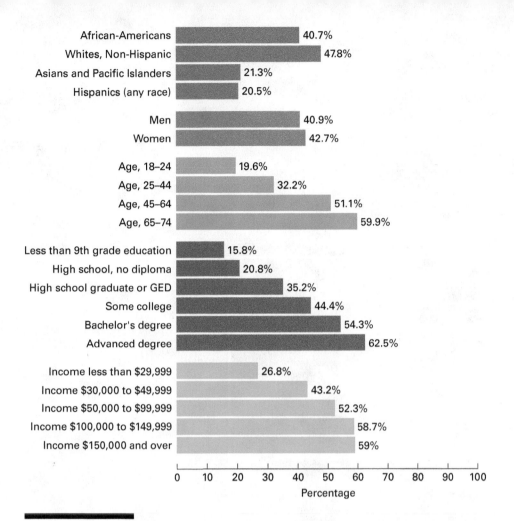

FIGURE 10.3 CONGRESSIONAL ELECTION TURNOUT BY SOCIAL GROUP, 2010 MIDTERM ELECTIONS

Age, education, race, ethnicity, income, and gender all affect voting behavior. Members of certain social groups are more likely to vote in elections than others. The Census Bureau warns that these numbers may be inflated because of people's tendency to want to report positive citizen behavior to interviewers. What is important here, however, is not necessarily the accuracy of the turnout totals but the comparison between groups of people. The relative turnout comparisons between groups fit the general picture available from other academic research and government sources.

Source: U.S. Bureau of the Census, Current Population Reports, October 2011.

about politics, are less troubled by registration requirements, and are more confident in their ability to affect political life.

Looking at political participation more broadly, citizens with lower incomes are also less likely to work in campaigns, give money, contact officials, and the like. Wealthier Americans, who have more time, more money, and more knowledge of how to get things done, tend to be much more active politically. As a result, they may have more political clout than their fellow citizens.

☐ Race and Ethnicity

In the past, fewer black people than whites voted, but now the proportions have become more nearly equal. Both non-Hispanic whites and blacks turned out at about 65 percent in 2008, with the black vote up five points from 2004, mostly because Barack Obama, the nation's first African American candidate for the presidency, was in the race. In 2010, a nonpresidential year, the differences between white and black turnout more closely resembled the pattern in 2004. About 41 percent of African Americans voted in 2010 compared to whites at 48 percent. Racial differences remain, then, but they are smaller than they have been historically. The gap can be attributed to African Americans' lower average levels of income and education. African Americans are at least equally likely to vote, and sometimes more likely, than non-Hispanic whites of similar educational and income backgrounds.

Who Votes and Who Doesn't?

Political scientists analyze voting patterns by group to find out why certain people are and are not voting. Hispanics, school dropouts, low-income citizens, and youth consistently vote less than other Americans. New policies, such as photo identification requirements, may make voting harder and might reinforce non-voting in these groups.

Explore on MyPoliSciLab

Who Didn't Vote in 2008?

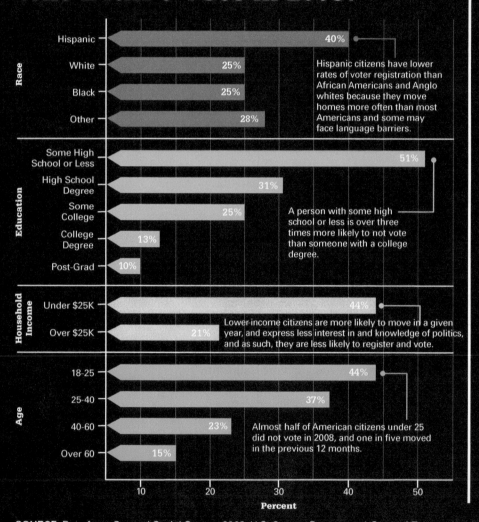

Race
- Hispanic — 40%
- White — 25%
- Black — 25%
- Other — 28%

Hispanic citizens have lower rates of voter registration than African Americans and Anglo whites because they move homes more often than most Americans and some may face language barriers.

Education
- Some High School or Less — 51%
- High School Degree — 31%
- Some College — 25%
- College Degree — 13%
- Post-Grad — 10%

A person with some high school or less is over three times more likely to not vote than someone with a college degree.

Household Income
- Under $25K — 44%
- Over $25K — 21%

Lower-income citizens are more likely to move in a given year, and express less interest in and knowledge of politics, and as such, they are less likely to register and vote.

Age
- 18-25 — 44%
- 25-40 — 37%
- 40-60 — 23%
- Over 60 — 15%

Almost half of American citizens under 25 did not vote in 2008, and one in five moved in the previous 12 months.

Percent (axis: 10, 20, 30, 40, 50)

Who Doesn't Have Photo ID in Texas?

A 2012 federal court trial challenging Texas's voter photo identification requirements found that African American and Hispanic Texans are nearly twice as likely as Anglo whites to lack necessary photo identification.

Percent Without Photo ID

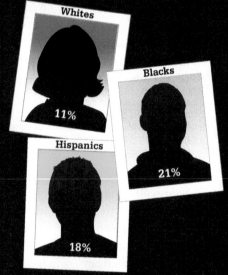

- Whites — 11%
- Blacks — 21%
- Hispanics — 18%

SOURCE: Data from General Social Survey, 2008; U.S. Census Bureau; and *State of Texas v. Holder*, 12-cv-128, District Court for the District of Columbia (2012).

Investigate Further

Concept Why does voting participation among groups matter? Members of groups have common experiences or circumstances that help us understand why they do or don't vote. For example, southern Jim Crow laws kept black voting rates low for decades.

Connection What do non-voting groups share in common? Hispanics, the poor, and the young are more likely to move from year to year, and less likely to be registered. Less-educated Americans confront literacy barriers to political information which also makes them less likely to vote.

Cause How might voter photo identification laws lead to less voting? Minority voters are less likely to have photo identification. In addition, members of highly mobile groups are less likely to have identification with a correct address.

Latinos have historically had very low participation rates; many are discouraged from participating by low incomes, language problems, or suspicion of government authorities. Although Latinos continue to vote at lower rates than other Americans with a similar income and educational profile, the number appearing at the polls has been increasing.[31] For example, while close to 50 percent voted in the 2008 presidential contest, this was a significant jump from 1996 when only 27 percent reported voting. In 2010, an off-year election when overall turnout is low for all Americans, you will recall, about 21 percent of Latinos voted, compared to 48 percent for non-Latino whites and 41 percent for African Americans. Significantly, Latinos in 2010 represented a larger share of the electorate at 6.9 percent than in any previous midterm election—lower than their share in the population, to be sure, but a significant increase nevertheless.[32] This recent jump in the turnout rate for Latinos has made a difference in states where Hispanic voters are concentrated. In 2008, Barack Obama and John McCain made special efforts to win over this group, especially in closely contested states such as Florida, Nevada, Colorado, and New Mexico—all won by Obama—demonstrating its rising importance. It may be that the harsh anti-immigrant legislation passed in the last few years by Alabama, Arizona, Georgia, Indiana, and South Carolina, which have angered Latinos, against whom these laws have been directed, may increase voting turnout among Latinos, as these things generally do. To have a big impact, however, Latinos would need to raise their rates of voter registration, which are well below those of other groups in the population. In 2012, for example, only 42 percent of eligible Latino voters in Nevada were registered, and only 35 percent were registered in Virginia, both important battleground states.[33]

Voting has also been relatively low among Asian Americans; about 21 percent reported voting in 2010, very similar to turnout for Latinos. Like Latinos, voting turnout has increased in recent elections, as have Asian American contributions to candidates and parties. Moreover, Asian American individuals and organizations have become more active in local politics.

☐ Age

Age is one of the most important variables when explaining why some people vote and others do not. The youngest groups of eligible voters go to the polls much less often than older voters. This was true even in the exciting 2008 presidential election when young people played such a visible role in the Obama campaign in organizing state and local campaign organizations and get-out-the-vote efforts. Though 2 million more 18- to 29-year-olds voted than in 2004, their voting turnout was still only 51 percent (up 2 percent from the previous presidential election, to be sure).[34] In comparison, turnout among older voters age 65 to 74 was 72 percent. In the 2010 midterm, less than 20 percent of those under 25 voted compared to 51 percent for those spanning the 45 to 64 age group. Interestingly, the turnout among those over 65 was more than three times that of the youngest voting-age Americans. The reasons for low turnout among young people may be that they tend to be less rooted in communities, less familiar with registration and voting procedures, less in the habit of voting, and less clear about what stake they have in elections.[35]

☐ Gender

Women were prevented from participating in politics for a large part of our history; they got the vote, by constitutional amendment, only in 1920. Not all women immediately took advantage of this new opportunity. For many years, women voted and participated in politics at lower rates than men—about 10 or 15 percent lower in the elections of the 1950s, for example. The gender gap in voting and other forms of political participation disappeared in the United States by the end of the 1980s.[36] In fact, by 2008, women voted at a significantly higher rate than men, around 66 percent compared to 62 percent in that year's presidential election and almost 43 percent to men's turnout of just under 41 percent in the 2010 midterm elections (see Figure 10.3). This marks a dramatic change over the past two or three decades and can probably be traced to the improvement in the educational attainments of women, the entrance

10.1
10.2
10.3
10.4
10.5
10.6

of more women than ever into the paid workforce, and the increased importance of issues such as pay equity and abortion on the American political agenda.

☐ Does It Matter Who Votes?

Some observers have argued that it doesn't matter if many people don't vote, because their preferences aren't much different from those who do; the results would be about the same if everyone voted. In some elections, nonvoters have shown support for the same candidate who won, so their votes would apparently have changed nothing,[37] and some surveys have indicated that nonvoters' policy preferences differ little from those of voters.

However, we should not be too quick to accept these arguments, just as few now accept the nineteenth-century view that there was no need for women to vote because their husbands could protect their interests. Even when the expressed preferences of nonvoters or nonparticipators do not look very distinctive, their objective circumstances, and therefore their needs for government services, may differ markedly.[38] Latinos, the young, and those with low incomes might benefit from government programs that are of less interest to other citizens.[39] A political system that included and mobilized these people vigorously might produce quite different government policies. There is a growing body of evidence, in fact, that high- and low-income people in the United States have very different preferences about what government should do and that elected officials are more likely to attend to the views of higher-income groups than others.[40] It is also known that government efforts to compensate people with low incomes in the rich democracies are associated with the degree to which low-income people vote, with the United States, where low-income people participate at far lower rates than others, doing the least in this area of government activity.[41]

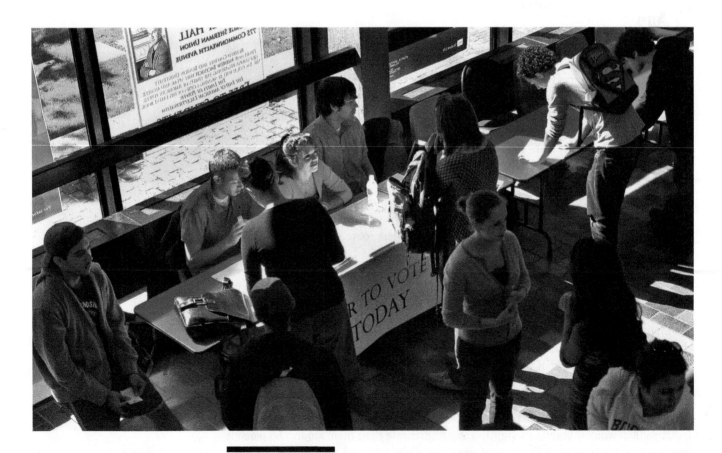

MOBILIZING THE YOUTH VOTE

Here College Democrats at Boston University register students to vote in the upcoming national elections, trying to match in 2012 the high turnout of the youth vote that occurred in 2008 that was so helpful to Democrats. They succeeded.

314

Campaigning for Office

Outline the process of campaigns for the presidency and Congress

superdelegates
Elected officials from all levels of government who are appointed by party committees to be delegates to the national convention of the Democratic Party; not selected in primary elections or caucuses.

The ideas we discussed about how elections might ensure democratic policymaking all depend in various ways on what sorts of choices are presented to the voters. It makes a difference what kind of people run for office, whether they take clear policy stands, whether those stands differ from each other, and whether they stand for what the average voter wants. In evaluating how democratic our elections are, therefore, we need to examine what kinds of alternatives are put before the voters in campaigns. We consider these issues in this section focusing on presidential elections only.

☐ Gaining the Nomination

The first step for someone seeking the presidency is winning the nomination of one's own party. (For sitting presidents seeking a second term, such as George Bush in 2004 and Barack Obama in 2012, this is normally not a serious problem; they are the presumptive nominees of their party.) In a formal sense, the Republican and Democratic presidential nominees are selected at their national conventions the summer before the presidential election. In both parties, the nomination goes to the winner of a majority of delegates to the national party convention mostly chosen in state primaries and caucuses (to be described later). The Democrats' popularly elected primary and caucus delegates are supplemented by **superdelegates**, usually party luminaries and elected officials, including members of Congress, and state and local officials. In 2012, about one-in-five delegates to the Democratic National Convention fell into this category. About the same proportion of delegates to the Republican National Convention were "unpledged," not called superdelegates, but playing the same role as superdelegates in the Democratic nominating process: allowing the party establishment to have a voice at the national convention, serving as a counterweight to delegates selected in primaries and caucuses dominated by the most ideologically committed party voters.

WHO HAS A CHANCE In any given presidential election, only a handful of candidates are serious possibilities. So far in American history, these have virtually always been middle-aged or elderly white men with extensive formal educations, fairly high incomes,[42] and substantial experience as public figures—usually as government officials (especially vice presidents, governors, or senators) or military heroes. The Democrats broke the white male mold in 2008 when Hillary Clinton came close to winning the nomination in a tight race with the eventual winner, Barack Obama, an African American. Movie stars, media commentators, business executives, and others who would be president almost always have to perform important government service before they are seriously considered for the presidency. Ronald Reagan, for example, most of whose career was spent acting in motion pictures and on television, served as governor of California before being elected president. In addition to being a successful businessman at Bain Capital, 2012 Republican presidential nominee Mitt Romney has served as governor of Massachusetts. His Republican rivals for the nomination also had extensive government experience. Rick Santorum was a former U.S. senator from Pennsylvania. Newt Gingrich, best known at the beginning of the 2011–2012 election cycle as a conservative media commentator, writer, and lobbyist, served in the 1990s as the Republican Speaker of the House.

The single best stepping-stone to becoming president has been the vice presidency, which is usually filled by former senators or governors. Since 1900, 5 of the 18 presidents have succeeded from the vice presidency after the president's death or resignation, and two others, Nixon and Bush (the elder), were former vice presidents elected in their own right.

It used to be the case that serious candidates for president almost invariably represented mainstream American values and policy preferences. Seldom had an "extreme"

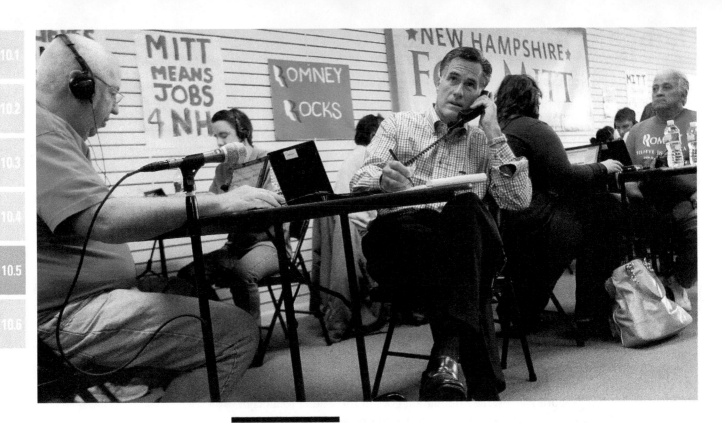

GATHERING VOTES

In addition to living room coffee klatches and rallies, contenders for the presidential nomination in each of the parties spend considerable time on the phones with potential voters trying to get them to the polls in primary states such as New Hampshire's in early 2012. Here eventual Republican nominee Mitt Romney asks a potential voter for his or her support. Must candidates engage in these forms of retail politics to gain the nomination or would television advertising, use of social media, and rallies be a better use of the time and resources of candidates?

candidate—that is, a candidate who appeals only to active partisans in a party—gotten very far. In the 2011–2012 election cycle, Newt Gingrich, and then Rick Santorum, made a serious run for the Republican nomination, having generated much excitement among the most conservative Republicans and Tea Party activists, but the nomination went to so-called establishment candidate Mitt Romney. Most of the time, serious candidates must be acceptable not only to the party base but to the business community and have enthusiastic support from at least some sectors of industry or finance. They also must be considered "presidential" by the news media and find some support among independent voters. And they must be attractive to those individuals and groups that fund campaigns. With the rise of super PACs, however, more nonmainstream candidates may be able to hang around longer. A big contribution by a rich contributor to a super PAC supporting such a candidate can keep him or her in a nomination contest even if that candidate has not won a string of state contests. That happened in the 2012 GOP nomination race when Newt Gingrich was supported by Winning Our Future, largely funded by Las Vegas gambling and hotel magnate Sheldon Adelson. Though he had only a handful of delegates and no chance of winning the Republican nomination, his rich backers allowed Gingrich to stay in the nomination race until late April.

GETTING STARTED A person who wants to run for the presidency usually begins at least two or three years before the election by testing the waters, asking friends and financial backers if they will support a run, and observing how people react to the mythical "Great Mentioner." A friendly journalist may write that Senator Blathers "has been mentioned" as a smart, attractive, strong candidate; Blathers waits to see whether anyone agrees. The would-be candidate may commission a national survey to check for name recognition and a positive image. He or she may put together an exploratory committee to round up private endorsements, commitments, and financial contributions, perhaps setting up private political action committees to gather money.

If all goes well in the early stages, the presidential aspirant becomes more serious, assembling a group of close advisers, formulating strategy, officially announcing his or her candidacy, forming a fund-raising operation, setting up campaign and personal websites, and putting together organizations in key states. Early money is crucial to finance organization and advertising.[43] Raising serious money from donors big and small—the latter, primarily through the Internet—is a clear sign to party bigwigs, associated interest and advocacy groups, and the news media that a candidate ought to be taken seriously. The relationship between money-raising and consideration as a serious candidate is now so important that it is commonly called the "invisible primary" and the "money primary."[44]

It is a vicious cycle of sorts. If a candidate can't raise money, she or he is not taken seriously. If a candidate is not taken seriously, then raising money becomes even more difficult. And with little money in the bank and not much coming in, failure in the first primaries and caucuses is inevitable. Candidates who can't raise money drop out early. In 2008, Bill Richardson, John Edwards, and Christopher Dodd were gone early from the Democratic nomination race, facing the awesome campaign finance machines of Hillary Clinton and Barack Obama, each of whom had raised about $100 million by the end of 2007 and each of whom was spending money almost as fast as it was coming in. In 2012, Mitt Romney easily won the money contest, persuading those without much money (or standing in the polls), such as Michele Bachmann, Jon Huntsman, and Tim Pawlenty to drop out. Texas governor Rick Perry was able to stay in the Republican nomination campaign for a time because he had such a large campaign war chest, even though his poll numbers had collapsed by late January 2012 into the single digits.

At one time, an important early decision was whether to be a part of the public campaign finance system—in which the federal government matches the first $250 from each individual donor on condition that candidates in the 2007–2008 election cycle limit preconvention campaign spending to around $50 million—or to go it alone, raise hard money contributions from individuals (limited to $2,500 in 2012) and PACs (limited to $5,000), and spend what they wish. But things began to change in 2000 when George W. Bush became the first serious candidate to eschew public financing since it was first established in 1976. Democrats John Kerry and John Dean, as well as Republican President Bush, skipped public funding in 2004. In the 2007–2008 election cycle, none of the leading contenders for the presidential nomination in either party, with the exception of John Edwards, chose public funding with its attendant spending limits, nor did any of the major contenders do so in the 2011–2012 cycle.

Public financing of presidential nomination campaigns seems to be going by the wayside for two reasons. First, the costs of running a credible campaign for the party presidential nomination have gone up much faster than the amount that candidates who choose the public funding route are allowed to spend. Most candidates do not want to handcuff themselves in this way. Second, it is easier now to raise money outside the public financing system. The campaign reform act in 2002 substantially increased the amount of money individuals can give to candidates. The Internet—typically e-mail blasts and appeals on social media sites such as Facebook—has proved to be an incredibly efficient and cost-effective device for raising lots of money from individual contributors, something Barack Obama did particularly well in both 2008 and 2012. And, though not officially part of their campaigns, super PACs and 501 advocacy organizations, often run by close associates and friends of the candidates, can raise unlimited amounts of money from corporations, unions, and wealthy individuals, then spend that money on advertising supporting that candidate and attacking his or her opponents.

Another important early decision involves which state primaries and caucus contests to enter. Each entry takes a lot of money, energy, and organization, and any loss is damaging; many candidates drop out after just a few early defeats, as John Edwards, Fred Thompson, and Mitt Romney did in 2008 and Michele Bachmann, Tim Pawlenty, and Rick Perry did in 2012. To win the nomination, it is generally necessary to put together a string of primary and caucus victories, something John McCain was able to do in 2008, starting with New Hampshire. By the end of the day on March 4, after winning the big primaries in Ohio and Texas, he had secured the nomination with a majority of Republican convention delegates pledged to him, an outcome made possible by the

10.1
10.2
10.3
10.4
10.5
10.6

winner-take-all rules then in effect in the Republican Party. With fewer winner-take-all state primaries and caucuses in effect in the Republican Party in 2012, and with many in the base of the party trying out first one, then another conservative alternative to Mitt Romney—Rick Perry, Newt Gingrich, Rick Santorum, and, for a dedicated handful, Ron Paul—it took much longer for Romney to emerge as the presumptive nominee.

PRESIDENTIAL PRIMARIES AND CAUCUSES Since 1952, no national party convention has taken more than one ballot to nominate its candidate for the presidency, and the pre-convention front-runner has always been the nominee.[45] Since the 1970s, a majority of the delegates to the conventions in each party have been chosen in state primary or caucus elections, with direct voting by citizens. A small majority of these primaries are closed, meaning they are open only to voters who have registered Republican or Democrat before the date of the primary; the others are open to all voters, who can decide on the day of the election which party's ballot they wish to take into the voting booth. Republicans had 12 open primaries or caucuses during the 2012 nomination season, while Democrats had 18. Parties have been known to encourage their supporters to enter the other party's primary in a bid to damage the opposition's front-runner. There were press reports in 2012, for example, that party officials were encouraging Democrats to vote for Rick Santorum in the Ohio primary as a way to deny a victory to the presumptive front-runner, Mitt Romney (it didn't work; Romney eked out a victory). Whether a primary is closed or open also can affect how candidates run their campaigns. Because closed primaries mean that the bulk of the voters likely will be party loyalists, candidates tend to pitch their appeal to the party base. (Thus the frequent attacks on government regulatory agencies such as the Environmental Protections Agency. See the "Can Government Do Anything Well?" feature.) In open primaries with more diverse voters, candidates tend to make broader appeals. Many states—most famously Iowa, with the first on the calendar—use caucuses, where active party members and officials gather in meetings to select the delegates to the national convention. To confuse matters even further, some states select convention delegates in primaries and caucuses.

It is especially important for a candidate to establish momentum by winning early primaries and caucuses. Early winners get press attention, financial contributions, and better standings in the polls as voters and contributors decide they are viable candidates and must have some merit if people in other states have supported them. All these factors—attention from the media, money, and increased popular support—help the candidates who win early contests go on to win more and more contests.[46]

Because the states and the parties—not Congress or the president—control this nominating process, the system is a disorganized, even chaotic one, and it changes from one election to the next. Some states have primaries for both parties on the same day (including the important New Hampshire primaries); others hold primaries for the parties on separate dates. States are particularly anxious that they are not ignored, so an increasing number of them have moved their primary and caucus dates forward in the calendar. States with late primaries, even very large ones such as California, discovered in recent elections that the winners of early primaries had, for all intents and purposes, sewed up the party nominations, discounting the importance of their own primaries and caucuses. As a result, the primary and caucus season started to get "front-loaded" in 2004, then accelerated in 2008 when it became a stampede, with states leap-frogging over the others to position themselves earlier in the calendar. The result in 2008 was that 20 states—including big ones such as New York, New Jersey, Illinois, Missouri, and California—held their primaries on February 5, only a little more than a month after the first caucus in Iowa on January 3 (always the first caucus by state law) and a little less than a month after the first-in-the-nation primary in New Hampshire (always the first primary by state law) on January 8. The large states of Florida and Michigan held their Democratic primaries in mid and late January, respectively, against the rules of the Democratic National Committee, and were penalized for doing so. Perhaps ironically, the Clinton–Obama race was so close that states with late primaries, such as North Carolina and Indiana, became very important in 2008.

Both parties passed rules after this to slow or reverse the trend toward front-loading and early winner-take-all primaries, but Florida, Michigan, and Arizona Republicans

Can Government Do Anything Well?

10.1
10.2
10.3
10.4
10.5
10.6

The Environmental Protection Agency

Candidates for the 2012 GOP presidential nomination couldn't get enough of the EPA. The agency came up in nearly every televised debate. Michele Bachmann said she wanted to "padlock the EPA's doors." Newt Gingrich proposed that the EPA be eliminated, as did Rick Santorum. Rick Perry proposed an immediate moratorium on new EPA regulations. (As Texas governor, Perry led a group of states in a lawsuit to prevent the EPA from issuing rules on greenhouse gas emissions from power plants, refineries, and mining operations.) Ron Paul saw no need for a significant federal role, believing that the proper tax incentives would allow the private sector to address CO_2 emissions and other pollutants. Mitt Romney, somewhat favorable at times to the EPA, still said he wanted the EPA to stop issuing regulations on CO_2 emissions.

The Environmental Protection Agency was created in 1970 during the presidency of Republican Richard Nixon. Its mission was to conduct or sponsor scientific research on the human impacts of air and water pollution and to issue regulations affecting private firms and government entities that emit pollutants. In issuing regulations, the agency is responsible for maintaining national standards set by federal statutes that limit air pollution, water pollution, and hazardous waste. From the beginning, business has been hostile to the agency, claiming that its rules make doing business more expensive, undercutting profits and destroying jobs. Over the years, the Republican Party has joined business in opposition to the EPA. Democrats, more supportive of an activist government primed to solve social and economic problems, have become champions of the agency.

What has widened the partisan divide even further was the declaration in 2009 by the EPA that greenhouse gas emissions posed a threat to human health because of their role in causing global warming and that it would issue rules regulating such emissions. Acting on a suit brought by a broad coalition of industry groups, the Supreme Court ruled in 2011 that the EPA was acting properly under authority granted to it by Congress. Needless to say, Republicans were not pleased, given the widespread belief among party supporters and activists that global warming does not exist and, if it does, is not caused by human activity, including CO_2 emissions.

Support for the claim that government can and should regulate air and water pollution and greenhouse gas emissions:

- The EPA has a solid record in regulating pollutants that degrade human health: lead in paints and gasoline, DDT and other harmful pesticides and herbicides, for example.
- EPA rules have forced local governments to provide safe drinking water.
- The EPA played in big role in the effort to eliminate ozone layer–depleting fluorocarbons in products.
- Agency rules forced a cutback in dumping sewage in coastal waters.
- Agency rules on emissions from chemical plants in 1997 led to the reduction of air pollutants from that source by 90 percent.
- Solid scientific research supports the move by the EPA, using its authority under the Clean Air Act, to define CO_2 emissions as harmful to human health and issue rules starting in 2011 to lower such emissions.

Rejection of the claim that government can and should regulate air and water pollution and greenhouse gas emissions:

- EPA regulations hurt business by increasing their operating expenses, and when businesses are hurting they do not hire.
- EPA regulations cost state and local governments a great deal of money to comply; this takes money away from other needs and raises taxes for the people.
- Like most regulatory agencies, the EPA over-regulates; it does more than what is optimal to guard against pollution and its effects.
- Many EPA regulations are based on poor science; this is especially true for the research linking CO_2 to global warming and to ill effects on humans.
- EPA regulations adversely affect economic growth, which is a key correlate of a healthy population; by slowing growth, the EPA adversely affects human well-being in the United States.
- EPA regulations are hurting the economic recovery from the Great Recession, the deepest since the Great Depression.

10.1

10.2

10.3

10.4

10.5

10.6

WHAT DO YOU THINK?

What do you think about the past, present, and future role of the EPA in regulating air and water pollution and greenhouse gas emissions?

- EPA policies and regulations have been beneficial to the United States as a whole, and the EPA should vigorously pursue its mandate in rule-making; funding should continue to be allocated to this important government agency.
- EPA policies and regulations have been net beneficial to the United States as a whole, but at times efforts have been contrary to business interests; it should rescind its most egregious regulations and refrain from issuing new ones that hurt the economy.
- EPA policies are almost always contrary to business interests and hurt the economy; the agency should have its budget drastically reduced or be abolished.

How would you defend your position to a fellow student? What would be your main line of argument? What evidence do you believe best supports your position? For help in developing your argument, please refer to the sources listed in the "Can Government Do Anything Well" feature in Chapter 2 on p. 48.

Additional sources for this feature: John M. Broder, "Bashing E.P.A. Is New Theme in G.O.P. Race," *The New York Times* (August 17, 2011), p. 1.

bucked party rules to hold their binding primaries in January and February during the 2012 nomination season even though doing so cost them one-half of their delegates at the Republican National Convention. Nevertheless, by dissuading a number of states from moving up in the calendar and with a number of states moving from a winner-take-all to proportional selection of delegates, the Republican nomination battle extended far later into the spring than usually is the case for the Republican Party. No candidate, including the early presumptive party nominee Mitt Romney, could deliver an early knockout blow and secure the nomination. Like Obama in 2008, Romney failed to win in the first two months after Iowa and New Hampshire but was able to slowly and steadily accumulate delegates over a longer period leading up to the convention.

THE PRESIDENTIAL NOMINATING CONVENTIONS Because the front-runner now comes to the national convention with enough delegates to win on the first ballot, the gathering has become a coronation ceremony in which pre-pledged delegates ratify the selection of the leading candidate, accept that candidate's choice for the vice presidency, and put on a colorful show for the media and the country. Enthusiasm and unity are staged for the national television audience. Barack Obama's acceptance speech before 80,000 wildly cheering supporters at Invesco Field in Denver drew a national television audience of more than 38 million. John McCain's "town hall–style" acceptance speech at the Republican National Convention in St. Paul, Minnesota, before an equally enthusiastic crowd, drew an even larger national television audience.

It is a disaster for a political party if serious conflicts break out or the timing of the elaborate nomination process goes wrong. The Democrats were in turmoil over the Vietnam War at their 1968 gathering, for example, with the conflict played out on the convention floor and in the streets of Chicago, carried live on television. By all accounts, the conflict and disunity played a role in Hubert Humphrey's loss in the general election to Republican Richard Nixon. In 1972, conflict between the eventual nominee George McGovern and Ted Kennedy, as well as procedural snafus, meant that McGovern didn't deliver his televised acceptance speech until early morning, well after most people on the East Coast and in the Midwest had gone to bed.

NOMINATING INCUMBENT PRESIDENTS We have been focusing on how outsiders and political challengers try to win party presidential nominations. Things are very different for incumbent presidents seeking reelection, like Bill Clinton in 1996 or George W. Bush in 2004 or Barack Obama in 2012. These candidates must also enter and win primaries and caucuses, but they have the machinery of government working for them and, if times are reasonably good, a unified party behind them. They also have an easier time getting campaign contributions, especially for the primaries when incumbent presidents only occasionally meet serious competition. They campaign on the job, taking credit for policy successes while discounting or blaming others, such as Congress, for failures. Winning renomination as president is usually easy, except in cases of disaster such as the 1968 Vietnam War debacle for Lyndon Johnson.

NOMINATION POLITICS AND DEMOCRACY What does all this have to do with democratic control of government? Several things. On the one hand, as we have indicated, the presidential nomination process has some success in coming up with candidates who take stands with wide popular appeal, much as electoral competition theories dictate. On the other hand, as the sharp differences between Republican and Democratic convention delegates suggest (see Table 9.2), Republican and Democratic nominees tend to differ in certain systematic ways, in responsible party fashion. Party platforms—the parties' official statements of their stand on issues—tend to include appeals to average voters but also distinctive appeals to each party's base constituencies.

Both these tendencies might be considered good for democracy. However, the crucial role of party activists and money-givers in selecting candidates means that nominees and their policy stands are chosen partly to appeal to party elites, financial contributors, and strong partisans rather than to ordinary voters. Thus, neither party's nominee may stand for what ordinary citizens want, the result being voter dissatisfaction and no ideal democratic outcome.

THE PUBLIC FACE OF PARTY CONVENTIONS

The impression conveyed by political conventions can have an important impact on elections. The apparent unhappiness of many anti–Vietnam War delegates with their party's selection at the 1968 Democratic convention in Chicago severely damaged the campaign of nominee Hubert Humphrey. In contrast, the 1984 Republican convention that selected Ronald Reagan as its nominee more nearly resembled a coronation and gave Reagan and the GOP a fast start in the fall campaign. Are party conventions still necessary? Might there be an easier way to certify each party's nominee? Do they still exist because of their pep-rally appeal?

10.1

10.2

10.3

10.4

10.5

10.6

☐ The General Election Campaign

The general election campaign pitting the candidates of the two major parties against one another, with an occasional third party thrown into the mix, is a very different sort of contest than the run for party nomination. It requires different things from the candidates, campaign organizations, and associated interest and advocacy groups, and has an entirely different tone and set of rules, both formal and informal. The general election campaign season, much like the nomination campaign season, has gotten much longer as well. For a discussion of the 2012 presidential campaign and election, please refer again to the chapter-opening story.

GETTING THE CAMPAIGN UP AND RUNNING In the not-too-distant past, the general election campaign generally began on or about Labor Day, some weeks after the Republican and Democratic conventions were done with their business. That's why it was referred to as the "autumn campaign" and the "fall campaign." Today, however, as we have suggested, the presidential nominees for both parties are known months before the conventions even convene and they begin to campaign for the presidency months before their formal nomination. Flush with campaign money and unworried about their no-longer-relevant challengers within their own party, each of the presumptive nominees—George W. Bush and Al Gore in 2000, Bush and John Kerry in 2004, and McCain in 2008—repositioned their campaigns by mid-spring to take on their general election foe: setting up a campaign organization in each state, sending aides to coordinate backers and local party leaders, and continuing the money-raising effort. Barack Obama swung into general election mode by early June in 2008 once he had bested Hillary Clinton for the nomination. In 2012, major advertising campaigns by the Obama and Romney camps were well underway in important swing states by late May, months before either was confirmed as the official nominee of his respective party.[47]

Once the post-convention autumn campaign begins in September, the candidates' staffs have the nominees making speeches in six or seven media markets each week, with the pace intensifying as the November election draws closer, concentrating on so-called battleground states, where the contest between the presidential candidates is deemed to be very close and could go either way (see the "Mapping American Politics" feature on campaign ad buys). In all of this, hired pollsters and campaign consultants are deeply involved, playing a role in virtually all tactical and strategic decision making.[48]

A new media blitz begins, with many brief spot commercials on television, including "attack" ads such as Democrat Bill Clinton's in 1992 mocking George H. W. Bush's "read my lips, no new taxes" pledge (which he did not keep). Political consultants use voter focus groups to identify hot-button emotional appeals. Negative advertising, whether print, on television, or on the Internet, has been heavily criticized as simplistic and misleading, but it has often proved effective and is difficult to control or counteract. (Some scholars even argue that such ads increase voter interest and provide needed information.)[49]

Each campaign uses micro-targeting techniques to identify and communicate with base supporters and persuadable voters who might be convinced to vote for the candidate. Sophisticated software allows campaign organizations to combine surveys, census tract data, and materials from marketing research firms to identify base and persuadable voters and to tailor messages to particular groups and people and deliver the message by mail, door-to-door canvassing, e-mail, and social-network tools. Republican messages are directed, for example, not only to well-off people but more specifically to those who subscribe to *Golf Weekly* and shop at Saks Fifth Avenue. Democratic messages, using the same micro-targeting, might be directed to members of teachers unions and contributors to the American Civil Liberties Union.[50]

In all of these activities, presidential candidates, with lots of help to be sure, run their own campaigns. They and not the political parties decide on campaign themes, schedules, and strategies. The national party organizations are there to help, running parallel advertising campaigns supporting their candidate and attacking the opponent, channelling money to state and local party organizations, and getting potential supporters registered and to the polls. Meanwhile, interest groups and advocacy

10.1
10.2
10.3
10.4
10.5
10.6

OBAMA ON THE CAMPAIGN TRAIL

Until the early years of the twentieth century, it was considered unseemly for a sitting president to campaign for his own reelection. Modern presidents, such as Barack Obama here in 2012, are deeply engaged in their campaigns, spending as much time as possible on television and video-friendly events available for broad distribution.

organizations run their own ad campaigns and get-out-the-vote efforts. Liberal advocacy organizations such as MoveOn.org, for example, run ads in support of the Democratic presidential candidate (and House and Senate Democratic candidates), raise money, and work on turning out Democrats, while conservative Christian groups and business-oriented organizations work to help the Republican side. Now, since *Citizens United v. Federal Election Commission* (2010), corporations, unions, and rich individuals can give without limit in support of or in opposition to candidates so long as they don't give money directly to the candidates' official campaign organizations.

INFORMING VOTERS What kinds of information do voters get in presidential campaigns? Among other things, voters get information on the candidates' stands on the issues, their past performances, and their personal characteristics.

Issues Some of the information voters get concerns issues. In accord with electoral competition theories, both the Republican and the Democratic candidates typically have tried to appeal to the average voter by taking similar, popular stands on a range of policies, whether it be support for federal student loan programs or proposals to create more jobs. In recent elections, however, intensification of partisanship has moved American presidential and congressional electoral campaigns in a more responsible party direction, with clear stands on the issues, differentiated from the other party. In 2008, Barack Obama and John McCain took decidedly different stands on major issues, especially on the wars in Iraq and Afghanistan, abortion, global climate change, and health care reform. On these issues, the Democratic candidate tends to take a more liberal (on both economic and social dimensions) stand than the Republican, just as Democratic Party identifiers, activists, money givers, and convention delegates tend to be more liberal than their Republican counterparts.

Past Performance Often candidates focus on past performance in their campaigns. The "outs" blame the "ins" for wars, recessions, and other calamities. The "ins" brag about how they have brought peace and prosperity and paint a warm picture of a glorious future, without saying exactly how it will come about. When these issues become the overriding theme in a campaign, the result is a "retrospective," "reward–punish" type of election. Democrat Franklin Roosevelt won a landslide victory in 1932, for example, because of popular discontent with government performance under Herbert Hoover in the face of the Great Depression; Republican Ronald Reagan capitalized on economic and foreign policy troubles under Jimmy Carter to win in 1980.

Personal Characteristics Most of all, however, voters get a chance during the general election campaign to learn about the real or alleged personal characteristics of the candidates. Even when the candidates are talking about something else, they give an impression of either competence or incompetence. Jimmy Carter, for example, emphasized his expertise as a "nuclear engineer," whereas Gerald Ford was haunted by films of him stumbling down airplane steps.

Candidates also come across as interpersonally warm or cold. Dwight D. Eisenhower's radiant grin appeared everywhere in 1952 and 1956, as Reagan's did in 1984, but Richard Nixon was perceived as cold and aloof in 1968, despite clever efforts at selling his personality.

Still another dimension of candidates' personalities is a candidate's presumed strength or weakness. George H. W. Bush overcame the so-called wimp factor in 1988 with his tough talk about crime and the flag. Merely by surviving many personal attacks in 1992 and 1996, Clinton appeared strong and resilient.

The sparse and ambiguous treatment of policy issues in campaigns, as well as the emphasis on past performance and personal competence, fits better with ideas about electoral reward and punishment than with responsible parties or issue-oriented electoral competition models of democratic elections. To be sure, candidate personalities are not irrelevant to the democratic control of government. Obviously, it is useful for voters to pick presidents who possess competence, warmth, and strength. And citizens may be more skillful in judging people than in figuring out complicated policy issues.

Voters can be fooled, however, by dirty tricks or slick advertising that sells presidential candidates' personalities and tears down the opponent. Moreover, the focus on personal imagery may distract attention from policy stands. If candidates who favor unpopular policies are elected on the basis of attractive personal images, democratic control of policymaking is weakened. By the purchase of advertising and the hiring of smart consultants, money may, in effect, overcome the popular will.

☐ Money in General Elections

Money plays a crucial role in American general election campaigns and elections. Not surprisingly, parties and candidates spend much of their time and effort raising money for campaigns.

THE SCALE OF CAMPAIGN MONEY AND WHERE IT COMES FROM Presidential campaigns cost a great deal of money, although the system is so complex that even seasoned observers can make only educated guesses about the total. We have good data on money coming from certain sources but not from others. For example, we know that federal candidates during the 2007–2008 election cycle spent around $5.3 billion,[51] and more than $6 billion during the 2011–2012 cycle,[52] but we are less sure about a wide range of other expenditures on their behalf by advocacy groups. What we do know is that, considering only monies officially reported (so-called hard money), the total that is raised and spent from one presidential election cycle to the next keeps increasing and shows no signs of slowing down (see Figure 10.4).

HARD MONEY Hard money refers to contributions to and spending by candidate and party committees that fall under the jurisdiction of the Federal Election Commission. The rules followed by the FEC are the result of two major reform bills—the Federal Election Campaign Act and its later amendments passed during the 1970s and the McCain–Feingold Campaign Reform Act of 2002—interpretations of this legislation by the Supreme Court, and administrative rulings by the Commission itself. Importantly, advocacy group advertising by corporations, unions, and rich individuals is becoming as important in campaigns as hard money flowing to and being spent by official campaign committees. This trend has been helped along by *Citizens United v. Federal*

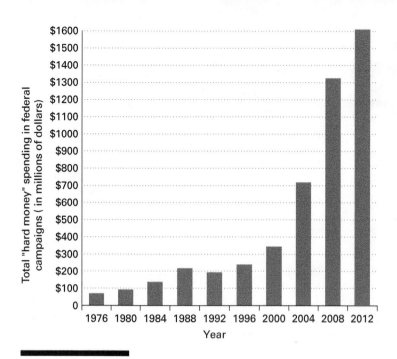

10.1

10.2

10.3

10.4

10.5

10.6

FIGURE 10.4 THE GROWTH IN SPENDING IN PRESIDENTIAL ELECTIONS*

*Spending by candidates, party, and independent committees as reported to the Federal Election Commission. All numbers are based on summary reports filed with the FEC. The 2012 election is based on preliminary estimates.

Source: The Center for Responsive Politics.

Election Commission (2010) in which the Court ruled that corporations and unions may not be limited on what they spend on advertising in support of or opposition to a candidate, nor can any pre-election advertising-free time period be imposed on them so long as they do not work in close collaboration with party or candidate committees. This means that corporations and unions likely will play a much bigger role than in the past in financing independent, parallel campaigns, from federal elections to local races.

Individuals The largest single source of hard money funding for presidential campaigns is from individual contributors, ranging from those who made small contributions to the candidates in response to an e-mail or letter solicitation or a call from a party worker, to wealthier individuals who gave the maximum amount allowed in 2008 of $2,400 to a single candidate (or a total of $42,700 to several candidates) and $28,500 to a national party committee per year. (See Table 10.1 for FEC rules on contributions limits for the 2011–2012 election cycle.) Before passage of the Federal Election Campaign Act (FECA), individuals could make contributions of unlimited size, and candidates and the parties depended on a handful of very rich individuals to fund their operations. After limits were placed on the size of allowable contributions, both parties invented a variety of ways to attract small contributions from hundreds of thousands of people, beginning with targeted mail and telephone solicitations, then adding Internet fund-raising, a development that fueled much of the funding for the Obama campaign. Indeed, roughly 55 percent of Obama's funds in 2008 came from individuals giving $200 or less.[53]

Candidates Candidates seeking a party's nomination will sometimes contribute or lend money to their campaigns; both John McCain and Hillary Clinton did this in 2007 and 2008. But once each party chooses its nominee for the presidency, presidential candidates have no need to use their personal resources. There are sufficient campaign monies coming from other sources to finance a full campaign.

Political Action Committees (PACs) You will recall that PACs are entities created by interest groups—whether business firms, unions, membership organizations, or liberal and conservative advocacy groups—to collect money and make contributions to candidates in federal elections (i.e., to candidates for the presidency, the House of Representatives, and the Senate). In 2012, PACs raised about $2 billion to contribute to presidential and congressional candidates, party committees, and their own electioneering campaigning (television, radio, and Internet advertising on the issues or candidates).[54]

10.1
10.2
10.3
10.4
10.5
10.6

TABLE 10.1 HARD MONEY CONTRIBUTION LIMITS 2011–2012

	To Each Candidate or Candidate Committee per Election	To National Party Committee per Calendar Year	To State, District, and Local Party Committee per Calendar Year	To Any Other Political Committee per Calendar Year	Special Limits
Individual	$2,500	$30,800	$10,000 (combined limit)	$5,000	$117,000 overall biennial limit: $46,200 to all candidates, $70,800 to all PACs and parties
National Party Committee	$5,000	No limit	No limit	$5,000	$43,100 to Senate candidate per campaign
State, District, and Local Party Committee	$5,000 (combined limit)	No limit	No limit	$5,000 (combined limit)	No limit
PAC (multicandidate)	$5,000	$15,000	$5,000 (combined limit)	$5,000	No limit
PAC (not multicandidate)	$2,500	$30,800	$10,000 (combined limit)	$5,000	No limit
Authorized Campaign Committee	$2,000	No limit	No limit	$5,000	No limit

Source: Federal Election Commission.

Political Parties The political parties also play an important role in helping out the party presidential nominee. Though campaign finance laws limit the amount of money that parties can give to the candidate's official campaign committee, the amount is not inconsiderable ($5,000 in 2011–2012). They also are allowed to spend a regulated amount on candidate services such as polling and advertising for get-out-the-vote efforts. More importantly, as described later, parties can also run very large and mostly unregulated "independent" campaigns on behalf of candidates. For these various campaign activities, the Republican National Committee raised almost $351 million in 2011–2012, while the Democratic National Committee raised a little more than $267 million.[55]

PUBLIC FUNDING Since 1971, and until recently, much of the money spent in the fall presidential campaign by the two presidential candidates' official campaign committees came from the federal treasury, paid by taxpayers. Taxpayers can check off a box on their tax returns to authorize a $3 contribution from public funds. The government uses these taxpayer contributions to provide matches for money contributors give to candidates during the primary and general election campaigns of those candidates who agree to spending limits. In 2004, the Kerry and Bush campaigns each received $74.4 million in public funds for the general election in the fall. Although Kerry and Bush refused public money for their nomination campaigns, both accepted it for the general election contest. Republican John McCain accepted public funding of roughly $84 million in 2008. But why, until quite recently, did candidates do such a thing, given that accepting public funding for their campaigns limits what they could spend?

- Because publicly provided funds were not inconsiderable.
- Because the two party presidential candidates get a great deal of free publicity simply by being the standard bearer of one of the two major parties.
- Because various state, local, and national party committees spend generously on the campaigns.
- Because corporations and unions spend heavily supporting or working against presidential candidates.
- Because interest groups and advocacy organizations spend lavishly on independent parallel campaigns.

Dramatically breaking with tradition, Democratic nominee Barack Obama chose in 2008 to reject public funding with its accompanying spending limits, primarily because of his remarkably successful fund-raising operation with monies coming to his campaign committee both from millions of small and medium-sized donations raised primarily online and from large donors. In doing so, he went back on a promise to use public funding and limit his spending, saying he needed to do so because of expected attacks from independent conservative advocacy groups and 527 and 501 organizations (explained in the next section). In 2012, neither Democrat Barack Obama nor Republican Mitt Romney accepted public funding, effectively killing the system.

OTHER MONEY After soft money to political parties was banned, 527, 501, and super PAC organizations gained favor.

527s So named because of where they are defined in the Tax Code, 527s are entities that can use unregulated money to talk about issues, mobilize voters, and praise or criticize candidates and office holders. There are no limits on contributions to them, nor are 527s limited in what they can spend. Many of these groups devoted to liberal or conservative causes and candidates sprouted up after passage of McCain–Feingold and played a very large role in the 2004 presidential election—Swift Boat Veterans for Truth (anti-Kerry) and MoveOn.org (anti-Bush) were the most prominent—and the 2006 congressional elections. Many of these groups depend on very large contributions from a handful of rich individuals; George Soros contributed more than $15 million to anti-Bush 527s in 2004, while Texas oilman T. Boone Pickens gave $4.6 million to anti-Kerry groups.

501s Although 527s are still around, they have lost favor. For one thing, both John McCain and Barack Obama condemned them in 2008 and informed 527 groups that they did not want their help. Perhaps more importantly, a better entity was discovered. 527s are required to report their total receipts and expenditures to the Internal Revenue Service (IRS) and report the identity of their contributors and how much they gave. 501 tax-exempt organizations—entities whose main purpose is to encourage "civic engagement"—must also report receipts and expenditures to the IRS, but less frequently than 527s, and they are not obligated to report the identities of their contributors. And,

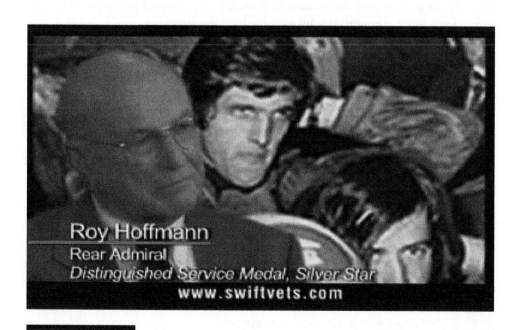

GETTING "SWIFT BOATED"

In the 2004 presidential campaign, 527 advocacy organizations became very important, mostly by running attack ads. One of the most effective was the Swift Boat group, which attacked Democratic candidate John Kerry's war record, calling his wartime awards and citations "dishonest and dishonorable." By law, such 527 groups are not allowed specifically to ask voters to vote for a particular candidate or to not vote for a particular candidate, though they can praise or criticize them. Is it truly possible or even reasonable for an organization to promote certain issues while not endorsing a candidate, or to praise or criticize a candidate without the same effect?

10.1

10.2

10.3

10.4

10.5

10.6

like 527s, there are no limits on how much money they can collect or spend. Not surprisingly, 501s have come to play a bigger role in the campaign finance system.

Super PACs These are nonprofit entities—usually organized as 527 organizations—that can accept unlimited amounts in donations from corporations, unions, groups, and individuals. They can use these monies to advocate issues and for and against candidates for public office, though (unlike PACs) they cannot give money directly to candidates. They must issue periodic reports to the Federal Election Commission and identify their donors, though donors may be 501 organizations that need not report who their donors are. Super PACs played a major role in the 2011–2012 election cycle, with conservative ones leading the way. They have become the favored vehicles of very rich individuals who are not worried about their identities being known. In 2012, Las Vegas gambling magnate Sheldon Adelson pledged $100 million to help Mitt Romney, giving mainly to the group Restore Our Future.

DOES MONEY TALK? Money matters a great deal in the presidential nomination process—aspirants for party nominations who cannot raise sizable funds always drop out of the race—but not so much during the post-convention run for the White House.[56] As we pointed out earlier, once a presidential campaign is under way, each of the major party candidates has at his or her disposal all of the organizational resources of the party organization and money from traditional party contributors and allied interest groups, 527s, 501s, and super PACs, and lots of free publicity from news organizations.

Money may talk at a later stage, however. It is widely believed, although difficult to prove, that contributors of money often get something back.[57] The point is not that presidential, House, and Senate candidates take outright bribes in exchange for policy favors. Indeed, exchanges between politicians and money-givers are complex and varied, sometimes yielding little benefit to contributors. Undeniably, however, cozy relationships do tend to develop between politicians and major money-givers. Contributors gain access to, and a friendly hearing from, those whom they help to win office. And, groups that spend lavishly on issue campaigns often influence the policy agenda in Washington. Though this influence is indirect rather than direct, it is surely considerable.

It is clear that money-givers are different from average citizens. They have special interests of their own. As we have indicated, a large amount of campaign money comes from large corporations, investment banking firms, wealthy families, labor unions, professional associations (e.g., doctors, lawyers, or realtors), and issue-oriented groups such as the National Rifle Association, Focus on the Family, and the National Abortion Rights Action League. The big contributors generally do not represent ordinary workers, consumers, or taxpayers, let alone minorities or the poor. Surveys show that the individuals who give money tend to have much higher incomes and more conservative views on economic issues than the average American.[58] This is true as well for those who contribute by way of the Internet.[59]

The result is political inequality. Those who are well organized or have a lot of money to spend on politics have a better chance of influencing policy than ordinary citizens do, and they tend to influence it in directions different from those the general public would want. The role of money in presidential and congressional nomination and election campaigns is a major problem for the working of democracy in the United States.

Election Outcomes

10.6   Assess how presidential elections are decided

fter the parties and candidates have presented their campaigns, the voters decide. Exactly how people make their voting decisions affects how well or how poorly elections contribute to the democratic control of government.

☐ How Voters Decide

Years of scholarly research have made it clear that feelings about the parties, the candidates, and the issues, as well as their own social characteristics, have substantial effects on how people vote.[60]

SOCIAL CHARACTERISTICS People's socioeconomic status, place of residence, religion, ethnic backgrounds, gender, and age are related to how they vote (see Figure 10.5). African Americans, Jews, and lower-income citizens for many years have tended to vote for Democrats, while white Protestants and upper-income Americans have voted for Republicans. Much of this stayed the same in 2012, but some things changed as well.

PARTY LOYALTIES To a great extent, these social patterns of voting work through long-term attachments to, or identification with, political parties. As indicated

10.1

10.2

10.3

10.4

10.5

10.6

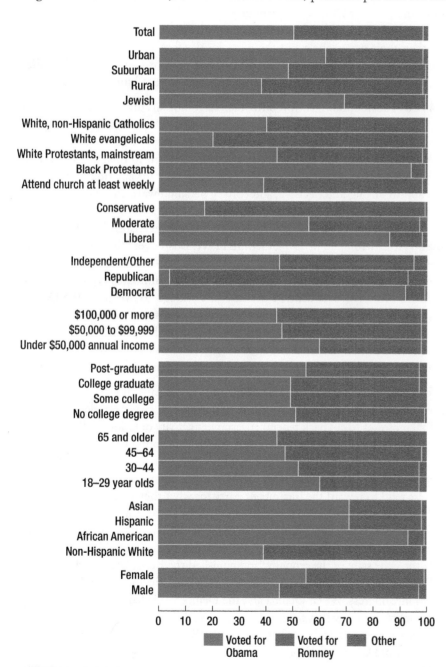

FIGURE 10.5 PRESIDENTIAL VOTE IN 2012, BY SOCIAL GROUP

Racial and ethnic minorities, urbanites, young people, liberals, people with post-graduate degrees, and women voted strongly for Democrat Barack Obama in the 2012 election, while white Catholics and Protestants, regular church-goers, and evangelicals rural people, conservatives, older people, and men favored Republican Mitt Romney.

Source: The Election Day Polls, Edison Research, November 6, 2012; and the Pew Research Center, November 7, 2012.

10.1
10.2
10.3
10.4
10.5
10.6

earlier, a majority of Americans still say they consider themselves Republicans or Democrats, especially if we include so-called "leaners." Party loyalties vary among different groups of the population, often because of past or present differences between the parties on policy issues, especially economic and social issues. For this reason, when people use their party identification as a shortcut for choosing a candidate, they are likely choosing a candidate who is close to them on the issues. The ability of party identification to serve as a useful tool for people to choose candidates that are close to them on the issues is further enhanced by the close linkages between the parties and ideologies, with Democrats generally more liberal (including party identifiers, activists, and candidates) and Republicans generally more conservative.

Again, as we pointed out earlier, party loyalties are very good predictors of how people will vote.[61] Those who say they consider themselves Republicans tend to vote for Republican candidates in one election after another, and those who consider themselves Democrats vote for Democratic candidates. This is especially true in congressional elections and in state and local races, where most voters know little more about the candidates than their party labels, but the party loyalty factor is extremely important in presidential elections as well. Thus, in 2012, 92 percent of Democratic identifiers voted for Obama, and 93 percent of Republican identifiers voted for Romney.

CANDIDATES Presidential election outcomes have not simply reflected the party balance in the country; if that were true, Democrats would have won most presidential elections during the post–World War II period given their persistent party ID advantage over Republicans. Voters also pay a lot of attention to their perceptions of the personal characteristics of candidates. They vote heavily for candidates who have experience, appear strong and decisive, and convey personal warmth. The Republican candidate in 1952 and 1956, Dwight D. Eisenhower, had a tremendous advantage in these respects over his Democratic opponent, Adlai Stevenson;[62] so did Ronald Reagan over Walter Mondale in 1984, George H. W. Bush over Michael Dukakis in 1988, and George W. Bush over John Kerry in 2004. In elections between 1952 and 1972, the contrast between Republican and Democratic candidates typically gained the Republicans four or five percentage points—just enough to overcome the Democrats' advantage in what political scientists call the *normal vote*: how votes would be cast if only party identification determined voters' choices for president. Democrats have won when they have managed to add attractive candidates to augment their lead in party identification; Bill Clinton in 1996 and Barack Obama in 2008 are examples.

ISSUES Voters also pay attention to issues. Sometimes this means choosing between different policy proposals for the future (as in the responsible party voting model), such as Reagan's 1980 promises to cut back federal government activity or Clinton's 1992 pledges of jobs and a middle-class tax cut. Most often, however, issue voting has meant retrospective voting (the electoral reward and punishment model), making judgments about the past, especially on major questions about the state of the economy and war and peace.

The voters tend to reward the incumbent party for what they see as good times and to punish it for what they see as bad times. In especially bad economic times, for example, Americans tend to vote the incumbent party out of office, as they did the Republicans during the Great Depression in 1932. In 1992 the electorate punished Republican George H. W. Bush for the poor state of the economy and punished the Republicans in the midst of the Great Recession in 2008 when Obama handily beat McCain and the Democrats won big majorities in Congress. When Obama and the Democrats failed to bring the country out of bad economic times when they were in control, the voters punished them in the 2010 congressional elections, and gave big gains to the Republicans. In 1996, on the other hand, it rewarded Bill Clinton for being president during good economic times.

Foreign policy can be important as well, especially when war and peace are at issue. Bitter disillusionment over the Korean War hurt the Democrats in 1952, just as the Vietnam War cost them in 1968, and unhappiness about American hostages in Iran and the Soviet intervention in Afghanistan hurt Jimmy Carter in 1980. During nearly all of the past half-century, in fact, Republican candidates have been seen as better at providing foreign policy strength and at keeping us out of war. The bloody, expensive, and drawn-out war in Iraq undermined traditional GOP advantages in this area in 2008, however. In most elections, though, foreign policy concerns take a back seat to domestic ones for most voters. Even in 2008, in the midst of war, economic troubles triggered by the sub-prime mortgage and credit crunch disasters trumped foreign policy issues for a majority of voters.

☐ The Electoral College

Determining the winner of House and Senate elections is straightforward: the candidate with the most votes in a statewide contest for the Senate and the candidate with the most votes in a House district is elected. It's different for presidential elections. In contrast, the outcome of presidential elections is determined not by the number of popular votes cast for each candidate but by the candidate who wins a majority in the Electoral College.

When Americans vote for a presidential candidate whose name appears on the ballot, they are actually voting for a slate of **electors** in their state—equal to the number of the state's U.S. senators and representatives—who have promised to support a party's presidential candidate. (Very rarely have electors reneged on their promises and cast ballots for someone else; there was one so-called "faithless elector" in 2000.) Nearly all states now have winner-take-all systems in which the winner of the popular vote wins the state's entire allotment of electoral votes; Maine and Nebraska, in slight variations, choose electors on a winner-take-all basis for each congressional district.

The "college" of electors from the different states never actually meets together; instead, the electors meet in their respective states and send lists of how they have voted to Washington, D.C. (see the Twelfth Amendment to the Constitution). The candidate who receives a majority of all the electoral votes in the country is elected president. Not since 1824 has it been necessary to resort to the odd constitutional provisions that apply when no one gets a majority of electoral votes: the House of Representatives chooses among the top three candidates, by majority vote of state delegations. Each state in this procedure has one vote.

Most of the time, this peculiar Electoral College system works about the same way as if Americans chose their presidents by direct popular vote, but it has certain features that are politically consequential.

- *It magnifies the popular support of winners.* A candidate who wins in many states, by a narrow margin in each, can win a "landslide" in the Electoral College. In 1996, for example, Bill Clinton's 49 percent of the popular vote translated into 379 electoral votes, or 70 percent of the total. Ordinarily, this magnification simply adds legitimacy to the democratic choice, especially when the winner has only a **plurality** of the popular vote, that is, more than anybody else but less than a majority of all votes. Many of our presidents have been elected by only a plurality and not a majority of votes cast—most recently, Clinton (1992 and 1996), Richard Nixon (1968), John Kennedy (1960), and Harry Truman (1948). (See Table 10.2.)

- *It may let the less popular candidate win.* A president can be elected who had *fewer* votes than an opponent, if those votes happened to produce narrow margins in many states. Such a result has occurred three times: in 1876, when Rutherford Hayes defeated Samuel Tilden; in 1888, when Benjamin Harrison beat the more popular Grover Cleveland; and in 2000, when George W. Bush defeated Al Gore. (Gore beat Bush by more than a half million votes nationally.) Several early-nineteenth-century presidents were probably chosen with only small fractions of the popular vote, although we cannot be sure because some of the statistics are unreliable. Most notably, in 1824, John Quincy Adams defeated the very popular Andrew Jackson in the House of Representatives after an election when no candidate won a majority of electoral votes.

- *It discourages third parties.* Our constitutional arrangements for a single president and single-member congressional districts (rather than proportional representation) already discourage third parties; if candidates cannot win a plurality, they get nothing. The Electoral College adds significantly to this disadvantage: a third party with substantial support may get no electoral votes at all if its support is scattered among many states. In 1992, for example, Ross Perot's impressive

electors
Representatives who are elected in the states to formally choose the U.S. president.

plurality
More votes than any other candidate but less than a majority of all votes cast.

10.1
10.2
10.3
10.4
10.5
10.6

TABLE 10.2 ELECTION RESULTS, 1980–2012

Year	Candidate	Party	Percentage of Popular Votes	Percentage of Electoral Votes
1980	Ronald Reagan	Republican	51%	91%
	Jimmy Carter	Democratic	41%	9%
	John Anderson	Independent	7%	0%
1984	Ronald Reagan	Republican	59%	98%
	Walter Mondale	Democratic	41%	2%
1988	George H. W. Bush	Republican	53%	79%
	Michael Dukakis	Democratic	46%	21%
1992	William Clinton	Republican	43%	69%
	George H. W. Bush	Democratic	37%	31%
	H. Ross Perot	Independent	19%	0%
1996	William Clinton	Democratic	49%	70%
	Robert Dole	Republican	41%	30%
	H. Ross Perot	Reform Party	8%	0%
2000	George W. Bush	Republican	48%	60.5%
	Albert Gore	Democratic	48%	49.5%
	Ralph Nader	Green Party	3%	0%
2004	George W. Bush	Republican	51%	53%
	John Kerry	Democratic	48%	47%
2008	Barack Obama	Democratic	53%	68%
	John McCain	Republican	46%	32%
2012	Barack Obama	Democratic	50%	62%
	Mitt Romney	Republican	48%	38%

Sources: Data from the Federal Election Commission and Harold Stanley and Richard C. Niemi, *Vital Statistics in American Politics 2011–2012* (Washington, D.C.: CQ Press, 2012) authors' calculations for 2012.

19 percent of the popular vote translated into zero electoral votes because he failed to win a plurality in any single state.

There have been many calls over the years to change the Electoral College system of electing the president.[63] Majorities of Americans have told pollsters repeatedly that they want a system based on direct popular vote. Simply count up the votes nationally, and the candidate with the most votes wins the presidency. Simple.

But perhaps it's not so simple. What if three, four, or five candidates run and the plurality winner only receives, let us say, 30 percent of the vote? Would Americans be comfortable with a president elected by so few people? One way to solve this, as they do in France, among other places, is to have a second-round run-off election between the top two candidates so that the person elected comes to office with majority support.

Another idea that has been floated around is to retain the Electoral College but to remove the "winner-take-all" feature whereby the winner of a state receives all of the state's Electoral College votes even if the win is by the slimmest of margins. Various methods for apportioning a state's electoral votes in a way that approximates the division in the popular vote in the state have been suggested.

One way to get to such a system would be for each of the states to act on its own. The Constitution leaves it up to the states to choose how they determine the distribution of their Electoral College votes. The problem here, of course, is that unless all states acted at the same time, the first movers would be disadvantaged. If a state were to divide up its electoral votes to approximate the popular vote division, it would no longer be such a prize for the candidates compared to those states that were still operating on a "winner-take-all" basis. First-movers would lose influence in national elections, and there would be no assurance that other states would live up to their reform promises down the road. So, a change in the Electoral College along these lines would require national action, perhaps even a constitutional amendment.

Additionally, some benefit from the current system and do not want to change it. Small states, for example, have more influence than they would have in a direct popular election system because the number of electoral votes a state has is determined by adding up its number of representatives (based on population) and senators (two for each state). Thus, small states have more weight in presidential elections than

Mapping American Politics

Ad Buys and Battleground States

Introduction

As you have seen, presidents are selected not by the people directly, but by votes in the Electoral College. The winner is that candidate who wins a majority of electoral votes. Campaigns are conducted on a state-by-state basis in a bid to put together a majority of electoral votes. With the exception of Nebraska and Maine, states use winner-take-all systems in which the candidate with the most votes (not necessarily a majority) wins all the state's electoral votes. Knowing this, campaign managers and their candidates focus on a relative handful of states where the contest is too close to call and where winning might affect the outcome of the presidential contest. They virtually ignore states that are not "in play," where the outcome is a foregone conclusion. In the 2012 election, for example, Democrats were in such a commanding position in California and New York that neither Democrats nor Republicans thought it wise to use scarce funds to campaign there. As well, Republicans were so far ahead in Texas, Utah, and Alabama that neither party thought it worthwhile to campaign there.

Mapping Ad Buys

The cartogram below, with the size of the states reflecting the number of electoral votes, highlights the states where the parties and campaign organizations bought the greatest number of television ads urging votes for their candidate in the month or so before the 2004 election. You can see that significant television ad buys occurred in only 10 states, but those 10 accounted for 88 percent of all such ads bought across the entire country. The focus of the campaign on battleground states is very evident. Note that several of the very largest Electoral College states were not among those 10, including California, Illinois, New Jersey, and New York (reliably Democratic) and Texas and the Deep South (reliably Republican), not including Florida. Ad buys occurred overwhelmingly in states where party and campaign professionals believed either party's presidential candidate had a chance to win. The cartogram below shows the final electoral vote outcome.

What Do You Think?

Taking a look at how the vote turned out in the battleground states, whose campaign seems to have done a better job of using ad buys effectively? Referring to the chapter-opening story, who did a better job in the battleground states in 2012? If you lived in a nonbattleground state, did it seem that there was very little campaign advertising on television? If you lived in a battleground state, did it seem that there was too much advertising? Is there any way to convince parties and presidential campaigns to wage the presidential battle on a nationwide basis so long as we use the Electoral College system for selecting presidents?

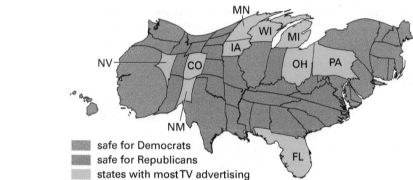

safe for Democrats
safe for Republicans
states with most TV advertising

States Sized by Electoral Vote Totals, Colored by Party Leanings and Ad Buys
Source: © 2006 M. D. Ward

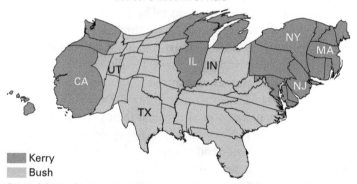

Kerry
Bush

States Sized by Electoral Vote Totals, Colored by Election Outcomes, 2004
Source: © 2006 M. D. Ward. Source for top left cartogram: "Presidential TV Advertising Battle Narrows to Just Ten Battleground States," Nielsen Monitor-Plus and the University of Wisconsin Advertising Project (press release, October 12, 2004).

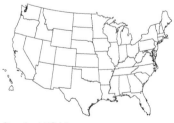

Standard US Map

Note: In cartograms, Alaska is not shown (although information is included in calculations), and Hawaii is moved closer to the mainland.

Source for top left cartogram: "Presidential TV Advertising Battle Narrows to Just Ten Battleground States," Nielsen Monitor-Plus and the University of Wisconsin Advertising Project (press release, October 12, 2004).

they would have if electoral votes were tied to the number of its seats in the House. Politicians and activists in battleground states also tend to like the Electoral College system because they gain attention—including visits, ad campaigns, and the like—from candidates and parties in close elections where a bloc of electoral votes might make the difference in the outcome of a national election. And, because a constitutional amendment requires ratification by three-fourths of the states, it would be very hard to make a change that small states and battleground states such as Ohio, Missouri, Florida, and Colorado, among others, are likely to oppose.

Using the DEMOCRACY STANDARD

Do voting and elections make government leaders listen to the people?

Elections and citizen political participation in the United States have been substantially democratized over the years, altering some of the constitutional rules introduced by the framers. For example, the Seventeenth Amendment, adopted in 1913, transformed the Senate into an institution whose members are elected directly by voters rather than by state legislatures. The manner of electing the president is completely different from what the framers thought they had created: an independent body for presidential selection. By custom or by law, virtually all electors today are pledged to a particular candidate before the presidential election, so that, for all intents and purposes, the president is directly elected by the people (although disparities between the electoral and popular vote occasionally happen, as in 2000). Equally important, the franchise has been so broadened—to include previously excluded racial minorities and women—that today almost all Americans 18 years and older are eligible to vote, something that few of the framers envisioned or would have found conducive to good government.

In addition to these institutional transformations, democratizing changes in the prevailing political culture have also been important. The spread of the ideas that political leaders ought to be responsible and responsive to the people, and that political leaders ought to pay attention to what the mass public wanted from them, represents a fundamental change from the prevailing view among the framers.

Elections are the most important means by which citizens can exert democratic control over their government. Although a variety of instruments help convey the people's wishes to officials—public opinion polls, interest groups, and social movements—it is ultimately the fact that officials must face the voters that keeps them in line. In terms of the responsible party idea, the fact that the Republican Party tends to be more conservative than the Democratic Party on a number of economic and social issues provides voters with a measure of democratic control by enabling them to detect differences and make choices about the future. Alternatively, through electoral punishment, voters can exercise control by reelecting successful incumbents and throwing failures out of office, thus making incumbents think ahead. Finally, electoral competition forces the parties to compete by nominating centrist candidates and by taking similar issue stands close to what most Americans want. This last force, in fact, may be the chief way in which citizens' policy preferences affect what their government does.

While U.S. elections help make the public's voice heard, they do not bring about perfect democracy. Far from it. Elections do not lead to a greater degree of democracy for a number of reasons: the low turnouts that characterize American elections at all levels, the educational and income biases in participation rates, and the role of interest groups and well-off contributors in campaign finance. Uneven participation and the influence of money on campaigns undermine political equality by giving some people much more political clout than others. Ever fiercer partisanship, moreover, increasingly is keeping candidates from choosing policies that reflect the wishes of the median voter in the electoral competition model, making this democracy-enhancing electoral mechanism less effective. So, notwithstanding the spread of democracy beyond the imaginings of the framers, those who support the democratic idea think we have some distance yet to travel.

Review the Chapter

 Listen to **Chapter 10** on **MyPoliSciLab**

Elections and Democracy

10.1 Evaluate three models of how elections can lead to popular control, p. 298

In theory, at least, elections are the most important means by which citizens can exert democratic control over their government by forcing elected officials to pay attention to the wishes of voters.

Three theoretical models of voting are at play in making elections a potentially democratic instrument of the people: responsible parties/prospective voting; reward and punishment/retrospective voting; and the electoral competition/median voter model. Elections matter not only when there is a clear choice but also when electoral reward or punishment occurs or when electoral competition forces both parties to take similar popular stands.

The Unique Nature of American Elections

10.2 Distinguish American elections from those in other countries, p. 301

There are more elections here than in other democratic countries. They are on a fixed date and the offices voted upon have a fixed term. Elections almost always are of the winner-take-all, first-past-the-post variety, encouraging a two-party system. And, elections are administered by state and local governments rather than the national government.

Voting in the United States

10.3 Analyze the importance of political participation in elections, p. 304

The right to vote, originally quite limited, was expanded in various historical surges to include nearly all adults and to apply to most major offices. The changes came about because of changes in American society and the struggle for democracy waged by various groups of Americans.

Who Votes?

10.4 Identify demographic factors that increase the likelihood of voting, p. 310

The higher the income and the higher the education a person has, the more likely that person is to vote. When education

and income are accounted for, the long-time differentiation between white and black turnout disappears.

Women now vote at a slightly higher rate than men.

Campaigning for Office

10.5 Outline the process of campaigns for the presidency and Congress, p. 315

Candidates for the party nomination for president start by testing the waters, raising money, and forming campaign organizations; in a series of state primaries and caucuses, they seek delegates to the national nominating conventions, which generally choose a clear front-runner or the incumbent president.

Candidates who cannot raise money or have money raised for them by others do not become serious contenders in the party nomination contests. Money differences between the candidates in the presidential contest in the general election are less important in determining the outcome because of public financing, party spending, interest and advocacy group spending, and intense and costless press coverage of the election.

The goal of presidential candidates in the fall campaign is to rally the party base and win over a substantial proportion of independent and moderate voters. Campaign activity and spending focus on battleground states.

Election Outcomes

10.6 Assess how presidential elections are decided, p. 328

Voters' decisions depend heavily on party loyalties, the personal characteristics of the candidates, and the issues, especially the state of the economy.

The president is selected not by direct popular vote but by a majority in the Electoral College vote.

responsible party, p. 298
prospective voting model, p. 298
electoral competition model, p. 299
median voter, p. 299
electoral reward and
    punishment, p. 300
retrospective voting, p. 300

provisional ballot, p. 301
franchise, p. 304
suffrage, p. 304
Electoral College, p. 305
party convention, p. 306
primary election, p. 306
party caucuses, p. 306

turnout, p. 306
referenda, p. 308
initiatives, p. 308
superdelegates, p. 315
electors, p. 331
plurality, p. 331

Test Yourself

 Study and **Review** the **Practice Tests**

Answer key begins on page T-1.

10.1 Evaluate three models of how elections can lead to popular control

1. In the electoral competition model of democratic elections, unified parties compete for votes by taking:

   a. The least popular position
   b. The middle-of-the-road position
   c. The most popular position
   d. The most controversial position
   e. The least controversial position

10.2 Distinguish American elections from those in other countries

2. Which of the following is a distinguishing feature of elections in the United States?

   a. Elections are infrequent
   b. Elections are all conducted around the same time
   c. Elected positions do not have fixed terms of office
   d. Inconsistent election procedures and vote-counting
   e. Elections are not held on a fixed date

10.3 Analyze the importance of political participation in elections

3. Most delegates to the Republican and Democratic national conventions are selected when party supporters and activists hold neighborhood and area-wide meetings to select delegates. These are called:

   a. State elections
   b. Party caucuses
   c. Primary elections
   d. Party conventions
   e. Local elections

10.4 Identify demographic factors that increase the likelihood of voting

4. What factor does NOT generally influence the likelihood of a person voting?

   a. Age
   b. Income
   c. Gender
   d. Race
   e. Location

10.5 Outline the process of campaigns for the presidency and Congress

5. Refers to contributions and spending that fall under the jurisdiction of the Federal Election Commission:

   a. Hard money
   b. Soft money
   c. Voter contribution
   d. Federal support
   e. Public funding

10.6 Assess how presidential elections are decided

6. When a candidate has more votes than any other candidate, but less than a majority of all votes cast, this is called:

   a. Majority vote
   b. Minority vote
   c. Plurality
   d. Majority election
   e. Landslide

Explore Further

INTERNET SOURCES

Democratic National Committee **www.democrats.org**
Official site of the Democratic Party, with information on party positions and candidates, how to work as a volunteer or contribute money, and more.

The Federal Election Commission **www.fec.gov**
Rules and data on campaign fund-raising and spending in federal elections.

The National Archives Electoral College Site **www.archives.gov/federal_register/electoral_college/index.html**
Everything there is to know about the law and practices of the Electoral College and the process by which it elects the president.

Voting America: United States Politics **www.americanpast.org/voting/**
A comprehensive collection of interactive maps detailing elections from 1840–2008. This site also has discussions by scholars on past elections and U.S. voting.

Open Secrets at the Center for Responsive Politics **www.opensecrets.org**
An especially good site for following the money trail—how campaign money is gathered and spent.

Project Vote Smart **www.vote-smart.org**
A political portal loaded with links to information about candidates, parties, election rules, and issues.

Intrade **www.intrade.com**
A futures market focusing on elections and public opinion about issues; extraordinarily accurate in predicting election outcomes.

Republican National Committee **www.rnc.org**
Official site of the Republican Party, with information on party positions and candidates, how to work as a volunteer or contribute money, and more.

A Plain Blog About Politics **plainblogaboutpolitics.blogspot.com**
Follow contemporary politics on this site through the eyes of practicing political scientists who bring disciplinary perspectives to bear on tough questions about democracy and governance.

SUGGESTIONS FOR FURTHER READING

Kamarck, Elaine C. *Primary Politics: How Presidential Candidates Have Shaped the Modern Nominating System.* Washington, D.C.: Brookings Institution Press, 2009.
A history of the changing presidential nominating process and how candidates take advantage of existing primary and caucus rules and try to change rules to their advantage.

Maisel, Sandy L. *American Political Parties: A Very Short Introduction.* New York: Oxford University Press, 2007.
The best brief book on American voting and elections; surprisingly insightful for such a short book.

Polsby, Nelson W., Steven E. Schier, and David A. Hopkins. *Presidential Elections,* 13th ed. Lanham, MD: Rowman & Littlefield, 2011.
A comprehensive textbook on the presidential nominating process, the general election, and voting.

Shea, Daniel M. *Let's Vote: The Essentials of the American Electoral Process.* New York: Pearson, 2013.
A lively and accessible account of the American electoral system, what is enduring about it, and what is changing.

Verba, Sidney, Kay Lehman Schlozman, and Henry E. Brady. *Voice and Equality: Civic Volunteerism in American Politics.* Cambridge, MA: Harvard University Press, 1995.
A comprehensive analysis of inequalities in political participation and their meaning for the quality of democracy in the United States.

Wattenberg, Martin P. *Where Have All the Voters Gone?* Cambridge, MA: Harvard University Press, 2002.
A clear-headed and accessible look at this perennial and complex question.

11

Congress

DIVIDED WE STAND

Unlike 2006, 2008, and 2010, 2012 was not a "wave election," a term used to designate shifts between the parties of 30 or more seats. After all the commotion, endless ads and phone calls, and the expenditure of 1.6 billion on congressional races, not much seems to have changed. The elections left the Democrats still in control of the Senate with a small, non-filibuster proof majority. Counting independent senators who caucus with the Democrats—Bernie Sanders of Vermont and Angus King of Maine—the Democrats enjoy a 55–45 majority. In the House, Republicans maintained their majority, losing only 7 seats in the elections at this writing, nowhere near the 25 seats Democrats needed to regain control, so Republicans remain in charge, much as they did in the 112th Congress.

Below the surface, however, a number of important and interesting things happened during this non-wave congressional election. For one thing, there was, as the saying goes, "the dog that didn't bark," suggesting things that don't happen when all evidence suggests that they should have. Take the gain in Senate seats for the Democrats. Going into campaign season, most political insiders expected the Democrats to lose their majority in the Senate for the simple reason that they had many more seats to defend than the Republicans, 23 of them, in fact, to only 10 for the GOP. As for the House, Democratic expectations until very late in the game was that they stood a very good chance of winning a "wave election" proportion of seats given the 60 seats Republicans had took away from the Democrats in 2010, many of them in districts that were traditionally Democratic. It was not unrealistic to expect that many of these districts would revert back to their historical norms. So what happened in the Senate and House?

Though we won't know the exact reasons until political scientists have the opportunity to scientifically examine the question, a number of reasons have been offered. In the Senate, at least four Democratic wins could be attributed to the nomination in the Republican primaries of Tea Party-backed, extreme conservative candidates, including Charlie Sumner in Maine, Rick Berg in North Dakota, Todd Akin in Missouri, and Richard Mourdock in Indiana, all of whom lost. Democrats were also successful in retaining seats in the key battleground states such as Ohio, Virginia, Pennsylvania, Wisconsin, where President Obama won and where his very effective ground operation helped bring Democratic voters to the polls.

11.1	11.2	11.3	11.4	11.5
Identify the ways in which the Constitution shapes Congress, p. 342	Assess how and to what extent the members of Congress represent their constituents, p. 344	Describe what leaders, political parties, and committees do in Congress, p. 357	Outline the process by which a bill becomes a law, p. 370	Explain why Congress is doing less oversight than in the past, p. 374

DEMOCRATS RECLAIM A SENATE SEAT Democrat Elizabeth Warren celebrates her victory in the 2012 Senate race in Massachusetts. The former Harvard professor and crusader for regulating Wall Street defeated Republican and Tea Party-favorite Senator Scott Brown. Warren's election helped increase the number of women in the Senate to its highest level ever.

MyPoliSciLab Video Series

The Big Picture Why is Congress the most despised branch of government? Author Edward S. Greenberg diagnoses Congress' dysfunction as a combination of today's extreme partisanship and Congress's original design by the framers.

The Basics Why do we have two houses of Congress? This video reveals the answer to this question and explores the differences between the two houses in their organization and procedures. You will also learn how a bill becomes a law, how Congress is organized, and how members of Congress represent you.

How does Congress pass laws?

In Context Discover the role that the framers expected Congress to serve in the U.S. government. Columbia University political scientist Greg Wawro discusses how Congress has become more expansive in its powers. Listen as Greg Wawro also delves into the process of creating coalitions in Congress to achieve policy results.

Think Like a Political Scientist Why has the United States become more polarized in the last decade? Columbia University political scientist Greg Wawro examines this central question and explains why polarization may be correlated to the income gap between the wealthy and the poor. He also explores recent research on the Senate as a super-majoritarian institution.

In the Real World Congress today is the most divided it has been since the end of WWII. It is also the least effective. Is compromise the answer? Real people consider the benefits and the dangers of compromise, and they discuss issues—like abortion—where compromise seems impossible.

So What? Who is to blame for Congress's inefficiencies? Are members distracted by the ongoing campaign for reelection that our system requires? Is it the Senate's recent reliance on filibusters? Author Edward S. Greenberg offers his explanations and encourages students to come up with some of their own.

As for the House, Republican loses were kept to a minimum not only by an effective national strategy by the Republican House Campaign Committee which targeted vulnerable "blue dog" Democrats (that is, moderate to conservative Democrats serving in strongly Republican states or areas, mainly in the South), but by the redistricting that occurred in the states after the 2010 census. As you will learn later in this chapter, House districts are redrawn after each census so that each district within a state has roughly the same number of people in it. While there are legislative and judicial restrictions on drawing lines that disadvantage racial and ethnic minorities, there are few restrictions on drawing lines that advantage or disadvantage one or the other political party. Fortunately for Republicans, their sweeping national election victory in 2010 extended to the states where they ended up in control of twice as many state legislatures as the Democrats. Legislatures control redistricting in most states, so it is hardly surprising that both Republicans and Democrats drew lines for the 2012 elections that were designed to protect their own candidates. Fortunately for the Republicans, they were in power in many more states. In North Carolina, for example, Republicans redrew the district of moderate Democrat Heath Shuler so much to his disadvantage that he decided to retire rather than face certain defeat. There is reason to believe that redistricting played a key role in maintaining the GOP majority given the even split nationally between Republicans and Democrats in votes for the House.[1]

One compelling outcome of the 2012 elections was that Congress is now much more representative of the nation's diverse population. Over 80 women were elected to the House, bringing the percentage of women there to 19 percent. Eight new members of the House are Latinos; four new members are Asian Americans. Five more African Americans joined the House as a result of the 2012 elections. There are also four new House members who are openly gay. Though some of these new members are Republicans, most are Democrats. In fact, for the first time in American history, a majority of the House Democratic Caucus is comprised of women and racial and ethnic minorities.[2]

Though the number of Democrats and Republicans has not changed much in the aftermath of the 2012 elections, there has been a substantial exodus of moderates in both parties. The number of "blue-dog" Democrats from the South, numbering as many as 54 as recently as 2010, is now down to 14, with only a single Democratic representative from the five states of the deep South. In the New England states there are only a handful of Republicans representative left, most of whom in the past were found in the moderate wing of the GOP. Much of the middle has disappeared in both the House and the Senate. What this portends, perhaps, is the continuation of gridlock in Congress as those willing and able to compromise are fewer in number.

Thinking Critically About This Chapter

In this chapter, we turn our attention to the Congress of the United States, examining how Congress works as both a representative and governing institution.

Using the Framework

In this chapter you will learn how the way in which Congress works is affected by other government actors and institutions; political linkage level factors such as interest groups, public opinion, the media, and elections; and structural factors, such as constitutional rules and economic and social change.

Using the Democracy Standard

Using the concept of democracy used in this book, you will be able to evaluate how well Congress acts as a democratic institution. You will see that the story of Congress and democracy is a mixed one: Congress is, at times and under certain circumstances, highly responsive to the American public; at other times and under other circumstances, it is most responsive to special interest groups and large contributors.

enumerated powers
Powers of the federal government specifically mentioned in the Constitution.

elastic clause
Article I, Section 8, of the Constitution, also called *the necessary and proper clause*; gives Congress the authority to make whatever laws are necessary and proper to carry out its enumerated powers and other of its powers vested in the Constitution.

bicameral
As applied to a legislative body, consisting of two houses or chambers.

Constitutional Foundations of the Modern Congress

11.1 Identify the ways in which the Constitution shapes Congress

 he framers of the Constitution were concerned about the possibility of government tyranny. Yet they also wanted an energetic government capable of accomplishing its assigned tasks. These multiple and sometimes conflicting objectives are reflected in the constitutional design of Congress.

☐ Empowering Congress

The framers began by empowering Congress, making the legislative branch the center of lawmaking in the federal government. In Article I, Section 1, of the Constitution, they gave Congress the power to make the laws: "All legislative power herein granted shall be vested in a Congress of the United States." For the framers, Congress was the main bearer of federal governmental powers. In listing its powers and responsibilities in Article I, Section 8—the **enumerated powers**—they were largely defining the powers and responsibilities of the national government itself.[3] The framers enhanced the enumerated powers by adding the **elastic clause**, granting broad power to Congress to pass whatever legislation was necessary to carry out its enumerated powers and other responsibilities vested in it from other sections of the Constitution.

☐ Constraining Congress

Worried that too strong a legislative branch would lead to tyranny, the framers also limited congressional power. They made Congress a **bicameral** body—divided into two chambers—so that legislation could occur only after patient deliberation. Single-house legislative bodies, they believed, would be prone to rash action. They then added provisions—Article I, Section 9—specifically to prohibit certain kinds of actions: bills of attainder, ex post facto laws, the granting of titles of nobility, and the suspension of the right of habeas corpus. In the 1st Congress, additional constraints on congressional action were added in the form of the Bill of Rights. Note that the First Amendment, perhaps the most important constitutional provision protecting political liberty, begins with the words "Congress shall make no law . . ."

We also learned in the chapter on the Constitution that the national government was organized on the basis of a "separation of powers" and "checks and balances" so that "ambition might check ambition" and protect the country from tyranny. This means that although the framers envisioned the legislative branch as the vital center of a vigorous national government, they wanted to make sure that Congress would be surrounded by competing centers of government power. We will see that this fragmentation of governmental power in the United States affects how Congress works and often makes it difficult for it to fashion coherent and effective public policies. In this regard, we will see in this chapter and the chapter on presidency how separation of powers invites a situation of conflict between the president and Congress, especially when divided party government exists. This was evident in the "budget ceiling" crisis in 2011 when the United States came close to defaulting on its debts for the first time in our history.

☐ Bicameralism and Representation

Congress is organized into two legislative chambers, each with its own principles of representation and constitutional responsibilities. While we often use the word "Congress" and think of it as a single institution, it is worth remembering that the House and Senate are very different from one another and are "virtually autonomous chambers."[4] Here are the most important things in the constitutional design of Congress that make the two chambers different from one another.

In what came to be known as the Great Compromise, the framers decided to apportion the House of Representatives on the basis of population and the Senate on the basis of equal representation of the states. Equal representation in the Senate of states that are highly unequal in terms of population, we will see, has important negative impacts on democracy in the United States.[5] The terms of office of the members of the House of Representatives were set at two years. The terms of the members of the Senate were set at six years, with only one-third of the seats up for election in each two-year election cycle. We learn in this chapter how these differences affect the legislative process.

The Constitution called for the election of senators by state legislatures, not by the people. The objective was to insulate one house of Congress from popular pressures and to make it a seat of deliberation and reflection. As James Madison put it, "The use of the Senate is to consist in its proceeding with more coolness . . . and with more wisdom than the popular branch."[6] The election of senators by the state legislatures could not survive the democratizing tendencies in the country, however. The Seventeenth Amendment, passed in 1913 after years of agitation for reform pressed by labor and farm groups and progressive reformers, gave the people the power to elect senators directly.

In addition to its general grants of power to Congress, the Constitution assigns particular responsibilities to each of the legislative chambers (see Table 11.1). For example, the House of Representatives has the power to impeach the president for "high crimes and misdemeanors," which it did in the case of Bill Clinton arising out of the Monica Lewinsky affair; the Senate has the power to conduct the trial of the president and remove him from office, if the impeachment charges are proved to its satisfaction (which they were not for Clinton).

☐ Federalism

Congress is also greatly affected by the federal design of the Constitution. In our federal system, some powers and responsibilities are granted to the national government, some are shared between the national government and the states, and some are reserved for the states. It is inevitable in such a system that conflicts will occur between state governments and the national government and its legislative branch. Such conflicts sometimes reach the Supreme Court for resolution. In *United States v. Lopez* (1995), for instance, the Court ruled that Congress had gone too far in the use of its commerce clause powers when it passed a law banning firearms in and around public schools. Although the goal of the law might be worthy, such a matter, in the opinion of the Court, was the business of the states, not Congress. In 2012, though the Court upheld the mandate in the Affordable Care Act for everyone to have health

TABLE 11.1 CONSTITUTIONAL DIFFERENCES BETWEEN THE HOUSE AND THE SENATE

	Senate	House of Representatives
Term	6 years	2 years
Elections	One-third elected in November of even-numbered years	Entire membership elected in November of even-numbered years
Number per state	2	Varies by size of state's population (minimum of 1 per state)
Total membership	100	435 (determined by Congress; at present size since 1910)
Minimum age for membership	30 years	25 years
Unique powers	Advice and consent for judicial and upper-level executive branch appointments	Origination of revenue bills
	Trial of impeachment cases	Bringing of impeachment charges
	Advice and consent for treaties	

delegate

According to the doctrine articulated by Edmund Burke, an elected representative who acts in perfect accord with the wishes of his or her constituents.

trustee

An elected representative who believes that his or her own best judgment, rather than instructions from constituents, should be used in making legislative decisions.

descriptive representation

Sometimes called *statistical representation*; the degree to which the composition of a representative body reflects the demographic composition of the population as a whole.

insurance, it rejected Congress's use of the commerce clause to justify the requirement. By doing so, the Court signalled that it was anxious to further cut back the powers of the national government relative to the states.

Federalism also infuses "localism" into congressional affairs.[7] Although Congress is charged with making national policies, we should remember that the members of the Senate and the House come to Washington as the representatives of states and districts. They are elected by and are beholden ultimately to the voters and interest groups at home and have voters' and important groups' interests and opinions in mind even as they struggle with weighty issues of national importance. This remains true even as rising partisanship and the increasing influence of ideologically oriented advocacy groups have forced representatives and senators to be more sensitive to issues beyond their electoral districts and states.

Representation and Democracy

11.2   Assess how and to what extent the members of Congress represent their constituents

Members of Congress serve as our legislative representatives. But do they carry out this representative responsibility in a way that can be considered democratic?[8] To answer this question, we need to look at several aspects of representation: styles of representation, how closely the demographics of members of Congress match the demographics of the population in general, and the electoral process.

☐ Styles of Representation

In a letter to his constituents written in 1774, English politician and philosopher Edmund Burke described two principal styles of representation. As a **delegate**, the representative tries to mirror perfectly the views of his or her constituents. As a **trustee**, the representative acts independently, trusting to his or her own judgment of how to best serve the public interest. Burke preferred the trustee approach: "Your representative owes you, not his industry only, but his judgment; and he betrays you, instead of serving you, if he sacrifices it to your opinion."[9]

Campaigning for Congress in Illinois several decades later, Abraham Lincoln argued otherwise: "While acting as [your] representative, I shall be governed by [your] will, on all subjects upon which I have the means of knowing what [your] will is."[10] (If only he had access to public opinion polls!)

Every member of the House and Senate chooses between these two styles of representation. Their choice usually has less to do with their personal tastes than it has to do with the relative safety of their seats and how often they must face the electorate. Senators with six-year terms face the electorate less often than members of the House, so they are generally freer than representatives to assume the trustee style. As they get closer to the end of their term and the prospect of facing the voters, however, senators edge toward the delegate style. Because members of the House must run for reelection every two years, and tend to be in campaign mode at all times, they are pushed almost inexorably toward the delegate style.[11]

☐ Race, Gender, and Occupation in Congress

Representation also implies that elected officials are like us in important ways—that they represent us because they are similar to us. Which raises the question: is the makeup of Congress in a demographic sense similar to that of the nation as a whole? This is often called **descriptive representation**. From the point of view of descriptive representation, the views of significant groups—let us say, women and African Americans—will only be taken into account in policymaking if members of these

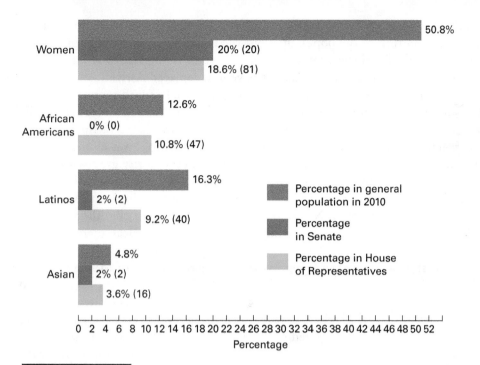

FIGURE 11.1 WOMEN AND MINORITIES IN THE 113TH CONGRESS, 2013–2014

Although their numbers in Congress have increased in recent years, women and racial minorities are still substantially underrepresented compared with their proportion in the American population. This graph compares the percentage of women and racial minorities in each house of the 113th Congress with their percentages in the population in the 2010 census. It reflects the big gains made my women and minorities in the 2012 elections.

Sources: U.S. Bureau of the Census; the website of the U.S. Senate at www.senate.gov; the website of the House of Representatives at www.house.gov.

groups hold seats in a legislative body in rough proportion to their size in the population. From this perspective, a perfectly representative legislative body would be similar to the general population in terms of race, sex, ethnicity, occupation, religion, age, and the like. In this sense, the U.S. Congress is highly *unrepresentative*.[12]

GENDER AND RACE Both women and racial minorities are significantly underrepresented in Congress, particularly in the Senate, despite important recent gains. We can see this in Figure 11.1 which compares the distribution of women and minorities in the 113th Congress (2013–2014) with their distribution in the country as a whole.

Black representation reached its peak during the post–Civil War Reconstruction period, when blacks played an important political role in several southern states. African Americans disappeared from Congress for many years after the reimposition of white supremacy and the creation of Jim Crow laws in the South at the end of the nineteenth century. Although a handful of black representatives from northern cities served during the first half of the twentieth century—Oscar De Priest from Chicago's predominantly black South Side and Adam Clayton Powell from New York City's Harlem, for example—very few African Americans were elected to Congress until the late 1960s. While there has been some improvement in representation of African Americans in the House of Representatives—from 26 to 47 between the 102nd (1991–1992) and 113th Congresses—their numbers are still well below what might be expected, given the proportion of African Americans in the population. All but four twentieth-century African American representatives were Democrats. There were no Republican African American representatives between the retirement of J. C. Watts in 2003 and the election of Allen West (R–FL) and Tim Scott (R–SC) in the 2010 Republican landslide. Because 40 of the 42 African American representatives were Democrats, they exercised little influence in the heavily Republican and tightly party-controlled House in 2011 and 2012. There are no African American senators in the Congress. Barack Obama (D–IL) left in 2008 to run for president. He was replaced for a short time by another African American, Roland Burris, who chose not to run for reelection in 2010.

Hispanics are even more poorly represented than African Americans relative to their proportion of the population, but the increase in their number in recent years has given the Hispanic caucus a greater voice in legislative affairs than in the past. Interestingly, while Hispanics have now replaced African Americans as the largest minority group in the population, they are less well represented than African Americans in Congress. Forty are serving in the House and two in the Senate in the 113th Congress; Ken Salazar (D–CO) and Mel Martinez (R–FL) were elected to the Senate in 2004; Robert Martinez (D–NJ) was elected in 2006 and Marco Rubio (R–FL) was elected in 2010. Other minority groups are represented in small numbers among members of the House. There were three Arab Americans, two of whom were Muslim, in the House in the 113th Congress, for example. There were no Native American senators—Ben Nighthorse Campbell (R–CO) retired in 2004—and only a single Native American member of the House.

The first woman to sit in Congress was Jeannette Rankin of Montana, a suffragist and pacifist, elected in 1916. The number of women in Congress increased during the 1990s, with a big gain coming in the 1992 elections (often called the "year of the woman"), which sent 48 women to the House and 7 to the Senate in the 103rd Congress (compared with only 29 and 2, respectively, in the 102nd Congress). There are a record number of women in Congress in the 113th, with 20 in the Senate and 81 in the House. Proportionally, however, female representation in Congress is quite low, compared either to the percentage of women in the American population (slightly more than one-half) or to the percentage of women in national legislative bodies in countries globally. On the latter point, as of late 2010, the United States ranked only 71st on the world list.[13] Leadership posts in Congress are overwhelmingly held by men, but a few women have gained important party and institutional leadership posts. Most notable is Nancy Pelosi (D–CA), who became the first female Speaker of the House in American history after the Democrats won the House in 2006. When Republicans regained control of the House in the 2010 elections she lost the speakership, but retained her position as Democratic leader. There were five female committee chairs in the House and Senate in the 113th Congress. Women also hold important party posts, including Patty Murray (D–WA), secretary of the Senate Democratic Conference, and Chair of the Senate Democratic Campaign Committee, and Debbie Stabenow (D–MI), chair of the Democratic Steering Committee.

INCOME AND OCCUPATION Members of Congress are far better educated than the rest of the population. They also are quite wealthy, having been born into high-income families, or earning it before entering Congress or even while serving in Congress (until 2012, members of Congress had not bound themselves with "insider trader" rules as they had bound Wall Street). Significantly, three-quarters of senators are millionaires, as are almost one-half of members of the House. By occupational background, members lean heavily toward the law or business occupations, though many have been career politicians. In recent Congresses, only about 15 percent came from working-class backgrounds, whether of the blue-collar or white-collar service variety, and there was no one who had been a farm laborer.[14]

Most members of Congress, however, did not step into their current posts directly from a profession or occupation. Before putting themselves up for election, representatives and senators, for the most part, had been career politicians or in some other form of public service. Strikingly, 112 members of the House in 2010 had been staffers in Congress.[15] More than a few representatives and senators came from the military, while senators included former governors and cabinet secretaries in previous administrations.

Does it matter that descriptive representation is so low in Congress, that its members are so demographically unrepresentative of the American people? Some political scientists and close observers of Congress think not. They suggest that the need to face the electorate forces lawmakers to be attentive to all significant groups

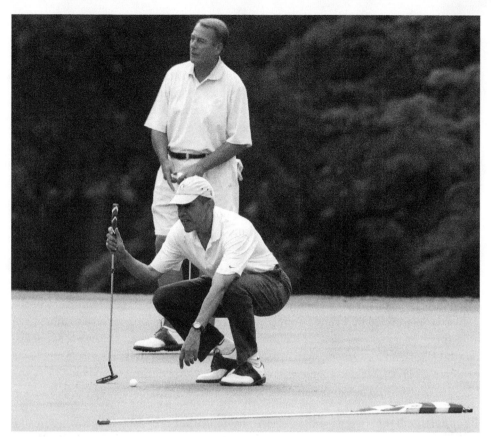

constituency
The district of a legislator.

constituent
A citizen who lives in the district of an elected official.

11.1
11.2
11.3
11.4
11.5

RELAXING ON THE LINKS
Like many leading members of Congress, House Speaker John Boehner, here playing a round of golf with President Obama as they tried (without success) to tone down the partisan rancor that paralyzed the 112th Congress, is a wealthy man with a background in business.

in their **constituency**. A representative from a farm district tends to listen to farm **constituents**, for example, even if that representative is not a farmer.[16]

Nevertheless, many who feel they are not well represented—women, African Americans, Asian Americans, Hispanics, blue-collar workers, gays and lesbians, those with disabilities, and the poor—often believe that their interests would get a much better hearing if their numbers were substantially increased in Congress. There is significant evidence supporting this view: women members of the House introduce more bills related to women's and children's issues than do their male colleagues.[17] The same has been found to be true for African American legislators and issues considered to be important to African Americans in the country.[18] As members of the upper 1 percent of income earners—senators' and representatives' salaries of roughly $175,000 and the considerable investments most of them have, place them solidly in that group—they don't have much in common, one would suspect, with the daily concerns of middle-income households. The demographic disparity between the American population and the makeup of Congress, then, suggests a violation of the norm of political equality, an important element of democracy.

☐ The Electoral Connection

Members of the House of Representatives and Senate have particular constituencies they represent in Congress. They get to represent these constituencies by virtue of election to office. We have suggested that elections are the principal instrument in a democracy for keeping representatives responsive and responsible to citizens—even, potentially, overcoming shortcomings in descriptive representation. Let's see how congressional elections affect the quality of representation in the United States.

reapportionment
The reallocation of House seats among the states, done after each national census, to ensure that seats are held by the states in proportion to the size of their populations.

redistricting
The redrawing of congressional district lines within a state to ensure roughly equal populations within each district.

THE STATE AS THE SENATE'S ELECTORAL UNIT Each state elects two senators for six-year terms (though not at the same time). This has important implications for politics in the United States, as well as the quality of democratic representation here. Equal representation gives extraordinary power in the Senate to states with small populations. Wyoming, our least-populous state, for example, has exactly the same number of senators as California, but it has less than one-seventieth of California's population; two senators in Wyoming in 2010, for example, represented only about 560,000 people, while the two senators from California represented just over 37 million. This means that a coalition of 51 senators from the 26 smallest-population states, representing a mere 18 percent of the American population, can pass a bill in the Senate. You will see later in this chapter that the Senate's rules and procedures give even more power in the body to a small minority of the population, magnifying the antimajoritarian qualities produced by the Constitution.

THE DISTRICT AS THE HOUSE'S ELECTORAL UNIT Each member of the House of Representatives is elected from a single-member geographical district (a 1967 law prohibits multimember districts). The number of representatives each state is entitled to in the House is determined by a state's population, with the proviso that each state must have at least one congressional district; the low-population states Alaska, Delaware, Montana, North Dakota, South Dakota, Vermont, and Wyoming fall into this category. The House of Representatives decided that, beginning in 1910, its upper limit would be 435 members (the House can change this number at any time, although it is highly unlikely).

Reapportionment Because the American population is constantly growing in size and changing where it lives, the 435 House representatives must be periodically redistributed among the states. **Reapportionment**, the technical name for this redistribution, occurs every 10 years, after the national census (see Figure 11.2 for the most recent changes). Based on the official census, some states keep the same number of seats; others gain or lose them depending on their relative population gains or losses. The big winner following the 2010 census count was Texas, which gained four additional seats in the House. Florida gained two seats, followed by Arizona, Georgia, Nevada, South Carolina, Utah, and Washington with one additional seat. The biggest losers were New Jersey, New York, and Ohio, which lost two seats each; Illinois, Louisiana, Massachusetts, Michigan, Missouri, and Pennsylvania each lost one seat.

Redistricting Except for states with only a single representative whose House district is the entire state, those states gaining or losing seats must redraw the boundary lines of their congressional districts so that they are of roughly equal population size.[19] Redrawing district lines within a state is known as **redistricting** and is done primarily by state legislatures, although the courts have been playing a more active role lately in cases which legislatures are unable to decide (redistricting is the job of a nonpartisan commission in 13 states). Very often in the past, because it was then legal to do so, legislatures created congressional districts of vastly different population sizes—in New York in the 1930s, some congressional districts had 10 times the population of others—and significantly overrepresented rural populations. The Supreme Court ruled in *Wesberry v. Sanders* (1964), however, that the principle of one person, one vote applies to congressional districts, meaning that congressional districts within a state must be of roughly equal population size. Because the distribution of the population changes in many states over the course of 10 years—some people moving from the cities to the suburbs; some people moving from rural areas to cities—many congressional district boundaries must be redrawn even in those states that have neither gained nor lost congressional seats due to reapportionment, because of the Supreme Court's ruling that districts within states must be roughly equal in population size.

Although congressional districts must hold approximately equal numbers of citizens, state legislatures are relatively free to draw district lines where they choose. The party that controls the state legislature and governorship usually tries to draw the lines in a way that will help its candidates win elections.[20] The results are often strange indeed. Rather

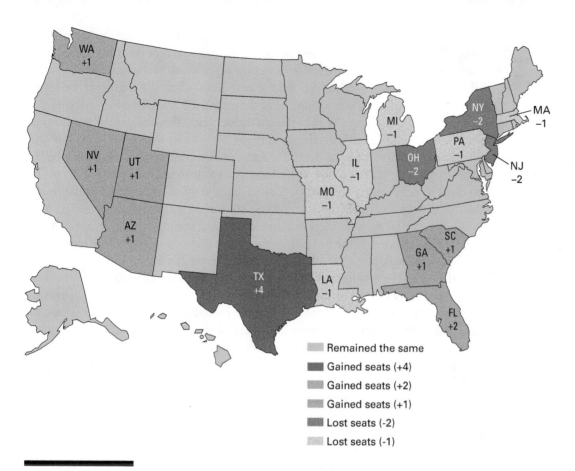

FIGURE 11.2 STATES GAINING AND LOSING CONGRESSIONAL SEATS FOLLOWING THE 2010 CENSUS

The number of representatives for each state in the House of Representatives is based on the size of its population. Because the relative sizes of the states' populations change over time while the number of representatives in the House is fixed, the number of representatives from each state is recalculated after each census. This process is called reapportionment. This map shows which states gained and lost seats after the 2010 census.

Source: "U.S. Census Population Estimates for 2011," press release, U.S. Census Bureau, December 2011 and January 2012.

than creating compact and coherent districts, neighborhoods, towns, and counties can be strung together in odd-looking ways in order to take full **partisan** advantage of the redistricting process. Taken to an extreme, the process is known as **gerrymandering**, after Governor Elbridge Gerry of Massachusetts, who signed a bill in 1811 that created a district that looked like a salamander. It made wonderful raw material for editorial cartoonists (see illustration on next page).

The tradition lives on. For example, Texas gained four additional House seats after the 2010 census, mostly because of the increase of its Hispanic population. The Republican-controlled state legislature in 2011 created a redistricting plan that added one super majority Hispanic district that would likely elect a Democrat, then created three other districts with so few Hispanics in them that they would likely elect Republicans. In the process of creating the oddly shaped and noncontiguous House District 35, running from Austin to San Antonio, Republicans refashioned House District 25, represented by liberal Democratic congressman Lloyd Doggett, diminishing his chances for reelection. (It removed areas from his district that included neighborhoods close to the University of Texas that tended to vote for Democrats.) Because Texas has had a long history of using redistricting to dilute the influence of minorities, it was forced under terms of the Voting Rights Act to submit its plan to the Justice Department for approval. Justice refused to accept it and a federal court in Washington ordered the Texas Court to come up with its own plan. Coming almost full circle, the Supreme Court then ordered the lower court to pay special heed to the redistricting map designed by the state legislature.

Though the Supreme Court sometimes has tried to prevent the most flagrant abuses, especially when some identifiable group of voters is disadvantaged—for example, a racial or ethnic group such as Hispanics in Texas as described above—it has turned a blind

partisan
A committed member of a party; also, seeing issues from the point of view of the interests of a single party.

gerrymandering
Redrawing electoral district lines in an extreme and unlikely manner to give an advantage to a particular party or candidate.

crack

The act of dividing a district where the opposing party has a large majority, rendering it a minority in both parts of the redrawn districts.

pack

The process of concentrating voters for the other party into fewer districts in order to weaken them elsewhere.

majority-minority districts

Districts drawn to ensure that a racial minority makes up the majority of voters.

eye to partisan redistricting in which parties try to draw district lines to their own advantage. The Court, along with most politicians, seems to accept the notion that "to the victor belongs the spoils." Partisan redistricting happens when the same party controls both houses of the state legislature and the governor's office, although even here there are sometimes conflicts if one or another of the party's incumbent House members feels that he or she has been hurt by the redrawn district lines. This situation of unified party control existed in 42 states when the states began to redistrict after the 2010 census, with Republicans in control of 24 of them. Parties in unified control of a state where the legislature draws district lines follow several strategies to gain seats on the rival party. One is to **crack** a district where the party enjoys too big a margin. Too large a majority wastes votes in a district where the party would win anyway, so legislators can spread its party voters across two or more districts in hopes of winning additional seats in a state's congressional delegation. On the flip side of the coin, a party that controls the redistricting machinery can **pack** voters for its rival party into fewer districts, giving the rival party bigger margins of victory in them, leading them to waste their strength.

Divided party control in the states was common during the post-2000 census period, but much less so in the post-2010 census period after the Republicans won big in the 2010 congressional elections. But where divided party control exists, intense partisan conflict and deadlock are often the result, with resolution coming in many states only after the matter is turned over to the courts. In states with divided party control, where neither party has sufficient strength to get its way, the two parties have increasingly made tacit bipartisan redistricting arrangements that protect their own incumbents, presumably on the grounds that the best each party can do is to protect its hard-won gains. In large states such as California, Illinois, Michigan, New York, and Ohio in recent elections, there is hardly a district anymore where the incumbent faces serious competition from the other party in the general election. Across the nation, incumbent-protection redistricting has become so extensive that only about 75 out of 435 seats in the 2008 elections to the House of Representatives, and about 100 in the 2010 elections, were actually competitive, where winners and losers were separated by 5 percentage points or less.[21]

The outcome of the decline in the number of competitive districts in House elections is that the vast majority of districts in the United States are safely Republican or safely Democratic where candidates need not appeal to the constituency in general but only to their partisan base to ensure that they show up at the polls. This has contributed to the ever-deepening partisan divide in Congress.

Majority-Minority Districts Amendments to the 1965 Voting Rights Act passed in 1982 encouraged the states to create House districts in which racial minorities would be in the majority. Sponsors of the legislation hoped that this would lead to an increase in the number of members of racial minority groups elected to the House. The result was the formation of 24 new **majority-minority districts**, 15 with African American majorities and 9 with Hispanic American majorities.[22] The creation of some of these districts has taken great imagination. North Carolina's Twelfth District, for instance, created after the 1990 census and shown on the previous page, linked a narrow strip of predominantly African American communities along 160 miles of Interstate 85 connecting Durham and Charlotte. After going back and forth on the issue, the Court accepted a slightly redrawn North Carolina Twelfth District map in *Hunt v. Cromartie* (2001), ruling that race can be a significant factor in drawing district lines "so long as it is not the dominant and controlling one." (For more insight into how district lines are drawn, see the "By the Numbers" feature).

The creation of these special majority-minority districts has contributed to the increase in the number of racial minority representatives in Congress; each of the districts has consistently elected a member of a racial minority group to the House. Ironically, however, the creation of such districts has undermined Democratic Party strength in other districts by taking traditionally Democratic-oriented minority group voters away from previously Democratic-dominated districts in order to form majority-minority ones. (One political scientist reports that after 1991 Republicans

By the Numbers

Can congressional districts be drawn in different ways to include equal numbers of voters yet favor one party over the other?

Here is a headline that might have appeared in any city newspaper in late 2011 or early 2012: "Legislature fails to reach agreement on congressional district lines; Issue to be decided by the state courts." What's going on? How difficult can it be to count people and draw congressional district lines? Actually, it is difficult and the issues are important.

Why It Matters
How congressional district lines are drawn has a lot to do with which political party will control the House of Representatives, at least until the next census.

Behind Redistricting
In the House of Representatives, seats are apportioned to each state based on the state's population. Thus, after a new census is taken, a state may gain or lose seats based on the current count of people residing there. To gain a seat means that a new congressional district must be carved out of the state; to lose a seat means that lines must be redrawn to fill in the gap. Even in states where the size of its congressional delegation has not changed, lines must always be redrawn because of population shifts within state boundaries (e.g., more people moving to the suburbs) and the Court's ruling that each congressional district within a state must be of roughly the same population size.

How District Lines Are Drawn
In theory, as long as district lines create congressional districts of roughly equal size, and as long as district lines do not unduly disadvantage racial and ethnic groups, congressional district lines can be drawn in any way that politicians choose. The politicians can be very imaginative in doing so, as they try to ensure that their own party and favored members of Congress are advantaged by the outcome.

Where the district lines are drawn is extremely important in determining the composition of the congressional delegation from each state. Note the following hypothetical example, which shows how easily district lines can be used to effect different outcomes. Let "D" stand for 100,000 Democratic voters; let "R" stand for 100,000 Republican voters; and let "A" stand for 100,000 African Americans, most of whom vote for Democrats. Taking the same number and locations of voters, district lines can be drawn one way to yield three Democratic seats and no Republican seats (the hypothetical map on the left) and another way to yield two Republican seats and one Democratic seat (the hypothetical map on the right).

Comment on the Process for Drawing District Lines
These alternative outcomes are somewhat exaggerated in order to make a point about how politicians strive for maximum flexibility in the redistricting process. In real life, the Court has also demanded that district lines not deviate too much from their historical patterns and that they be relatively compact, putting people who live near each other in the same district. The federal courts also have

Congressional Districts

Result: districts equal in size (1.4 million each); three Democratic seats, zero Republican seats.

Result: districts equal in size (1.4 million each); one Democratic seat carved out to create a position for an African American and two Republican seats.

D = 100,000 white Democrats   R = 100,000 white Republicans
A = 100,000 African Americans, mostly Democrats
Different Congressional District Lines, Different Party Outcomes
Source: State of California.

(Continued)

rejected districting maps that disadvantage protected minorities such as African Americans and Hispanics.

What to Watch For
Redistricting is one of the most important things that goes on in our political system, yet it is virtually invisible to the general public. Pay attention to the debates over redistricting in your state and determine what political alliances appear and what political bargains are being struck.

What Do You Think?
What might be a nonpartisan, scientific method to draw district lines that would avoid the sometimes unseemly process of reshaping congressional districts to suit political parties and interested groups? If there was such a method, do you think it would be better than our current system? Why or why not?

open-seat election
An election in which there is no incumbent officeholder.

won and held every congressional seat in which redistricting had reduced the African American population by 10 percentage points or more.[23]) Naturally, Republicans have been eager to support minority group efforts to form their own districts. Concentrating black voters in homogeneous districts—packing them, as it were—has tipped the balance to Republicans in many congressional districts in the South. One result was that policies favored by African Americans were less likely to be enacted when Republicans were in the majority because of the decreased strength of Democrats in the House, this despite an increase in the number of African American representatives.[24]

MONEY AND CONGRESSIONAL ELECTIONS Running for the House or the Senate is a very expensive proposition, and it keeps getting more expensive. House and Senate candidate campaigns do not receive public funding and, by virtue of that fact, face no limits on what they can spend in the general election. To fill their campaign coffers, they rely on contributions from individuals (who are limited in what they can contribute), PACs, and political party committees. In 2010, 59 percent of contributions to House campaigns came from individual contributors (including the candidates themselves), 38 percent was from PACs, and 3 percent from party committees. The numbers for the Senate were 77 percent from individuals, 15 percent from PACs, and 8 percent from party committees.[25] More than a few rich individuals self-fund a portion of their campaign expenses. Democrat John Corzine set the record in 2000 with contributions of $62 million to his campaign, which he won narrowly. Many congressional candidates also receive campaign contributions from

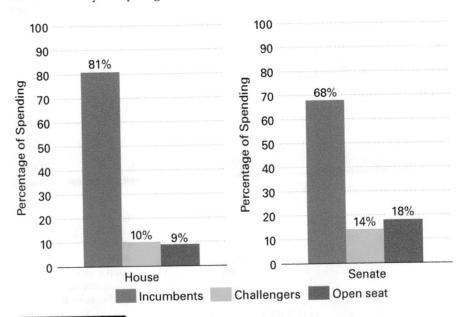

FIGURE 11.3 CAMPAIGN MONEY RAISED BY INCUMBENTS, CHALLENGERS, AND OPEN-SEAT CANDIDATES, 2009–2010 ELECTION CYCLE

Because campaign contributors want access to important decision-makers in Congress, contributors tend to give a disproportionate share of campaign contributions to incumbents and to those open-seat candidates who have a good chance to win their elections.

Source: Federal Election Commission.

Note: at this writing, the Federal Election Commission has not reported on campaign money raised in the 2012 congressional elections. Please check MyPoliSciLab for updates.

PACs associated with congressional party leaders such as House Speaker John Boehner (R–OH) and Senate Majority Leader Harry Reid (D–NV). Similar to presidential campaigns, contributions to PACs are dominated by business corporations and trade associations, while individual contributors to congressional campaigns come primarily from top income earners and wealth holders.

Not to be overlooked, parties, committees, interest groups, corporations, unions, and advocacy organizations spend lavishly on issue and candidate ad campaigns and get-out-the-vote efforts that are extremely helpful to congressional candidates. In the 2011–2012 cycle, following the groundbreaking *Citizen's United* decision, corporations and unions—especially the former—increased their spending in direct support of or in opposition to particular Senate and House candidates. Super-wealthy individuals did the same by way of large contributions to Super PACs. (Refer to the chapter-opening story for more details.)

Incumbents, especially in the House, have an easier time raising money than their challengers and spend more (see Figure 11.3). The reasons are fairly obvious: those who give want access to senators and representatives and, because incumbents are reelected at very high rates, the smart play is to donate to those in power and likely to remain in power. **Open-seat election** races, in which no incumbent is involved, also attract and use lots of money, especially in the Senate, because the stakes are so high for each of the parties and allied interest and advocacy groups, with control of Congress hanging in the balance at nearly every election. For example, in the 2009–2010 cycle, the average open-seat candidate in House and Senate races raised 46 percent more than challengers to incumbents.[26] Moreover, being a member of the majority party in Congress serves as a magnet for money because contributors generally want to be able to have access to those in power.[27] These money sources are for what is called "hard" or "regulated" money that goes into the treasuries of the official campaign committees of House and Senate candidates. It is but the tip of a very large iceberg, however, as you have seen. Much more money is spent independently on issue ads and get-out-the-vote campaigns by interest and advocacy groups and by 501 and 527 organizations and Super PACs that indirectly pump up the resources that support congressional candidate campaigns.

THE INCUMBENCY FACTOR As we have seen, incumbents in Congress—current office holders—win at very high rates, especially in the House (see Figure 11.4), meaning that the overwhelming majority of electoral contests for Congress are not really

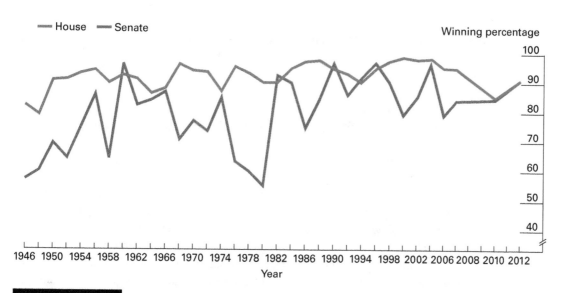

FIGURE 11.4 RATES OF INCUMBENT REELECTION IN CONGRESS

The probability that incumbents will be reelected remains at historic highs. This does not mean, however, that the membership of Congress is stagnant. Turnover in membership is substantial because of retirements and the defeat of incumbents in primary elections.

Sources: Congressional Quarterly Weekly Reports (November and December 2008); "Norm Colman Concedes," Associated Press (June 30, 2009); and "Incumbent reelection over the years," Center for Responsive Politics," (www.opensecrets.org), November 10, 2012.

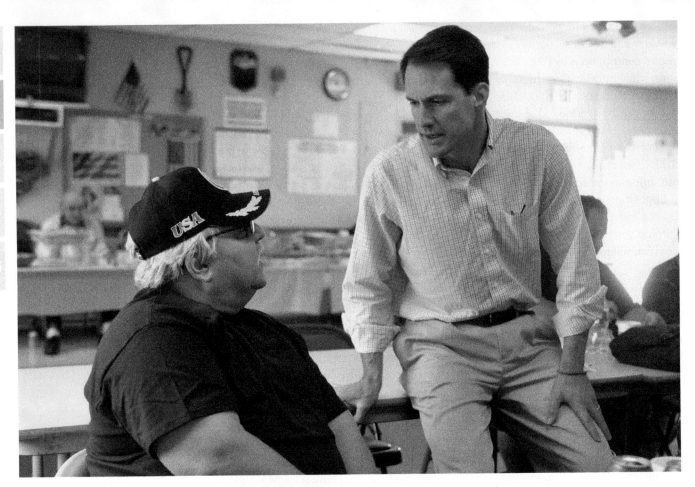

IN THE HOME DISTRICT

Members of Congress must spend considerable time staying in personal touch with their constituents, even when Congress is in session. Here Connecticut representative Jim Himes talks with a constituent at a VFW gathering in his home district. Should representatives spend less time staying in touch and more time legislating, or is this an important role for representatives in a democracy?

franking privilege
Public subsidization of mail from the members of Congress to their constituents.

competitive; for the most part, seats in the House today are considered "safe," with the incumbent facing little serious challenge from the opposition party candidate. Since the end of World War II, in fact, on average, 93 percent of House incumbents have been reelected and 80 percent of Senate incumbents have done the same. Incumbents won at very high rates even in big party swing elections as in 1994 and 2006. In 1994, when Republicans took over control of Congress, incumbent losses were concentrated in Democratic districts and states; in 2006, when the Democrats took control, most incumbent losses were among Republicans. To be sure, there is still turnover in the House and Senate—some members retire, especially when prospects in the next election are not encouraging, others lose to challengers in their party's primary, and a few die—but those who choose to stay and run usually win.

There are several reasons incumbents almost always win when they seek reelection. The most important, of course, is that the redistricting process in many states in recent years—reviewed earlier in this chapter—has been fashioned to protect incumbents in each of the parties. On the face of it, this process has been very effective.

Incumbents also have the advantage of attracting and spending much more campaign money than their rivals. Many contributors look at campaign contributions as an "investment" in access to key members of Congress.[28] To contribute to a challenger is to jeopardize access if the challenger loses, which is most often the case.

Incumbents also use the congressional machinery to help their reelection chances.[29] Already well known to voters because they garner so much free media coverage, members of Congress have many ways to advertise their accomplishments and keep their names before the public. For example, the **franking privilege** allows them to mail

Using the FRAMEWORK

Why can't our government seem to solve our most pressing national problems?

Background: During the last several years, Congress and the president have, as the saying goes, "kicked the can down the road" on nearly every important national issue. Whether considering health care reform, job creation in the midst of the worst economy since the Great Depression, global climate change, and deficits and the long-term national debt, one must be struck by the lack of progress. We have failed to address the rising costs of health care, already the highest in the world. We have shied away from short-term stimulus measures that might address unemployment. We have backtracked on market-based approaches to cutting down on carbon emissions. And we cannot seem to agree on the mix of government program cuts and additional taxes that are required to cut into the national debt. Things are so bad that major business groups such as the World Economic Forum and the World Bank recently have downgraded the United States on the quality of its governance. Why has this happened? Taking a broad look at how structural, political linkage, and governmental factors affect what government does will help explain the situation.

Government Action

Late and short-term fixes with no long-term solutions to big national problems: program cuts but none on Medicare or defense, and no tax increases on the wealthy to deal with national debt; no economic stimulus or other job-creation actions; no action on climate change; no action on cost containment in health care.

Government

Senators and representatives of both parties pay disproportionate attention to their most well-off constituents and those who fund their campaigns. ➡ Business and trade association groups help write legislative bills and have an important presence in committee hearings and bill markups. ➡ Divided government in 2011 and 2012, with the anti-tax, anti-regulation Tea Party caucus dominating the House GOP, and a Democratic president (Obama) in office who seems willing to trade away taxes on upper income groups for the sake of compromise. ➡ Speaker Boehner cannot carry through on bargains he has negotiated with the Senate and the president because of Tea Party resistance.

Political Linkage

Decline of labor union density weakens voice of working and middle classes in politics. ➡ Political influence of corporations and upper income groups increases. ➡ 501 and 527 groups, regular PACs, and super PACs representing entrenched interests, dominate campaign finance. ➡ Bitter partisanship increases, with the GOP less and less inclined to nominate candidates for any office who would consider new government regulations or increasing taxes, especially on the wealthy. ➡ Media buys into the "deficit is the problem" narrative, with little attention to other problems, especially jobs.

Structure

Income and wealth inequality soars. ➡ Default positions of American political culture are anti-government and pro-market.

Productivity-enhancing technological change puts pressure on jobs. ➡ Global outsourcing puts pressure on jobs. ➡ Declining manufacturing sector undermines middle-class lifestyles. ➡ Rise of financial sector and CEO compensation funnels much of national income to the top.

casework

Services performed by members of Congress for constituents.

pork

Also called *pork barrel*; federally funded projects designed to bring to the constituency jobs and public money for which the members of Congress can claim credit.

newsletters, legislative updates, surveys, and other self-promoting literature free of charge. The House and the Senate also provide travel budgets for lawmakers to make periodic visits to their states or districts. Because members believe that time spent in their districts helps their electoral chances, they spend lots of time back home.[30] Some manage to spend three or four days a week in their districts or states, meeting constituents, giving speeches, raising money, and keeping in the public eye. The congressional leadership helps by scheduling important legislative business for the Tuesday-to-Thursday period and cutting down the number of hours Congress is in session.

Incumbents also use their offices to "service the district." One way is through **casework**, helping constituents cut through the red tape of the federal bureaucracy, whether it be by speeding up the arrival of a late Social Security check or expediting the issuance of a permit for grazing on public land.[31] Generous budgets for establishing and staffing offices in the constituency help representatives and senators do casework. Another way to service the district is to provide **pork**—federal dollars for various projects in the district or state. In 2005, for example, Congress passed a massive $286 billion highway and mass transit bill that, in addition to whatever improvements it might bring for the safety and convenience of Americans, poured lots of federal construction money into the constituencies of senators and representatives for highway and bridge projects, rail and bus improvements, urban bike paths, and more. Even Tea Party newcomers to Congress, elected on promises to end earmarks and cut government spending, have come to appreciate pork. For example, Steven Palazzo (R–MI), after voting to cut defense spending in 2011, sponsored an amendment to put back $150 million for a combat ship being built at a shipyard in his district.[32]

☐ How Representative?

There are several respects in which Congress may not be broadly representative of the American people. For one thing, as we have seen, women and members of minority racial and ethnic groups are vastly underrepresented in the ranks of House and Senate members compared with their proportions in the population. We have learned, as well, that senators and representatives by a very wide margin are more financially well off than the average American. For another thing, we have seen that people in very small states have much more voice than people in large states in the U.S. Senate because of the constitutional provision mandating two senators for each state. This feature of the Constitution means that the 12 smallest states, with only about 7 percent of the American population, elect almost one-fourth of all senators.[33] Elections and attentiveness to public opinion on the part of lawmakers help rectify some of this, but imperfectly.

But representatives and senators pay a great deal of attention to the interests and the preferences of the people in their districts and states. Because they are worried about being reelected—even incumbents tend to run scared, perhaps afraid of being the exception that proves the rule—they try to see as many people as they can during their frequent visits home, and they pay attention to their mail and the public opinion polls. Moreover, they vote on and pass laws in rough approximation to public opinion. Members of Congress vote in a manner that is consistent with public opinion in their districts and states about two-thirds of the time, and Congress produces laws that are consistent with national public opinion at about the same rate. Having said that, however, it is also the case that members of Congress are very skilled at shaping public opinion in their districts[34] and at shaping legislation in ways that seem to address public concerns without actually doing so.[35] For example, responding to the widespread public concern about the state of private pension plans, Congress set about reforming the system in 2006. In the end, it gave companies more leeway in escaping pension obligations and lowered the amount of money companies had to contribute to the federal pension bailout program.[36] This may reflect the very large amounts of money spent by business and trade groups on lobbying and making contributions to congressional campaigns, and the tendency for senators and representatives to listen to the wealthiest people in their constituencies.[37]

In a substantial number of cases, moreover, Congress does *not* follow public opinion, even on highly visible issues. If members of Congress follow public opinion two-thirds of the time on important bills, that still leaves one-third of the time that they go their own way. Moreover, on many issues of high complexity or low visibility, such as securities and telecommunications regulation, the public may have no well-formed opinions at all. It is in these areas that we can most fully see the influence of money and interest groups at work.

One of the reasons members of Congress have some latitude in representing public opinion in their districts—indeed, in the nation—is that, as we have shown, most come to Congress from relatively "safe" districts where being turned out by the voters is not common. Consequently, House elections do not adequately fulfill the role assigned to elections in democratic theory: as the principle instrument for keeping elected leaders responsive and responsible.[38] A case could be made, however, that despite these shortcomings, Congress has done a great deal to make voting and citizenship more inclusive (see the "Can Government Do Anything Well?" feature).

How Congress Works

11.3 Describe what leaders, political parties, and committees do in Congress

Congress is a vital center of decision making and policymaking in our national government. It is not a place where the executive's bills are simply rubber-stamped, as it is in legislative bodies in many parliamentary systems. By all accounts, Congress is the most influential and independent legislative body among the Western democratic nations. In this section, we turn our attention to how Congress is organized and how it functions as a working legislative body.[39]

There are a number of very important things to keep in mind as we examine how Congress is organized and operates. First, while they are alike in many ways, the House and Senate are very different institutions. They differ in size, the nature of the constituencies they represent, the terms of office of their members, and their constitutional responsibilities; together, these differences give each chamber a distinctive character.

Second, both the House and Senate have had a tendency over the years to succumb to centrifugal forces, always seemingly on the verge of flying apart, with each representative and senator tempted to go his or her own way. The task of running each body has been likened to "herding cats." The reasons are fairly obvious: representatives and senators in some sense are like independent contractors. Congressional leaders lack the normal tools of organizational leadership to force compliance with their wishes; they cannot order members about, they cannot hire or fire them (this is the role of voters), nor can they control the size of their paychecks or benefits. Moreover, in our candidate-centered form of politics, congressional leaders traditionally have had little control over the reelection of representatives and senators who run their own campaigns.

Between 1995 and 2006, however, Republicans used party resources and leadership positions to gain a great deal of control over legislative affairs, especially in the House of Representatives. Republicans not only granted more formal powers to the office of the Speaker but learned to channel campaign money from their own PACs, party campaign committees, and conservative groups and individuals to maintain discipline among members who might be tempted to stray too far from where legislative party leaders want them to be on important matters. The process of centralization of leadership in the Senate did not advance as far as in the House but, given leadership influence over the flow of campaign money from diverse sources, some centralization occurred there as well.[40]

Can Government Do Anything Well?

How Congress made voting and citizenship in America more inclusive

The framers had a fairly narrow definition of who might be best suited to vote and hold public office. For the most part, they left the question of voting eligibility to the states, with full knowledge that the states did not allow access to women, Native Americans, slaves, free blacks, or young people. Many required a poll tax or evidence of property ownership. A few even required people to belong to an established church. A majority of people residing in the United States when the Constitution was ratified in 1788 were not eligible to vote in American federal elections.

Over the broad course of American history, the suffrage has expanded to include virtually every excluded group. These democratizing actions took place first at the state level, where poll taxes were gradually eliminated (later reinstituted for African Americans in the South during the Jim Crow period), as were property qualifications and religious tests. By the late 1820s, white male suffrage was universal in the United States. Then, a series of constitutional amendments gradually incorporated other excluded groups. First, male former slaves were granted the right to vote, then women, and finally 18- to 21-year-olds. In all of this, the Congress of the United States played a central role, as it must in the process of amending the Constitution.

Support for the claim that Congress has played the central role in making voting and citizenship in America more inclusive:

- For a few years after the end of the Civil War, Congress was controlled by radical Republicans who were committed to refashioning the slave system of the South, with the protection of former slaves and their enfranchisement as full citizens among their primary goals. To ensure that the Emancipation Proclamation was not regarded as a temporary war measure, Congress passed the Thirteenth Amendment in 1864 abolishing slavery, sending it to the states for ratification, which happened in 1865. When it became clear that many Southern states were instituting harsh measures of near servitude to control their African American population—called Black Codes—Republicans in Congress passed the Fourteenth Amendment making all persons born or naturalized in the United States full citizens of the nation and of the states where they live, with the full rights and obligations of all other citizens, with rights to due process and equal protection (meaning the right to equal treatment by government). The Amendment was ratified in 1868. The Fifteenth Amendment, passed by Congress and ratified in 1870, was the third and last of the so-called "Reconstruction Amendments" and the one of most interest to us in this feature on making voting more inclusive. In it, Congress specified that the vote could not be denied on the basis of race, color, or previous condition of servitude. With passage of the Fourteenth and Fifteen Amendments, Congress and the states effectively overruled the *Dred Scott* (1857) case in which the Supreme Court said that African Americans, whether free or slave, had no rights that others were obliged to respect.

- In 1920, the House and Senate passed the Nineteenth Amendment, stating that neither state governments nor the federal government could deny a citizen the right to vote based on that citizen's sex. The Amendment was passed during a special session of Congress called specifically to consider it, and was ratified by the requisite number of states that same year.

- The Twenty-Sixth Amendment, passed by Congress and ratified by the states in 1971, set the minimum voting age in the United States at 18, and stipulated that no state government nor the federal government could deny the vote to anyone 18 years or older strictly on the account of his or her age. The measure passed during the Vietnam War, in which most of the fighting was being done by people who could not vote in U.S. elections.

- A Democratic-controlled Congress passed and President Bill Clinton signed the National Voter Registration Act in 1993. Also known as the "Motor Voter" act, the law required that the states allow people to register to vote when they were applying for their driver's license or social services such as food stamps or welfare benefits. The new law had been pushed by civil rights organizations and organized labor and was enacted after Democrats regained unified control of the federal government in the 1992 national elections.

Rejection of the claim that Congress has played the central role in making voting and citizenship in America more inclusive:

- There is no denying that Congress played an important role in passage of each of the voting inclusion initiatives described above. In some sense it could not be otherwise; when it comes to amending the Constitution, Congress necessarily is involved because the main alternative route to changing our founding document—an Amendment proposed by a national constitutional convention called by two-thirds of the states then ratified by the state legislatures of three-fourths of the states—is so fraught with difficulties that it has only been used once. The question of Congress's "centrality," however, is another matter. And so too is the degree to which Congress stopped short of what it might have done better or acted only after a very long period of time, pressed hard by social movements and voters to finally move ahead.

(Continued)

■ With respect to the Fifteenth Amendment, Congress failed to include under its protection at least one-half of former slaves, namely women. This was no oversight. Though women and women's suffrage organizations had been prominent in the abolitionist movement to end slavery, many among them had allowed themselves to be convinced by congressional leaders that granting the right to vote to former slaves and to women at the same time would be too radical a step and would endanger suffrage for African Americans.

■ Again, with respect to the Fifteenth Amendment, Congress did little for almost a century to put federal muscle behind African Americans' right to vote in the South. It would take the Voting Rights Act of 1965 to make the promise of the Fifteenth Amendment real.

■ With respect to women's right to vote, Congress had rejected proposals similar to that of the Nineteenth Amendment in 1887, 1914, 1915, 1918, and 1919. It was finally enacted after pressure was brought to bear by a militant women's suffrage movement, the coming to power in Washington of a political class born in the progressive movement (with Woodrow Wilson as president), and an agreement by suffragettes to cease their disruptions during World War I and to actively support the war effort in trade for a constitutional amendment.

■ The Twenty-Sixth Amendment was passed not only in the midst of the Vietnam War, perhaps recognizing the sacrifice and service of many 18- to 21-year-olds fighting in Southeast Asia, but also at the height of the antiwar movement that was disrupting cities and campuses across the country. Support for it began to build after a model amendment was crafted by students and faculty at Dartmouth College with the express purpose of moving young people from the streets into the voting booth. It was seen as a way to have young people's voices heard and to fashion a more viable democracy in the midst of an unpopular war. Congress passed the proposed Amendment, to be sure, but the initiative and energy behind it was from elsewhere.

■ Republicans have accused Democrats of passing the Motor Voter Act as a way to enhance its chances in local, state, and national elections by allowing more people from its electoral base to register to vote, namely young people (at motor vehicle departments), racial and ethnic minorities, and the poor in particular. Partly to counter this, Republicans later began to champion efforts for voter ID laws, claiming that such laws would stymie vote fraud. Democrats rightly or wrongly have interpreted such proposed statutes as a device to decrease the voting participation of people likely to vote Democratic.

WHAT DO YOU THINK?

What do you think about the past, present, and future role of Congress in making voting and citizenship more inclusive? Which of the following positions is closest to your own?

● Congress has played an admirable role in making voting and citizenship more inclusive and should continue to look for ways to improve matters further.

● Congress has played an admirable role in making voting and citizenship more inclusive, but only at the bequest of voters and activists; further progress can only come if such people continue to press Congress.

● Congress has played an admirable role in making voting and citizenship more inclusive, but there is not much more to be done.

● Congress has been late to the party and has not done as much as it might to make voting and citizenship more inclusive. We really cannot count on it.

How would you defend this position to a fellow student? What would be your main line of argument? What evidence do you believe best supports your position? For help in developing your argument, please refer to the sources listed in the "Can Government Do Anything Well?" feature in Chapter 2 on p. 48.

Additional sources for this feature: James MacGregor Burns and Stewart Burns, *A People's Charter: The Pursuit of Rights in America* (New York: Knopf, 1991).

When they regained control of Congress after the 2006 elections, Democrats tried with some success to become more centralized and coordinated as well, using the political party and congressional leadership positions as its main tools. But the game remains one of "herding cats," typified by Majority Leader Harry Reid's months-long effort to put together the 60 Democratic votes he needed to break a Republican filibuster and pass a health insurance reform bill on the morning of Christmas Eve, 2009. Gaining the votes of Ben Nelson (D–NE) and Joe Lieberman (I–CT) didn't happen until a few days before the final vote and required big leadership concessions to them. For Lieberman, it meant removing the "public option" from the bill.

party conference

An organization of the members of a political party in the House or Senate.

caucus

A regional, ethnic, racial, or economic subgroup within the House or Senate. Also used to describe the party in the House and Senate, as in Republican caucus.

Republicans retook the House in the 2010 elections. But the large new crop of Tea Party-backed freshman refused to toe the leadership line. On several occasions, as in the debt ceiling and payroll tax cut extension, they embarrassed House Speaker John Boehner by refusing to support the compromise agreements he had reached with Senate Democratic leaders and President Obama.

☐ Political Parties in Congress

Political parties have a very strong presence in Congress. Its members come to Washington, D.C., as elected candidates of a political party. At the start of each session, they organize their legislative business along political party lines. At the start of each new Congress, each **party conference**—all the members of a political party in the House or the Senate (although House Democrats use the term **caucus** rather than conference)—meets to select its leaders; approve committee assignments, including committee and subcommittee chairs; and reach agreement on legislative objectives for the session. The majority party in the House selects the Speaker of the House, while the majority party in the Senate selects the president pro tempore (usually its most senior member) and the majority leader. The minority party in each chamber also selects its leaders. Political parties, as we shall see, also are influential in what policies representatives and senators support and how they cast their votes on important bills. So, political parties are at the very core of legislative business in the United States and are becoming ever more important as the partisan divide between Democratic and Republican voters, activists, advocacy groups, and elected officials gets steadily wider.[41]

PARTY VOTING IN CONGRESS The political parties provide important glue for the decentralized fragments of Congress and the legislative process. Party labels are important cues for members of Congress as they decide how to vote on issues before the

PARTY DIVISION

Democratic administrative and congressional leaders applaud the president during his State of the Union address to the nation in January 2010, while Republicans "sit on their hands." This graphically illustrates how Congress operated in the first years of the Obama administration: Democrats largely supported major legislation while Republicans were nearly unanimous in saying no. In spite of this, President Obama and the Democrats produced a historic legislative record: an economic stimulus, health care reform, and financial industry regulation, among other things. Is this development of party government a good thing or something to be worried about? Why?

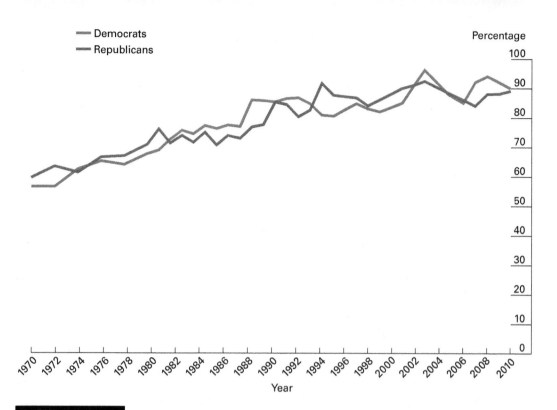

FIGURE 11.5 PARTY VOTING IN CONGRESS

Partisanship has been growing in Congress. One indicator is the increase in the percentage of times the average Democrat and Republican in the House and Senate sided with his/her party on partisan votes—those votes when a majority of Democrats voted against a majority of Republicans.

Source: Davidson, Roger H., Walter J. Oleszek, and Frances E. Lee. Congress and Its Members, 13th ed. Washington, D.C.: CQ Press, 2012.

committees and on the floor of the House and the Senate. Indeed, it has been shown that party affiliation is the best predictor of the voting behavior of members of the Congress and that it is becoming ever more important. In the words of several leading congressional scholars, following what party leaders and other party legislators want is the default position of most senators and representatives.[42]

One way to track partisanship is a statistic showing how often the average Democrat and Republican voted with his or her party in partisan votes in Congress (see Figure 11.5). You can see that partisanship has been rising steadily since the early 1970s and is evident today in about 9 out of 10 votes. In 2009, for example, Democratic leaders were only able to muster three Republican votes in the Senate for President Obama's emergency economic stimulus package and none at all for the final health care bill in 2010.

One result is that reaching bipartisan agreements is becoming more difficult. Then-Maine Republican Senator Olympia Snowe observed, "The whole Congress has become far more polarized and partisan so it makes it difficult to reach bipartisan agreements. The more significant the issue, the more partisan it becomes."[43]

WHY PARTY-LINE VOTING IN CONGRESS HAS INCREASED There are a number of reasons partisanship is increasing.[44] One factor is the changing regional bases of the parties, particularly the historic transformation of the Deep South from a solidly Democratic region at the congressional level to a solidly Republican one.[45] In 2010, Republicans won every contested Senate seat and virtually all competitive House seats. In the 112th Congress, only four Democratic senators and thirty Democratic representatives from the former Confederate states remained.

Another reason that partisanship is on the rise in Congress is that partisan conflict has been on the rise nationally, especially among party activists and party-associated advocacy groups. The inevitable result is that members of Congress have been facing an ever-more partisan-divided electorate and interest group environment.

It is not entirely clear whether party voting differences are caused directly by party affiliation or indirectly by the character of constituencies or by the preexisting ideological commitments of members of Congress. Some scholars have found strong independent party effects regardless of constituency or ideology. Others argue that the tendency of people in the same party to vote together is simply a reflection of the fact that Democratic lawmakers tend to come from districts and states that are similar to one another and that Republican lawmakers come from places that are different from the constituencies of Democrats. For example, compared to Democrats, Republicans generally come from districts where more people go to church on a regular basis. Democratic districts, in turn, tend to contain more union members and racial minorities or large university campuses.[46] The strongest tie, in this line of argument, is between the member of Congress and the constituency, not between the member and the party.

Increasingly, however, internal party unity and conflict between the parties seem attributable to ideology. Both in the electorate and among the members of Congress and other political elites, Democrats have become somewhat more liberal, while Republicans have become much more consistently conservative.[47] Political scientist and former Democratic representative from Oklahoma Mickey Edwards observes the following about the ideological tendencies of members of Congress: "Most people who run for office have . . . [strong] feelings not only about specific issues but about general philosophical concepts, such as the proper role of government, the impact of taxation on investment and savings, and the reasons for crime and poverty."[48]

While our parties are more ideological and unified in Congress than at any time in recent memory, senators and representatives can and do stray from the party turf, even on important matters. Republicans in Congress were unwilling in 2007 to support President Bush on his proposal for a road to citizenship for millions of undocumented immigrants, for example. But most of the time, members of each party in each chamber stick closely to one another.

☐ Congressional Leadership

The political parties work through the leadership structure of Congress because the leaders of the majority political party are, at the same time, the leaders of the House and the Senate.[49] As Congress becomes more partisan, party becomes ever more important in shaping the actions of House and Senate leaders.[50]

LEADERSHIP IN THE HOUSE The leader in the House of Representatives is the Speaker of the House. This position is recognized in the Constitution and stands second in the line of succession to the presidency, immediately after the vice president.

Until 1910, the Speaker exercised great power over the House legislative process. The bases of his power were his right to appoint committees and their chairs and his position as chair of the powerful Rules Committee, which controls the flow of legislation in the House. The revolt of the rank and file against Speaker "Uncle Joe" Cannon in 1910 resulted in the Speaker's removal from the Rules Committee and the elimination of the Speaker's power to appoint committees and their chairs.

From 1910 until the early 1970s, the weakened Speaker competed with a handful of powerful committee chairs for leadership of the House. A few Speakers, such as Sam Rayburn of Texas, were able to lead by sheer dint of their personalities and legislative skills, but power tilted toward the committee chairs most of the time.

The Democratic Caucus staged a revolt against the committee system after 1974 and restored some of the powers of the Speaker, especially in making committee assignments. The Democratic Conference also gave the Speaker more power to refer bills to committee, control the House agenda, appoint members to select committees, and direct floor debate. This change gave Speakers Tip O'Neill, Jim Wright, and Tom Foley considerable leadership resources.

In 1995, the Republican Caucus gave even more power to control the House legislative process to their first Speaker since 1954, Newt Gingrich. Some scholars suggest that Gingrich's speakership was the most powerful one since Cannon's.[51] Unexpected losses of Republican House seats in the 1998 elections, after a campaign featuring a Gingrich-designed advertising blitz to impeach the president, led to his resignation of the speakership and from the House.

Democrat Nancy Pelosi (D–CA) exercised a strong hand as Speaker of the House from 2007 through 2010, when the Republicans took over. She believed in and was adept at top-down, energetic leadership. She largely controlled the Democratic message in the House, leaned on committee chairs to push her agenda, and used the levers of campaign finance—the Democratic Congressional Campaign Committee and her own leadership PAC, which reportedly gave $40 million to Democratic House candidates in the 2007–2008 election cycle—to influence representatives in her then-majority party. To advance the Democratic agenda in the 111th Congress, she pushed through several important rules in 2009, one to make it harder for representatives—in practice, aimed at Republican members of the House—to bring a motion to send a bill back to committee from the floor.[52] She is generally credited with convincing the president, several of his advisers, and other Democratic congressional leaders to make a final push for health care reform when they were wavering—and eventually prevailed.[53] When the Republicans regained their majority in the House in the 2010 elections, John Boehner (R–OH) became Speaker.

No matter which party is the majority, the Speaker has more power and influence in the legislative branch than any other representative or senator. This power and influence has come about because of House rules and political party rules that have evolved since the 1970s that give the Speaker important powers and prerogatives in determining the flow of legislative business. The Speaker names conference committee members, appoints members to the powerful Rules Committee, and exercises strong influence over the appointment of the chairs of other committees and referral of bills to committees for hearings and review. The Speaker appoints the leaders of the majority party's organizations, including the campaign finance committee and the party caucus. The Speaker also has the power to recognize (or not recognize) people to speak during floor debates and is in charge of the House's schedule, which can be used to encourage favored bills and stop others.[54] The Speaker's power is not absolute, however. Note again that on several occasions in 2011 and 2012, the members of the Tea Party caucus in the Republican Party refused to support compromises that Boehner had negotiated with the Senate and the president.

The majority party in the House also selects a majority leader to help the Speaker plan strategy and manage the legislative business of the House, and a majority **whip**. Neither House nor party rules spell out their precise responsibilities. The nature of these jobs depends very much on what the Speaker wants, on the majority leader's talents and energy, and on what the Speaker and majority leader want the whip to do. In general, however, the Speaker may be likened to the chairman of the board in a business corporation, while the majority leader may be likened to the chief executive officer, responsible for the day-to-day operations of the enterprise.[55] The whip is the majority leader's deputy, carrying out many of the tasks of getting bills passed, including counting votes and twisting arms. Lest one think that this arrangement runs like a well-oiled machine, personality and ideological differences, and conflicting ambitions—the majority leader may think that he would make a better Speaker than the incumbent—sometimes get in the way. During many of the tense negotiations between President Obama and Speaker Boehner to increase the debt ceiling and avoid default on the nation's debt in 2011, for example, Majority Leader Eric Cantor (R–VA), second in the leadership hierarchy to Boehner, was noticeably cool to the initial compromise and failed to support it in the Republican caucus.

The minority party elects a minority leader, who acts as the chief spokesperson and legislative strategist for the opposition. The minority leader not only tries to keep the forces together but also seeks out members of the majority party who might be willing to vote against the House leadership on key issues, although this is getting

whip
A political party member in Congress charged with keeping members informed of the plans of the party leadership, counting votes before action on important issues, and rounding up party members for votes on bills.

more difficult to do because of rising partisanship. The House minority leader in the 111th Congress (and Speaker in the 112th) was John Boehner (R–OH), a strong conservative who used his position to harshly criticize the Democrats and rally the Republican base in the electorate.

LEADERSHIP IN THE SENATE Leadership in the Senate is less visible. Senators with formal leadership titles, such as the president pro tempore, exercise little influence. The Senate majority leader is as close as one comes to a leader in this body, but the powers of the office pale before those of the Speaker of the House. The Senate majority leader has some influence in committee assignments, office space designation, and control of access to the floor of the Senate. The majority leader is also important in the scheduling of the business of the Senate. The degree of actual influence is based less on formal powers, however, than on skills of personal persuasion, the respect of colleagues, visibility in the media as majority party spokesperson, and a role at the center of many of the various communication networks. In addition, campaign contributors often take the advice of the majority leader in how they allocate money for incumbents seeking reelection, giving the majority leader additional influence.

The power of the position is personal and not institutional; it cannot be passed on to the next leader. The Senate remains a body of independent, relatively equal members loosely tied together by threads of party loyalty, ideology, and mutual concern about the next election. It is not an environment conducive to decisive leadership, although a few, such as Lyndon Johnson, managed to transcend the limits of the office. And, with partisanship on the rise in the Senate, it is increasingly difficult for any majority leader to push the majority party's agenda, because important bills now require 60 votes to pass due to the increasing use of the filibuster by the minority party. Remarkably, however, the majority leader in the 111th Congress, Harry Reid (D–NV), was able to keep together the 60 votes on his side of the aisle that he needed to pass health insurance reform legislation and the bill to regulate the financial industry in 2010, something few observers thought possible.

☐ Congressional Committees

Much of the work of Congress takes place in its many committees and subcommittees. Committees are where many of the details of legislation are hammered out and where much of the oversight of the executive branch takes place. As recently as the 1960s and 1970s, committees and their chairs were relatively autonomous, exercising great power over the course of legislation, because parties were not unified and House and Senate leaders had little power. As partisanship rose in the country and Congress, however, Republicans and Democrats decided, as we have seen, to give much more power to the Speaker and some additional powers to the majority leader in the Senate, especially over committee appointments and most especially to appointments to the most important committees. The result is a dramatic decline in the power of committees and of committee chairs in the legislative process and an increase in the influence of the parties and their leaders.[56] Sometimes, and most especially in the House, leaders will completely bypass the committee process, creating special party task forces to consider important bills or bringing bills to the floor directly by the leadership team. This direct leadership-to-floor consideration of legislation happened with the pay equity bill passed early in 2009, for example.

WHY CONGRESS HAS COMMITTEES Committees serve several useful purposes. For one thing, they allow Congress to process the huge flow of business that comes before it. The committees serve as screening devices, allowing only a small percentage of the bills put forward to take up the time of the House and the Senate.

Committees are also islands of specialization, where members and staff develop the expertise to handle complex issues and to meet executive branch experts on equal terms. The Ways and Means Committee of the House can go toe-to-toe with the

Treasury Department, for instance, on issues related to taxation. Committee expertise is one of the reasons Congress remains a vital lawmaking body.

Members of Congress also use their committee positions to enhance their chances for reelection. Rational lawmakers usually try to secure committee assignments that will allow them to channel benefits to their constituents or to advance an ideological agenda popular in their district or state.

TYPES OF COMMITTEES IN CONGRESS There are several kinds of committee, each of which serves a special function in the legislative process.

Standing committees are set up permanently, as specified in the House and Senate rules. These committees are the first stop for potential new laws. The ratio of Democrats to Republicans on each committee is set for each house through a process of negotiation between the majority and minority party leaders. The majority party naturally enjoys a majority on each of the committees and controls the chair, as well as a substantial majority on the most important committees, such as the Budget and Finance Committee in the Senate and the Rules Committee and the Ways and Means Committee in the House. Not surprisingly, the ratio of Democrats and Republicans on committees is a point of considerable contention between the two parties, especially when they are evenly divided.

The avalanche of legislative business cannot be managed and given the necessary specialized attention in the full House and Senate standing committees. For most bills, **hearings**, negotiations, and **markup** take place in subcommittees. It is in the subcommittees, moreover, that most oversight of the executive branch takes place.

Select committees are usually temporary committees created by congressional leaders to conduct studies or investigations. Their distinguishing feature is that they have no power to send bills to the House or Senate floor. They exist to resolve matters that standing committees cannot or do not wish to handle. Often the issues before select committees are highly visible and gain a great deal of public attention for their members. Select committees investigated the Watergate scandal, the Iran-Contra affair, and intelligence failures regarding the 9/11 attacks and the run-up to the war in Iraq.

Joint committees, with members from both houses, are organized to facilitate the flow of legislation. The Joint Budget Committee, for instance, helps speed up the normally slow legislative process of considering the annual federal budget.

Before a bill can go to the president for signature, it must pass in identical form in each chamber. Most often, the committee that irons out the differences between House and Senate versions is called a **conference committee**. A conference committee is created as needed for each piece of major legislation. Members are selected by the Speaker of the House and the Senate majority leader in consultation with the chairs of the committees that originally considered the bills in each chamber and sometimes with the leaders of the minority party. Although they are supposed to reconcile versions of bills coming out of the House and the Senate, conference committees sometimes add, subtract, or amend provisions that are of great consequence. Much of the power of conference committees comes from the fact that bills reported by them to the House and Senate must be voted up or down; no new amendments are allowed. During the early and mid-2000s, Republican leaders often excluded their Democratic counterparts from conference committees considering important bills, making conference a place to work out differences among House and Senate Republicans. Given the unanimous opposition of Senate Republicans to the health reform bill, and the near unanimous opposition to it by House Republicans, Democrats did not include GOP members on the conference committee for this legislation in 2010.

COMMITTEE CHAIRS AND RANKING MEMBERS For most of the twentieth century before the 1970s, appointment by **seniority** was an unbreakable rule. The most senior committee member of the majority party automatically became chair of the committee; the most senior member of the minority party automatically became the **ranking minority member**. After 1974, however, both Republicans and Democrats

standing committees
Relatively permanent congressional committees that address specific areas of legislation.

hearings
The taking of testimony by a congressional committee or subcommittee.

markup
The process of revising a bill in committee.

select committees
Temporary committees in Congress created to conduct studies or investigations; they have no power to report bills.

joint committees
Congressional committees with members from both the House and the Senate.

conference committees
Ad hoc committees, made up of members of both the Senate and the House of Representatives, set up to reconcile differences in the provisions of bills.

seniority
The principle that one attains a position on the basis of length of service.

ranking minority member
The highest-ranking member of the minority party on a congressional committee.

in the House instituted the secret ballot among party members for the election of chairs, and seniority was occasionally ignored. Seniority became even less important in the 1990s when Speaker Newt Gingrich began to bypass the most senior committee members in favor of members who would support his conservative legislative program. Appointment of committee chairs in the House remains firmly in the hands of majority party leaders today. Speaker Nancy Pelosi followed suit when the Democrats took over the House in 2007. In the Senate, however, seniority continues to be an important criterion for appointment to a chairmanship position although, even there, party leaders and members increasingly are demanding more ideological and policy conformity as a condition of appointment.

Not long ago, chairs of committees were the absolute masters of all they surveyed. From the early twentieth century to the early 1970s, the heads of congressional committees went virtually unchallenged. They hired and assigned staff, controlled the budget, created or abolished subcommittees at will, controlled the agenda, scheduled meetings, and reported (or refused to report) bills to the floor. Things are different today. As we have shown, much of the power of committee chairs over legislation has migrated to the party leadership in each house. The upshot is that decisions that were entirely the province of the chair in the past have now been greatly diminished and are shared with others.[57] Committee chairs and ranking minority members—oftentimes in the past, mavericks opposed to their own parties who were protected by seniority—now must be attentive to the party caucus and party leaders or risk losing their positions.[58] Still, committee chairs remain the most influential and active members within their committees, being at the center of all of the lines of communication, retaining the power to schedule meetings and organize the staff, having an important say on the committee's agenda and appointments to conference committees, and often winning deference as the most experienced members of their committees.

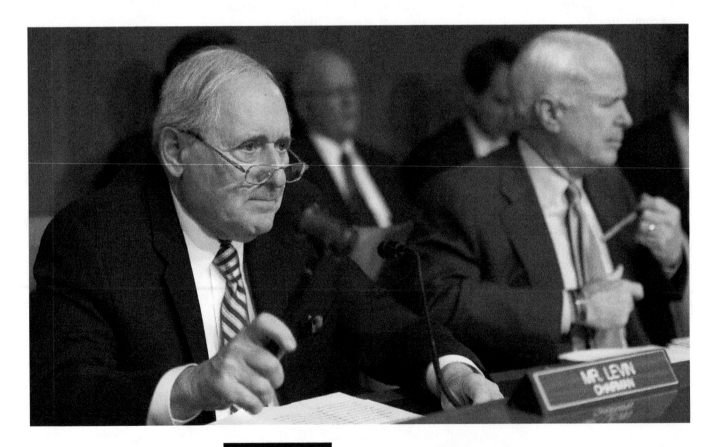

POWER COMMITTEE

The Senate Armed Services Committee, here chaired by Senator Carl Levin (D-Mich), is one of the committees that ambitious senators try to join during their legislative careers. Not only are important national security issues on the committee's agenda, garnering senators much appreciated attention and giving them influence on important policy matters, but the size of the defense budget and the needs of the Defense Department affords ample opportunity for senators to shape the flow of defense contracts to their states.

Rules and Norms in the House and Senate

Like all organizations, Congress is guided by both formal rules and informal norms of behavior.[59] Rules specify precisely how things should be done and what is not allowed. Norms are generally accepted expectations about how people ought to behave and how business ought to proceed.

Traditionally, members of the House have been expected to become specialists in some area or areas of policy and to defer to the judgment of other specialists on most bills. This mutual deference is known as **reciprocity**. While reciprocity is still common, deference to specialists—usually chairs or ranking members of committees—is declining in favor of deference to the wishes of party leaders. In the Senate, the norm of reciprocity was always less prevalent than it was in the House. Because there are fewer members in the Senate, because senators are elected on a statewide basis, and because the Senate has been the breeding ground for many presidential candidacies, a senator has more prestige, visibility, and power than a member of the House. As a result, senators are generally unwilling to sit quietly for a term or two, waiting their turn. It is not unusual for a first-term senator to introduce major bills and make important speeches. In the House, such a thing was very unusual in the past. There the old rule held sway: "To get along, go along."

Legislative life is much more rule-bound in the House of Representatives, because of its large size, than in the Senate; it tends to be more organized and hierarchical (see Table 11.2). Leaders in the House have more power, the majority party exercises more control over legislative affairs, the procedures are more structured, and the individual members have a harder time making their mark. It is geared toward majority rule, with the minority playing a lesser role. The Senate tends to be a more open and fluid place, and it lodges less power in its leaders than the House does. Each senator is more of an independent operator than his or her House colleagues. The Senate is a much more relaxed place, one that accommodates mavericks (though less so than in the past), tolerates the foibles of its members, and pays more attention to members of the minority party. It is a place where the minority and individual senators play important roles in the legislative process.

Differences between the House and the Senate are especially apparent in floor debate. Bills are scheduled for floor debate in the Senate, for instance, not by a powerful committee but by **unanimous consent**, meaning that business can be blocked by a single dissenter. Outgoing Senator Jim Bunning (R–KY) blocked Senate consideration of an unemployment insurance extension for a whole week in early 2010 by responding "no" to the majority leader Harry Reid's request for unanimous consent to bring the bill to the floor. In the Senate, moreover, each senator has the power to place a **hold** on a bill or nomination to delay consideration by the whole body. While holds cannot be found

reciprocity
Deferral by members of Congress to the judgment of subject-matter specialists, mainly on minor technical bills.

unanimous consent
Legislative action taken "without objection" as a way to expedite business; used to conduct much of the business of the Senate.

hold
A tactic by which a single senator can prevent action on a bill or nomination; based on an implied threat of refusing to agree to unanimous consent on other Senate matters or willingness to filibuster the bill or nomination.

TABLE 11.2 DIFFERENCES BETWEEN HOUSE AND SENATE RULES AND NORMS

Senate	House
Informal, open, nonhierarchical	Rule-bound, hierarchical
Leaders have only a few formal powers	Leaders have many formal powers
Members may serve on two or more major committees	Members restricted to one major committee
Less specialized	More specialized
Unrestricted floor debate	Restricted floor debate
Unlimited amendments possible	Only limited amendments possible
Amendments need not be germane	Amendments must be germane
Unlimited time for debate unless shortened by unanimous consent or halted by invocation of cloture	Limited time for debate
More prestige for each member	Less prestige for each member
More reliance on staff	Less reliance on staff
Minority party plays a larger role; hard to put majority rule into effect	Minority party plays a smaller role; majority rule drives legislative process

filibuster

A parliamentary device used in the Senate to prevent a bill from coming to a vote by "talking it to death," made possible by the norm of unlimited debate.

cloture

A vote to end a filibuster; requires the votes of three-fifths of the membership of the Senate.

in the formal rules of the Senate, they have become part of the many informal customs of the body. Their use is regulated only by the majority leader, who may decide on whether to grant holds and how long they can be in effect, but only by using complex and time-consuming procedural mechanisms. In 2009, Senator Jim DeMint (R–SC) held up President Obama's nominee to head the Transportation Safety Administration (TSA) for months in an effort to block TSA employees from joining a union. Later that same year, Senator Richard Shelby of Alabama blocked consideration of 70 nominees submitted by the president, using the hold as a tool to force the Obama administration to put a new FBI lab in his state and to award a military tanker contract to a firm in Alabama. Unlike the House, moreover, where debate on a bill is strictly regulated regarding the number and kinds of amendments as well as time limits for debate (determined by the Rules Committee with the agreement of the Speaker), the Senate's tradition allows for unlimited numbers of amendments—that need not be germane to the bill under consideration—and unlimited debate.

Senators in the minority have increasingly used this tolerance of unlimited amendments and debate to good effect. Because limiting debate is so difficult in the Senate, the opponents of a bill can tie up legislative business by refusing to stop debating its merits. This practice is known as the **filibuster**. In the past, senators engaged in a filibuster had to be on the floor of the Senate addressing the body. Senators trying to hold up a bill often talked for hours through night and day, working together in shifts. Under Senate rules, filibustering senators did not even have to talk about the bill itself; some read from novels or quoted verse, others told stories about their children, and still others quoted long lists of sports statistics. The purpose was serious, however: to force the majority to give up the fight and move on to other business. This tactic was highly successful but used only occasionally because it was so hard to pull off; filibustering senators had to hold the floor for hours and days, fending off challenges to end debate. And, it held up all other business in the Senate.

Today, it is much easier to filibuster because a group of senators can simply announce a filibuster—not actually engage in the act of filibustering, that is to say—and a bill is stopped in its tracks unless 60 votes to end the filibuster can be mustered (Senate Rule XXII). Needless to say, the motion to end debate, known as **cloture**, is very hard to pass in an evenly divided Senate, where a party with a small majority must attract several members of the minority party to reach the 60-vote threshold. Or, in the rare case when the majority party has 60 or more votes—which the Democrats had in 2009 and 2010—cloture is possible only if the leadership can prevent defections from its side. This gives enormous power to a handful of senators who can threaten defection.

Not surprisingly, given the power that the filibuster gives to the minority party and to a handful of senators in the majority party, the number of filibusters and the number of cloture votes to end them have multiplied dramatically. Political scientist Barbara Sinclair has shown that "extended debate" tactics—filibusters threatened or used—affected 8 percent of important bills during the 1960s, 27 percent during the 1980s, and a staggering 70 percent after the Democrats took control of the Senate in 2007.[60]

Senators' positions on the filibuster depend somewhat on whether one's party is in the majority or the minority. When Republicans were in the majority in 2005 and Democrats were holding up President Bush's judicial nominations, Republicans threatened passage of a rule that came to be called the "nuclear option" that would end the use of the filibuster entirely on matters of judicial appointments. When they were in the minority from 2007 through 2010, however, Republicans used the filibuster repeatedly to slow or stop majority Democrats from passing bills to change Iraq war policy, provide stimulus spending and tax relief, reform the health care system, regulate the financial industry, and slow emissions of greenhouse gases. Whatever one thinks of the filibuster—some condemn it as a device that undermines majority rule; others praise it as a device that guarantees that the voice of the minority is heard—it is inescapably the case today, given the deep partisan divisions between the parties and the difficulty of acting in a bipartisan fashion, that most major bills need a super-majority of 60 votes to pass rather than a simple majority (51 votes). For more on the status of the majority and the minority in filibusters and cloture, see the "Mapping American Politics" feature.

Mapping American Politics

Majorities, Minorities, and Senate Filibusters

Introduction

Unlimited debate is a tradition in the U.S. Senate. Senate rules make it very difficult to end debate on a proposed bill and bring it to a vote if a number of senators wish to continue deliberations. Increasingly, senators try to kill a bill by "filibustering"—talking it to death, if you will—by not allowing other business to be taken up on the floor of the Senate. Filibusters can only be ended by passage of a cloture motion, which requires 60 votes, so the votes of only 41 senators can keep a filibuster going. The filibuster is often defended as an important instrument of deliberative democracy, because it allows the minority in the Senate to have an important say in legislative matters and not be steamrolled by the majority. Critics of the filibuster, whether Democrats or Republicans, liberals or conservatives, usually claim that filibusters are contrary to the principle of majority rule. Who is right?

Different Maps; Different Stories

Both are right and wrong. The filibuster can be considered to serve the minority or the majority, depending on who we think the senators represent. Sustaining a filibuster, while requiring the votes of only 41 of 100 senators, may involve senators representing a large majority of the American population, a small minority, or anything

in between. A filibuster sustained by a coalition of 41 senators from the most populous states would represent about 76 percent of Americans (red states on the cartogram), but a filibuster sustained by a coalition of 41 senators from the least populous states would represent only about 11 percent of Americans (green states). The cartogram, with states drawn to reflect the sizes of their populations, shows this very clearly.*

Today, of course, the filibuster usually is the tool of the minority party. In the first year of the 112th Congresss, for example, 40 GOP senators forced cloture votes on nearly every major piece of legislation. These 40 senators represented about 36 percent of the American population.

What Do You Think?

When they were a majority in the Senate, Republicans wanted to change the filibuster rule, especially on votes that involve judicial appointments on which the Senate has constitutional "advise and consent" responsibilities. Their argument was that a minority should not be able to block this important constitutional role. But what if the minority in the Senate actually represents states with a majority of the population? Some have suggested that a filibuster should be sustained only when the 41 senators supporting it represent a majority of Americans. What do you think about this idea?

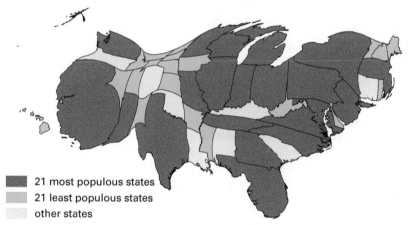

- 21 most populous states
- 21 least populous states
- other states

States Sized by Population

Source: © 2006 M.D. Ward; updated by authors through 2012.

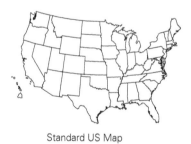

Standard US Map

*41 senators represent 20½ states, but there is no way reasonably to draw one-half of a state. In this cartogram, the large-state bloc and the small-state block each is composed of 21 states.

Legislative Responsibilities: How a Bill Becomes a Law

11.4 Outline the process by which a bill becomes a law

Explore on
MyPoliSciLab
Simulation
You Are a Consumer Advocate

We can put much of what we have learned to work by seeing how a bill moves through the legislative labyrinth to become a law. The path by which a bill becomes a law is so strewn with obstacles that few bills survive; in fact, only about 6 percent of all bills that are introduced are enacted. To make law is exceedingly difficult; to block bills from becoming laws is relatively easy. At each step along the way (see Figure 11.6), a "no" decision can stop the passage of a bill in its tracks. As one account points out, members of the House or the Senate have "two principal functions: to make laws and to keep laws from being

FIGURE 11.6 HOW A BILL BECOMES A LAW

This diagram shows the path by which major bills introduced in Congress become law. As explained in the text, the road that bills must travel is complex and difficult, and few bills survive it. A bill can be derailed at any stop in its passage. A subcommittee can refuse to report a bill; a bill may be defeated on the floor of each chamber; a conference committee may fail to reach an agreement on a compromise; the conference bill may be defeated in either chamber; or the president may veto the bill.

made. The first of these [they] perform only with sweat, patience, and a remarkable skill in the handling of creaking machinery; but the second they perform daily, with ease and infinite variety."[61]

What follows describes how major bills become law most of the time. Minor bills are often considered in each house under special rules that allow shortcuts. Thus, in the House, the "suspension calendar" and the "corrections calendar" set aside certain times for consideration of minor matters. It is also worth noting that bills involving the federal budget—authorization and appropriations bills—have several unique aspects to them, which need not concern us here. And, more importantly, on some major bills, House and Senate leaders have made changes in bills coming out of committee on their way to floor action, or made important changes to bills in conference committees. Some observers claim that these "unorthodox" routes for lawmaking are becoming more and more common.[62]

hopper
The box in the House of Representatives in which proposed bills are placed.

discharge petition
A petition signed by 218 House members to force a bill that has been before a committee for at least 30 days while the House is in session out of the committee and onto the floor for consideration.

☐ Introducing a Bill

A bill can be introduced only by a member of Congress. In reality, bills are often written in the executive branch or by interest groups. The initial draft of the bill that became the Tax Reform Act of 1986, for instance, was fashioned in the Treasury Department by a committee headed by the department's secretary, James Baker. Industry trade groups, to take another example, wrote substantial parts of bills designed to roll back timber and mining regulations in 1995, while pharmaceutical industry trade group representatives wrote key portions of the Medicare drug benefit bill that went into effect in 2006.

With the exception of tax bills (which must originate in the House), a bill may be introduced in either the House or the Senate. In the House, a member introduces a bill by putting it into the **hopper** (a box watched over by one of the House clerks). In the Senate, a member must announce a bill to the body after being recognized by the presiding officer. The bill is then assigned a number, with the prefix *H.R.* in the House or *S.* in the Senate.

☐ Committee Action on a Bill

The presiding officer in the Senate or the Speaker in the House refers the bill to the appropriate standing committee. In the majority of cases, referral to committee is routine; the subject matter of the bill clearly indicates the appropriate committee. Revenue bills go automatically to the Ways and Means Committee in the House and to the Finance Committee in the Senate, for instance. In a small but still significant number of cases, however, the relevant committee is not so obvious because of overlapping committee jurisdictions. For example, the House Committee on International Relations is in charge of "international policy," whereas the Commerce Committee is in charge of "foreign commerce generally." In such cases, the Speaker can make multiple referrals, that is, send a bill to more than one committee for consideration. In the Senate, bills must go to a single committee, regardless of any ambiguity that may exist about its exact content. Needless to say, the more bills there are without an obvious committee destination, the more discretionary power there is in the hands of the Speaker of the House and the Senate majority leader. Where they decide to send such bills often determines whether bills will survive the legislative process and what form they will take in the end.

Committee chairs normally pass the bill on to the appropriate subcommittee for hearings. Many a bill dies at this stage, when either the subcommittee or the full committee declines to consider it further. A bill quietly killed in committee can reach the floor only by a device called a **discharge petition**, which is rarely successful.

If a bill is accepted for consideration, the subcommittee generally holds hearings, taking testimony from people for and against it. Subcommittee staff not only help prepare representatives and senators for the questioning but also often take part in the questioning themselves. The subcommittee may then forward the bill as rewritten by the staff and subcommittee members to the full committee, or it can decide to allow the bill to go no further.

Rewriting the bill in committee is called the *markup* (discussed earlier), which usually occurs amid very intense bargaining and deal making, with an eye toward fashioning a bill that will muster majority support in the full committee and on the floors of the House and the Senate and that will gain the support of the president. The staff plays a central role in the markup.

The subcommittee reports its action to the full committee. The committee chair, in consultation with other important members of his or her committee, may opt for the committee to hold its own hearings and markup sessions, may decide to kill the bill outright, or may simply accept the action of the subcommittee. If the subcommittee has done its job well and has consulted with the most important players on the full committee (especially the chair), the committee will simply rubber-stamp the bill and move it along for floor action.

FLOOR ACTION ON A BILL If a bill is favorably reported from committee, congressional leaders schedule it for floor debate. In the House, major bills must first go to the Rules Committee, which decides where bills will appear on the legislative calendar and the terms under which bills will be debated by the House. A rule specifies such things as the amount of time for debate and the number (if any) and nature of amendments allowed. The Rules Committee may choose not to issue a rule at all or to drag its feet, as it did with civil rights bills until the mid-1960s. This has happened less often in recent years because both Democratic and Republican Speakers have had more power over Rules Committee appointments. The committee can also grant a "closed rule," allowing only a yes or no vote without amendments, as it generally does with tax bills.

PUBLIC WHIPPING

John Mack, chairman of Morgan Stanley, tries to explain to members of the Senate Finance Committee in January 2010 why the financial collapse happened, why industry profits were soaring, and why bonuses were being paid, even as loan money for small businesses and homeowners was scarce. The chief executives of other leading financial firms wait their turns to testify. What role in our political system do congressional hearings play? Do they lead to substantive changes in regulations and laws, or are they more often opportunities to play to the anger or frustration of the public?

an Congress Get
nything Done?

overnment cannot operate without a budget, revenue, or appropriations. But over the past thirty years,
embers of Congress have grown so polarized that they cannot agree on a budget or much of anything
olarization occurs when members of both parties move away from the moderate middle and share
ingly less common ground. Since 2001, Congress failed to pass a budget eight times, succeeding only in
ing temporary budgets to keep government running. As the parties grow more polarized, Congress is less
pass a permanent budget and the national debt increases.

ty **Polarization**

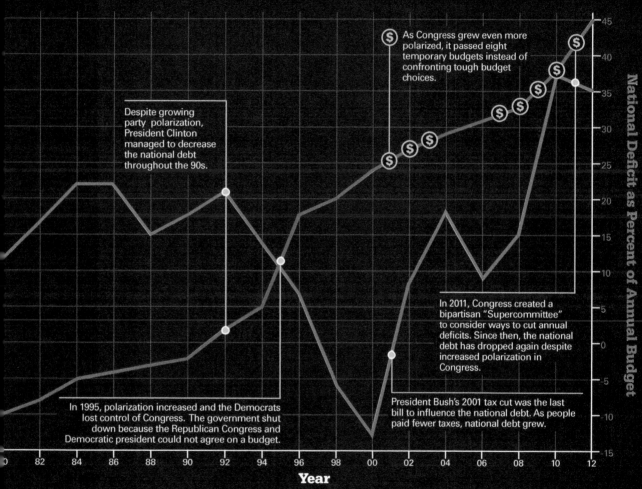

As Congress grew even more polarized, it passed eight temporary budgets instead of confronting tough budget choices.

Despite growing party polarization, President Clinton managed to decrease the national debt throughout the 90s.

In 2011, Congress created a bipartisan "Supercommittee" to consider ways to cut annual deficits. Since then, the national debt has dropped again despite increased polarization in Congress.

In 1995, polarization increased and the Democrats lost control of Congress. The government shut down because the Republican Congress and Democratic president could not agree on a budget.

President Bush's 2001 tax cut was the last bill to influence the national debt. As people paid fewer taxes, national debt grew.

Year

82   84   86   88   90   92   94   96   98   00   02   04   06   08   10   12

National Deficit as Percent of Annual Budget

45 40 35 30 25 20 15 10 5 0 -5 -10 -15

tion is measured as the distance between the two parties' ideological scores as computed from data at Voteview.com.
Data from Voteview and the U.S. Government Accountability Office.

estigate **Further**

ept What is political polariza-
arization occurs when members of
tical parties consistently vote along
al lines. Political scientists track
on because it has nearly doubled
st thirty years, and it tends to
he government's ability to function.
is a product of the 2001 and 2003
cuts, the unpaid-for wars in Iraq

Connection Is polarization related
to greater annual debt? On a yearly basis,
polarization is largely independent of the debt
incurred by the United States—notice, for
example, during the Clinton presidency how
polarization grew even as debt decreased.
However, as a long-term trend, both national
debt and polarization in Congress do increase
together.

Cause Does polarization impede
Congress's ability to create annual
budgets? Yes. The more polarized
Congress becomes, the more likely the
disagreements over permanent budget
solutions lead to temporary resolutions that
barely stave off government shutdown.

11.1

11.2

11.3

11.4

11.5

veto

Presidential disapproval of a bill that has been passed by both houses of Congress. The president's veto can be overridden by a two-thirds vote in each house.

pocket veto

Rejection of a bill if the president takes no action on it for 10 days and Congress has adjourned during that period.

oversight

Congressional responsibility for monitoring the actions of executive branch agencies and personnel to ensure conformity to federal statutes and congressional intent.

Floor debate in the Senate, where rules do not limit debate as in the House, is much more freewheeling. Floor debate is also more important in the Senate in determining the final form a bill will take because Senate committees are less influential than House committees. Senators are also less likely to defer to committee judgments. Also, the threat of a hold or a filibuster means that the minority in the Senate plays an important role in determining the final shape of legislation.

After floor debate, the entire membership of the chamber votes on the bill, either as reported by the committee or (more often) after amendments have been added. If the bill receives a favorable vote, it then goes through the same obstacle course in the other chamber or awaits action by the other house if the bill was introduced there at the same time.

CONFERENCE COMMITTEE Even if the bill makes it through both houses, its journey is not yet over. Bills passed by the House and the Senate almost always differ from one another, sometimes in minor ways and sometimes in quite substantial ways. Before the bill goes to the president, its conflicting versions must be rewritten so that a single bill gains the approval of both chambers of Congress. This compromise bill usually is fashioned in a conference committee made up of members from both the House and the Senate appointed by the Speaker and the Senate majority leader, customarily from the relevant committees but not always. Increasingly, House and Senate leaders appoint people who will write a final bill that will be acceptable to them and to their party. Sometimes a conference committee is not used; separate House and Senate versions of a bill can be reconciled by the two trading amendments until they are similar, for example, or one chamber can simply defer to the other and accept that version of a bill.

A bill from a conference committee must be voted up or down on the floors of the House and the Senate; no amendments or further changes are allowed. If, and only if, both houses approve it, the bill is forwarded to the president for consideration.

PRESIDENTIAL ACTION Because the president plays an important constitutional role in turning a bill into a law, he or his assistants and advisers are usually consulted throughout the legislative process, especially if the president is of the same party that controls Congress. If the president approves the bill, he signs it and it becomes law. If he is not particularly favorable but does not want to block the bill, it becomes law after 10 days if he takes no action. He can also **veto** the bill and return it to Congress. A bill can still become law by a two-thirds vote of each house, which will override the president's veto. A president can also kill a bill at the end of a congressional session if he takes no action and Congress adjourns before 10 days pass. This is known as a **pocket veto**.

Legislative Oversight of the Executive Branch

11.5   Explain why Congress is doing less oversight than in the past

 Oversight is another important responsibility of Congress. Oversight involves keeping an eye on how the executive branch carries out the provisions of the laws that Congress has passed and on possible abuses of power by executive branch officials, including the president.

Oversight is primarily the province of the committees and subcommittees of Congress, and it is among Congress's most visible and dramatic roles, guided by the wishes of House and Senate leaders and the majority party caucus in each. High-profile examples of legislative probes of alleged administrative malfeasance or incompetence include Watergate, the Iran-Contra affair, the savings-and-loan collapse and bailout, corporate accounting scandals, intelligence failures, the federal response to the Hurricane Katrina disaster in New Orleans, and the sub-prime mortgage meltdown.

In these highly partisan times, whether oversight hearings take place and the relative vigor with which they are carried out depend increasingly on which party controls which branch of government. In the years 2003 through 2006, when Republicans controlled both houses of Congress and Republican George W. Bush was president, Congress did not probe very deeply into a number of troublesome areas, including failed prewar intelligence on weapons of mass destruction in Iraq or warrantless searches and eavesdropping on American citizens. Asked why not much oversight took place during these years, representative Chris Shays (R–CT) remarked that fellow Republicans asked him, "Why do we want to embarrass the administration?"[63] After the 2006 elections, when Democrats won majorities in both chambers, oversight hearings ratcheted up on a wide range of issues, including the alleged use of harsh interrogation methods like waterboarding on detainees and access to the courts for terrorism detainees being held at Guantanamo Bay. Democrats, apparently, were not as concerned as Republicans about embarrassing a Republican administration. After Barack Obama came to office, Democrats in Congress were less aggressive in their use of the oversight tools, though they held hearings in 2009 on bank bailouts and approval of lucrative bonuses to many of their executives, in 2010 on the TSA's and the Department of Homeland Security's failure to detect a suicide bomber (whose bomb failed to detonate) on a flight from Europe to the United States, and on BP's oil blowout in the Gulf of Mexico.

Overall, however, the number of committee hearings has declined dramatically since 1980, with only slightly more than half the number of hearings in the 2011 as there were then. This is probably because committee chairs have less power now, with less independence from the leadership on what they may do in committee.[64] Members also spend more time raising money for their reelection campaigns.[65] Still, hearings are an important part of the oversight process. Testimony is taken from agency officials, outside experts, and congressional investigatory institutions such as the Government Accounting Office and the Office of Technology Assessment. The hearings are not simply information-gathering exercises, however. As often as not, they are designed to send signals from committee members to the relevant part of the bureaucracy. Hearings that focus on the overly aggressive efforts of Internal Revenue Service agents to collect taxes, for example, are a clear signal to IRS officials that they had better rein in their agents before the next round of hearings on the budget.

Congress's final instrument of oversight of the executive branch is **impeachment** (responsibility of the House) and trial and removal from office (responsibility of the Senate) of high executive officials, including the president. This is a blunt tool, rarely used, except in the most partisan atmosphere or in cases involving truly egregious executive behavior. Over the course of American history, only seven executives have been removed from office by the Senate. No president has ever been convicted and removed from office, but the impeachment processes in the House of presidents Andrew Johnson, Nixon, and Clinton were deeply divisive, so Congress treads very cautiously in this area.

impeachment
House action bringing formal charges against a member of the executive branch or the federal judiciary that may or may not lead to removal from office by the Senate.

Using the DEMOCRACY STANDARD

Is Congress out of touch with the American people?

Although Congress was significantly democratized by passage of the Seventeenth Amendment in 1913, which transferred the election of senators from state legislatures to voters, the institution is still significantly shaped by the antimajoritarian constitutional design of the framers. Most important in this regard is its bicameral nature, the equal representation of the states in the Senate, Senate rules on the filibuster and cloture, and its immersion in a system of checks and balances.

The framers settled on bicameralism for two reasons. First, it was the only way to break the deadlock between large and small states at the constitutional convention. Had the Connecticut Compromise not been agreed to, the convention would most likely have adjourned without completing its historic task. Second, bicameralism conformed to the framers' belief that the legislative branch—the center of policymaking for government—ought to be a place where the public's business is deliberated carefully and slowly, free from the pressure of fickle public opinion. As any observer of our national legislature can report, this part of the vision was fulfilled; Congress is a place where the legislative process grinds slowly, with only a few pieces of major legislation produced in each Congress and most bills never seeing the light of day. The need for legislation to pass through two powerful chambers—one upper and one lower, each organized in different ways and each tuned to different election cycles and constituencies—is the central reason for the slow pace of this process.

As noted earlier, equal representation of the states in the Senate violates the democratic principle of political equality. Small-population states such as Wyoming, Nevada, and North Dakota have the same number of senators as large-population states such as California, New York, Texas, and Florida, meaning that the people in each of the states are unequally represented. This characteristic affects much of what the Senate does and does not do. For example, a coalition of 41 senators from the smallest population states, representing a mere 11 percent of the American population, can block any bill in the Senate (because 60 votes are needed to override a filibuster). To say that the Senate enshrines unequal representation is no exaggeration.

We must not forget, moreover, the antimajoritarian effects of the system of checks and balances within which Congress operates. Designed by the framers as the most "popular" branch—and not very "popular" at that in its original design—Congress finds itself continually hemmed in by the other two branches. Even on those rare occasions when it acts vigorously in response to public opinion, it may not always have the support it needs from the president and the courts. Further, the balance against democracy in Congress is even more disproportionate once one takes into account the important role played by interest groups and campaign contributors in its affairs.

It appears, then, that Congress has not drifted very far from what the framers had envisioned. To be sure, senators are now elected directly by the people. Also, senators and members of the House are more prone than in the past to pay attention to public opinion. Nevertheless, it remains an institution that the framers would recognize as their own creation.

Review the Chapter

 Listen to **Chapter 11** on **MyPoliSciLab**

Constitutional Foundations of the Modern Congress

11.1 Identify the ways in which the Constitution shapes Congress, p. 342

The framers of the Constitution granted Congress legislative power, gave it an existence independent of the executive branch, enumerated an impressive range of powers, and gave it elastic powers sufficient to carry out its enumerated ones. However, they also gave the other branches powers to check legislative excesses, created a bicameral body, and strictly denied certain powers to Congress.

Representation and Democracy

11.2 Assess how and to what extent the members of Congress represent their constituents, p. 344

Congress is a representative institution but not necessarily fully democratic; its members are constantly balancing the preferences of the people in their constituencies and important interest groups and contributors as well as their own conceptions of the public interest.

Because elections are the most important mechanism for representation, and because they are the way in which members attain office, elections dominate the time and energy of lawmakers and shape how Congress organizes itself and goes about its business.

How Congress Works

11.3 Describe what leaders, political parties, and committees do in Congress, p. 357

Nearly every aspect of congressional organization and operations are defined by political parties. Leadership in each of the chambers, committee leadership and membership, and the agenda are determined by the majority party.

The House invests great powers in its leaders, with the Speaker of the House acting very much like a leader in a parliamentary system. Leadership in the Senate is much more elusive; each senator has a great deal of independent power and must be persuaded to side with party leaders.

Most of the business of the House and Senate takes place in committees and their subcommittees. Here hearings are held on bills, negotiations on bills take place, and members of Congress can bring their subject matter expertise to bear.

Over the past several decades, however, each of the political parties has given its leaders more powers, reducing that of committees and their chairs.

To conduct its business, Congress depends on an elaborate set of norms and rules and a web of committees and subcommittees, political parties, legislative leaders, and an extensive staff.

Legislative Responsibilities: How a Bill Becomes a Law

11.4 Outline the process by which a bill becomes a law, p. 370

After they are introduced, bills are referred to committee. Only a few make it out of committee for consideration by the entire membership of the House or Senate. In the House, the Rules Committee must issue a rule for a bill to reach the floor for debate.

If related bills pass each chamber, but in different forms, differences must be resolved in a conference committee. The report of the conference committee cannot be amended and must be voted up or down in the House and the Senate. If a bill makes it this far, it goes to the president for his signature or veto.

A bill becomes law if the president signs it, or absent his signature, if 10 days pass while Congress is in session, or if both the House and the Senate vote by a two-thirds majority to override a veto.

Legislative Oversight of the Executive Branch

11.5 Explain why Congress is doing less oversight than in the past, p. 374

Oversight is a way for members of Congress to bring attention to issues and to turn the spotlight on the performance of executive branch agencies. Oversight is done through committee or subcommittee hearings.

When there is unified government, Congress is reluctant to embarrass a president of its own party.

When there is divided government in today's partisan charged atmosphere, most other political actors and the media know that hearings are more about gamesmanship than about serious oversight of the executive.

Learn the Terms

Study and **Review** the **Flashcards**

enumerated powers, p. 342
elastic clause, p. 342
bicameral, p. 342
delegate, p. 344
trustee, p. 344
descriptive representation, p. 344
constituency, p. 347
constituent, p. 347
reapportionment, p. 348
redistricting, p. 348
partisan, p. 349
gerrymandering, p. 349
crack, p. 350
pack, p. 350

majority-minority districts, p. 350
open-seat election, p. 352
franking privilege, p. 354
casework, p. 356
pork, p. 356
party conference, p. 360
caucus, p. 360
whip, p. 363
standing committees, p. 365
hearings, p. 365
markup, p. 365
select committees, p. 365
joint committees, p. 365
conference committees, p. 365

seniority, p. 365
ranking minority member, p. 365
reciprocity, p. 367
unanimous consent, p. 367
hold, p. 367
filibuster, p. 368
cloture, p. 368
hopper, p. 371
discharge petition, p. 371
veto, p. 374
pocket veto, p. 374
oversight, p. 374
impeachment, p. 375

Test Yourself

Study and **Review** the **Practice Tests**

Answer key begins on page T-1.

11.1 Identify the ways in which the Constitution shapes Congress

1. Congress is organized into
   a. One legislative chamber.
   b. Two legislative chambers.
   c. Three legislative chambers.
   d. Four legislative chambers.
   e. Five legislative chambers.

11.2 Assess how and to what extent the members of Congress represent their constituents

2. This happens when the same party controls both houses of the state legislature and the governor's office.
   a. Packing
   b. Partisan redistricting
   c. Gerrymandering
   d. Reapportionment
   e. Partisan advantage

11.3 Describe what leaders, political parties, and committees do in Congress

3. These types of committees are usually temporary, and created by congressional leaders to conduct studies or investigations.
   a. Hearing committees
   b. Joint committees
   c. Conference committees
   d. Select committees
   e. Standing committees

11.4 Outline the process by which a bill becomes a law

4. A bill quietly killed in committee can reach the floor only by a device called
   a. Discharge petition.
   b. Hopper petition.
   c. Favorable vote.
   d. Oversight.
   e. Presidential action.

11.5 Explain why Congress is doing less oversight than in the past.

5. Why do members of Congress spend less time than in the past questioning members of the executive branch about their activities and practices?
   a. They are of a generation that does not like to work very hard at their jobs.
   b. They find that agencies such as the GAO can do a better job.
   c. They spend more time than in the past raising money for their reelection campaigns.
   d. They are more interested in national defense policies than in domestic policies.
   e. Under a unified government, members of Congress do not want to embarrass their president.

Explore Further

INTERNET SOURCES

CongressLink at the Dirksen Center **www.congresslink.org**

Designed for teachers of American government, history, and civics, this is a very rich information site on Congress. Features include access to information on pending legislation, legislative schedules, caucuses, committees, rules, histories of the House and Senate, ways to contact members of Congress, and much more.

National Atlas **nationalatlas.gov/printable/congress.html**

Maps of all House districts.

Congress.org by Capitol Advantage **www.congress.org**

Congressional news, legislation, issues, personalities, and more, as well as information on how to have your voice heard on Capitol Hill.

CQ MoneyLine/Federal Election Commission **moneyline.cq.com/pml/home.do**

Information on campaign finance for presidential and congressional elections.

Office of the Clerk **houselive.gov**

Streaming video from the floor proceedings since the 111th Congress.

THOMAS **thomas.loc.gov**

Expansive repository of information on the House of Representatives, including the full text and progress of bills, the Congressional Record, legislative procedures and rules, committee actions, and more.

U.S. House of Representatives home page **www.house.gov**

House schedule, House organization and procedures, links to House committees, information on contacting representatives, and historical documents on the House of Representatives.

U.S. Senate Home Page **www.senate.gov**

Similar to the House of Representatives home page, focused on the Senate. One exciting new feature is a virtual tour of the Capitol.

SUGGESTIONS FOR FURTHER READING

Adler, E. Scott, and John S. Lapinski, eds. *The Macropolitics of Congress.* Princeton, NJ: Princeton University Press, 2006.

A collection of research by leading scholars on the impact of congressional lawmaking on American society.

Caro, Robert. *The Years of Lyndon Johnson.* New York: Knopf, 1982.

This classic and award-winning biography of Lyndon Baines Johnson of Texas reveals more about how Congress worked in the "old days" than virtually any academic treatise.

Davidson, Roger H., Walter J. Oleszek, and Frances E. Lee. *Congress and Its Members*, 13th ed. Washington, D.C.: CQ Press, 2012.

The classic textbook on Congress, now in its 12th edition.

Oleszek, Walter J. *Congressional Procedures and the Policy Process*, 8th ed. Washington, D.C.: CQ Press, 2010.

The most comprehensive compilation yet published of the rules and operations of the legislative process in Congress, written by a scholar who served as the policy director of the Joint Committee on the Organization of Congress.

Quirk, Paul J., and Sarah A. Binder. *The Legislative Branch.* New York: Oxford University Press and the Annenberg Foundation Trust, 2005.

A very accessible compendium of essays by leading scholars on every aspect of Congress and the legislative process.

Sinclair, Barbara. *Unorthodox Lawmaking: New Legislative Processes in the U.S. Congress*, 3rd ed. Washington, D.C.: CQ Press, 2007.

Argues that the traditional textbook rendition of "how a bill becomes a law" has dramatically changed over the past two decades.

Specialized newspapers and journals: *The Hill, Roll Call, Congressional Quarterly, National Journal.*

Valuable sources for up-to-the-minute, in-depth coverage of what is happening in Congress.

12

The Presidency

PRESIDENT OBAMA USES HIS UNITARY POWERS

Barack Obama inherited a range of national problems that were almost unprecedented in their depth and complexity when he became president of the United States. When he took the oath of office on January 20, 2009, the nation was involved in two armed conflicts abroad and involved in a prolonged conflict in many places (Pakistan, Yemen, and Somalia, among others) against Al Qaeda and related jihadist groups. The country was also stuck in the deepest and most prolonged economic crisis since the Great Depression, devastated by the collapse of the financial system that froze credit and wiped out the savings of many ordinary Americans, hit hard by the bursting of a massive real estate bubble and rising foreclosures, and uncertain about its future global economic role in the face of a rising China and a falling dollar. Barack Obama promised in his campaign and in his inaugural address to boldly take on these problems, to bring "change we can believe in," using an energized and activist government to make the promised changes happen.

Working with a Democratic-controlled Congress, and initially making overtures to moderate Republicans in the House and Senate, Obama pressed for a number of major legislative initiatives. He succeeded on several very important ones. Congress passed his massive $787 billion economic stimulus bill within one month of his swearing-in (no House Republicans and only three Senate Republicans supported the measure); about one-half of the cost of the bill was in tax cuts, with the other half in new spending for school construction, student loans, scientific research, transportation infrastructure, alternative energy development, and extended unemployment insurance payments. Two months later, the president signed the $3.4 trillion fiscal year 2010 budget, which included monies not only for ongoing domestic, military and national security programs, but also for a massive new national health insurance program, a cap-and-trade system

12.1	12.2	12.3	12.4	12.5
Trace the expansion of presidential responsibilities and power, p. 384	Identify the many roles presidents play, p. 390	Outline the functions filled by the president's many advisers and helpers, p. 399	Analyze the conflict between presidents and Congress, p. 402	Assess how democratic the presidency is and whether presidents respond to the public, p. 405

THANKS FOR GETTING BIN LADEN President Obama can act more decisively in foreign and military affairs than he can on domestic matters. Here he thanks Vice Admiral William McRaven, the operational commander of the SEAL raid into Pakistan that killed Osama Bin Laden in 2011. Obama had ordered the secret operation.

The Big Picture What actions can the president take without the approval of Congress, the voters, or the judiciary branch? A lot more than you would think. Author Edward S. Greenberg discusses the unitary powers of the president, and he traces how these powers have developed over time.

The Basics What do presidents do? The simple answer is "an awful lot." In this video, you'll hear what ordinary people think about what presidents should do. In the process, you'll discover why there is often a gap between what we expect and what we get.

What makes a great president?

In Context Uncover the historical context that led the framers to fear a strong executive. In this video University of Oklahoma political scientist Glen Krutz not only reveals the reason behind the framers' apprehension, but also explores how this fear still restricts presidents today as they struggle to create new policies.

Think Like a Political Scientist Why do presidents try to persuade you to support their policies? In this video, University of Oklahoma political scientist Glen Krutz discloses why persuasion is vital to a president's success and how technology has created obstacles and opportunities for presidents.

In the Real World Should President Obama have used an executive order to change immigration policy? The president bypassed Congress to implement his own agenda. Find out why some people believe the president abused his powers and others think he was entirely justified.

So What? How has the role of the president changed since the writing of the Constitution? Author Edward S. Greenberg gives examples of different presidents who expanded their powers to accomplish what they felt needed to be done, and he discusses how subsequent presidents have interpreted their actions for their to reduce carbon consumption, aid to financially stressed states, and increased spending on research and development and education. The budget also provided for an extension of middle-class tax cuts.

But passing bills in Congress to establish new programs on which to spend these new monies proved to be a more difficult task. Passage of the health care reform bill took a full year to pass Congress before it could be signed into law by President Obama. His proposal to impose new regulations on the financial and mortgage industries to prevent another crisis met stiff resistance from Republicans and a few senators from his own party, and took a year and a half to make its way through Congress. His cap-and-trade carbon emissions initiative was unsuccessful; the battles over the stimulus, health care, and financial regulation were so partisan, brutal, and drawn out that the cap-and-trade proposal never got off the ground as the 2010 elections loomed. Things got even tougher after the 2010 elections when Republicans made big gains, winning control of the House and diminishing the Democratic majority in the Senate from 60 seats to 53. Because of this, 2011 and 2012 were marked by bitter partisan combat, legislative gridlock, and brinksmanship on matters such as the debt ceiling fight in 2011, with government closure and national default barely averted.

Passing multiple bills that transform major elements of American public policy is a very difficult thing to do at any time, given our constitutional system of separated powers and checks and balances. Our system, as you have learned, is better geared to stopping big policy changes than to encouraging them. Making big policy changes in a bitterly partisan environment, especially in the Senate where major bills now routinely must garner a super-majority of 60 votes to pass, is even more difficult. When divided government is thrown into the mix, the degree of difficulty increases even more. Is it any wonder, then, that Barack Obama, like all modern presidents, has made liberal use of the unitary powers of the presidency to move public policies in a direction he wants? As commander in chief, for example, he shifted the attention of the military from Iraq to Afghanistan and the Pakistan border area without the need to ask Congress. He not only increased troop levels there, but dramatically increased the number of drone attacks on Al Qaeda sites in the region and authorized special forces actions against radical jihadist groups in Somalia and Yemen. He also authorized the Navy Seal raid that killed Osama Bin Laden. As chief executive—that is, the administrative head of the executive branch of government—he issued a string of executive orders to various bureaucratic agencies, reversing Bush administration policies on stem-cell research, climate change, and the use of torture in the interrogation of enemy combatants; ordered the Department of Transportation to allow states to impose emissions requirements that exceed those of the federal government; and overturned the ban on government contributions to international organizations that offer family planning services that include abortion. He supported the Environmental Protection Agency when it issued rules increasing gas mileage requirements on cars, and issued an executive order formalizing a negotiated agreement between the EPA, the Department of Transportation, and the auto companies in 2011 to dramatically increase gas mileage requirements on cars, SUVs, and trucks by 2025. Saying he couldn't wait for Congress to act, he also issued an executive order mobilizing a number of federal agencies to help overcome a serious shortage of important prescription drugs in the country.

President Obama, like all presidents, must gain the cooperation of Congress on many matters if he is to achieve the major elements of his policy agenda and fulfill the promises made during his campaign for office, in his inauguration speech to the nation, and in his State of the Union addresses. What many people fail to appreciate, however, is the degree to which presidents can act first and on their own, without Congress, on many important matters. This is usually referred to as the unitary powers of the president and encompasses a broad range of tools, including executive orders, executive agreements, signing statements, presidential proclamations, national security directives, and regulatory review, as well as his authority over the armed forces and American foreign policy.[1] In this chapter we will examine the key features of the modern presidency, including the broad range of the office's unitary powers, the rise of the office to a position of preeminence in American government, and why it happened.

Thinking Critically About This Chapter

This chapter is about the American presidency, how it has evolved, and what role it plays in American politics and government.

Using the Framework

You will see in this chapter how the presidential office has changed substantially from how the framers envisioned it, primarily because of changes in America's international situation, the nature of its economy, and popular expectations. You will also see how presidents interact with other governmental institutions (such as Congress and the Court) and with political linkage–level actors (such as political parties, public opinion, the mass media, and interest groups), and how these interactions influence what presidents do.

Using the Democracy Standard

You will see in this chapter how the presidential office, although not envisioned by the framers to be a democratic one, has become more directly connected to and responsive to the American people. On the other hand, you will be asked to think about whether presidents' growing ability to influence the thinking of the public and shape their perceptions of public events undermines democracy.

The Expanding Presidency

12.1 Trace the expansion of presidential responsibilities and power

The American presidency has grown considerably since our nation's beginning. The increase has occurred in presidential responsibilities, burdens, power, and impact.

When George Washington took office as the first president, he had a total budget (for 1789–1792) of just over $4 million. Washington had only a handful of federal employees. Even by 1801, there were only about 300 federal office-holders in the capital. Washington's cabinet consisted of only five officials: the secretaries of state, war, and the treasury; a postmaster general; and an attorney general (who acted as the president's personal attorney, rather than as head of a full-fledged Justice Department). The entire Department of State consisted of one secretary, one chief clerk, six minor clerks, and one messenger. In 1790, only about 700 Americans were in uniform, and they had no way to project force around the world. Federal government functions were few. The entire United States consisted of the 13 original eastern and southeastern states, with only 864,746 square miles of land area; the population was only about 4 million persons, most living on small farms.[2]

When Barack Obama was first sworn into office 220 years later, he presided over a federal budget with more than $2.7 trillion in annual expenditures and a federal bureaucracy with approximately 2.7 million civilian employees (postal workers accounted for 656,000 employees). He was commander in chief of the armed forces, with about 1.5 million men and women in active-duty service; hundreds of military bases at home and scattered throughout the world; and about 10,000 nuclear warheads, 2,600 of which are operational, enough to obliterate every medium-sized or large city in the world many times over.[3] The United States in early 2009 had a population of almost 307 million diverse people; a gross domestic product of more than $14 trillion; and a land area of some 3.8 million square miles, stretching from Alaska to Florida and from Hawaii to Maine.[4]

☐ The Framers' Conception of the Presidency

The Founders certainly had in mind a presidency more like Washington's than Obama's. Article II of the Constitution provided for a single executive who would be strong, compared with his role under the Congress-dominated Articles of Confederation, but

WASHINGTON REVIEWS THE TROOPS

The presidency has grown in scale and responsibility. As commander in chief of the armed forces, President George Washington, here reviewing his troops during his first year as president, commanded an army of just over 700 soldiers and had little to do with affairs outside the United States. Today, the president commands a force of about 1.4 million active duty personnel stationed all over the world. How has this change in the role of the president affected the relative balance of power among the three branches of government?

the Constitution's sparse language declaring that "The executive power shall be vested in a President of the United States," barely hinted at the range of things twentieth- and twenty-first-century presidents would do.[5] The Constitution made the president "commander in chief" of the armed forces, for example, without any suggestion that there would be a vast standing army that presidents could send abroad to fight without a declaration of war. It empowered presidents to appoint and to "require the opinion in writing" of executive department heads without indicating that a huge federal bureaucracy would evolve. The Constitution provided that presidents could from time to time "recommend . . . measures" to Congress without specifying that these proposals would very often come to dominate Congress's agenda. Still, the vague language of the Constitution proved flexible enough to encompass the great expansion of the presidency.

☐ The Dormant Presidency

From the time of George Washington's inauguration at Federal Hall in New York City to the end of the nineteenth century, the presidency, for the most part, conformed to the designs of the Founders. The presidency did not, by and large, dominate the political life of the nation. Presidents saw their responsibility as primarily involving the execution of policies decided by Congress. Congress was a fully equal branch of government, or perhaps more than equal. But the office changed after that.

STRUCTURAL FACTORS Why does the early presidency seem so weak in comparison with the contemporary presidency? Surely it is not because early presidents were less intelligent, vigorous, or ambitious; indeed, this era produced some of our greatest presidents—as well as some who are largely forgotten. A more reasonable answer is that the nation did not often require a very strong presidency before the twentieth century, particularly in the key areas of foreign policy and military leadership. Only in the twentieth century did the United States develop into a world power, involved in military, diplomatic, and economic activities around the globe. With that *structural* development came a simultaneous increase in the power and responsibility of the president.

It was not until the late nineteenth century, moreover, that the economy of the United States was transformed from a simple free market economy of farmers and small firms to a corporate-dominated economy, with units so large and interconnected

habeas corpus
The legal doctrine that a person who is arrested must have a timely hearing before a judge.

that their every action had social consequences. This transformation eventually led to demands for more government supervision of the American economic system. As this role of government grew, so did the president's role as chief executive of the federal government.

Although the presidency was largely dormant until the end of the nineteenth century, events and the actions of several presidents during the early period anticipated what was to happen to the office in our own time. Presidential actions created precedents for their successors; what the public and political elites expected of presidents changed; and new laws were passed that gradually enhanced presidential responsibilities and powers.

IMPORTANT EARLY PRESIDENTS The war hero George Washington solidified the prestige of the presidency at a time when executive leadership was mistrusted.[6] Washington also affirmed the primacy of the president in foreign affairs and set a precedent for fashioning a domestic legislative program. Thomas Jefferson, although initially hostile to the idea of a vigorous central government, boldly concluded the Louisiana Purchase with France, which roughly doubled the size of the United States and opened the continent for American settlement. Andrew Jackson, elected with broader popular participation than ever before, helped transform the presidency into a popular institution, as symbolized by his vigorous opposition to the Bank of the United States (which was seen by many ordinary Americans as a tool of the wealthy).

James Polk energetically exercised his powers as commander in chief of the armed forces, provoking a war with Mexico and acquiring most of what is now the southwestern United States and California. Abraham Lincoln, in order to win the Civil War, invoked emergency powers based on his broad reading of the Constitution: he raised and spent money and deployed troops on his own initiative, with Congress acquiescing only afterward; he temporarily suspended the right of *habeas corpus* and allowed civilians to be tried in military courts; and he unilaterally freed the slaves in the Confederate states by issuing the Emancipation Proclamation justifying it as a war measure under his commander-in-chief powers.

☐ The Twentieth-Century Transformation

More enduring changes in the presidency came only in the twentieth century, when new structural conditions made an expanded presidency both possible and necessary. Theodore Roosevelt vigorously pushed the prerogatives and enhanced the powers of the office as no president had done since Lincoln. Roosevelt was happiest when he was deploying the troops as commander in chief or serving as the nation's chief diplomat to protect American economic and political interests. On the domestic front, Roosevelt pushed for regulation of the new and powerful business corporations, especially by breaking up trusts, and he established many national parks. (See the "Can Government Do Anything Well?" feature.) In Theodore Roosevelt, we see the coming together of an energetic and ambitious political leader and a new set of structural factors in the United States, particularly the nation's emergence as a world power and an industrialized economy. The interplay of these three factors expanded the power and responsibilities of the presidency.

Woodrow Wilson's presidency marked further important steps in the expansion of the federal government and the presidency. Wilson's "New Freedom" domestic program built on the Progressive Era measures of Theodore Roosevelt, including further regulation of the economy by establishment of the Federal Reserve Board (1913) and the Federal Trade Commission (1914). Under Wilson, World War I brought an enormous increase in activity: a huge mobilization of military personnel and a large, new civilian bureaucracy to oversee the production and distribution of food, fuel, and armaments by the American "arsenal of democracy."

It was Franklin D. Roosevelt, however, who presided over the most significant expansion of presidential functions and activities in American history and changed American expectations about the office. In response to the Great Depression, Roosevelt and the Democratic majority in Congress pushed into law a series of measures for

Can Government Do Anything Well?

The National Park System

Taking a break from a presidential tour of the country during April 1903 in which he was to deliver two hundred speeches (presumably the same speech at each stop in this time before radio, television, and the Internet), President Theodore Roosevelt wanted some time alone. In the vicinity of Yellowstone National Park, TR left his entourage and protectors behind and spent a day riding through the wilderness with the army officer in charge of the park (the army was given this task since there was no state government). On the same trip, he visited the Grand Canyon, not yet a national park. A month after his stay in Yellowstone, he camped in Yosemite National Park for three nights with conservationist John Muir, who wanted Roosevelt to add the beautiful Yosemite Valley to the park.

Roosevelt was no neophyte in the wilderness. He spent much of his youth watching and categorizing birds, writing a major book on the subject before he entered Harvard. He spent years during his teen and adult life working in and around wilderness areas, switching off between being a cowboy, a big-game hunter, and a rancher, and even put in a stint as a marshal chasing outlaws through the badlands of North Dakota. He loved the wilderness and thrived in its solitude. He was moved and saddened when Muir described how much of the natural world was fast disappearing as the country was filling up. Convinced by Muir that action was required before a point of no return was reached, Roosevelt acted boldly on his return to Washington. From then until the end of his presidency in 1909, Roosevelt signed bills creating 5 new national parks; issued executive orders under the Antiquities Act creating 18 new national monuments, including the Grand Canyon, Muir Woods, the Devil's Tower, and Chaco Canyon; and set aside over 100 million acres of public land as national forests.

The National Park System, now numbering 58 parks with almost 80 million acres, and administered since 1916 by the National Park Service, is among the most appreciated accomplishments of the national government. The parks are heavily used—some say too heavily used—by Americans and visitors from other countries, with more than 281 million visits in 2010.

Support for the claim that the federal government has been successful in creating and managing a system of national parks:

- Consistently positive evaluations by the public in surveys, the number of annual visitors to the park system, and the degree to which the U.S. system has been copied around the world suggest that the national parks are a significant achievement.

- The creation of national parks was part and parcel of a larger conservation movement that helped preserve tens of millions of acres of national forests and wilderness, making the natural world accessible to America's people.

- The National Park Service employs just over 20,000 people to administer the parks, but 10 times that many volunteers pitch in, making the operation more cost effective.

- The park service has taken on the difficult task of restoring ecosystems and has made much progress in projects such as the South Florida Restoration Initiative that are beyond the means of state and local governments.

Rejection of the claim that the federal government has been successful in creating and managing a system of national parks:

Rejection of the concept of wilderness protection in principle (from the Cato Institute)

- A free country needs a wide diffusion of private property; the government already holds and manages too much land, so there should be no further expansion of the national parks or wilderness areas in general. Private ownership is the most efficient way to manage land use and the best way to preserve our freedom.

- Restricted access to the energy and mineral wealth in the parks lessens GDP growth and hurts the standard of living of Americans.

The private sector would be better at park administration

- The NPS often does a poor job maintaining and protecting national parks and national monuments. For example, the Organ Pipe Cactus National Monument in Arizona has been so degraded that it has lost its "wilderness" character.

- Given budget constraints, the park service cannot keep up with maintenance and upgrading needs as well as the other obligations Congress has assigned to it, even though its budget has been gradually increasing.

- Private enterprise is the best solution to resource and management problems; more extensive public–private partnerships would do much to improve the state of the parks, which are finding it increasingly difficult to maintain and improve visitor facilities and amenities.

(Continued)

WHAT DO YOU THINK?

What do you think about the past, present, and future role of the federal government in creating and managing the national park system?

- The federal government (i.e., the National Park Service) has been very successful in its administration and protection of national parks throughout the United States and no private intervention is necessary.
- The federal government (i.e., the National Park Service) has been successful in its administration and protection of national parks throughout the United States, but because of budget problems, some private sector involvement would be helpful.
- The federal government (i.e., the National Park Service) has not been successful in its administration and protection of national parks throughout the United States and should rely substantially on the private sector to rectify the current problems.

How would you defend your position to a fellow student? What would be your main line of argument? What evidence do you believe best supports your position? For help in developing your argument, please refer to the sources listed in the "Can Government Do Anything Well" feature in Chapter 2 on p. 48.

economic relief that grew into vast programs of conservation and public works, farm credit, business loans, and relief payments to the destitute. Roosevelt's New Deal also established a number of independent commissions to regulate aspects of business (the stock market, telephones, utilities, airlines) and enacted programs such as Social Security, which provided income support for retired Americans, and the Wagner Act, which helped workers join unions and bargain collectively with their employers. As Congress created these and many other new agencies in the executive branch, the role of the presidency grew because of his constitutional powers as chief executive.

Even bigger changes, however, resulted from World War II, when the government mobilized the entire population and the whole economy for the war effort. With the end of World War II, the United States was established as a military superpower. Since the time of Franklin Roosevelt, all U.S. presidents have administered a huge national security state with large standing armed forces, nuclear weapons, and bases all around the world.

Although he accomplished little on the legislative front during his brief time in office—he did introduce the 1964 Civil Rights Act, passed after his death—John F. Kennedy was the first president to appreciate the importance of television as both a campaign tool and as an instrument for influencing the public and political actors in Washington, the states, and other countries. His televised speeches and press conferences, where his charm, intelligence, and sense of humor were clearly evident, became one of his most effective governing tools. Presidents after him tried to follow his lead, but only Ronald Reagan, Bill Clinton, and Barack Obama matched Kennedy's mastery of the medium.

In the 1980s, Ronald Reagan managed to bring many of the main items of the conservative agenda to fruition: a massive tax cut to stimulate the economy, cutbacks in the number of regulations that affect business, cuts in a wide range of domestic social programs, and a substantial buildup of U.S. armed forces. Perhaps more importantly, he showed the American people and others around the world that a vigorous and popular presidency was still possible after the failed presidency of Richard Nixon, and the relatively weak presidencies of Gerald Ford and Jimmy Carter.

After the 9/11 terrorist attacks on the United States, George W. Bush pushed what many consider to be among the most expansive readings of presidential power in American history. In order to protect the United States against future terrorist attacks, President Bush felt it both necessary and constitutionally permissible, for example, to advise the armed forces and the CIA to ignore the Geneva Convention on the treatment of detainees captured in the war on terrorism. He claimed the right, moreover, to keep detainees indefinitely without trial or hearings, even if they were American citizens. He also authorized warrantless surveillance of American citizens by the National Security Agency, which the agency is forbidden to do without the permission of a special court. It remains to be seen whether future presidents after him will return to the Bush model if a major terrorist attack should occur again on American soil.[7]

REAGAN AND GORBACHEV IN RED SQUARE

Whether rightly or wrongly, Ronald Reagan—whose foreign policies included a dramatic arms buildup followed by proposals to refashion the basic relationship between the two superpowers—is often given credit for ending the Cold War and nurturing the collapse of the Soviet Union. Here, President Reagan and Soviet leader Mikhail Gorbachev enjoy the sun and meet people in Red Square. How do world events shape the president's popularity in the United States?

☐ How Important Are Individual Presidents?

We cannot be sure to what extent presidents themselves caused this great expansion of the scope of their office. Clearly, they played a part. Lincoln, Wilson, and Franklin Roosevelt, for example, not only reacted vigorously to events but also helped create events; each had something to do with the coming of the wars that were so crucial in adding to their activities and powers. Yet these great presidents were also the product of great times; they stepped into situations that had deep historical roots and dynamics of their own.

Lincoln found a nation in bitter conflict over the relative economic and political power of North and South and focused on the question of slavery in the western territories; war was a likely, if not inevitable, outcome. Wilson and Franklin Roosevelt each faced a world in which German expansion threatened the perceived economic and cultural interests of the United States and in which U.S. industrial power permitted a strong response. The Great Depression fairly cried out for a new kind of presidential activism. Kennedy faced an international system in which the Soviet Union had become especially strident and menacing. George W. Bush was president when the 9/11 terrorist attacks on the United States occurred, allowing him to make the broadest claims possible concerning the president's powers to defend the nation. Thus, the great upsurges in presidential power and activity were, at least in part, a result of forces at the *structural* level, stimulated by events and developments in the economy, American society, and the international system.

We see, then, that it is this mixture of a president's personal qualities (personality and character) and deeper structural factors (such as the existence of military, foreign policy, or economic crises) that determines which presidents transform the office.

THE WAR LEADER

President George W. Bush imposed a strong national defense orientation on nearly every aspect of American foreign policy in the wake of the 9/11 terrorist attacks. As foreign policy leader and commander-in-chief, the president had sufficient tools to move the United States in this direction. Secretary of Defense Donald Rumsfeld (left) and Vice President Richard Cheney (center) were strong and able advocates of such an orientation in foreign affairs.

Most of these big presidential transformations become part of the presidency as an institution. Presidents want and need the powers accumulated by their predecessors, and use the precedents set by them. The American people have tended to support—and in crisis situations, demand—strong presidential leadership. Congress has passed laws over the years in response to new challenges that directly or indirectly increase presidential responsibilities and power. And the courts, with some notable exceptions to be mentioned elsewhere in this book, generally have accepted the development path the presidency has taken as it became the preeminent office in American government.

The Powers and Roles of the President

12.2 Identify the many roles presidents play

Explore on
MyPoliSciLab
Simulation
You Are a First-Term President

T he American presidency has assumed powers and taken on roles unimaginable to the Founders. Each touches on the daily lives of everyone in the United States and affects tens of millions of people around the world as well. In this section, we examine the many roles of the president and see how each role has a set of responsibilities associated with it as well as a set of powers that have become more expansive over the years.

☐ Chief of State

The president is both the chief executive of the United States—responsible for the executive branch of the federal government—and the chief of state, a symbol of national authority and unity. In contrast to European parliamentary democracies such as Britain or Norway, where a monarch acts as chief of state while a prime minister serves as head of the government, in the United States the two functions are combined. It is the president who performs many ceremonial duties (attending funerals of important people, proclaiming official days, lighting the national Christmas tree, honoring heroes, celebrating national holidays) that are carried out by members of royal families in other nations. As one journalist once put it, "The office of President is such a bastardized thing, half royalty and half democracy, that nobody knows whether to genuflect or spit."[8] Because it adds to their prestige and standing with other government officials and the public, presidents have always found the chief of state role to be a useful tool in their political arsenal, enabling them to get their way on many important issues. Especially in times of armed conflict, criticism of the president seems to many Americans to amount to criticism of the country itself and the troops who are in harm's way, something skilled presidents can and do use to maximize support for their policies.

☐ Domestic Policy Leader

The president has taken on important responsibilities on the domestic front that were probably not anticipated by the framers. These include his role as the nation's legislative leader and manager of the economy.[9]

LEGISLATIVE LEADER While the Constitution seems to give primary responsibility for the legislative agenda of the United States to Congress, over time, the initiative for proposing big policy changes and new programs has shifted significantly to the president and the executive branch. The bases of this change may be found in the Constitution, statutes passed by Congress, and the changing expectations of the American people. The Constitution, for example, specifies that the president must, ". . . from time to time give the Congress information on the state of the union, and recommend to their consideration such measures as he shall judge necessary and expedient." Until Woodrow Wilson's presidency, the "**State of the Union**" took the form of a written report sent every year or every two years to Congress for its consideration. These reports often gathered dust in the House and Senate clerks' offices. Wilson, a strong believer in the role of the president as chief legislative leader similar to the prime minister in a parliamentary system, began the practice of delivering the State of the Union to Congress in an address to a joint session of the House and Senate, in which the president sets out his agenda for congressional legislation. Wilson correctly sensed that the American people were in the mood for vigorous legislative leadership from the president, given the enormous technological, economic, and social changes that were happening in the United States and the problems that were being generated by these changes.

In modern times, the State of the Union address has become one of the most important tools by which presidents gain the attention of the public and other public officials for what they want to accomplish. The State of the Union is now a very dramatic and visible event, delivered before a joint session of Congress, with members of the Supreme Court, the president's cabinet, and the military joint chiefs in attendance, and a national television audience. In the State of the Union, presidents, much as Wilson did, set out what issues they hope Congress will address, with a promise that detailed proposals for legislation will be forthcoming. In doing so, presidents now have the biggest say in defining the political agenda for the nation.

The president's legislative role also was enhanced by the Budget Act of 1921, which requires the president to submit an annual federal government budget to Congress for its consideration, accompanied by a budget message setting out the president's rationale and justifications. Prior to the Act, the budget of the United States was prepared initially in Congress. This change in the location of where initial decisions were to be made about proposed spending for government programs and agencies from the

State of the Union
Annual report to the nation by the president, now delivered before a joint session of Congress, on the state of the nation and his legislative proposals for addressing national problems.

executive order

A rule or regulation issued by the president that has the force of law, based either on the constitutional powers of the presidency as chief executive or commander in chief or on congressional statutes.

legislative to the executive branch represented a formidable enhancement in both the responsibilities and power of the president.

Although the House and Senate often take action on their own with regard to the nation's legislative agenda, what is striking is the degree to which Congress waits for and acts in response to presidential State of the Union addresses, budgets, and legislative proposals to meet various national problems. Indeed, the twentieth century is dotted with presidential labels on broad legislative programs: Wilson's New Freedom, Roosevelt's New Deal, Truman's Fair Deal, Kennedy's New Frontier, and Johnson's Great Society. On the other hand, presidents invite trouble when they fail to lead on major pieces of legislation about which they care deeply. Barack Obama, for example, left it almost entirely to Congress in 2009 to fashion a health care reform bill without much guidance from the White House. The result was a bitter, year-long struggle in Congress that dismayed the public and undermined presidential and congressional popularity, and produced a bill which the president signed that satisfied few, even its supporters.[10]

MANAGER OF THE ECONOMY We now expect presidents to "do something" about the economy when things are going badly. The Great Depression taught most Americans that the federal government has a role to play in fighting economic downturns, and the example of Franklin Roosevelt convinced many that the main actor in this drama ought to be the president. Congress recognized this in 1946 when it passed the Employment Act, requiring the president to produce an annual report on the state of the economy, assisted by a new Council of Economic Advisers, with a set of recommendations for congressional action to maintain the health of the American economy. The role is now so well established that even conservative presidents like Ronald Reagan and George W. Bush felt compelled to involve the federal government in the prevention of bank failures, the stimulation of economic growth, and the promotion of exports abroad. George W. Bush, for example, supported an economic stimulus package in 2008 to fight a growing recession and the collapse of the real estate market. He also authorized the Treasury Department to work with the Federal Reserve to reorganize investment banks, provide bailouts to big commercial banks, and take over failing mortgage giants Freddie Mac and Fannie Mae to avert a financial collapse. Though he came to office in the midst of recession, a credit freeze, mounting foreclosures, and rising unemployment, President Obama's popularity was damaged badly as his actions failed to visibly change the situation for average Americans by the end of his first two years in office, leading to massive losses to the Republicans in the 2010 national elections.

☐ Chief Executive

Although he shares influence over the executive branch of the federal government with Congress and the courts, the president is the chief executive of the United States, charged by the Constitution and expected by the American people to ensure that the nation's laws are efficiently and effectively carried out by bureaucratic agencies such as the Justice, Interior, and Commerce Departments; the National Aeronautics and Space Administration (NASA); and the National Weather Service. When an agency fails, as the Federal Emergency Management Agency (FEMA) did spectacularly in the aftermath of the Katrina disaster, and the Department of the Interior and the Minerals Management Service did in the face of the BP oil blowout in the Gulf of Mexico, the president invariably takes the heat. The problem is that presidents have something less than full control over the federal bureaucracy, so they cannot be certain that agency leaders and personnel will do what presidents want them to do.[11] Nevertheless, presidents exercise more influence over executive branch agencies than any other government actor or set of actors.

Presidents have various tools to shape the behavior of executive branch agencies. Sometimes presidents try to get federal bureaucrats to act by issuing **executive orders**— formal directives to executive branch departments and agencies that have the force of law. These orders take many forms, including presidential proclamations, decision memoranda, and national security directives. The legitimacy of such orders is based sometimes on the constitutional positions of the president as chief executive and commander in chief, sometimes on discretionary authority granted to the president by Congress in statutes, and often on precedents set by past presidents. Executive orders are not only about minor administrative matters; many have been issued by presidents to institute important federal policies and programs.[12] Thomas Jefferson executed the Louisiana Purchase by proclamation (though he needed money appropriated by Congress to complete the agreement with France), and Abraham Lincoln did the same when he ordered the emancipation of slaves held in states that were in revolt against the United States during the Civil War. Franklin Roosevelt ordered the internment of Japanese Americans during World War II. His successor, Harry Truman, ordered the end of racial segregation in the armed forces. Bill Clinton issued orders to set aside millions of acres of land as national monuments off-limits to logging and roads. President George W. Bush issued executive orders to, among other things, establish the White House Office of Faith-Based and Community Initiatives and restrict stem-cell research supported by federal funds. President Obama issued scores of executive orders in his first two months in office rescinding many of Bush's orders, but adding many of his own (increasing fuel mileage requirements on cars and trucks, for example). Some scholars worry that the use of executive orders has become so important in fashioning government policies that it amounts to unilateral presidential rule, legislating, as it were, without need of Congress or public support.[13]

Believing that the presidency had been crippled by too much congressional and judicial interference in recent decades, members of George W. Bush's administration and many conservatives revived and gave a very expansive reading to a long-dormant constitutional theory known as the **unitary executive** in an attempt to "unstymie" the office. The concept is based on Article II's "vesting" ("The executive Power shall be vested in a President of the United States of America.") and "take care" clauses ("The President shall take care that the laws be faithfully executed . . .") to suggest that the office is free to exercise command and authority over the executive branch in all respects. Presidential adviser and Justice Department official John Yoo proposed early in the Bush administration that the Constitution created a unified and hierarchical executive branch under the direct control of the president, who has all authority necessary to control the actions of federal bureaucracy personnel and units without interference from the other federal branches, including the courts.[14]

Under this doctrine, the president has the sole authority, for example, to direct the actions of agencies such as the Central Intelligence Agency (CIA), the National Security Agency (NSA) and the armed forces in the defense of the nation. He alone can interpret, in his signing statements, the meaning of laws passed by Congress for executive branch personnel and units. He alone can determine the degree to which departmental and agency personnel cooperate with Congress, in terms of the release of documents or testimony before congressional committees, for example. And, he can order the review of all regulations issued by regular and independent regulatory agencies for their consistency with the law as interpreted by the president. The doctrine of the unitary executive is, to say the least, controversial, and it is not broadly accepted among constitutional scholars or by the courts.

The reality of politics on the ground, however, is that the president cannot entirely control what the executive branch does. In the day-to-day operations of the federal bureaucracy, direct command is seldom feasible. Too much is going on in hundreds of agencies. Presidents cannot keep track personally of each one of the millions of government officials and employees. Most of the time, the president can only issue general guidelines and pass them down the chain of subordinates, hoping that his wishes will be followed faithfully. But lower-level officials, protected by civil service status from being fired, may have their own interests, their own institutional norms and practices, that lead them to do something different. President Kennedy was painfully reminded of this during the Cuban Missile Crisis of 1962, when Soviet Premier Khrushchev demanded that U.S. missiles be removed from Turkey in return for the removal of Soviet missiles from Cuba: Kennedy was surprised to learn that the missiles had not already been taken out of Turkey, because he had ordered them removed a year earlier. The people responsible for carrying out this directive had not followed through.[15] In 2009, President Obama was frustrated by the amount of time it took federal agencies to arrange for the production and distribution of the H1N1 flu vaccine, despite his demand for swift action.

12.1 12.2 12.3 12.4 12.5

unitary executive
Constitutional doctrine that proposes that the executive branch is under the direct control of the president, who has all authority necessary to control the actions of federal bureaucracy personnel and units without interference from the other federal branches.

CLOSE CALL

The American destroyer USS Vesole escorts a Soviet cargo ship carrying nuclear missiles away from Cuba after President Kennedy and Soviet Premier Nikita Khrushchev reached an agreement to end what came to be known as the Cuban Missile Crisis 1962. The two nuclear powers came very close to war, but the two leaders managed to pull back from the brink despite a number of advisors on each side urging military action.

treaty
A formal international agreement between two or more countries; in the United States, requires the "advice and consent" of the Senate.

To a significant extent, a president cannot simply order things to be done to accomplish his goals but must also *persuade* executive branch officials and personnel to do things. He must bargain, compromise, and convince others that what he wants is in the country's best interest and in their own interest as well. One prominent presidential scholar has said, "Presidential power is the power to persuade."[16] Of course, presidents can do many things besides persuade: appoint top officials to executive branch departments and agencies who share the president's goals; put White House observers in second-level department positions; reshuffle, reorganize, or even—with the consent of Congress—abolish agencies that are not responsive; influence agency budgets and programs through Office of Management and Budget review; and generate pressure on agencies by Congress and the public.[17]

☐ Foreign Policy and Military Leader

Although the framers gave a role to Congress in fashioning foreign and military policies—note congressional control of the federal purse strings, its role in declaring war, and the Senate's "advice and consent" responsibilities with respect to treaties and appointment of ambassadors—they wanted the president to be the major player in these areas. What they could not have anticipated was that the United States would develop into the world's superpower, with global responsibilities and commitments, a development that enormously expanded the power of the presidency in the federal government.

FOREIGN POLICY LEADER In a case decided in 1936, the Supreme Court confirmed the president's position as the nation's preeminent foreign policy maker, saying: ". . . the president is the sole organ of the federal government in the field of international relations."[18] The president's role as foreign policy leader is rooted in the diplomatic and treaty powers sections of Article II of the Constitution, as well as in his role as commander in chief of the armed forces.[19]

The Constitution specifies that the president shall have the power to appoint and receive ambassadors and to make **treaties**. Although these formal constitutional powers may seem minor at first glance, they confer on the president the main

OUTREACH TO THE MUSLIM WORLD
President Obama made reaching out to the world's 1.5 billion Muslims one of the main priorities of his foreign policy agenda. Here, he is greeted in Cairo by Egyptian Foreign Minister Ahmed Abul Gheit in June 2009. The president later gave a historic and widely televised speech before Egypt's parliament to say the United States and Muslims were not enemies. But presidents cannot always control events. In the wake of the Arab Spring, anti-Americanism grew as Islamists gained more political influence in important Arab countries such as Egypt and Libya.

responsibility for fashioning American foreign policy. Take the power to appoint and receive ambassadors. From the very beginning of the American republic, presidents have used this provision as a tool for recognizing or refusing to recognize foreign governments. In 1793, for example, George Washington refused to accept the credentials of the French ambassador, Citizen Edmond Genet, signaling that the United States did not recognize the legitimacy of the French revolutionary government. In the twentieth century, presidents Wilson, Harding, Coolidge, and Hoover refused to recognize the revolutionary communist government of the Soviet Union, a policy that was reversed by Franklin D. Roosevelt in 1933. The Chinese communist government went unrecognized by the United States for 23 years after it came to power, a policy that was eventually reversed by Richard Nixon. The president's sole power to proclaim U.S. policy in this area is suggested by the following: neither Franklin D. Roosevelt nor Richard Nixon required the permission of any other government institution or public official—whether Congress or the courts or state legislatures, for example—to change American policy with respect to the Soviet Union or Communist China. The decision was the president's alone to make.

The power to initiate the treaty-making process is also a powerful tool of presidential diplomacy and foreign policymaking. By virtue of this power, the president and the foreign policy officials in the State, Treasury, Commerce, and Defense departments that report to him consult, negotiate, and reach agreements with other countries. Sometimes the agreements with other countries take the form of treaties—the Paris Treaty ending the Revolutionary War is an example, as are the various arms control, human rights, trade, and environmental treaties to which the United States is a party. More often, however, international agreements take the form of **executive agreements** entered into by the president and one or more foreign governments, without the need to get the "advice and consent" of the Senate. Originally understood to be agreements about minor or technical details associated with a treaty, executive agreements eventually began to be used for very important matters. In 2002, for example, President Bush entered into an executive agreement with Russia that committed the two countries to reducing the size of their nuclear stockpiles.[20]

A TOAST TO A NEW ERA

President Richard Nixon reestablished diplomatic relations with China in 1972. The two countries had been estranged since the Communists came to power in China in 1949 after defeating a long-time ally of the United States. The president did not require any action by Congress, the courts, or the American people to make this momentous change in policy, though most eventually welcomed it. Here he joins a toast to the new era with Chinese foreign minister Zhou Enlai.

COMMANDER IN CHIEF Article II, Section 2, of the Constitution specifies that the president is the commander in chief—without saying anything at all about what this actually means. On the other hand, Article I, Section 8, specifies that Congress has the power to declare war. What the framers seemed to have had in mind was a distinction between defensive war and offensive war, with the president the primary decision maker with respect to the former and Congress preeminent with respect to the latter. Thus, the president was given the power to deploy and use the armed forces in order to protect the United States against external invasions and internal insurrections; Congress was given the power to declare war against another country.[21] Over the years, this distinction between offensive and defensive war disappeared; American forces are now sent into hostilities abroad, deployed by presidents without a formal declaration of war by Congress, in the name of defending the United States. In fact, there have been only five war declarations in American history—the last came in December 1941 after the Japanese attack on Pearl Harbor. Here is what seems to have been going on: as the United States became a global power, presidents, other American leaders, and the public came to believe that defending the United States required more than simply defending against cross-border invasions from other countries. Other threats seemed to many to be equally dangerous, including communism, nationalist threats to American economic interests, drug trafficking, and, most recently, terrorism.

Here is a sampling of how presidents have used American military power abroad since the Second World War. In the early 1950s, Harry Truman fought a bitter war in Korea against North Korean and Chinese forces, without a declaration of war from Congress, in the name of halting communist aggression. Presidents Eisenhower, Kennedy, Johnson, and Nixon did the same in Vietnam. Ronald Reagan used American forces in Grenada and Nicaragua to fight communism and launched an air attack against Libya to punish it for its involvement in terrorism. George H. W. Bush launched an invasion of Panama to capture its president and drug lord Manuel Noriega, and in 1991 used more than 500,000 U.S. troops in Operation Desert Storm to push Iraq out of Kuwait. President Bill Clinton sent several thousand American troops as peacekeepers to Bosnia in 1995, Haiti in 1996, and Kosovo in 1999 and waged an air war against Serbia to try to prevent further "ethnic

Using the FRAMEWORK

How was President Obama able to wage a war of drone strikes against jihadist targets in the Afghanistan–Pakistan border areas?

Background: The strategy of the United States to root out the Taliban from Afghanistan and to help install a stable government in Kabul in the wake of the 9/11 attacks on America was long frustrated by the Taliban's (and Al Qaeda's) use of the Afghanistan–Pakistan tribal areas as bases to launch attacks. Because Pakistan has been a quasi-ally of the United States during the Afghanistan operation, direct ground attacks on Taliban base areas were out of the question because it would have embarrassed the Pakistan military and roused anti-American feelings among that nation's public. The rapid advance in the technology of drone aircraft that can observe potential targets on the ground and attack with missiles when deemed appropriate allowed the United States to wage war across the border, with a fairly high success rate against those defined as enemies, though many innocents were killed as well either because of incorrect targeting or as "collateral damage" (that terrible term) in otherwise successful operations. But how is it that President Obama was able to have the armed forces wage such a military campaign inside an allied country without authorization from Congress or oversight of the operation? We can better understand how by looking at structural, political linkage, and governmental factors that were at play.

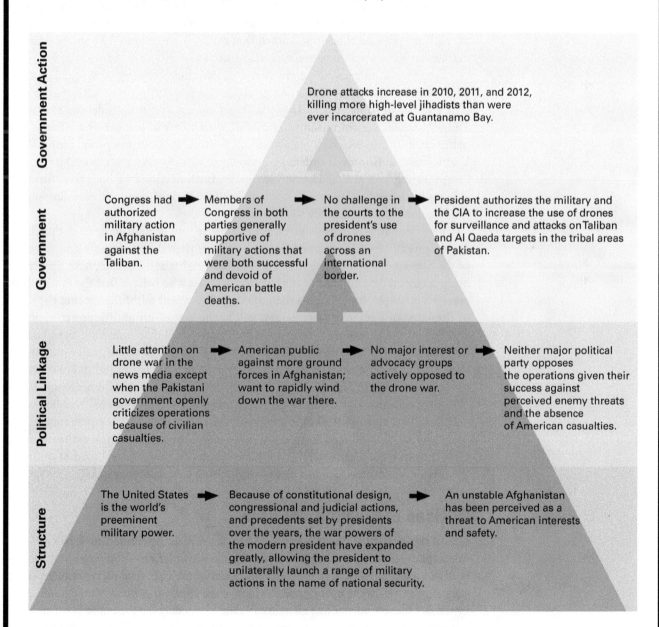

Government Action

Drone attacks increase in 2010, 2011, and 2012, killing more high-level jihadists than were ever incarcerated at Guantanamo Bay.

Government

Congress had authorized military action in Afghanistan against the Taliban. ➡ Members of Congress in both parties generally supportive of military actions that were both successful and devoid of American battle deaths. ➡ No challenge in the courts to the president's use of drones across an international border. ➡ President authorizes the military and the CIA to increase the use of drones for surveillance and attacks on Taliban and Al Qaeda targets in the tribal areas of Pakistan.

Political Linkage

Little attention on drone war in the news media except when the Pakistani government openly criticizes operations because of civilian casualties. ➡ American public against more ground forces in Afghanistan; want to rapidly wind down the war there. ➡ No major interest or advocacy groups actively opposed to the drone war. ➡ Neither major political party opposes the operations given their success against perceived enemy threats and the absence of American casualties.

Structure

The United States is the world's preeminent military power. ➡ Because of constitutional design, congressional and judicial actions, and precedents set by presidents over the years, the war powers of the modern president have expanded greatly, allowing the president to unilaterally launch a range of military actions in the name of national security. ➡ An unstable Afghanistan has been perceived as a threat to American interests and safety.

cleansing" in its province of Kosovo. After the September 11, 2001, attacks on the United States, George W. Bush launched a military campaign against the Taliban regime and the Al Qaeda terrorist network in Afghanistan, then invaded and occupied Iraq in 2003 to protect the country against the Iraqi regime's purported weapons of mass destruction program and ties to the 9/11 terrorists (both claims proved, in the end, to be untrue). President Barack Obama, as we have seen, increased the number of troops in Afghanistan, upped the number of drone attacks on terrorist targets along the Pakistani border, and used special forces in operations in Somalia and Yemen. In none of these or related cases was Congress called upon to pass a formal declaration of war nor were they notified under terms of the War Powers Act that the United States was engaged in hostilities.

To be sure, when presidents choose to use American military power, they ordinarily consult widely with members of Congress and other government and opinion leaders. They do everything they can, moreover, to enlist the support of the public. They may even at times ask that Congress pass a resolution of support authorizing presidential use of the armed forces to defend the national security of the United States, although they are not legally bound to do so. Thus, President George H. W. Bush asked Congress to pass a resolution supporting Desert Storm in 1991, which it did. Likewise, in 2002, his son, President George W. Bush, asked Congress for a resolution supporting military action against Saddam Hussein's Iraq, which it did. Tellingly, each of the Bush presidents let it be known that military action would be forthcoming no matter the outcome of congressional deliberations.

Some presidents also have claimed that the office's commander in chief powers allow them to take extraordinary actions on the home front that seemingly violate civil liberties of some Americans, if such actions are required to defend the nation. Thus, Abraham Lincoln used military tribunals to try a number of southern sympathizers during the Civil War, Woodrow Wilson censored the press during World War I, Franklin Roosevelt ordered placement of Japanese Americans into internment camps during World War II, and George W. Bush detained without trial American citizens he defined as "enemy combatants" and authorized domestic eavesdropping by the National Security Agency to find terrorists.

President Bush's actions after 9/11 at home and abroad to defend the United States, several of which seemed contrary to laws passed by Congress and to rulings of the Supreme Court on the protected status of rights and liberties, have been vigorously defended by a number of conservative scholars who believe that the president has emergency powers based on his oath of office (". . . I will faithfully execute the Office of President of the United States, and will to the best of my ability, preserve, protect, and defend the Constitution of the United States . . .") that transcend the Constitution itself. They have suggested that some provisions of the Constitution might for a time need to be set aside or ignored in order to defend the nation and its constitutional order.[22] As Abraham Lincoln once asked regarding his own use of emergency powers, "Was it possible to lose the nation, and yet preserve the constitution?" Needless to say, other scholars and political observers worry that the use of such emergency powers over time might well lead to tyranny.[23] John Yoo, then an attorney with the Justice Department, was a particularly influential and vocal advocate of the broadest reading of the president's commander-in-chief powers during the presidency of George W. Bush.

☐ Head of His Political Party

One of the great difficulties all presidents face is the seeming contradiction between their role as president of all the people—as commander in chief, chief diplomat, and chief executive, for example—and their role as the leader of their political party seeking partisan advantage as well as the public good.[24] Much of the apparent contradiction has been eased by the fact that presidents, like all political leaders, generally see the public good and commitment to party principles and programs as one and the same. Thus, Ronald Reagan, as leader of the Republican party and as president, believed that the public good and his own party's prospects in upcoming elections were well served by his successful efforts to increase defense spending, deregulate the economy, and decrease domestic spending. For his part,

Lyndon Johnson, as the leader of the Democratic Party and as president, believed that the public and his party would benefit from programs to end racial discrimination and reduce poverty. Sometimes, however, the public reacts negatively when a president plays his party leader role too vigorously, seeing it as perhaps unpresidential. In 1938, in an oft-cited example, Franklin Roosevelt's effort to campaign for Democratic congressional candidates was not well received and his party won fewer seats than expected. George W. Bush's campaign involvement in the 2006 congressional elections did not prevent Democrats from winning control of both houses of Congress, nor did Obama's do much for the Democrats in 2010.

The President's Support System

12.3 Outline the functions filled by the president's many advisers and helpers

institutional presidency
The permanent bureaucracy associated with the presidency, designed to help the incumbent of the office carry out his responsibilities.

chief of staff
A top adviser to the president who also manages the White House staff.

national security adviser
A top foreign policy and defense adviser to the president who heads the National Security Council.

 ach of the president's functions is demanding; together, they are overwhelming. Of course, presidents do not face their burdens alone; they have gradually acquired many advisers and helpers. The number and responsibilities of these advisers and helpers have become so extensive, and the functions they perform so essential, that they have come to form what some call the **institutional presidency**.[25]

☐ The White House Staff

The White House staff, for example, which is specially shaped to fit the particular needs of each president, includes a number of close advisers.

One top adviser, usually designated **chief of staff**, tends to serve as the president's right hand, supervising other staff members and organizing much of what the president does. Presidents use their chiefs of staff in different ways. Franklin Roosevelt kept a tight rein on things himself, granting equal but limited power and access to several close advisers in a *competitive* system. Dwight Eisenhower, on the other hand, used to the *hierarchical* army staff system, gave overall responsibility to his chief of staff, Sherman Adams.

Another important staff member in most presidencies is the **national security adviser**, who is also head of the president's National Security Council, operating out of the White House. The national security adviser generally meets with the president every day to brief him on the latest events that might affect the nation's security and offer advice on what to do. Several national security advisers, including Henry Kissinger (under Nixon) and Zbigniew Brzezinski (under Carter), have been strong foreign policy managers and active, world-hopping diplomats who sometimes clashed with the secretaries of state and defense. Most recent presidents, however, have appointed team players who have closely reflected the president's wishes and quietly coordinated policy among the various executive departments. This was true of President Obama's first national security advisor, former Marine Corps commandant James Jones.

Most presidents also have a top domestic policy adviser who coordinates plans for new domestic laws, regulations, and spending, although this role is often subordinate to that of the chief of staff and is not usually very visible. Close political advisers, often old comrades of the president from past campaigns, may be found in a number of White House or other government posts (e.g., James Baker served as George H. W. Bush's secretary of state, while Karen Hughes served as White House counselor to the younger Bush during his first term) or may have no official position at all (such as consultant Dick Morris, who crafted Clinton's 1996 reelection strategy). Prominent in every administration is the press secretary, who holds press conferences, briefs the media, and serves as the voice of the administration. All have a legal counsel. There are also one or more special assistants who act as a liaison with Congress, deal with interest groups, handle political matters, and consult on intergovernmental relations. Facing a deep recession and continuing financial crisis when he came to office, President Obama appointed a team of economic advisers, led by Larry Summers, to try to keep him abreast of daily developments.

Executive Office of the President (EOP)

A group of organizations that advise the president on a wide range of issues; includes, among others, the Office of Management and Budget, the National Security Council, and the Council of Economic Advisers.

Office of Management and Budget (OMB)

An organization within the Executive Office of the President that advises on the federal budget, domestic legislation, and regulations.

Council of Economic Advisers (CEA)

An organization in the Executive Office of the President made up of a small group of economists who advise on economic policy.

National Security Council (NSC)

An organization in the Executive Office of the President made up of officials from the State and Defense Departments, the CIA, and the military, who advise on foreign and security affairs.

However, the exact shape of the White House staff changes greatly from one presidency to another, depending on the preferences and style of the president. What was particularly striking about President George W. Bush's management style was his penchant for setting overall goals and policies but giving his staffers a great deal of freedom and latitude in getting the job done.[26] Presidents Clinton and Obama were more closely involved in the day-to-day work of their staffs.

☐ The Executive Office of the President

One step removed from the presidential staff, and mostly housed in the Executive Office Building next door to the White House, is a set of organizations with more than 1,800 employees that forms the **Executive Office of the President (EOP)**.

Most important of these organizations is the **Office of Management and Budget (OMB)**. The OMB advises the president on how much the administration should propose to spend for each government program and where the money will come from. The OMB also exercises legislative clearance; that is, it examines the budgetary implications of any proposed bills that will be sent to Congress and sometimes kills proposals it deems too expensive or inconsistent with the president's philosophy or goals. The OMB director often is a very powerful player in the White House and in Washington politics; good examples include David Stockman and Peter Orszag, the one serving Ronald Reagan, the other Barack Obama.

The **Council of Economic Advisers (CEA)** advises the president on economic policy. Occasionally, the head of the council exercises great influence, as Walter Heller did during the Kennedy administration. However, Obama economic czar Lawrence Summers and Treasury Secretary Tim Geithner, skilled bureaucratic infighters, made sure that CEA head Christina Romer was not much of a factor in the administration's response to the Great Recession because they disagreed with her on the size of the stimulus necessary to revive the economy (she wanted a much bigger one).[27]

The Executive Office of the President also includes the **National Security Council (NSC)**, a body of leading officials from the Departments of State and Defense, the Central Intelligence Agency (CIA), the military, and elsewhere who

A UNIQUELY POWERFUL VICE PRESIDENT

Richard Cheney is generally acknowledged to be the most engaged and influential vice president in American history, playing especially prominent roles in the development of doctrines and policies ranging from the use of American military power to the treatment of prisoners detained in the "war on terrorism" and the particulars of national energy policy. Is it important to the nation and presidents that vice presidents play a central role in fashioning administration policies, or should they stay more in the background?

advise the president on foreign affairs. The NSC has been particularly active in crisis situations and covert operations. The NSC staff, charged with various analytical and coordinating tasks, is headed by the president's national security adviser.

Increasingly important in the effort to protect the United States against terrorist attacks is the **Intelligence Advisory Board**, which provides information and assessments to the president's director of national intelligence and to the president directly. This agency was criticized for failing to "connect the dots" that allowed Nigerian national Umar Farouk Abdulmutallab to carry explosives onto a Delta Air Lines flight from London to Detroit on Christmas Day 2009.

Intelligence Advisory Board
An organization in the Executive Office of the President that provides information and assessments to the president's director of national intelligence and to the president directly.

☐ The Vice Presidency

In 1804, the Twelfth Amendment fixed the flaw in the original Constitution in which the person with the second most electoral votes became the vice president. Under the old rules, Aaron Burr, Thomas Jefferson's running mate in 1800, had tied Jefferson in electoral votes and tried, in the House of Representatives, to grab the presidency for himself. Since then, vice presidents have been elected specifically to that office on a party ticket with their presidents. But now there is also another way to become vice president. The Twenty-Fifth Amendment (ratified in 1967) provides for succession in case of the temporary or permanent inability of a president to discharge his office. It also states that if the vice presidency becomes vacant, the president can nominate a new vice president, who takes office on confirmation by both houses of Congress. This is how Gerald Ford became vice president in 1973 when Spiro Agnew was forced to resign because of a scandal, and how Nelson Rockefeller became vice president in 1974, when Ford replaced Richard Nixon as president.

Until quite recently, the vice presidency has not been a highly regarded office. John Nance Garner, Franklin Roosevelt's first vice president, has been quoted as saying in his earthy Texan way that the office was "not worth a pitcher of warm piss."[28] Within administrations, vice presidents were considered to be fifth wheels, not fully trusted (because they could not be fired) and not personally or politically close to the president. Vice presidents used to spend much of their time running minor errands of state, attending funerals of foreign leaders not important enough to demand presidential attention, or carrying out limited diplomatic missions. Some vice presidents were virtually frozen out of the policymaking process. For example, while vice president, Harry Truman was never informed of the existence of the Manhattan Project, which built the atomic bomb. He learned of the bomb only months before he was obligated to make a decision on using it to end the war against Japan, soon after he became president on the death of Franklin D. Roosevelt.

Recent presidents, however, have involved their vice presidents more.[29] Bill Clinton gave Al Gore important responsibilities, including the formulation of environmental policy, coping with Ross Perot's opposition to NAFTA, and the ambitious effort to "reinvent government." Barack Obama's vice president, Joe Biden, for many years a prominent senator, played a particularly important role in foreign policy, meeting with many foreign leaders, and in the several difficult budget negotiations with Congress during the period of divided government in 2011 and 2012. More than any other vice president in American history, however, Dick Cheney was at the center of the policymaking process in the White House, serving (by all accounts) as President George W. Bush's principal adviser on both domestic and foreign policy, the key player within the administration on long-range policy planning and selection of Supreme Court justices, the main liaison to Republicans in Congress,[30] an important consumer of information from the intelligence community,[31] the chief advocate for a war against Iraq, and the leading advocate of a muscular interpretation of presidential war powers.[32]

☐ The Cabinet

The president's cabinet is not mentioned in the Constitution. No legislation designates the composition of the cabinet, its duties, or its rules of operation. Nevertheless, all presidents since George Washington have had one. It was Washington who established the practice of meeting with his top executive officials as a group to discuss policy matters. Later presidents continued the practice, some meeting with the cabinet

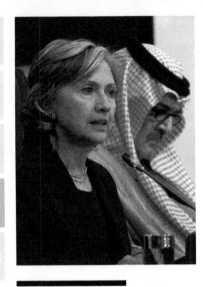

PRESSING AMERICAN INTERESTS
Secretary of State Hillary Clinton meets with her Saudi counterpart in February 2010 to gain Saudi Arabian cooperation with imposing new U.N. sanctions on Iran for the development of its nuclear weapons program. Clinton's considerable impact as secretary of state came not only because she is an appointee of the president and a member of his cabinet, but because of the considerable stature she brought to the office as a former senator and contender for the Democratic Party's presidential nomination. How might foreign leaders be affected by dealing with secretaries of state who have their own independent standing in politics?

as often as twice a week, and others paying it less attention or none at all. Today, the cabinet usually consists of the heads of the major executive departments, plus the vice president, and whichever other officials the president deems appropriate, including the Director of National Intelligence and the White House Chief of Staff.

Presidents do not rely on the cabinet as a decision-making body. Not only is there no constitutional warrant for such a body to make policies, presidents know that they alone will be held responsible for decisions, and they alone keep the power to make them. According to legend, when Abraham Lincoln once disagreed with the entire cabinet, he declared, "Eight votes for and one against; the nays have it!"

Most recent presidents have convened the cabinet infrequently and have done serious business with it only rarely. Ronald Reagan held only a few cabinet meetings each year, and those were so dull and unimportant that Reagan was said to doze off from time to time. Bill Clinton, with his "policy wonk" mastery of details, thoroughly dominated cabinet discussions. Barack Obama hardly ever met with his full cabinet, preferring instead to consult with advisers and department secretaries only when he needed their specific expertise.

One reason for the weakness of the cabinet, especially in recent years, is simply that government has grown large and specialized. Most department heads are experts in their own areas, with little to contribute elsewhere. It could be a waste of everyone's time to engage the secretary of Health and Human Services in discussions of military strategy. Another reason is that cabinet members occupy an ambiguous position: they are advisers to the president but also represent their own constituencies, including the permanent civil servants in their departments and the organized interests that their departments serve. They may have substantial political stature of their own—consider Hillary Clinton, Obama's secretary of state—somewhat independent of the president's.

The President and Congress: Perpetual Tug-of-War

Analyze the conflict between presidents and Congress

he president and Congress are often at odds. This is a *structural* fact of American politics, deliberately intended by the authors of the Constitution.[33]

☐ Conflict by Constitutional Design

The Founders created a system of separation of powers and checks and balances between Congress and the president, setting "ambition to counter ambition" in order to prevent tyranny. Because virtually all constitutional powers are shared, there is a potential for conflict over virtually all aspects of government policy; our system is quite exceptional in this regard. In parliamentary systems such as Great Britain, Germany, Sweden, and Japan, there is no separation of powers between the executive and legislative branches. Recall that in such systems the prime minister and cabinet—who together make up the government, what we would call the executive branch—are themselves parliamentarians selected by the majority party or a majority coalition of parties in parliament. The executive and legislative functions thus are fused in such systems, not separated. The government—the prime minister and the cabinet—serves at the behest and will of parliament and can be dissolved by it. So checks and balances between the executive and legislative powers do not exist because the executive and the legislative are one and the same. Not so in the United States; separated powers and mutual checks are real and consequential for what government does; even though presidents have, as we have seen, dramatically expanded their powers by increasing their use of signing statements, executive orders, and executive agreements, and interpreting their war powers quite expansively.

SHARED POWERS Under the Constitution, presidents may propose legislation and can sign or veto bills passed by Congress, but both houses of Congress must pass any laws and can (and sometimes do) override presidential vetoes. Presidents can appoint ambassadors and high officials and make treaties with foreign countries, but the Senate must approve them. Presidents nominate federal judges, including U.S. Supreme Court justices, but the Senate must approve the nominations. Presidents administer the executive branch, but Congress appropriates funds for it to operate, writes the legislation that defines what it is to do, and oversees its activities.

divided government
Control of the executive and the legislative branches by different political parties.

Presidents cannot always count on the members of Congress to agree with them. The potential conflict written into the Constitution becomes real because the president and Congress often disagree about national goals, especially when there is **divided government**, that is, when the president and the majority in the House and/or the Senate belong to different parties. Bill Clinton was impeached by the Republican-controlled House of Representatives in late 1998, for example, while George W. Bush's Iraq War policies were bitterly opposed by a Democratic-dominated Congress in the last two years of his presidency. The Republican House's opposition to Barack Obama's budget plans and priorities in 2011 was so strident that it almost led to the United States defaulting on the national debt, courting financial disaster for the country and the global economy. It is not uncommon, however, for presidents to clash with members of Congress even if they are of the same party. George W. Bush ran into trouble with co-partisans on a number of issues during his second term, especially on the issue of a path to citizenship for undocumented immigrants (Bush favored such a path).

SEPARATE ELECTIONS In other countries' parliamentary systems, the national legislatures choose the chief executives so that unified party control is ensured. But in the United States, there are separate elections for the president and the members of Congress. Moreover, our elections do not all come at the same time. In presidential election years, two-thirds of the senators do not have to run and are insulated from new political forces that may affect the choice of a president. In nonpresidential, "off" years, all members of the House and one-third of the senators face the voters, who sometimes elect a Congress with views quite different from those of the president chosen two years earlier. In 1986, for example, halfway through Reagan's second term, the Democrats recaptured control of the Senate and caused Reagan great difficulty with Supreme Court appointments and other matters. The Republicans did the same thing to Clinton in 1994 after they gained control of Congress. Obama ran into trouble with his programs in Congress after the 2010 election, when Republicans gained control of the House and reduced the Democrat's majority in the Senate.

OUTCOMES In all these ways, our constitutional structure ensures that what the president can do is limited and influenced by Congress, which in turn reflects various political forces that may differ from those that affect the president. At its most extreme, Congress may even be controlled by the opposing party. This divided government situation always constrains what presidents can do and may sometimes lead to a condition called "gridlock," in which a president and Congress are locked in battle, neither able to make much headway. This is hardly surprising; a president is not only the chief executive and commander in chief of the United States but the leader of his party, so members of the opposition are not inclined to give him what he wants on the chance that it will benefit his election prospects or those of his party in Congress. Right after the 2010 Republican landslide victory, Senate Minority Leader Mitch McConnell, explaining his party's strategy, said his goal was to ensure that Barack Obama would be a one-term president. This hardly offered the promise of compromise on important legislative issues.

☐ What Makes a President Successful with Congress?

A number of political scientists have studied presidents' successes and failures in getting measures that they favor enacted into law by Congress and have suggested reasons some presidents on some issues do much better than others.[34]

PARTY AND IDEOLOGY The most important factor is a simple one: when the president's party controls both houses of Congress, he is much more likely than at other times to find that he gets his way in terms of legislation, approval of his appointments, and more gentle handling of executive branch problems by congressional oversight committees.[35] The president's success under this condition of unified control does not come from the president ordering party members around. Rather, the president and the members of his party in Congress tend to be like-minded on a wide range of issues, sharing values and policy preferences and a common interest in reelection. For these reasons, members of Congress tend to go along most of the time with a president of their own party.[36]

Because the parties have become so ideologically cohesive since the mid-1990s, presidents can get their way with Congress even when they have only a very slim party majority in the House and a small but somewhat larger majority in the Senate—where 60 votes are needed to get past the filibuster barrier. Between 2001 and 2006, for example, George W. Bush enjoyed many legislative successes though Republican majorities in the House and Senate were paper-thin. He was able to do this because the highly cohesive and disciplined Republican Party in the Senate was joined by a handful of moderate Democrats on many bills, making Democratic filibusters rare events. Because Barack Obama enjoyed bigger party majorities in Congress than did George W. Bush during his first two years in office—with a 60–40 margin in the Senate (counting two independents who caucused with the Democrats)—and because the Democratic Party stayed cohesive when it came to decisive votes in Congress, he was able to put together a very substantial legislative record in his first two years. According to the *Congressional Quarterly (CQ)*, Obama forged the highest presidential success score with Congress since *CQ* began keeping score in 1953.[37] The result was victory for the president on a wide range of matters, including a massive economic stimulus bill, a historic overhaul of health insurance in the United States, and wide-ranging regulation of the financial services industry. After the GOP gained seats in the Senate and gained control of the House in the 2010 elections, Obama's success with Congress sank dramatically in 2011 and 2012, with congressional Republicans doing everything they could to try to meet their goal of making Obama a one-term president. Not only did Obama-favored legislation die in the legislative branch, but so did a record number of presidential appointees to the federal courts and executive branch departments and agencies. Reciprocating, Obama made the "do nothing Congress" (a phrase coined by Harry Truman in the 1948 election) a main theme in his campaign for reelection.

FOREIGN POLICY AND NATIONAL SECURITY ISSUES Presidents tend to do better with Congress on foreign policy issues than on domestic ones, mainly because Americans want to appear united when dealing with other countries and because members' constituents pay less attention to events abroad than to what is going on in the United States. Political scientist Aaron Wildavsky went so far as to refer to "two presidencies," domestic and foreign, with the latter presidency much more dominant.[38]

This difference between domestic and foreign policy success by the president has decreased since the Vietnam War, but it remains significant. Although there was significant dissent, Congress voted in January 1991, despite many misgivings, to authorize President George H. W. Bush to use force against Iraq, once again illustrating presidential primacy in foreign affairs. Congress eventually supported Clinton's decision to send U.S. forces to Haiti, Bosnia, and Kosovo as part of multinational peacekeeping operations, despite considerable initial grumbling.

It is also the case, as you saw in the section on presidential war powers, that Congress may not be able to alter or stop presidential actions when it involves national security threats, real or perceived, even when it may want to do so. Presidents can simply act unilaterally when it comes to the deployment and use of U.S. armed forces, particularly when the public supports the overall mission.

The generalization about presidents having an easier time with Congress on foreign policy issues than on domestic ones does not hold, however, when foreign policy concerns trade and other global economic issues that directly affect constituents. Nor does it hold when foreign policy and military action go wrong. In 2005 and 2006, as news of prisoner abuse and secret prisons for suspected terrorism detainees held by the United States began to trouble increasing numbers of Americans and to prompt criticism from friendly governments, Congress passed laws outlawing harsh and inhumane treatment and requiring periodic reports from the administration on such prisons and prisoners. Though Bush signed the legislation into law, he issued signing statements suggesting he would carry them out only to the extent that they did not conflict with his responsibilities of ensuring national security.

VETOES[39] When the issue is a presidential veto of legislation, the president is again very likely to prevail.[40] Vetoes have not been used often, except by certain "veto-happy" presidents, such as Franklin Roosevelt, Truman, and Ford. But when vetoes have been used, they have seldom been overridden—only 5 percent of the time for Truman and only 1.5 percent for Roosevelt. Bill Clinton did not use the veto at all during his first two years in office, when he had a Democratic majority in Congress, but he used it 11 times in 1995 alone during his budget battles with the Republican-controlled 104th Congress. Because Republicans committed to the president's agenda controlled the House from 2001 through 2006 and the Senate between 2003 and 2006, George W. Bush did not resort to the veto at all during this period. However, he used the veto several times in 2007 and 2008, most especially on bills from the Democratic-controlled Congress setting a timetable for withdrawal of American forces from Iraq and for expanding the number of children covered by the Children's Health Insurance Program (CHIP). With his party in control of Congress, Barack Obama did not use the veto in 2009 and vetoed only two minor bills in 2010. With his party in control of the Senate, nothing emerged from Congress in 2011 or 2012 that generated a veto.

POPULARITY Most scholars and observers of Washington politics, as well as elected officials and political operatives, agree that presidential effectiveness with Congress is significantly affected by how popular a president is with the American people.[41] The reasons are not hard to fathom. Voting against proposals from a very popular president may encourage quality challengers in the next election, for example, or slow the flow of campaign funds to one's war chest, whether the president is of one's party or not. Voting with a popular president, on the other hand, can offer protective cover for a member of Congress who favors the proposal but whose constituents may not ("This is a vote for the president").[42] When a president's popular approval collapses—as George W. Bush's did after 2004—even members of his own party are loath to follow executive leadership. Bush was unable to win his own party's approval in Congress, for example, for policies he favored on immigration, Social Security reform, and the bank bailout bill.

The President and the People: An Evolving Relationship

12.5 Assess how democratic the presidency is and whether presidents respond to the public

 The special relationship between the president and the general public has evolved over many years to make the presidency a more democratic and powerful office. Let's look at several aspects of this relationship.

☐ Getting Closer to the People

The Founders thought of the president as an elite leader, relatively distant from the people, interacting with Congress often but with the people only rarely. Most nineteenth-century presidents and presidential candidates thought the same. They seldom made speeches directly to the public, for example, generally averaging no more than 10 such speeches per year.[43] In the earliest years of the American Republic, presidents were not even chosen directly by the voters but by electors chosen by state legislators or, in case no one got

What Influences a President's Public Approval?

Political scientists watch a president's approval because it shows how much political capital is available to h indicates how the public endorses the executive's performance, and helps us relate popular support to po success, such as dealing with foreign crises or managing the economy. Gallup approval ratings of two recent presidents are shown below; you can see how presidential approval can be shaped by the economy and by eve

Bill Clinton was president during one of the largest economic expansions in American history and his popularity climbed with the tech-driven economic boom.

Public support for **George W. Bush** soared to record levels after the 9/11 terrorist attacks, but steadily dropped from that point onward. As economic growth slowed, and after a botched response to Hurricane Katrina in 2005, Bush's approval ratings never recovered.

SOURCE: Data from the Gallup Presidential Job Approval Center.

Investigate Further

Concept Do presidents gain or lose popularity over the course of their term? For President Clinton, an initial loss of popularity—due in part to economic recession—was followed by durable gains in public support. George W. Bush's popularity peaked with the 9/11 attacks then systematically fell off

Connection Is popularity tied to economic performance? Clearly Bill Clinton's popularity moved with the economy. As it grew, so too did Clinton's job approval. For President Bush, there may be correlation between economic approval and popularity, but it is masked for much of his term by the effects of

Cause How do events shape the popularity of President Bush? The 9/ terrorist attacks led to a rally-round-the-f effect which defined George W. Bush's presidency. For a brief period, success in the Iraq war boosted Bush's popularity until war fatigue and failure to manage other crises pulled his approval ratings an electoral college majority, by the House of Representatives. The Constitution thus envisioned very indirect democratic control of the presidency.

As we have also seen, however, this system quickly evolved into one in which the people played a more direct part. The two-party system developed, with parties nominating candidates and running pledged electors and the state legislators allowing ordinary citizens to vote on the electors. Presidential candidates began to win clear-cut victories in the Electoral College, taking the House of Representatives out of the process. Voting rights were broadened as well. Property and religious qualifications were dropped early in the nineteenth century. Later, slaves were freed and male former slaves were granted the right to vote; still later, women, Native Americans, and 18-year-olds won the franchise.

By the beginning of the twentieth century, presidents began to speak directly to the public. Theodore Roosevelt embarked on a series of speech-making tours in order to win passage of legislation to regulate the railroads. Woodrow Wilson made appeals to the public a central part of his presidency, articulating a new theory of the office that highlighted the close connections between the president and the public. Wilson saw the desires of the public as the wellspring of democratic government: "As is the majority, so ought the government to be."[44] He argued that presidents are unique because only they are chosen by the entire nation. Presidents, he said, should help educate the citizens about government, interpret their true will, and faithfully respond to it.

Wilson's theory of the presidency has been followed more and more fully in twentieth- and twenty-first-century thought and practice. All presidents, especially since Franklin Roosevelt, have attempted to both shape and respond to public opinion; all, to one degree or another, have attempted to speak directly to the people about policy.[45]

More and more frequently, presidents go public, using television and the Internet to bypass the print media and speak to the public directly about policy. They have held fewer news conferences with White House correspondents (where awkward questions cannot be excluded).[46] Richard Nixon pioneered prime-time television addresses, at which Ronald Reagan later excelled. Bill Clinton was more interactive with citizens, appearing on radio and TV talk shows and holding informal but televised "town hall meetings." George W. Bush liked to appear before carefully screened audiences of supporters. Barack Obama was most comfortable doing speeches and town hall–style meetings, but he also depended upon the same Internet-based technologies, especially social media, that he used so successfully in his 2008 campaign to get his message to the public, unfiltered by the news media.

☐ Leading Public Opinion

Especially since the rise of television, modern presidents have enhanced their power to shape public opinion. Some studies have indicated that when a popular president takes a stand in favor of a particular policy, the public's support for that policy tends to rise.[47] But there are many cases where presidents have tried but failed to move public opinion in a favorable direction, despite strong efforts to build public support for favored programs.[48] Barack Obama gave a televised address from the Oval Office to build support for his approach to the BP oil crisis in the Gulf in June 2010, but he was unable to improve his own flagging job ratings or build much enthusiasm or political support for his program of alternative energy development or a proposed "cap-and-trade" system to fight global warming.

Although not as likely to happen as is often believed, the power to lead the public also implies a power to *manipulate* public opinion if a president is so inclined— that is, to deceive or mislead the public so that it will approve policies that it might oppose if it were fully informed.[49] It is useful to remember that every modern White House has had communications specialists adept at getting out the administration's views, whether through formal channels—such as press releases, the daily briefing for reporters, and materials posted on the White House website—or informal ones, including leaks to favored journalists and in-house-written but anonymous news stories and commentaries for use in newspapers, television news broadcasts, and weblogs.[50] Especially in foreign affairs, presidents can sometimes control what information the public gets, at least in the short run.

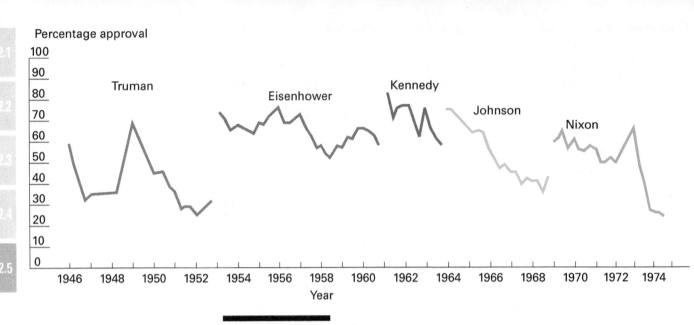

Percentage approval

FIGURE 12.1 TRENDS IN PRESIDENTIAL JOB APPROVAL, 1946–2012

Ratings of how well presidents are doing their jobs rise and fall in response to political, social, and economic events.

Source: Gallup surveys (graph based on average job approval for each year through summer, 2012).

presidential job approval

The percentage of Americans who believe the president is doing a good job.

☐ Responding to the Public

Besides trying to lead the people, presidents definitely tend to respond to public opinion. Electoral competition produces presidents who tend to share the public's policy preferences. Moreover, most presidents want to be reelected or to win a favorable place in history, and they know that they are unlikely to do so if they defy public opinion on many major issues. Usually, they try to anticipate what the public will want in order to win electoral reward and avoid electoral punishment.

There is plenty of evidence that presidents pay attention to what the public is thinking. At least since the Kennedy administration, presidents and their staffs have carefully read the available public opinion surveys and now have full-blown polling operations of their own.[51] Although such polling is often deplored, it helps presidents choose policies that the American public favors and change or discard those that are unpopular. It is worth considering another view about the role of presidential polling, however: that its purpose is to uncover not what the public wants but what words and symbols can be used by a president to sell a program.[52]

☐ Presidential Popularity

Presidential job approval affects how influential a president is with Congress, the judicial branch, and elected officials at the state and local level. Since the 1930s, Gallup and other poll takers have regularly asked Americans whether they approve or disapprove of "the president's handling of the job." The percentage of people who approve varies from month to month and year to year, and as time passes, these varying percentages can be graphed in a sort of fever chart of how the public has thought the president was doing (see Figure 12.1). A number of factors seem to be especially important in determining presidential popularity, including the stage in the president's term of office, the state of the economy, and foreign policy crises.[53]

Historically, most presidents have begun their terms of office with a majority of Americans—usually 60 percent or more—approving of how they are handling their job. Most presidents have tended to lose popularity as time passes. But this loss of popularity does not represent an inexorable working of time: Eisenhower, Reagan, and Clinton actually gained popularity during their second terms. Those who lose popularity do so in response to bad news. Good news generally makes presidents more popular.[54]

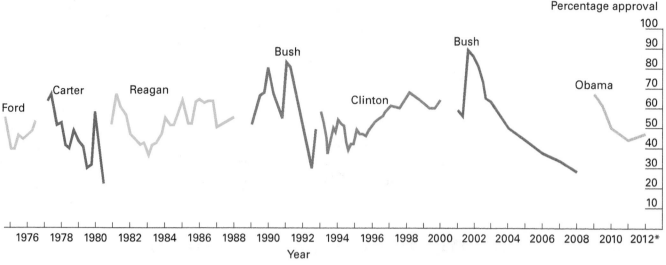

* 2012 is through July 15th.

One of the most serious kinds of bad news involves economic recession. When the economy goes sour, fewer Americans approve of the job the president is doing. This happened to George H. W. Bush in mid-1991, as the economy faltered. Barack Obama, too, after initial support from the public, felt the sting of the public's disapproval when unemployment stayed high and disposable income stagnated, even though he had inherited a deep recession and financial crisis when he became president.

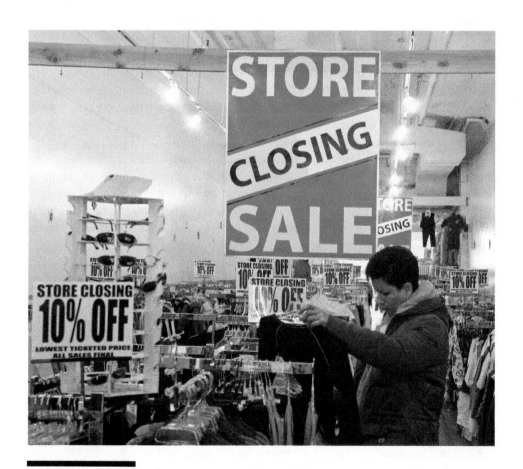

BAD ECONOMY, POOR PRESIDENTIAL JOB APPROVAL

Here, a woman in New York City in late 2009 shops for bargains before yet another retail store closed in this section of the city. The scene could have been repeated in cities and towns across the country as the nation suffered through a deep recession and jobless recovery from late 2007 through 2012. As is almost always the case, a bad economy, especially joblessness and declining disposable income, led to blows to public approval of the president and his party. Is this fair? Should we judge presidents mainly on the state of the economy, or are there other matters that are equally as important?

Successful military actions may sometimes add to presidential popularity, as Ronald Reagan happily discovered after the U.S. invasion of Grenada in 1982. The senior Bush's approval rating soared during the 1991 Gulf War, while the junior Bush's initial success in Afghanistan sustained his popularity. Conversely, an unsuccessful war is bad news for a president, as president Harry Truman learned regarding the Korean War. Bad news from Iraq—perhaps in combination with the administration's apparent failures in the Katrina disaster—steadily eroded George W. Bush's public approval after 2003. Bad news on the war and economic fronts at the same time can be especially lethal to a president's approval, as George W. Bush learned in 2008 when his rating reached a historic low in presidential polling, and Barack Obama did in 2010 as economic troubles and a sputtering war in Afghanistan combined to undermine his standing with the American public.

Using the DEMOCRACY STANDARD

Presidents and the American People

When considering the role of the chief executive, the framers never intended that it be a democratic office. In creating the Electoral College, for example, they imagined an independent body whose members (or electors) would be chosen in a manner decided by state legislatures. For the most part, they understood that state legislatures would leave the responsibility of selecting electors to themselves rather than the people. The electors from the states would then meet to elect the president from among the nation's leading citizens, free from the pressures of public opinion. As Alexander Hamilton put it in *The Federalist Papers*, No. 68, "The immediate election [of the president] should be made by men most capable of analyzing the qualities adapted to the station, and acting under circumstances favorable to deliberation, and to a judicious combination of all the reasons and inducements which were proper to govern their best choice." Because a president chosen in such a manner would not be beholden to the people for his election or reelection, he would not be overly concerned with or unduly influenced by the views of the mass public.

In addition, when designating the powers and responsibilities of the president in Article II of the Constitution, the framers evidently envisioned an office somewhat detached from national policymaking, something like a constitutional monarchy, in which the office holder would symbolize the nation but not do much in the way of running it. Although they gave the president important powers for conducting foreign affairs and defending the nation against civil unrest and invasion by foreign powers, they placed most national policymaking powers in Congress.

More than any other of the three branches of government in the Constitution created by the framers, the presidency has been democratized, with the changes so dramatic that the office would be hardly recognizable to them. As we have described this situation at various places in this chapter, the presidency has become a popular office, tied to the American people in a variety of important ways. Although the Electoral College remains in place—and can still have antimajoritarian democratic outcomes, as in the 2000 election—for all intents and purposes, presidents are elected directly by the American people as a whole, the only national office (other than the vice president) carrying this distinction. As such, modern presidents are prone to claim the mandate of the people when governing, and the American people are prone, for their part, to see the president as the center of governance and the locus for their hopes and aspirations for the nation. Presidents have used these ties to the people as the foundation for expanding presidential powers in the course of responding to national problems and emergencies.

We also know that modern presidents pay close attention to what the public wants, following public opinion polls closely and commissioning their own. To be sure, presidents sometimes manipulate the public, especially in foreign and military affairs, where presidential constitutional powers are considerable and public scrutiny is lower, but in the end, presidents cannot succeed unless they enjoy strong public support.

Review the Chapter

The Expanding Presidency

12.1 Trace the expansion of presidential responsibilities and power, p. 384

The American presidency began small; only a few nineteenth-century presidents (among them Jefferson, Jackson, Polk, and Lincoln) made much of a mark.

In the twentieth century, however, as a result of the problems of industrialization, two world wars and the Cold War, and the Great Depression, presidential powers and resources expanded greatly. The presidency attained much of its modern shape during Franklin Roosevelt's presidency.

The constitutional bases of the expansion of presidential responsibilities and power lie in the president's roles as chief executive, commander in chief, and chief diplomat.

Additional sources of presidential expansion come from public expectations, legislative grants of power, and the office's role as de facto legislative leader of the nation.

The Powers and Roles of the President

12.2 Identify the many roles presidents play, p. 390

Presidents play many roles, including that of chief of state, chief executive, domestic policymaking leader, foreign policy and military leader, and head of their political party.

Some of the president's roles are formally inscribed in the Constitution, but others have evolved through precedent, public expectations, and congressional actions.

The President's Support System

12.3 Outline the functions filled by the president's many advisers and helpers, p. 399

The job of the president has become so complex and the range of the office's responsibilities so broad that the occupant needs a great deal of help carrying out his duties. The staff and agencies in the White House and the Executive Office Building that help him carry out his duties have grown to such an extent that they have come to be called the institutional presidency.

White House staff members are numerous and do such things as advise the president on domestic and national security policies, maintain relationships with Congress, convey the president's views to the media and the public, and help fashion legislation.

The main agencies in the Executive Office of the President advise and help the president carry out policies regarding the economy, the federal budget, and national security.

The President and Congress: Perpetual Tug-of-War

12.4 Analyze the conflict between presidents and Congress, p. 402

The tug-of-war between the president and Congress is an inherent part of the constitutional design of our government as embodied in the separation of powers and checks and balances.

Presidents also have different constituencies than members of the House and Senate, the president being the only nationally elected office.

Representatives and senators often are elected at times when the president is not a candidate, so they may come to office propelled by a different public mood than that which prevailed when the president was elected.

Conflict is exacerbated when there is divided government and high levels of partisanship.

The President and the People: An Evolving Relationship

12.5 Assess how democratic the presidency is and whether presidents respond to the public, p. 405

The presidency has become a far more democratic office than the framers envisioned: the people play a more important role in the election of the president, and research shows that presidents listen to public opinion and respond to it most of the time (though they sometimes do not).

habeas corpus, p. 386
State of the Union, p. 391
executive order, p. 392
unitary executive, p. 393
treaty, p. 394
executive agreement, p. 395
institutional presidency, p. 399

chief of staff, p. 399
national security adviser, p. 399
Executive Office of the President
    (EOP), p. 400
Office of Management and Budget
    (OMB), p. 400

Council of Economic Advisers
    (CEA), p. 400
National Security Council
    (NSC), p. 400
Intelligence Advisory Board, p. 401
divided government, p. 403
presidential job approval, p. 408

Test Yourself

 Study and **Review** the **Practice Tests**

Answer key begins on page T-1.

12.1 Trace the expansion of presidential responsibilities and power

1. This president provoked a war with Mexico, thus acquiring most of the southwestern United States and California.

   a. Thomas Jefferson
   b. Andrew Jackson
   c. George Washington
   d. Abraham Lincoln
   e. James Polk

12.2 Identify the many roles presidents play

2. In American history the United States has only declared war:

   a. Two times
   b. Four times
   c. Five times
   d. Ten times
   e. Twelve times

12.3 Outline the functions filled by the president's many advisers and helpers

3. This organization advises the president on how much the administration should propose to spend on each government program and where the money will come from.

   a. Office of Management and Budget
   b. Council of Economic Advisers
   c. Intelligence Advisory Board
   d. Executive Office of the President
   e. National Security Council

12.4 Analyze the conflict between presidents and Congress

4. What factors have the ability to make a president successful with Congress?

   a. Party, foreign policy, religious background
   b. Foreign policy, party, popularity
   c. Party, leadership style, religious background
   d. Party, effective speeches, charisma
   e. Leadership style, foreign policy, effective speeches

12.5 Assess how democratic the presidency is and whether presidents respond to the public

5. This president thought that a president should help educate the citizens about government, interpret their true will, and faithfully respond to it.

   a. George Washington
   b. Theodore Roosevelt
   c. Franklin Roosevelt
   d. Woodrow Wilson
   e. Abraham Lincoln

Explore Further

INTERNET SOURCES

Executive Orders **www.archives.gov/federal-register/executive-orders/index.html**

A complete list with full text of presidential executive orders from the National Archives, from Herbert Hoover through Barack Obama.

Miller Center's "American President" website **www.millercenter.virginia.edu/academic/americanpresident**

A site full of historical documents, current developments, and descriptions of how the role of the president has changed.

POTUS **www.potus.com**

Biographies and other information about every American president.

National Archives Presidential Libraries **www.archives.gov/presidential_libraries/addresses/addresses.html**

Access to presidential addresses, libraries, and other information about the office.

Office of the Clerk **artandhistory.house.gov/house_history/vetoes.aspx**

Information and concise tables showing the number of vetoes, as well as the type, used by all the presidents of the United States.

PollingReport.com **www.pollingreport.com**

Collection of all major presidential job performance and popularity polls.

White House **www.whitehouse.gov**

Information on the first family, recent presidential addresses and orders, text from news conferences, official presidential documents, and ways to contact the White House.

PBS's American Experience: the Presidents **www.pbs.org/wgbh/americanexperience/collections/presidents**

Online streaming of first-rate documentary films on the lives and works of selected presidents.

SUGGESTIONS FOR FURTHER READING

Crenson, Matthew, and Benjamin Ginsberg. *Presidential Power, Unchecked and Unbalanced.* New York: Norton, 2007.

The authors submit that the American system has been sliding toward "presidentialism," a system in which presidents are no longer checked by the other branches of government, the press, or the public.

Edwards III, George C., and Stephen J. Wayne. *Presidential Leadership: Politics and Policy Making.* Belmont, CA: Cengage Wadsworth, 2009.

A comprehensive textbook on the American presidency by two of the leading scholars of the office.

Fisher, Louis. *Defending Congress and the Constitution.* Lawrence: University of Kansas Press, 2011.

A rigorous yet passionate defense of Congress's central role in the decision to go to war and how and why modern presidents have illegitimately bypassed Congress.

Howell, William G. *Power Without Persuasion: The Politics of Direct Presidential Action.* Princeton, NJ: Princeton University Press, 2003.

Rejecting the common view among political scientists that presidential power is based primarily on the president's ability to persuade, Howell suggests instead that presidents have many tools for taking unilateral action to get their way.

Pfiffner, James, and Roger H. Davidson, eds. *Understanding the Presidency*, 6th ed. New York: Pearson Longman Publishers, 2011.

A comprehensive anthology of recent scholarship on all aspects of the presidency and its place in the American political system.

Suskind, Ron. *Confidence Men.* New York: Harper, 2011.

An inside and devastating look at the first two years of the Obama presidency with a focus on the role of influential staff in shaping a presidency (not always for the best).

Wills, Gary. *Bomb Power: The Modern Presidency and the National Security State.* New York: Penguin Press, 2010.

Traces the rise in presidential powers to the rise of the national security state associated with nuclear weapons and the secrecy surrounding them, suggesting that these developments are dangerous to democracy and liberty, and unconstitutional.

Yoo, John. *The Powers of War and Peace: The Constitution and Foreign Affairs After 9/11.* Chicago: University of Chicago Press, 2005.

An argument for expansive and unitary presidential powers in the post–9/11 world by one of the architects of Bush administration policies on the treatment of detainees during war.

14

The Courts

THE BATTLE FOR THE COURTS

T ension filled the hearing room as Samuel Alito, President Bush's nominee for a position on the U.S. Supreme Court, began testifying before the Senate Judiciary Committee on January 9, 2006. Knowing that federal courts were deciding cases having to do with the most contentious issues of the day—including presidential powers in times of war, affirmative action, gay rights, the relationship between church and state, the role of the federal government in relationship to the states, and more—Republican and Democratic partisans and conservative and liberal advocacy groups were mobilized to contest Alito's nomination. Lurking in the background was the issue of the judicial filibuster. Republicans believed the filibuster could not be properly used when the Senate was exercising its constitutional duty to "advise and consent" on judicial nominations. Most Democrats believed it was the only way to prevent the accession of judges to the federal bench who would threaten hard-won rights and protections, particularly a woman's right to terminate her pregnancy. Would the Democrats use it to block Alito? If they did, would Republicans ban the practice, using their majority in the Senate to redefine the chamber's rules?

Partisan tensions over the judicial filibuster had been festering for years. Things first came to a head on November 14, 2003, when, after 40 hours of continuous debate, Republicans fell seven votes short of the 60 votes needed to end Democratic filibusters blocking Senate votes on several very conservative Bush federal judicial nominees, including Priscilla Owen for the Fifth Circuit. Republicans were furious. Senate Judiciary Chairman Orrin Hatch (R–UT) fumed, "This is petty politics . . . cheap politics . . . and can lead to more partisan division in the Senate."[1]

Democrats were not impressed, pointing out that Republicans had blocked many Clinton nominees during the 1990s but had not needed the filibuster because, as the majority, they could stop nominations in the Judiciary Committee, never allowing them to reach the floor of the Senate. As chair of that committee during the Clinton years, the very same Orrin Hatch, who insisted in 2003 that every nominee was entitled to an "up or down" vote, refused to hold hearings for several Clinton nominees and delayed hearings for others for up to 18 months.

CHANGING THE BALANCE OF THE COURT When strong conservative Samuel Alito joined the Court in 2006, replacing moderate conservative Sandra Day O'Conner, it changed the ideological balance of the Court on a wide range of issues. Because the stakes were so high, the battle in the Senate over his confirmation was contentious and attracted a large audience to his televised testimony before the Judiciary Committee.

MyPoliSciLab Video Series

The Big Picture How is it that the Supreme Court's most profound power—judicial review—is not mentioned in the Constituion? Author Edward S. Greenberg, details exactly what Article 3 says about our court system and where these additional responsibilities came from.

The Basics Do you have confidence in the U.S. court system? Watch this video to discover what the founders did to make sure the federal judiciary would be independent of political influence. You'll also learn about an important check the Supreme Court has on the other two branches of U.S. government.

How do cases get to the Supreme Court?

In Context Discover how the Supreme Court gained a check on the other two branches after the U.S. Constitution was written. East Central University political scientist Christine Pappas discusses Marbury v. Madison and analyzes how the power of judicial review has impacted campaign finance law.

Think Like a Political Scientist Why do legal scholars and political scientists disagree over how judges make decisions? East Central University political scientist Christine Pappas analyzes this and other questions scholars study. She explains how the other branches of government limit the role of the judiciary in public policy-making, and discusses research on how public opinion influences the courts.

In the Real World Should the Supreme Court have the power to knock down popular laws? This segment uses the Supreme Court's decision in U.S. v. Arizona (2012) to illustrate the tension between protecting the law and having a government that's run by the people.

So What? Though the Supreme Court decides only about 70 cases per year, they are exceedingly important ones. Author Edward S. Greenberg explains why it is a mistake to call the judiciary the "least dangerous branch" as Supreme Court Justices have more power than you might think.

The issue was revived when President Bush renominated Priscilla Owen in early 2005. When Democrats announced they would again use the filibuster to block the nomination, Majority Leader Frist warned that he would ask the presiding officer of the Senate—Vice President Richard Cheney—to disallow it. If Democrats appealed, Republicans would approve the ruling by a simple majority vote—a filibuster cannot be used on issues related to rulings by the presiding officer—which they could easily muster. Democrats warned that if this so-called nuclear option was imposed by Republicans, they would tie up the business of the Senate for the foreseeable future, something they could easily do, given that much of the Senate's business is done through unanimous consent. Partisans on both sides in the Senate and the country were itching for a fight on this issue because they believed the stakes had never been higher. A train wreck loomed.

Into the fray stepped the so-called gang of 14, a group of Republican and Democratic moderates who worked out a compromise in May 2005. Wielding enormous power because their 14 votes would be decisive on any vote related to this issue, whether on a cloture vote to end a filibuster or a vote on rulings from the presiding officer, they agreed that the judicial filibuster could be used only in undefined "extraordinary circumstances." Under the agreement, the Senate confirmed the long-delayed nominations of Priscilla Owen and two other nominees, but took no action on two other nominees who presumably fit the "extraordinary circumstances" requirement that would allow Democrats to use the filibuster.

Most observers believed that the agreement was just a temporary truce that might break down at any time, especially when it came to nominations to the Supreme Court. The agreement held, however, when John Roberts was nominated for the post of Chief Justice after the death of Chief Justice William Rehnquist in late 2005, perhaps because he was a conservative jurist replacing the conservative Rehnquist. Conservative judge Samuel Alito was another matter entirely, because President Bush nominated him to replace the retiring Sandra Day O'Connor, a relatively moderate voice and swing vote on the Court who played an important role in protecting abortion rights and affirming the use, under certain circumstances, of affirmative action in higher education admissions. In the end, however, the Democrats were unable to mount much of a challenge to Alito, and calls for a filibuster by a few Democratic senators failed to gain traction. His nomination was confirmed on January 31, 2006.

As predicted by almost everyone, Alito's ascension to the Court swung it sharply in a conservative direction on issues ranging from civil rights to environmental protection, regulation of abortions, class-action lawsuits, and the role of corporations in campaign finance,[2] matters to be examined in greater detail later in this and later chapters. The fundamental balance on the Court was not affected much when Obama nominee Sonia Sotomayor joined the Court in 2009, because she was a liberal replacing a liberal, David Souter, who retired. The same thing was true regarding the appointment of Elena Kagan in 2010; she was a liberal replacing a liberal stalwart, John Paul Stevens, so the balance on the Court was unaffected. The key appointment remained that of Alito replacing O'Connor in 2006, which created a solid conservative 5–4 majority under the able leadership of Chief Justice Roberts.[3] In 2012, this very same majority coalition severely restricted Congress's power to use the Commerce Clause, the basis of many federal regulations and programs. In *Knox v. Service Employees International Union*, it made it harder for public sector labor unions to gather money to fight political campaigns. While rejecting most of Arizona's law on illegal immigration as an unconstitutional intrusion on federal powers, the 5-4 conservative majority nevertheless upheld the law's requirement that police making legitimate stops determine the immigration status of suspects (*Arizona, et. al. v. the United States*).

In the system of separated powers and federalism created by the framers, the judicial branch, most especially the Supreme Court, assesses, in cases that come before it, the legitimacy of actions taken by the other two branches and by the states in light of the Constitution. Although the Supreme Court does not legislate or regulate on its own, its decisions strongly influence the overall shape of federal and state policies in a number of important areas. As such, the Supreme Court is a key national policymaker, and an important political actor in Washington, every bit as much a part of the governing process as the president and Congress.[4]

judicial review
The power of the Supreme Court to declare actions of the other branches and levels of government unconstitutional.

Thinking Critically About This Chapter
This chapter is about the judicial branch of the federal government, with a special focus on the Supreme Court. We examine how the federal judiciary and Supreme Court are organized, what they do in the American political and government systems, and what effects their actions have on public policies and American democracy.

Using the Framework
You will see in this chapter that the Court is embedded in a rich governmental, political linkage, and structural environment that shapes its behavior. The other branches of government impinge on and influence its composition, deliberations, and rulings; political linkage institutions such as elections, interest groups, and social movements matter; and structural factors such as economic and social change influence its agenda and decisions.

Using the Democracy Standard
You will see in this chapter that an unelected Court makes important decisions about public policies, raising questions about the degree to which popular sovereignty and majority rule prevail in our system. You will also see that the Court often turns its attention to cases that involve issues of political equality and liberty, so essential to the existence of a healthy representative democracy.

The Foundations of Judicial Power

14.1 Trace the evolution of judicial power in the United States

The judicial Power of the United States shall be vested in one supreme Court, and in such inferior Courts as the Congress may from time to time ordain and establish.

—U.S. Constitution, Article III, Section 1

We are under a Constitution, but the Constitution is what the judges say it is, and the judiciary is the safeguard of our liberty and our property under the Constitution.

—Chief Justice Charles Evans Hughes (1907)

☐ Constitutional Design
The Constitution speaks only briefly about the judicial branch and doesn't provide much guidance about what it is supposed to do or how it is supposed to go about its job. The document says little about the powers of the judicial branch in relationship to the other two federal branches or about its responsibilities in the area of constitutional interpretation. Article III is considerably shorter than Articles I and II, which focus on Congress and the president. It creates a federal judicial branch, it creates the office of "chief justice of the United States," it states that judges shall serve life terms, it specifies the categories of cases the Court may or must hear (to be explained later), and it grants Congress the power to create additional federal courts as needed. Article III of the Constitution is virtually devoid of detail.[5]

☐ Judicial Review
Extremely interesting is the Constitution's silence about **judicial review**, the long-established power of the Supreme Court to declare state and federal laws and actions null and void when they conflict with the Constitution. Debate has raged for many years over the question of whether the framers intended that the Court should have this power.[6]

14.1

14.2

14.3

14.4

14.5

14.6

The framers surely believed that the Constitution ought to prevail when other laws were in conflict with it. But did they expect the Supreme Court to make the decisions in this matter? Jefferson and Madison thought that Congress and the president were capable of rendering their own judgments about the constitutionality of their actions. Alexander Hamilton, however, believed that the power of judicial review was inherent in the notion of the separation of powers and was essential to balanced government. As he put it in *The Federalist*, No. 78 (see the Appendix), the very purpose of constitutions is to place limitations on the powers of government, and it is only the Court that can ensure such limits in the United States. The legislative branch, in particular, is unlikely to restrain itself without the helping hand of the judiciary.

There is reason to believe that Hamilton's view was the prevailing one for a majority of the framers.[7] They were firm believers, for instance, in the idea that there was a "higher law" to which governments and nations must conform. Their enthusiasm for written constitutions was based on their belief that governments must be limited in what they could do in the service of some higher or more fundamental law, such as that pertaining to individual rights. The attitudes of the time, then, strongly supported the idea that judges, conversant with the legal tradition and free from popular pressures, were best able to decide when statutory and administrative laws were in conflict with fundamental law.[8]

MARBURY v. MADISON Chief Justice John Marshall boldly claimed the power of judicial review for the U.S. Supreme Court in the case of *Marbury v. Madison* in 1803.[9] The case began with a flurry of judicial appointments by President John Adams in the final days of his presidency, after his Federalist Party had suffered a resounding defeat in the election of 1800. The apparent aim of these so-called midnight appointments was to establish the federal courts as an outpost of Federalist Party power (federal judges are appointed for life) in the midst of Jeffersonian control of the presidency and the Congress.

William Marbury was one of the midnight appointments, but he was less lucky than most. His judgeship commission was signed and sealed, but it had not been delivered to him before the new administration took office. Jefferson, knowing what Adams and the Federalists were up to, ordered Secretary of State James Madison not to deliver the commission. Marbury sued Madison, claiming that the secretary of state was obligated to deliver the commission, and asked the Supreme Court to issue a *writ of mandamus* to force Madison to do so.

Marshall faced a quandary. If the Court decided in favor of Marbury, Madison would almost surely refuse to obey, opening the Court to ridicule for its weakness. The fact that Marshall was a prominent Federalist political figure might even provoke the

ADVOCATES OF JUDICIAL REVIEW

Although the Constitution is silent on the issue of judicial review, many of the Founders probably agreed with Alexander Hamilton (left), who argued that the Supreme Court's power to interpret the Constitution and declare state and federal laws and actions unconstitutional is inherent in the notion of the separation of powers. However, it was not until the Supreme Court's 1803 *Marbury v. Madison* decision that Chief Justice John Marshall (right) affirmed the Court's power of judicial review. How might a lack of the power of judicial review hinder the classic American system of checks and balances?

Jeffersonians to take more extreme measures against the Court. But if the Court ruled in favor of Madison, it would suggest that an executive official could defy without penalty the clear provisions of the law.

Marshall's solution was worthy of Solomon. The Court ruled that William Marbury was entitled to his commission and that James Madison had broken the law in failing to deliver it. By this ruling, the Court rebuked Madison. However, the Court said it could not compel Madison to comply with the law because the section of the Judiciary Act of 1789 that granted the Court the power to issue writs of mandamus was unconstitutional. It was unconstitutional, he said, because it expanded the **original jurisdiction** of the Supreme Court as defined in Article III, which could not be done except by constitutional amendment.

On the surface, the decision was an act of great modesty. It suggested that the Court could not force the action of an executive branch official. It suggested that Congress had erred in the Judiciary Act of 1789 by trying to give the Supreme Court too much power. Beneath the surface, however, was a less modest act: the claim that judicial review was the province of the judicial branch alone. In Marshall's words in his written opinion, "It is emphatically the province and duty of the judicial department to say what the law is." In making this claim, he was following closely Hamilton's argument in *The Federalist*, No. 78.

Until quite recently, the Supreme Court used the power of judicial review with great restraint, perhaps recognizing that its regular use would invite retaliation by the other branches. Judicial review of a congressional act was not exercised again until 54 years after *Marbury* and was used to declare acts of Congress unconstitutional only about 230 times from then until 2007. However, the Court has been much less constrained about overruling the laws of the states and localities; it did so more than 1,100 times during this same period.[10] During the 1990s and early 2000s, the Rehnquist Court was much more inclined to review and overturn congressional actions, especially in cases involving federalism and the powers of Congress under the commerce clause, trimming back the power of the federal government relative to the states. Indeed, it

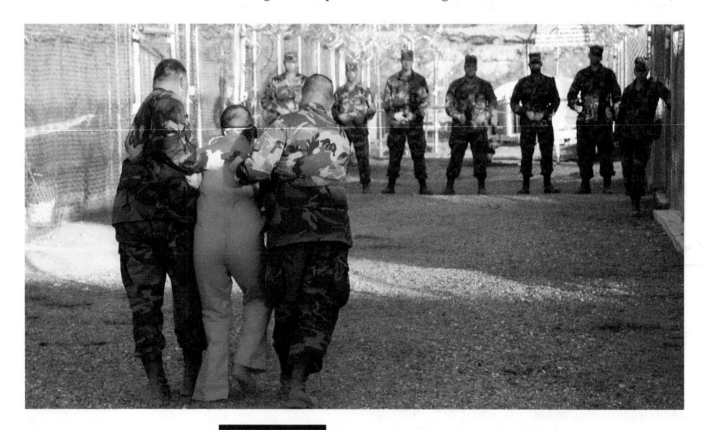

DETENTION

Though the Supreme Court ruled at first in favor of greater access of suspected terrorism detainees to the American judicial system, it has increasingly deferred to the president, military authorities, and Congress on how such detainees should be treated and how long they can be held in custody. Here a detainee is escorted to his cell at Guantanamo Bay, Cuba by military police.

invalidated congressional actions at a rate double that of the Warren Court of the 1960s, considered by many to be the most "activist" Court since the early 1930s.[11]

The Court has been less inclined to exercise judicial review on presidential actions, though some important ones have occurred during our history.[12] Between 2004 and 2008, however, the Court four times invalidated presidential actions pertaining to the treatment of detainees designated as enemy combatants.[13]

JUDICIAL REVIEW AND DEMOCRACY Judicial review involves the right of a body shielded from direct accountability to the people—federal judges are appointed, not elected, and serve for life (barring impeachment for unseemly, unethical, or illegal behavior)—to set aside the actions of government bodies whose members are elected. Many believe that judicial review has no place in a democratic society. One prominent democratic theorist has described the issue this way:

> But the authority of a high court to declare unconstitutional legislation that has been properly enacted by the coordinate constitutional bodies— . . . in our system, the Congress and the president—is far more controversial . . . The contradiction remains between imbuing an unelected body—or in the American case, five out of nine justices on the Supreme Court—with the power to make policy decisions that affect the lives and welfare of millions of Americans. How, if at all, can judicial review be justified in a democratic order?[14]

Political scientists and legal scholars use the phrase the "counter-majoritarian difficulty," coined by Alexander Bickel in 1962, to describe this enduring problem in the American political system; Bickel described judicial review as a "deviant institution in American democracy."[15] On the other hand, some observers believe that judicial review is the only way to protect the rights of political and racial minorities, to check the potential excesses of the other two government branches and the states, and to preserve the rules of the democratic process.

Many political scientists believe that the problem of democratic accountability of a nonelected judiciary with life tenure is less dire than it seems on the surface because the Supreme Court and other federal courts are influenced directly and indirectly by elected officials, public opinion, and other important actors in American society.[16] We come back to this issue later in this chapter.

The U.S. Court System: Organization and Jurisdiction

14.2 Outline the organization of the U.S. court system

Our country has one judicial system for the national government (the federal courts) and another in each of the states. In each state, courts adjudicate cases on the basis of the state's own constitution, statutes, and administrative rules.[17] In total, the great bulk of laws, legal disputes, and court decisions (roughly 99 percent) are located in the states. Most important political and constitutional issues, however, eventually reach the federal courts. In this chapter, our focus is on these federal courts. In the following sections, we'll look at the source of the federal court's power and the organization of its system.

☐ Constitutional Provisions

The only court specifically mentioned in the Constitution's Article III is the U.S. Supreme Court. The framers left to Congress the tasks of designing the details of the Supreme Court and establishing "such inferior courts as the Congress may from time to time ordain and establish." Beginning with the Judiciary Act of 1789, Congress has periodically reorganized the federal court system. The end result is a three-tiered

14.1

14.2

14.3

14.4

14.5

14.6

constitutional courts
Federal courts created by Congress under the authority of Article III of the Constitution.

legislative courts
Highly specialized federal courts created by Congress under the authority of Article I of the Constitution.

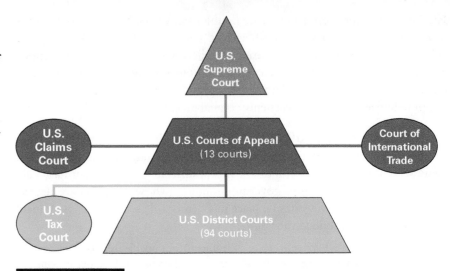

FIGURE 14.1 THE U.S. FEDERAL COURT SYSTEM

The federal court system is a three-tiered pyramidal system, with the Supreme Court at the top. Below it are 13 federal courts of appeal and 94 district courts, with at least one district in each state. Additional courts exist to hear cases in highly specialized areas, such as taxes, international trade, and financial claims against the U.S. government.

Source: Administrative Office of the U.S. Courts.

pyramidal system (see Figure 14.1), with a handful of offshoots. At the bottom are 94 U.S. federal district courts, with at least one district in each state. In the middle are 13 courts of appeal. At the top of the pyramid is the Supreme Court. These courts are called **constitutional courts** because they were created by Congress under Article III, which discusses the judicial branch. Congress has also created a number of courts to adjudicate cases in highly specialized areas of concern, such as taxes, patents, and maritime law. These were established under Article I, which specifies the duties and powers of Congress, and are called **legislative courts**.

Article III does not offer many guidelines for the federal court system, but the few requirements that are stated are very important. The Constitution requires, for instance, that federal judges serve "during good behavior," which means, in practice, until they retire or die in office, as Chief Justice William Rehnquist did in 2005 at the age of 81. Because impeachment by Congress is the only way to remove federal judges, the decision about who will be a judge is an important one because they are likely to serve for a very long time. Article III also states that Congress cannot reduce the salaries of judges once they are in office. This provision was designed to maintain the independence of the judiciary by protecting it from legislative intimidation.

Article III also specifies the subject matter of cases that are solely the province of the federal courts:

- The Constitution (e.g., disputes involving the First Amendment or the commerce clause).
- Federal statutes and treaties (including disputes involving ambassadors and other diplomats).
- Admiralty and maritime issues (disputes involving shipping and commerce on the high seas).
- Controversies in which the U.S. government is a party.
- Disputes between the states.
- Disputes between a state and a citizen of another state.
- Disputes between a state (or citizen of a state) and foreign states or citizens.

☐ Federal District Courts

Most cases in the federal court system are first heard in one of the 94 district courts. District courts are courts of original jurisdiction, that is, courts where cases are first heard; they do not hear appeals from other courts. They are also trial courts; some use juries—either **grand juries**, which bring indictments, or **petit (trial) juries**, which decide cases—and in some, cases are heard only by a judge.

Most of the business of the federal courts takes place at this level. In 2011, about 379,000 cases were filed; roughly 76 percent of them were civil cases, and 24 percent were criminal cases.[18] Civil cases include everything from antitrust cases brought by the federal government, to copyright infringement suits (as when Apple sued Amazon for its use of the term "Appstore" on the Amazon website), and commercial and contract disputes between citizens (or businesses) of two or more states. Criminal cases include violations of federal criminal laws, such as bank robbery, interstate drug trafficking, and kidnapping.

Most civil and criminal cases are concluded at this level. In a relatively small number of disputes, however, one of the parties to the case may feel that a mistake has been made in trial procedure or in the law that was brought to bear in the trial, or one of the parties may feel that a legal or constitutional issue is at stake that was not taken into account at the trial stage or was wrongly interpreted. In such cases, one of the parties may appeal to a higher court—a Court of Appeals.

□ U.S. Courts of Appeal

The United States is divided into 12 geographic **circuit courts** (see the map in Figure 14.2) that hear appeals from federal district courts. The one for Washington, D.C., not only hears appeals from the federal district court there but also is charged with hearing cases arising from rule-making by federal agencies like the Securities and Exchange Commission and the National Labor Relations Board. There is also a 13th circuit court, called the U.S. Court of Appeals for the Federal Circuit, located in Washington, D.C., that hears cases from all over the nation on patents and government contracts. In 2011, about 55,000 cases were filed in the federal appeals courts, although only

grand juries
Groups of citizens who decide whether there is sufficient evidence to bring an indictment against accused persons.

petit (trial) juries
Juries that hear evidence and sit in judgment on charges brought in civil or criminal cases.

circuit courts
The 12 geographical jurisdictions and one special court that hear appeals from the federal district courts.

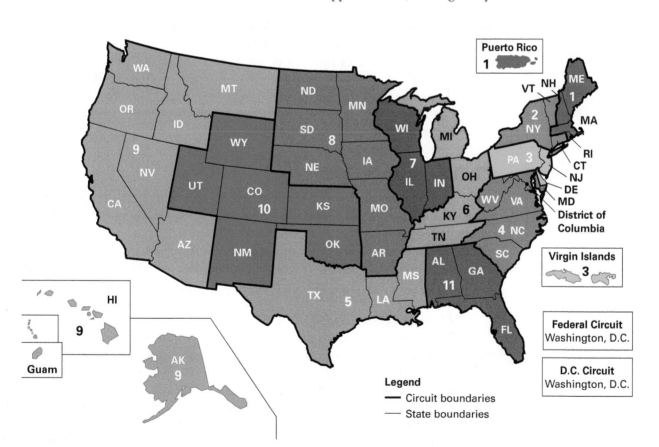

FIGURE 14.2 U.S. FEDERAL CIRCUIT COURTS

The United States is divided into 12 geographic regions (including the D.C. Circuit Court), each housing a federal circuit court of appeals. One additional circuit court of appeal, the Federal Circuit Court, is located in Washington, D.C.

Source: Administrative Office of the U.S. Courts.

appellate courts

Courts that hear cases on appeal from other courts.

briefs

Documents setting out the arguments in legal cases, prepared by attorneys and presented to courts.

opinion

The explanation of the majority's and the minority's reasoning that accompanies a court decision.

precedents

Past rulings by courts which guide judicial reasoning in subsequent cases.

stare decisis

The legal doctrine that says precedent should guide judicial decision making.

about 8,000 reached the formal hearing stage (most of these end in negotiated settlements without going to trial).[19] Cases cannot originate in these courts but must come to them from district courts. Because they exist only to hear appeals, they are referred to as **appellate courts**. New factual evidence cannot be introduced before such courts; no witnesses are called or cross-examined. At the appellate level, lawyers do not examine witnesses or introduce new evidence; instead, they submit **briefs**, which set out the legal issues at stake. Judges usually convene as panels of three (on important cases, there are more—sometimes seven members) to hear oral arguments from the lawyers on each side of the case and to cross-examine them on points of law. Weeks or even months later, after considerable study, writing, and discussion among the judges, the panel issues a ruling. In important cases, the ruling is usually accompanied by an **opinion** that sets forth the majority side's reasoning for the decision.

Once appellate decisions are published, they become **precedents** that guide the decisions of other judges in the same circuit. Although judges do not slavishly follow precedents, they tend to move away from them only when necessary and only in very small steps. This doctrine of closely following precedents as the basis for legal reasoning is known as **stare decisis**.

It is important to know that the decisions of the 12 geographic circuit courts determine the meaning of laws for the people who live in the states covered by each circuit. They have become more important as they have ruled on ever more cases recently, without review by the Supreme Court, which decides fewer than 80 cases each year.

Sometimes particular circuits play a more important role than others in changing constitutional interpretation. For example, the Fourth Circuit Court, based in Richmond, Virginia, has been a leader in the trend toward reasserting the power of the states in the federal system.[20] The Ninth Circuit Court, which sits in San Francisco, on the other hand, is known to be especially liberal on civil rights and civil liberties cases. Because the Supreme Court considers only a relative handful of cases from the appeals courts each term, the rulings of the Fourth Circuit are binding for almost 24 million people in the southeastern United States, while the rulings of the Ninth Circuit Court of Appeals hold for roughly 61 million people in the western United States, including California. Although it has had several of its rulings reversed in recent years by the more conservative U.S. Supreme Court, the Ninth Circuit's rulings, nevertheless, cover about 20 percent of the American population.

☐ The Supreme Court

Congress decides how many judges sit on the Supreme Court. The first Court had six members. The Federalists, however, reduced the number to five in 1801 to prevent newly elected president Thomas Jefferson from filling a vacancy. In 1869, Congress set the number at its present nine members (eight associate justices and the chief justice). It has remained this way ever since, weathering the failed effort by President Franklin Roosevelt to "pack" the Court with more politically congenial justices by expanding its size to 15.

The Supreme Court is both a court of original jurisdiction and an appellate court. That is, some cases must first be heard in the Supreme Court. Disputes involving ambassadors and other diplomatic personnel, as well as disputes between two or more states, must start in the Supreme Court rather than in some other court, though the Court is not obliged to hear such cases.[21]

The Supreme Court also, in its most important role, serves as an appellate court for the federal appeals courts and for the highest courts of each of the states. Cases in which a state or federal law has been declared unconstitutional can be heard by the Supreme Court, as can cases in which the highest state court has denied a claim that a state law violates federal law or the Constitution (see Figure 14.3).

There is a popular misconception that the Supreme Court only takes cases having to do with constitutional questions. This is not correct. The Court can and does hear cases about the interpretation of statutes and regulations. For example, in *Grove City*

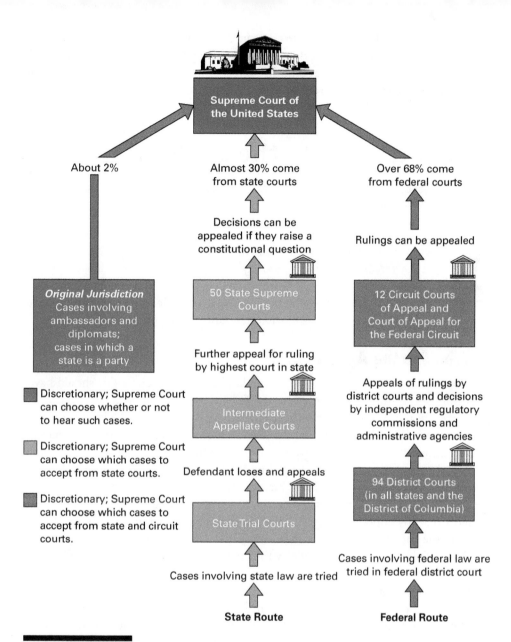

14.1
14.2
14.3
14.4
14.5
14.6

FIGURE 14.3 HOW CASES GET TO THE SUPREME COURT

The vast majority of cases that reach the Supreme Court come to it from the federal court system. Most of the others come on appeal from the highest state courts. A handful originate in the Supreme Court itself.

Source: Adapted from *Storm Center: The Supreme Court in American Politics*, Seventh Edition, by David M. O'Brien. Copyright © 2005, 2003, 2000, 1996, 1993, 1990, 1986 by David O'Brien. Used by permission of W. W. Norton & Company, Inc.

College v. Bell (1984), the Court ruled that Title IX of the Federal Education Act did not mean that institutions of higher education receiving federal funds would lose all federal funding if they practiced gender discrimination (as Congress clearly intended). Rather, it ruled that only the discriminating program or department would lose funding, say the athletic department or the physics department. To take another example, the Court ruled in 2011 that the Environmental Protection Agency was acting properly under the Clean Air Act when it designated greenhouse gases a health hazard, and such emissions subject to regulation.

Congress determines much of the appellate jurisdiction of the Court. In 1869, following the Civil War, a Congress controlled by radical Republicans removed the Court's power to review cases falling under the Reconstruction program for the South. In 1995, responding to a plea from Chief Justice Rehnquist to lighten the Court's caseload, Congress dropped the requirement that the Supreme Court *must* hear cases in which a state court declares a federal statute unconstitutional. It can choose, but is not obligated, to do so.

Because it is the highest appellate court in the federal court system, the decisions and opinions of the Supreme Court become the main precedents on federal and constitutional questions for courts at all other levels of jurisdiction. It is for this reason that Supreme Court decisions receive so much attention from other political actors, the media, and the public.

Appointment to the Federal Bench

Describe the background of appointees to the federal bench and the process by which they are appointed

ecause federal judges are appointed for life and make important decisions, it matters in a democratic society who they are and how they get to the bench. If they are isolated from popular influence, democracy is at risk. If they are too responsive, they ignore their judicial role to act as neutral arbiters of the meaning of the Constitution in political and government affairs.

☐ Who Are the Appointees?

The Constitution offers no advice on what qualifications a federal judge should have. By custom and tradition, appointees to the federal bench must be lawyers, but until quite recently, they did not have to have judicial experience. Indeed, almost one-half of all Supreme Court justices during the twentieth century had no prior experience as judges. Among the ranks of the "inexperienced" are some of the most prominent and influential justices in our history, including John Marshall, Louis Brandeis, Harlan Stone, Charles Evans Hughes, Felix Frankfurter, and Earl Warren.[22] Former Chief Justice William Rehnquist also came to the bench without judicial experience, as did the most recently appointed justice, Elena Kagan, who served in the Clinton White House in the late 1990s after years in private practice and law school teaching.

As the federal courts—particularly the circuit courts and the Supreme Court—have become more important in determining American public policies, and as partisan and ideological conflicts have become more pronounced in the country, having judicial experience has become more important in the nomination and confirmation process. Because the stakes seem so high to many people—whether *Roe v. Wade* (1973) will be overturned, let us say, or what constitutional limits can be placed on the president during a war—they want to know the judicial philosophies and general ideological outlooks of the people who will become Supreme Court and appeals court judges. One way to know this is to examine the rulings and written opinions of nominees who have been judges. The new, though unwritten, rules about prior judicial experience became apparent in the firestorm that erupted within Republican and conservative circles after President Bush nominated Harriet Miers in late 2005 to fill the Sandra Day O'Connor vacancy. Many people who were normally Bush supporters were upset by the fact that Miers was an unknown in terms of constitutional law, having never served as a judge. They could not be sure they could trust her on the central issues of the day. They were much more comfortable with Bush nominees John Roberts and Samuel Alito, who had established extensive conservative records on the federal bench.[23]

Like most lawyers, federal judges tend to come from privileged backgrounds. Moreover, federal judges, and particularly Supreme Court justices, come from the most elite parts of the legal profession. For most of our history, they have been white male Protestants from upper-income or upper-middle-class backgrounds, who attended the most selective and expensive undergraduate and graduate institutions.[24] The current Supreme Court has moved entirely away from the almost exclusive Protestant membership that marked its history—indeed three current members, Ginsburg, Breyer, and Kagan, are Jewish and six, Scalia, Thomas, Kennedy, Roberts,

Alito, and Sotomayor, are Catholic—and is more diverse in terms of race and gender than has been true for most of its history as well. On the current Supreme Court, there is one African American (Clarence Thomas), one Hispanic (Sotomayor), and three women (Ginsburg, Sotomayor, and Kagan). The racial and gender representativeness of judicial appointees at the circuit and district court levels is better, and improving rapidly, but it is still a long way from reflecting the composition of the legal profession, much less the American people as a whole.

The Appointment Process

Federal judges assume office after they have been nominated by the president and confirmed by the Senate in a process that has become ever more contentious as national politicians have become more partisan.[25] Presidents pay special attention to judicial appointments, because they are a way for presidents to affect public policy long after their presidential term is up.[26]

Presidents take many things into consideration besides merit.[27] No president wants a nomination rejected by the Senate, for example, so the president and presidential advisers consult with key senators, especially those on the Judiciary Committee, before nominations are forwarded. Nominations for district court judgeships are subject to what is called **senatorial courtesy**, the practice of allowing the senior senator from the president's party to approve nominees from the state where the district court is located. Senatorial courtesy does not operate, however, in appointments to the circuit courts, whose jurisdictions span more than a single state, or to the Supreme Court, whose jurisdiction is the entire nation. Nevertheless, presidents must be extremely attentive to the views of key senators, even those in the opposing party when the opposing party controls the Senate.

On occasion, despite presidential efforts to placate it, the Senate has refused to give its consent. Of the 143 nominees for the Supreme Court since the founding of the Republic, the Senate has refused to approve 28 of them, although only five of these

senatorial courtesy
The tradition that a judicial nomination for a federal district court seat be approved by the senior senator of the president's party from the state where a district court is located before the nominee is considered by the Senate Judiciary Committee.

14.1
14.2
14.3
14.4
14.5
14.6

BORK REJECTED
The Democratic Senate's rejection in 1987 of conservative legal scholar Robert Bork, President Reagan's nominee for a vacant seat on the Supreme Court, helped trigger the long ideological and partisan battle over the composition of the Supreme Court that persists to the present day. Here Bork explains his judicial philosophy to members of the Senate Judiciary Committee.

14.1

14.2

14.3

14.4

14.5

14.6

standing

Authority to bring legal action because one is directly affected by the issues at hand.

executive privilege

A presidential claim that certain communications with subordinates may be withheld from Congress and the courts.

refusals have occurred since 1900. Rejection of nominees has usually happened when the president was weak or when the other party was in control of the Senate. The defeat of Ronald Reagan's nominee, Robert Bork, was the product of deep ideological differences between a Republican president and a Democratic-controlled Senate. There have also been several near defeats. George H. W. Bush's nominee, Clarence Thomas, was confirmed by a margin of only four votes after questions were raised about his legal qualifications and about sexual harassment charges brought by law professor Anita Hill.

As the chapter-opening story shows, Senate confirmations of judicial nominees, especially for the federal appeals court and the Supreme Court, have become very contentious. Battles over presidential judicial nominees raged during the Clinton presidency and during the Bush presidency, culminating in the Democrats' use of the filibuster on several judicial nominations, Republican threats to use the nuclear option to end judicial filibusters, and the fight in the Senate and among advocacy groups over the nomination of Samuel Alito in early 2006.

Although presidents must be concerned about the merit of their candidates and their acceptability to the Senate, they also try by their appointments to make their mark on the future. Presidents go about this in different ways.

For the most part, presidents are interested in nominating judges who share their ideological and program commitments.[28] John Adams nominated John Marshall and a number of other judges to protect Federalist principles during the ascendancy of the Jeffersonians. Franklin Roosevelt tried to fill the courts with judges who favored the New Deal. Ronald Reagan favored conservatives who were committed to rolling back affirmative action and other civil rights claims, abortion rights, protections for criminal defendants, and broad claims of **standing** in environmental cases. Both George H. W. Bush and his son George W. Bush carried on the Reagan tradition of nominating conservative judges to the federal courts.

Bill Clinton, eager to avoid a bitter ideological fight in the Senate, where he was trying to forge a bipartisan coalition to support the North American Free Trade Agreement and a national crime bill, nominated two judges with reputations as moderates for the high court—Ruth Bader Ginsburg and Stephen Breyer—in the first years of his administration. The Ginsburg nomination was also indicative of Clinton's apparent commitment to diversifying the federal court system. (More than one-half of federal court nominees during his presidency were women and minorities.)

Diversity was also important to President Barack Obama. During his first year in office, he nominated 12 people for federal circuit court positions. Of these 12, nine were women and/or minorities. He also was anxious to appoint the first Hispanic to the Supreme Court, and did so in 2009, choosing Sonia Sotomayor.[29] He added another woman to the Court when he nominated Elena Kagan in 2010. Both were liberal on social issues but relatively favorable to business.

Presidents are often disappointed in how their nominees behave once they reach the Court. Dwight Eisenhower was dumbfounded when his friend and nominee, Earl Warren, led the Court in a liberal direction by transforming constitutional law regarding civil rights and criminal procedure. Richard Nixon was stunned when Chief Justice Warren Burger voted with a unanimous Court to override the president's claim of **executive privilege** and forced him to give up the documents that would seal his fate in the Watergate affair. He and other Court observers were also surprised by the odyssey of his nominee Harry Blackmun, who, despite a conservative judicial record before joining the Court, had become one of its most liberal justices by the time of his retirement in 1994 (he wrote the majority opinion in *Roe v. Wade* [1973]). The elder George Bush no doubt was surprised when his nominee, David Souter, refused to vote for the overturn of *Roe* in *Planned Parenthood v. Casey* (1992). Despite these dramatic examples, the past political and ideological positions of federal court nominees are a fairly reliable guide to their later behavior on the bench.[30] No one was surprised that the Court moved in a very conservative direction after Bush nominees Roberts and Alito joined the Court, given the record of their past political activities and judicial opinions.

The Supreme Court in Action

14.4 Outline how the Supreme Court decides cases

separate but equal doctrine
The principle articulated in *Plessy v. Ferguson* (1896) that laws prescribing separate public facilities and services for nonwhite Americans are permissible if the facilities and services are equal to those provided for whites.

superprecedents
Landmark rulings that have been reaffirmed by the Court over the course of many years and whose reasoning has become part of the fabric of American law.

 he Supreme Court meets from the first Monday in October until late June or early July, depending on the press of business. Let's see how it goes about deciding cases.[31]

☐ Norms of Operation

A set of unwritten but clearly understood rules of behavior—called *norms*—shapes how the Court does things. One norm is *secrecy*, which keeps the conflicts between justices out of the public eye and elevates the stature of the Court as an institution. Justices do not grant interviews very often, though several recently have authored books. Reporters are not allowed to stalk the corridors for a story. Law clerks are expected to keep all memos, draft opinions, and conversations with the justices they work for confidential. Justices are not commonly seen on the frantic Washington, D.C., cocktail party circuit. When meeting in conference to argue and decide cases, the justices meet alone, without secretaries or clerks. Breaches of secrecy have occurred only occasionally. As a result, we know less about the inner workings of the Court than about any other branch of government.

Seniority is another important norm. Seniority determines the assignment of office space, the seating arrangements in open court (the most junior are at the ends), and the order of speaking in conference (the chief justice, then the most senior, and so on down the line). Speaking first allows the senior members to set the tone for discussion.

Finally, the justices are expected to stick closely to *precedent* when they decide cases. When the Court departs from a precedent, it is essentially overruling its own past actions, in effect, exercising judicial review of itself. In most cases, departures from precedent come in only very small steps over many years. For example, several decisions chipped away at the **separate but equal doctrine** of *Plessy v. Ferguson* (1896) before it was decisively reversed in *Brown v. Board of Education of Topeka* (1954) to end state and local laws requiring racial segregation. Times may be changing, however, as the Court has become more divided along partisan lines. When it came to its *Citizens United* ruling in 2010 allowing corporations to spend unlimited money in funding issue advertising during election campaigns, for example, the Roberts Court showed no inclination to move slowly; it simply over-ruled a series of its previous rulings, one being but three years old.

Some legal theorists, both conservative and liberal, have begun to talk of **superprecedents** or super–*stare decisis* landmark rulings, that have been reaffirmed by the Court over the course of many years and whose reasoning has become part of the fabric of American law, making them especially difficult to reverse. Senator Arlen Specter, chair of the Senate Judicial Committee at the time, asked Chief Justice nominee John Roberts during his confirmation hearings in 2005 where he stood on this issue. While Roberts agreed that such fundamental rulings exist, he was unwilling to say whether *Roe v. Wade* (1973) was one of them, leaving observers unsure how he would eventually stand on the abortion issue. Other legal thinkers and jurists, however, are not impressed with this idea of superprecedents; cases that are wrongly decided, they say, should not be protected against reversal, no matter how many times they have been affirmed in the past by the Court.[32]

☐ Controlling the Agenda

The Court has a number of screening mechanisms to control what cases it will hear so that it can focus on cases that involve important federal or constitutional questions.[33]

Several technical rules help keep the numbers down. Cases must be *real* and *adverse;* that is, they must involve a real dispute between two parties. The disputants in a case must have *standing;* that is, they must have a real and direct interest in the issues that are raised. The Court sometimes changes the definition of *standing* to make access for **plaintiffs** easier or more difficult. The Warren Court (1956–1969) favored an expansive definition; the Rehnquist Court (1986–2005), a restricted one. Cases must also be *ripe;* that is, all other avenues of appeal must have been exhausted, and the injury must already have taken place (the Court will not accept hypothetical cases). Appeals must also be filed within a specified time limit, the paperwork must be correct and complete, and a filing fee of $300 must be paid. The fee may be waived if a petitioner is poor and files an affidavit *in forma pauperis* ("in the manner of a pauper"). One of the most famous cases in American history, *Gideon v. Wainwright* (1963), which established the right of all defendants to have lawyers in criminal cases, was submitted *in forma pauperis* on a few pieces of lined paper by a Florida State Penitentiary inmate named Clarence Earl Gideon. The Rehnquist Court was less friendly to indigent petitions than previous Courts and took several steps to cut down what the Chief Justice called "frivolous" suits by "jailhouse lawyers."

The most powerful tool that the Court has for controlling its own agenda is the power to grant or not to grant a **writ of certiorari**. A grant of "cert" is a decision of the Court that an appellate case raises an important federal or constitutional issue that it is prepared to consider.[34] Under the **rule of four**, petitions are granted cert if at least four justices vote in favor. There are several reasons a petition may not command four votes, even if the case involves important constitutional issues: it may involve a particularly controversial issue that the Court would like to avoid, or the Court may not yet have developed a solid majority and may wish to avoid a split decision. Few petitions survive all of these hurdles. Of the 10,000 or so cases that are filed in each session, the Court today grants cert for fewer than 80 (this number varies a bit year to year), down from the 150 that was typical in the 1970s and 1980s. In cases denied cert, the decision of the federal appeals court or the highest state court stands.

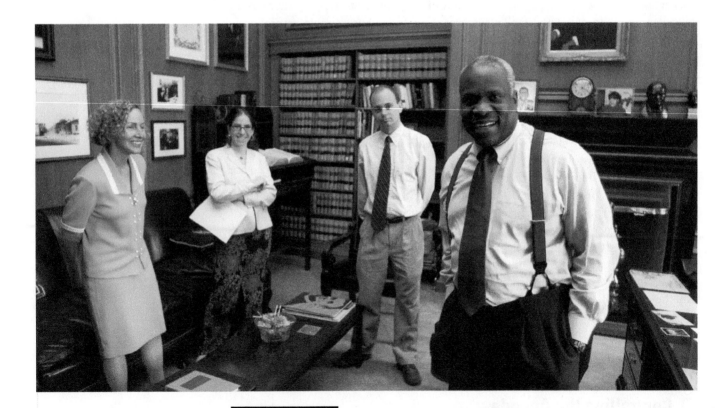

CLERKING FOR JUSTICE THOMAS

Law clerks play an extremely important role at the Supreme Court, with each justice selecting his or her own from among graduates of the nation's leading law schools. Here, Justice Clarence Thomas relaxes with three of his clerks after a long day. What is the importance of clerks to the effectiveness of the justices?

Deciding how freely to grant cert is a tricky business for the Court. Granted too often, it threatens to inundate the Court with cases. Granted too sparingly, it leaves in place the decisions of 13 different federal appeals courts on substantial federal and constitutional questions, as well as the decisions of state supreme courts, which often leads to inconsistent constitutional interpretations across the country. Because the Court now takes so few cases, more influence than ever is being exercised by the 13 federal circuit courts. For many important cases, the federal circuit courts have become the judicial forum of last resort. When the Supreme Court wants to reach out and settle differences in decisions in lower federal courts or among the states, however, it is entirely free to do so; it controls its own agenda. In 2011, it granted cert to appeals involving several very controversial issues, including state laws trying to control illegal immigration and the constitutionality of parts of the new health care reform law.

amicus curiae
Latin for "a friend of the court"; describes a brief in which individuals not party to a suit may have their views heard.

☐ Deciding Cases

Almost all cases granted cert are scheduled for oral argument (about 10 to 15 are decided without oral argument, depending on the session). Lawyers on each side are alerted to the key issues that the justices wish to consider, and new briefs are invited. Briefs are also submitted on most important cases by other parties who may be interested in the disputes. These "friend of the court," or *amicus curiae*, briefs may be submitted by individuals, interest groups, or some agency of the federal government, including the Justice Department or even the president.

Each case is argued for one hour, with 30 minutes given to each side in the dispute. Oral argument is not so much a presentation of arguments, however, as it is a give-and-take between the lawyers and the justices and among the justices themselves. When the federal government is a party to the case, the solicitor general or one of his or her deputies presents the oral arguments. Some justices—Antonin Scalia and Chief Justice John Roberts, for example—are famous for their relentless grilling of lawyers. Ruth Bader Ginsburg often asks that lawyers skip abstract legal fine points and put the issues in terms of their effect on ordinary people.

After hearing oral arguments and reading the briefs in the case, the justices meet in conference to reach a decision. The custom is for each justice to state his or her position, starting with the chief justice and moving through the ranks in order of seniority. Chief justices of great stature and intellect, such as John Marshall and Charles Evans Hughes, used the opportunity to speak first as a way of structuring the case and of swaying votes. Those who did not command much respect from the other justices (e.g., Warren Burger) were less able to shape the decision process.[35]

Political scientists have tried to determine what factors are most important in predicting how the justices will vote.[36] One approach looks at the ideological predilections of the justices and manages to explain a great deal about their voting behavior that way.[37] Another approach looks at the strategic behavior of judges, using the diaries and personal papers of retired justices to show that a great deal of negotiating and "horse trading" goes on, with justices trading votes on different cases and joining opinions they do not like so that they can have a hand in modifying them.[38] Another approach tries to link voting behavior to social background, types of previous judicial experience, and the political environment of family upbringing.[39] Still another believes that justices vote strategically, departing from their own policy preferences when they believe a particular decision will enhance the influence of the Court in the federal government and American society.[40] Finally, others believe that justices often vote out of a sense of duty, committed to preserving the standing of the Court and their sense of professional responsibility. None of these approaches has been totally successful, though the ideological models seem to do the best over the long term.[41] We cannot know for certain because the other approaches require access to information that is not directly available to researchers because much of what the Court does in conference is secret and can be only imperfectly reconstructed.

About all one can say is that the justices tend to form relatively stable voting blocs over time, with ideology increasingly the most important factor.[42] For example,

opinion of the Court
The majority opinion that accompanies a Supreme Court decision.

concurring opinion
The opinion of one or more judges who vote with the majority on a case but wish to set out different reasons for their decision.

dissenting opinion
The opinion of the judge or judges who are in the minority on a particular case before the Supreme Court.

during the 1990s and early 2000s, the Rehnquist Court, on many cases involving federalism and the rights of criminal defendants, divided into two blocs, a five-member conservative one (Justices Scalia, Thomas, Rehnquist, Kennedy, and O'Connor) and a four-member liberal one (Justices Stevens, Breyer, Ginsburg, and Souter). The Roberts Court is dominated by a solid conservative majority, as has been shown, even though the Chief Justice surprisingly sided with his liberal colleagues in upholding the Affordable Care Act in 2012.

The vote in conference is not final, however. As Justice John Harlan once explained, "The books on voting are never closed until the decision finally comes down."[43] The justices have an opportunity to change their votes in response to the opinion supporting the majority decision. An opinion is a statement of the legal reasoning that supports the decision of the Court. There are three kinds of opinions. The **opinion of the Court** is the written opinion of the majority. A **concurring opinion** is the opinion of a justice who supports the majority decision but has different legal reasons for doing so. A **dissenting opinion** presents the reasoning of the minority. Dissenting opinions sometimes become the basis for future Court majorities.

If he votes with the majority in conference, the chief justice assigns the writing of the opinion. He can assign it to any justice in the majority; chief justices often write majority opinions themselves. Some jurists and scholars believe that this power to assign is the most important role of the chief justice, and it is guarded jealously. Warren Burger was so eager to play a role in opinion assignments that, much to the distress of his colleagues, he would often delay announcing his vote so that he could place himself with the majority. Justice William Douglas angrily charged that Burger voted with the majority in *Roe* only so that he could assign the case to a justice who was closer to the minority view.[44] If the chief justice's opinion is with the minority, the opinion is assigned by the most senior member of the majority.

The justice assigned to write the opinion does not work in isolation. He or she is assisted by law clerks and other justices, who helpfully provide memoranda suggesting wording and reasoning. Justices also consider the legal reasoning presented to the Court in *amicus curiae* briefs.[45] Most opinions go through numerous revisions and are subject to a considerable amount of bargaining among the justices.

Only when an opinion is completed is a final vote taken in conference. The justices are free to change their earlier votes: they may join the majority if they are now persuaded by its reasoning, or a concurring opinion may be so compelling that the majority may decide to replace the original majority opinion with it.

The Supreme Court as a National Policymaker

14.5 Evaluate the Supreme Court as a national policymaker

Explore on MyPoliSciLab
Simulation
You Are a Supreme Court Clerk

People often say that the Court should settle disputes and not make policy. But because the disputes it settles involve contentious public issues (such as abortion rights and affirmative action) and fundamental questions about the meaning of our constitutional rules (such as the extent of presidential powers in wartime), the Court cannot help but make public policy.

It seems likely that the Court recognizes and cultivates its policymaking role. In the main, the Court does not see itself as a court of last resort, simply righting routine errors in the lower courts or settling minor private disputes. It sees itself, instead, as the "highest judicial tribunal for settling policy conflicts" and constitutional issues and chooses its cases accordingly.[46] The fact that decisions are not simply handed down but come with an opinion attached for the purpose of guiding the actions of other courts, litigants, and public officials is another demonstration that the Court recognizes its policymaking role. Let's look at judicial policymaking—which takes the form of the

Court's constitutional interpretations as revealed in its decisions—and see how it has evolved over time.

□ Structural Change and Constitutional Interpretation

Scholars generally identify three periods in the history of constitutional interpretation by the Supreme Court in the United States, one stretching from the early 1800s to the Civil War, the next from the end of the Civil War to the Great Depression, and the last from World War II to the mid-1980s.[47] We would add a fourth, covering the years from 1991 to the present (see Figure 14.4). We will see how changes in constitutional law have been influenced by structural factors, particularly economic change.

PERIOD 1: NATIONAL POWER AND PROPERTY RIGHTS The United States experienced significant growth and change during the first 75 years of its existence. This growth was accompanied by changes in constitutional law. Chief Justice John Marshall, who presided over the Supreme Court from 1801 to 1835, was the key judicial figure during this important period in our history.[48] Marshall was a follower of the doctrines of Alexander Hamilton, who believed that American greatness depended on a strong national government, a partnership between government and business in which industry and commerce were encouraged, and a national market economy free of the regulatory restraints of state and local governments. In a string of opinions that have shaped the fundamentals of American constitutional law—especially important are *Fletcher v. Peck* (1810), *Dartmouth College v. Woodward* (1819), *McCulloch v. Maryland* (1819), and *Gibbons v. Ogden* (1824), discussed elsewhere in this text— Marshall interpreted the Constitution to mean "maximum protection to property rights and maximum support for the idea of nationalism over states' rights."[49]

PERIOD 2: GOVERNMENT AND THE ECONOMY The Industrial Revolution and the Civil War triggered the development of a mass-production industrial economy dominated by the business corporation. Determining the role to be played by government in such an economy was a central theme of American political life in the late nineteenth and early twentieth centuries. The courts were involved deeply in this rethinking. At the beginning of this period, the Supreme Court took the position that the corporation was to be protected against regulation by both the state and federal governments; by the end, it was more sympathetic to the desire of the people and the political branches for the expansion of government regulation and management of the economy during the crisis of the Great Depression.

The main protection for the corporation against regulation came from the Fourteenth Amendment. This amendment was passed in the wake of the Civil War to guarantee the citizenship rights of freed slaves. The operative phrase was from Section 1: "Nor shall any state deprive any person of life, liberty, or property without due process of law"—on its face, hardly relevant to the world of the corporation. But in one of the great ironies of American history, the Court took up this expanded federal power over the states to protect rights and translated it to mean that corporations (considered "persons" under the law) and other forms of business should have increased protection from state regulation.

This reading of **laissez-faire** economic theory into constitutional law made the Supreme Court the principal ally of business in the late nineteenth and early twentieth centuries.[50] Keeping the government out of the economy in general, the Court overturned efforts by both the state and federal governments to provide welfare for the poor; to regulate manufacturing monopolies; to initiate an income tax; to regulate interstate railroad rates; to provide scholarships to students; to regulate wages, hours, and working conditions; and to protect consumers against unsafe or unhealthy products. The Court also supported the use of judicial injunctions to halt strikes by labor unions.

The business–Supreme Court alliance lasted until the Great Depression. Roosevelt's New Deal reflected a new national consensus on the need for a greatly expanded federal government with a new set of responsibilities: to manage the economy;

laissez-faire

The political-economic doctrine that holds that government ought not interfere with the operations of the free market.

14.1

14.2

14.3

14.4

14.5

14.6

469

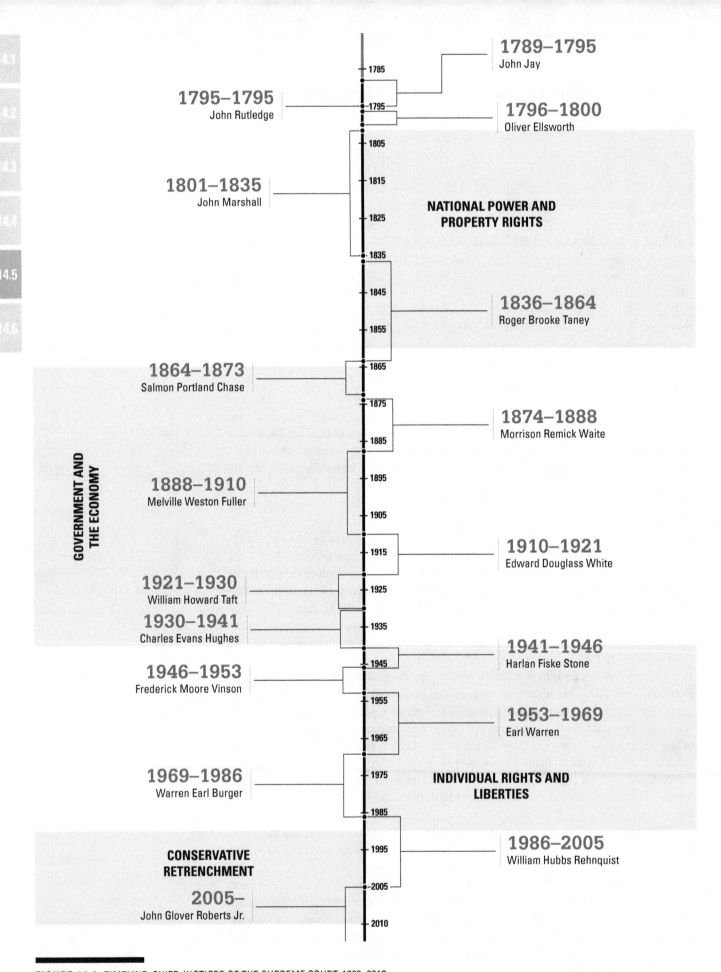

1789–1795
John Jay

1795–1795
John Rutledge

1796–1800
Oliver Ellsworth

NATIONAL POWER AND PROPERTY RIGHTS

1801–1835
John Marshall

1836–1864
Roger Brooke Taney

GOVERNMENT AND THE ECONOMY

1864–1873
Salmon Portland Chase

1874–1888
Morrison Remick Waite

1888–1910
Melville Weston Fuller

1910–1921
Edward Douglass White

1921–1930
William Howard Taft

1930–1941
Charles Evans Hughes

1941–1946
Harlan Fiske Stone

1946–1953
Frederick Moore Vinson

1953–1969
Earl Warren

1969–1986
Warren Earl Burger

INDIVIDUAL RIGHTS AND LIBERTIES

1986–2005
William Hubbs Rehnquist

CONSERVATIVE RETRENCHMENT

2005–
John Glover Roberts Jr.

FIGURE 14.4 TIMELINE: CHIEF JUSTICES OF THE SUPREME COURT, 1789–2013

Source: United States Supreme Court.

Who Are the Activist Judges?

In practice, an activist judge—liberal or conservative—is one who overturns a law as unconstitutional. Even though the current Supreme Court hands down fewer decisions, 19 out of 408 decisions declared laws unconstitutional between 2005 and 2010. The data below shows which judges are most responsible for these controversial decisions.

Supreme Court Decisions

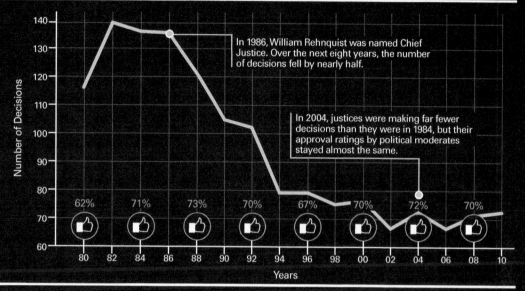

In 1986, William Rehnquist was named Chief Justice. Over the next eight years, the number of decisions fell by nearly half.

In 2004, justices were making far fewer decisions than they were in 1984, but their approval ratings by political moderates stayed almost the same.

Supreme Court Approval Rating by Moderates

62% 71% 73% 70% 67% 70% 72% 70%

Number of Decisions

Years

Judicial Activism on the Roberts Court

Justice Kennedy voted with the majority in nearly all of the cases declaring laws unconstitutional. The majority of judicial activism comes from conservative judges.

During Souter's career he voted with the majority of the Court to overturn laws 40% of the time. He was considered a conservative appointee, but he gradually voted less with his fellow conservative judges as he grew more liberal.

Justices Sotomayor, Ginsburg, and Breyer voted with the majority at least 40% of the time, meaning that activism on the Court can be bipartisan.

Kennedy Roberts Scalia Thomas Alito Sotomayor Ginsburg Breyer Kagan Stevens Souter

■ Republican ■ Democratic ■ Retired Judges

SOURCE: Data from the United States Supreme Court and the General Social Survey, 1980-2010.

Investigate Further

Concept Why is judicial activism controversial? By declaring a law unconstitutional, judicial activism overturns legislation that is a product of the democratic process. It sets precedents

Connection Does judicial activism affect public confidence? Over two-thirds of American moderates continued to express confidence in the Court, even as it became less active and more conservative in

Cause Is judicial activism conservative or liberal? On the Roberts Court, the decisions that overturn laws can be bipartisan, but they are usually decided by the conservative justices

14.1
14.2
14.3
14.4
14.5
14.6

Can Government Do Anything Well?

Protecting the Due Process Rights of the Accused

By the mid-1960s, billboards screaming "Impeach Earl Warren" dotted the highways of the American South. Though most of the anger there was generated by Warren Court decisions declaring much of the South's elaborate system of segregation unconstitutional (especially *Brown v. Board of Education* [1954]), additional anger there and in much of the rest of the country was generated by a series of Court decisions broadening the protections for those suspected or accused of a felony crime. The Court, for example, ruled that police could not coerce confessions from the accused and that evidence gathered by illegal searches and seizures was not admissible in court. Police would henceforth be bound by the requirement of obtaining a search warrant from a judge. The Court ruled that the accused must be read their rights upon being taken into custody—the list of rights is widely known as the Miranda warnings—including the right to remain silent and the right to have legal counsel. The indigent were to be provided with an attorney if they could not hire one on their own.

"Law and order" advocates sharply criticized the Warren Court, saying that rulings expanding the rights of those suspected or accused of a crime were handcuffing the police and would undermine civic order. Police echoed these complaints, though they complied with the new order in most cases. Even dissenting members of the Court on the *Miranda* decision were outraged; Byron White wrote in his dissenting opinion that "the decision would return a killer, rapist, or other criminal to the streets to repeat his crime whenever it pleases him." The novelist Truman Capote (*In Cold Blood*) wondered, "Why do they seem to totally ignore the rights of the victims and the potential victims?" For his part, Richard Nixon made the decline of "law and order" the central theme of his winning presidential campaign in 1968, drawing away from the Democrats many working-class whites upset by urban riots and escalating violent crime rates in their cities. This drift of non–college-educated whites, as well as southern whites, to the Republican column would eventually reshape American politics.

Support for the claim that government has protected the due process rights of the accused without endangering the rights of others:

- The framers believed that due process rights were among the most important liberties they aimed to protect in the Constitution; due process protections are found in Article I and in five of the ten amendments that comprise the Bill of Rights.

- Police departments in every region of the United States had been regularly forcing confessions from the accused, violating the privacy of the homes of people suspected of crimes, and detaining people for long periods of time without access to an attorney.

- Police are not hampered by adhering to a set of standards that protect all persons suspected or accused of a felony crime; these standards protect the innocent as well as the guilty.

- Even in the rare case when a guilty party is set free, this is a better outcome than one in which an innocent is falsely punished for a crime he or she did not commit.

- While crime rates increased after the Warren Court rulings, this was a product of crowded and poverty-stricken ghettos in American cities. Crime rates eventually declined beginning in the 1990s as economic conditions improved for racial and ethnic minorities.

Rejection of the claim that government has protected the due process rights of the accused without endangering the rights of others:

- The framers intended due process protections in the Constitution to be confined to those suspected of and accused of a crime by federal authorities; the framers did not bind the states to these specific standards.

- The Warren Court wrongly used the 14th Amendment to restrict the states (and localities) in fighting crime.

- The Warren Court rulings paid no heed to the rights of victims of crimes.

- The due process rulings undermined law and order in the United States.
  - Police were hampered in crime-fighting.
  - Crime rates soared after the rights of the accused were expanded.

- Crime rates only declined later as first the Burger Court, then the Rehnquist Court, began to chip away at the Warren Court rulings, giving some powers back to the police.

WHAT DO YOU THINK?

What do you think about the past, present, and future role of the government in protecting the due process rights of those suspected or accused of a crime?

- Government should protect the due process rights of those suspected or accused of a crime as one of its top priorities.
- Government should protect the due process rights of those suspected or accused of a crime, though this should be balanced against other priorities like maintaining law and order.
- Government has gone much too far in protecting the due process rights of those suspected or accused of a crime, which has made the United States a much less safe society. Many of these rights are due to judicial over-interpretation and should be rolled back.

How would you defend your position to a fellow student? What would be your main line of argument? What evidence do you believe best supports your position? For help in developing your argument, please refer to the sources listed in the "Can Government Do Anything Well?" feature in Chapter 2 on p. 48.

Additional sources for this feature: Rick Perlstein, *Nixonland: The Rise of a President and the Fracturing of America* (New York: Scribner, 2008).

to provide a safety net for the poor, the unemployed, and the elderly; to protect workers' rights to form labor unions; and to regulate business in the public interest. The Supreme Court, however, filled with justices born in the nineteenth century and committed to the unshakable link between the Constitution and laissez-faire economic doctrine, was opposed to the national consensus and in 1935 and 1936 declared unconstitutional several laws that were part of the foundation of the New Deal. In an extraordinary turn of events, however, the Supreme Court reversed itself in 1937, finding the Social Security Act, the Labor Relations Act, and state minimum wage laws acceptable. It is not entirely clear why the so-called switch-in-time-that-saved-nine occurred, but surely Roosevelt's landslide reelection in 1936, the heightening of public hostility toward the Court, and Roosevelt's threat to expand and "pack the Court" all played a role. Whatever the reason, the Court abandoned its effort to prevent the government from playing a central role in the management of the economy and the regulation of business, and it came to defer to the political linkage branches of government on such issues by the end of the 1930s. In doing so, it brought another constitutional era to a close.

PERIOD 3: INDIVIDUAL RIGHTS AND LIBERTIES Three fundamental issues of American constitutional law—the relationship of the states to the nation, the nature and extent of private property rights, and the role of government in the management of the economy—were essentially settled by the time World War II broke out. From then until the mid- to late 1980s, the Court turned its main attention to the relationship between the individual and government.[51]

Later chapters tell the story on civil liberties and civil rights. For now, it is sufficient to point out that the Court, especially during the tenure of Chief Justice Earl Warren, decided cases that expanded protections for free expression and association, religious expression, fair trials, and civil rights for minorities. (For more about the role of the Supreme Court in protecting the due process rights of those accused of a crime, see the "Can Government Do Anything Well?" feature). In another series of cases dealing with the apportionment of electoral districts, the Court declared for political equality, based on the principle of "one person, one vote." In many of its landmark decisions, the Court applied the Bill of Rights to the states. Although the Court's record was not without blemishes during and after World War II—see the "Using the Framework" feature on *Korematsu v. United States* (1944)—it made significant strides in expanding the realm of individual freedom.

PERIOD 4: CONSERVATIVE RETRENCHMENT A new conservative majority emerged on the Supreme Court in the early 1990s, fashioned by the judicial nominations of Presidents Ronald Reagan and George H. W. Bush, and the patient efforts of

14.1
14.2
14.3
14.4
14.5
14.6

Using the FRAMEWORK

If the Supreme Court exists to protect individual rights, why did it allow the military to keep Japanese Americans in internment camps during World War II?

Background: On the advice of the U.S. military, President Franklin Roosevelt signed a series of executive orders in early 1942 authorizing the relocation of 112,000 Japanese Americans living on the West Coast, 70,000 of whom were citizens, into internment camps. In 1944, the Supreme Court in *Korematsu v. United States* upheld the legality of the exclusion and confinement orders. Constitutional scholar Edward Corwin described the internment and the Court's action as "the most drastic invasion of the rights of citizens of the United States by their own government" in modern American history. Taking a broad overview of structural, political linkage, and governmental factors that influenced the Supreme Court's decision will help explain this situation.

Government Action

The Supreme Court announces its decision allowing the internment of Japanese Americans in *Korematsu v. United States* (1944).

Government

President Franklin Roosevelt, troubled by the action, but fully aware of the feelings of the public and the wishes of military leaders in wartime, signed the necessary executive orders. ➡ The Supreme Court, unwilling to act against opinion of military leaders that Japanese Americans living on the West Coast posed a national security threat, supported the exclusion order in a case brought by Fred Korematsu.

Military authorities believed that Japanese Americans living on the West Coast posed a national security threat to the United States; asked the president to authorize curfews, relocation, and confinement. ➡ Congress passed supporting legislation making relocation and internment possible.

Political Linkage

Anti-Japanese attitudes were widespread among the public, particularly in the West Coast states, whose populations feared a Japanese invasion. ➡ Public opinion strongly supported the war against Japan and whatever military policies were necessary to win it. ➡ The media whipped up hysteria about a possible Japanese invasion.

Structure

Japanese immigrants to the United States in the late nineteenth and early twentieth centuries settled mainly in the West Coast states. ➡ The Japanese attack on Pearl Harbor on December 7, 1941, plunged the United States into World War II. ➡ The Constitution vests enormous powers in the president as commander-in-chief during wartime.

vociferously concerned about an overly activist judiciary, it was the most conservative members of the Court who most frequently voted to overturn congressional statutes during these years.[57] The Roberts Court seems to be even more aggressively moving in this direction. These trends in the use of judicial review suggest that the Court over time has become more willing to monitor the activities of other governmental entities.

The aggressive use of judicial review in recent years, as well as the fairly broad claims in several of its opinions that it and it alone has the final say on the meaning of the Constitution, has prompted talk among many legal scholars about "judicial imperialism" and "judicial supremacy."[58] Ironically, perhaps, it is now mainly liberal scholars who worry that the Court, dominated by a solid conservative majority, is too frequently reversing the actions of popularly elected bodies—Congress and state legislatures—a position once held mostly by conservatives.[59] Liberals worry that the Court will exercise judicial review on matters such as federal, state, and local governments' affirmative action programs as a violation of the "equal protection" clause of the Fourteenth Amendment.

REVERSING THE DECISIONS OF PAST SUPREME COURTS Despite the norm of precedent (*stare decisis*) that guides judicial decision making, the Warren, Burger, Rehnquist, and Roberts Courts overturned a number of previous Court decisions. The most dramatic instance was the reversal by the Warren Court of *Plessy v. Ferguson* (1896), which had endorsed legal segregation in the South, by *Brown v. Board of Education* (1954), which removed segregation's legal underpinnings. The Rehnquist Court overturned a number of previous Court decisions that had expanded the rights of criminal defendants and that had supported the extension of federal government power, reviewed earlier. When the Roberts Court upheld the federal Partial-Birth Abortion Ban Act, it reversed its own position on an identical Nebraska law it had declared unconstitutional in 2000. In *Citizens United v. Federal Election Commission* (2010), the Court overturned three of its own precedents, including cases from 1990, 2003, and 2007. In his dissent in this case, read from the bench as a sign of his deep displeasure with the majority, Justice John Paul Stevens lamented what he took to be the overly broad and ambitious reach of the majority, saying "essentially, five justices were unhappy with the limited nature of the case before us, so they changed the case to give themselves an opportunity to change the law." To be sure, the Court so far has been reluctant to overturn so-called superprecedents, but it can do so if it so chooses.

DECIDING "POLITICAL" ISSUES Critics claim that the Court is taking on too many matters that are best left to the elected branches of government. An oft-cited example is the Court's willingness to become increasingly involved in the process of drawing congressional electoral district boundaries in the states. Defenders of the Court argue that when such basic constitutional rights as equality of citizenship are at peril, the Court is obligated to protect these rights, no matter what other government bodies may choose to do. The Court's intervention in the 2000 presidential election generated widespread criticism for its meddling in politics, although its many defenders insist that the Court's decision in *Bush v. Gore* saved the nation from a constitutional crisis.

REMEDIES The most criticized aspect of judicial activism is the tendency for federal judges to impose broad remedies on states and localities. A **remedy** is what a court determines must be done to rectify a wrong. Since the 1960s, the Court has been more willing than in the past to impose remedies that require other governmental bodies to take action. Some of the most controversial of these remedies include court orders requiring states to build more prison space and mandating that school districts bus students to achieve racial balance. Such remedies often require that governments spend public funds for things they do not necessarily want to do. Critics claim that the federal judiciary's legitimate role is to prevent government actions that threaten rights and liberties, not to compel government to take action to meet some policy goal.

ORIGINAL INTENT Much of the debate about the role of the Court centers on the issue of the original intent of the framers.[60] Advocates of **original intent** believe that the Court must be guided by the original intent of the framers and the exact words

remedy
An action that a court determines must be taken to rectify a wrong done by government.

original intent
The doctrine that the courts must interpret the Constitution in ways consistent with the intentions of the framers rather than in light of contemporary conditions and needs.

14.1

14.2

14.3

14.4

14.5

14.6

strict construction

The doctrine that the provisions of the Constitution have a clear meaning and that judges must stick closely to this meaning when rendering decisions.

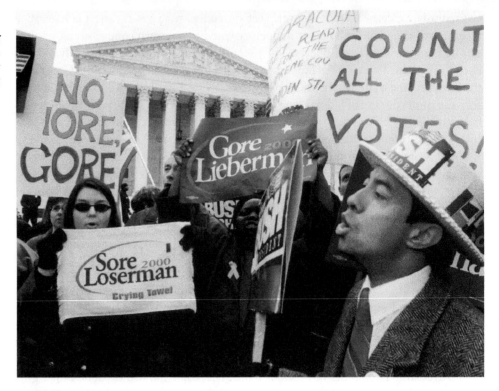

DECIDING THE 2000 PRESIDENTIAL ELECTION

The outcome of the closely fought 2000 presidential election was not finally decided until the Supreme Court stopped the recount in Florida, giving the state's electoral votes to George W. Bush. Here, passionate supporters of Bush and Al Gore demonstrate in front of the Supreme Court building while awaiting its decision. Do you think the Court's intervention was in the nation's best interests?

found in the Constitution, using **strict construction** as a way to stay close to its true meaning. Originalists believe that the expansion of rights that has occurred since the mid-1960s—such as the new right to privacy that formed the basis of the *Roe v. Wade* decision and rights for criminal defendants—is illegitimate, having no foundation in the framers' intentions or the text of the Constitution. Justices Antonin Scalia and Clarence Thomas are the strongest originalists on today's Court.

Critics of original intent and strict construction believe that the intentions of the framers are not only impossible to determine but also unduly constricting. As to the first assertion,[61] critics point out that original intent cannot be known, mostly because the only record of the debates at the constitutional convention are Madison's notes, which incorporated only about 10 percent of what was said, according to scholars. Moreover, it is not entirely clear how to define the framers. Is it all who attended the convention? All who signed the document? And what about the ratification conventions in the states? Do we include them among what we might call the Founders, knowing that there were several states that voted against the Constitution and many who dissented from the majority in those state conventions which voted to ratify? As to the second, critics suggest that sticking to a very narrow understanding of what the framers and Founders intended is unduly constricting in light of the great transformations that have occurred in American society in the years since ratification. What seems more reasonable, in this view, is to have jurists try to reconcile the fundamental principles of the Constitution with changing conditions in the United States and the democratic aspirations of the American people.[62]

Clearly, the modern Supreme Court is more activist than it was in the past; most justices today hold a more expansive view of the role of the Court in forging national policy than did their predecessors. And because the Court is likely to remain activist under Chief Justice John Roberts, the debate about judicial activism is likely to remain important in American politics.

Outside Influences on the Court

Assess the factors and players that influence Supreme Court decisions

T he courts make public policy and will continue to do so, but they do not do so in splendid isolation; many other governmental and political linkage actors and institutions influence what they do. Indeed, many scholars suggest that what the federal courts do reflects the prevailing politics and opinion of the day. Judges, after all, are nominated by presidents and confirmed by senators whose views are known to the public and who are elected by them. As new coalitions come to power in American politics, they make appointments to the federal courts that are in tune with the electoral coalition supporting the president and a majority of the Senate. A highly politicized judiciary, whose decisions become entangled in and engaged with the prevailing issues of the day and whose decisions reflect the views of the winners, in this view, is not to be lamented but celebrated as a reflection of democratic politics. Aggressive use of judicial review by the Supreme Court, in the view of several leading scholars, is simply a way for the new majority in the country to clear the way for its own policies.[63] Critics of this view would point out, however, that the courts might be out of touch with the mood of the country for long periods of time because federal judges serve life terms and are slow to be replaced (see Table 14.1).

Government and political influences on the Court come not only during times of partisan realignment and the appearance of new electoral coalitions but on an everyday basis. Here are important ways this happens.

☐ Governmental Influences

The Supreme Court must coexist with other governmental bodies that have their own powers, interests, constituencies, and visions of the public good. Recognizing this, the Court usually tries to stay somewhere near the boundaries of what is acceptable to other political actors. Being without "purse or sword," as Hamilton put it in *The Federalist*, No. 78, the Court cannot force others to obey its decisions. It can only hope that respect for the law and the Court will cause government officials to do what it has mandated in a decision. If the Court fails to gain voluntary compliance, it risks a serious erosion of its influence, for it then appears weak and ineffectual.

THE PRESIDENT The president, as chief executive, is supposed to carry out the Court's decrees. However, presidents who have opposed particular decisions or been lukewarm to them have dragged their feet, as President Eisenhower did on school desegregation after the Court's *Brown* decision in 1954.

TABLE 14.1 SUPREME COURT JUSTICES, 2012

Justice	Born	Sworn In	Appointed By
Chief Justice John Roberts	1955	2005	George W. Bush
Antonin Scalia	1936	1986	Ronald Reagan
Anthony M. Kennedy	1936	1988	Ronald Reagan
Clarence Thomas	1948	1991	George H. W. Bush
Ruth Bader Ginsburg	1933	1993	Bill Clinton
Stephen G. Breyer	1938	1994	Bill Clinton
Samuel A. Alito Jr.	1950	2006	George W. Bush
Sonia Sotomayor	1954	2009	Barack Obama
Elena Kagan	1960	2010	Barack Obama

The president has constitutional powers that give him some degree of influence over the Court. In addition to the Court's dependence on the president to carry out its decisions (when the parties to a dispute do not do it voluntarily), for example, the president influences the direction of the Court by his power to nominate judges when there are vacancies. He can also file suits through the Justice Department, argue cases before the Court, or introduce legislation to alter the Court's organization or jurisdiction (as Franklin Roosevelt did with his Court-packing proposal).

CONGRESS Although Congress can alter the size, organization, and appellate jurisdiction of the federal courts, it rarely does so.[64] The size of the Court, for example, has not changed since 1860. Nor, since that time, has Congress changed its jurisdiction as a reaction to its decisions, despite the introduction of many bills over the years to do so. In 2003, for example, a bill was introduced by Republicans in the House to take away the Court's jurisdiction to hear cases challenging the inclusion of the phrase "under God" in the Pledge of Allegiance. In 2004 a resolution was introduced in the House decrying the citation of the opinions of foreign and international courts and international law in U.S. judicial pronouncements—something Justice Kennedy had done in his majority opinion in a case overturning the state of Texas's antisodomy statute in *Lawrence v. Texas* (2003)—and threatening impeachment for any federal judge doing so. (Neither bill passed.) Congress is more likely to bring pressure to bear on the courts by being unsympathetic to pleas from the justices for pay increases or for a suitable budget for clerks or office space. The Senate also plays a role in the appointment process, as we have learned, and can convey its views to the Court during the course of confirmation hearings. Finally, Congress can change statutes or pass new laws that specifically challenge Supreme Court decisions, as it did when it legislated the Civil Rights Act of 1991 to make it easier for people to file employment discrimination suits.[65] All of this matters. There is evidence that throughout American history, the Supreme Court exercises a great deal of restraint in its judicial review of congressional actions when Congress is clearly hostile to the Court.[66]

☐ Political Linkage Influences

The Supreme Court is influenced not only by other government officials and institutions, but also by what we have termed political linkage factors.

GROUPS AND MOVEMENTS Interest groups, social movements, and the public not only influence the Court indirectly through the president and Congress but often do so directly. An important political tactic of interest groups and social movements is the **test case**. A test case is an action brought by a group that is designed to challenge the constitutionality of a law or an action by government. Groups wishing to force a court determination on an issue that is important to them will try to find a plaintiff on whose behalf they can bring a suit. When Thurgood Marshall was chief counsel for the NAACP in the 1950s, he spent a long time searching for the right plaintiff to bring a suit that would drive the last nail into the coffin of the *Plessy* separate-but-equal doctrine that was the legal basis for southern segregation. He settled on a fifth-grade girl named Linda Brown who was attending a segregated school in Topeka, Kansas. Several years later, he won the landmark case *Brown v. Board of Education of Topeka* (1954).

Many test cases take the form of **class-action suits**. These are suits brought by an individual on behalf of a class of people who are in a similar situation. A suit to prevent the dumping of toxic wastes in public waterways, for example, may be brought by an individual in the name of all the people living in the area who are adversely affected by the resulting pollution. Class-action suits were invited by the Warren Court's expansion of the definition of *standing* in the 1960s. The Rehnquist Court later narrowed the definition of *standing*, making it harder to bring class-action suits. As you learned above, the Roberts Court further limited the ability of similarly situated people to bring such suits.

Interest groups often get involved in suits brought by others by filing *amicus curiae* briefs.[67] Pro-abortion and anti-abortion groups submitted 78 such briefs in *Webster v. Reproductive Health Services* (1989), a decision that allowed states to regulate and limit abortion availability.[68] These briefs set out the group's position on the constitutional issues or talk about some of the most important consequences of deciding the case one way or the other. In a sense, this activity is a form of lobbying. Some scholars believe that the Court finds such briefs to be a way to keep track of public and group opinion on the issues before it, which is helpful to its work.[69]

Remember that business power in politics is substantial, ranging across a wide range of political activities, from campaign advertising to lobbying Congress and regulatory agencies in Washington. It is also large corporations within the business sector that have the means—money, subject matter specialists, outside lawyers, and in-house lawyers—to bring suits in state and federal courts against government attempts to regulate their activities. As we saw above, they have enjoyed considerable success before the Supreme Court.

LEADERS The Supreme Court does not usually stray very far from the opinions of public and private sector leaders when a consensus exists among them.[70] Social and economic leaders use their influence in a number of ways. As we learned in earlier chapters, their influence is substantial in the media, the interest group system, party politics, and elections at all levels. It follows, then, that elites play a substantial role in the thinking of presidents and the members of Congress as they, in turn, deal with the Court.

In addition to this powerful but indirect influence, the Court is also shaped by developments on issues and doctrine within the legal profession as these are expressed by bar associations, law journals, and law schools. To take but one example, Justice O'Connor, in her opinion in the 2004 Michigan Law School affirmative action case, justified her vote by pointing out that the use of race as one criterion among many in law school admission decisions was now widely accepted in the university and legal communities, as was the legitimacy of the goal of "diversity" in higher education.

PUBLIC OPINION We might think that the Supreme Court is immune from public opinion, because the justices are appointed for life and do not need to face the electorate. There is reason to believe, however, that what the Court does and what the public wants—at least as expressed in public opinion polls—are highly correlated; a substantial body of research shows that Court rulings and public opinion are consistent with one another about two-thirds of the time, about the same level of consistency with the public as the president and Congress.[71] There does not seem to be a yawning gap, then, between the public and the Supreme Court. We cannot say for sure, however, that public opinion causes the Court to act in particular ways when making decisions.[72] Indeed, it is just as likely that third factors—such as major events, political developments, and cultural changes conveyed in the media—shape the perceptions of judges and citizens alike. Nevertheless, the close association between Court decisions and public opinion is good news in a society that aspires to be democratic.

Having said that, it also is important to point out that there have been times during our history when the Court was so influenced by other political actors that it set aside, if only for a short while, its responsibility to protect the rights and liberties of all citizens. Although the Court has played an important role in advancing rights and liberties in the United States, it has not been entirely immune from pressure brought to bear by the public, other government officials, and private sector leaders to punish suspect groups. For example, the Court went along with local, state, and federal actions to punish dissident voices during the McCarthy era's anti-Communist hysteria of the 1950s. It also approved the forced relocation and internment of Japanese Americans during World War II, as discussed earlier in the "Using the Framework" feature.

14.1
14.2
14.3
14.4
14.5
14.6

CIVIL RIGHTS CHAMPION

Social movements often use test cases to challenge the constitutionality of laws and government actions. After a long search, NAACP attorney Thurgood Marshall—shown here in front of the Supreme Court, where he would later sit as a justice—selected Linda Brown, a fifth-grader from Topeka, Kansas, who was not permitted to attend the school closest to her house because it was reserved for whites, as the principal plaintiff in *Brown v. Board of Education of Topeka*, the historic case that successfully challenged school segregation. How else has the Court been a vehicle for social change?

14.1
14.2
14.3
14.4
14.5
14.6

Using the DEMOCRACY STANDARD

Does the Supreme Court enhance American democracy?

The framers designed the Supreme Court as an institution that would serve as a check on the other branches, most especially on Congress, the only semi-democratic institution of the lot in their original design. They also structured the Court to be the least democratic of the branches in the new federal government, with justices appointed rather than elected and serving for life rather than for a fixed term of office. The framers wanted the judiciary to function as a referee who stands above the fray, preserving the rules, overseeing the orderly changing of some rules when the situation demands it, protecting minorities against the potentially tyrannical behavior of the majority, and protecting individuals in the exercise of their constitutionally guaranteed rights. From the perspective of democratic theory, however, it is unacceptable that one of the three main branches of the federal government in the United States—with the power to override the decisions of presidents, Congress, and state legislatures and to make binding decisions for the nation as a whole—is staffed with members who never face the judgment of the voters.

Although designed as an antimajoritarian institution, the Supreme Court is much more responsive to majoritarian political actors and to the public than the framers ever imagined would be the case. For example, we have seen that the Supreme Court does not often stray very far from what is acceptable to the president and Congress or to private elites; we have seen, also, that the Court acts consistently with public opinion about as often as Congress and the president do. Moreover, the chapters on civil rights and civil liberties show that the Court plays an important and positive role in the protection of minority rights and liberties in the United States, although it has often been inconsistent and slow in doing so.

The overall view suggests that, whatever the intention of the framers, the Court has not acted consistently as an antimajoritarian institution, though it has sometimes done so. In fact, it has often protected popular democracy.

Review the Chapter

The Foundations of Judicial Power

14.1 Trace the evolution of judicial power in the United States, p. 454

Despite the fact that Article III of the Constitution is quite vague about the powers and responsibilities of the U.S. Supreme Court, the Court has fashioned a powerful position for itself in American politics, coequal with the executive and legislative branches.

Under Justice John Marshall in the early nineteenth century, the Court first claimed its right to rule on the constitutionality of state and federal legislation. The Court exercised its power of judicial review in the nineteenth century primarily over state actions, with particular regard to preventing regulation of business.

The Court became much more aggressive in overturning federal legislation during the New Deal and vigorously used the Fourteenth Amendment's due process and equal protection clauses starting in the 1960s to overrule state practices that restricted civil liberties and civil rights.

The Rehnquist and Roberts Courts regularly overruled Congress and the president in the 1990s and 2000s.

The U.S. Court System: Organization and Jurisdiction

14.2 Outline the organization of the U.S. court system, p. 457

The federal court system is made up of three parts. At the bottom are 94 federal district courts, in which most cases originate. In the middle are 13 appeals courts. At the top is the Supreme Court, with both original and appellate jurisdiction. Only a relative handful of the thousands of cases filed in the federal district courts make it to the Supreme Court.

Appointment to the Federal Bench

14.3 Describe the background of appointees to the federal bench and the process by which they are appointed, p. 462

Until quite recently, the federal judiciary was dominated by white Protestant men from top law firms and law schools or government service.

Today, many more women and racial and ethnic minorities serve in the federal judiciary, with two women, one African American, and one Hispanic woman on the Supreme Court. A majority on today's high court is Catholic.

The appointment process is highly political and increasingly contentious, with presidents trying to leave their mark in the Courts, the political parties bringing ideological views to the process, and interest and advocacy groups fully engaged.

The Supreme Court in Action

14.4 Outline how the Supreme Court decides cases, p. 465

The Supreme Court operates on the basis of several widely shared norms: secrecy, seniority, and adherence to precedent. The Court controls its agenda by granting or not granting a writ of certiorari to cases filed with it.

Cases before the Court wend their way through the process in the following way: submission of briefs, oral argument, initial consideration in conference, opinion writing, and final conference consideration by the justices.

Published opinions serve as precedents for other federal courts and future Supreme Court decisions.

The Supreme Court as a National Policymaker

14.5 Evaluate the Supreme Court as a national policymaker, p. 468

The Supreme Court is a national policymaker of considerable importance. Its rulings settle disputes between political actors on critical matters and help define the meaning of the Constitution for others in the political system.

The Court often serves as the referee of the democratic process and the rights of minorities, although it has sometimes failed to do this.

Outside Influences on the Court

14.6 Assess the factors and players that influence Supreme Court decisions, p. 479

The decisions of the Court are influenced not only by the judicial philosophies of the justices themselves, but also by the actions and preferences of other political actors such as the president and Congress, as well as by interest groups and public and elite opinion.

Increasingly the ideological predispositions of the justices are determinative. The Supreme Court is now dominated by a conservative majority.

Learn the Terms

judicial review, p. 454
original jurisdiction, p. 456
constitutional courts, p. 458
legislative courts, p. 458
grand juries, p. 459
petit (trial) juries, p. 459
circuit courts, p. 459
appellate courts, p. 460
briefs, p. 460
opinion, p. 460
precedents, p. 460

stare decisis, p. 460
senatorial courtesy, p. 463
standing, p. 464
executive privilege, p. 464
separate but equal doctrine, p. 465
superprecedents, p. 465
plaintiff, p. 466
in forma pauperis, p. 466
writ of certiorari, p. 466
rule of four, p. 466
amicus curiae, p. 467

opinion of the Court, p. 468
concurring opinion, p. 468
dissenting opinion, p. 468
laissez-faire, p. 469
judicial activism, p. 476
remedy, p. 477
original intent, p. 477
strict construction, p. 478
test case, p. 480
class-action suit, p. 480

Test Yourself

Answer key begins on page T-1.

14.1 Trace the evolution of judicial power in the United States

1. From 1803 to 2007 judicial review of a congressional act was only used about:

   a. 2 times
   b. 150 times
   c. 230 times
   d. 1,100 times
   e. 2,000 times

14.2 Outline the organization of the U.S. court system

2. Which of these is NOT a subject matter solely the province of the federal courts?

   a. Maritime issues
   b. The Constitution
   c. Disputes between the states
   d. Disputes between citizens
   e. Federal statutes and treaties

14.3 Describe the background of appointees to the federal bench and the process by which they are appointed

3. During President Barack Obama's first year in office he nominated 12 people for federal court positions, of which this number were women and/or minorities:

   a. 3
   b. 4
   c. 9
   d. 11
   e. 12

14.4 Outline how the Supreme Court decides cases

4. Which of the following are the norms, or the clearly understood rules of behavior, that shape how the Court does things?

   a. Seniority, standing, and secrecy
   b. Precedent, record, and standing
   c. Secrecy, precedent, and record
   d. Secrecy, seniority, and precedent
   e. Standing, merit, and seniority

14.5 Evaluate the Supreme Court as a national policymaker

5. The most criticized aspect of judicial activism is the tendency for federal judges to:

   a. Impose remedies
   b. Decide political issues
   c. Reverse past Supreme Court decisions
   d. Impose judicial review
   e. Use strict construction

14.6 Assess the factors and players that influence Supreme Court decisions

6. An action brought by a group that is designed to challenge the constitutionality of a law or an action by government is called a:

   a. Class-action suit
   b. Public opinion ruling
   c. Leader designation
   d. Constitution test
   e. Test case

Explore Further

INTERNET SOURCES

Federal Courts Home Page **www.uscourts.gov**
Information and statistics about the activities of U.S. district courts, circuit courts of appeal, and the Supreme Court.

Legal Information Institute, Cornell University Law School **www.law.cornell.edu**
The gateway to a world of information and links to associated law and court sites on the Web. Among its sections you will find the following: the Supreme Court calendar; biographies and opinions of the justices; directories of law firms, law schools, and legal associations; constitutions and codes, including U.S. statutes, regulations, and judicial rules of procedure; and court opinions, including those of state supreme courts.

The Oyez Project **www.oyez.org/oyez/frontpage**
A website that archives multimedia material concerning the U.S. Supreme Court (including recordings of oral arguments).

Certiorari Grants at Duke Law **www.law.duke.edu/publiclaw/ supremecourtonline/certgrants/**
A website describing all recent cases that were granted a writ of certiorari and links to opinions for those cases that have been decided.

C-SPAN Judicial and Legal Resources **http://www.c-span.org/ Resources/Supreme-Court-Judiciary**
A treasure trove of links to sites having to do with the law and the courts.

Senate Judiciary Committee **judiciary.senate.gov/nominations/ judicial.cfm**
Track the status of federal judicial nominations and confirmations.

Scotus Blog **www.scotusblog.com**
A blog on the inner workings of the Supreme Court administered by one of the nation's most experienced Supreme Court attorneys.

The Supreme Court **www.supremecourtus.gov/**
The official website of the Supreme Court, with a wealth of information about the Court's docket and decisions.

SUGGESTIONS FOR FURTHER READING

Barnett, Randy E. *Restoring the Lost Constitution: The Presumption of Liberty.* Princeton, NJ: Princeton University Press, 2003.
A conservative case for understanding the Constitution as a legal framework for the protection of individual rights.

Breyer, Stephen. *Active Liberty: Interpreting Our Democratic Constitution.* New York: Knopf, 2005.
The Justice's attempt to define a coherent doctrine of a "Living Constitution."

Greenburg, Jan Crawford. *Supreme Conflict: The Inside Story of the Struggle for Control of the United States Supreme Court.* New York: Penguin, 2007.
A fascinating account of the politics behind the conservative transformation of the Supreme Court.

McCloskey, Robert G. *The American Supreme Court,* 5th ed. Chicago: University of Chicago Press, 2010.
First published 45 years ago, and revised for the 2005 and 2010 editions by noted legal scholar Sanford Levinson, this remains the classic interpretation of the Supreme Court's role in shaping the meaning of the Constitution.

Schwartz, Bernard. *Decision: How the Supreme Court Decides Cases.* New York: Oxford University Press, 2005.
A revealing behind-the-scenes look at how the Supreme Court considers and decides the cases before it.

Steven, John Paul. *Five Chiefs: A Supreme Court Memoir.* New York: Little Brown, 2011.
An unusually candid and insightful look inside the Supreme Court by one of its most influential justices.

Wittington, Keith E. *Political Foundations of Judicial Supremacy: The Presidency, the Supreme Court, and Constitutional Leadership in U.S. History.* Princeton, NJ: Princeton University Press, 2007.
A provocative book that suggests that the Supreme Court has not so much taken power over the course of U.S. history but has had power thrust upon it by presidents and senators as a way to advance their own political interests and agendas.

15

Civil Liberties: The Struggle for Freedom

CAMPUS SPEECH CODES AND FREE SPEECH

- Stanford University enacted a speech code in 1990 that prohibits "personal vilification of students on the basis of their sex, race, color, handicap, religion, sexual orientation, or national and ethnic origin." The code was strongly opposed by Stanford's eminent constitutional scholar Gerald Gunther, who claimed that hate speech should not be banned but vigorously rejected "with more speech, with better speech, with repudiation and contempt."

- Campus newspapers across the nation in 2001 refused to accept a paid advertisement from conservative activist David Horowitz in which he opposed reparations for slavery. Many of the handful of newspapers that ran the ad "Ten Reasons Why Reparations for Slavery Is a Bad Idea—and Racist Too" faced angry demonstrations, vandalism of their offices, and theft of the papers containing the offending ads.

- During a class at the University of Michigan, a student argued that homosexuality could be treated with psychotherapy. He was accused of violating a campus rule against victimizing people on the basis of their sexual orientation.

- At Southern Methodist University, a student was sentenced to work for 30 hours with minority organizations because, among other things, he sang "We Shall Overcome" in a sarcastic manner.[1]

- At Washington State University in 2005, a group of student protestors disrupted the performance of a play that poked fun at "political correctness" and that purposely offended

15.1	15.2	15.3	15.4
Identify civil liberties protections in the Constitution, p. 490	Trace the evolution of civil liberties in the nineteenth century, p. 490	Outline the liberties guaranteed by the Bill of Rights and their gradual application to the states by the Supreme Court, p. 494	Analyze how concerns about terrorism may affect civil liberties, p. 516

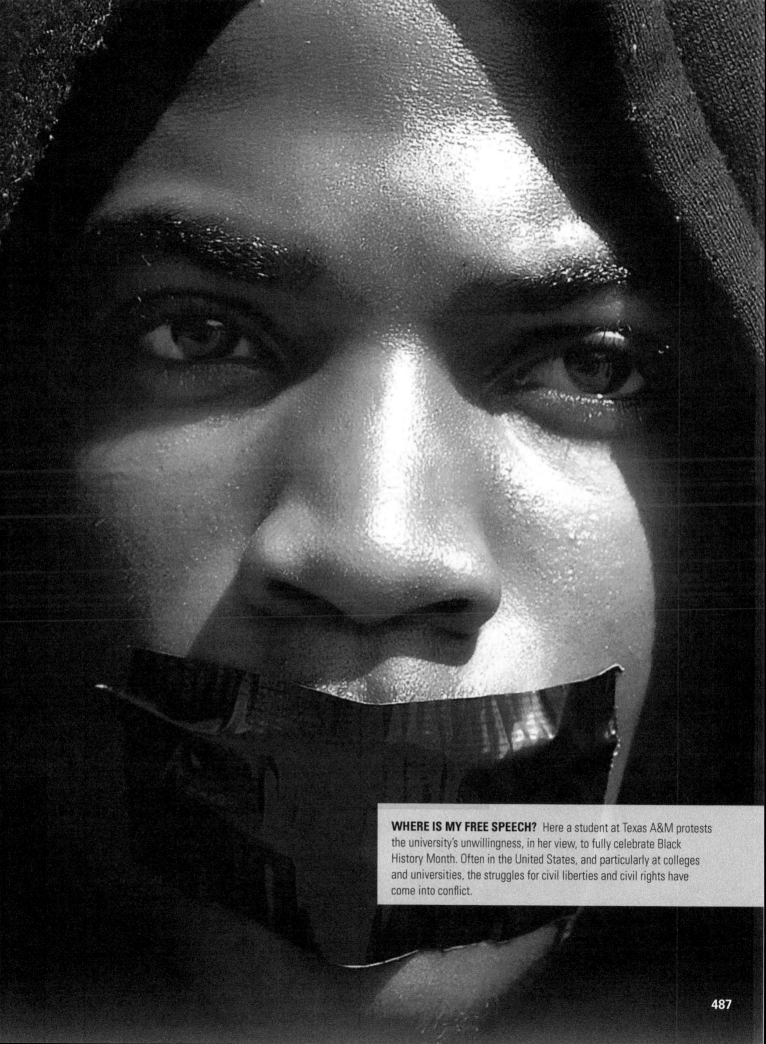

WHERE IS MY FREE SPEECH? Here a student at Texas A&M protests the university's unwillingness, in her view, to fully celebrate Black History Month. Often in the United States, and particularly at colleges and universities, the struggles for civil liberties and civil rights have come into conflict.

MyPoliSciLab Video Series

Watch on MyPoliSciLab

The Big Picture Did you know that before the 20th century, someone could be arrested by their state government for protesting on a street corner? Author Edward S. Greenberg discusses the significance of the fourteenth amendment, which required states to enforce the Bill of Rights and the civil liberties it protects.

The Basics What are civil liberties and where do they come from? In this video, you will learn about our First Amendment guarantees and about protections the Bill of Rights provides those accused of crimes. In the process, you'll discover how our liberties have changed over time to reflect our changing values and needs.

In Context Uncover the importance of civil liberties in a changing American society. University of Massachusetts at Boston political scientist Maurice T. Cunningham identifies the origins of our civil liberties and evaluates the clash between national security and civil liberties in a post 9/11 age.

Think Like a Political Scientist What are some of the challenges facing political scientists in regards to civil liberties? In this video, University of Massachusetts at Boston political scientist Maurice T. Cunningham raises some of the thought provoking questions regarding civil liberties that have arisen during the last decade.

In the Real World The American legal system and the American people have both struggled over whether the death penalty should be imposed in this country. In this segment, we'll hear what citizens have to say about the death penalty.

So What? Which civil liberty do you most value? Using the example of freedom of speech in the aftermath of 9/11, author Edward S. Greenberg admires the degree to which the government still values a person's right to say whatever he wants, wherever he wants.

gays, Jews, Christians, Muslims, and others. Responding to critics, the university's president suggested that the disruptive students had been simply expressing their First Amendment rights and were doing so in a responsible fashion.

- At Brandeis University in 2007, a professor was formally admonished for racial harassment for analyzing for his students the origin of the derogatory term "wetback."

- At the University of Florida, the institution's 2011 "Student Rights and Responsibilities" policy says that disciplinary actions can be taken against "organizations or individuals who upset the delicate balance of communal living . . ." without specifying what actions or speech might be subject to review.

- In 2011, the University of Southern California's policy on "Advertising, Promotion, and Literature Distribution" states that materials distributed by students may not have "derogatory language or material that is aimed at harming a specific person or an organization's reputation." Elsewhere USC says it is committed to vigorously preserving First Amendment rights.

The college campus has become one of the most visible battlegrounds in the continuing struggle over the meaning of free speech in the United States, as traditional notions of liberty come into conflict with newer and equally valued notions of equal citizenship (or civil rights, to be discussed in the next chapter). Campus speech codes, today more likely to be called "harassment" or "diversity" policies, have been instituted at many colleges and universities across the country in an effort to rid campuses of speech that may offend women and members of various minority groups. Many civil libertarians, like Gerald Gunther, although protective of the rights of women and minority students to have a supportive learning environment, have fought hard against such codes in the service, they say, of free speech and a free society. While state and lower federal courts generally have sided with the civil libertarians—in 1995, the California Supreme Court agreed with Gunther's position, saying that the Stanford code unconstitutionally restricts free speech rights under the First Amendment to the Constitution[2] —colleges and universities have continued to revise and issue rules to reduce gender, sexual orientation, and minority harassment on campus and to provide a supportive environment for these students. These well-intentioned efforts, however, from the civil libertarians' point of view, puts free speech at risk. Getting the balance right between liberties and equal rights is difficult, to say the least. The Supreme Court has not as yet taken a case that would settle the constitutional validity of such codes and rules and offer guidelines on where the proper balance might lie between the two.

Thinking Critically About This Chapter

This chapter is about civil liberties in the United States, with special attention on how historical developments, politics, and government policies have influenced the degree to which Americans can and do exercise their freedoms.

Using the Framework

You will see in this chapter how structural, political linkage, and governmental factors influence the meaning and practice of civic freedoms. Although the decisions of the Supreme Court are particularly important in determining the status of civil liberties at any particular moment in American history, you will learn how they are also the product of influences from a wide range of actors, institutions, and social processes.

Using the Democracy Standard

You will see in this chapter how the expansion of the enjoyment of civil liberties in the United States has been a product of the struggle for democracy and how civil liberties are fundamental to the democratic process itself.

civil liberties

Freedoms found primarily in the Bill of Rights, the enjoyment of which are protected from government interference.

habeas corpus

The legal doctrine that a person who is arrested must have a timely hearing before a judge.

bill of attainder

A governmental decree that a person is guilty of a crime that carries the death penalty, rendered without benefit of a trial.

ex post facto law

A law that retroactively declares some action illegal.

economic liberty

The right to own and use property free from unreasonable government interference.

Civil Liberties in the Constitution

15.1 Identify civil liberties protections in the Constitution

he framers were particularly concerned about establishing a society in which liberty might flourish. While government was necessary to protect liberty from the threat of anarchy, the framers believed that government might threaten liberty if it became too powerful. **Civil liberties** are freedoms protected by constitutional provisions, laws, and practices from certain types of government interference. As embodied in the Bill of Rights, civil liberties are protected by prohibitions against government actions that threaten the enjoyment of freedom. These liberties fall into two major groups: first, those associated with freedoms of expression, belief, and association; and second, those involving protections for people accused of committing a crime.

In the Preamble to the Constitution, the framers wrote that they aimed to "secure the Blessings of Liberty to ourselves and our Posterity." But in the original Constitution, they protected few liberties from the national government they were creating and almost none from state governments. To safeguard against tyranny, the framers preferred to give the national government little power with which to attack individual liberties. Rather than listing specific prohibitions against certain kinds of actions, then, they believed that a republican constitutional design that fragmented government power and that included separation of powers, checks and balances, and federalism would best protect liberty. Still, the framers singled out certain freedoms as too crucial to be left unmentioned. For example, the Constitution prohibits Congress and the states from suspending the writ of **habeas corpus**, except when public safety demands it because of rebellion or invasion, and from passing **bills of attainder** or **ex post facto laws** (see Table 15.1 for an enumeration).

Many citizens found the proposed Constitution too stingy in its listing of liberties, so that the Federalists were led to promise a "bill of rights" as a condition for passing the Constitution. The Bill of Rights was passed by the 1st Congress in 1789 and was ratified by the required number of states by 1791. Passage of the Bill of Rights made the Constitution more democratic by specifying protections of political liberty and by guaranteeing a context of free political expression that makes popular sovereignty possible.

Reading the Constitution and its amendments, however, reveals how few of our most cherished liberties are to be found in this document. Decisions by government officials and changes brought about by political leaders, interest groups, social movements, and individuals remade the Constitution in the long run; hence many of the freedoms we expect today are not specifically mentioned there. Some extensions of protected liberties were introduced by judges and other officials. Others have evolved as the culture has grown to accept novel and even once-threatening ideas. Still other liberties have secured a place in the Republic through partisan and ideological combat. The key to understanding civil liberties in the United States, then, is to follow their evolution over the course of our nation's history.

Rights and Liberties in the Nineteenth Century

15.2 Trace the evolution of civil liberties in the nineteenth century

uring the nineteenth century, the range of protected civil liberties in the United States was somewhat different from their range today. Especially noteworthy were the special place of **economic liberty** and the understanding that the Bill of Rights did not apply to state governments.

TABLE 15.1 CIVIL LIBERTIES IN THE U.S. CONSTITUTION

The exact meaning and extent of civil liberties in the Constitution are matters of debate, but here are some freedoms spelled out in the text of the Constitution and its amendments, or clarified by early court decisions.

Constitution

Article I, Section 9

Congress may not suspend habeas corpus.

Congress may not pass bills of attainder or ex post facto laws.

Article I, Section 10

States may not pass bills of attainder or ex post facto laws.

States may not impair obligation of contracts.

Article III, Section 2

Criminal trials in national courts must be jury trials in the state in which the defendant is alleged to have committed the crime.

Article III, Section 3

No one may be convicted of treason unless there is a confession in open court or testimony of two witnesses to the same overt act.

Article IV, Section 2

Citizens of each state are entitled to all privileges and immunities of citizens in the several states.

The Bill of Rights

First Amendment

Congress may not make any law with respect to the establishment of religion.

Congress may not abridge the free exercise of religion.

Congress may not abridge freedom of speech or of the press.

Congress may not abridge the right to assemble or to petition the government.

Second Amendment

Congress may not infringe the right to keep and bear arms.

Third Amendment

Congress may not station soldiers in houses against the owner's will, except in times of war.

Fourth Amendment

Citizens are to be free from unreasonable searches and seizures.

Federal courts may issue search warrants based only on probable cause and specifically describing the objects of search.

Fifth Amendment

Citizens are protected against double jeopardy (being prosecuted more than once for the same crime) and self-incrimination.

Citizens are guaranteed against deprivation of life, liberty, or property without due process of law.

Citizens are guaranteed just compensation for public use of their private property.

Sixth Amendment

Citizens have the right to a speedy and public trial before an impartial jury.

Citizens have the right to face their accuser and to cross-examine witnesses.

Eighth Amendment

Excessive bail and fines are prohibited.

Cruel and unusual punishments are prohibited.

☐ Economic Liberty in the Early Republic

Liberty may be understood as protection against government interference in certain kinds of private activities. Among the few such protections mentioned in the original Constitution was one that concerned the use and enjoyment of private property. This is hardly surprising; recall that the constitutional convention was convened, in part, because many of the new nation's leading citizens by the mid-1780s were growing ever more alarmed by threats to their holdings represented by passage of stay laws and the production of cheap paper money in several states, and insurrections like Shays' Rebellion. Property rights protections are stated most directly in the Constitution in the language of contracts (i.e., the freedom to enter into binding private agreements about many things, including the use of one's property): "No State shall . . . pass any . . . Law impairing the Obligation of Contracts" (Article I,

Section 10).[3] The framers protected private property in a number of other constitutional provisions as well, including provisions that created a system for recognizing intellectual property (patents and copyrights) and for safeguarding property in the form of slaves by requiring Americans to return runaway slaves to their owners. The **full faith and credit** clause (Article IV, Section 1), moreover, obligated each state to recognize contracts and other legal obligations entered into by its citizens with citizens or legal bodies in other states. The so-called takings clause of the Fifth Amendment—ratified in 1791 with other amendments that constitute the Bill of Rights—declares that "private property [shall not] be taken for public use, without just compensation." The importance of property rights as a fundamental liberty in the body of the Constitution and its Amendments was reinforced by more than a century of judicial interpretation.[4]

THE MARSHALL COURT (1801–1835) Although the Supreme Court ruled (in *Barron v. Baltimore*, 1833) that the Bill of Rights did not apply to the states, it ruled on several occasions that the **contract clause** in the Constitution directly applied against unwarranted state action. In the hands of Chief Justice John Marshall, the clause became an important defense of property rights against interference by the states. In *Fletcher v. Peck* (1810), for example, the Marshall Court upheld a sale of public land, even though almost all of the legislators who had voted for the land sale had been bribed by the prospective purchasers. Chief Justice Marshall wrote in his majority opinion that even a fraudulent sale created a contract among private individuals that the state could not void. In *Dartmouth College v. Woodward* (1819), Marshall argued in his majority opinion that New Hampshire could not modify the charter of Dartmouth College because the original charter constituted a binding contract, the terms of which could not be changed without impairing the obligations in the original contract. The framers' attempt to protect the contractual agreements of private parties ballooned in the hands of the Marshall Court to bar virtually any and all changes by the states of established property relations.[5] This expansion of property rights protections under the contract clause made it very difficult for states to regulate business activities because any such regulation could be interpreted as interfering with those binding contracts by which businesses were established and operated.

HISTORIC RULING

An important Supreme Court ruling solidifying property rights under the Constitution involved Dartmouth College, shown here in a drawing from 1819, the same year *Dartmouth College v. Woodward* was decided. Why did the framers and the Supreme Court place such importance on property rights?

SLAVES BRINGING IN THE COTTON CROP

Prior to passage of the Thirteenth and Fourteenth Amendments after the Civil War, African American slaves were considered to be nothing more or less than the private property of their owners. How did the framers make the Constitution amenable to the practice of slavery?

due process clause
The section of the Fourteenth Amendment that prohibits states from depriving anyone of life, liberty, or property "without due process of law," a guarantee against arbitrary or unfair government action.

THE TANEY COURT (1836–1864) Under the leadership of Chief Justice Roger Taney, the Court began to make a distinction between private property used in ways that encouraged economic growth and private property used for simple enjoyment. In landmark cases, the Taney Court issued rulings favoring the former when the two concepts of property conflicted.[6] In *Charles River Bridge v. Warren Bridge* (1837), investors who had secured a contract from the Massachusetts legislature for the construction of the Charles River Bridge charged that the state had violated its contract by chartering the construction of a competing bridge less than a decade later. In the majority opinion, Chief Justice Taney argued that the original charter for the Charles River Bridge did not imply a monopoly that closed off competitors. He ruled that Massachusetts could charter the rival Warren Bridge because the states should encourage economic competition and technological advances. It did not matter that the second bridge would result in financial losses for stockholders in the Charles River Bridge. Taney argued that the "creative destruction" of established but idle property in a dynamic market economy is the price of economic and social progress.

The Court's defense of property rights was especially and tragically strong when it came to slavery. Until the Civil War, courts in the North and the South consistently upheld the right of slaveholders to recapture fugitive slaves. In his opinion in *Dred Scott v. Sandford* (1857)—a case that helped bring on the Civil War because it declared that Congress could not regulate slavery in any way, voiding the "Missouri Compromise" that had balanced the interests of free states and slave states as the country expanded westward—Chief Justice Taney declared that slaves who traveled to free states (nonslave) with their masters could not sue for their freedom because that would mean depriving slave owners of their property. Slaves, in this view, like land and tools, were nothing more nor less than private property belonging to their owners, not people in a legal sense.

☐ Economic Liberty After the Civil War

The Fourteenth Amendment, passed after the Civil War, was designed to guarantee the citizenship rights of the newly freed slaves. It included a clause—the **due process clause**—stating that no state "may deprive a person of life, liberty, or property, without due process of law." Strangely, the Supreme Court in the late

selective incorporation
The gradual and piecemeal spread of the protections of the Bill of Rights to the states by the U.S. Supreme Court.

nineteenth century began to interpret this clause as a protection for businesses against the regulatory efforts of the national government and the states. In the view of the Court in *Santa Clara County v. Southern Pacific Railroad* (1886), corporations were "persons" in the eyes of the law and were subject to the same protections provided by the Fourteenth Amendment for any other "persons" in the United States.

The Court's most famous decision in this regard was *Lochner v. New York* (1905). Lochner ran a bakery in Utica, New York. He was convicted of requiring an employee to work more than 60 hours per week, contrary to a New York State maximum-hours statute. But Justice Rufus Peckham wrote for a 5–4 Supreme Court majority that the right of employer and employee to negotiate hours of work was part of the "liberty" of which, under the Fourteenth Amendment, no person could be deprived without due process of law. In other words, New York State had no right to regulate the hours of labor.

The nineteenth century was an era in which the rights of property were expanded, refined, and altered to become consistent with an emerging, dynamic industrial economy. The twentieth century would bring new approaches to property rights and to political liberties in general. These new approaches would be triggered by structural transformations in the economy and culture, the efforts of new political groups and movements, and the actions of government officials, all of which we will examine in greater detail.

Nationalization of the Bill of Rights

    Outline the liberties guaranteed by the Bill of Rights and their gradual application to the states by the Supreme Court

Explore on
MyPoliSciLab
Simulation
You Are a Police Officer

Americans rightly understand the Bill of Rights to be a foundation of American freedom. Until the twentieth century, however, the protections of the Bill of Rights did not apply to the states, only to the national government. The Supreme Court only gradually applied the Bill of Rights to the states through a process known as **selective incorporation**.[7]

The framers were worried more about national government intrusions on individual freedom than about state government intrusions. Most of the states, after all, had bills of rights in their own constitutions, and, being closer to the people, state governments would be less likely to intrude on the people's freedom, or so the framers believed. This reading of the Bill of Rights as a prohibition of certain actions by the national government seems explicit in the language of many of the first 10 amendments. The first, for instance, starts with the words "*Congress shall make no law. . . .*" This understanding of the Bill of Rights as a set of prohibitions against certain actions by the national government and not the states was confirmed by Chief Justice John Marshall in *Barron v. Baltimore* (1833). As he put it:

> The Constitution was ordained and established by the people of the United States for themselves, for their own government, and not for the government of the individual states.

After the Civil War, the majority in Congress very clearly wanted to change the reach of the Bill of Rights, extending it to the states. It did so by approving the Fourteenth Amendment in 1866, which was ratified by the states by 1868. After declaring that "all persons born or naturalized in the United States are citizens of both the United States and the states in which they reside," the Amendment's three key clauses specify that the states cannot violate the rights and liberties of the people living in them:

- The **privileges and immunities clause** specifies that no *state* "shall make or enforce any law which shall abridge the privileges or immunities of citizens of the United States."

- The due process clause specifies that no *state* shall "deprive any person of life, liberty, or property, without due process of law."

- The **equal protection clause** requires states to provide equal treatment for all persons within their boundaries.

Although Congress wrote the Fourteenth Amendment to guarantee that states would protect all of U.S. citizens' rights and liberties, including those found in the Bill of Rights, the Supreme Court was very slow in **nationalizing** or **incorporating** the Bill of Rights, making it binding on the state governments. Indeed, the Supreme Court has not yet fully incorporated or nationalized the Bill of Rights. Rather, it has practiced selective incorporation, only slowly adding, step by step, even traditional civil liberties to the constitutional obligations of the states. Several Amendments have not been incorporated, including the Third on quartering troops, the Fifth on a right to a grand jury hearing, the Seventh on a right to a jury trial in civil suits, and the Eighth's prohibition against excessive bail and fines.

The Second Amendment's right of gun ownership was declared a fundamental individual right by the Court in 2008 in *District of Columbia v. Heller* and was incorporated—that is, made incumbent upon the states to not unreasonably restrict the enjoyment of this right—soon after in *McDonald v. Chicago* (2010). The prevailing view in the courts until then had been that the wording of the Second Amendment protects a collective right to form militias rather than an individual right to have guns. Gun advocates such as the National Rifle Association and libertarian organizations like the Cato Institute, on the other hand, had long held that the Amendment is not a collective right but a fundamental individual right, which the Court affirmed in *Heller*. Strangely perhaps, a handful of influential liberal constitutional scholars such as Sanford Levinson, Akhil Reed Amar, and Lawrence Tribe had come around to this "individual rights" understanding of the Second Amendment as well.[8] The issue of gun rights is not entirely settled, however; just how much state and local regulation of gun ownership the Court will allow remains an open question.

How does the Supreme Court decide whether to incorporate some portion of the Bill of Rights? That is, what standard does the Court use to protect a liberty specified in the Bill of Rights from violation by a state government? The answer is quite simple and is spelled out, strange as it may seem, in footnote 4 of the opinion of the Court in *United States v. Carolene Products Company* (1938), written by Justice Harlan Fiske Stone, where he set out the legal standards the Court had been using in this area of constitutional interpretation, which he hoped and expected future justices would follow. Stone suggested in his footnote that most legislative enactments by states would fall under what he called **ordinary scrutiny**, meaning that the Court would assume, unless convinced otherwise, that its actions were constitutional. However, the footnote declares, three types of state actions would automatically be presumed unconstitutional, the burden being on the states to prove otherwise. When state actions are presumed to be unconstitutional, the Court is said to be exercising **strict scrutiny**. The three types of suspect state actions that bring strict scrutiny are the following:

- Those that seem to contradict specific prohibitions in the Constitution, including those in the Bill of Rights.

- Those that seem to restrict the democratic process.

- Those that seem to discriminate against racial, ethnic, or religious minorities.

The first of these is the subject matter of this chapter. The second has been addressed at several points in the text; for example in the cases establishing "one person, one vote." In the remainder of this chapter, we focus on specific civil liberties, clarifying their present status in both constitutional law and political practice.

It is important to note in the course of these discussions that the freedoms guaranteed in the Bill of Rights and in other sections of the Constitution hold and have always held with respect to actions of the national government; incorporation is about the process of extending these protections against government violations of freedom on the part of state and local governments. When the Supreme Court exercises strict scrutiny with respect to some law or statute or regulation, it can focus its displeasure at the federal level—for example, bills passed by Congress and signed into law by the president—or at state and local governments—for example, actions by governors, legislators, mayors, and police departments.

☐ Freedom of Speech

Congress shall make no Law . . . abridging the freedom of speech.

—First Amendment to the U.S. Constitution

Speech can take many forms. The Court has had to consider which forms of speech are protected under the Constitution. (See Figure 15.1 for a timeline on milestones in free expression, of which speech is a key component.)

POLITICAL SPEECH For many people, the right to speak one's mind is the first principle of a free and democratic society. Democratic theorists have argued, by and large, that a democratic society is based not only on popular sovereignty, but on the existence of a range of freedoms that allow free and open conversations among the people about the kind of government that is best for them and the sorts of public policies they consider most appropriate. Central among these freedoms is speech, the idea being that public conversations about government and politics depend on the ability and willingness of people to express their views, even if it means saying unpopular, even inflammatory things. Justice Oliver Wendell Holmes described the centrality of this "marketplace of ideas" in a free society in his famous and influential dissenting opinion in *Abrams v. United States* (1919).

Given the centrality of free speech to democracy, it is perhaps odd that free speech was not incorporated (made applicable to state governments) by the Supreme Court until 1925 in *Gitlow v. New York* (1925). Benjamin Gitlow had published *The Left Wing Manifesto,* which embraced a militant, revolutionary socialism to mobilize the proletariat to destroy the existing order in favor of communism. Gitlow did not advocate specific action to break the law, but he was nonetheless convicted of a felony under the New York Criminal Anarchy Law (1902).

The Supreme Court majority held that New York State was bound by the First Amendment—thus incorporating the First Amendment, making it binding on all states—but then argued that even the First Amendment did not prohibit New York from incarcerating Gitlow for his publishing and distributing his pamphlet because it represented a danger to peace and order for which, said Justice Edward Sanford, "A single revolutionary spark may kindle a fire that, smoldering for a time, may burst into a sweeping and destructive conflagration. It cannot be said that the State is acting . . . unreasonably when . . . it seeks to extinguish the spark without waiting until it has enkindled the flame or blazed into the conflagration." In his famous dissent, Justice Oliver Wendell Holmes said, "Every idea is an incitement. . . . Eloquence may set fire to reason. But whatever may be thought of the redundant discourse before us, it had no chance of starting a present conflagration."

Freedom of speech has grown in the ensuing years so that far more speech is protected than is not. In general, no U.S. government today—whether federal, state, or local—can regulate or interfere with the content of speech without a compelling reason. For a reason to be compelling, a government must show that the speech poses a "clear and present danger"—the standard formulated by Holmes in

Amendment Key: First • Second • Fourth •
Fifth • Sixth • Eighth • Ninth •

1897
Payment of compensation
for the taking of private property
Chicago, Burlington and Quincy R. Co. v. Chicago

1925
Freedom of speech
Gitlow v. New York

1931
Freedom of the press
Near v. Minnesota

1937
Freedom of assembly
Dejonge v. Oregon

1939
Freedom to petition
Hague v. CIO

1940
Free exercise of religion
Cantwell v. Connecticut

1947
Cruel and unusual punishment
Louisiana ex rel. Francis v. Resweber

1947
Establishment of religion
Everson v. Board of Education

1948
Due notice
Cole v. Arkansas

1948
Public trial
In re Oliver

1949
Unreasonable search and seizure
Wolf v. Colorado

1961
Exclusionary rule
Mapp v. Ohio

1963
Right to counsel (felonies)
Gideon v. Wainwright

1964
Self-Incrimination
Malley v. Hogan

1965
Confrontation and cross-
examination of adverse witness
Pointer v. Texas

1965
Privacy*
Griswold v. Connecticut

1967
Speedy trial
Klopfer v. North Carolina

1967
Compulsory process to obtain witnesses
Washington v. Texas

1969
Double jeopardy
Benton v. Maryland

1968
Jury trial
Duncan v. Louisiana

1978
When jeopardy attaches
Crist v. Bretz

1972
Right to counsel (misdemeanor)
when jail is possible
Argersinger v. Hamlin

2010
Free speech for corporations
and unions in campaigns
Citizens United v. Federal Election Commission

2008
Right to own a firearm
D.C. v. Heller

FIGURE 15.1   TIMELINE: MILESTONES IN INCORPORATION OF THE BILL OF RIGHTS

ª"Privacy" does not appear in the Ninth Amendment, only reference to "other rights retained by the people."

Source: United States Supreme Court

Schenck v. United States (1919)—that it has a duty to prevent. The danger, moreover, must be very substantial, and the relationship between the speech and the danger must be direct, such as falsely yelling "Fire!" in a crowded theater. The danger must also be so immediate that the people responsible for maintaining order cannot afford to tolerate the speech. As the Court put it in *Brandenburg v. Ohio* (1969), in a case involving an appeal of the conviction of a leader of the Ku Klux Klan under Ohio's criminal syndicalism law, ". . . the constitutional guarantees of free speech . . . do not permit a State to forbid or proscribe advocacy of the use of force or of law violation except where such advocacy is directed to incitement or producing imminent lawless action and is likely to incite or produce such action." Abstract advocacy of ideas, even ideas considered dangerous by police, politicians, or popular majorities, is protected unless it meets both conditions.

In the name of free speech the Court has been gradually taking apart legislative efforts to restrict campaign spending in federal elections. In *Buckley v. Valeo* (1976) it invalidated parts of the Federal Election Campaign Act, most significantly, a restriction on how much money a candidate for federal office might put into his or her own campaign. In *Federal Election Commission v. Wisconsin Right to Life* (2007), the Court ruled that restrictions on media advertising by corporations and labor unions in the period immediately before an election which had been prohibited by the Bipartisan Campaign Reform Act of 2002 (McCain–Feingold) is an unconstitutional restriction on free speech. In *Citizens United v. Federal Election Commission* (2010), a bitterly divided Court ruled in the name of free speech that government could not restrict in any way what corporations and unions collect and spend on advertising expressing their ideas during campaigns.[9] Soon after, the D.C. Circuit Court of Appeals ruled in *SpeechNow v. FEC* that political committees could accept unlimited money from people, unions, and corporations for the purpose of independent (that is, not formally tied to or coordinated with a particular candidate) political spending. These quickly came to be called super PACs and played a big role in the GOP primaries during the 2011–2012 election cycle and in the general election that followed. The foundation for the *Wisconsin*, *Citizens United*, and *SpeechNow* rulings is that money spent in campaigns expressing political ideas is speech that must be protected and that corporations and unions are "persons" under the Constitution with the same liberties as natural persons.[10]

Not all political speech is protected against government restriction. The Supreme Court has allowed governments to restrain and punish speakers whose words can be shown to lead or to have led directly to acts of violence or vandalism, interfered with the constitutional rights of others (e.g., blocking access to an abortion clinic), disrupted a legitimate government function (e.g., a sit-in demonstration in the House chambers), talked to others of information contained in classified documents, or trespassed on private or public property, whether people's businesses and homes or a secured defense installation. The Court has also allowed some restrictions on speech during time of war. But over the years, the Court has been careful to keep the leash tight on government officials who have tried to quiet the voice of citizens. Any attempt to restrict political speech must be content neutral (i.e., it cannot favor some views over others), serve a legitimate government purpose, be narrowly tailored to address a specific problem (i.e., it cannot be vague), and not have a chilling effect on other people's willingness to exercise their free speech rights. All in all, then, freedom of speech has gained powerful legal foundations over the years and is an important component of democracy in the United States.[11]

ACTIONS AND SYMBOLIC SPEECH Difficult questions about free expression persist, of course. Speech mixed with *conduct* may be restricted if the restrictions are narrowly and carefully tailored to curb the conduct while leaving the speech unmolested. Symbolic expressions (such as wearing armbands or picketing) may also receive less protection from the Court. The use of profanity or words that are likely to cause violence ("fighting words") may be regulated in some cases, as may symbolic actions that prevent others from carrying out legitimate activities. Still, freedom of speech throughout the United States has grown to the point at which contenders wrestle with relatively peripheral issues, leaving a large sphere of expressive freedom. *Texas v. Johnson* (1989) shows just how far the protection of free speech has expanded. In this case, Gregory Johnson challenged a Texas state law against flag desecration under which he had been convicted for burning an American flag as part of a demonstration at the 1984 Republican convention. Although dominated by a conservative majority, the Rehnquist Court overturned the Texas law, saying that flag burning falls under the free expression protections of the Constitution unless imminent incitement or violence is likely. In response, some members of Congress have tried on several occasions, without success, to pass an anti–flag desecration constitutional amendment for consideration by the states.

SUPPRESSION OF FREE EXPRESSION   A major exception to the expansion of freedom of expression has been the periodic concern among the authorities about internal security and national defense.[12] Fearing a rise of radicalism inflamed by the French Revolution, Congress passed the Sedition Act of 1798 to forbid criticism of the government and its leaders. The Civil War saw some restrictions on speech by the states, although the national government remained surprisingly lenient on this score (the Lincoln administration did, however, jail some rebel sympathizers without trial and used military tribunals to try civilians accused of actively helping the southern cause). Censorship of dissent and protests occurred during and after World War I; 32 states enacted laws to suppress dangerous ideas and talk, and local, state, and national officials led raids on the offices of "radicals." Hoping to become president, Attorney General A. Mitchell Palmer conducted raids on the headquarters of suspect organizations in 1919 and 1920, sending the young J. Edgar Hoover out to collect information on suspected anarchists and communists.

A similar period of hysteria followed World War II. Its foundations were laid when the Democrat-controlled House of Representatives created the House Un-American Activites Committee (generally referred to as the HUAC). When the Republicans won control of the Congress in 1952, they professed to see security risks in the Truman administration, labor unions, and Hollywood. Soon Democrats and Republicans alike were exploiting the "Red scare" for political gain. The greatest gain (and, subsequently, the hardest fall) was for Senator Joseph McCarthy (R–WI). McCarthy brandished lists of purported communists and denounced all who opposed him as traitors.[13]

SOUNDING THE ALARM ON THE COMMUNIST THREAT

Senator Joseph McCarthy made his reputation and career sounding the alarm bell about communists and communist sympathizers in every nook and cranny of the federal government. Though he was almost always wrong in his assertions, and ruined the lives and careers of many, he did not stir the wrath of other elites until he took on the Army in 1954. Army counsel Joseph Welch listens in disbelief as the junior senator from Wisconsin points out the location of the latest threats during a committee hearing.

prior restraint
The government's power to prevent publication, as opposed to punishment afterward.

Many civil libertarians also worry about the possible chilling effect on free speech and privacy violations of new laws passed to fight what George W. Bush called the war on terrorism. Most important is the USA Patriot Act—passed in 2001 and renewed in 2006 with a few small changes to allow for a little more judicial oversight—granting the federal government access to Americans' private and business records. Revelations that the FBI and the NSA had been conducting secret and warrantless searches of phone conversations (land lines and cell phones), financial transactions, and Internet communications ever since 9/11 led to intense press scrutiny, public condemnation, and congressional probes in early 2006, but the opposition was unable to block renewal of the Patriot Act. In 2007, in a revelation that came too late to affect congressional deliberations on renewal, FBI director Robert Mueller reported to Congress that, since 2001, his agents had improperly and sometimes illegally obtained personal information on thousands of American citizens by overzealously using tools provided by the Act.[14] To the disappointment of many of his supporters, President Barack Obama continued many of the policies instituted during the Bush years, including searching business records and roving wiretaps, something we explore in a later section of this chapter.

☐ Freedom of the Press

Congress shall make no law . . . abridging the freedom . . . of the press.

—FIRST AMENDMENT TO THE U.S. CONSTITUTION

In an aside in the opinion of the Court in *Gitlow v. New York* (1925), the Supreme Court included freedom of the press as a freedom guaranteed against state interference by the Fourteenth Amendment. Incorporation of this aspect of the Bill of Rights seems reasonable in light of the importance of the free flow of information in a society that aspires to freedom and democracy.

PRIOR RESTRAINT In *Near v. Minnesota* (1931), the Court made good on the promise of *Gitlow* by invalidating the Minnesota Public Nuisance Law as a violation of freedom of the press.[15] Jay Near published the *Saturday Press*, a scandal sheet that attacked local crime, public officials, and a few other groups that he disliked: Jews, Catholics, blacks, and unions, for example. Near and his associates were ordered by a state court not to publish, sell, or possess the *Saturday Press*. This sort of state action is called **prior restraint** because it prevents publication before it has occurred. Freedom of the press is not necessarily infringed if publishers are sued or punished for harming others after they have published, but Minnesota was trying to keep Near and his associates from publishing in the future.

The prohibition of prior restraint on publication remains the core of freedom of the press.[16] Freedom of the press and freedom of speech tend to be considered together as freedom of expression, so the general principles applicable to free speech apply to freedom of the press as well. Thus, the Court will allow the repression of publication only if the state can show some "clear and present danger" that publication poses, similar to its position on free speech. In *New York Times v. United States* (1971), the Court ruled that the U.S. government could not prevent newspapers from publishing portions of the Pentagon Papers, secret government documents revealing the sordid story of how the United States had become involved in the Vietnam War. A major expansion of freedom of the press in *New York Times v. Sullivan* (1964) protects newspapers against punishment for trivial or incidental errors when they are reporting on public persons. This limits the use or threat of libel prosecutions by officials because officials can recover damages only by showing that the medium has purposely reported untruths or has made no effort to find out if what is being reported is true.

PROTECTING SOURCES Many reporters and executives in news organizations believe that reporters must be able to protect their sources if they are to have access to insider information that the public needs to know. Without protection of sources, newspeople suggest, the stream of information that the public requires in a democracy will flow more slowly. This is the argument that *New York Times* reporter Judith Miller made when she went to jail for 85 days in 2005 for refusing to testify about her source in the administration who had revealed the identity of CIA operative Valerie Plame, who happened to be the wife of a vocal critic of President Bush's reasons for going to war in Iraq. Although most states have shield laws allowing reporters to protect their sources, there is no such federal law, and the Supreme Court has rejected the argument that constitutional doctrines on freedom of the press give reporters immunity from testifying when they have been issued a subpoena by a court (see *Branzburg v. Hayes*, 1972).

OFFENSIVE MEDIA *Pornography* is a nonlegal term for offensive sexual materials; the legal term is **obscenity**. Although the courts have held that *obscenity* is unprotected by the First Amendment, the definition of obscenity has provoked constitutional struggles for half a century. Early disputes concerned the importation and mailing of works that we regard today as classics: James Joyce's *Ulysses* and D. H. Lawrence's *Lady Chatterley's Lover*, for example.[17] Although the justices admitted that principled distinctions sometimes eluded them (Justice Potter Stewart once famously said that he did not know how to define hard-core pornography but that he knew it when he saw it), a reasonably clear three-part test emerged from *Miller v. California* (1973):

1. The average person, applying contemporary community standards, must find that the work as a whole appeals to the prurient interest (lust).

2. The state law must specifically define what depictions of sexual conduct are obscene.

3. The work as a whole must lack serious literary, artistic, political, or scientific value.

If the work survives even one part of this test, it is not legally obscene and is protected by the First Amendment. Community standards, applied by juries, are used to judge whether the work appeals to lust and whether the work is clearly offensive. However, literary, artistic, political, and scientific value (called the *LAPS test*, after the first letter of each of the four values) is *not* judged by community standards but by the jury's assessment of the testimony of expert witnesses. If, and only if, all three standards are met, the Supreme Court will allow local committees to regulate the sale of obscene materials. Because these tests are not easily met in practice, the *Miller* ruling has done little to stem the tide of sexually explicit material in American popular culture.[18] The Court has ruled, however, in *New York v. Ferber* (1982) that states can prohibit the production, distribution, and sale of child pornography.

Recently, many Americans have begun to worry about the availability to minors of sexually offensive material on the Internet. Responding to this concern, Congress and President Clinton cooperated in 1996 to pass the Communications Decency Act, which made it a crime to transmit over the Internet or to allow the transmission of indecent materials to which minors might have access. The Supreme Court, in *Reno, Attorney General of the United States v. American Civil Liberties Union* (1997), ruled unanimously that the legislation was an unconstitutional violation of the First Amendment, being overly broad and vague and violative of the free speech rights of adults to receive and send information (the Court reaffirmed this ruling in 2004). The strong and unambiguous words of the opinion of the Court make it clear that government efforts to regulate the content of the Internet, as well as cable television, will not get very far. Because the government licenses a limited number of airwaves (there are only so many frequencies available at any one time) and they are considered public property, broadcast television falls under different rules. Thus, the Court has allowed the Federal Communications Commission to ban cursing and nudity on broadcast TV, something it cannot do with respect to other electronic or print media or cable television. The Court went further in affirming new media press freedoms in 2011 when it ruled that efforts by governments to ban violent video games are constitutionally

15.1

15.2

15.3

15.4

obscenity
As defined by the Supreme Court, the representation of sexually explicit material in a manner that violates community standards and is without redeeming social importance or value.

CONTROVERSIAL ART

The distinction between art and obscenity can be very difficult to establish, and battles over the banning of controversial works, such as Robert Mapplethorpe's homoerotic photographs, are quite common in American communities. How does the Court decide what constitutes obscenity?

---

free exercise clause

That portion of the First Amendment to the Constitution that prohibits Congress from impeding religious observance or impinging upon religious beliefs.

---

unacceptable. As Justice Scalia wrote in *Brown v. Entertainment Merchants Association* (2011), "Like the protected books, plays and movies that preceded them, video games communicate ideas—and even social messages—through familiar literary devices (such as characters, dialogue, plot and music) and through features distinctive to the medium (such as the player's interaction with the virtual world). That suffices to confer First Amendment protection."

☐ Religious Freedom

For much of our history, Congress did not impede the exercise of religion because it did not legislate much on the subject. Because the states were not covered by the First Amendment, the free exercise of religion was protected by state constitutions or not at all. The Supreme Court was content to defer to the states on issues of religious freedom.

As late as 1940, in *Minersville School District v. Gobitis*, the Supreme Court upheld the expulsion of two schoolchildren who refused to salute the flag because it violated their faith as Jehovah's Witnesses. Justice Harlan Stone wrote a stinging dissent:

> The Constitution expresses more than the conviction of the people that democratic processes must be preserved at all costs. It is also an expression of faith and a command that freedom of mind and spirit must be preserved, which government must obey, if it is to adhere to that justice and moderation without which no free government can exist.

Stone's dissent, as well as a series of decisions deferring to state restrictions on Jehovah's Witnesses in 1941 and 1942, eventually moved other justices to Stone's side. In *West Virginia v. Barnette* (1943), the Court reversed *Gobitis* and firmly established free exercise of religion as protected against infringement by the states.

FREE EXERCISE OF RELIGION

Congress shall make no law . . . prohibiting the free exercise [of religion].

—First Amendment to the U.S. Constitution

The core of the **free exercise clause** today is that neither the federal government nor state governments may interfere with religious *beliefs*. This is one of the few absolutes in U.S. constitutional law. Religious *actions*, however, are not absolutely protected. Here the issue involves whether people with sincere religious beliefs are exempt from laws and regulations that hold for others in the course of practicing their religion. The Court has upheld state laws, for instance, outlawing the use of peyote (an illegal hallucinogen) in Native American religious ceremonies (*Employment Division v. Smith*, 1990). Congress and President Clinton tried to overturn this decision with the Religious Freedom Restoration Act in 1993, but the Act was declared unconstitutional in *City of Boerne v. Flores* (1997) because the act, in view of the Court majority, unduly extended national government power over the states. By and large, then, people are free in the United States to believe what they want to believe religiously, and to worship as they wish unless worship practices violate general statutes that serve some compelling public purpose, such as state and federal drug laws or local public health ordinances (which in most locales do not permit such religious practices as animal sacrifice).

ESTABLISHMENT OF RELIGION

Congress shall make no law respecting an establishment of religion.

—First Amendment to the U.S. Constitution

Many countries in the world have an official state religion. Sometimes this means that religious law trumps secular law in almost every instance, as in Saudi Arabia and Iran. Sometimes this means that religious law takes precedence in a narrow range of matters, usually involving family matters like marriage and divorce, as in Israel. Often, a state church will exist but not affect everyday life in many ways, playing more of a symbolic role. In most Western European democracies that have monarchies, for example, the king or queen must be a member in good standing of the state church. For example, monarchs in Great Britain must be members of the Church of England.

There is no state church in the United States but many churches (and mosques and synagogues and temples) and many religious people. What allows them to peacefully coexist, in the view of many, is not only the broad freedom to worship or not worship as one pleases under the terms of the "free exercise" clause of the First Amendment, but keeping religion and government at arm's length from one another. Freedom of conscience, it is often argued, requires that government not favor one religion over another by granting it special favors, privileges, or status, or interfering in the affairs of religious institutions. It requires, in Jefferson's famous terms, "a wall of separation between church and state." The framers were mindful of the violent history in Europe and Great Britain involving which Christian religious denomination, Catholicism or Protestantism, would be supreme in the state. The Thirty Years' War, the Inquisition, the struggle over the British crown following the reign of Henry VIII, and conflicts within Protestantism that contributed to the English Civil War were the sad results. Many people who settled in the New World were fleeing these religious conflicts.[19]

Nevertheless, despite general support for the doctrine of "separation of church and state," incorporation of the **establishment clause** by the Court proved to be a particularly messy matter. In *Everson v. Board of Education* (1947), Justice Hugo Black for the Supreme Court determined that no state could use revenues to support an institution that taught religion, thus incorporating the First Amendment ban into the Fourteenth Amendment. But the majority in that case upheld the New Jersey program that reimbursed parents for bus transportation to parochial schools. A year later, Justice Black wrote another opinion incorporating the establishment clause in *McCollum v. Board of Education* (1948). This time, a program for teaching religion in public schools was found unconstitutional. In *Zorach v. Clauson* (1952), however, the Court upheld a similar program in New York State that let students leave school premises early for religious instruction. The establishment clause had been incorporated, but the justices long have had a difficult time determining what "separation of church and state" means in practice.

establishment clause
The part of the First Amendment to the Constitution that prohibits Congress from establishing an official religion; the basis for the doctrine of the separation of church and state.

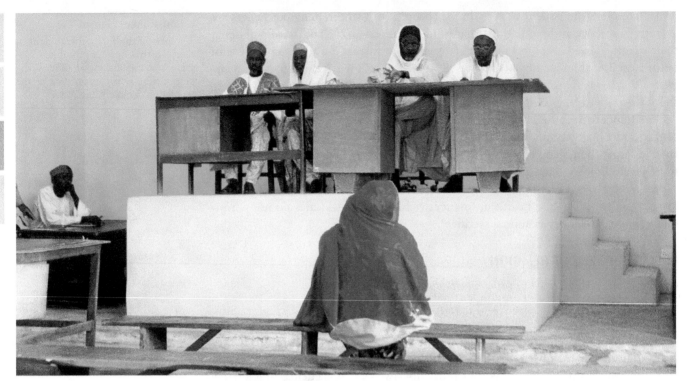

NO SEPARATION OF CHURCH AND STATE

This young woman was sentenced to death by stoning for having committed adultery by a Sharia Islamic court in Nigeria in 2002. The man in the adulterous relationship was not charged with a crime. Her sentence was overturned by Nigerian authorities after the case sparked international outrage and censure. What might our country look like if the majority's religious preferences became the basis for constitutional law and statutes?

THE *LEMON* TEST The Warren Court (1953–1969) brought together a solid church–state separationist contingent whose decisions the early Burger Court (1969–1973) distilled into the major doctrine of the establishment clause: the "*Lemon* test." In *Lemon v. Kurtzman* (1971), Chief Justice Warren Burger specified three conditions that every law must meet to avoid "establishing" religion:

1. The law must have a secular *purpose*. That secular purpose need not be the only or primary purpose behind the law. The Court requires merely some plausible non-religious reason for the law.

2. The *primary effect* of the law must be neither to advance nor to retard religion. The Court will assess the probable effect of a governmental action for religious neutrality.

3. Government must never foster *excessive entanglements* between the state and religion.

While the *Lemon* test would seem to have erected substantial walls that bar mixing church and state, the Court has not been entirely consistent over time in applying it to real cases.[20] For example, while the Rehnquist Court took some bricks out of the wall separating church and state, it was not altogether predictable in its rulings. In *Rosenberger v. University of Virginia* (1995), it ruled that the university (a state-supported institution) must provide the same financial subsidy to a student religious publication that it provides to other student publications. In 2002, in *Zelman v. Simmons-Harris,* decided by a 5–4 vote, the Court approved Cleveland's program of school vouchers that provides public money to parents who want to send their children to private schools, whether secular or religious. The Court majority based its ruling on the fact that public monies do not go directly to religious schools in the Cleveland program but rather to parents who are free to choose their children's school(s). In other cases, the Rehnquist Court ruled that public monies can go to parochial schools if they are for programs that are similar to ones in public schools and not used to advance religious instruction. This would include things such as funds to purchase science books or support drug education programs.[21] However, the Rehnquist Court was unwilling to depart too far from the principle of separation of church and state; in 2004, for example, the Court ruled that the state of Washington had done no constitutional harm when it denied a state-funded scholarship to a student studying for the ministry.

With regard to religious displays in courthouses and other public buildings, the Rehnquist Court seemingly adopted Justice Sandra Day O'Connor's somewhat vague proposition that the establishment clause does not forbid religious displays in courthouses and other public buildings unless a "reasonable observer would view them as endorsing religious beliefs or practices."[22] The Court seems to have decided that it will need to look at such things as religious displays—lights, manger scenes, and the like—at public buildings on a case-by-case basis. In 2005, it ruled in one instance that hanging framed copies of the Ten Commandments in a courthouse in Kentucky went too far in promoting a particular set of religious beliefs (*McCreary County, Kentucky, et al. v. ACLU*). As Justice David Souter put it in his majority opinion, "The reasonable observer could only think that the counties meant to emphasize and celebrate the religious message. . . . The display's unstinting focus was on religious passages [posted with the Commandments], showing that the counties posted the Commandments precisely because of their sectarian content." In another ruling handed down the same day (*Van Orden v. Perry*), the Court allowed a display of a six-foot-high monument of the Ten Commandments in front of the state capitol in Austin because it was one of 40 monuments and historical markers that, in the words of Justice Stephen Breyer, ". . . served a mixed but primarily nonreligious purpose."

In 2012, in *Hosanna-Tabor Church v. Equal Employment Opportunity Commission*, the Court ruled unanimously that employees of religious organizations who carry out some religious duties—leading services, teaching bible classes, and the like—cannot bring job discrimination suits under federal law. Arguing for a "ministerial exception" to federal employment laws, the justices said their enforcement would be an unconstitutional intrusion of government into the affairs of religious institutions, breaking the wall of separation between church and state. Religious organizations from virtually all denominations in the United States hailed the decision, though worries were expressed by many others that this might mean that teachers of theology in religious-affiliated colleges, let us say, might not be able to bring suits under federal law for age discrimination or sexual harassment at work.[23] Such issues no doubt will be litigated in the years ahead.

Waiting in the wings are a range of issues involving the separation of church and state that the Court will eventually consider, given the number of cases that are working their way up from state courts and federal district courts. These include the legitimacy of the words "one nation under God" in the Pledge of Allegiance, and the acceptability of the nondenominational prayers that open the daily sessions in Congress. The point here is fairly straightforward: the debate over where to draw the line that separates church and state is a continuing one in America and is unlikely to ever be resolved once and for all.

RELIGION IN PUBLIC SCHOOLS One of the most controversial aspects of constitutional law regarding the establishment of religion concerns school prayer. Although a majority of Americans support allowing a nondenominational prayer or a period of silent prayer in the schools, the Court has consistently ruled against such practices since the early 1960s, perhaps believing that children in school settings, as opposed to adults in other areas of life, are more likely to feel pressure from those conveying religious messages. In *Engel v. Vitale* (1962), the Court ordered the state of New York to suspend its requirement that all students in public schools recite a nondenominational prayer at the start of each school day. In *Stone v. Graham* (1980), the Court ruled against posting the Ten Commandments in public school classrooms. In *Lee v. Weisman* (1992), it ruled against allowing school-sponsored prayer at graduation ceremonies. In *Santa Fe Independent School District v. Doe* (2000), the Court ruled that student-led prayers at school-sponsored events such as football games are not constitutionally permissible because they have the "improper effect of coercing those present to participate in an act of religious worship." In these and other cases the Court has consistently ruled against officially sponsored prayer in public schools as a violation of the separation of church and state.

Returning prayer to the public schools and making schools less secular are very high on the agenda of religious conservatives. Bills supporting voluntary classroom prayer (such as a moment of silent contemplation) are constantly being introduced into Congress and state legislatures, with little success so far. Christian conservatives have also tried without success to pass a school prayer constitutional amendment. In several very religious communities, school officials have simply ignored the Supreme Court and continue to allow prayer in public classrooms.

An important battle about religion in the schools concerns attempts by some committed believers to either exclude Darwinian evolutionary biology from the school curriculum or to balance it with alternative interpretations such as "creationism" (the idea that God created the earth as described in the Bible) or "intelligent design" (the idea that the natural world is so complex that it could not have evolved as scientists propose, advocated by the Discovery Institute in Seattle). Because courts at all levels have rejected the teaching of "creationism" in the science curriculum as an improper intrusion of religion into public education, many religious activists have pushed "intelligent design" as an alternative approach that might pass court muster. The Dover, Pennsylvania, school board tried this strategy but lost in federal court. As Judge John Jones put it in his opinion in *Kitzmiller v. Dover Area School District* (2005), ". . . we conclude that the religious nature of ID [intelligent design] would be readily apparent to an objective observer, adult, or child. . . . The overwhelming evidence at trial established that ID is a religious view, a mere relabeling of creationism, and not a scientific theory."

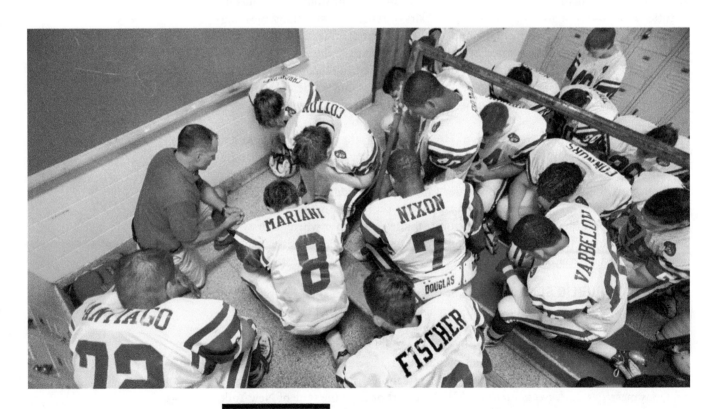

PRAY AND PLAY

Here, a high school coach leads his team in prayer before a game. This practice, quite common across America, raises important questions about the "establishment" clause, especially the degree to which local school authorities in many communities are willing to comply with the doctrine of "separation of church and state." Should the federal government take a harder line against such practices, or should they be left alone as long as no one complains?

With no sign that the tide of religious feeling is about to recede in the United States, debates over school prayer, religious displays in school, and the teaching of evolution will continue for the foreseeable future. The main reason these issues will linger is that neither the courts nor the American people are entirely certain where the line between church and state should be drawn.

☐ Privacy

The freedoms addressed so far—speech, press, and religion—are listed in the First Amendment. The freedom to be left alone in our private lives—what is usually referred to as the *right to privacy*—is nowhere mentioned in the First Amendment or any of the other amendments that make up the Bill of Rights. Nevertheless, most Americans consider the right to privacy to be one of our most precious freedoms; most believe we ought to be spared wiretapping, e-mail snooping, and the regulation of consensual sexual activities in our own homes, for instance. Many (though not all) constitutional scholars believe, moreover, that a right to privacy is inherent in the Bill of Rights, even if it is not explicitly stated; note the prohibitions against illegal searches and seizures and against quartering of troops in our homes, as well as the right to free expression and conscience. Such scholars also point to the Ninth Amendment as evidence that the framers believed in the existence of liberties not specifically mentioned in the Bill of Rights: "The enumeration in the Constitution of certain rights, shall not be construed to deny or disparage others retained by the people." The Supreme Court agreed with this position in *Griswold v. Connecticut* (1965), in which it ruled that a constitutional right to privacy exists when it struck down laws making birth control illegal.

Most jurists and legal scholars have come to accept that a fundamental right to privacy exists, though a group of "original intent" conservatives like Justice Clarence Thomas do not agree. Even among those who accept the fundamental right to privacy, there is disagreement on its specific applicability in the areas of abortion, gay and lesbian rights, the right to die, and the security of interpersonal communications during wartime.

ABORTION *Griswold*'s right to privacy doctrine became the basis for Justice Harry Blackmun's majority opinion in the landmark case *Roe v. Wade* (1973), in which the Court ruled in favor of a woman's right to terminate her pregnancy. Blackmun's opinion in *Roe* prohibited the states from interfering with a woman's decision to have an abortion in the first two trimesters of her pregnancy and prohibited any state actions in the third trimester that might threaten the life or health of the mother. The ruling transformed abortion from a legislative issue into a constitutional issue, from a matter of policy into a matter of rights. It remains one of the most contentious issues in American politics.

The background to the ruling was a changing attitude towards abortion in many parts of the United States. By the time *Roe* was decided, 11 states already had reformed their statutes to allow women to have abortions when the woman's health, fetal abnormalities, or rape or incest were involved. Four more states (Alaska, Hawaii, Washington, and New York) had already gone further and repealed all prohibitions of abortion. In most state legislatures, however, progress was slow or nonexistent.

The litigation over abortion reflected changes in public opinion, pressure by interest groups, and persisting inequities against women. Disapproval of abortion decreased and discussion of abortion increased during the 1960s, even among Roman Catholics.[24] Numerous groups worked to reform or to eliminate abortion laws before *Roe* was decided.[25] The pro-choice team benefited from 42 *amicus curiae* briefs. The medical profession, which had been instrumental in making abortion a crime in the nineteenth century,[26] supported reform in the 1960s.

The Court's decision hardly resolved matters. Anti-abortion groups, energized by the repeal of abortion laws, struck back after *Roe*. Single-issue, anti-abortion politics surfaced in the 1976 and subsequent elections and became an important factor in the emergence of a conservative movement in American politics and the rising political power of the Republican Party. In this environment, and with the appointment of several Supreme Court justices concerned about the sweeping character of the *Roe* ruling, many states began to place restrictions on abortion, ranging from parental notification to waiting periods, counseling about alternatives to abortion, and prohibitions on the use of public money for the procedure. In *Webster v. Reproductive Health Services* (1989), the Court seemed to invite these restrictions. A few years later, however, in *Planned Parenthood v. Casey* (1992), the Court ruled that these restrictions cannot go so far as to make abortion impossible to obtain. In the words of Justice Sandra Day O'Connor, while some restrictions are acceptable, none could "place an undue burden" on a woman's fundamental right to terminate a pregnancy. Furthermore, the Court has ruled in a number of cases since *Casey*, most recently in 2006, that state and federal laws and regulations restricting abortions must always contain exceptions for situations in which the life or health of the mother is at risk.

Many abortion opponents, however, now believe that a direct challenge to *Roe* might be successful given the addition of two more conservatives to the Court (Roberts in 2005 and Alito in 2006). Friends of *Roe* were alarmed and its foes were encouraged by the Court's 5–4 ruling in 2007 upholding the federal Partial-Birth Abortion Act, the first time a specific abortion method had been banned. A similar ban by the state of Nebraska had been rejected by the Court in 2000 when Justice Sandra Day O'Connor was a member. Also, following the sweeping victory of the GOP in the 2010 national elections, several Republican-controlled state legislatures became quite aggressive in passing new laws restricting access to abortion. Five states, for example, simply banned abortions after 20 weeks of gestation on the grounds that fetuses can feel pain at that point in a pregnancy. Eight states now require that a woman seeking an abortion be shown an ultrasound of her fetus—some, such as Texas, mandating vaginal ultrasounds—while three other states made it illegal for private health insurance policies to cover abortion services. Sixteen states said that coverage purchased in the health insurance exchanges created under the new health care reform act could not be used for abortions. Challenges to these laws eventually will make their way to the Supreme Court. There, the justices will have to determine which of these restrictions pass the "undue burden" test.

PRIVATE SEXUAL ACTIVITY The Supreme Court had ruled as recently as 1986 in *Bowers v. Hardwick* that private sexual activity between consenting adults was not a protected right under the constitution. States could, in its view, continue to outlaw certain sexual acts, particularly those involving homosexuals, as the state of Georgia continued to do after winning *Bowers*. Things changed after privacy was recognized as a fundamental right in *Griswold*. In *Lawrence v. Texas* (2003) the Court ruled that state anti-sodomy laws prohibiting consensual gay and lesbian sexual relations are unconstitutional. "Private lives in matters pertaining to sex," declared Justice Anthony Kennedy in his majority opinion, "are a protected liberty." This reversal of its own ruling in so short a period of time is unusual in the history of the Court; though, as we saw in this chapter's section on free speech, it did so recently in the campaign finance case, *Citizens United v. Federal Election Commission* (2010).

THE RIGHT TO DIE It is relatively unclear yet whether the courts will support a privacy-based "right to die." So far the Supreme Court has refused to endorse or reject the existence of such a right. The status of this potential right was at the heart of the case of Terri Schiavo, a comatose heart attack victim with extensive brain damage, who was dependent on a feeding tube to keep her alive, albeit in a "persistent vegetative state." The Florida courts had ruled on several occasions that the feeding tube could be removed, per her husband's wishes; her parents were fighting that decision. A law passed in record time by Congress and signed by President Bush in 2005 insisted that the federal courts take up jurisdiction in the case. But both federal district and circuit courts supported the position of the Florida Supreme Court.

In 2004, the Ninth Circuit Court of Appeals upheld Oregon's assisted suicide law (called the Death with Dignity Act) passed by voters in 1994. In its opinion the justices strongly criticized Attorney General John Ashcroft's announcement that any doctor prescribing drugs that are used by patients to end their lives would be subject to prosecution under the federal Controlled Substances Act, saying that his action "far exceeds the scope of his authority under federal law." The Supreme Court upheld the ruling of the Ninth Circuit in 2006 in *Gonzales v. Oregon*. Interestingly, the ruling was based on very narrow grounds—whether the attorney general could prosecute doctors for prescribing end-of-life drugs—but did not consider whether doctor-assisted suicide was a protected privacy-based right. The Court's ruling leaves the matter, at least for the time being, in the hands of the states, unless Congress chooses to legislate on the issue. In 2009, the state of Washington passed an assisted suicide law closely modeled on Oregon's.

PRIVATE COMMUNICATIONS Finally, there are issues relating to government intrusion on private communications. News in late 2005 about the government's extensive surveillance operations targeting American citizens in the name of the war on terrorism—whether in a fashion authorized by the USA Patriot Act or in secret, warrantless phone and Internet searches by the NSA—created a firestorm of criticism about possible violation of fundamental American liberties. We will look at this in more detail later in this chapter.

So, a right to privacy is well established in principle. Disagreements continue to exist, however, on what this means in practice.

☐ Rights of Those Accused of a Crime

The framers were so concerned about protections for individuals suspected, accused, or convicted of a crime that they included important protections in the main body of the Constitution. Article I, as you have learned, prohibits Congress, and by implication, the federal government, from issuing bills of attainder, passing ex post facto laws, or suspending the right of habeas corpus (this last is much in the news because of the types of hearings used for terrorism detainees, something we will look at later in the chapter). Further indication of their concern for the rights of those accused of a crime is the fact that 5 of the 10 amendments that make up the Bill of Rights are about providing such protections. Most Americans today treasure the constitutional rights and liberties that protect innocent individuals—what are generally termed *due process* protections—from wrongful prosecution and imprisonment. But most Americans also want to control crime as much as possible. The latter concern seems to be winning out; although the United States accounts for a little less than 5 percent of the world's population, it has almost one-fourth of the world's total prison population.[27]

When reading about the status of protections for those accused of a crime, it is well to keep in mind the discussion of constitutional eras.[28] The general pattern on constitutional protections in this area of the law follows the pattern on many other rights issues. Warren Court (1953–1969) rulings greatly expanded protections, Burger Court (1969–1986) rulings trimmed protections for defendants, and the Rehnquist Court (1987–2004) quickened the pace of favoring prosecutors. It remains too early to predict the direction of the Roberts Court, though the strongly unified conservative majority and the addition to the Court of Obama nominee and former prosecutor Sonia Sotomayor suggests that further movement away from the Warren Court on protections for those accused of a crime may be coming.

UNREASONABLE SEARCHES AND SEIZURES The Fourth Amendment secures the right of all persons against unreasonable searches and seizures and allows the granting of search warrants only if the police can specify evidence of serious lawbreaking that they reasonably expect to find. Until the Warren Court compelled the states to abide by the Fourth Amendment in 1961, they had frequently used searches and seizures that the federal courts would consider "unreasonable" in an effort to control

exclusionary rule

A standard promulgated by the Supreme Court that prevents police and prosecutors from using evidence against a defendant that was obtained in an illegal search.

probable cause

Legal doctrine that refers to a reasonable belief that a crime has been committed.

crime. In *Mapp v. Ohio* (1961), the Supreme Court enunciated that the **exclusionary rule** to prevent the police and prosecutors from using evidence that had been gained through warrantless and unreasonable searches to convict people must be followed by the states. A majority of the justices believed that the threat of perpetrators' being freed in cases where unreasonable searches had been conducted eventually would force the police to play by the constitutional rules while conducting their investigations.

The Warren Court (1953–1969) demanded that the police get warrants whenever the person to be subjected to a search had a "reasonable expectation of privacy."[29] The Burger Court (1969–1986) limited the places in which privacy could be reasonably expected, allowing searches of moving cars stopped even for routine traffic infractions and of garbage cans set out for collection. The Burger Court authorized a "good-faith" exception to the exclusionary rule, under which prosecutors may introduce evidence obtained illegally if they can show that the police had relied on a warrant that appeared valid but later proved to be invalid.[30] The Court allowed another exception for illegally gathered evidence that would have been discovered eventually without the illegal search.[31] The Rehnquist Court went well beyond these exceptions. In *Murray v. United States* (1988), it allowed prosecutors to use products of illegal searches if other evidence unrelated to the illegal evidence would have justified a search warrant. The combination of "good faith," "inevitable discovery," and "retroactive probable cause" considerably narrowed the exclusionary rule. The Rehnquist Court (1986–2005) further narrowed the exclusionary rule when it held in *Wyoming v. Houghton* (1999) that police who have **probable cause** to search an automobile for illegal substances may also search personal possessions (in this case, a purse) of passengers in the car. In *Hudson v. Michigan* (2005), the Roberts Court ruled that police need not knock or announce their presence when entering a house with a search warrant.

However, the Court has stopped short of taking the exclusionary rule back to pre–Warren Court days. It ruled, for example, that police could not search every driver or car involved in petty traffic offenses. Thus, a bag of marijuana discovered in a search incident to a speeding ticket in *Knowles v. Iowa* (1998) was excluded as the product of an illegal search. Moreover, the Court ruled in *Kyllo v. United States* (2001) that police could not use high-technology thermal devices to search through the walls of a house to check for the presence of high-intensity lights used for growing marijuana. Justice Scalia was especially incensed, saying in his opinion that to allow such searches "would leave the homeowner at the mercy of advancing technology . . ." And, in 2009, the Court ruled that the police needed to demonstrate a threat to public safety or a need to preserve evidence to search a compartment in someone's car. Trying to reconcile the digital age with the traditional protections of the Fourth Amendment, the Court ruled in early 2012 that police had violated a suspect's protection against unreasonable searches when it attached a GPS tracking device to his car and followed his movements for a month.

SELF-INCRIMINATION The Warren Court was instrumental in incorporating Fifth Amendment protections against self-incrimination. It determined, for example, that the privilege not to be forced to incriminate oneself was useless at trial if the police coerced confessions long before the trial took place. To forestall "third-degree" tactics in the station house, the Court detailed a stringent set of procedural guarantees: the famous rights established in *Miranda v. Arizona* (1966). Once detained by authorities, all persons had to be informed of their rights to remain silent and to consult with an attorney. Although the Burger Court upheld *Miranda,* it allowed exceptions: it allowed the use of information obtained without "Mirandizing" suspects if the suspects took the stand in their own defense. It also allowed the use of information obtained without *Miranda* warnings if some immediate threat to public safety had justified immediate questioning and postponing warnings.[32] The Rehnquist Court went beyond these exceptions when it held that a coerced confession may be "harmless error" that does not constitute self-incrimination.[33] The main principle of the *Miranda* decision was upheld by the Rehnquist Court, however, in *Dickerson v. United States* (2000) and reaffirmed in three 2004 decisions.

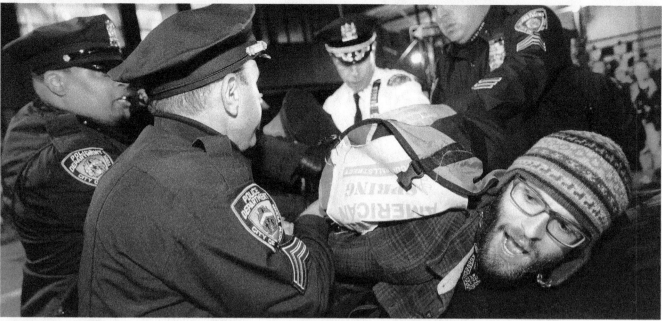

"YOU HAVE THE RIGHT TO REMAIN SILENT"

An Occupy Wall Street demonstrator in 2012 is arrested and read his rights as defined by the landmark Supreme Court ruling *Miranda v. Arizona* (1966). Though the requirement that arrestees be notified of their rights has been challenged by police departments ever since the ruling, Miranda remains solidly in place. How have police adjusted to the restrictions on their actions required by Miranda?

THE RIGHT TO COUNSEL The Sixth Amendment's right to counsel was incorporated in two landmark cases. In *Powell v. Alabama* (1932)—the famed Scottsboro Boys prosecution—the Court ruled that legal counsel must be supplied to all indigent defendants accused of a **capital crime** (any crime in which the death penalty can be imposed). Before this decision, many poor people in the southern states, especially African Americans, had been tried for and convicted of capital crimes without the benefit of an attorney. Thirty-one years later, in *Gideon v. Wainwright* (1963), the Court ruled that defendants accused of any felony in state jurisdictions are entitled to a lawyer and that the states must supply a lawyer when a defendant cannot afford to do so. Justice Black wrote the following for a unanimous Court:

> Not only . . . precedents but also reason and reflection require us to recognize that in our adversary system of criminal justice, any person hauled into court, who is too poor to hire a lawyer, cannot be assured of a fair trial unless counsel is provided for him. This seems to be an obvious truth.

By incorporating the Sixth Amendment's guarantee of legal counsel, the Court has ensured that every criminal defendant in the United States can, at least in theory, mount a defense regardless of socioeconomic status.

CAPITAL PUNISHMENT The Burger Court examined capital punishment in the states under the Eighth Amendment's prohibition of "cruel and unusual punishment." In *Furman v. Georgia* (1972), a split Court found that the death penalty, as used in the states, constituted "cruel and unusual punishment" because the procedures by which states were sentencing people to death sentence were, in its words, "capricious and arbitrary." Responding to the Court's criticisms, Congress and 35 states passed new authorizations of the death penalty aimed at rectifying procedural problems identified by the Court. The Burger Court held in *Gregg v. Georgia* (1976), after states had changed their sentencing procedures, that capital punishment was not inherently cruel or unusual so long as procedures were nonarbitrary and nondiscriminatory. However, the Court tended to create an "obstacle course" of standards that the states had to meet if they wanted to use the death penalty. Basically, the Court insisted that defendants be given every opportunity to show mitigating circumstances so that as few convicts as possible would be killed.

capital crime
Any crime for which death is a possible penalty.

Should the Government Apply the Death Penalty?

The United States is the only advanced democracy that practices capital punishment. Proponents arg[ue] death penalty is a deterrent to violent crimes, but since 1992, public support for it has declined. A m[ajority] Americans still believe the death penalty should exist, but there are racial differences among supporters[.]

Death Penalty Supporters by Race

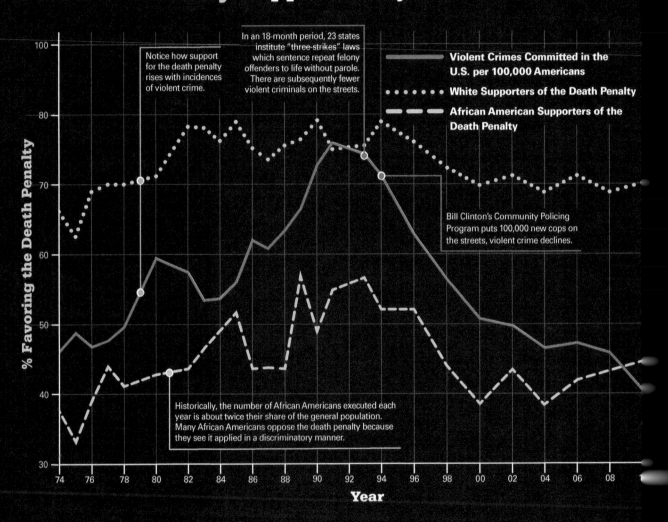

Notice how support for the death penalty rises with incidences of violent crime.

In an 18-month period, 23 states institute "three-strikes" laws which sentence repeat felony offenders to life without parole. There are subsequently fewer violent criminals on the streets.

— Violent Crimes Committed in the U.S. per 100,000 Americans

• • • • • White Supporters of the Death Penalty

– – – – African American Supporters of the Death Penalty

Bill Clinton's Community Policing Program puts 100,000 new cops on the streets, violent crime declines.

Historically, the number of African Americans executed each year is about twice their share of the general population. Many African Americans oppose the death penalty because they see it applied in a discriminatory manner.

% Favoring the Death Penalty (y-axis: 30, 40, 50, 60, 70, 80, 100)

Year (x-axis: 74, 76, 78, 80, 82, 84, 86, 88, 90, 92, 94, 96, 98, 00, 02, 04, 06, 08)

SOURCE: Data from General Social Survey, 1972-2010; Bureau of Justice Statistics, U.S. Department of Justice.

Investigate Further

Concept How widespread is American support for using the death penalty? A majority of Americans endorse capital punishment, but support is stronger among whites than African Americans. The racial disparities are due in part to the fact that African Americans are more likely to be on death row than whites.

Connection Is support for the death penalty related to lower crime rates? When violent crime goes up nationally, so does support for the death penalty because supporters believe it will decrease the crime rate. However, this effect is contested by death penalty opponents and those who see other explanations for less crime.

Cause Are there any co[mmon] explanations for the decline of the death penalty? There are at [least three] non-death penalty related reas[ons for the] decline of crime: increased fed[eral money] to put more cops on the street, stiffer sentencing for repeat fel[ons,] and the aging of the populatio[n.]

Before Clarence Gideon won his case before the Supreme Court in 1963, states did not have to provide attorneys for people accused of a felony. Gideon wrote his appeal letter—shown here—from his prison cell in Florida. The Court agreed with Gideon, incorporating this part of the Sixth Amendment. How did the Court support its decision?

The Rehnquist Court at first expedited the use of the death penalty. (Some of the reasons are examined in the "Using the Framework" feature.) In *McCleskey v. Kemp* (1987), the Court said that statistical evidence that blacks who kill whites are four times more likely to be sentenced to death than whites who kill blacks is not sufficient to prove racism in death penalty cases; individual defendants, it ruled, must show that racism played a role in their specific cases. In *Penry v. Lynaugh* (1989), the Court allowed the execution of a convicted murderer who had the intelligence of a seven-year-old. In *Stanford v. Kentucky* (1989), it allowed the execution of a minor who had been convicted of murder. The Rehnquist Court also limited avenues of appeal and delay in death penalty cases. In *McCleskey v. Zant* (1991), it made delays much less likely by eliminating many means of challenging capital convictions. In *Keeney v. Tamayo-Reyes* (1992), the Court limited the right of "death row" inmates convicted in state courts to appeal to the Supreme Court.

From the middle of the 1960s to the late 1990s, political leaders and public opinion strongly supported the use of the death penalty. In this environment, the Court removed most of the obstacles to its use. It is hardly surprising, then, that the number of people executed in the United States in 1999 reached its highest level (98) since 1976, when the Court reinstated the death penalty, with Texas accounting for more than one-third of the total (see Figure 15.2).[34]

Much to the surprise of seasoned observers, the Rehnquist Court began in 2002 to pull back from its unstinting support for the death penalty. In *Atkins v. Virginia* (2002), the Court followed the lead of 18 states in banning the use of the death penalty for mentally retarded defendants, saying, in Justice John Paul Stevens's majority opinion, that "a national consensus now rejects such executions as excessive and inappropriate" and that "society views mentally retarded offenders as categorically less culpable than the average criminal." In *Ring v. Arizona* (2002), the Court overruled the death sentences of more than 160 convicted killers, declaring that only juries, and not judges, can decide on the use of the death penalty for those convicted of capital crimes. In 2005, the Supreme Court struck down death penalty convictions in cases

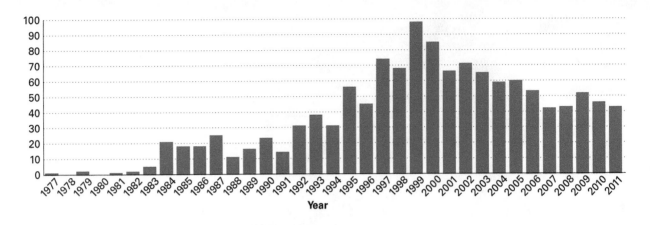

FIGURE 15.2 EXECUTIONS IN THE UNITED STATES, 1977–2011

Fueled by fear of violent crime, executions in the United States increased dramatically from the early 1980s to the late 1990s but declined significantly after that as public concerns rose about how fairly the death penalty is used.

Source: Bureau of Justice Statistics, "Capital Punishment 2012."

in which it was convinced that a defendant had inadequate legal defense, another in which a defendant was brought to a death penalty sentencing hearing in shackles (terming it "inherently prejudicial"), and yet another in which the defendant was under the age of 18.

The Roberts Court has sent mixed signals about the nature of the hurdles it will accept in death sentencing and executions. In 2006, the Court ruled unanimously that states cannot deny the introduction of evidence in capital cases that suggests a person other than the defendant had committed the crime. In 2007, however, it made it easier than it had been for prosecutors to exclude from juries people who were unsure about the appropriateness and morality of the death penalty. In 2008, the Roberts Court ruled in a case involving the state of Kentucky that the most widely used method of execution by lethal injection was constitutionally permissible, rejecting the argument that it caused unacceptable pain. Chief Justice John Roberts wrote in his opinion that states using lethal injection protocols "substantially similar" to Kentucky's would be immune from challenge, leading many to assume that the pace of executions will again pick up. However, after jumping to 52 in 2009, executions fell to 43 in 2011.

Although still strongly in favor of capital punishment in principle, the public and many elected officials and judges seem to be having second thoughts about how fairly it is used in practice. Most of the rethinking about the death penalty is based on concerns about the quality of legal defense for those accused of murder, the fairness of the system toward racial minorities, and the desire to see a wider use of DNA evidence where relevant. The exoneration of several death row inmates by the use of DNA evidence in the early 2000s, as well as a long-term drop in the violent crime rate in the United States, have also had an effect on public opinion. A large majority of Americans still favors the death penalty—61 percent in 2009— but about one-half of those who are not opposed in principle to the death penalty say they support life sentences without the possibility of parole as an alternative to the death penalty.[35] President George W. Bush asked Congress to look at this alternative to the death penalty in federal cases in his 2005 State of the Union message. By 2005, 28 of 37 death penalty states, including Texas, had legislated life without parole as a sentence that juries might consider in capital cases. (See the "Mapping American Politics" feature for a consideration of how death penalty sentencing is related to the incidence of violent crime.) Other states have abolished the death penalty by statute. In 2012 Connecticut became the 17th state to do so, following four other states that had banned the practice since 2008. Other states are considering similar bans.

Mapping American Politics

Violent Crime and the Death Penalty

Introduction

It is well known that the United States has more prisoners on death row and executes more prisoners annually than any other rich democratic country. (The death penalty has been abolished in virtually all of them; in fact, abolition is a condition of membership in the European Union and the Council of Europe.) However, the use of the death penalty is not distributed uniformly across the United States. State-by-state variations are extraordinarily high. Why this is the case is not entirely obvious. One reason could be that the frequency of violent crime—including murder—varies substantially among the states. Or it could be that violent crime does not vary much, but that the responses to it by the public, prosecutors, and juries vary a great deal. Some states, that is to say, may be more inclined than others to use the ultimate penalty in response to crime. We examine the two explanations in these cartograms.

Crime and Punishment Maps

The cartogram on top shows the rate of violent crime for each state per 100,000 people. States are expanded or diminished from their normal size by incidence of violent crime. If the violent crime rates were relatively uniform across the country, the cartogram would appear undistorted, similar to a standard map. We can see that the cartogram is only slightly distorted. To be sure, Oklahoma, Louisiana, Florida, South Carolina, Tennessee, Maryland, and Delaware are enlarged a bit because they suffer from more violent crime than other states, and California, Texas, and New York are smaller because their crime rates are lower than those of other states. Nevertheless, the variation among the states is not great. In the cartogram on the bottom, in contrast, each state is expanded or diminished by how many prisoners it has on death row per 100,000 people (the number of annual executions in the

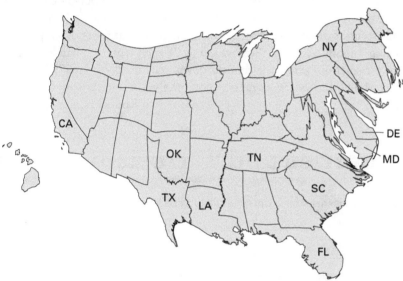

States Sized by Violent Crime Rate per 100,000 People

Standard US Map

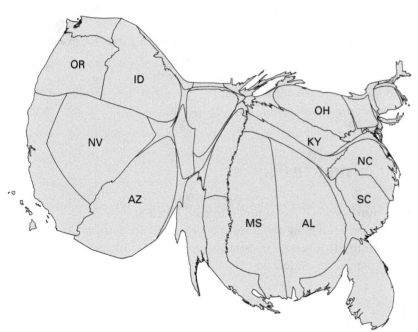

States Sized by Prisoners on Death Row per 100,000 People

United States is not high enough to allow for statistical analysis of the sort being used here). This cartogram suggests that the imposition of capital sentences has little to do with levels of violent crime and much more to do with state-by-state differences in political cultures, legal codes, prosecutorial practices, and jury behaviors. States that are especially prone to impose death penalty sentences include many states of the Deep South (Texas, Mississippi, Arkansas, Alabama, South Carolina, and Georgia), as well as Nevada, Missouri, Oregon, Rhode Island, Connecticut, Maryland, and Delaware. Relative to their violent crime rates, Minnesota, Wisconsin, Maine, and Vermont have few people on death row, and Washington and California are quite low as well.

What Do You Think?

Why is it acceptable, or unacceptable, that the penalty for a crime in one state might be different from that in another state? What kinds of federal statutes or guidelines would ensure national uniformity in sentencing for felony crimes, including the imposition of the death penalty? Or should the people in each state be free, as they are now, to treat crime in a way that seems most appropriate to them? How about your state? Does it have a relatively high death row population or a low one? Why do you think that might be the case?

SOURCES: U.S. Bureau of the Census, *Statistical Abstract of the United States, 2010*, Table 297 (violent crime); and Bureau of Justice Statistics, "Prisoners under Sentence of Death, by Region, Jurisdiction, and Race, 2007 and 2008."

Of course, the main evidence supporting the proposition that beliefs about the death penalty are changing among the public (whose members make up juries), lawyers (whether prosecutors or defense attorneys), and judges is that fewer death penalty sentences are being imposed. In 2011 there were only 78 such sentences handed out in state and federal jurisdictions across the country, down dramatically from 277 in 1999. Having said that, the United States remains among the world's leaders in the use of the death penalty along with China, Iran, Yemen, and North Korea.[36]

Civil Liberties and Terrorism

15.4 Analyze how concerns about terrorism may affect civil liberties

Because involvement in war raises public and governmental concerns about public safety and national security and tends to encourage patriotic sentiments and feelings of national unity, wars have almost always led to some restrictions on civil liberties in democratic countries, including the United States, particularly for those who vocally dissent from the war effort and those who seem to be associated with the enemy in one way or another.[37] Note, for example, the Sedition Act of 1798, which made criticism of government officials and their policies off limits, the use of military tribunals for civilians during the Civil War, the Red Scare following World War I, the forced internment of Japanese Americans during World War II, and the McCarthy anticommunist hysteria in the early years of the Cold War with the Soviet Union.[38]

☐ Bush Administration Policies

Actions by President Bush to fight what he and others called the war on terrorism produced significant restrictions on civil liberties in the United States. Many Americans believed that what had been done was a reasonable price to pay in perilous times.[39] Civil libertarians worried and continue to worry that these restrictions represent a serious long-term danger for American freedom. Here are some of the actions that were taken.

- The USA Patriot Act, passed soon after the 9/11 attacks on the United States, gave the federal government expanded powers to use wiretapping and electronic surveillance, impose stricter penalties for harboring or financing terrorists,

Using the FRAMEWORK

Why did executions in the United States peak in the 1990s, then decline?

Background: Between the reinstatement of the death penalty by the Supreme Court in 1976 and the end of 2001, 737 inmates were executed in the United States. Of the total, 619 (84 percent) took place in the 1990s. In 1999, 98 executions were carried out, the highest total since 1951, with Texas, Virginia, and Florida leading the way. During the first decade of the twenty-first century, however, the number of executions declined. By 2011, the number had fallen to 43. We can understand better why this is so by looking broadly at how structural, political linkage, and governmental factors have influenced the death penalty issue.

Government Action

Illinois, New Jersey, New Mexico, and New York drop the death penalty, joining 12 existing non–death penalty states. ➤ The number of executions declines from its high point in 1999. ➤ Fewer inmates on death row.

Government

Between 1976 and 2002, Supreme Court supports most state efforts to reinstate the death penalty. ➤ After that, Supreme Court tightens some rules on the use of the death penalty. ➤ Juries increasingly choose "life without parole" as alternative to death penalty when available as an option. ➤ Prosecutors after mid-2000s less willing to ask for imposition of the death penalty. ➤ Many state governments in financial difficulties because of the Great Recession begin to rethink death penalty given high costs of death rows.

Political Linkage

Long history of public support of death penalty; increases as crime wave hits. ➤ Political candidates, in response, run on "get tough on crime" platform. ➤ Some advocacy and religious groups come out against death penalty as number of executions increases in 1990s. ➤ A number of death row inmates are exonerated by DNA evidence, leading many to worry about fairness of capital punishment sentencing.

Structure

For the most part, states are responsible for criminal statute writing, prosecution, and punishment of law-breakers. ➤ Though the Constitution prohibits "cruel and unusual punishment," there is little evidence that the framers considered the death penalty to be such. ➤ Violent crime increased in 1970s and 1980s, but decreases thereafter. ➤ Advances made in the science of DNA. ➤ Increasing numbers of countries ban death penalty.

monitor the bank accounts and e-mail of suspect individuals and organizations, turn away from our borders anyone who endorses terrorism, and detain without a hearing any noncitizens living in the United States whom the attorney general deemed to be a threat to national security.

- By executive order, the president expanded the use of a little-known and little-used law created in the 1970s to give the FBI secret access to customer, telephone, and financial records of U.S. citizens. Between 2002 and 2005, almost 150,000 such "national security letters" were issued.[40] Under terms of the law, people were given no notice of the request, firms were obligated to comply, and no one was permitted to make public the fact that such requests had been made. Issuance of these letters required approval by the Office of Intelligence Policy and Review in the Justice Department; there was no judicial oversight.[41]

- The president authorized the indefinite detention without hearings of American citizens discovered to have been fighting against U.S. troops in Afghanistan or aiding Al Qaeda, designating them "enemy combatants."

- The administration instituted secret deportation hearings for detainees held on immigration violations and indefinite detention without a hearing for people designated "material witnesses" in terrorism cases.

- The president authorized a vast eavesdropping and data-mining operation by the National Security Agency on the electronic and wire communications of American citizens. Under terms of the Foreign Intelligence Surveillance Act, NSA eavesdropping on American citizens requires a warrant granted by a special court. When it was revealed in late 2005 that the NSA had been doing this without warrants, the president claimed he had the power to do so as the commander in chief charged with protecting the country and by congressional post-9/11 legislation cited in the previous paragraph.

Despite strong criticism of the USA Patriot Act by civil libertarians, it was renewed by Congress in 2006, with only minor changes in its original provisions. In 2008, Congress passed a bill proposed by President Bush to allow more latitude in the use of wiretaps and to immunize phone companies against lawsuits for their cooperation with the government. That the USA Patriot Act was renewed with so few changes and that a Democratic Congress gave a Republican president more authority to use wiretaps are probably testament to the public's strong support for government actions that prevent terrorist attacks. By a 40–36 margin in 2009, Americans said they are more concerned that the government has not gone far enough in protecting the country as compared with not going far enough to protect civil liberties.[42]

□ Obama Administration Policies

Though Barack Obama campaigned against many of these Bush-era policies and made some stabs at improving the civil liberties climate—he released some documents related to the treatment of detainees, dropped the designation "enemy combatants" for people held without trial, drastically cut back the use of national security letters to gather information, and ended the use of most harsh interrogation techniques—he ended up continuing many of the policies bequeathed to him by the Bush administration. Congressional Republicans blocked his efforts to close the prison at Guantanamo and to try 9/11 conspirators in civilian courts. But he also fought efforts to reveal information about secret NSA wiretapping, and he asked Congress to reauthorize the Patriot Act, perhaps thinking that it had proved effective in preventing terrorist attacks (see the "Can Government Do Anything Well?" feature on this issue). His administration also successfully pressed the courts to prevent terrorism suspects at U.S. bases abroad from having access to American federal courts to review their confinement. In 2011, he signed a defense appropriations bill that had Republican-sponsored riders attached to it stripping the FBI, federal prosecutors, and the federal courts of powers to arrest and prosecute suspected terrorists, handing these off to the military.

Can Government Do Anything Well?

The Patriot Act and protecting citizens against terrorist attacks

There has been no major terrorist attack on American soil since 9/11. There have been several close calls, to be sure. There was, for example, the Nigerian man on a flight from Amsterdam to Detroit who tried to explode a bomb over Detroit in late 2009. In 2010, a car bomb placed near Times Square by Faisal Shahzad ignited but failed to detonate. In that same year, large plastic explosives placed by Al Qaeda operatives were discovered on two cargo planes bound for the United States. There also have been others that managed to kill or came close to killing several people in the name of religion, though no links to terrorist organizations have been discovered regarding them. In 2009, a Muslim Army psychiatrist, likely mentally unstable, gunned down 13 soldiers at Ft. Hood in Texas. A Muslim convert claiming he was trying to stop a war by the United States against Islam shot two soldiers at a military recruiting station in Little Rock, Arkansas. Also in 2010, a pipe bomb exploded in a mosque in Jacksonville, Florida, but no one was hurt.

All in all, this seems to represent a solid record of achievement on the part of the federal government in protecting the American people since 9/11 against jihadist organizations that say they want to do great harm on American soil. At this writing in mid-2012, this has not happened. To what should we attribute this outcome? Those who credit federal government efforts point to a variety of things. There is the stepped-up intelligence capacities of the NSA, the CIA, and the uniformed services. There are the operations by Special Forces and unmanned drone aircraft that capture or kill leaders of jihadist organizations in Pakistan, Afghanistan, Yemen, and Somalia. There was the preventive detention and harsh interrogation of suspects at Guantanamo and other prisons. And, there is the Patriot Act, which allows security agencies of the government to track potential terrorist threats by gaining access to the financial, telecommunications, business, library, and other records of American citizens who may be plotting or be in contact with others plotting attacks. Much of this, to say the least, has been highly controversial, with widespread concern that these initiatives are damaging our liberties. We focus here on the Patriot Act (described in more detail in this chapter).

Support for the claim that the government's use of the Patriot Act has been effective without undermining the civil liberties of Americans:

- The world remains a dangerous place and intelligence and police agencies need tools to stay ahead of those trying to do harm to the country.
- In war—which this is—there is always some trade-off between civil liberties and security.
- Compared to the civil liberties trade-offs of the Alien and Sedition period, the Civil War, World War I, and World War II, the current retreat of some civil liberties is mild, affecting few Americans.
- The Act simply gives counterintelligence agencies the same powers that police have in investigating criminal cases.
- The Act specifies that Americans cannot be investigated for exercising their First Amendment rights.

Rejection of the claim that the government's use of the Patriot Act has been effective without undermining the civil liberties of Americans:

- The operating presumption of federal authorities today is that purported terrorists are guilty until proven innocent; people are detained under "material witness" claims or deported by immigration authorities on the slimmest of evidence of terrorist involvement.
- There is no real judicial oversight of federal agency requests for bank and library records; the Foreign Intelligence Surveillance Court routinely grants requests, which are overused.
- A 2007 report from the inspector general of the Justice Department said that the FBI used tools of the Patriot Act against many people who had no evident association with terrorism.
- People can be and have been prosecuted for "material support" of terrorist organizations when giving speeches or writing articles in support of such organizations, violating many peoples' conception of free speech.
- Terrorists only need to succeed once; the American people cannot be assured that they will be protected against future attacks because of the Patriot Act.

WHAT DO YOU THINK?

What do you think about the past, present, and future role of the government in preventing terrorist attacks on the United States?

- The government has done an excellent job of protecting Americans without undermining their liberties.
- The government has done an excellent job of protecting Americans, though there has been a necessary price to pay in diminished liberty.
- The government has done an excellent job of protecting Americans, but the cost in undermining our liberty has been too high.
- There is no way of knowing how effective the government will be in protecting Americans against a terrorist attack.

How would you defend your position to a fellow student? What would be your main line of argument? What evidence do you believe best supports your position? For help in developing your argument, please refer to Geoffrey R. Stone, *Perilous Times: Free Speech in Wartime* (New York: W. W. Norton, 2004).

☐ The Court Responds

Naturally, the courts have been wrestling with the issue of the proper balance between national security and civil liberties at a time when people feel legitimately threatened by terrorism. For the most part, they have supported government national security concerns, but they have, at the same time, rejected overly broad claims of presidential war powers. In a stunning blow to the Bush administration's claim of extraordinary executive power in wartime, for example, the Supreme Court ruled in 2004 (*Hamdi v. Rumsfeld*) that both foreigners and American citizens detained as "enemy combatants" have a right to a hearing to contest the basis of their detentions. In her opinion in the case, Justice Sandra Day O'Connor reminded everyone, "We have long since made clear that a state of war is not a blank check for the president when it comes to the rights of the nation's citizens." In 2007, the Ninth Circuit Court ruled that enemy combatants could not be held indefinitely in military detention in the United States.

The Roberts Court has also been troubled by the legal treatment of foreign detainees. In 2006, the Court ruled that all detainees held at Guantanamo Bay and elsewhere are entitled to protections guaranteed under the Geneva Convention. It also ruled that the military tribunal-style hearings used at Guantanamo were unacceptable because they had not been authorized by Congress. In response, Congress passed the Military Commissions Act of 2006, which set up a system of tribunals but, almost provocatively, added language to the effect that no court would be allowed to consider habeas corpus petitions from foreigners held as enemy combatants. Perhaps seeing this "habeas" provision as a direct challenge by the legislative branch to the independent powers of the judicial branch, the Court rejected this in 2008 when it ruled that foreign detainees held at Guantanamo have a constitutional right to take their cases to the federal courts to challenge their detention.

With the exception of those instances when the executive branch seems to be challenging the authority and legitimacy of the judicial branch, the Court has granted broad leeway to the government in fighting terrorism. In the first test of the constitutionality of the Patriot Act's "material support" provision, for example, the Court ruled in 2010 that the government has very broad authority and can prosecute people for seemingly benign activities—for example, providing legal services and expert advice to government-designated terrorist organizations seeking to overturn their designation.

The direction that civil liberties will take as a result of the effort to protect the United States against terrorism is hard to predict. All we can say with any degree of certainty at this point is that some restrictions will exist for the duration of the campaign to contain terrorism, and that the severity of these restrictions will be directly related to the degree to which the American people feel afraid that further attacks will occur and their judgment about how much freedom they are willing to trade for security. So far, we have not taken as harsh a line as several other rich democracies including Australia, Canada, and Great Britain, which have instituted the practice of preventive detention—incarceration of terrorism suspects who are citizens or otherwise legally in the country without charges or hearings—and placed strict limits on subversive speech.[43]

Using the DEMOCRACY STANDARD

Has the state of American freedom improved?

The protection of individual freedom—civil liberty—is a foundational principle of both the eighteenth-century republican philosophy of the framers and of democratic theory. For the framers, protection of individual freedom was not only an essential feature of good government and the good society, but also the very reason republican government was formed in the first place. Political liberty is also an essential feature of democratic theory, because it is necessary for both popular sovereignty and political equality. Popular sovereignty cannot be guaranteed if people are prevented from participating in politics or if opposition to the government is crushed by the authorities. Popular sovereignty cannot prevail if the voice of the people is silenced and if citizens are not free to argue and debate, based on their own ideas, values, and personal beliefs, and to form and express their political opinions. Political equality is violated if some people can speak out but others cannot.

Both the framers and more recent democratic theorists are committed to civil liberties, but each has taken a somewhat different approach concerning how civil liberties might be enjoyed by Americans. Recall that the framers focused their attention on the potential for violations of liberty by the national government and paid little attention to the states, believing that freedom in the states was well protected. Note as well that many of the framers and most political leaders who followed during the long course of the nineteenth century seemed most concerned about protecting property rights, or economic liberty. Civil liberties, broadly understood, became widely available to Americans only in the twentieth century in response to the spread of democratic aspirations in politics and of democratic ideas in the culture, the efforts of individuals and groups to struggle for liberty, and a federal judiciary that finally agreed to nationalize most of the protections of the Bill of Rights.

There has been an enormous expansion of freedom in the United States; the freedoms of speech, association, press, conscience, and religion, as well as the rights of those accused of a crime, are far more extensively developed and protected in the United States today than they were in the past. However, we must also recognize a serious flaw in the current status of civil liberties. While civil liberties today are fairly well protected against intrusions by government, not all people have the capacities and resources to use their liberties effectively. Substantial income and wealth inequality often creates political inequality. Thus, only a privileged few can make substantial campaign contributions; form political lobbying organizations; and run ads for their favorite candidates, parties, and issues.

We cannot say with total confidence, moreover, that freedom cannot and will not be violated by government at some point in the future. In the past, waves of hysteria among political leaders and the public have led to the violation of civil liberties. Given the right conditions—war, civil unrest, economic depression—the same might happen again. Many worry, with some justification, that the war on terrorism may represent just such a setting for the suppression of civil liberties. What makes the possibility especially troubling is the indeterminate time period of such a war. One can imagine it stretching on into the indefinite future. We can only hope that such a suppression of civil liberties will not happen and that people will struggle for democracy if it does.

Review the Chapter

Civil Liberties in the Constitution

15.1 Identify civil liberties protections in the Constitution, p. 490

The formal foundation of American liberties is found in the Constitution and its amendments, particularly the Bill of Rights and the Fourteenth Amendment, but the degree to which civil liberties have been enjoyed in practice during our history has depended upon the actions of courts, the behavior of government officials, and the struggle for democracy by the American people.

Rights and Liberties in the Nineteenth Century

15.2 Trace the evolution of civil liberties in the nineteenth century, p. 490

During the nineteenth century, the Supreme Court concerned itself mainly with protecting property rights. Somewhat belatedly, it used the Fourteenth Amendment to make the protections in the Constitution and the Bill of Rights apply to state and local governments. This considerably expanded Americans' enjoyment of the familiar liberties of expression, association, press, and religion.

The Court's changing interpretation of the meaning of liberty was influenced by changing attitudes among the public and elected officials, as well as by the nation's leading law journals.

Nationalization of the Bill of Rights

15.3 Outline the liberties guaranteed by the Bill of Rights and their gradual application to the states by the Supreme Court, p. 494

American history has witnessed an expansion of the boundaries of liberties, with the Supreme Court gradually incorporating the Bill of Rights based on the Fourteenth Amendment under terms described in a footnote in the *Carolene* case. This footnote suggested that the Court would apply "strict scrutiny" to government actions that seemed to violate democracy, failed to offer equal protection to minorities, or prevented the enjoyment of liberties spelled out in the Bill of Rights.

The broadest expansion of due process protections and equal protection came during the Warren and Burger Court years.

The expansion of the rights of the accused was always a hotly disputed political issue, and the conservative orientation of the Rehnquist and Roberts Courts resulted in the reversal of many of the due process innovations of the Warren and Burger Courts. The Roberts Court also ruled against a number of government efforts to expand civil rights protections to racial minorities.

Civil Liberties and Terrorism

15.4 Analyze how concerns about terrorism may affect civil liberties, p. 516

The fight against terrorism has resulted in the widespread surveillance of American citizens and restrictions of the civil liberties of noncitizens living legally in the United States. How long these restrictions remain in place will depend on the severity of terrorist threats and public perceptions about these threats.

Learn the Terms

 Study and **Review** the **Flashcards**

civil liberties, p. 490
habeas corpus, p. 490
bill of attainder, p. 490
ex post facto law, p. 490
economic liberty, p. 490
full faith and credit, p. 492
contract clause, p. 492
due process clause, p. 493

selective incorporation, p. 494
privileges and immunities clause, p. 495
equal protection clause, p. 495
nationalizing, p. 495
incorporation, p. 495
ordinary scrutiny, p. 495
strict scrutiny, p. 495

prior restraint, p. 500
obscenity, p. 501
free exercise clause, p. 502
establishment clause, p. 503
exclusionary rule, p. 510
probable cause, p. 510
capital crime, p. 511

Test Yourself

Answer key begins on page T-1.

15.1 Identify civil liberties protections in the Constitution

1. In this amendment, citizens are protected from double jeopardy, or being prosecuted more than once for the same crime.

   a. Second Amendment
   b. Third Amendment
   c. Fourth Amendment
   d. Fifth Amendment
   e. Sixth Amendment

15.2 Trace the evolution of civil liberties in the nineteenth century

2. This clause obligated each state to recognize contracts and other legal obligations entered into by its citizens with citizens or legal bodies in other states.

   a. Takings clause
   b. Full faith and credit clause
   c. Fundamental liberty clause
   d. Rebellion clause
   e. Contract clause

15.3 Outline the liberties guaranteed by the Bill of Rights and their gradual application to the states by the Supreme Court

3. The right to privacy is covered in this amendment:

   a. The First Amendment
   b. The Second Amendment
   c. The First and Second Amendment
   d. It is not covered in the Bill of Rights
   e. It is implied in almost every Amendment

15.4 Analyze how concerns about terrorism may affect civil liberties

4. Congress passed this act that set up a system of tribunals for foreign detainees, but added in that no court would be allowed to consider habeas corpus petitions from foreigners held as enemy combatants.

   a. Military Commissions Act of 2006
   b. Roberts–Guantanamo Act of 2006
   c. National Citizens Act of 2007
   d. The USA Patriot Act
   e. Civil Liberties and Terrorism Act of 2006

Explore Further

INTERNET SOURCES

The American Civil Liberties Union **www.aclu.org**
Website of the long-time defender of civil liberties in the United States.
Bureau of Justice Statistics **www.ojp.usdoj.gov/bjs/**
Official statistics on crimes, trials, incarceration rates, and executions are available at this site.
The Cato Institute **www.cato.org**
A comprehensive site covering civil liberties issues from the conservative libertarian point of view.
The Death Penalty Information Center **www.deathpenaltyinfo.org**
Information on the death penalty around the world.
Findlaw Supreme Court Opinions **www.findlaw.com/casecode/ supreme.html**
Find historical and contemporary Supreme Court decisions and opinions on civil liberties at this site.
First Amendment Center **www.firstamendmentcenter.org**
Rich source of history and recent developments related to First Amendment freedoms.
Financial Crimes Enforcement Network **www.fincen.gov/ statutes_regs/patriot/index.html**
This site contains the official wording and full text of the USA Patriot Act.
The Bill of Rights **billofrightsinstitute.org/founding-documents/ bill-of-rights/**
A site dedicated to the Bill of Rights and the Constitution, along with full text of both of these documents.
The Library of Congress: Military Commissions Act **thomas.loc .gov/cgi-bin/query/z?c109:S.3930**:
Links to four versions of the Military Commissions Act of 2006.

SUGGESTIONS FOR FURTHER READING

Abraham, Henry J., and Barbara A. Perry. *Freedom and the Court*, 8th ed. Lawrence: University of Kansas Press, 2003.
A trusted introduction to the study of civil rights and liberties for more than 30 years.
Barker, Lucius J., Twiley W. Barker Jr., Michael W. Combs, Kevin L. Lyles, and H. W. Perry Jr. *Civil Liberties and the Constitution: Cases and Commentaries*. New York: Longman, 2011.
Encyclopedic overview of American civil liberties presented in an engaging style.
Epstein, Lee, and Thomas G. Walker. *Rights, Liberties, and Justice*. Washington, DC: CQ Press, 2010.
An exhaustive and compelling examination of the rulings that have shaped the status of civil liberties in the United States.
Fallon, Richard. *The Dynamic Constitution: An Introduction to American Constitutional Law*. New York: Cambridge University Press, 2005.
An accessible introduction to all aspects of American constitutional law.
Lewis, Anthony. *Freedom for the Thought We Hate: A Biography of the First Amendment*. New York: Basic Books, 2007.
A celebration of the expansion of First Amendment freedoms and the story of how it happened.
Stone, Geoffrey R. *Perilous Times: Free Speech in Wartime*. New York: W. W. Norton, 2004.
A history of the tension between free speech and national security during American conflicts.
Zimring, Franklin. *The Contradictions of American Capital Punishment*. New York: Oxford University Press, 2003.
Examines the question of why Americans so strongly support the death penalty compared with people in other rich democracies.

16

Civil Rights: The Struggle for Political Equality

THE RETURN OF SEGREGATED SCHOOLS

"I don't know why they left," said one fourth-grader at Reid Park Elementary School in Charlotte, North Carolina. "Maybe they didn't like it here."[1] She was referring to the virtual disappearance of white children at her school where, only one year earlier, about one-third of her schoolmates had been white. What was happening at Reid Park Elementary was happening all over the South at the turn of the new century. Fifty years after the Supreme Court had ruled in *Brown v. Board of Education* (1954) that "separate but equal" was unconstitutional, schools were becoming more segregated. By 2003, only 29 percent of black children in the South were in schools that were majority white, a decrease from 44 percent as recently as 1988. By 2007, matters had grown worse.[2]

For those Americans committed to a racially integrated society, there was much to be proud of in the record of desegregation of public education in the United States after the *Brown* decision, especially in the South where school segregation was official policy from the early twentieth century until the Court's 1954 decision. After a slow start for a few years following *Brown*, school integration took off in the mid-1960s and gained steadily until it reached its peak in the late 1980s. By 1988, only one in four black children were in schools that were

16.1	16.2	16.3	16.4
Trace the evolution of civil rights protections for racial minorities and women to the twentieth century, p. 528	Assess the present status of civil rights protections for racial minorities, p. 532	Assess the present status of civil rights protections for women, p. 542	Analyze the expansion of civil rights protections to the elderly, the disabled, and gays and lesbians, p. 547

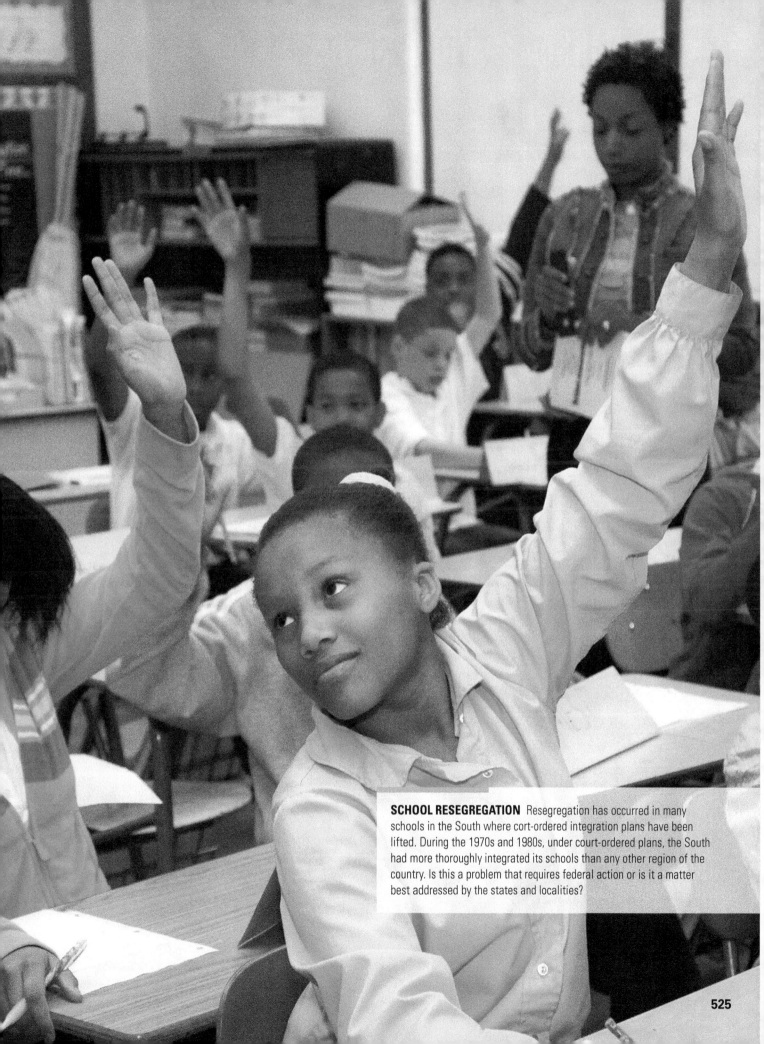

SCHOOL RESEGREGATION Resegregation has occurred in many schools in the South where cort-ordered integration plans have been lifted. During the 1970s and 1980s, under court-ordered plans, the South had more thoroughly integrated its schools than any other region of the country. Is this a problem that requires federal action or is it a matter best addressed by the states and localities?

MyPoliSciLab Video Series

1 **The Big Picture** When author Edward S. Greenberg was growing up in DC, he could not go to school with many of his African American friends. Learn how African Americans and others have used social movements to make America more equal, just, and democratic.

The Basics Discover whether we have always had civil rights and whether all American citizens have them. Watch as ordinary people answer questions about where our civil rights come from and how we won them. Consider what equal treatment and protection under the law means today.

Have all Americans always had civil rights?

2

3 **In Context** Discover how civil rights issues have permeated our society since the United States was founded. In the video, University of Oklahoma political scientist Alisa H. Fryar talks about how civil rights has expanded in scope since the Civil Rights Movement of the twentieth century.

Think Like a Political Scientist Where are we headed in terms of civil rights research in the United States? University of Oklahoma political scientist Alisa H. Fryar discusses how current research on voting rights, municipal election methods, and education address civil rights issues.

4

5 **In the Real World** The Defense of Marriage Act declares that the federal government does not recognize same-sex marriage. Is that constitutional? Hear real people argue both sides as they discuss their beliefs about same-sex marriage, and find out how public opinion has changed dramatically over the years.

So What? In the search for equality, which comes first—changed public opinion or new legislation? Using affirmative action and same-sex marriage as examples, author Edward S. Greenberg explains how both can be the

6

90 to 100 percent black, a far cry from the pre-*Brown* years when virtually all black children were in such schools. During the 1990s, however, the trend reversed all over the South, with more black children going to school where there were few whites or none at all and where white children had less contact with African American children than in many years.[3]

As troubling as the picture might be, the South is still doing better on the school integration front than other parts of the country. In the Northeast, for example, more than one-half of all African American children are in schools that are 90 to 100 percent black, closely followed by the states in the Midwest. In addition, black children are least exposed to white children in public schools in New York, Illinois, Michigan, California, Maryland, and New Jersey and are most exposed to their white counterparts in the South and the border states. And, as in the South, school segregation in every region of the nation has become more pronounced.[4]

So why did the trend in the South toward a more integrated public school system first level off, then recede during the 1990s and 2000s? The answer is fairly straightforward: The federal courts, following the lead of the Supreme Court in *Dowell v. Oklahoma City* (1991)—which ruled that school districts that had made lengthy good-faith efforts to end the effects of previously legal school segregation in their jurisdictions had fulfilled their constitutional obligations for equal protection of the races in education—began to lift court-ordered desegregation plans that required busing and other methods to integrate schools across local jurisdictions. About 40 school districts over the past 12 years have been relieved of such orders, and it is precisely in these districts where the reversals in school integration trends are most evident.

But that still leaves the question of why lifting federal court orders would lead to such a development. Again, the answer is fairly straightforward: when most whites and most blacks live in racially homogeneous neighborhoods—as they do because of white flight to the suburbs and the existence of informally segregated housing markets—local neighborhood schools, absent busing or other student assignment strategies designed to foster integration, will also be racially homogeneous.[5]

It remains to be seen what the outcomes of these changes will be. Many whites and African Americans believe that integrated schooling, whether achieved voluntarily or under court order, is important for children's educational achievement and for teaching tolerance in a racially diverse society. However, other whites and African Americans believe that integration by itself does little to increase academic achievement, and that court-ordered busing mainly leads to intergroup tensions and wasted tax money. Many African Americans who think this way have become attracted to the idea of school vouchers that allow children to use public funds to go to either a public or private school as a way to improve schools in predominantly black neighborhoods. Many others are being attracted to charter schools as an alternative within public schools. The thinking here is that competition for students between public and private schools, as well as competition between different kinds of public schools, will force schools to offer a better educational product.

Civil rights are government guarantees of equality for people in the United States regarding judicial proceedings, the exercise of political rights, treatment by public officials, and access to and enjoyment of the benefits of government programs. (The terms *equal citizenship* and *civil rights* often are used interchangeably, which is our practice in this textbook.) The expansion of civil rights protections for African Americans as well as for other racial, ethnic, and religious minorities and for women is one of the great achievements of American history. Gays and lesbians have not gained "equal protection" status in the courts as of this writing and have suffered many recent political setbacks, but they have attained a level of rights protections never before achieved in our history, though fewer than gay and lesbian advocates have hoped for. These changes on the civil rights front have not come easily or quickly; it took the struggle of millions of Americans to force change from political leaders and government institutions. The result has been a significant democratization of the republican constitutional system of the framers. As this opening story suggests, however, the expansion of civil rights protection in the United States is neither complete nor free of problems and controversy. And, there continue to be setbacks.

civil rights
Guarantees of equal treatment by government officials regarding political rights, the judicial system, and public programs.

Thinking Critically About This Chapter
This chapter is about civil rights in the United States and how politics and public policies have affected the status of equal protection and equal treatment for all Americans.

Using the Framework
In this chapter, you will see that the meaning of civil rights has changed over the course of American history, and you will learn how structural, political linkage, and governmental factors, taken together, explain that change.

Using the Democracy Standard
In this chapter, you will learn how civil rights are at the very center of our understanding of democracy in the United States. You will see how the struggle for democracy helped expand civil rights protections. You also will see how the expansion of civil rights has enhanced formal political equality in the United States, one of the basic foundations of a democratic political order.

Civil Rights Before the Twentieth Century

16.1 Trace the evolution of civil rights protections for racial minorities and women to the twentieth century

 ivil rights for racial minorities and women were a comparatively late development in the United States, and most major advances were not evident until well into the twentieth century. In this section, we look at the period before the expansion of civil rights.

☐ An Initial Absence of Civil Rights

Neither the original Constitution nor the Bill of Rights said anything about equality beyond insisting that all Americans are equally entitled to due process in the courts.[6] Indeed, the word *equality* does not appear in the Constitution at all. Nor did state constitutions offer much in the way of guaranteeing equality other than equality before the law. Americans in the late eighteenth and early nineteenth centuries seemed more interested in protecting individuals against government than in guaranteeing certain political rights through government.[7] For most racial or ethnic minorities and women, equality eluded constitutional protection until the twentieth century, although the groundwork was laid earlier.

The inequality of African Americans and women before the Civil War is quite striking. In the South, African Americans lived in slavery, with no rights at all. Outside the South, although a few states allowed African Americans to vote, the number of states doing so actually declined as the Civil War approached, even as universal white male suffrage was spreading. In many places outside the slave South, African Americans were denied entry into certain occupations, required to post bonds guaranteeing their good behavior, denied the right to sit on juries, and occasionally threatened and harassed by mobs when they tried to vote or to petition the government. Chief Justice Roger Taney, in *Dred Scott v. Sandford* (1857), went so far as to claim that the Founders believed that blacks had no rights that whites or government were bound to honor or respect. As for women, no state allowed them to vote, few allowed them to sit on juries, and a handful even denied them the right to own property or enter into contracts.

Many African Americans and women refused to play a passive political role, however, even though the pre–Civil War period was not conducive to their participation in politics. African Americans, for instance, voted in elections where they were allowed, helped organize the Underground Railroad to smuggle slaves out of the South, and were prominent in the abolitionist movement against slavery. Both black and white women played an important role in the abolitionist movement—the antislavery speaking tours of Angelina and Sarah Grimké caused something of a scandal in the 1840s when women's participation in public affairs was considered improper—and a few began to write extensively on the need for women's emancipation and legal and political equality. In 1848, Elizabeth Cady Stanton issued her call for a convention on women's rights to be held at the village of Seneca Falls, New York. The Declaration of Sentiments and Resolutions issued by the delegates to the convention stands as one of the landmarks in women's struggle for political equality in the United States:

> *All men and women are created equal . . . but the history of mankind is a history of repeated injuries and usurpations on the part of man toward woman, having in direct object the establishment of a direct tyranny over her. . . . [We demand] that women have immediate admission to all the rights and privileges which belong to them as citizens of the United States.*

☐ The Civil War Amendments

In the years following the Civil War, Congress passed a number of constitutional amendments that essentially created the foundations for civil rights as we understand them today.

ADVOCATING FOR WOMEN'S RIGHTS

In 1848, Elizabeth Cady Stanton helped organize the Seneca Falls Convention on women's rights. The resulting Declaration of Sentiments and Resolutions was patterned after the Declaration of Independence, stating that "all men and women are created equal," and included a list of the injustices of men against women. Stanton remained an activist for many years, helping to found the National Women's Suffrage Association in 1896 to press for the vote for women, and became the first president of the National American Woman Suffrage Association in 1890. Why did it take so many years of such outspoken activism for women to finally be granted the right to vote?

16.1

privileges and immunities clause

The portion of Article IV, Section 2 of the Constitution which states which citizens from out of state have the same legal rights as local citizens in any state; also in the Fourteenth Amendment assuring national citizenship.

16.2

16.3

due process clause

The section of the Fourteenth Amendment that prohibits states from depriving anyone of life, liberty, or property "without due process of law," a guarantee against arbitrary or unfair government action.

16.4

equal protection clause

The section of the Fourteenth Amendment requiring states to provide equal treatment to all people within their boundaries.

Jim Crow

Popular term for the system of state-sanctioned racial segregation that existed in the American South until the middle of the twentieth century.

poll tax

A tax to be paid as a condition of voting; used in the South to keep African Americans away from the polls.

literacy test

A device used by the southern states to prevent African Americans from voting before the passage of the Voting Rights Act of 1965, which banned its use; usually involved interpretation of a section of a state's constitution.

- The Thirteenth Amendment to the Constitution, ratified in 1865, outlawed slavery throughout the United States, settling once and for all the most divisive issue of our early history as a nation.

- The Fourteenth Amendment (1868) reversed *Dred Scott* by making all people who are born or naturalized in the United States, black or white, citizens both of the United States and of the states in which they reside. To secure the rights and liberties of recently freed slaves, Article I of the amendment further provided that "no State shall make or enforce any law which shall abridge the privileges or immunities of citizens of the United States" (the **privileges and immunities clause**); "nor shall any State deprive any person of life, liberty, or property, without due process of law" (the **due process clause**); "nor deny to any person within its jurisdiction the equal protection of the laws" (the **equal protection clause**). As imposing as this constitutional language sounds, the Supreme Court would soon transform it into a protection for property rights, but not for African Americans, women, or Native Americans.

- The Fifteenth Amendment (1870) said states could not prevent people from voting on the grounds of "race, color, or previous condition of servitude" (former slaves).

UNDERMINING THE CIVIL WAR AMENDMENTS In the two decades following their passage, the Supreme Court blocked the promise of equal citizenship for African Americans found in the Civil War amendments. During this time, when many Americans in the northern states had grown weary of efforts to reconstruct the South and uplift and protect former slaves, white supremacists were regaining control in many areas of the South, and racist attitudes were widespread across the nation, the Supreme Court struck against key provisions of the amendments. For example, the *Slaughterhouse Cases* (1873) rendered the privileges and immunities clause virtually meaningless. Writing for the Court, Justice Samuel Miller found that the clause did not guarantee citizenship rights against violations by state governments, only against violations by the federal government. The Court ruled that it was powerless to protect African Americans against abuses by state governments, including barriers to voting and office holding. Within five years of its passage, then, this section of the Fourteenth Amendment was seriously compromised by the Court, foiling the attempt by the post–Civil War radical Republican Congress to amend the Constitution in favor of equality.

Though the equal protection clause of the Fourteenth Amendment survived the *Slaughterhouse Cases*, it soon lost all practical meaning as a guarantor of equality for African Americans. First, the Court ruled in the *Civil Rights Cases* (1883) that the Fourteenth Amendment gave Congress no power to prohibit discrimination unless it was practiced by state government. "Equal protection of the laws" did not, therefore, preclude race discrimination by private owners or managers of restaurants, theaters, hotels, and other public accommodations. Then the Court made even government-sponsored discrimination constitutional in *Plessy v. Ferguson* (1896). The Court said that the states could separate the races in intrastate railways if they provided "equal" facilities for the races. This ruling gave the doctrine of "separate but equal" full constitutional status and legitimacy, and provided the legal underpinnings for the segregation of the races in nearly every area of life throughout the South. This system of racial segregation—usually referred to as **Jim Crow**—would remain in force until *Plessy* was overturned in *Brown v. Board of Education of Topeka* (1954) more than half a century later.

The Fifteenth Amendment's voting guarantees were also rendered ineffectual—this time by a variety of devices invented to prevent African Americans from voting in the former states of the Confederacy. The **poll tax** was a tax required of all voters in many states, and it kept many African Americans away from the polls, given their desperate economic situation in the South in the late nineteenth and early twentieth centuries. Several states required voters to pass a **literacy test** devised

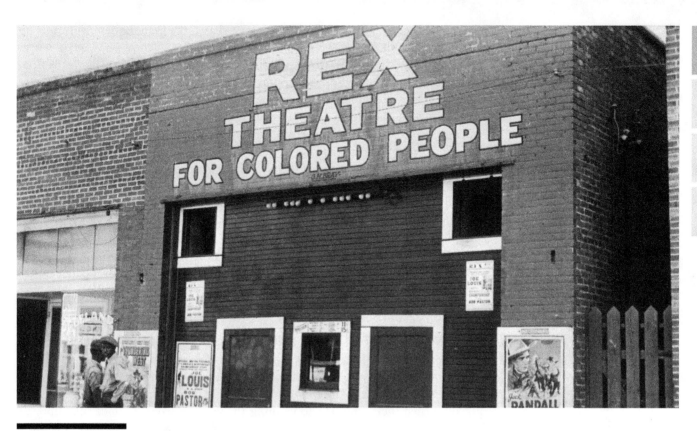

JIM CROW

For more than half a century, until the Court's 1954 *Brown* decision, the civil rights movement, and the 1964 Civil Rights Act ended it, the Jim Crow system of racial segregation of public facilities was virtually universal in the southern states. Should states have been left alone to address how to change this system or was federal intervention essential?

and administered by local officials (see Table 16.1). The evaluation of test results was entirely up to local officials, who rarely passed blacks, even those with a college education or a PhD. If white voters failed the literacy test, many states allowed them to vote anyway under the **grandfather clause**, which provided that anyone whose ancestors had voted prior to 1867 could vote as well. Because the ancestors

grandfather clause
A device that allowed whites who had failed the literacy test to vote anyway by extending the franchise to anyone whose ancestors had voted prior to 1867.

TABLE 16.1 SELECTED ITEMS FROM THE ALABAMA LITERACY TEST

These 10 questions are part of the 68-question Alabama Literacy Test used to decide on the eligibility of voters in that state. The test and others like it were declared illegal by the 1965 Voting Rights Act. Most white voters who were unable to pass this or similar tests in the states of the Deep South were protected by a "grandfather clause" allowing people to vote whose grandfathers had done so.

1. A person appointed to the U.S. Supreme Court is appointed for a term of _____.

2. If a person is indicted for a crime, name two rights which he has.

3. Cases tried before a court of law are of what two types: civil and _____.

4. If no candidate for president receives a majority of the electoral vote, who decides who will become president?

5. If no person receives a majority of the electoral vote, the vice president is chosen by the Senate. True or False?

6. If an effort to impeach the President of the United States is made, who presides at the trial?

7. If the two houses of Congress do not agree to adjournment, who sets the time?

8. A president elected in November takes office the following year on what date?

9. Of the original 13 states, the one with the largest representation in the first Congress was _____.

10. The Constitution limits the size of the District of Columbia _____.

Answers: (1) good behavior; life; (2) jury trial, protection against self incrimination, right to counsel, speedy trial, protection against excessive bail; (3) criminal; (4) the House of Representatives; (5) true; (6) although not stipulated in the Constitution, the House has always turned to its Judiciary Committee to manage the impeachment process; (7) the president; (8) January 20; (9) Virginia; (10) not to exceed 10 miles square.

white primaries

Primary elections open only to whites in the one-party South where the only elections that mattered were the Democratic Party's primaries; this effectively disenfranchised blacks.

strict scrutiny

The assumption that actions by elected bodies or officials violate the Constitution.

of African Americans in the South had been slaves, the grandfather clause was no help to them at all.

Several states instituted **white primaries** that excluded African Americans from the process of nominating candidates for local, state, and national offices. The states argued that excluding blacks from primaries was acceptable because political parties were private associations that could define their own membership requirements, including skin color. In the one-party (Democratic) South at the time, the actual election of public officials happened in the state Democratic primaries, leaving those few African Americans who voted in the November general elections without any voice at all. And, for those African Americans who might try to vote anyway in the face of the poll tax, the literacy test, and the white primary, there was always the use of terror as a deterrent: night riding, bombings, and lynchings were used with regularity, especially during times when blacks showed signs of assertiveness.

The statutory devices for keeping African Americans away from the polls were consistently supported by state and federal courts until well into the twentieth century. Terror as a means of preventing voting remained a factor until the 1960s, when the civil rights movement and federal intervention finally put an end to it.

WOMEN AND THE FIFTEENTH AND NINETEENTH AMENDMENTS Politically active women were stung by their exclusion from the Fifteenth Amendment's extension of the right to vote, as the amendment said only that no state could exclude people on the grounds of "race, color, or previous condition of servitude." Thus, they quickly turned their attention to winning the vote for women. Once the Supreme Court had decided, in *Minor v. Happersett* (1874), that women's suffrage was not a right inherent in the national citizenship guarantees of the Fourteenth Amendment, many women abandoned legal challenges and turned to more direct forms of political agitation: petitions, marches, and protests. After years of struggle, the efforts of the women's suffrage movement bore fruit in the Nineteenth Amendment, ratified in 1920: "The right of citizens of the United States to vote shall not be denied or abridged by the United States or by any State on account of sex."

The Contemporary Status of Civil Rights for Racial and Ethnic Minorities

16.2   Assess the present status of civil rights protections for racial minorities

Explore on **MyPoliSciLab**
Simulation
You Are a Mayor

The Supreme Court, using the guidelines written by Justice Harlan Fiske Stone in *United States v. Carolene Products Company* (1938), gradually extended the protections of the Bill of Rights to the states, based on the Fourteenth Amendment. Recall that among the actions by the states that would trigger **strict scrutiny** under the *Carolene* guidelines were those that either "restricted the democratic process" or "discriminated against racial, ethnic, or religious minorities." This reading of the Fourteenth Amendment, particularly the equal protection clause, lent judicial support to the gradual advance of civil rights guarantees for African Americans and other minorities and eventually (although less so) for women. In the following sections, we look at the extension of the civil rights of racial and ethnic minorities, women, and other groups, including gays and lesbians. Here we concentrate mainly (although not exclusively) on Supreme Court decisions,[8] the actions of other branches of government regarding civil rights, and the standing of these groups in American politics. As you consider these materials, recall the important role that protest and social movements played in improving the civil rights of a broad range of Americans. Without these movements and the pressures they brought to bear on public opinion, elected officials, and the courts, many of the changes we now take for granted would surely not have happened.

Two basic issues have dominated the story of the extension of civil rights for African Americans since the mid-1960s:

- The ending of legally sanctioned discrimination, separation, and exclusion from citizenship.

- The debate over what actions to take that would remedy the past wrongs done to African Americans.

We examine both in this section.

Ending Government-Sponsored Separation and Discrimination

We reviewed earlier how the Constitution was long interpreted to condone slavery and segregation. In the twentieth century, however, the legal and political battles waged by the civil rights movement eventually pushed the Supreme Court, the president, and Congress to take seriously the equal protection clause of the Fourteenth Amendment. The "Can Government Do Anything Well?" feature looks closely at the role of the federal government in this story.

In 1944, amid World War II (a war aimed in great part at bringing down the racist regime of Adolf Hitler) and the NAACP's campaign to rid the nation of segregation, the Supreme Court finally declared that race was a **suspect classification** that demanded strict judicial scrutiny. This meant that any local ordinance, or state

suspect classification
The invidious, arbitrary, or irrational designation of a group for special treatment by government, whether positive or negative; historically, a discriminated against, visible minority without the power to protect itself.

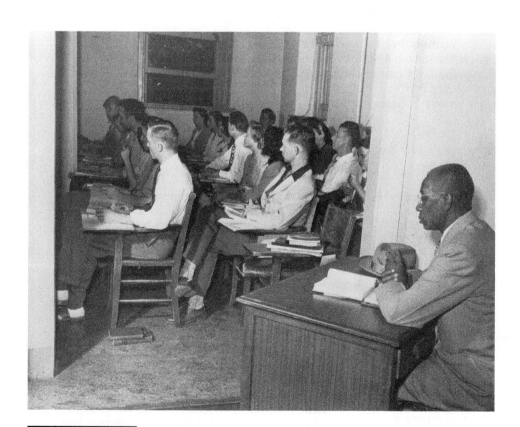

GRUDGING INTEGRATION

The erosion of official segregation in education came slowly and reluctantly in many parts of the nation. When ordered by a federal court in 1948 to admit a qualified black applicant, the University of Oklahoma law school did so but forced the lone student to sit separated from other students. Did the ruling truly allow for the university to so blatantly discriminate against minority students, or did the university follow the law by just admitting them?

Can Government Do Anything Well?

Making "equal protection" a reality

It required federal government intervention and oversight of the states of the former Confederacy to fulfill the promise of the "equal protection" clause of the Fourteenth Amendment for African Americans. Passed in the wake of the Civil War, the Fourteenth Amendment was intended to make former slaves (in effect, males only, since the states did not allow women to vote) full citizens of the United States and of the states in which they lived, with all the rights and privileges of other citizens. Beginning in 1877 when the federal government withdrew its troops from the South marking the end of Reconstruction, the Southern states imposed a system of racial separation and subordination, called Jim Crow, that was similar to the apartheid system of South Africa. Under this system, African Americans were barred from "white only" establishments (restaurants, taverns, hotels, boarding houses, and the like), had separate sections to which they were confined on public conveyances such as trains and buses, had separate and inferior schools, were denied access to certain occupations, enjoyed few protections from the police, and were denied the right to vote and to hold public office.

By the 1960s, national leaders became persuaded that Jim Crow would have to end and that the South would not or could not do it on its own. There are many reasons why they reached this conclusion. They were embarrassed by the existence of racial segregation when we were in a Cold War struggle with the Soviet Union for the "hearts and minds" of people in the Third World, most of whom had dark skin. There was the fact, as well, that African Americans outside the South had the right to vote and used it effectively, especially in states where they lived that had lots of electoral votes (Illinois, New York, Pennsylvania, and California, among others), something to which elected leaders paid attention. The civil rights movement gained strength in the 1950s and reached full fruition in the 1960s, bringing moral pressure on national leaders to end Jim Crow, but also the political muscle of organized labor. So here is a partial list of what the national government did to end Jim Crow. In 1954, the Supreme Court ruled in *Brown v. Board of Education* that "separate but equal" in schools, and by implication other areas of social life, was constitutionally unacceptable. In follow-up cases, the Court pressed the southern states to end segregated schools "with all deliberate speed" and, when they violently resisted in some instances, presidents sent in troops to carry out court orders—President Eisenhower sent the 101st Airborne to Little Rock, Arkansas, in 1957, and President Kennedy sent troops to Oxford, Mississippi, in 1962. President Johnson used the FBI to infiltrate and disrupt the KKK in the mid-1960s. In 1964, Congress and the president passed the Civil Rights Act to end segregation in public accommodations. In 1965, the Voting Rights Act declared illegal the various devices used by the southern states to keep African Americans from the polls, provided for federal officials to take over the voting registration process, and forced the states in the South that had done the most to keep African Americans from voting to seek approval from the Justice Department when they legislated anything to do with the voting process.

Support for the claim that the federal government has been necessary for the provision of "equal protection" for African Americans:

- All citizens are guaranteed equal protection by the Constitution. The Fourteenth Amendment requires states to do this, but the southern states failed to do this for their African American citizens for three-quarters of a century after its adoption. It is the responsibility of the federal government to enforce the Constitution and court orders related to it.

- Southern states, especially in the Deep South, showed no signs of ending segregation on their own, even into the 1960s.

- After 1965, African Americans began to vote in the South, electing African Americans across all levels of government, from representatives in Congress, to members of state legislatures, city council members, and county sheriffs.

- By the end of the 1960s, de jure segregation of the races in restaurants, taverns, theaters, buses, trains, and hotels had disappeared.

Rejection of the claim that the federal government has been necessary for the provision of "equal protection" for African Americans:

- The various actions described above are a violation of states' rights under our federal Constitution; a solution to the equal protection problem should have been left to the states.

- The Supreme Court failed to practice stare decisis in their *Brown* decision, overturning historic precedents preserving states' rights in the area of race relations.

- Presidents and Congresses, in passing the Civil Rights Act and the Voting Rights Act, were practicing social engineering, and brought unwanted change to an entire region of the United States.

- Rapid changes in race relations wrought by federal government action led to social tensions, violent street protests, and more crime.

- As often happens when the federal government gets involved, the push for equal protection went too far, morphing into affirmative action and racial quotas to redress past discrimination and bring more diversity.

WHAT DO YOU THINK?

What do you think about the past, present, and future role of the federal government in providing equal protection for African Americans and other minorities?

- The federal government needed to take actions to force states to provide equal protection and must continue to do so as some states seek ways to limit the participation of African Americans in the voting process.
- The federal government needed to take actions to force states to provide equal protection but no further action is needed as African Americans are now fully integrated into American life and politics.
- The federal government was never needed to force states to provide equal protection for its African American citizens and it violated the letter and spirit of federalism in doing so. It certainly is no longer needed as African Americans are now fully integrated into American life and politics.

How would you defend your position to a fellow student? What would be your main line of argument? What evidence do you believe best supports your position? For help in developing your argument, please refer to the sources listed in the "Can Government Do Anything Well" feature in Chapter 2 on p. 48.

Additional sources for this feature: James MacGregor Burns and Stewart Burns, *A People's Charter* (New York: Knopf, 1991).

or national statute, using racial criteria was presumed to be unconstitutional unless it could be shown that such an ordinance or statute was both necessary and compelling. Pressed by the legal efforts of the NAACP, the Court gradually chipped away at the *Plessy* "separate but equal" doctrine and the edifice of segregation it helped create. In *Smith v. Allwright* (1944), the Court declared that the practice of excluding nonwhites from political-party primary elections was unconstitutional. Then the Court ruled that the states' practice of providing separate all-white and all-black law schools was unacceptable. Many of the key cases before the Supreme Court that eroded the official structure of segregation were argued by Thurgood Marshall—later a justice of the Supreme Court—for the NAACP.[9]

The great legal breakthrough for racial equality came in *Brown v. Board of Education of Topeka* (1954), also argued on the plaintiffs' side by Thurgood Marshall. The Court declared that "separate but equal" was inherently contradictory and that segregation imposed by state and local laws was constitutionally unacceptable in public schools because it violated guarantees of equal protection. Chief Justice Earl Warren, speaking for a unanimous Court, said that education was "perhaps the most important function of state and local governments" and that segregation in education communicated the message that blacks were inferior and deserving of unequal treatment. "In the field of education [in Warren's words] the doctrine of 'separate but equal' has no place."[10] *Brown* was a constitutional revolution, destined to transform racial relations law and practices in the United States, because it struck down the foundations of segregation and discrimination.[11]

The white South did not react violently at first, but it did not desegregate either. Once recognition spread that the Court was going to enforce civil rights, however, massive resistance to racial integration gripped the South. Citizens Councils (white) committed to imposing economic sanctions and boycotts on anybody who supported desegregation had over 250,000 members by 1956. Membership in the KKK increased dramatically, along with beatings, cross-burnings, and killing of blacks and their white supporters.[12] This resistance was what Dr. Martin Luther King Jr. and others had to work (and die) to overcome. The Court—even with many follow-up cases—was able to accomplish little before the president and Congress backed up the justices with the 1964 Civil Rights Act and the 1965 Voting Rights Act. The civil rights movement and supportive changes in American public opinion in favor of protections for blacks helped spur these legislative and judicial actions.

The drive to protect the rights of racial minorities has occupied the nation ever since. The prevailing legal doctrine on racial discrimination is straightforward: Any use

THE MARCH ON WASHINGTON

Dr. Martin Luther King Jr. waves to a crowd of an estimated half-million people at the March on Washington at the Lincoln Memorial after delivering his "I Have a Dream" speech on August 28, 1963. This event, one of the high points of the civil rights movement, helped convince Congress to pass the Civil Rights Act of 1964.

de jure discrimination

Unequal treatment based on government laws and regulations.

de facto discrimination

Unequal treatment by private individuals, groups, and organizations.

of race in law or government regulations to discriminate—sometimes called **de jure discrimination**—will trigger strict scrutiny (a presumption of unconstitutionality) by the courts. Recall from our earlier discussion that a state or the federal government can defend its acts under strict scrutiny only if it can produce a *compelling* government interest for which the act in question is a *necessary* means. Almost no law survives this challenge; laws that discriminate on the basis of race are dead from the moment of passage. In *Loving v. Virginia* (1967), for example, the Court ruled that Virginia's law against interracial marriage served no compelling government purpose that would justify unequal treatment of the races. Needless to say, other racial minority groups in addition to African Americans—Latinos, Asian Americans, and Native Americans—have benefited from the constitutional revolution that has occurred.[13]

To say that racial discrimination in the law is no longer constitutionally acceptable does not mean that discrimination against racial minorities has disappeared from the United States. **De facto discrimination**—unequal treatment by private individuals, groups, and organizations—remains a fact of life, although its exact extent is hard to measure accurately. For example, 68 percent of African Americans and 52 percent of Latinos tell pollsters they have experienced a specific instance in which they felt discriminated against, while 51 percent of blacks claim that there is job discrimination in their community.[14]

Moreover, there remain perceptions among minority group members that discriminatory treatment by public officials has not disappeared. For example, all minorities report bad experiences with racial profiling by police. Fifty-two percent of black men and 25 percent of Latino and Asian men claim to have been stopped by police for no apparent reason. Although various police departments have taken steps to stop these practices, the courts have never defined racial profiling as suspect, especially if some important law enforcement need is being met by it.[15] But sometimes profiling may go too far. In Arizona, according to a report from the Justice Department, the Maricopa County Sheriff's office, led by "America's toughest sheriff" (his self-description) Joe Arpaio, has systematically targeted Latinos for traffic violations—Latinos were stopped four to nine times more than whites—repeatedly conducted illegal searches during these stops, and routinely mistreated Spanish-speaking inmates in the county's jails.[16]

The examples just given are actions or perceived actions by government officials that have discriminatory effects without any explicit reference to race or ethnicity in regulations, ordinances, and statutes. Sheriff Joe Arpaio claims, for instance, that the target of his department's aggressive policing has been illegal immigrants, not Latinos. Likewise, new voter identification laws in scores of states, purportedly aimed at ending voter fraud, may have the effect of keeping poor African Americans and Latinos from the polls, along with 18- to 25-year-olds and the elderly, those least likely to have government-issued ID cards. (Using this argument, Attorney General Eric Holder blocked South Carolina's voter ID law in 2012 under provisions of the Voting Rights Act that prohibit state actions that are likely to have a discriminatory effect on the right to vote.) And, the recent near-hysteria over illegal immigrants has resulted in rather draconian measures in a number of states that have drawn not only undocumented people to police attention but also law-abiding Hispanic citizens and noncitizen visa holders. One section of a recent Alabama statute, for example, *requires* law enforcement officials to determine the immigration status of people they stop for routine traffic violations if they have a "reasonable suspicion" they may be undocumented. The law also specifies that "willful failure" to carry immigration papers by noncitizens is a felony, persuading many Hispanic citizens in the state to carry papers at all times for fear of being whisked off to a detention center until matters might be cleared up.[17] Ruling in 2012 on a similar law in Arizona, the Supreme Court allowed police to inquire about immigration status of people during stops but disallowed the other provisions. The Court also made it clear that while it would allow states to have their police make such inquiries, they would need to do so on a non-discriminatory basis. It remains to be seem how all this will be sorted out.

☐ Affirmative Action

Despite these examples of real or perceived mistreatment by governments, it is now widely accepted that the Constitution protects racial minorities against any discrimination or disadvantage that is sanctioned or protected by law or government action. The issues are not as clear-cut, however, in the area of government actions that *favor* racial and ethnic minorities (and women) in **affirmative action** programs designed to rectify past wrongs.[18]

ORIGINS OF AFFIRMATIVE ACTION The main goal of the civil rights movement of the 1950s and 1960s was to remove barriers to equal citizenship for black Americans. This goal was largely accomplished by Court decisions, passage of the 1964 Civil Rights Act and the Voting Rights Act of 1965 and by broad changes in public attitudes about race. But even with these important changes, the economic and social situations of African Americans did not seem to be improving much. It seemed to an increasing number of people that ending discrimination was a start, but that more proactive government actions would be required if African Americans were to escape the conditions that years of discrimination had put them in. President Lyndon Johnson, Robert Kennedy, and Martin Luther King Jr., among others, eventually came to believe that the advancement of black Americans could happen only if there was a broad societal effort to eradicate poverty by equipping the poor, black and white, with the tools for success. This led to the founding of the Johnson administration's Great Society and War on Poverty and programs such as Head Start.

After Martin Luther King's assassination, however, and the urban riots that followed, many people in government, the media, higher education, and the major foundations began to support the notion that progress for African Americans would happen only if government encouraged proactive efforts to increase the levels of black representation in private and public sector jobs and contracting, and in colleges and universities.[19] Somewhat surprisingly, it was Richard Nixon, not generally thought of as a booster of civil rights, who took the most important step, requiring in his 1969 Philadelphia Plan that construction companies with federal contracts and the associated construction trade unions hire enough blacks and other minorities to achieve "racial balance" (a proportion roughly equal to the racial distribution in the community).

affirmative action
Programs of private and public institutions favoring minorities and women in hiring and contracting, and in admissions to colleges and universities, in an attempt to compensate for past discrimination or to create more diversity.

16.1
16.2
16.3
16.4

Are All Forms of Discrimination the Same?

In the 1967 *Loving v. Virginia* decision, the Supreme Court ruled unconstitutional all laws that restricted marriage based solely on race. Today, a similar debate revolves around marriage for same-sex couples. Public opposition to interracial marriage had been declining steadily before the Court ruling and continued after the Court issued its ruling — as shown in the 1972 and 1988 data. Has opinion about same-sex marriage changed in a similar way?

"Should Interracial Marriage Be Legal?"

1972

REGION	YES	NO
Northeast	71%	26%
Midwest	61%	35%
South	43%	53%
Rocky Mountains	54%	41%
Pacifc Coast	74%	24%

1988

REGION	YES	NO
Northeast	85%	11%
Midwest	76%	21%
South	62%	35%
Rocky Mountains	89%	11%
Pacifc Coast	87%	12%

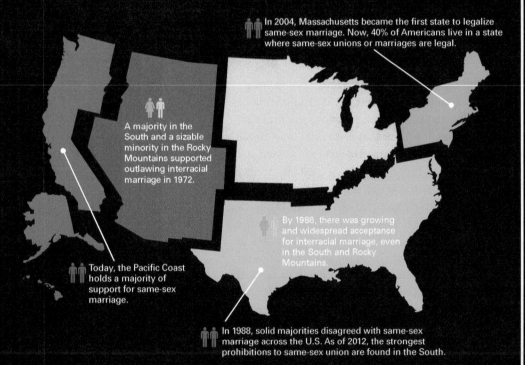

In 2004, Massachusetts became the first state to legalize same-sex marriage. Now, 40% of Americans live in a state where same-sex unions or marriages are legal.

A majority in the South and a sizable minority in the Rocky Mountains supported outlawing interracial marriage in 1972.

By 1988, there was growing and widespread acceptance for interracial marriage, even in the South and Rocky Mountains.

Today, the Pacific Coast holds a majority of support for same-sex marriage.

In 1988, solid majorities disagreed with same-sex marriage across the U.S. As of 2012, the strongest prohibitions to same-sex union are found in the South.

"Should Same-Sex Marriage Be Legal?"

1988

REGION	YES	NO
Northeast	12%	63%
Midwest	12%	66%
South	8%	78%
Rocky Mountains	12%	63%
Pacifc Coast	16%	62%

2010

REGION	YES	NO
Northeast	54%	30%
Midwest	50%	41%
South	38%	46%
Rocky Mountains	45%	44%
Pacifc Coast	52%	33%

SOURCE: General Social Survey data from 1972, 1988, and 2010.

Investigate Further

Concept How do we measure discrimination regarding interracial and same-sex marriage? Pollsters ask if a person agrees or disagrees with policy proposals, such as laws that recognize same-sex or interracial marriage. By watching the responses over time, we are able to determine changes in attitudes across the country.

Connection How does geography help predict public opinion on interracial marriage and same-sex marriage? The American South and Rocky Mountains are historically more conservative regions, and more resistant to changing definitions of marriage. But, even in these regions, opinion on marriage became much more liberal over time.

Cause Does opinion about marriage influence policy or vice versa? After the Supreme Court settled the matter of interracial marriage in 1967, majority opinions followed suit across the country, though public opinion had been changing even before the Court ruled. Support for same-sex marriage has also changed over time, but policies vary by state. Legalization is more common where public opinion is most favorable, and bans are most common where support lags.

Although initially skeptical of racial preferences, Justices William Brennan, Byron White, Thurgood Marshall, and Harry Blackmun supported temporary programs to remedy the effects of past discrimination. Joined by Justice Lewis Powell, they formed the majority in *Regents v. Bakke* (1978), in which the Court authorized a compromise on affirmative action programs. The Constitution and federal law prohibited employers and admissions committees from using strictly racial quotas, the Court said, but it saw no problem with the use of race as one factor among several in hiring or college admissions.

Since *Bakke*, government and higher education racial outreach programs, which were preferred at that time, have become relatively permanent rather than temporary, and their aim has shifted from providing remedies for past discrimination to enhancing diversity. The proliferation of diversity programs, diversity training, and diversity offices has become commonplace in colleges and universities, in government, and in the corporate world.

WHY AFFIRMATIVE ACTION?[20] For the most part, according to proponents, affirmative action programs that promote diversity are needed for the following reasons:

- The effects of past discrimination disadvantage, to one degree or another, all members of discriminated-against groups, so simply removing barriers to advancement is insufficient. When government policies themselves have had profound and lasting effects—slavery being the most obvious, but also state-sanctioned segregation, and racial discrimination in major benefit programs such as the post–World War II GI Bill[21]—the proper remedy is to prefer members of such groups in hiring, contracts, and education until such time as they reach parity with the majority.

- In a diverse society such as the United States, tolerance and a sense of community can develop only if we work together in educational, workplace, and government institutions that are diverse.

- People from disadvantaged and discriminated-against groups will improve themselves only if they have experience with successful role models in important institutions.

Critics of affirmative action are not convinced by these arguments. They believe:

- Affirmative action violates one of the most basic American principles: that people be judged, rewarded, and punished as individuals, not because they are members of one group or another.

- Affirmative action benefits those within each preferred group who are already advantaged and need little help. Thus, the main beneficiaries of affirmative action in higher education have been middle-class African Americans, not the poor.

- Affirmative action seeks to remedy the effects of past discrimination by discriminating against others today—most notably, white males—simply because they belong to nonpreferred groups.

- Affirmative action increases intergroup and interracial tension by heightening the saliency of group membership. That is, social friction is increased by encouraging people to think of themselves and others as members of groups and to seek group advantages in a zero-sum game in which one group's gain is another group's loss.

PUBLIC OPINION ON AFFIRMATIVE ACTION In survey after survey, a vast majority of Americans say they approve of the diversity goals of affirmative action—special programs to help those who have been discriminated against get ahead; outreach programs to hire minority workers and find minority students—but disapprove of racial preferences in hiring, awarding of government contracts, and admission to colleges.[22] Most polling organizations show the following pattern: when asked whether they generally support affirmative action, about 50 to 60 percent of Americans say they approve; when the survey asks whether they favor affirmative action programs that involve preferential treatment or "set-asides" for racial minorities and women, support erodes dramatically. Not surprisingly, perhaps, racial differences on the issue of preferential treatment are wide; in 2009, 58 percent of African Americans and 53 percent

AFFIRMATIVE ACTION AT MICHIGAN

These two University of Michigan room mates expressed their surprise to journalists that the Supreme Court had ruled the university's undergraduate admissions process unconstitutional because of its overt and mechanical use of race in the admitting decision in the landmark case *Gratz v. Bollinger* (2003). Should some form of affirmative action continue so long as deep racial disparities in higher education continue or should other methods be found for overcoming such disparities?

of Latinos supported affirmative action programs that involved preferential treatment, whereas only 22 percent of whites did, a drop from 27 percent in 2007.[23]

American discomfort with affirmative action programs can perhaps be best seen in actions in several of the states. For example, referenda banning affirmative action in any state and local government activity were passed in California (1996), Washington (1997), and Michigan (2006)—three very liberal states—and other states have severely restricted affirmative action by executive order of their governors.[24] In 2008, Nebraska voters approved a measure that bans government use of affirmative action; Colorado voters narrowly rejected a ban, the first time affirmative action bans at the state level had failed at the polls.

THE SUPREME COURT ON AFFIRMATIVE ACTION   The Supreme Court has been grappling for years with the issue of which forms of affirmative action, if any, are constitutionally permissible. Recall that the prevailing constitutional doctrine on matters of race holds that any mention of race in a government statute, ordinance, or rule is subject to strict scrutiny—that is, unconstitutional—unless the government can show some compelling and necessary reason for it. Historically, of course, there is good reason for the Court to take this position, given the fact that laws mentioning race were usually designed to deny equal protection to African Americans and other racial and religious minorities. But what about government actions meant to compensate African Americans and others for past discriminatory actions? Or initiatives to increase diversity in a broad range of institutions such as police departments and universities?

Since the mid-1980s, the Supreme Court has been moving gradually toward the position that laws and other government actions that are not colorblind should be subject to strict scrutiny. In *Wygant v. Jackson Board of Education* (1986) and *Richmond v. Croson Co.* (1989), the Supreme Court said programs that narrowly redress specific violations will be upheld as constitutional but that broader affirmative action programs that address society's racism will be struck down. In *Adarand Constructors v. Peña* (1995), the Court ruled by a 5–4 majority that the federal government must abide by the strict standards for affirmative action programs imposed on the states in the *Richmond* case and could not award contracts using race as the main criterion. In *Miller v. Johnson* (1995), the Court ruled, again by a 5–4 majority, that race could not be used as the basis for drawing House district lines in an effort to increase the number of racial minority members in Congress.[25] In 1997, the Court refused to overturn a ruling of the Ninth Circuit Court that California's anti–affirmative action Proposition 209 was constitutionally permissible. In 2001, the Court let stand a decision by the Eleventh U.S. Circuit Court of Appeals that disallowed a Fulton County, Georgia, program setting annual goals for awarding county contracts to blacks, Latinos, Asians, Native Americans, and women.

Given these rulings by the Rehnquist Court, civil rights organizations were braced for a decision by the Supreme Court that would render affirmative action admissions policies unconstitutional once and for all. When the Court agreed to hear two admissions cases involving the University of Michigan—one involving its undergraduate program, the other its law school—liberals dreaded the outcome, while conservatives could hardly wait for the ruling. The Court stunned virtually every political observer when it ruled by a 5–4 vote in late June 2003 that universities could take race into consideration when considering applications for admission, so long as the consideration of race was not done in a mechanically quantitative manner or used as part of a racial and ethnic quota system, reaffirming, as it were, its position in the 1978 *Bakke* decision. (See the "Using the Framework" feature for more on why this happened.) In its twin decisions, the Court rejected the University of Michigan's undergraduate admissions affirmative action program—because it automatically assigned extra points to each minority applicant—but accepted the law school's—whose admissions process uses race as but one among several factors in a holistic examination of each applicant's file. What surprised observers the most, perhaps, was not the decision itself, but the broad language that Justice Sandra Day O'Connor used in her majority opinion, in which she stressed that achieving diversity in universities, and especially in its elite law schools, was indeed a compelling reason for not applying strict scrutiny by the Court:

> In order to cultivate a set of leaders with legitimacy in the eyes of the citizenry, it is necessary that the path to leadership be visibly open to the talented and qualified individuals of every race and ethnicity. . . . Access to legal education (and thus the legal profession) must be inclusive of talented and qualified individuals of every race and ethnicity so that all members of our heterogeneous society may participate in the educational institutions that provide the training and education necessary to succeed in America. . . . Cross-racial understanding helps to break down racial stereotypes and better prepares graduates for the working world. . . . The law school's educational judgment that such diversity is essential to its educational mission is one to which we defer.[26]

After the University of Michigan cases, here is where affirmative action stood as of Fall 2012, when the Supreme Court took up the case of *Fisher v. Texas* challenging its Michigan rulings:

- Any program by a government entity that uses race to define who receives or does not receive benefits or services is subject to strict scrutiny—that is, considered unconstitutional unless compelling and necessary reasons for the policies are proved. This holds whether or not such policies are designed to discriminate against or favor racial minorities.

- With respect to the award of government contracts and government hiring—whether federal, state, or local—affirmative action programs are acceptable only if they are narrowly tailored to rectify past discriminatory actions by that particular government agency. In the view of the Court, rectifying past racist actions by a particular government agency is a compelling reason. Such programs, however, must be temporary efforts to transcend past practices and not a permanent feature of hiring and contracting. Affirmative action in hiring and contracting is not valid if it is designed simply to increase diversity or to decrease racism in society.

- With respect to admission to educational institutions—into undergraduate and graduate programs, law schools, and medical schools—actions to rectify past discriminatory admissions policies by a particular higher education institution are compelling and necessary, and are permitted.

- With respect to higher education admissions, the goal of achieving a diverse student body is a compelling reason to have affirmative action programs. However, race can only be used if it is one among several factors in a holistic consideration of each applicant's file; formulas in which students of a particular race or ethnicity automatically receive a set number of points are not permissible.

With Justice O'Connor now retired and replaced by Samuel Alito, a strong conservative, and with the Supreme Court now led by Chief Justice John Roberts, on record as opposing the use of affirmative action for increasing diversity or fixing societal wrongs, many civil rights advocates had been worried that even the narrow opening provided by the Michigan decisions would not stand for long. They worried with reason that any use of race in government programs would trigger strict scrutiny, even if such programs are designed to rectify a long history of exclusion. This almost happened in 2007; by a 5–4 margin, the Roberts Court ruled in two paired cases that race-based systems for making primary and secondary school assignments in Seattle and Louisville were unconstitutional.[27] Although the Chief Justice and three of his colleagues wanted to exercise strict scrutiny in both—as Roberts put it, "The way to stop discrimination on the basis of race is to stop discriminating on the basis of race"—Justice Anthony Kennedy, who cast the deciding votes on these cases, refused to go this far. He simply stated in his majority opinions that the Seattle and Louisville systems were not sufficiently tailored to remedy past discrimination in these particular school districts. Opponents of affirmative action waited eagerly for the Court's ruling in Fisher that would clarify the legal status of race in education.

Outside of education, the Roberts Court edged very close in *Ricci v. DeStefano* (2009) to ending the use of race at all in government programs except in manifest cases of overt discrimination. The case was brought by 18 New Haven firefighters (1 Hispanic, 17 white) who claimed they were denied the opportunity for promotion when the city threw out promotion examination results because no African American was in the top group. The city decided not to promote anyone. The Supreme Court agreed with the firefighters that the city of New Haven had practiced reverse discrimination in throwing out the examination results, overturning New Haven's victories at the district and appeals court levels. Significantly, the Court based its ruling on narrow grounds, rather than on broad constitutional ones, saying that New Haven was guilty of "disparate treatment based on race," which was contrary to the Civil Rights Act. Justice Antonin Scalia was not happy, saying in his concurring opinion that the Court was simply postponing the inevitable day when race-based laws and programs would be deemed unconstitutional under the "equal protection" clause of the Fourteenth Amendment.[28]

Affirmative action programs in the United States have been designed to help not only African Americans, of course, but other racial and ethnic minorities as well, including Latinos, Asian Americans, and Native Americans. Most of the programs also have included women as beneficiaries. The present Supreme Court guidelines on affirmative action described here apply to all of these groups, not only African Americans. So the extreme narrowing of the acceptability by the Court of affirmative action affects each of these groups.

The Contemporary Status of Civil Rights for Women

16.3 Assess the present status of civil rights protections for women

s the civil rights movement helped put the issue of equality for African Americans on the nation's political agenda, so did several women's rights movements advance civil rights protections for women. The struggle for women's suffrage, for example, was long and hard, finally succeeding in 1920. Fifty years later, the women's movement of the 1970s and 1980s helped win civil rights protections for women and broaden the participation of women in all aspects

Using the FRAMEWORK

Why did the Supreme Court dramatically narrow the scope of affirmative action programs?

Background: During the 1990s, the Supreme Court rendered a number of decisions that narrowed the use of racial preferences in the areas of government hiring and contracting, congressional redistricting, and university admissions. It therefore came as a great surprise to both proponents and critics of affirmative action when the Supreme Court ruled by a 5–4 vote in a pair of cases involving the University of Michigan in 2003 that affirmative action of a certain kind—one that uses race as only one among several factors in a holistic consideration of each individual's file—is permissible in university admissions. The ruling was made possible by the emergence in the late 1990s of a new Court majority, on certain issues, led by Sandra Day O'Connor. After she was replaced by Samuel Alito in 2006, the Court veered sharply again against affirmative action.

Government Action

The Roberts Court ruled that race cannot be used in school assignments in primary and secondary schools. ➡ The Roberts Court ruled in *Ricci* that "reverse discrimination" is illegal under the Civil Rights Act.

The Supreme Court rejected diversity as a compelling state interest in programs involving government jobs and contracting, and in congressional districting. ➡ The Rehnquist Court ruled in 2003 that the use of race in university admissions is permissible if it is not used as part of a mechanical, quantitative formula.

Government

A slim new majority, led by Sandra Day O'Connor that supported affirmative action in important institutions to increase diversity had emerged by the late 1990s. O'Connor retired in 2006 and was replaced by committed conservative Samuel Alito.

Republican presidents Reagan and Bush nominated conservatives to the Court. ➡ The Senate approved the nominees. ➡ A narrow but firm conservative majority under the leadership of Chief Justice William Rehnquist controlled the Court on many issues during the early 1990s.

Political Linkage

Anti-government conservatives gained political influence in the 1980s. ➡ Republicans, whose platform rejects affirmative action, reached parity with Democrats in national elections. ➡ Republicans won control of the Senate from 1981–1986 and from 1995 to 2000.

The political influence of civil rights organizations declined in the 1980s and 1990s. ➡ The majority white population reported in polls that it believed the goals of the civil rights movement had been met. ➡ A substantial majority of Americans reported support for nondiscrimination laws but distaste for laws that give minorities and women special advantages in college admissions, jobs, and government contracts.

Structure

The Fourteenth Amendment's promise of "equal protection" bars government discrimination against groups of citizens but is unclear about the need for remedies for past discrimination. ➡ The political culture honors individual rather than group rights and responsibilities. ➡ The white middle and working classes suffered economic reverses during the 1980s and early 1990s, creating a climate that was generally hostile to affirmative action programs.

Mapping American Politics

Comparing Women's Progress

Introduction

There are many ways to evaluate how well women are doing in the United States at the beginning of the twenty-first century. One way is to look at various over-time measures comparing women and men in the United States. On a number of these measures, cited at various points in this book, we have noted many signs of progress, as well as areas where the news is not so good. On the plus side of the ledger, women have improved their relative position with men on measures such as median income; median income within occupations and professions; representation among the ranks of the professions, especially medicine, law, higher education, and journalism; and improved legal protections. Not as much progress has been made, however, in breaking the "glass ceiling" in the corporate and financial worlds or in reaching parity in the holding of elective offices. To be sure, there are several women who have been or are in politically powerful positions, including former House Speaker Nancy Pelosi and Obama's Secretary of State and leading contender for the 2008 Democratic nomination, Hillary Clinton. And, Sarah Palin was the GOP nominee for vice president in 2008.

Another way to look at women's relative standing is to compare the situation in the United States to the situation in the rest of the world. Taking that approach, using the particular measure reflected in this cartogram, women in the United States are doing very well indeed.

Mapping Women Managers and Professionals

This cartogram shows each country's share of the world's 130 million female managers and professionals.

Managers and professionals are defined in the data set used to draw the cartogram—from the United Nation's 2004 Human Development Report—as people who are technical workers, senior officials in the public and private sectors, managers, or legislators, and making more than $30,000 a year. What the cartogram shows is that virtually all the world's female managers and professionals are located in the United States and Western Europe. Indeed, according to the data from the Human Development Report, almost one-half of all women managers and professionals in the world live and work in the United States. Doing particularly poorly on this measure are such emerging economic powers as China, India, and Russia and the oil-producing states of the Middle East.

What Do You Think?

How have women's situation and standing in the United States been improving? Where do they still need improving? Does it matter how women are doing relative to women elsewhere, or do you think we should concentrate on how well women are doing in our own country relative to men over time? In what areas of American life are women doing better, and in what areas are they doing worse? If you see room for improvement, what role do you think government should play in helping out? Or, do you think matters such as this are best left to the private sector?

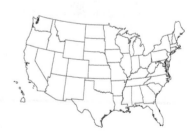

Standard US Map

SOURCE: Worldmapper, map number 133. The SASI Group (University of Sheffield) and Mark Newman (University of Michigan) 2006. (www.worldmapper.org).

of American society, economy, and politics. Although the movement did not win one of its main objectives—passage of the Equal Rights Amendment (ERA) to the U.S. Constitution—the broad advance of women in gaining equal treatment and respect on virtually all fronts in the United States attests to its overall effectiveness.[29] Issues such as pay equity, family leave, sexual harassment, and attention to women's health problems in medical research are now a part of the American political agenda. Women have made important gains economically and are becoming more numerous in the professions, corporate managerial offices (although there is evidence that a glass ceiling remains blocking many women from the most senior posts in corporations; in 2011, only 12 CEOs of *Fortune* 500 companies were women), and political office. (See the "Mapping American Politics" feature for more about how women's standing in the private sector in the United States compares with their standing in other countries.) Having said that, it remains the case that a wage gap still exists between men and women, and that the poverty rate for women is considerably higher than it is for men.

In terms of constitutional law, however, the expansion of civil rights protections for women has taken a path that differs decidedly from that for African Americans.[30]

☐ Intermediate Scrutiny

By 1976 the proposed Equal Rights Amendment (ERA) to the Constitution to guarantee full legal equality for women had stalled, falling short of the required three-fourths of the states. Moreover, the Supreme Court did not have the necessary votes for a strict scrutiny interpretation of gender classification. There was support, however, for the new doctrine that came to be called **intermediate scrutiny.** In *Craig v. Boren* (1976), six justices supported Justice William Brennan's compromise, which created a more rigorous scrutiny of gender as a *somewhat* suspect classification. In the view of the justices, the use of strict scrutiny would endanger traditional sex roles, while the use of ordinary scrutiny would allow blatant sex discrimination to survive. The Burger Court defined a test that it believed to be "just right." Under intermediate scrutiny, government enactments that relied on gender would be constitutional if the use of gender were *substantially related* to an *important objective.*[31] The test in *Craig* was refined in *United States v. Virginia* (1996), when the Court ruled that a male-only admissions policy at the state-supported Virginia Military Institute was unacceptable in that it discriminated against women. In this case, the standard to be met when men and women are treated differently in statutes and state government practices became "an exceedingly persuasive justification." Intermediate scrutiny defines a legal test, then, somewhere between strict and lax. Thus, for example, certain laws protecting pregnant women from dangerous chemicals in the workplace have passed this test. The improvement of women's rights under the doctrine of intermediate scrutiny is less than what many in the women's movement wanted.

Thus, women's rights have not followed the path of other rights and liberties. The nation has not restructured civil rights for women based on the courts' expansive reading of the equal protection clause of the Fourteenth Amendment. Rather, advances have come by virtue of changing societal attitudes about the role of women in society, increased involvement of women in politics (see Figure 16.1), and new statutes designed to equalize women's opportunities. In the private sector, women have made important advances in the corporate world and in the professions. Women now outnumber men among law school and medical school students, and more women than men go to college and graduate. While wage disparities still exist between men and women, the gap is narrowing, especially among college graduates between the ages of 25 and 34.[32] (In some cities—including New York, Chicago, Boston, and Minneapolis—young women under 30 actually earn more than their male counterparts.[33])

intermediate scrutiny
A legal test falling between ordinary and strict scrutiny relevant to issues of gender; under this test, the Supreme Court will allow gender classifications in laws if they are *substantially* related to an *important* government objective.

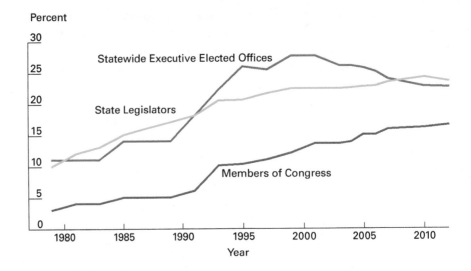

FIGURE 16.1 PERCENTAGE OF ELECTIVE OFFICES HELD BY WOMEN, 1979–2012

Although accounting for more than one-half the American population, women hold a much smaller proportion of elected federal, state, and local offices across the nation than men. However, the percentage of offices held by women has been increasing steadily since the 1970s. Given rising education and incomes among women, as well as changing social attitudes toward women's role in society, the proportion of elected offices held by women is likely to continue to increase.

Source: Center for American Women and Politics, Rutgers University (January 2012).

Women have also successfully pushed for laws that compensate for past injustices. One example of such a law is Title IX of the Civil Rights Act of 1964, which prohibits discrimination against women at federally funded institutions, including universities. Title IX is generally credited with enhancing funding for women's sports programs in colleges and dramatically improving the quality of women's athletics in the United States. Another example is the Lilly Ledbetter Fair Pay Restoration Act, signed into law by President Barack Obama in January 2009 only days after his inauguration, which makes it easier for women and others to sue their companies over pay discrimination and may serve to narrow the pay gap between men and women. The new law was designed to override the Supreme Court's ruling in *Ledbetter v. Goodyear Tire & Rubber Co.* (2007), which made pay discrimination lawsuits exceedingly difficult to mount.

☐ Abortion Rights

For many women (and men), the right of women to abort an unwanted pregnancy is a central element of the civil rights agenda falling under the equal protection clause of the Fourteenth Amendment. (To be sure, many others are against abortion on religious grounds.) That may well be, but the Supreme Court, in a number of important cases beginning with *Roe v. Wade* (1973), has based a woman's right to terminate a pregnancy on privacy grounds rather than equal protection grounds. It is for this reason that we have addressed the abortion issue, with its contentious politics and string of Court rulings revising and refining *Roe*, in the previous chapter. Please refer to that section to see more on the politics and law of the struggle over abortion in the United States.

☐ Sexual Harassment and Hostile Environment

Another issue of concern to many women (and many men) is sexual harassment in the workplace. One poll reported that 20 percent of women say they have experienced sexual harassment of one kind or another at work.[34] Many have filed complaints with the Equal Employment Opportunity Commission (EEOC), which reported that more than 11,000 complaints for sexual harassment (16 percent of them from men) were filed with the agency in fiscal year 2011.

People disagree, of course, about what kinds of behavior constitute sexual harassment, although the courts, regulatory agencies, and legislative bodies are gradually

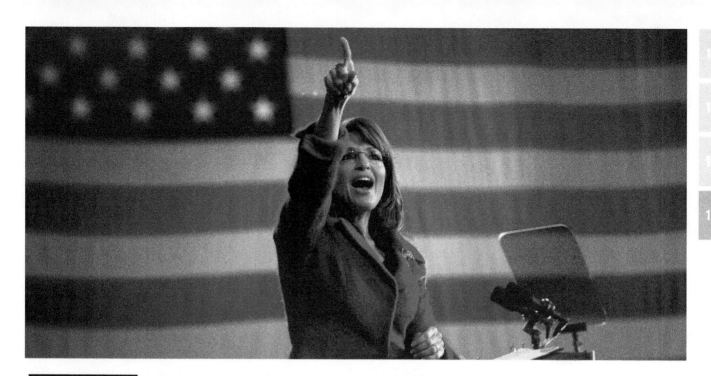

VICE PRESIDENTIAL CANDIDATE SARAH PALIN

Sarah Palin was the first women vice presidential candidate in the Republican Party, nominated to join presidential candidate John McCain on the 2008 ticket. Here she campaigns in Hershey, Pennsylvania.

defining the law in this area. In 1980, the EEOC ruled that making sexual activity a condition of employment or promotion violates the 1964 Civil Rights Act, a ruling upheld by the Supreme Court. The EEOC also ruled that creating "an intimidating, hostile, or offensive working environment" is contrary to the law. The U.S. Supreme Court took a major step in defining sexual harassment when it ruled unanimously, in *Harris v. Forklift Systems Inc.* (1993), that workers do not have to prove that offensive actions make them unable to do their jobs or cause them psychological harm, only that the work environment is hostile or abusive. In a pair of rulings in June 1998, the Court broadened the definition of sexual harassment by saying that companies were liable for the behavior of supervisors even if top managers were unaware of harassing behavior. However, companies were offered a measure of protection by the Court when it ruled that companies with solid and well-communicated harassment policies could not be held liable if victims failed to report harassment in a reasonable period of time.

An increase in public awareness about sexual harassment has triggered an increase in lawmaking by state legislatures to erase sexual harassment in the workplace. Moreover, most major corporations and state and local government entities (including public colleges and universities) have sexual harassment and hostile environment prohibitions in place and require their employees to participate in training programs to lessen their incidence.

Broadening the Civil Rights Umbrella

16.4   Analyze the expansion of civil rights protections to the elderly, the disabled, and gays and lesbians

 he expansion of civil rights protections for women and racial minorities encouraged other groups to press for expanded rights protections.

16.1

16.2

16.3

16.4

civil union

A legal status in which same-sex couples have the same rights, benefits, and protections as married couples.

☐ The Elderly and the Disabled

Interest groups for the elderly have pressed for laws barring age discrimination and have enjoyed some success in recent years. Several federal and state laws, for instance, now bar mandatory retirement. And, the Age Discrimination in Employment Act passed in 1967 prohibits employers from discriminating against employees over the age of 40 in pay, benefits, promotions, and working conditions. The courts also have begun to strike down hiring practices based on age unless a compelling reason for such age requirements can be demonstrated. But problems persist; downsizing companies often lay off older workers first because the pay and benefits of older workers are almost always higher than those of younger workers. And, because people are living longer and worried about the size of their pensions and the rising costs of medical care (even with Medicare), many more Americans say they want to work, at least part time, beyond the normal retirement age.

Disabled Americans have also pushed for civil rights and other protections and have won some notable victories, including passage of the Americans with Disabilities Act (ADA) of 1990. The act prohibits employment discrimination against the disabled and requires that reasonable efforts be made to make places of employment and public facilities (such as concert halls, restaurants, retail shops, schools, and government offices) accessible to them. The proliferation of wheelchair ramps and wheelchair-accessible toilet facilities is a sign that the legislation is having an important effect. Several advocates for the disabled, however, claim that the act depends too much on voluntary compliance.

In 2001, the Supreme Court dramatically narrowed the reach of the ADA, saying that state employees could not sue states for damages arising from violations of the act, as provided for in the legislation. Advocates for the rights of the disabled worried that this judicial ruling expanding the scope of state immunity from congressional actions means that other sections of the ADA act are doomed, including the requirement that state governments make their services and offices accessible to people with disabilities. Others worried that a wide range of civil rights laws that require nondiscriminatory behavior by state agencies—schools and hospitals, for example—may be at risk, as well, because the basis of the Court's decision was that Congress had gone beyond its authority in telling the states what to do under the interstate commerce clause.[35] If the states are immune from the requirements of the Americans with Disabilities Act, the reasoning goes, why should they not be immune from the provisions of other civil rights laws passed by Congress? In *Tennessee v. Lane* (2004), the Court ruled that the disabled could sue a state for money damages in federal court if the state fails to make its courts fully accessible. Congress responded to the Court by extending the protections of the ADA in new legislation passed in 2008.

☐ Gays and Lesbians

The gay and lesbian civil rights movement began in earnest following the 1969 "Stonewall rebellion"—three days of rioting set off by police harassment of the patrons of a popular gay bar in Greenwich Village, New York. The movement picked up steam as the gay community reacted to the powerful inroads of AIDS and in response to the Supreme Court's decision in *Bowers v. Hardwick* (1986) upholding Georgia's ban against homosexual sexual relations. The movement was also inspired by and borrowed many of the tactics of the civil rights and women's movements. The goal was to gain the same civil rights protections under the law enjoyed by African Americans and other minority groups and women and to gain respect from the public. The tactics have ranged from patient lobbying and voting to mass demonstrations and deliberately shocking actions by groups such as ACT-UP. While some important gains have been made by the gay and lesbian movement, its open advocacy for civil rights for homosexuals, especially **civil unions** and same-sex marriage, has triggered strong counterattacks over the years by groups strongly opposed to its objectives, such as the American Family Association, Concerned Women for America, and Focus on the Family.

Gays and lesbians have moved toward equal treatment in a variety of settings in the private sector. Gains in the areas of high culture and mass entertainment have been important. Sympathetic gay and lesbian characters appear regularly on network television (*Ugly Betty, The Office, Glee, Modern Family*) and cable (*The L Word, South Park, Nip/Tuck, Project Runway*), as well as in movies and plays (*Brokeback Mountain, Angels in America, Rent*).[36] Not surprisingly, given the advances made in the arts and mass entertainment, public attitudes about gays and lesbians are growing steadily more tolerant. Fewer Americans today than in the past think that gay and lesbian relationships are wrong. Indeed, a 2011 Pew survey reported that 60 percent of respondents agreed with the proposition that "homosexuality should be accepted" (to be sure, 91 percent of respondents in Spain and 87 percent in Germany agreed with the proposition).[37] Substantial majorities, moreover, favor ending discrimination against gays and lesbians in jobs, housing, and education and favor passing hate-crime legislation. Fully 53 percent of Americans believe that same-sex couples should be allowed to marry, up from 27 percent in 1996, a remarkable change in public attitudes in so short a time. Among the 18–34 age group, fully 70 percent say they favor extending equality of marriage rights to same-sex couples.[38]

Successes on the public policy front for gay and lesbian equality has not mirrored the broad changes in American public opinion. The movement's political efforts have had mixed success, that is to say. In presidential politics, partial advances have been the order of the day. When Bill Clinton was a presidential candidate, for example, he promised to lift the ban on gay people in the military, but as president he was forced to reverse course in 1993 because of the hostile reaction from Congress and the armed services. The resulting "don't ask, don't tell, don't pursue" policy satisfied very few people, though it remained in place under his successor George W. Bush. True to his campaign promise, President Barack Obama persuaded Congress in late 2010 to repeal the policy, allowing gays and lesbians to openly serve in the military.

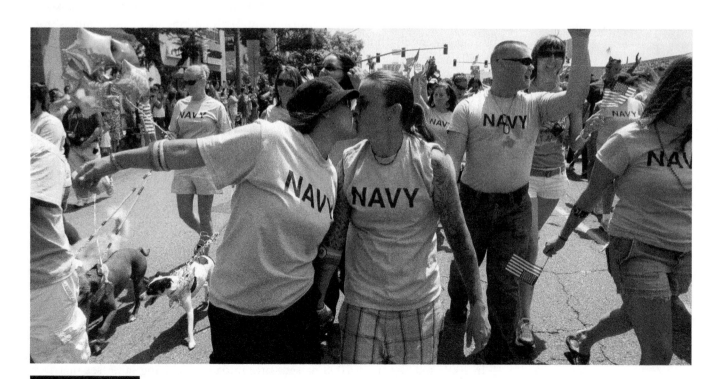

GAYS IN THE MILITARY

After a long period when homosexuals were not allowed to serve in the military at all, then an almost two-decade long period of "don't ask, don't tell, don't pursue" during which gays and lesbians could serve so long as their sexual orientation stayed hidden, President Obama and Congress agreed on a bill in late 2010 that allowed homosexuals to openly serve their country. Here two active-duty sailors demonstrate their feelings during a Gay Pride parade in San Diego in 2011.

After considerable Pentagon study and preparation, the new policy went into effect in September 2011.

With the exception of the bill authorizing gay and lesbian service in the military, Congress has not been too sympathetic over the years to gay and lesbian civil rights claims. In 1993—responding to decisions by several major universities to bar military recruiters from campus because the military would not allow openly practicing homosexuals to serve—Congress passed the Solomon Amendment which bars federal money to colleges and universities that deny military recruiters the same campus access as other private and public employers. In 1996, Congress passed the Defense of Marriage Act (referred to as DOMA), defining marriage as a union of a man and a woman and declaring that states are under no legal obligation to recognize same-sex marriages performed in other states. (A federal judge ruled this unconstitutional in 2010, suggesting that the Act was an inappropriate federal intrusion on states' traditional prerogatives regarding marriage; the issue is sure to reach the Supreme Court at some point). It also barred same-sex couples in civil unions or marriages from receiving federal benefits like Social Security in the same way as heterosexual couples. However, President Obama issued an executive order in 2011 that directed the Justice Department to stop defending DOMA in court.

Important civil rights gains for gays and lesbians have occurred in the courts. At the state level, Vermont's high court ruled in 2003 that same-sex couples must have the same legal rights, protections, and benefits as heterosexual married couples, including matters such as joint tax returns, property ownership, insurance benefits, and medical decisions involving a spouse. In 2004, the Massachusetts high court ruled that same-sex couples have the same right to marry as heterosexual couples, citing the state constitution's provision for equal rights for all citizens. In 2008, the Supreme Courts of California and Connecticut ruled that bans on same-sex marriages in their states were unconstitutional. (California voters reversed their Court in the November elections; the issue is now being adjudicated in the courts.)

Gays and lesbians also have won important Supreme Court cases. The Court ruled in *Romer v. Evans* (1996), for example, that state laws designed to deny basic civil rights to gays and lesbians are unconstitutional. In this case, the Court looked at Colorado's provision (known as Amendment 2) prohibiting local communities from passing gay antidiscrimination ordinances. The Court ruled that the law was constitutionally unacceptable because not only was there was no rational basis for the law but, as Justice Anthony Kennedy declared in his opinion, "a state cannot so deem a class of persons [gays and lesbians] a stranger to its laws." And, in a stunning and highly unexpected decision in 2003, the Supreme Court overturned its own *Bowers* decision from 1986 and ruled in *Lawrence v. Texas* that state anti-sodomy laws designed to make homosexual sexual relations illegal were unconstitutional. Justice Kennedy again gave the ruling a very expansive reading in his majority opinion, declaring that gay people "were entitled to freedom, dignity, and respect for their private lives." Interestingly, neither of these major cases was based on the equal protection clause of the Fourteenth Amendment, which is the foundation for equal treatment of racial and religious minorities.

Gays and lesbians have won significant civil rights protections in a handful of states—Massachusetts, New York, Vermont, New Hampshire, Connecticut, Washington, Maine, Maryland, and Iowa permit same-sex marriage; New Jersey and Nevada allow civil unions and mandate that people in such unions receive the same state rights and benefits as people in heterosexual marriages; Oregon permits same-sex civil partnerships but with fewer rights and benefits as those of married couples; and Illinois bars discrimination based on sexual orientation. However, 13 states in 2004, 8 in 2006, and 3 more in 2008 passed voter initiatives banning same-sex marriage. 39 states have laws or constitutional provisions defining marriage as between one man and one woman.[39]

Until 2012 same-sex marriage faired poorly with voters. Only Colorado and Minnesota voters have rejected bans on same-sex marriage. Even voters in states considered to be liberal on social issues have surprised same-sex marriage advocates. In California, for example, voters passed Proposition 8 in 2008 overturning the California Supreme Court's decision allowing such marriages. Voters in Maine repealed a law passed by its legislature legalizing same-sex marriage in 2009; Maine voters reversed themselves in 2012, passing a gay marriage initiative. As of 2011, almost 60 percent of Americans lived in states where there was no legal recognition of same-sex couples; this despite the movement in favor of homosexual equality in public opinion.[40]

It is evident that the struggle over gay and lesbian civil rights will remain an important part of the American political agenda for a long time to come. The eventual outcome remains very much in doubt, however. While gays and lesbians have made important advances, to be sure, many religious conservatives have been politically mobilized by the possibility that state courts and the U.S. Supreme Court might eventually sanction same-sex marriage as a basic civil right, though that seems like a remote possibility today given the political leanings of the Roberts Court.

Using the DEMOCRACY STANDARD

Is equal citizenship a reality in the United States?

It is with respect to civil rights—guarantees of equality for people in the United States with regard to judicial proceedings, the exercise of political rights, treatment by public officials, and access to and enjoyment of the benefits of government programs—that the differences between the ideas of the framers and the demands of democracy theory are most evident. It is with respect to civil rights, moreover, that democratic aspirations and the struggle for democracy have most altered the original Constitution of the United States. Recall that the framers not only paid scant attention to guarantees of equality, but they also included a number of provisions in the Constitution that accepted and sustained the institution of slavery as well as the noncitizen status of Native Americans. Further, in leaving voting and office-holding requirements largely to the states, the framers implicitly accepted prevailing practices in the states, including the exclusion of women from political life, but also property qualifications and religious tests for voting and office holding. For the framers, civil rights guarantees—other than equality in the courts—were not among the first principles of good government. In fact, the framers worried a great deal about "leveling tendencies" in society that might lead to too much equality and a system of governance in which people of virtue, character, and education would not be in control. In democratic theory, on the other hand, equal citizenship—another way of saying civil rights—is the very essence of good government, one of the three essential pillars of democracy, joining popular sovereignty and liberty. Absent equal citizenship, democracy cannot be said to exist.

The glaring absence of a strong constitutional foundation for the principle of equal citizenship—buttressed for much of U.S. history by a popular culture that favored broad political inclusion for white males but not for other groups—meant that the spread of civil rights protections has been slow and uneven. Thus, women were denied the vote well into the twentieth century. Most African Americans were slaves until passage of the Thirteenth Amendment after the Civil War and were not admitted into full citizenship across the nation until at least 1965, after passage of the Civil Rights and Voting Rights Acts. Even today, women, racial and ethnic minorities, and gays and lesbians fail to play a role in the political process commensurate with their numbers in the population.

Having said that, it is undeniably true that civil rights dramatically increased in the United States during the second half of the twentieth century as guarantees of equal citizenship were extended—unevenly to be sure—to women, African

Americans, other racial and ethnic minorities, and partially to gays and lesbians. These developments were a product of the struggle for democracy by previously excluded groups who insisted on their right to full citizenship, the emergence of a more egalitarian society and culture in the United States, the rational behavior of elected public officials responding legislatively to a public increasingly supportive of civil rights, and changes in the judicial interpretation of equal citizenship in a country turned more favorable to claims of equality.

This advance of civil rights protections since the end of World War II has enriched American democracy because it has made political equality more of a reality in the United States. This is not to say that racial and ethnic minorities and women have attained full social or material equality; many areas of American life, from wealth holding to representation in the professions and in Congress, remain unequal and unrepresentative. Nor is this to say that all civil rights issues are settled; note the continuing disagreements over same-sex marriages and affirmative action. Nevertheless, the attainment of formal political equality is real and something about which many Americans take a great deal of pride.

Review the Chapter

Civil Rights Before the Twentieth Century

16.1 Trace the evolution of civil rights protections for racial minorities and women to the twentieth century, p. 528

The original Constitution and the Bill of Rights were relatively silent on equality other than providing for equality before the law.

The Fourteenth Amendment that was adopted after the Civil War was a foundation for later civil rights advances.

Although the Court paid little attention to civil rights during the nineteenth century, structural changes in society, the transformation of attitudes about race and gender, and the political efforts of racial and ethnic minority group members and women of all races finally prompted the Court to begin to pay attention by the middle of the twentieth century. These contributed to important civil rights gains for racial and religious minorities and women.

The Contemporary Status of Civil Rights for Racial and Ethnic Minorities

16.2 Assess the present status of civil rights protections for racial minorities, p. 532

It is now settled law that discrimination of any kind against racial minorities in the statutes and administrative practices of federal, state, or local government is unconstitutional. It is also settled law that governments may use affirmative action to rectify the past discriminatory practices of a particular public entity such as a fire department in its hiring practices or county government in letting road-building contracts. The status of affirmative action programs meant to achieve general societal progress for minorities (or women) or to enhance diversity, however, remains unsettled, though the Court is leaning strongly against such efforts.

The Contemporary Status of Civil Rights for Women

16.3 Assess the present status of civil rights protections for women, p. 542

The Court has taken the position that laws mentioning gender fall under the doctrine of "intermediate scrutiny," signaling that it will allow more latitude than it does to race to federal, state, and local governments that wish to give gender special attention.

Recent political, social, and economic gains by women are the result of changes in social attitudes, the political efforts of women, and the changing occupational needs of the American economy, rather than the product of a series of favorable Court rulings about gender equality.

Broadening the Civil Rights Umbrella

16.4 Analyze the expansion of civil rights protections to the elderly, the disabled, and gays and lesbians, p. 547

The civil rights movement gave impetus not only to the women's movement but also to a range of other groups of Americans who felt they were discriminated against, including the elderly, the disabled, and gays and lesbians. Statutes have been passed at all levels of government addressed to the equal protection needs of the elderly and the disabled, though compliance has been very uneven.

The question of whether lesbians and gay men can be discriminated against in housing, employment, and education has been largely settled in law and increasingly in social practice. Gays and lesbians can now openly serve in the military. However, the issue of same-sex marriage remains the subject of considerable political debate and legal disputation.

Learn the Terms

 Study and **Review** the **Flashcards**

civil rights, p. 528
privileges and immunities clause,
  p. 530
due process clause, p. 530
equal protection clause, p. 530
Jim Crow, p. 530

poll tax, p. 530
literacy test, p. 530
grandfather clause, p. 531
white primaries, p. 532
strict scrutiny, p. 532
suspect classification, p. 533

de jure discrimination, p. 536
de facto discrimination, p. 536
affirmative action, p. 537
intermediate scrutiny, p. 545
civil union, p. 548

Test Yourself

 Study and **Review** the **Practice Tests**

Answer key begins on page T-1.

16.1 Trace the evolution of civil rights protections for racial minorities and women to the twentieth century

1. This amendment reversed the *Dred Scott* case by making all those born in the United States both citizens of the United States and of the states they live in.

  a. First Amendment
  b. Fourth Amendment
  c. Fourteenth Amendment
  d. Fifteenth Amendment
  e. Sixteenth Amendment

16.2 Assess the present status of civil rights protections for racial minorities

2. Which of the following is NOT a reason affirmative action programs are needed:

  a. Past discrimination
  b. Current discrimination
  c. A need for a diverse environment in work and school
  d. A need for tolerance and a sense of community
  e. A need to educate the less wealthy

16.3 Assess the present status of civil rights protections for women

3. The U.S. Supreme Court ruled in *Harris v. Forklift Systems Inc.* that workers do not have to prove that offensive actions make them unable to do their jobs, only that the work environment:

  a. Is hostile and abusive
  b. Causes psychological harm
  c. Is uncomfortable
  d. Is unprofessional
  e. Causes unneeded stress

16.4 Analyze the expansion of civil rights protections to the elderly, the disabled, and gays and lesbians

4. Which of these states does NOT permit same sex marriage?

  a. New York
  b. Massachusetts
  c. Alabama
  d. Iowa
  e. Vermont

Explore Further

INTERNET SOURCES

Civil Rights Project **www.civilrightsproject.ucla.edu**
Cutting-edge research on race in America.
Infoplease Civil Rights Timeline: Milestones in the Modern
  Civil Rights Movement **www.infoplease.com/spot/**
  civilrightstimeline1.html
A richly detailed timeline of the African American civil rights
  movement.
Cornell Legal Information Institute **www.law.cornell.edu**
Links to the Constitution, landmark and recent Supreme
  Court civil rights decisions, international treaties on human

rights, the Civil Rights Division of the Justice Department,
  and more.
Equal Opportunity Employment Commission **www.eeoc.gov**
Statistics and reports about and rulings on employment discrimination.
Issues: Gay Rights **www.politics1.com/issues-gay.htm**
Links to organizations in favor of and opposed to advancing gay
  and lesbian civil rights.
Martin Luther King Jr. and the Civil Rights Movement
  seattletimes.nwsource.com/mlk
Created by the *Seattle Times*, the site includes study guides on
  King and the civil rights movement, interactive exercises,

audios of King speeches, and links to other King and civil
rights websites.

Yahoo/Civil Rights **http://www.yahoo.com/Society_and_Culture/
Issues_and_Causes/Civil_Rights/**

Links to a vast compendium of information on civil rights and
to organizations devoted to the protection and expansion of
domestic and international rights.

United States Department of Labor: Affirmative Action **http://
www.dol.gov/dol/topic/hiring/affirmativeact.htm**

Links to official laws and information regarding affirmative action
and hiring people with disabilities.

The Woman's Rights Movement **utc.iath.virginia.edu/abolitn/
wmhp.html**

A site focusing on the link between the woman's rights movement
and abolitionism with multiple links to valuable texts on the
subject.

SUGGESTIONS FOR FURTHER READING

Baer, A. Judith, and Leslie Friedman Goldstein. *The Constitutional and
Legal Rights of Women.* Belmont, CA: Roxbury Publishing, 2006.
A rich blend of judicial politics, the women's movement, and
constitutional interpretation.

Barry, Brian. *Culture and Equality.* Cambridge, MA: Harvard
University Press, 2001.
An assault on multiculturalism in the name of liberal egalitarianism
by a distinguished political philosopher.

Bowen, William G., and Derek C. Bok. *The Shape of the River:
Long-Term Consequences of Considering Race in College and
University Admissions.* Princeton, NJ: Princeton University
Press, 1998.
Based on surveys of more than 60,000 white and African American
students at highly selective colleges and universities, Bowen
and Bok argue that affirmative action in college and university
admissions has had substantial and widespread positive effects
on American society.

Branch, Taylor. *At Canaan's Edge: America in the King Years, 1965–
1968.* New York: Simon and Schuster, 2006.
The third volume in Taylor Branch's brilliant and award-winning
biographies of Martin Luther King; focuses not only on King
in this volume but on the transformation of race relations and
American politics during this decisive period.

Gates, Henry Louis, Jr. *America Behind the Color Line.* New York:
Warner Books, 2004.
An examination of the legacy of the civil rights movement for
African Americans.

Katznelson, Ira. *When Affirmative Action Was White: An Untold
History of Racial Inequality in Twentieth-Century America.* New
York: W. W. Norton, 2005.
An eye-opening look at how a long list of federal government
programs, beginning in the New Deal, favored whites over
blacks.

O'Brien, David M. *Constitutional Law and Politics: Civil Rights and
Civil Liberties.* New York: W. W. Norton, 2011.
The 8th edition of a leading textbook on civil liberties and civil
rights, mixing cases with revealing commentaries about the
cases and their impact on American society and politics.

GLOSSARY

A

active partisans People who identify with a party, vote in elections, and participate in additional party and party-candidate activities.

advocacy group An interest group organized to support a cause or ideology.

affirmative action Programs of private and public institutions favoring minorities and women in hiring and contracting, and in admissions to colleges and universities, in an attempt to compensate for past discrimination or to create more diversity.

agency A general name used for a subunit of a cabinet department.

agenda setting Influencing people's opinions about what is important.

agents of socialization Those institutions and individuals that shape the core beliefs and attitudes of people.

Aid to Families with Dependent Children (AFDC) The federal entitlement program that provided income support for poor families until it was replaced by TANF in 1996.

amicus curiae Latin for "friend of the court"; a legal brief in which individuals not party to a suit may have their views heard in court.

Anti-Federalists Opponents of the Constitution during the fight over ratification.

appellate courts Courts that hear cases on appeal from other courts.

appropriation Legal authority for a federal agency to spend money from the U.S. Treasury.

appropriations committees The committees in the House and Senate that set specific spending levels in the budget for federal programs and agencies.

Articles of Confederation The first constitution of the United States, adopted during the last stages of the Revolutionary War, created a system of government with most power lodged in the states and little in the central government.

asymmetric warfare Unconventional tactics used by a combatant against an enemy with superior conventional military capabilities.

B

balance of payments The annual difference between payments and receipts between a country and its trading partners.

beat The assigned location where a reporter regularly gathers news stories.

bias Deviation from ideal standards such as representativeness or objectivity.

bicameral As applied to a legislative body, consisting of two houses or chambers.

bill of attainder A governmental decree that a person is guilty of a crime that carries the death penalty, rendered without benefit of a trial.

Bill of Rights The first 10 amendments to the U.S. Constitution, concerned with the protection of basic liberties.

block grants Federal grants to the states to be used for general activities.

briefs Documents setting out the arguments in legal cases, prepared by attorneys and presented to courts.

budget deficit The amount by which annual government expenditures exceed revenues.

bureau Generally, a subunit of a cabinet department.

bureaucracy A large, complex organization characterized by a hierarchical set of offices, each with a specific task, controlled through a clear chain of command, and where appointment and advancement of personnel is based on merit.

bureaucrat A person who works in a bureaucratic organization.

C

capital crime Any crime for which death is a possible penalty.

capitalism An economic system characterized by private ownership of productive assets where most decisions about how to use these assets are made by individuals and firms operating in a market rather than by government.

casework Services performed by members of Congress for constituents.

categorical grants Federal aid to states and localities clearly specifying what the money can be used for.

caucus A regional, ethnic, racial, or economic subgroup within the House or Senate. Also used to describe the party in the House and Senate, as in Republican caucus.

checks and balances The constitutional principle that each of the separate branches of government has the power to hinder the unilateral actions of the other branches as a way to restrain an overreaching government and prevent tyranny.

chief of staff A top adviser to the president who also manages the White House staff.

Children's Health Insurance Program (CHIP) Program that pays for health care services for children in households above the poverty line but below 133 percent to 400 percent of the poverty line, depending on the state.

circuit courts The 12 geographical jurisdictions and one special court that hear appeals from the federal district courts.

civil disobedience Intentionally breaking a law and accepting the consequences as a way to publicize the unjustness of the law.

civil liberties Freedoms found primarily in the Bill of Rights, the enjoyment of which are protected from government interference.

civil rights Guarantees of equal treatment by government officials regarding political rights, the judicial system, and public programs.

civil servants Government workers employed under the merit system; not political appointees.

civil service Federal government jobs held by civilian employees, excluding political appointees.

civil union A legal status in which same-sex couples have the same legal rights, benefits, and protections as married couples.

Civil War Amendments The Thirteenth, Fourteenth, and Fifteenth Amendments to the Constitution, adopted immediately after the Civil War, each of which represented the imposition of a national claim over that of the states.

class-action suit A suit brought on behalf of a group of people who are in a situation similar to that of the plaintiffs.

cloture A vote to end a filibuster; requires the votes of three-fifths of the membership of the Senate.

Cold War The period of tense relations between the United States and the Soviet Union from the late 1940s to the late 1980s.

collective public opinion The political attitudes of the public as a whole, expressed as averages, percentages, or other summaries of many individuals' opinions.

concurrent powers Powers under the Constitution that are shared by the federal government and the states.

concurring opinion The opinion of one or more judges who vote with the majority on a case but wish to set out different reasons for their decision.

conditional grants Federal grants with provisions requiring that state and local governments follow certain policies in order to obtain funds.

confederation A loose association of states or territorial divisions in which very little power or no power at all is lodged in a central government.

conference committees Ad hoc committees, made up of members of both the Senate and the House of Representatives, set up to reconcile differences in the provisions of bills.

Congressional Budget Office (CBO) An agency of the U.S. Congress that provides technical support and research services on budget issues for its members and committees.

Connecticut Compromise Also called the *Great Compromise*; the compromise between the New Jersey and Virginia plans formulated by the Connecticut delegates at the Constitutional Convention; called for a lower legislative house based on population size and an upper house based on equal representation of the states.

consciousness-raising groups Meetings of small groups of women designed to raise awareness of discrimination against women and to encourage involvement in movement activities.

conservative The political position, combining both economic and social dimensions, that holds that the federal government ought to play a very small role in economic regulation, social welfare, and overcoming racial inequality, that abortion should be illegal, and that family values and law and order should guide public policies.

constituency The district of a legislator.

constituent A citizen who lives in the district of an elected official.

constitution The basic framework of law for a nation that prescribes how government is to be organized, how decisions are to be made, and what powers and responsibilities government shall have.

constitutional courts Federal courts created by Congress under the authority of Article III of the Constitution.

contract clause The portion of Article I, Section 10 of the Constitution that prohibits states from passing any law "impairing the obligations of contracts."

cooperative federalism Federalism in which the powers and responsibilities of the states and the national government are intertwined and in which they work together to solve common problems; said to have characterized the 1960s and 1970s.

core beliefs The most fundamental beliefs in a national population about human nature, the country, government, and the economy.

core beliefs (political) Individuals' views about the fundamental nature of human beings, society, the economy, and the role of government; taken together, they comprise the political culture.

cost-benefit analysis A method of evaluating rules and regulations by weighing their potential costs against their potential benefits to society.

Council of Economic Advisers (CEA) An organization in the Executive Office of the President made up of a small group of economists who advise on economic policy.

crack The act of dividing a district where the opposing party has a large majority, rendering it a minority in both parts of the redrawn districts.

D

de facto discrimination Unequal treatment by private individuals, groups, and organizations.

de jure discrimination Unequal treatment based on government laws and regulations.

dealignment A gradual reduction in the dominance of one political party without another party supplanting it.

delegate According to the doctrine articulated by Edmund Burke, an elected representative who acts in perfect accord with the wishes of his or her constituents.

democracy A system of government in which the people rule; rule by the many.

demographic Pertaining to the statistical study and description of a population.

departments Generally the largest units in the executive branch, each headed by a cabinet secretary.

depression A severe and persistent drop in economic-activity.

deregulation The process of diminishing regulatory requirements for business.

descriptive representation Sometimes called *statistical representation*; the degree to which the composition of a representative body reflects the demographic composition of the population as a whole.

devolution The delegation of power over and responsibilities for federal programs to state and/or local governments.

direct democracy A form of political decision making in which policies are decided by the people themselves, rather than by their representatives, acting either in small face-to-face assemblies or through the electoral process as in initiatives and referenda in the American states.

discharge petition A petition signed by 218 House members to force a bill that has been before a committee for at least 30 days while the House is in session out of the committee and onto the floor for consideration.

discretionary spending That part of the federal budget that is not tied to a formula that automatically provides money to some program or purpose.

dissenting opinion The opinion of the judge or judges who are in the minority on a particular case before the Supreme Court.

disturbance theory A theory positing that interest groups originate with changes in the economic, social, or political environment that threaten the well-being of some segment of the population.

divided government Control of the executive and the legislative branches by different political parties.

dual federalism An interpretation of federalism in which the states and the national government have separate jurisdictions and responsibilities.

due process clause The section of the Fourteenth Amendment that prohibits states from depriving anyone of life, liberty, or property "without due process of law," a guarantee against arbitrary or unfair government action.

E

earmarking Practice of appropriating money for specific pet projects of members of Congress, usually done at the behest of lobbyists, and added to bills at the last minute with little opportunity for deliberation.

economic conservatives People who favor private enterprise and oppose government regulation of business.

economic liberals People who favor government regulation of business to protect the public from harm, and government spending for social programs.

economic liberty The right to own and use property free from unreasonable government interference.

elastic clause Article I, Section 8 of the Constitution, also called the *necessary and proper clause*; gives Congress the authority to make whatever laws are necessary and proper to carry out its enumerated responsibilities.

Electoral College Representatives selected in each of the states, their numbers based on each state's total number of its senators and representatives; a majority of Electoral College votes elects the president.

electoral competition model A form of election in which parties seeking votes move toward the median voter or the center of the political spectrum.

electoral reward and punishment The tendency to vote for incumbents when times are good and against them when times are bad; same as retrospective voting.

electors Representatives who are elected in the states to formally choose the U.S. president.

entitlements Government benefits that are distributed automatically to citizens who qualify on the basis of a set of guidelines set by law; for example, Americans over the age of 65 are entitled to Medicare coverage.

enumerated powers Powers of the federal government specifically mentioned in the Constitution.

equal protection clause The section of the Fourteenth Amendment that provides for equal treatment by government of people residing within the United States and each of its states.

Equal Rights Amendment (ERA) Proposed amendment to the U.S. Constitution stating that equality of rights shall not be abridged or denied on account of a person's gender; it failed to win the approval of the necessary number of states.

establishment clause The part of the First Amendment to the Constitution that prohibits Congress from establishing an official religion; the basis for the doctrine of the separation of church and state.

ex post facto law A law that retroactively declares some action illegal.

exclusionary rule A standard promulgated by the Supreme Court that prevents police and prosecutors from using evidence against a defendant that was obtained in an illegal search.

executive agreement An agreement with another country signed by the president that has the force of law, like a treaty; does not require Senate approval; originally used for minor technical matters, now an important tool of presidential power in foreign affairs.

Executive Office of the President (EOP) A group of organizations that advise the president on a wide range of issues; includes, among others, the Office of Management and Budget, the National Security Council, and the Council of Economic Advisers.

executive order A rule or regulation issued by the president that has the force of law, based either on the constitutional powers of the presidency as chief executive or commander in chief or on congressional statutes.

executive privilege A presidential claim that certain communications with subordinates may be withheld from Congress and the courts.

externalities The positive and negative effects of economic activities on third parties.

F

factions Madison's term for groups or parties that try to advance their own interests at the expense of the public good.

federal Describing a system in which significant governmental powers are divided between a central government and smaller territorial units, such as states.

federal bureaucracy The totality of the departments and agencies of the executive branch of the national government.

Federal Reserve Board (Fed) The body responsible for deciding the monetary policies of the United States.

federalism A system in which governmental powers are divided between a central government and smaller units, such as states.

federalists Proponents of the Constitution during the ratification fight; also the political party of Hamilton, Washington, and Adams.

filibuster A parliamentary device used in the Senate to prevent a bill from coming to a vote by "talking it to death," made possible by the norm of unlimited debate.

fiscal federalism That aspect of federalism having to do with federal grants to the states.

fiscal policy Government efforts to affect overall output and incomes in the economy through spending and taxing policies.

foundation An entity of the executive branch that supports the arts or sciences and is designed to be somewhat insulated from political interference.

framing Providing a context for interpretation.

franchise The legal right to vote; see suffrage.

franking privilege Public subsidization of mail from the members of Congress to their constituents.

free enterprise An economic system characterized by competitive markets and private ownership of a society's productive assets; a form of capitalism.

free exercise clause That portion of the First Amendment to the Constitution that prohibits Congress from impeding religious observance or impinging upon religious beliefs.

full faith and credit The provision in Article IV, Section 1 of the Constitution which provides that states must respect the public acts, laws, and judicial rulings of other states.

G

General Agreement on Tariffs and Trade (GATT) An international agreement that requires the lowering of tariffs and other barriers to free trade.

general revenue sharing Federal aid to the states without any conditions on how the money is to be spent.

gerrymandering Redrawing electoral district lines in an extreme and unlikely manner to give an advantage to a particular party or candidate.

global climate change The upset of historical climate patterns, with rising temperatures and more extreme climate events, tied to the increase in atmospheric carbon whether caused by human activities or naturally occurring cycles.

globalization The increasing tendency of information, products, and financial capital to flow across national borders, with the effect of more tightly integrating the global economy.

government corporation A unit in the executive branch that operates like a private business but provides some public service.

grand juries Groups of citizens who decide whether there is sufficient evidence to bring an indictment against accused persons.

grandfather clause A device that allowed whites who had failed the literacy test to vote anyway by extending the franchise to anyone whose ancestors had voted prior to 1867.

grants-in-aid Funds from the national government to state and local governments to help pay for programs created by the national government.

grassroots lobbying The effort by interest groups to mobilize local constituencies, shape public opinion to support the group's goals, and bring that pressure to bear on elected officials.

Great Depression The period of economic crisis that lasted in the United States from the stock market crash of 1929 to America's entry into World War II.

gridlock A situation in which things cannot get done in Washington, usually because of divided government.

gross domestic product (GDP) Monetary value of all goods and services produced in a nation each year, excluding income residents earn abroad.

H

habeas corpus The legal doctrine that a person who is arrested must have a timely hearing before a judge.

hearings The taking of testimony by a congressional committee or subcommittee.

hegemon Term used to refer to the dominant power during various historical periods that takes on responsibilities for maintaining and protecting a regional or global system.

hold A tactic by which a single senator can prevent action on a bill or nomination; based on an implied threat of refusing to agree to unanimous consent on other Senate matters or willingness to filibuster the bill or nomination.

hopper The box in the House of Representatives in which proposed bills are placed.

horizontal federalism Term used to refer to relationships among the states.

I

impeachment House action bringing formal charges against a member of the executive branch or the federal judiciary that may or may not lead to removal from office by the Senate.

in forma pauperis Describing a process by which indigents may file a suit with the Supreme Court free of charge.

incorporation The process by which the Supreme Court has made most of the provisions of the Bill of Rights binding on the states. See *nationalizing*.

independent executive agency A unit of the executive branch outside the control of executive departments.

independent regulatory commission An entity in the executive branch that is outside the immediate control of the president and Congress that issues rules and regulations to protect the public.

industrialization The transformation of a society's economy from one dominated by agricultural pursuits to one dominated by manufacturing.

inflation A condition of rising prices and reduced purchasing power.

infotainment The merging of hard news and entertainment in news presentations.

initiatives Procedures available in some states for citizens to put proposed laws and constitutional amendments on the ballot for voter approval or rejection.

institutional presidency The permanent bureaucracy associated with the presidency, designed to help the incumbent of the office carry out his responsibilities.

integration Policies encouraging the interaction between different races in schools or public facilities.

Intelligence Advisory Board An organization in the Executive Office of the President that provides information and assessments to the president's director of national intelligence and to the president directly.

interest groups A private organization or voluntary association that seeks to influence public policy as a way to protect or advance its interests.

intermediate scrutiny A legal test falling between ordinary and strict scrutiny relevant to issues of gender; under this test, the Supreme Court will allow gender classifications in laws if they are *substantially* related to an *important* government objective.

interstate compacts Agreements among states to cooperate on solving mutual problems; requires approval by Congress.

iron triangles An enduring alliance of common interest among an interest group, a congressional committee, and a bureaucratic agency.

isolationism The policy of avoiding undue involvement in the affairs of other countries and multilateral institutions.

issue networks Broad coalitions of public and private interest groups, policy experts, and public officials that form around particular policy issues; said to be more visible to the public and more inclusive.

J

Jim Crow Popular term for the system of legally sanctioned racial segregation that existed in the American South until the middle of the twentieth century.

Joint Chiefs of Staff (JCS) The military officers in charge of each of the armed services.

joint committees Congressional committees with members from both the House and the Senate.

judicial activism Actions by the courts that purportedly go beyond the role of the judiciary as interpreter of the law and adjudicator of disputes.

judicial review The power of the Supreme Court to declare actions of the other branches and levels of government unconstitutional.

K

Keynesians Advocates of government programs to stimulate economic activity through tax cuts and government spending.

L

laissez-faire The political-economic doctrine that holds that government ought not interfere with the operations of the free market.

leak Inside or secret information given to a journalist or media outlet by a government official.

leaners People who claim to be independents but consistently favor one party over another.

legislative courts Highly specialized federal courts created by Congress under the authority of Article I of the Constitution.

liberal The political position, combining both economic and social dimensions, that holds that the federal government has a substantial role to play in providing economic justice and opportunity, regulating business in the public interest, overcoming racial discrimination, protecting abortion rights, and ensuring the equal treatment of gays and lesbians.

liberal democracy Representative democracy characterized by popular sovereignty, liberty, and political equality.

literacy test A device used by the southern states to prevent African Americans from voting before the passage of the Voting Rights Act of 1965, which banned its use; usually involved interpretation of a section of a state's constitution.

lobbying Effort by an interest or advocacy group to influence the behavior of a public official.

lobbyists A person who attempts to influence the behavior of public officials on behalf of an interest group.

M

macroeconomic policy Policy that has to do with the performance of the economy as a whole.

majority rule The form of political decision making in which policies are decided on the basis of what a majority of the people want.

majority tyranny Suppression of the rights and liberties of a minority by the majority.

majority-minority districts Districts drawn to ensure that a racial minority makes up the majority of voters.

mandate A formal order from the national government that the states carry out certain policies.

markup The process of revising a bill in committee.

mass mobilization The process of involving large numbers of people in a social movement.

means-tested Meeting the criterion of demonstrable need.

media monopoly Term used to suggest that media corporations are so large, powerful, and interconnected that the less economically and politically powerful cannot have their views aired.

median household income The midpoint of all households ranked by income.

median voter The voter at the exact middle of the political issue spectrum.

medicaid Program administered by the states that pays for health care services for the poor; jointly funded by the federal government and the states.

medicare Federal health insurance program for the elderly and the disabled.

Millennium Challenge Account A Bush administration initiative to distribute development aid on the basis of a country's degree of improvement in areas such as the rule of law, women's rights, protection of property rights, anticorruption measures, and political and civil rights.

monarchy Rule by the one, such as where power rests in the hands of a king or queen.

monetarists Advocates of a minimal government role in the economy, limited to managing the growth of the money supply.

monetary policy Government efforts to affect the supply of money and the level of interest rates in the economy.

multilateralist The stance toward foreign policy which suggests that the United States should seek the cooperation of other nations and multilateral institutions in pursuing its goals.

multilateralists Those who believe the United States should use its military and diplomatic power in the world in cooperation with other nations and international organizations.

multiparty system A political system in which three or more viable parties compete to lead the government; because a majority winner is not always possible, multiparty systems often have coalition governments where governing power is shared among two or more parties.

N

national debt The total outstanding debt of the federal government; the sum total of all annual budget deficits and surpluses.

national interest What is of benefit to the nation as a whole.

national security adviser A top foreign policy and defense adviser to the president who heads the National Security Council.

National Security Council (NSC) An organization in the Executive Office of the President made up of officials from the State and Defense Departments, the CIA, and the military, who advise on foreign and security affairs.

nationalist position The view of American federalism that holds that the Constitution created a system in which the national government is supreme, relative to the states, and that it granted that government a broad range of powers and responsibilities.

nationalizing The process by which provisions of the Bill of Rights become incorporated. See *incorporation*.

nativist Antiforeign; applied to political movements active in the nineteenth century in the United States.

necessary and proper clause Article I, Section 8, of the Constitution, also known as the *elastic clause*; gives Congress the authority to make whatever laws are necessary and proper to carry out its enumerated powers and the responsibilities mentioned in the Constitution's preamble.

New Deal The programs of the administration of President Franklin D. Roosevelt.

New Deal coalition The informal electoral alliance of working-class ethnic groups, Catholics, Jews, urban dwellers, racial minorities, and the South that was the basis of the Democratic party dominance of American politics from the New Deal to the early 1970s.

New Jersey Plan Proposal of the smaller states at the Constitutional Convention to create a government with slightly more power in a central government than under the Articles, with the states equally represented in a unicameral national legislature.

news management The attempt by those in political power to put the presentation of news about them and their policies in a favorable light.

newsworthy Worth printing or broadcasting as news, according to editors' judgments.

North American Free Trade Agreement (NAFTA) An agreement among the United States, Canada, and Mexico to eliminate nearly all barriers to trade and investment among the three countries.

nuclear proliferation The spread of nuclear weapons to additional countries or to terrorist groups.

nullification An attempt by states to declare national laws or actions null and void.

O

objective journalism News reported with no evaluative language and with opinions quoted or attributed to a specific source.

obscenity As defined by the Supreme Court, the representation of sexually explicit material in a manner that violates community standards and is without redeeming social importance or value.

Office of Management and Budget (OMB) An organization within the Executive Office of the President that advises on the federal budget, domestic legislation, and regulations.

oligarchy Rule by the few, where a minority holds power over a majority, as in an aristocracy or a clerical establishment.

open-seat election An election in which there is no incumbent officeholder.

opinion The explanation of the majority's and the minority's reasoning that accompanies a court decision.

opinion of the Court The majority opinion that accompanies a Supreme Court decision.

ordinary scrutiny The assumption that the actions of elected bodies and officials are legal under the Constitution.

original intent The doctrine that the courts must interpret the Constitution in ways consistent with the intentions of the framers rather than in light of contemporary conditions and needs.

original jurisdiction The authority of a court to be the first to hear a particular kind of case.

oversight Congressional responsibility for monitoring the actions of executive branch agencies and personnel to ensure conformity to federal statutes and congressional intent.

P

pack The process of concentrating voters for the other party into fewer districts in order to weaken them elsewhere.

partisan A committed supporter of a political party; also, seeing issues from the point of view of a single party.

party caucuses The process for selecting delegates to the national party conventions characterized by neighborhood and area-wide meetings of party supporters and activists.

party conference An organization of the members of a political party in the House or Senate.

party convention A gathering of delegates who nominate a party's presidential candidate.

party identification The sense of belonging to one or another political party.

party platform A party's statement of its positions on the issues of the day passed at the quadrennial national convention.

patronage The practice of distributing government offices and contracts to the supporters of the winning party; also called the *spoils system*.

payroll tax Tax levied on salaries and wages for Social Security and Medicare.

petit (trial) juries Juries that hear evidence and sit in judgment on charges brought in civil or criminal cases.

plaintiff One who brings suit in a court.

pluralism The political science position that American democracy is best understood in terms of the interaction, conflict, and bargaining of groups.

plurality More votes than any other candidate but less than a majority of all votes cast.

pocket veto Rejection of a bill if the president takes no action on it for 10 days and Congress has adjourned during that period.

podcasts Digital audio and video files made readily available to interested people via computers and portable devices.

policy preferences Citizens' ideas about what policies they want government to pursue.

political action committees (PACs) An entity created by an interest group whose purpose is to collect money and make contributions to candidates in federal elections.

political attitudes Individuals' views and preferences about public policies, political parties, candidates, government institutions, and public officials.

political culture The set of core beliefs in a country that help shape how people behave politically and what they believe government should do.

political efficacy The sense that an individual can affect what government does.

political equality The principle that each person carries equal weight in the conduct of the public business.

political ideology A system of interrelated and coherently organized political beliefs and attitudes.

political liberty The principle that citizens in a democracy are protected from government interference in the exercise of a range of basic freedoms, such as the freedoms of speech, association, and conscience.

political party An organization that tries to win control of government by electing people to office who carry the party label.

political socialization The process by which individuals come to have certain core beliefs and political attitudes.

poll tax A tax to be paid as a condition of voting; used in the South to keep African Americans away from the polls.

popular sovereignty The basic principle of democracy that the people are the ultimate source of government authority and of the policies that government leaders make.

populism The belief that the common person is every bit as good as those with wealth and power.

pork Also called *pork barrel*; federally funded projects designed to bring to the constituency jobs and public money for which the members of Congress can claim credit.

poverty line The federal government's calculation of the amount of income families of various sizes need to stay out of poverty. In 2010 it was $22,314 for a family of four.

precedents Past rulings by courts that guide judicial reasoning in subsequent cases.

preemption Exclusion of the states from actions that might interfere with federal authority or statutes.

presidential job approval The percentage of Americans who believe the president is doing a good job.

presidential job approval rating A president's standing with the public, indicated by the percentage of Americans who tell survey interviewers that they approve a president's "handling of his job."

primary election Statewide elections in which voters choose delegates to the national party conventions.

prior restraint The government's power to prevent publication, as opposed to punishment afterward.

private interests An interest group that seeks to protect or advance the material interests of its members.

privatizing Turning over certain government functions to the private sector.

privatization The process of turning over certain government functions to the private sector.

privileges and immunities clause The portion of Article IV, Section 2 of the Constitution that says that citizens from out of state have the same legal rights as local citizens in any state; also in the Fourteenth Amendment assuring national citizenship.

probable cause Legal doctrine that refers to a reasonable belief that a crime has been committed.

progressive taxation A tax system in which higher-income individuals are taxed at a higher rate than those who make less.

proportional representation The awarding of legislative seats to political parties to reflect the proportion of the popular vote each party receives.

prospective voting model A theory of democratic elections in which voters decide what government will do in the near future by choosing one or another responsible party.

provisional ballot A vote that is cast but not counted until determination is made that the voter is properly registered.

public interests An interest group that works to gain protections or benefits for society at large.

public opinion The aggregated political attitudes of ordinary people as revealed by surveys.

pundits Somewhat derisive term for print, broadcast, and radio commentators on the political news.

Q

quasi-governmental organization An organization that has governmental powers and responsibilities but has substantial private sector control over its activities.

R

random sampling The selection of survey respondents by chance, with equal probability of being selected, to ensure their representativeness of the whole population.

ranking minority member The highest-ranking member of the minority party on a congressional committee.

rational public The notion that collective public opinion is rational in the sense that it is generally stable and consistent and that when it changes it does so as an understandable response to events, to changing circumstances, and to new information.

realignment The process by which one party supplants another as the dominant party in a two-party political system.

reapportionment The reallocation of House seats among the states, done after each national census, to ensure that seats are held by the states in proportion to the size of their populations.

recess appointments Presidential action to temporarily fill executive branch positions without the consent of the Senate; done when Congress is adjourned.

recession Two quarters or more of declining gross domestic product.

reciprocity Deferral by members of Congress to the judgment of subject-matter specialists, mainly on minor technical bills.

red tape Overbearing bureaucratic rules and procedures.

redistricting The redrawing of congressional district lines within a state to ensure roughly equal populations within each district.

referenda Procedures available in some states by which state laws or constitutional amendments proposed by the legislature are submitted to the voters for approval or rejection.

regressive taxation A tax system in which lower-income individuals are taxed at a higher rate than those who make more.

regulation The issuing of rules by government agencies with the aim of reducing the scale of negative externalities produced by private firms.

remedy An action that a court determines must be taken to rectify a wrong done by government.

representative democracy Indirect democracy, in which the people rule through elected representatives.

republicanism A political doctrine advocating limited government based on popular consent, protected against majority tyranny.

reservation clause Part of the Tenth Amendment to the Constitution that says powers not given to Congress are reserved to the states or to the people.

responsible party The notion that a political party will take clear and distinct stands on the issues and enact them as policy once elected to office.

retrospective voting A form of election in which voters look back at the performance of a party in power and cast ballots on the basis of how well it did in office.

revolving door The common practice in which former government officials become lobbyists for interests with whom they formerly dealt in their official capacity.

rule of four An *unwritten* practice that requires at least four justices of the Supreme Court to agree that a case warrants review by the Court before it will hear the case.

S

sample survey An interview study asking questions of a set of people who are chosen as representative of the whole population.

scope of conflict Refers to the number of groups involved in a political conflict; a narrow scope of conflict involves a small number of groups, and a wide scope of conflict involves many.

secularization The spread of nonreligious values and outlooks.

select committees Temporary committees in Congress created to conduct studies or investigations; they have no power to report bills.

selective incorporation The gradual and piecemeal spread of the protections of the Bill of Rights to the states by the U.S. Supreme Court.

senatorial courtesy The tradition that a judicial nomination for a federal district court seat be approved by the senior senator of the president's party from the state where a district court is located before the nominee is considered by the Senate Judiciary Committee.

seniority The principle that one attains a position on the basis of length of service.

separate but equal doctrine The principle articulated in *Plessy v. Ferguson* (1896) that laws prescribing separate public facilities and services for nonwhite Americans are permissible if the facilities and services are equal to those provided for whites.

separation of powers The distribution of government legislative, executive, and judicial powers to separate branches of government.

signing statement A document sometimes issued by the president in connection with the signing of a bill from Congress that sets out the president's understanding of the new law and how executive branch officials should carry it out.

sit-down strike A form of labor action in which workers stop production but do not leave their job site.

social (lifestyle) conservatives People who favor traditional social values; they tend to support strong law-and-order measures and oppose abortion and gay rights.

social (lifestyle) liberals People who favor civil liberties, abortion rights, and alternative lifestyles.

social contract The idea that government is the result of an agreement among people to form one, and that people have the right to create an entirely new government if the terms of the contract have been violated by the existing one.

social contract A philosophical device, used by Enlightenment thinkers such as Locke, Rousseau, and Harrington, to suggest that governments are only legitimate if they are created by a voluntary compact among the people.

social insurance Government programs that provide services or income support in proportion to the amount of mandatory contributions made by individuals to a government trust fund.

social movement A loosely organized group that uses unconventional and often disruptive tactics to have their grievances heard by the public, the news media, and government leaders.

Social Security Social insurance program that provides income support for the elderly, those with disabilities, and family survivors of working Americans.

soft power Influence in world affairs that derives from the attractiveness to others of a nation's culture, products, and way of life.

spin The attempt by public officials to have a story reported in terms that favor them and their policies; see news management.

spoils system The practice of distributing government offices and contracts to the supporters of the winning party; also called *patronage*.

standing Authority to bring legal action because one is directly affected by the issues at hand.

standing committees Relatively permanent congressional committees that address specific areas of legislation.

stare decisis The legal doctrine that says precedent should guide judicial decision making.

State of the Union Annual report to the nation by the president, now delivered before a joint session of Congress, on the state of the nation and his legislative proposals for addressing national problems.

states' rights position The view of American federalism that holds that the Constitution created a system of dual sovereignty in which the national government and the state governments are sovereign in their own spheres.

stay acts Laws forbidding farm foreclosures for nonpayment of debts.

strict construction The doctrine that the provisions of the Constitution have a clear meaning and that judges must stick closely to this meaning when rendering decisions.

strict scrutiny The assumption that actions by elected bodies or officials violate the Constitution.

sub-governments Another name for an iron triangle.

suffrage The legal right to vote; see franchise.

Sun Belt States of the Lower South, Southwest, and West, where sunny weather and conservative politics have often prevailed.

superdelegates Elected officials from all levels of government who are appointed by party committees to be delegates to the national convention of the Democratic Party; not selected in primary elections or caucuses.

superpower A nation with the military, economic, and political resources to project force anywhere in the world.

superprecedents Landmark rulings that have been reaffirmed by the Court over the course of many years and whose reasoning has become part of the fabric of American law.

supremacy clause The provision in Article VI of the Constitution that the Constitution itself and the laws and treaties of the United States are the supreme law of the land, taking precedence over state laws and constitutions when they are in conflict.

suspect classification The invidious, arbitrary, or irrational designation of a group for special treatment by government, whether positive or negative; historically, a discriminated against, visible minority without power to protect itself.

T

Temporary Assistance to Needy Families (TANF) Program that provides income and services to many poor families; has benefit time limits and a work requirement.

Tenth Amendment Part of the Bill of Rights, the Amendment says that those powers not given to the federal government and not prohibited to the states by the Constitution are reserved for the states and the people.

terrorism The use of deadly violence against civilians to further some political goal.

test case A case brought to force a ruling on the constitutionality of some law or executive action.

treaty A formal international agreement between two or more countries; in the United States, requires the "advice and consent" of the Senate.

trustee An elected representative who believes that his or her own best judgment, rather than instructions from constituents, should be used in making legislative decisions.

turnout The proportion of either eligible or all voting-age Americans who actually vote in a given election; the two ways of counting turnout yield different results.

two-party system A political system in which two parties vie on relatively equal terms to win national elections and in which each party governs at one time or another.

tyranny The abuse of the inalienable rights of citizens by government.

unanimous consent Legislative action taken "without objection" as a way to expedite business; used to conduct much of the business of the Senate.

unicameral A legislative body with a single chamber.

unified government Control of the executive and legislative branches by the same political party.

unilateralists Those who believe the United States should vigorously use its military and diplomatic power to pursue American national interests in the world, but on a "go it alone" basis.

unitary executive Constitutional doctrine that proposes that the executive branch is under the direct control of the president, who has all authority necessary to control the actions of federal bureaucracy personnel and units without interference from the other federal branches.

unitary system A system in which a central government has complete power over its constituent units or states.

urbanization The movement of people from rural areas to cities.

veto Presidential disapproval of a bill that has been passed by both houses of Congress. The president's veto can be overridden by a two-thirds vote in each house.

Virginia Plan Proposal by the large states at the Constitutional Convention to create a strong central government with power in the government apportioned to the states on the basis of population.

watchdog The role of the media in scrutinizing the actions of government officials.

weapons of mass destruction Nuclear, biological, or chemical weapons with the potential to cause vast harm to human populations.

whip A political party member in Congress charged with keeping members informed of the plans of the party leadership, counting votes before action on important issues, and rounding up party members for votes on bills.

whistle-blowers People who bring official misconduct in their agencies to public attention.

white primaries Primary elections open only to whites in the one-party South where the only elections that mattered were the Democratic Party's primaries; this effectively disenfranchised blacks.

wire services Organizations such as the Associated Press and Reuters that gather and disseminate news to other news organizations.

World Trade Organization (WTO) An agency designed to enforce the provisions of the General Agreement on Tariffs and Trade and to resolve trade disputes between nations.

writ of certiorari An announcement that the Supreme Court will hear a case on appeal from a lower court; its issuance requires the vote of four of the nine justices.

NOTES

1

1. William H. Chafe, *The Unfinished Journey: America Since World War II* (New York: Oxford University Press, 1986), p. 304; Howard Zinn, *SNCC: The New Abolitionists* (Boston: Beacon Press, 1964), p. 64.
2. Chafe, *Unfinished Journey*, p. 305.
3. Pei-te Lien, Dianne M. Pinderhughes, Carol Hardy-Fanta, and Christine M. Sierra, "The Voting Rights Act and the Election of Non-white Officials," *PS: Political Science and Politics* (July 2007), pp. 489–494.
4. Michael Coppedge and John Gerring, "Conceptualizing and Measuring Democracy," *Perspectives on Politics* 9, no. 2 (June 2011), pp. 247–267.
5. See summary of polls at Latinobarometro at http://www.latinobarometro.org/, Asiabarometer at https://www.asiabarometer.org, and the PEW Center for the People and the Press at http://www.pewresearch.org/.
6. See the Freedom House report, *Freedom in the World, 2012* (Washington, D.C.: Freedom House, 2012). It is online at www.freedomhouse.org.
7. James Surowiecki, *The Wisdom of Crowds* (New York: Doubleday, 2004).
8. For a fuller treatment of the claims in this paragraph, as well as supporting evidence for them, see Robert A. Dahl, *Democracy and Its Critics* (New Haven, CT: Yale University Press, 1989); Robert A. Dahl, *On Democracy* (New Haven, CT: Yale University Press, 1998). Also see Benjamin Radcliff, "Politics, Markets, and Life Satisfaction: The Political Economy of Human Happiness," *American Political Science Review* 95 (December 2001), pp. 939–952.
9. Robert A. Dahl, "James Madison: Republican or Democrat?" *Perspectives on Politics* 3, no. 3 (September 2005), pp. 439–448.
10. John Dewey, *The Public and Its Problems* (New York: Holt, 1927).
11. Charles Tilly, *Democracy* (Cambridge, UK: Cambridge University Press, 2007), p. 59.
12. Tilly, *Democracy*, pp. 26–28. Also see Josiah Ober, "What the Ancient Greeks Can Tell Us About Democracy," *The Annual Review of Political Science* 11 (2008), pp. 67–91.
13. Dahl, *Democracy and Its Critics*, p. 13; Dahl, "James Madison: Republican or Democrat?"
14. See Robert A. Dahl, *After the Revolution: Authority in the Good Society* (New Haven, CT: Yale University Press, 1970); Dahl, *Democracy and Its Critics*; Jane Mansbridge, *Beyond Adversary Democracy* (New York: Basic Books, 1980). Also see Kevin O'Leary, *Saving Democracy* (Stanford, CA: Stanford University Press, 2006), ch. 1.
15. See Benjamin Barber, *Strong Democracy: Participatory Democracy for a New Age* (Berkeley, CA: University of California Press, 1984); Peter Bachrach, *The Theory of Democratic Elitism* (Boston: Little, Brown, 1967); Robert A. Dahl, *A Preface to Economic Democracy* (Berkeley, CA: University of California Press, 1985); Edward S. Greenberg, "Spillovers from Cooperative and Democratic Workplaces," in Brandon Sullivan and John Sullivan, eds., *Cooperation as the Basis of Individual and Group Functioning* (Minneapolis, MN: University of Minnesota Press, 2006); Edward S. Greenberg, *Workplace Democracy: The Political Effects of Participation* (Ithaca, NY: Cornell University Press, 1986); C. B. MacPherson, *Democratic Theory: Essays in Retrieval* (Oxford, UK: Clarendon Press, 1973); Carole Pateman, *Participation and Democratic Theory* (London: Cambridge University Press, 1970).
16. Esther Dyson, *Release 2.0* (New York: Broadway Books, 1997); Lawrence K. Grossman, *The Electronic Republic: Reshaping Democracy in the Information Age* (New York: Viking Press, 1995); Jerome Armstrong and Markos M. Zuniga, *Crashing the Gate: Netroots, Grassroots, and the Rule of People-Powered Politics* (White River Junction, VT: Chelsea Green Publishing Co., 2006).
17. For the very mixed evidence on the degree to which the Internet and digital communications have enhanced democracy, see Michael Margolis and Gerson Moreno-Riano, *The Prospect of Internet Democracy* (London: Ashgate Publishing, 2009).
18. Christian Welzel and Ronald Inglehart, "The Role of Ordinary People in Democratization," *Journal of Democracy* 19, no. 1 (2008), p. 126.
19. On deliberation and democracy, see Jason Barabas, "How Deliberation Affects Policy Opinions," *American Political Science Review* 98 (2004), pp. 687–701; Seyla Benhabib, "Toward a Deliberative Model of Democratic Legitimacy," in Seyla Benhabib, ed., *Democracy and Difference* (Princeton, NJ: Princeton University Press, 1996); John Dryzek, *Discursive Democracy* (Cambridge, UK: Cambridge University Press, 1990); Nancy Fraser, "Rethinking the Public Sphere," in Craig Calhoun, ed., *Habermas and the Public Sphere* (New Brunswick, NJ: Rutgers University Press, 1992), pp. 109–142; Amy Guttman and Dennis Thompson, *Democracy and Disagreement* (Cambridge, UK: Belknap Press, 1996); Jurgen Habermas, *The Structural Transformation of the Public Sphere* (Cambridge, MA: MIT Press, 1989).
20. Kenneth May, "A Set of Independent, Necessary, and Sufficient Conditions for Simple Majority Decision," *Econometrical* 20 (1952), pp. 680–684, shows that only majority rule can guarantee popular sovereignty, political equality, and neutrality among policy alternatives. See also Douglas W. Rae, "Decision Rules and Individual Values in Constitutional Choice," *American Political Science Review* 63 (1969), pp. 40–53; Phillip D. Straffin Jr., "Majority Rule and General Decision Rules," *Theory and Decision* 8 (1977), pp. 351–360. On the other hand, Hans Gersbach argues in *Designing Democracy* (New York: Springer Publishers, 2005) that larger majorities ought to be required for more important decisions.
21. Mark Warren, "Democracy and the State," in John S. Dryzek, Bonnie Honig, and Ann Phillips, eds., *The Oxford Handbook of Political Theory* (Oxford, UK: Oxford University Press, 2006), pp. 385–386; and Gordon S. Wood, *The Idea of America: Reflections on the Birth of the United States* (New York: Penguin Press, 2011), ch. 6, "The Making of American Democracy," pp. 189–212.
22. For a review of contemporary research on this issue, see Larry M. Bartels, *Unequal Democracy: The Political Economy of the New Gilded Age* (New York: Russell Sage Foundation, 2008); Seymour Martin Lipset and Jason M. Lakin, *The Democratic Century* (Norman, OK: University of Oklahoma Press, 2004); Tilly, *Democracy*.
23. Dahl, *A Preface to Economic Democracy*, p. 68.

24. "Trends in the Distribution of Household Income Between 1979 and 2007," (Washington, D.C.: Congressional Budget Office, October 2011).

25. Robert A. Dahl, "On Removing Certain Impediments to Democracy in the United States," *Political Science Quarterly* 92, no. 1 (Spring 1977), p. 14; Elaine Spitz, *Majority Rule* (Chatham, NJ: Chatham House, 1984), p. 83; Dahl, *Democracy and Its Critics*, p. 170.

26. See Marc Plattner, "Liberalism and Democracy," *Foreign Affairs* (March–April 1998), pp. 171–180. On the inevitability of tension between and the necessity of balancing the claims of liberty and majority rule, see Adam Przeworski, "Self-Government in Our Times," *The Annual Review of Political Science* 12 (2009), pp. 88–90; and Michael Coppedge and John Gerring, "Conceptualizing and Measuring Democracy."

27. David Caute, *The Great Fear* (New York: Simon & Schuster, 1978); Victor Navasky, *Naming Names* (New York: Viking, 1980); Michael Rogin, *The Intellectuals and McCarthy* (Cambridge, MA: MIT Press, 1967).

28. Fareed Zakaria, *The Future of Freedom: Illiberal Democracy at Home and Abroad* (New York: Norton, 2004).

29. See Bartels, *Unequal Democracy*; Bernard R. Berelson, Paul F. Lazarsfeld, and William N. McPhee, *Voting* (Chicago: University of Chicago Press, 1954); V. O. Key Jr., *Public Opinion and American Democracy* (New York: Knopf, 1961); Herbert McClosky and Alida Brill, *Dimensions of Tolerance* (New York: Russell Sage Foundation, 1983); Robert Weissberg, *Polling, Policy, and Public Opinion: The Case Against Heeding the Voice of the People* (New York: Palgrave Press, MacMillan, 2003); Robert Weissberg, "Politicized Pseudo-Science," *PS* (January 2006), pp. 39–42; Alan Wolfe, *Does American Democracy Still Work?* (New Haven, CT: Yale University Press, 2006). But see, in rebuttal, James L. Gibson, "Political Intolerance and Political Repression during the McCarthy Red Scare," *American Political Science Review* 82 (1988), pp. 511–529; Benjamin I. Page and Robert Y. Shapiro, *The Rational Public: Fifty Years of Trends in Americans' Policy Preferences* (Chicago: University of Chicago Press, 1992).

30. Katherine Brandt, "Madisonian Majority Tyranny, Minority Rights, and American Democracy" (paper presented at the annual meetings of the Midwest Political Science Association, April 2004); Dahl, *A Preface to Democratic Theory*; and Desmond S. King and Rogers M. Smith, *Still a House Divided: Race and Politics in Obama's America* (Princeton, NJ: Princeton University Press, 2011).

31. Dahl, Democracy and Its Critics, p. 161.

32. Thanks to Professor Larry Martinez of the California State University, Long Beach, for this insight.

33. Philip A. Klinkner with Rogers M. Smith, *The Unsteady March: The Rise and Decline of Racial Equality in America* (Chicago: The University of Chicago Press, 1999).

2

1. The White House. Washington, D.C., January 14, 2005.

2. A bill also can become a law after 10 days if the president has not signed the bill and Congress is still in session.

3. www.whitehouse.gov/ (posted January 31, 2005).

4. January 4, 2006, p. 1.

5. Charlie Savage, "Obama Looks to Limit Impact of Tactic Bush Used to Sidestep New Laws," *The New York Times* (March 9, 2009), p. 1.

6. Charlie Savage, "Obama's Embrace of a Bush Tactic Riles Congress," *The New York Times* (August 9, 2009), p. 1.

7. Richard Bushman, "Revolution," in Eric Foner and John A. Garraty, eds., *The Reader's Companion to American History* (Boston: Houghton Mifflin, 1991), p. 936; Gordon S. Wood,

The Creation of the American Republic (New York: Norton, 1972), p. 12.

8. Joseph J. Ellis, Founding Brothers: The Revolutionary Generation (New York: Alfred A. Knopf, 2001), pp. 212–213; Roger Wilkins, Jacob's Pillow: The Founding Fathers and the Dilemma of Black Patriotism (Boston: Beacon Press, 2002).

9. Sarah M. Evans, *Born for Liberty: A History of Women in America* (New York: Free Press, 1997); John Hope Franklin and Alfred A. Moss Jr., *From Slavery to Freedom* (New York: Knopf, 1967).

10. See Hannah Arendt, *On Revolution* (New York: Viking, 1965).

11. Page Smith, *A People's History of the Young Republic: Vol. 3, The Shaping of America* (New York: McGraw-Hill, 1980).

12. Richard Hofstadter, *The American Political Tradition* (New York: Vintage Books, 1948), p. 4.

13. For a review of thinking about relevance of republicanism in our own time, see Frank Lovett and Philip Pettit, "Neorepublicanism: A Normative and Institutional Research Program," *Annual Review of Political Science* 12 (2009), pp. 11–29.

14. Kevin O'Leary, *Saving Democracy* (Stanford, CA: Stanford University Press, 2006), ch. 3; and Gordon S. Wood, *The Idea of America: Reflections on the Birth of the United States* (New York: The Penguin Press, 2011), ch. 4.

15. Alexander Hamilton, James Madison, and John Jay, *The Federalist Papers*, ed. Clinton Rossiter (New York: New American Library, 1961), No. 10. (Originally published 1787–1788.)

16. See Gordon S. Wood, *The Radicalism of the American Revolution* (New York: Knopf, 1992).

17. Wood, Creation of the American Republic, pp. 311–318.

18. Ibid., ch. 8.

19. Samuel Eliot Morison, *The Oxford History of the American People* (New York: Oxford University Press, 1965), p. 274.

20. See Wood, Creation of the American Republic, p. 400.

21. Smith, *The Shaping of America*, pp. 24–26.

22. Quoted in Jackson Turner Main, *The Anti-Federalists* (Chapel Hill: University of North Carolina Press, 1961), p. 62.

23. David Brian Robertson, "Madison's Opponents and Constitutional Design," *American Political Science Review* 99 (May 2006), pp. 225–243.

24. Melvin I. Urofsky, *A March of Liberty* (New York: Knopf, 1988), p. 89.

25. Quoted in *The Washington Post* (May 7, 1987). Also see Lee Epstein and Thomas G. Walker, *Constitutional Law for a Changing America* (Washington, D.C.: CQ Press, 2000), p. 6.

26. Charles Beard, *An Economic Interpretation of the Constitution* (New York: Macmillan, 1913). For a more recent work broadly supporting Beard's interpretation, see Robert A. McGuire, *To Form a More Perfect Union: A New Economic Interpretation of the United States Constitution* (New York: Oxford University Press, 2003).

27. See Robert Brown, *Charles Beard and the Constitution* (Princeton, NJ: Princeton University Press, 1956); Hofstadter, *The American Political Tradition*; Leonard Levy, *Constitutional Opinions* (New York: Oxford University Press, 1986); Robert A. McGuire and Robert L. Ohsfeldt, "An Economic Model of Voting Behavior over Specific Issues at the Constitutional Convention of 1787," *Journal of Economic History* 66 (March 1986), pp. 79–111; James A. Morone, *The Democratic Wish* (New York: Basic Books, 1990); Forrest McDonald, *We the People: The Economic Origins of the Constitution* (Chicago: University of Chicago Press, 1958); Gordon S. Wood, *The Convention and the Constitution* (New York: St. Martin's Press, 1965); Wood, *Creation of the American Republic*.

28. Wood, The Idea of America, p. 131.

29. Quoted in Wood, Creation of the American Republic, p. 473.

30. Ibid., p. 432.

31. Charles Stewart, "Congress and the Constitutional System," in Paul J. Quirk and Sarah A. Binder, eds., *The Legislative*

Branch (New York: Oxford University Press, Institutions of American Democracy Series, 2005).

32. See Robertson, "Madison's Opponents and Constitutional Design," for more information on how the Great Compromise shaped the Constitution as a whole.

33. Ellis, *Founding Brothers*, p. 110.

34. Max Farrand, *The Records of the Federal Convention of 1787* (New Haven, CT: Yale University Press, 1937).

35. Hamilton, Madison, and Jay, *The Federalist*, No. 10.

36. "The Invention of Centralized Federalism," in William H. Riker, ed., *The Development of Centralized Federalism* (Boston: Kluwer Academic, 1987).

37. Robert A. Dahl, "On Removing the Impediments to Democracy in the United States," *Political Science Quarterly* 92 (Spring 1977), p. 5.

38. Akhil Reed Amar, *America's Constitution: A Biography* (New York: Random House, 2005), p. 14.

39. Hamilton, Madison, and Jay, *The Federalist Papers*, No. 51.

40. Thomas Jefferson, *Notes on the State of Virginia*, ed. Thomas Perkins Abernathy (New York: Harper & Row, 1964), p. 120.

41. In a letter to James Madison dated November 18, 1788, in Adrienne Koch and William Peden, eds., *The Life and Selected Writings of Thomas Jefferson* (New York: Random House/The Modern Library, 1944), p. 452.

42. See Main, *The Anti-Federalists*; Wood, *Creation of the American Republic*; Smith, *The Shaping of America*, p. 99; Herbert Storing, *What the Anti-Federalists Were For* (Chicago: University of Chicago Press, 1981), p. 71; Robertson, "Madison's Opponents and Constitutional Design."

43. See Cass R. Sunstein, *A Constitution of Many Minds: Why the Founding Document Doesn't Mean What It Meant Before* (Princeton, NJ: Princeton University Press, 2009) for a particularly compelling statement of this idea.

44. On the undemocratic Constitution, see Sanford Levinson, *Our Undemocratic Constitution: Where the Constitution Goes Wrong* (New York: Oxford University Press, 2006).

3

1. Sources for this chapter-opening story include the following: Jonathon Adler, "*NFIB*," (the Volokh Conspiracy blog (www.folokh.com, posted on July 12, 2012); Paul M. Barrett, "John Roberts, CEO," *Bloomberg/BusinessWeek* (July 3, 2012), p. 23; Pamela S. Karlan, "No Respite for Liberals," *The New York Times* (June 30, 2012), p. 1; David Kopel, "The Bar Review Version of *NFIB v. Sebelius* (SCOTUSblog, www.scotusblog.com, posted July 6, 2012); and James B. Stewart, "In Obama's Victory, a Loss for Congress," *The New York Times* (June 29, 2012), p. 1.

2. William H. Riker, *The Development of American Federalism* (Boston: Kluwer Academic, 1987), pp. 56–60.

3. Gabriel A. Almond, G. Bingham Powell Jr., Russell J. Dalton, and Kaare Strom, *Comparative Politics Today: A World View*, updated 9th ed. (New York: Pearson Longman, 2010), p. 108.

4. Mark Rush, "Voting Power in Federal Systems: Spain as a Case Study," *PS: Political Science and Politics* XL, no. 4 (October 2007), pp. 715–720.

5. Rodney Hero, *Faces of Inequality: Social Diversity in American Politics* (New York: Oxford University Press, 1998). Also see Regina P. Branton and Bradford S. Jones, "Reexamining Racial Attitudes: The Conditional Relationship Between Diversity and Socioeconomic Environment," *American Journal of Political Science* 49, no. 2 (April 2005), pp. 359–372.

6. Dale Krane, "The Middle Tier in American Federalism: State Government Policy Activism During the Bush Presidency,"

Publius: The Journal of Federalism 37, no. 3 (2007), pp. 453–477.

7. John Schwartz, "After New York, New Look at Defense of Marriage Act," *The New York Times*, June 27, 2011, p. 1.

8. The study of the complex constitutional, legal, fiscal, and political links between states and the national government is often called the study of *intergovernmental relations* (the ever-changing constitutional, legal, fiscal, and political linkages among the states and the national government). For more on this, see B. G. Peters and J. Pierre, "Developments in Intergovernmental Relations: Towards Multi-Level Governance," *Policy and Politics* 29 (2001), pp. 131–141; R. B. Albritton, "American Federalism and Intergovernmental Relations," in Gillian Peele, Christopher J. Bailey, Bruce Cain, and B. Guy Peters, eds., *Developments in American Politics* (New York: Palgrave, 2008).

9. Thomas Gais and James Fossett, "Federalism and the Executive Branch," in Joel D. Aberbach and Mark A. Peterson, eds., *The Executive Branch* (New York: Oxford University Press, Institutions of American Democracy Series, 2005).

10. Hero, *Faces of Inequality*, pp. 31–34.

11. Robert G. McCloskey, *American Supreme Court*, 4th ed., ed. Sanford Levinson (Chicago: University of Chicago Press, 2004), pp. 49–51.

12. See the special "Symposium on Preemption" in *PS: Political Science and Politics* (Washington, D.C.: The American Political Science Association, July 2005), pp. 359–378.

13. McCloskey, *American Supreme Court*, pp. 104–107, 118–119.

14. "A Partisan Public Agenda: Opinion of Clinton and Congress Improves" (Washington, D.C.: Pew Research Center, 1997); "How Americans View Government: Deconstructing Distrust" (Washington, D.C.: Pew Research Center, 1998); "National Omnibus Survey" (Cambridge, MA: Cambridge Reports/Research International, 1982).

15. Tim Conlan and John Dinan, "Federalism, the Bush Administration, and the Transformation of American Conservatism," *Publius: The Journal of Federalism* 37, no. 3 (2007), pp. 279–303.

16. Krane, "The Middle Tier in American Federalism."

17. Shama Gamkhar and J. Mitchell Pickerill, "The State of American Federalism, 2010–2011," *Publius: The Journal of Federalism* 41, no. 3, pp. 361–394.

18. For example, in *Bond v. United States*, the Court ruled that individuals can sue the federal government when Congress goes too far in creating statutes that intrude on the legitimate authority of the states. In *Sossamon v. Texas*, it ruled that states do not give up their sovereign immunity against monetary lawsuits from their own citizens for violating a federal law when states accept federal funds under that law.

19. Ann O. M. Bowan and George A. Krause, "Power Shift: Measuring Policy Centralization in U.S. Intergovernmental Relations, 1947–1998," *American Politics Research* 31, no. 3 (May 2003), pp. 301–313; B. Guy Peters, *American Public Policy: Promise and Performance* (Washington, D.C.: CQ Press, 2009), pp. 24–29; Robert Nagel, *The Implosion of American Federalism* (New York: Oxford University Press, 2002).

20. Morton Grodzins, *The American System* (New Brunswick, NJ: Transaction Books, 1983).

21. Riker, *The Development of American Federalism*; David B. Walker, *Toward a Functioning Federalism* (Cambridge, MA: Winthrop. 1981), pp. 60–63.

22. Paul E. Peterson, Barry G. Rabe, and Kenneth Wong, *When Federalism Works* (Washington, D.C.: Brookings Institution, 1986), p. 2.

23. Gamkhar and Pickerill, "The State of American Federalism," p. 363.

24. Ed Gillespie and Bob Schellhas, eds., *Contract with America: The Bold Plan by Rep. Newt Gingrich, Rep. Dick Armey and the House Republicans to Change the Nation* (New York: Random House, 1994), p. 125.

25. "Symposium on Preemption," *PS*. Also see the "Preemption Monitor" of the National Conference of State Legislatures at http://www.ncsl.org/standcomm/sclaw/PreemptionMonitor_Index.htm.

26. William H. Riker, *Federalism: Origin, Operation, Significance* (Boston: Little, Brown, 1964), ch. 6.

27. Paul E. Peterson, *City Limits* (Chicago: University of Chicago Press, 1981); Paul E. Peterson, *The Price of Federalism* (Washington, D.C.: Brookings Institution, 1995).

4

1. Adam Cort, "Living the Dream," *Assembly Magazine* (www.assemblymag.com, August 1, 2006).

2. Dominic Gates, "A Prescient Warning to Boeing on 787 Trouble," *The Seattle Times* (February 5, 2011), p. 1.

3. John Newhouse, *Boeing versus Airbus: The Inside Story of the Greatest International Competition in Business* (New York: Knopf, 2007); and Gates, "A Prescient Warning . . ."

4. Boeing Commercial Airplanes Chief Jim Arbaugh, quoted in Gates.

5. For a detailed examination of how these changes at Boeing affected the health and well-being of its employees, see Edward S. Greenberg, Leon Grunberg, Sarah Moore, and Pat Sikora, *Turbulence: Boeing and the Future of American Workers and Managers* (New Haven, CT: Yale University Press, 2010).

6. See Grant D. Aldonas, *Globalization and the American Worker* (Washington, D.C.: CSIS Press, 2009); Richard Sennett, James O'Toole, and Edward E. Lawler III, *The New American Workplace* (New York: Palgrave, MacMillan, 2006); and Robert B. Reich, *Aftershock: The Next Economy and America's Future* (New York: Alfred A. Knopf, 2010).

7. Though the United States fell slightly below replacement level during the Great Recession. See "Births," *National Vital Statistics Reports* (Washington, D.C.: U.S. Department of Health and Human Services, 2010).

8. For a history of immigration and government policies regarding immigrations see Aristide R. Zolberg, *A Nation by Design: Immigration Policy in the Fashioning of America* (Cambridge, MA: Harvard University Press, 2006).

9. "2010 American Community Study," U.S. Census Bureau.

10. U.S. Department of Homeland Security, *Yearbook of Immigration Statistics* (Washington, D.C.: U.S. Government Printing Office, 2012).

11. U.S. Bureau of the Census, "2010 Quick Facts" (Washington, D.C.: U.S. Government Printing Office, 2011).

12. Ibid.

13. "Population Projections, 2005–2025" (Washington, D.C.: The Pew Research Center, February 11, 2008).

14. Richard Florida, *The Flight of the Creative Class* (New York: HarperBusiness, 2005).

15. Jeff S. Passel and D'Vera Cohn, "U.S. Unauthorized Immigration Flows Are Down Sharply Since Mid-Decade," (Washington, D.C.: The Pew Hispanic Center, September 1, 2010).

16. Pew Research Center for the People and the Press, press release, October 15, 2009.

17. "Public Favors Tougher Border Controls and Path to Citizenship; Most Oppose Ending 'Birthright Citizenship.' " (Washington, D.C: The Pew Research Center, survey report, February 24, 2011).

18. Daniel J. Tichenor, *Dividing Lines: The Politics of Immigration Control in the United States* (Princeton, NJ: Princeton University Press, 2002), p. 284; and "The Latino Electorate in 2010," (Washington, D.C.: The Pew Hispanic Center, April 26, 2011).

19. "The Census: Minority Report," *The Economist* (April 2, 2011), p. 25; and "The 2010 Census Data," (Washington, D.C.: Census Bureau, 2012).

20. U.S. Bureau of the Census, "Age and Sex Composition, 2010."

21. "Recession Turns a Graying Office Grayer" (Washington, D.C.: The Pew Research Center, September 3, 2009), p. 1.

22. U.S. Bureau of the Census, "Older Population in the United States," 2008.

23. Based on purchasing power.

24. *Human Development Report, 2011* (New York: The United Nations, 2012).

25. See the article by Brenda Cronin reporting statistics from Sentier Research based on Census Bureau data, "Slow Recovery Feels Like Recession," *The Wall Street Journal*, October 31, 2011, p. 1.

26. Ianthe Jeanne Dugan, "Returning Workers Face Steep Pay Cuts," *The Wall Street Journal* (November 12, 2009), p. 1.; and Shobhana Chandra and Steve Matthews, "Having A Job Ain't What It Used to Be," *Bloomberg/Businessweek* (October 17–October 23, 2011), pp. 19–20.

27. Census Bureau, reported in Conor Dougherty, *The Wall Street Journal*, September 13, 2011, p. 1.

28. Stanley B. Greenberg, *Middle-Class Dreams* (New York: Times Books, 1995); Susan J. Tolchin, *The Angry American* (Boulder, CO: Westview Press, 1999). On the more general relationship between income growth and political mood, see Benjamin M. Friedman, *The Moral Consequences of Economic Growth* (New York: Knopf, 2005).

29. David Leonhardt and Marjorie Connelly, "81 Percent in Poll Say Nation Is on the Wrong Track," *The New York Times* (April 4, 2008), p. A1. Also see Brian Blackstone, "Economy Sheds Jobs in March, Fueling Fears of Recession," *The Wall Street Journal* (April 4, 2008), p. 1

30. Bureau of the Census, "Poverty: 2009 and 2010," October 2011.

31. Bureau of the Census, "The Research Supplemental Poverty Measure: 2010," issued November 2011.

32. Bureau of the Census, "Income, Poverty, and Health Insurance Coverage in the United States: 2010," issued September 2011.

33. Ibid.

34. William Julius Wilson, *When Work Disappears: The World of the New Urban Poor* (New York: Vintage, 1997).

35. Florence Jaumotte, Subir Lall, and Chris Papageorgiou, "Rising Income Inequality: Technology, or Trade and Financial Globalization," (Washington, D.C.: International Monetary Fund, July 2008).

36. Emmanuel Saez, "Striking It Richer," working paper, update with 2007 estimates (August 5, 2009); Thomas Piketty and Emmanuel Saez, "Income Inequality in the United States," *Quarterly Journal of Economics* 118, no. 1 (2003), pp. 1–39.

37. Lawrence Mishel, Jared Bernstein, and Sylvia Allegretto, *The State of Working America, 2006* (Ithaca, NY: Economic Policy Institute and Cornell University Press, 2006); and Josh Bivens, "CEOs distance themselves from the average worker," The Economic Policy Institute, November 9, 2011 (http://www.epi.org/publication/ceo-ratio-average-worker).

38. Natasha Singer, "In Executive Pay, a Rich Game of Thrones," *The New York Times* (April 7, 2012), p. 1.

39. "CEO Pay Sinks Along with Profits," *The Wall Street Journal* (April 3, 2009), p. A1.

40. "CEO Pay Rebounds," *Bloomberg/Businessweek* (September 12, 2011), p. 35.

41. Singer, "In Executive Pay, a Rich Game of Thrones," p. 1.

42. Edward Wolff, "Recent Trends in Household Wealth in the United States," Bard College, Levy Economics Institute (June 2007). Also see Larry M. Bartels, *Unequal Democracy: The Political Economy of the New Gilded Age* (New York and Princeton, NJ: The Russell Sage Foundation and Princeton University Press, 2008), ch. 1.

43. Joseph E. Stiglitz, "Of the 1%, by the 1%, for the 1%," *Vanity Fair* (May 2011), p. 75.

44. "Income Inequality," Bureau of the Census, 2011.

45. The research is summarized and discussed in Jacob S. Hacker and Paul Pierson, *Winner-Take-All Politics* (New York: Simon and Schuster, 2010); and Robert B. Reich, *Aftershock: The Next Economy and America's Future* (New York: Knopf, 2010), ch. 7.

46. Raymond Boudon and Francois Bourricaud, *A Critical Dictionary of Sociology* (Chicago: The University of Chicago Press, 1989), pp. 340–346.

47. U.S. Bureau of the Census, *Current Population Reports*, 2012.

48. See the research cited and summarized in Hacker and Pierson, *Winner-Take-All Politics*, ch. 1; Jacob S. Hacker, *The Great Risk Shift* ((New York: Oxford University Press, 2006); and Reich, *Aftershock*.

49. Gerald F. Seib, "Populist Movements Rooted in Same Soil," *The Wall Street Journal* (November 15, 2011), Capital Journal, p. 1.

50. Reich, *Aftershock*, Part II, "Backlash."

51. David Coen, Wyn Grant, and Graham Wilson, "Perspectives on Business and Government (Political Science)," in David Coen, Wyn Grant, and Graham Wilson, eds., *The Oxford Handbook of Business and Government* (New York: Oxford University Press, 2010).

52. On the different forms of capitalism in the modern world, see William J. Baumol, Robert E. Litan, and Carl J. Schramm, *Good Capitalism, Bad Capitalism and the Economics of Growth and Prosperity* (New Haven, CT: Yale University Press, 2007); Gosta Esping-Andersen, "The Three Political Economies of the Welfare State," *Canadian Review of Sociology and Anthropology* 26 (1989), pp. 10–36; Bob Hancke, "Varieties of Capitalism and Business," in Coen, Grant, and Wilson, eds., *The Oxford Handbook of Capitalism and Business*; Jonas Pontusson, "The American Welfare State in Comparative Perspective," *Perspectives on Politics* 4, no. 2 (June 2006); pp. 315–326. Harold L. Wilensky, *Rich Democracies: Political Economy, Public Policy, and Performance* (Berkeley, CA: University of California Press, 2002).

53. U.S. Department of Commerce, *International Direct Investment* (Washington, D.C.: U.S. Government Printing Office, 1984), p. 1.

54. For entertaining yet highly informative critiques of extreme pro-globalization advocates and extreme anti-globalization advocates, see Michael Veseth, *Selling Globalization: The Myth of the Global Economy* (Boulder, CO: Lynne Rienner, 1998); Michael Veseth, *Globaloney: Unraveling the Myths of Globalization* (Lanham, MD: Rowman & Littlefield, 2005).

55. Robert B. Reich, *Supercapitalism: The Transformation of Business, Democracy, and Everyday Life* (New York: Alfred A. Knopf, 2007).

56. Louis Uchitelle, "Is Manufacturing Falling Off the Radar?" *The New York Times* (September 10, 2011), Business, p. 1; and Anton Troianovski, "Wireless Jobs Vanish," *Wall Street Journal* (July 18, 2011), Technology, p. 1.

57. Chandra and Matthews, "Having A Job Ain't What It Used to Be."

58. "Confidence in Obama Lifts U.S. Image Around the World," (Washington, D.C.: Pew Global Attitudes Project, July 23, 2009); "Obama More Popular Abroad Than at Home, Global Image of U.S. Continues to Benefit" (Washington, D.C.: Pew Global Attitudes Project, June 17, 2010).

59. See Seymour Martin Lipset, *American Exceptionalism: A Double-Edged Sword* (New York: Norton, 1996); Jennifer L. Hochschild, *Facing Up to the American Dream* (Princeton, NJ: Princeton University Press, 1995), ch. 1; John Micklethwait and Adrian Wooldridge, *The Right Nation: Conservative Power in America* (New York: Penguin Press, 2004), part IV. For a contrary view—namely, that America is divided into distinct political cultural traditions—see Rogers M. Smith, *Civic Ideals: Conflicting Visions of Citizenship in U.S. History* (New Haven, CT: Yale University Press, 1997). For an answer to Smith that defends the idea that the American political culture is of a single large cloth, see Marc Stears, "The Liberal Tradition and the Politics of Exclusion," *Annual Review of Political Science* 10 (2007), pp. 85–101.

60. For a contrary view of the place of individualism in American life, see Desmond King, *The Liberty of Strangers: Making the American Nation* (New York: Oxford University Press, 2004).

61. See Jennifer L. Hochschild, *What's Fair? American Beliefs about Distributive Justice* (Cambridge, MA: Harvard University Press, 1981); Herbert McClosky and John R. Zaller, *The American Ethos: Public Attitudes Toward Capitalism and Democracy* (Cambridge, MA: Harvard University Press, 1984); Sidney Verba and Gary R. Orren, *Equality in America* (Cambridge, MA: Harvard University Press, 1985). See Benjamin I. Page and Lawrence R. Jacobs, *Class War: What Americans Really Feel About Inequality* (Chicago: University of Chicago Press, 2009), however, which shows that public support exists for programs to lessen inequality.

62. See Joel F. Handler and Yeheskel Hasenfeld, *Blame Welfare, Ignore Poverty and Inequality* (Cambridge, UK: Cambridge University Press, 2007). For arguments suggesting that Americans are uncomfortable with income inequality and are willing to let government do something about making it less extreme, see Page and Jacobs, *Class War*.

63. Verba and Orren, *Equality in America*, p. 255.

64. Page and Jacobs, *Class War*, pp. 96–97.

65. The Gallup Poll, February 24, 2009.

66. "Support for Health Care Principles, Opposition to Package" (Washington, D.C.: Pew Research Center, October 8, 2009).

67. John Judis, "Anti-Statism in America," *The New Republic* (November 11, 2009), p. 2.

68. Russell Hanson, *The Democratic Imagination in America* (Princeton, NJ: Princeton University Press, 1985).

69. McClosky and Zaller, *The American Ethos*, p. 18; "Views of a Changing World 2003" (Washington, D.C.: Pew Research Center, 2003).

70. Alan Wolfe, *Does American Democracy Still Work?* (New Haven, CT: Yale University Press, 2006).

71. Gary Wills, *Under God: Religion and American Politics* (New York: Simon and Schuster, 1991); Micklethwait and Wooldridge, *The Right Nation*; Kevin Phillips, *American Theocracy: The Peril and Politics of Radical Religion, Oil, and Borrowed Money in the 21st Century* (New York: Viking, 2006).

72. "Views of a Changing World 2003."

73. Micklethwait and Wooldridge, *The Right Nation*.

5

1. Joseph C. Goulden, *Truth Is the First Casualty: The Gulf of Tonkin Affair—Illusion and Reality* (Chicago: Rand McNally, 1969). Also see Scott Stane, "Vietnam War Intelligence Deliberately Skewed, Secret Study Says," *The New York Times* (December 2, 2005), p. A1.

2. All public opinion polls cited in this chapter-opening story are from John E. Mueller, *War, Presidents and Public Opinion* (New York: Wiley, 1973).

3. U.S. Department of Defense, OASD (Comptroller), *Selected Manpower Statistics* (Washington, D.C.: Government Publications, June 1976), pp. 59–60.

4. Alexander Hamilton, James Madison, and John Jay, *The Federalist Papers*, ed. Clinton Rossiter (New York: New American Library, 1961; originally published 1787–1788). See Benjamin I. Page and Robert Y. Shapiro, *The Rational Public: Fifty Years*

of *Trends in Americans' Policy Preferences* (Chicago: University of Chicago Press, 1992), chs. 1 and 2.

5. Walter Lippmann, *Public Opinion* (New York: Macmillan, 1922), p. 127.

6. Philip E. Converse, "The Nature of Belief Systems in Mass Publics," in David Apter, ed., *Ideology and Discontent* (New York: Free Press, 1964), pp. 206–261; Philip E. Converse, "Attitudes and Non-Attitudes: Continuation of a Dialogue," in Edward R. Tufte, ed., *The Quantitative Analysis of Social Problems* (Reading, MA: Addison-Wesley, 1970), pp. 168–189. Also see Larry M. Bartels, *Unequal Democracy: The Political Economy of the Gilded Age* (New York and Princeton, NJ: Russell Sage Foundation and Princeton University Press, 2008), for an argument that people find it hard to understand whether public policies are consistent with their values and wishes.

7. Bartels, *Unequal Democracy*.

8. Bryan Caplan, *The Myth of the Rational Voter: Why Democracies Choose Bad Policies* (Princeton, NJ: Princeton University Press, 2007).

9. Robert S. Erikson and Kent L. Tedin, *American Public Opinion: Its Origins, Content, and Impact*, 8th ed. (New York: Pearson Longman, 2011), table 2.1. This book offers an excellent introduction to how surveys are done.

10. Ibid., p. 42.

11. George F. Bishop, *The Illusion of Public Opinion: Fact and Artifact in American Public Opinion Polls* (Lanham, MD: Rowman & Littlefield Publishers, 2004).

12. For a review of the research literature on political socialization see Erikson and Tedin, *American Public Opinion*, ch. 5.

13. M. Kent Jennings, "Political Socialization," in Russell Dalton and Hans-Dieter Klingman, eds., *The Oxford Handbook of Political Behavior* (Oxford: Oxford University Press, 2004); M. Kent Jennings, L. Stoker, and J. Bowers, "Politics Across Generations: Family Transmission Reconsidered," *The Journal of Politics* 71, pp. 782–799; and Laura Stoker and Jackie Bass, "Political Socialization," in Robert Shapiro and Lawrence R. Jacobs, eds., *The Oxford Handbook of Public Opinion and the Media* (Oxford: Oxford University Press, 2011).

14. Doris A. Graber, *Mass Media and American Politics*, 8th ed. (Washington, D.C.: CQ Press, 2010), pp. 161–166.

15. For data on how the economic prospects of young people have changed for the worse and on how their political attitudes differ from other age cohorts see "The Rising Age Gap in Economic Well-Being" (Washington, D.C.: Pew Research Center, released November 7, 2011) and "The Generation Gap and the 2012 Election" (Washington, D.C.: Pew Research Center, released November 3, 2011).

16. For articulations on how we are divided see Henry E. Brady, "The Art of Political Science: Spatial Diagrams as Iconic and Revelatory," *Perspectives on Politics* (June 2011), volume 9, number 2, pp. 311–331; and Desmond S. King and Rogers M. Smith, *Still a House Divided: Race and Politics in Obama's America* (Princeton: Princeton University Press, 2011).

17. Paul Sniderman and Thomas Piazza, *Black Pride and Black Prejudice* (Princeton, NJ: Princeton University Press, 2002), pp. 175–179; and Erikson and Tedin, *American Public Opinion*, pp. 199–200.

18. "Trends in Political Values and Core Attitudes: 1987–2009" (Washington, D.C.: Pew Research Center for the People and the Press, report released May 21, 2009); Laura R. Olson and John C. Green, *Beyond Red State, Blue State: Electoral Gaps in the Twenty-First Century American Electorate* (New York: Pearson Prentice-Hall, 2009).

19. "Trends in Political Values and Core Attitudes: 1987–2009," pp. 78–79.

20. This and the votes of other groups reported in this section are from "The National Election Pool Exit Poll" (Washington, D.C.: Edison Media Research and Mitofsky International, November 4, 2008).

21. Fredrick C. Harris, "The Contours of Black Public Opinion," in Shapiro and Jacobs, *The Oxford Handbook of American Public Opinion and the Media*.

22. Pew Research Center, "Trends in Political Values and Core Attitudes: 1987–2009."

23. Ibid., section 9; and Erikson and Tedin, *American Public Opinion*, pp. 200–201.

24. Ibid., p. 87. Hispanic Protestants, however, are even more conservative on social issues according to research reported by Rodolfo O. de la Garza and Seung-Jin Jang, "Latino Public Opinion," in Shapiro and Jacobs, *The Oxford Handbook of American Public Opinion and the Media*.

25. S. K. Ramakrishnan, J. S. Wong, T. Lee, and J. Junn, "Race-Based Considerations and the Obama Vote: Evidence from the 2008 National Asian American Survey," *Du Bois Review* 6, no. 1 (2009), 219–238.

26. Pew Research Center, January 10, 2012.

27. Nolan McCarty, Keith T. Poole, and Howard Rosenthal, *Polarized America: The Dance of Ideology and Unequal Riches* (Cambridge, MA: MIT Press, 2006), p. 107; Bartels, *Unequal Democracy*.

28. See "Trends in Political Values and Core Attitudes: 1987–2009," p. 24. For pre-2009 data see Erikson and Tedin, *American Public Opinion*, pp. 191–199, using over-time reports from the National Election Study surveys; McCarty, Poole, and Rosenthal, *Polarized America*.

29. "Trends in Political Values and Core Attitudes: 1987–2009," section 2.

30. Leslie McCall and Jeff Manza, "Class Differences in Social and Political Attitudes in the United States, " in Shapiro and Jacobs, *The Oxford Handbook of American Public Opinion and the Media*.

31. Earl Black and Merle Black, *The Rise of Southern Republicans* (Cambridge, MA: Harvard University Press, 2002); Earl Black and Merle Black, *Divided America: The Ferocious Power Struggle in American Politics* (New York: Simon and Schuster, 2007).

32. General Social Survey, 2008.

33. Ibid.

34. Larry J. Sabato, *Pendulum Swing* (New York: Pearson Education, 2011).

35. General Social Survey, 2008; Erikson and Tedin, *American Public Opinion*, pp. 213–218.

36. Morris P. Fiorina, *Culture War: The Myth of a Polarized America* (New York: Pearson Longman Publishers, 2005); Morris P. Fiorina and Samuel J. Abrams, "Political Polarization in the American Public," *The Annual Review of Political Science* 11 (2008), pp. 563–588; and Erikson and Tedin, *American Public Opinion*, pp. 214–215.

37. Erikson and Tedin, *American Public Opinion*, p. 195.

38. Ibid., pp. 196–197.

39. "Trends in Political Values and Core Attitudes: 1987–2009," p. 21. The Pew Research Center had the gender gap at 16 percent in 2009. Also see Julie Dolan, Melissa Deckman, and Michele L. Swers, *Women and Politics: Paths to Power and Influence* (New York: Longman Publishers, 2011), pp. 59–62.

40. Fiorina, *Culture War*, pp. 34–35, 66–76; Karen M. Kaufman, "The Gender Gap," *PS: Political Science and Politics* 39, no. 3 (2006), pp. 447–453. For a contrary view see Janet M. Box-Steffensmeier, Suzanna De Boef, and Tse-Min Lin, "The Dynamics of the Partisan Gender Gap," *American Political Science Review* 98, no. 3 (August 2004), pp. 515–528.

41. Mark Schlesinger and Caroline Heldman, "Gender Gap or Gender Gaps?" *The Journal of Politics* 63, no. 1 (February 2001), pp. 59–92; Erikson and Tedin, *American Public Opinion*, pp. 219–223; General Social Survey, 2008; and Leonie Huddy and Erin Cassese, "On the Complex and Varied Political Effects of Gender," in Shapiro and Jacobs, *The Oxford Handbook of American Public Opinion and the Media*.

42. Fiorina, *Culture War*, pp. 66–69.

43. Pew, "Trends in Political Values and Core Attitudes: 1987–2009."

44. ABC News/*Washington Post* poll, March 2011.

45. Pew Research Center, "Trends in Political Values and Core Attitudes: 1987–2009," section 4; Nicholas L. Danigelis, Melissa Hardy, and Stephen J. Cutler, "Population Aging, Intracohort Aging, and Sociopolitical Attitudes," *American Sociological Review* 72 (2007), pp. 812–830.

46. For detailed information on the size, beliefs, and political attitudes of various religious denominations in the United States see "The U.S. Religious Landscape Survey" (Washington, D.C.: Pew Forum on Religion and Public Life, November 9, 2009). All of the survey data in this section, unless otherwise noted, comes from this source.

47. Black and Black, *Divided America*.

48. Pew, "The U.S. Religious Landscape Survey."

49. Toni Johnson, "Muslims in the United States," (New York: The Council on Foreign Relations, September 19, 2011).

50. The data in this section is from *Trends, 2005* (Washington, D.C.: The Pew Research Center for the People and the Press, 2005).

51. Fiorina, *Culture War*; Fiorina and Abrams, "Political Polarization in the American Public."

52. King and Smith, Still a House Divided.

53. Erikson and Tedin, *American Public Opinion*, pp. 83–84.

54. Michael X. Delli Carpini and Scott Keeter, *What Americans Know About Politics and Why It Matters* (New Haven, CT: Yale University Press, 1996); Alan Wolfe, *Does American Democracy Still Work?* (New Haven, CT: Yale University Press, 2006).

55. See Erikson and Tedin, *American Public Opinion*, table 3.1, for full details. Also see Page and Shapiro, *The Rational Public*, pp. 9–14; Wolfe, *Does American Democracy Still Work?* pp. 24–30.

56. "Political Knowledge Update," (Washington, D.C.: Pew Research Center, March 31, 2011).

57. Jacob S. Hacker and Paul Pierson, *Winner-Take-All Politics* (New York: Simon and Schuster, 2010), pp. 154–155; and Bartels, *Unequal Democracy*.

58. Suzanne Mettler, *The Submerged State: How Invisible Government Policies Undermine American Democracy* (Chicago: University of Chicago Press, 2011).

59. Ibid.

60. "Public Knowledge of Current Affairs: Little Changed by News and Information Revolutions What Americans Know: 1989–2007" (Washington, D.C: Pew Research Center, April 15, 2007).

61. Paul M. Sniderman, Richard A. Brody, and Philip E. Tetlock, *Reasoning and Choice: Explorations in Political Psychology* (New York: Cambridge University Press, 1991). See also Carpini and Keeter, *What Americans Know About Politics*; Samuel Popkin, *The Reasoning Voter* (Chicago: University of Chicago Press, 1991). For the view that it matters a great deal that Americans don't know many of the details about what is going on in Washington see Bartels, *Unequal Democracy*; Caplan, *The Myth of the Rational Voter*; Wolfe, *Does American Democracy Still Work?*

62. Robert E. Lane, *Political Ideology: Why the American Common Man Believes What He Does* (New York: Free Press, 1962); Jennifer L. Hochschild, *What's Fair? American Beliefs about Distributive Justice* (Cambridge, MA: Harvard University Press, 1986); Carroll J. Glynn, Susan Herbst, Garrett O'Keefe, and Robert Y. Shapiro, *Public Opinion* (Boulder, CO: Westview Press, 1999), ch. 8.

63. Binyamin Appelbaum and Robert Gebeloff, "Even Critics of Safety Net Increasingly Depend on It," *The New York Times* (February 11, 2012), p. 1.

64. Page and Shapiro, *The Rational Public*. Also see Doris A. Graber, "Re-Measuring the Civic IQ: Decline, Stability, or Advance?" (paper prepared for presentation at the annual meeting of the American Political Science Association, Boston, August 28–31, 2008); Taeku Lee, *Mobilizing Public Opinion: Black Insurgency and Racial Attitudes in the Civil Rights Era* (Chicago: University of Chicago Press, 2002); Erikson and Tedin, *American Public Opinion*, pp. 93–94. This view is strongly rejected by Caplan, *The Myth of the Rational Voter*, who believes that, at least on issues related to economic policies, errors by the public are systematic rather than random so that they do not balance out.

65. Robert Y. Shapiro and Lawrence R. Jacobs, "The Democratic Paradox," in Shapiro and Jacobs, *The Oxford Handbook of American Public Opinion and the Media*, pp. 720–722.

66. Harris Poll, June 2004.

67. "The American-Western European Values Gap," (Washington, D.C.: Pew Reseach Center, released November 17, 2011), p. 6.

68. Pew, "Trends in Political Values and Core Attitudes: 1987–2009," p. 78.

69. "Trust in Government, 1958–2010," (Washington, D.C.: Pew Research Center for the People and the Press, March 2010).

70. *The New York Times*/CBS News poll, reported October 25, 2011.

71. See the November 2011 surveys reported by Polling Report (http://www.pollingreport.com/).

72. *The New York Times*/CBS News poll, reported October 25, 2011.

73. The Gallup Poll, November 15–17, 2011.

74. Vanessa Williamson, Theda Skocpol, and John Coggin, "The Tea Party and the Remaking of Republican Conservatism," *Perspectives on Politics* (2011), volume 9, number 1, pp. 25–43.

75. *The New York Times*/CBS News poll, reported October 25, 2011.

76. Steven Kull, *Americans and Foreign Aid: A Study of American Public Attitudes* (Washington, D.C.: Program on International Policy Attitudes, 1995).

77. Pew Research Center, April 18, 2010.

78. Pew, "Trends in Political Values and Core Attitudes: 1987–2009," p. 39.

79. CBS News Poll (September 28–October 2, 2011); and the ABC News/*Washington Post* Poll (July 14–17, 2011).

80. "Broad Approval for New Arizona Immigration Law" (Washington, D.C.: Pew Research Center for the People and the Press, May 12, 2010).

81. "Confidence in U.S. Foreign Policy Index, 2010," *Public Agenda Online and Foreign Affairs Magazine* (http://www.publicagenda.org/pages/foreign-policy-index-2010).

82. William Caspary, "Then 'The Mood Theory': A Study of Public Opinion and Foreign Policy," *American Political Science Review* 64 (1970), pp. 536–547; John E. Reilly, ed., *American Public Opinion and U.S. Foreign Policy, 1995* (Chicago: Chicago Council on Foreign Relations, 1995), p. 13; Princeton Survey Associates/Pew Research Center, October 1999. Also see Pew, "Trends in Political Values and Core Attitudes: 1987–2009," section 6.

83. *Time*/CNN Survey, December 7, 1994.

84. Gallup Poll, conducted for CNN and *USA Today*, September 2001.

85. Gallup Poll, conducted for CNN and *USA Today*, September 2005.

86. ABC News/*Washington Post* Poll. June 2–5, 2011.

87. Summary of polls on American foreign policy reported at *The Public Agenda Online* at http://www.publicagenda.org/; Benjamin I. Page with Marshall M. Bouton, *The Foreign Policy Disconnect: What Americans Want from Our Leaders But Don't Get* (Chicago: University of Chicago Press, 2006).

88. This seems to be the case in foreign and national defense issues as well. See John H. Aldrich, Christopher Gelpi, Peter Feaver, Jason Reifler, and Kristin Tompson Sharp, "Foreign

Policy and the Electoral Connection," *Annual Review of Political Science* 9 (2006), pp. 477–502.

89. For a summary of the evidence see Erikson and Tedin, *American Public Opinion*, pp. 305–312.

90. Alan D. Monroe, "Consistency Between Public Preferences and National Policy Decisions," *American Politics Quarterly* 7 (January 1979), pp. 3–19; Benjamin I. Page and Robert Y. Shapiro, "Effects of Public Opinion on Policy," *American Political Science Review* 77 (1983), pp. 175–190.

91. James A. Stimson, *Public Opinion in America: Moods, Cycles and Swings* (Boulder, CO: Westview Press, 1991).

92. Paul Burstein, "The Impact of Public Opinion on Public Policy: A Review and an Agenda," *Political Research Quarterly* 56, no. 1 (March 2003). Also see Vincent L. Hutchings, *Public Opinion and Democratic Accountability: How Citizens Learn About Politics* (Princeton, NJ: Princeton University Press, 2003).

93. The various arguments for this are summarized in Benjamin I. Page, "The Semi-Sovereign Public," in Jeff Manza, Fay Lomax Cook, and Benjamin I. Page, eds., *Navigating Public Opinion: Polls, Policy, and the Future of American Democracy* (New York: Oxford University Press, 2002); and in Shapiro and Jacobs, "The Democratic Paradox," in Shapiro and Jacobs, *The Oxford Handbook of American Public Opinion and the Media*.

94. For the argument that public opinion is largely a media creation see W. Lance Bennett, "News Polls: Constructing an Engaged Public," in Shapiro and Jacobs, *The Oxford Handbook of American Public Opinion and the Media*.

95. Lawrence R. Jacobs and Robert Y. Shapiro, *Politicians Don't Pander: Political Manipulation and the Loss of Democratic Responsiveness* (Chicago: University of Chicago Press, 2000); Shapiro and Jacobs, "The Democratic Paradox," in Shapiro and Jacobs, *The Oxford Handbook of American Public Opinion and the Media*; John Zaller, *The Nature and Origins of Mass Opinion* (New York: Cambridge University Press, 1992); and Wolfe, *Does American Democracy Still Work?*

96. W. Lance Bennett, Regina G. Lawrence, and Steven Livingston, *When the Press Fails: Political Power and the News Media From Iraq to Katrina* (Chicago: University of Chicago Press, 2007), ch. 5.

97. Page with Bouton, *The Foreign Policy Disconnect*. Also see Lawrence R. Jacobs and Benjamin I. Page, "Who Influences Foreign Policy," *American Political Science Review* 99, no. 1 (February 2005), pp. 107–124. On the elite–mass public disconnect also see Daniel W. Drezner, "The Realist Tradition in American Public Opinion," *Perspectives on Politics* 6, no. 1 (March 2008), pp. 51–70.

98. Bartels, *Unequal Democracy*.

99. Public opinion scholar Larry Bartels suggests that the 2001 tax cut (the largest in two decades, with tax relief going overwhelmingly to upper-income people) was supported by the public out of sheer ignorance and confusion about the impact of changes in the Tax Code. See Larry M. Bartels, "Homer Gets a Tax Cut: Inequality and Public Policy in the American Mind," *Perspectives on Politics* 3, no. 1 (March 2005), pp. 15–29. In the same issue (pp. 33–53), Jacob Hacker and Paul Pierson disagree; they suggest in their article "Abandoning the Middle: The Bush Tax Cuts and the Limits of Democratic Control," that manipulation and deception were prominent in the successful effort to raise public support for the 2001 tax cuts.

6

1. Material for this chapter opener is from W. Lance Bennett, Regina G. Lawrence, and Steven Livingston, *When the Press Fails: Political Power and the News Media from Iraq to Katrina* (Chicago: University of Chicago Press, 2007), pp. 13–45.

2. Adam Schiffer, "Blogswarms and Press Norms: News Coverage of the Downing Street Memos" (Washington, D.C.: paper presented at annual meetings of the American Political Science Association, August 31–September 3, 2006).

3. Bennett, Lawrence, and Livingston, *When the Press Fails*, p. 27.

4. Dana Milbank, "Democrats Play House to Rally Against the War," *The Washington Post* (June 6, 2005), p. 17.

5. Doris Graber, *Mass Media and American Politics*, 8th ed. (Washington, D.C.: Congressional Quarterly Press, 2010), pp. 16–19.

6. Joseph Cappella and Kathleen Hall Jamieson, *Spiral of Cynicism: The Press and the Public Good* (New York: Oxford University Press, 1997); Larry J. Sabato, Mark Stencel, and S. Robert Lichter, *Peepshow: Media and Politics in an Age of Scandal* (Boulder, CO: Rowman & Littlefield Publishers, 2000).

7. *The State of the News Media, 2008* (Washington, D.C.: Pew Research Center, Project for Excellence in Journalism, 2008).

8. For a description and a review of a group of thinkers celebrating the birth of a new journalism see Dean Starkman, "Confidence Game: the Limited Vision of the News Gurus," *Columbia Journalism Review* (November 9, 2011), at www.cjr.org, accessed February 20, 2012.

9. "Broadband and Dial-Up Adoption," *Trend Data, November 2011*, Pew Research Center at http://pewinternet.org/Trend-Data, accessed February 20, 2012.

10. Statistical Division, Organization of Economic Cooperation and Development (2011).

11. "Internet usage," *Infoplease*, www.infoplease.com (accessed November 30, 2011).

12. Andrew Kohut, *Internet's Broader Role in Campaign 2008* (Washington, D.C.: Pew Research Center, 2008).

13. Tom Rosenstiel and Amy Mitchel, "Overview: The State of the Media, 2011," Pew Research Center at http://stateofthenewsmedia.org/2011/overview, accessed on February 20, 2010.

14. "Big Is Best," *The Economist* (October 31, 2009), pp. 75–76; Shira Ovide, "U.S. Newspaper Circulation Falls," *The Wall Street Journal Online*, posted October 26, 2009 (http://online.wsj.com/).

15. Alex S. Jones, *Losing the News: The Future of the News That Feeds Democracy* (New York: Oxford University Press, 2009), pp. 180–181.

16. *Audience Segments in a Changing News Environment* (Washington, D.C.: The Pew Research Center, press release, August 17, 2008).

17. Rosenstiel and Mitchell, "Overview: The State of the Media, 2011;" and the Pew Research Center poll, release date February 7, 2012.

18. Bennett, Lawrence, and Livingston, *When the Press Fails*, pp. 57–59.

19. Matthew Hindman, *The Myth of Digital Democracy* (Princeton, NJ: Princeton University Press, 2009), ch. 6.

20. "The People Formerly Known as the Audience," *The Economist* (July 7, 2011), pp. 25–28.

21. Rosenstiel and Mitchell, "Overview: The State of the Media, 2011."

22. Graber, Mass Media and American Politics, pp. 36–37.

23. "Who Owns the News Media," *The State of the Media, 2011*," Pew Research Center.

24. "Who Owns What," *Columbia Journalism Review Online*, the Media," http://www.cjr.org/resources/ (updated and accessed, June 18, 2010).

25. "Read All About It," *The New Yorker* (August 13, 2007), p. 21.

26. W. Lance Bennett, *News: The Politics of Illusion* (New York: Pearson Longman, 2011), pp. 231–246, reviews the debate. The term *media monopoly* is from University of California–Berkeley journalism professor Ben Bagkikian's book, *Media Monopoly*, 5th ed. (Boston: Beacon Press, 1997).

27. Bennett, *News,* pp. 242–244.

28. Ibid., p. 241.

29. Jones, *Losing the News,* p. 7.

30. Doug Underwood, "Market Research and the Audience for Political News," in Doris Graber, Denis McQuail, and Pippa Norris, eds., *The Politics of News: The News of Politics* (Washington, D.C.: CQ Press, 1998), p. 171; also see Bennett, *News,* ch. 7.

31. Graber, Mass Media and American Politics, pp. 87–91.

32. Leon V. Sigal, Reporters and Officials: The Organization and Politics of News Reporting (Lexington, MA: Heath, 1973), p. 124.

33. Bennett, *News,* pp. 112–114; Steven Livingston and W. Lance Bennett, "Gatekeeping, Indexing, and Live Event News," *Political Communication,* 20, no. 4 (October–December 2003), pp. 363–380; Graber, *Mass Media and American Politics,* pp. 79–82.

34. Bennett, *News,* pp. 164–167.

35. Ibid., pp.127–134.

36. Mark Hertsgaard, *On Bended Knee* (New York: Farrar, Straus & Giroux, 1988), p. 5.

37. Anne E. Kornblut, "Administration Is Warned About Its News Videos," *The New York Times* (January 19, 2005), p. A9; Anne E. Kornblut, "Third Journalist Was Paid to Promote Bush Policies," *The New York Times* (January 29, 2005), p. A13; Charlie Savage and Alan Wirzbicki, "White House-Friendly Reporter Under Scrutiny," *The Boston Globe* (February 2, 2005), p. A1; "Source Watch," *Center for Media and Democracy* (http://www.prwatch.org/cmd/index.html), February 2005.

38. The Audit, "Learning Journalism Lessons of the Past," *Columbia Journalism Review* (posted June 5, 2009 at http://www.cjr.org/the_audit/learning_journalism_lessons_of.php).

39. David Murray, Joel Schwartz, and S. Robert Lichter, *It Ain't Necessarily So: How Media Make and Unmake the Scientific Picture of Reality* (Lanham, MD: Rowman & Littlefield Publishers, 2001), pp. 29–30.

40. Journalism.org (accessed, November 30, 2011).

41. Graber, Mass Media and American Politics, ch. 11.

42. For the best analysis of why and how this happens and its unfortunate impact on the democratic process, see Bennett, Lawrence, and Livingston, *When the Press Fails.*

43. Eric Alterman, *What Liberal Media?* (New York: Basic Books, 2003). Also see the online site FAIR (Fairness and Accuracy in Reporting) at www.fair.org for a liberal point of view about press bias.

44. Bernard Goldberg, *Bias in the News* (Washington, D.C.: Regnery, 2001); and the online conservative site AIM (Accuracy in Media) at www.aim.org.

45. Pew Research Center poll, released February 7, 2012.

46. For a review of this literature see Robert S. Erikson and Kent L. Tedin, *American Public Opinion: Its Origins, Content, and Impact* (New York: Pearson Longman, 2011), p. 239.

47. Neal Hickey, "Is Fox News Fair?" *Columbia Journalism Review,* 31 (March/April 1998), pp. 30–35; David Weaver and G. Cleveland Wilhoit, *The American Journalist* (Mahwah, NJ: Lawrence Erlbaum, 1996); Graber, *Mass Media and American Politics,* pp. 86–89; and Erikson and Tedin, *American Public Opinion,* pp. 233–234.

48. Bennett, *News,* pp. 34–35; Graber, *Mass Media and American Politics,* pp. 76–77; Thomas E. Patterson and Wolfgang Donsbach, "News Decisions: Journalists as Partisan Actors," *Political Communications* 13 (October–December 1996), pp. 455–468.

49. Erikson and Tedin, *American Public Opinion,* pp. 238–239.

50. Carmen M. Reinhart and Kenneth Rogoff, *This Time Is Different: Eight Centuries of Financial Folly* (Princeton, NJ: Princeton University Press, 2009); John Cassidy, *How Markets Fail* (New York: Farrar, Straus, and Giroux, 2009).

51. John Zaller, *A Theory of Media Politics* (Chicago: University of Chicago Press, 2004).

52. Bennett, *News,* pp. 238–241; Graber, *Mass Media and American Politics,* pp. 97–100; Jones, *Losing the News,* p. 51; and James Fallows, "Learning to Love the (Shallow, Divisive, Unreliable) New Media," *The Atlantic Monthly* (April, 2011).

53. News Index, *Project for Excellence in Journalism* (2007), at www.journalism.org.

54. "Coverage of Jackson's Death Seen as Excessive" (Washington, D.C.: Pew Research Center, July 1, 2009).

55. Bennett, *News,* pp. 238–240.

56. Alan Wolfe, *Does American Democracy Still Work?* (New Haven, CT: Yale University Press, 2006), pp. 108–110.

57. For a review of the literature on the subject, see Samuel L. Popkin, "Changing Media, Changing Politics," *Perspectives on Politics* (June 2006), pp. 327–341; Wolfe, *Does American Democracy Still Work?,* ch. 5.

58. David L. Paletz, "The Media and Public Policy," in Doris Graber, Denis McQuail, and Pippa Norris, eds., *The Politics of News: The News of Politics* (Washington, D.C.: CQ Press, 1998),

59. Shanto Iyengar and Donald R. Kinder, *News That Matters* (Chicago: University of Chicago Press, 1987); also see Erikson and Tedin, *American Public Opinion,* pp. 247–248, for a review of the research on news media agenda setting.

60. W. Lance Bennett, "News Polls: Constructing an Engaged Public," in Robert Y. Shapiro and Lawrence R. Jacobs, eds., *The Oxford Handbook of American Public Opinion and the Media* (Oxford: Oxford University Press, 2011).

61. G. Ray Funkhauser, "The Issues of the Sixties: An Exploratory Study in the Dynamics of Public Opinion," *Public Opinion Quarterly* 37 (Spring 1973), pp. 62–75.

62. George C. Edwards, "Who Influences Whom? The President, Congress and the Media," *The American Political Science Review* 93 (June 1999), pp. 327–344.

63. Bennett, Lawrence, and Livingston, *When the Press Fails.*

64. On framing, see Thomas E. Nelson, "Issue Framing," in Shapiro and Jacobs, *The Oxford Handbook of American Public Opinion and the Media.*

65. Shanto Iyengar, *Is Anyone Responsible? How Television News Frames Political Issues* (Chicago: University of Chicago Press, 1991); Kathleen Hall Jamieson and Paul Waldman, *The Press Effect* (Washington, D.C.: CQ Press, 2002).

66. Paul M. Kellstedt, *The Mass Media and the Dynamics of American Racial Attitudes* (Cambridge, UK: Cambridge University Press, 2003).

67. Benjamin I. Page, Robert Y. Shapiro, and Glenn R. Dempsey, "What Moves Public Opinion?" *American Political Science Review* 81 (1987), pp. 23–43.

68. Joseph Cappella and Kathleen Jamieson, *Spiral of Cynicism: The Press and the Public Good* (New York: Oxford University Press, 1997); Stephen C. Craig, ed., *Broken Contract: Changing Relations Between Americans and Their Government* (Boulder, CO: Westview Press, 1996); Mark J. Hetherington, "Declining Trust and Shrinking Policy Agenda," in Robert Hart and Daron R. Shaw, eds., *Communications in U.S. Elections* (Lanham, MD: Rowman & Littlefield, 2001); Bennett, *News*; Thomas E. Patterson, "Bad News, Period," *PS* (March 1996), pp. 17–20.

69. John A. Ferejohn and James H. Kuklinski, eds., *Information and Democratic Processes* (Urbana, IL: University of Illinois Press, 1990); Benjamin I. Page, *Who Deliberates? Mass Media in Modern Democracy* (Chicago: University of Chicago Press, 1996).

7

1. Information for this story is from the following sources: David Barstow, Laura Dodd, James Glanz, Stephanie Sauo, and Ian Urbina, "Regulators Failed to Address Risks in Oil

Rig Fail-Safe Device," *The New York Times* (June 20, 2010), p. 1; Ian Urbina, "Inspector General's Inquiry Faults Regulators," *The New York Times* (May 24, 2010), p. 1; "The Oil Well and the Damage Done," *The Economist Online* (June 17, 2010). www .economist.com/node/16381032; "How Did This Happen and Who Is to Blame," *Bloomberg/Businessweek* (June 14–20, 2010), pp. 60–64.

2. On the most recent deregulation movement in American politics and the thinking behind it, see Richard Harris and Sidney Milkis, *The Politics of Regulatory Change* (New York: Oxford University Press, 1989); John Cassidy, *How Markets Fail* (New York: Farrar, Straus and Giroux, 2009). Also see Marver Bernstein, *Regulation by Independent Commission* (Princeton, NJ: Princeton University Press, 1955); Grant McConnell, *Private Power and American Democracy* (New York: Vintage Books, 1966); James Buchanan and Gordon Tullock, "Polluters, Profits and Political Responses: Direct Control versus Taxes," *American Economic Review* 65 (1975), pp. 139–147; Murray Weidenbaum, *The Costs of Government Regulation of Business* (Washington, D.C.: Joint Economic Committee of Congress, 1978); Kevin P. Phillips, *The Politics of Rich and Poor: Wealth and the American Electorate in the Reagan Aftermath* (New York: Random House, 1990).

3. Jeffrey M. Berry and Clyde Wilcox, *The Interest Group Society*, 5th ed. (New York: Pearson Longman, 2009), pp. 4–6.

4. Alexander Hamilton, James Madison, and John Jay, *The Federalist Papers*, ed. Clinton Rossiter (New York: New American Library, 1961), No. 10. (Originally published 1787–1788.)

5. The classics of the pluralist tradition include Arthur F. Bentley, *The Process of Government* (Chicago: University of Chicago Press, 1908); David Truman, *The Governmental Process* (New York: Knopf, 1951); V. O. Key Jr., *Politics, Parties, and Pressure Groups* (New York: A. Crowell, 1952); Robert A. Dahl, *A Preface to Democratic Theory* (Chicago: University of Chicago Press, 1956); Robert A. Dahl, *Who Governs?* (New Haven, CT: Yale University Press, 1961). For a summary treatment of the pluralist tradition and its thinking about interest groups see Berry and Wilcox, *The Interest Group Society*, ch. 1.

6. E. E. Schattschneider, *The Semi-Sovereign People* (New York: Holt, Rinehart & Winston, 1960).

7. Robert B. Reich, Supercapitalism: *The Transformation of Business, Democracy, and Everyday Life* (New York: Knopf, 2007), pp. 80–86; Jeffrey M. Berry, *The New Liberalism: The Rising Power of Citizen Groups* (Washington, D.C.: Brookings, 1999); Thomas Byrne Edsall, *The New Politics of Inequality* (New York: Norton, 1984); Michael Goldfield, *The Decline of Organized Labor in the United States* (Chicago: University of Chicago Press, 1987); Edward S. Greenberg, *Capitalism and the American Political Ideal* (Armonk, NY: Sharpe, 1985); David Vogel, *Fluctuating Fortunes: The Political Power of Business in America* (New York: Basic Books, 1989), ch. 8.

8. U.S. Bureau of Labor Statistics, press release, January 21, 2011.

9. Reich, *Supercapitalism*. A country's institutional and legal structure also matter. The proportion of workers in labor unions actually increased over the past several decades in the Scandinavian countries. See Lyle Scruggs and Peter Lange, "Where Have All the Workers Gone? Globalization, Institutions, and Union Density," *The Journal of Politics* 64, no. 1 (February 2002), pp. 126–153.

10. Kenneth McLennan, "What Do Unions Do? A Management Perspective," in James T. Bennett and Bruce E. Kaufman, eds., *What Do Unions Do? A Twenty-Year Perspective* (New Brunswick, NJ: Transaction Publishers, 2007).

11. Jeffrey M. Berry, *Lobbying for the People* (Princeton, NJ: Princeton University Press, 1977), p. 7; Berry and Wilcox, *The Interest Group Society*, pp. 24–26; Berry, *The New Liberalism*, p. 2.

12. Ronald Brownstein, *The Second Civil War: How Extreme Partisanship Has Paralyzed Washington and Polarized America* (New York: The Penguin Press, 2007), pp. 106–112; Berry, *Lobbying for the People;* David Broder, *Changing the Guard* (New York: Simon & Schuster, 1980); Hugh Heclo, "Issue Networks and the Executive Establishment," in Anthony King, ed., *The New American Political System* (Washington, D.C.: American Enterprise Institute, 1978); Kay Lehman Schlozman and John A. Tierney, *Organized Interests and American Democracy* (New York: Harper and Row, 1986); Jack L. Walker Jr., "The Origins and Maintenance of Interest Groups in America," *American Political Science Review* 77 (1983), pp. 390–406; Theda Skocpol, *Diminished Democracy: From Membership to Management in American Civil Life* (Norman, OK: University of Oklahoma Press, 2003).

13. Skocpol, *Diminished Democracy;* Theda Skocpol, "Associations Without Members," *The American Prospect* 10, no. 4 (July/August 1999), pp. 66–73; Theda Skocpol, "Voice and Inequality: The Transformation of American Civil Democracy," *Perspectives on Politics* 2, no. 1 (March 2004), pp. 3–20.

14. The numbers above are from Roger H. Davidson, Walter J. Oleszek, and Francis E. Lee, *Congress and Its Members*, 13th ed. (Washington, D.C.: CQ Press, 2012), p. 373.

15. Ibid., p. 374; and the Center for Responsive Politics, "Lobbying Expenditures," based on required reports to the House and Senate, 2011.

16. David Coen, Wyn Grant, and Graham Wilson, "Political Science Perspectives on Business and Government," in David Coen, Wyn Grant, and Graham Wilson, eds., *The Oxford Handbook of Business and Government* (Oxford: Oxford University Press, 2010).

17. Reich, *Supercapitalism*, pp. 143–148; Ken Auletta, "The Search Party," *The New Yorker* (January 14, 2008), pp. 30–37.

18. Gary J. Andres, *Lobbying Reconsidered* (New York: Pearson Longman, 2009), ch. 4.

19. Reich, *Supercapitalism*, pp. 144–146.

20. Truman, *The Governmental Process*.

21. Jack L. Walker Jr., *Mobilizing Interest Groups in America* (Ann Arbor, MI: University of Michigan Press, 1991).

22. Jacob S. Hacker and Paul Pierson, "Winner-Take-All Politics: Public Policy, Political Organization, and the Precipitous Rise of Top Incomes in the United States," *Politics & Society* (2010), volume 38, number 2, p. 172.

23. "Pork and Scandals," *The Economist* (January 28, 2006), p. 29.

24. From the watchdog group Public Citizen, reported in a press release dated April 19, 2010. Also see the Center for Public Integrity, "Annual Lobbying Reports," at www.publicintegrity .org.

25. Frank Rich, "The Rabbit Ragu Democrats," *The New York Times* online (www.nytimes.com), October 4, 2009.

26. Mark A. Smith, *Business and Political Power: Public Opinion, Elections and Democracy* (Chicago: University of Chicago Press, 2000). Also see Pepper D. Culpepper, *Quiet Politics and Business Power* (New York: Cambridge University Press, 2011), ch. 1.

27. Schattschneider, *The Semi-Sovereign People*.

28. Frank R. Baumgartner, Jeffrey M. Berry, Marie Hojnacki, David C. Kimball, and Beth L. Leech, *Lobbying and Policy Change: Who Wins, Who Loses, and Why* (Chicago: University of Chicago Press, 2009), pp. 150–155; and Davidson, Oleszek, and Lee, *Congress and Its Members*, pp. 377–386.

29. Berry and Wilcox, *The Interest Group Society*, p. 138.

30. Glen Justice, "New Rules on Fund-Raising Bring Lobbyists to the Fore," *The New York Times*, April 20, 2004, p. A1.

31. Peter Katel, "The Lobbying Boom," (Washington, D.C.: CQ Researcher, July 22, 2005), p. 1.

32. Berry and Wilcox, *The Interest Group Society*, pp. 142–145.

33. Baumgartner et al., *Lobbying and Policy Change*, pp. 155–157.

34. Berry and Wilcox, *The Interest Group Society*, pp. 118–120.

35. Schattschneider, *The Semi-Sovereign People*.

36. Berry, T*he New Liberalism*.

37. Schlozman and Tierney, *Organized Interests and American Democracy*, p. 175.

38. Bruce Bimber, *Information and American Democracy* (New York: Cambridge University Press, 2003).

39. For a comprehensive examination of interest group involvement in campaigns see Michael M. Franz, *Choices and Changes: Interest Groups in the Electoral Process* (Philadelphia: Temple University Press, 2008).

40. Timothy Werner and Graham Wilson, "Business Representation in Washington," in Coen, Grant, and Wilson, eds., *The Oxford Handbook of Business and Government*.

41. Berry, *Lobbying for the People*; Skocpol, "Voice and Inequality"; Dara Strolovitch, "Do Interest Groups Represent the Disadvantaged? Advocacy at the Intersections of Race, Class, and Gender," *Journal of Politics* 68, no. 4 (November 2006), pp. 894–910; Hacker, "Winner-Take-All Politics," pp. 180–181.

42. Werner and Wilson, "Business Representation in Washington"; and Jacob S. Hacker and Paul Pierson, *Winner-Take-All Politics* (New York: Simon and Schuster, 2010).

43. Jim Drinkard, "Drugmakers Go Further to Sway Congress," *USA Today* (April 26, 2005), p. 2B; Leslie Wayne and Melody Petersen, "A Muscular Lobby Rolls Up Its Sleeves," *The New York Times* (November 4, 2001), p. 1.

44. Eric Dash and Nelson D. Schwartz, "As Reform Takes Shape, Some Relief on Wall St.," *The New York Times* (May 23, 2010), p. 1.

45. The Center for Responsive Politics, 2011.

46. "Money Talks, Congress Listens," *The Boston Globe* (December 12, 1982), p. A24.

47. Adam Liptak, "Justices, 5–4, Reject Corporate Spending Limit," *The New York Times* (January 21, 2010), p. 1; "Unbound: The Supreme Court Undermines Convoluted Campaign Finance Rules," *The Economist* (January 30, 2010), p. 39.

48. For elaboration of the points made in this paragraph and the supporting scholarly evidence see Gregory C. Shaffer, "Law and Business," in Coen, Grant, and Wilson, eds., *The Oxford Handbook of Business and Government*, pp. 66–70.

49. "The Trillion-Dollar Tax Holiday," *Bloomberg/Businessweek* (October 3-9, 2011), pp. 66–67.

50. The term "issue networks" is from Heclo, "Issue Networks." For a review and evaluation of the scholarly debate over sub-governments and issue networks see Baumgartner et al., *Lobbying and Policy Change*, pp. 57–67. Also see Berry and Wilcox, *The Interest Group Society*, pp. 163–165; Berry, *The New Liberalism*; Ainsworth, *Analyzing Interest Groups*; Allan J. Cigler, "Interest Groups," in William Crotty, ed., *Political Science: Looking to the Future*, Vol. 4 (Evanston, IL: Northwestern University Press, 1991); Robert H. Salisbury, John P. Heinz, Edward O. Laumann, and Robert L. Nelson, "Triangles, Networks, and Hollow Cores," and Mark P. Petracca, "The Rediscovery of Interest Group Politics," both in Mark P. Petracca, ed., *The Politics of Interests: Interest Groups Transform* (Boulder, CO: Westview Press, 1992); Robert M. Stein and Kenneth Bickers, *Perpetuating the Pork Barrel: Policy Subsystems and American Democracy* (Cambridge, UK: Cambridge University Press, 1995).

51. Shaffer, "Law and Business," pp. 66–67.

52. Charles Lindblom, *Politics and Markets* (New York: Basic Books, 1977), p. 356.

53. Neil J. Mitchell, *The Conspicuous Corporation: Business, Public Policy and Representative Democracy* (Ann Arbor, MI: University of Michigan Press, 1997), p. 167.

54. Dan Clawson, Alan Neustadt, and Mark Weller, *Dollars and Votes* (Philadelphia: Temple University Press, 1998), pp. 26–28, 64–71, 97–99; Berry and Wilcox, *The Interest Group Society*, pp. 184–185.

55. Jeffrey A. Winters and Benjamin I. Page, "Oligarchy in the United States?" *Perspective on Politics*, volume 7, number 4, pp. 731–751.

56. The full story of what has happened is told in Hacker and Pierson, "Winner-Take-All Politics."

57. Vogel, *Fluctuating Fortunes*, p. 291.

58. Coen, Grant, and Wilson, "Political Science: Perspectives on Business and Government"; and Werner and Wilson, "Business Representation in Washington, D.C.," both in Coen, Grant, and Wilson, eds., *The Oxford Handbook of Business and Government*.

59. Hacker and Pierson, *Winner-Take-All Politics*.

60. For a comparison of U.S. lobbying rules with other democracies see Raj Chari, Gary Murphy, and John Hogan, "Regulating Lobbyists: A Comparative Analysis of the United States, Canada, Germany, and the European Union," *Political Quarterly* 78, no. 3 (July–September 2007), pp. 422–438.

8

1. James MacGregor Burns and Stewart Burns, *A People's Charter: The Pursuit of Rights in America* (New York: Knopf, 1991), ch. 5; E. McGlen and Karen O'Connor, *Women's Rights* (New York: Praeger, 1983), ch. 3; Sarah M. Evans, *Born for Liberty: A History of Women in America* (New York: Free Press, 1997).

2. Sidney Tarrow, *Power in Movement* (New York: Cambridge University Press, 1998); David S. Meyer and Sidney Tarrow, eds., *The Social Movement Society* (Lanham, MD: Rowman & Littlefield Publishers, 1997); Doug McAdam, John D. McCarthy, and Mayer N. Zald, "Social Movements," in Neil J. Smelser, ed., *Handbook of Sociology* (Newbury Park, CA: Sage, 1994); Doug McAdam, *Political Process and the Development of Black Insurgency* (Chicago: University of Chicago Press, 1982); Doug McAdam, Sidney Tarrow, and Charles Tilly, *Dynamics of Contention* (Cambridge, UK: Cambridge University Press, 2001).

3. Sidney Tarrow, "Social Movements as Contentious Politics," *American Political Science Review* 90 (1996), pp. 853–866; Ronald R. Aminzade, Jack A. Goldstone, Doug McAdam, Elizabeth J. Perry, William H. Sewell Jr., and Sidney Tarrow, eds., *Silence and Voice in the Study of Contentious Politics* (New York: Cambridge University Press, Cambridge Studies in Contentious Politics, 2001).

4. Our focus is on social movements in politics and their impact on public policies. For a review of the scholarly literature on social movements more broadly considered see Edwin Amenta, Neal Caren, Elizabeth Chiarello, and Yang Su, "The Political Consequences of Social Movements," *The Annual Review of Sociology* (2010), volume 36, pp. 287–307; Elizabeth A. Armstrong and Mary Bernstein, "Culture, Power, and Institutions: A Multi-Institutional Approach to Social Movements," *Sociological Theory* 26, no. 1 (March 2008), pp. 74–99.

5. Malcolm X was a complex and compelling character who changed political course during his active political lifetime. See Manning Marable, *Malcolm X: A Life of Redefinition* (New York: Viking Press, 2011).

6. CBS News telecast, February 16, 2003.

7. Jackie Smith, "Globalizing Resistance: The Battle of Seattle and the Future of Social Movements," *Mobilization: An International Journal* 6, no. 1 (2000), pp. 1–19.

8. Mark Penn, *Microtrends: The Small Forces Behind Tomorrow's Big Changes* (New York: Twelve, Hachette Book Group. 2007), pp. 43–52.

9. "Public Divided Over Occupy Wall Street," Pew Research Center poll, released October 24, 2011.

10. E. E. Schattschneider, *The Semi-Sovereign People* (New York: Holt, Rinehart & Winston, 1960), p. 142.

11. Richard Polenberg, *One Nation Divisible* (New York: Penguin, 1980), p. 268; Craig A. Rimmerman, *From Identity to Politics: The Lesbian and Gay Movements in the United States* (Philadelphia, PA: Temple University Press, 2002), ch. 1.

12. Frances Fox Piven, *When Movements Matter: How Ordinary People Change America* (Lanham, MD: Rowman & Littlefield, 2006).

13. Theodore J. Lowi, *The Politics of Disorder* (New York: Basic Books, 1971), p. 54.

14. Piven, *When Movements Matter.*

15. Aminzade et al., *Silence and Voice in the Study of Contentious Politics;* Meyer and Tarrow, *The Social Movement Society;* McAdam et al., "Social Movements"; Sidney Tarrow, *Social Movements, Collective Action, and Politics* (New York: Cambridge University Press, 1994).

16. Neil J. Smelser, *Theory of Collective Behavior* (New York: Free Press, 1962); Elaine Walker and Heather J. Smith, *Relative Deprivation: Specification, Development, and Integration* (Cambridge, UK: Cambridge University Press, 2001).

17. Barbara Sinclair Deckard, *The Women's Movement* (New York: Harper & Row, 1983); Ethel Klein, *Gender Politics: From Consciousness to Mass Politics* (Cambridge, MA: Harvard University Press, 1984), ch. 2.

18. Donald P. Haider-Markel, "Creating Change—Holding the Line," in Ellen D. B. Riggle and Barry L. Tadlock, eds., *Gays and Lesbians in the Political Process* (New York: Columbia University Press, 1999).

19. Rimmerman, From Identity to Politics.

20. William Gamson, *The Strategy of Social Protest* (Homewood, IL: Dorsey, 1975); John D. McCarthy and Mayer N. Zald, "Resource Mobilization and Social Movements: A Partial Theory," *American Journal of Sociology* 82 (1977), pp. 1212–1241.

21. Jo Freeman, *The Politics of Women's Liberation* (New York: McKay, 1975); Nancy Burns, "Gender: Public Opinion and Political Action," in Ira Katznelson and Helen V. Milner, eds., *Political Science: The State of the Discipline* (New York: W. W. Norton, 2002), pp. 472–476.

22. Bruce Bimber, *Information and American Democracy: Technology and the Evolution of Political Power* (New York: Cambridge University Press, 2003), chs. 3 and 5.

23. Amenta, Caren, Chiarello, and Su, "The Political Consequences of Social Movements," p. 299; McAdam, *Political Process;* Tarrow, *Social Movements, Collective Action, and Politics;* Peter K. Eisenger, "The Conditions of Protest Behavior in American Cities," *American Political Science Review* 67 (1973), pp. 11–28.

24. Frances Fox Piven and Richard A. Cloward, *Poor People's Movements* (New York: Vintage, 1979), ch. 3.

25. Klein, *Gender Politics*, pp. 90–91.

26. National Opinion Research Center, General Social Survey, 1972.

27. *Trends in Political Values and Core Attitudes: 1987–2009* (Washington, D.C.: The Pew Research Center for the People and the Press, May 21, 2009).

28. Economic Mobility Project, Pew Research Center, 2011.

29. G. William Domhoff, *The Higher Circles* (New York: Random House, 1970); Edward S. Greenberg, *Capitalism and the American Political Ideal* (Armonk, NY: Sharpe, 1985); Gabriel Kolko, *The Triumph of Conservatism* (Chicago: Quadrangle, 1967); James Weinstein, *The Corporate Ideal in the Liberal State* (Boston: Beacon Press, 1968).

30. Carol A. Horton, *Race and the Making of American Liberalism* (New York: Oxford University Press, 2005), pp. 140–141.

31. Rimmerman, *From Identity to Politics.*

32. Piven, *When Movements Matter.*

33. Taylor Branch, *Parting the Waters: America in the King Years* (New York: Simon and Schuster, 1986); William H. Chafe, *The Unfinished Journey: America Since World War II* (New York: Oxford University Press, 2003).

34. Amenta, Caren, Chiarello, and Su, "The Political Consequences of Social Movements," pp. 294–298.

35. Jane Mansbridge, *Why We Lost the ERA* (Chicago: University of Chicago Press, 1986).

36. Christian Davenport, Hank Johnson, and Carol Mueller, eds., *Mobilization and Repression* (Minneapolis: University of Minnesota Press, 2005).

37. See David Caute, *The Great Fear* (New York: Simon & Schuster, 1978); Robert Justin Goldstein, *Political Repression in Modern America* (Cambridge, MA: Schenkman, 1978); Alan Wolfe, *The Seamy Side of Democracy* (New York: McKay, 1978).

38. Greenberg, *Capitalism and the American Political Ideal.*

39. Mart Martin, *The Almanac of Women and Minorities in American Politics* (Boulder, CO: Westview Press, 2002); Penn, *Microtrends*, pp. 43–52.

40. Desmond S. King and Rogers M. Smith, *Still a House Divided: Race and Politics in Obama's America* (Princeton, NJ: Princeton University Press, 2011), pp. 268–280.

41. Chafe, *The Unfinished Journey: America Since World War II*, pp. 430–468; Deckard, *The Women's Movement;* Klein, *Gender Politics*, ch. 2; Freeman, *Politics of Women's Liberation.* Also see debates on the relative progress of women in the United States collected in Dorothy McBride Stetson, *Women's Rights in the United States: Policy Debates and Gender Roles* (London: Routledge, 2004).

42. McKinsey Consultancy, reported in *The Economist* (November 26, 2011), p. 35.

9

1. Schumpeter, "American Idiocy," *The Economist* (August 13, 2011), p. 38.

2. "Special Report: How Washington Took the U.S. to the Brink," Reuters, August 4, 2011.

3. Ronald Brownstein, *The Second Civil War: How Extreme Partisanship Has Paralyzed Washington and Polarized America* (New York: Penguin Press, 2007); Nicol C. Rae, "Be Careful What You Wish For: The Rise of Responsible Parties in American National Politics," *Annual Reviews, Political Science* 10 (2007), pp. 169–191.

4. E. E. Schattschneider, *Party Government* (New York: Holt, Rinehart & Winston, 1942), p. 208.

5. Marjorie Randon Hershey, *Party Politics in America*, 14th edition (New York: Pearson Longman, 2011), p. 7.

6. Robert A. Dahl, *On Democracy* (New Haven, CT: Yale University Press, 1998); Marjorie Randon Hershey, *Party Politics in America*, pp. 1–2.

7. Schattschneider, *Party Government*, p. 208. Also see Jonathan White and Lea Ypi, "On Partisan Political Justification," *American Political Science Review* 105, no. 2 (May 2011).

8. See Hershey, *Party Politics in America*, ch. 1; A. James Reichley, *The Life of the Parties: A History of American Political Parties* (Lanham, MD: Rowman & Littlefield, 2002), ch. 1.

9. Steven J. Rosenstone and John Mark Hansen, *Mobilization, Participation, and Democracy in America* (New York: Macmillan, 1993).

10. E. E. Schattschneider, *The Semi-Sovereign People* (New York: Holt, Rinehart & Winston, 1960).

11. John H. Aldrich and John D. Griffin, "Parties, Elections, and Democratic Politics," in Jan E. Leighley, ed., *The Oxford Handbook of American Elections and Political Behavior* (Oxford, UK: Oxford University Press, 2010). Also see John H. Aldrich, *Why Parties? A Second Look* (Chicago: University of Chicago Press, 2011).

12. The classic statement on electoral rules is Maurice Duverger, *Political Parties* (New York: Wiley, 1954).

13. Ibid.

14. Marjorie Randon Hershey, "Like a Bee: Election Law and the Survival of Third Parties," in Matthew J. Streb, ed., *Election Law and Electoral Politics* (Boulder, CO: Lynn Rienner, 2004); Hershey, *Party Politics in America*, pp. 37–38.

15. Much of this discussion is drawn from Steven J. Rosenstone, Roy L. Behr, and Edward H. Lazarus, *Third Parties in America*, 2nd ed. (Princeton, NJ: Princeton University Press, 1996). Also see Paul S. Herrnson and John C. Green, *Multiparty Politics in America* (Lanham, MD: Rowman & Littlefield, 2002); Hershey, *Party Politics in America*, p. 37–40; John F. Bibby and Sandy Maisel, *Two Parties or More?* (Boulder, CO: Westview, 2003); Shigeo Hirano and James M. Snyder Jr., "The Decline of Third-Party Voting in the United States, *The Journal of Politics* 69, no. 1 (February 2007), pp. 1–16.

16. Ibid.

17. On realignment, see Walter Dean Burnham, *Critical Elections and the Mainsprings of American Politics* (New York: Norton, 1970); Jerome Clubb, William H. Flanigan, and Nancy H. Zingale, *Partisan Realignment* (Newbury Park, CA: Sage, 1980); V. O. Key Jr., "A Theory of Critical Elections," *The Journal of Politics* 17 (1955), pp. 3–18; Hershey, *Party Politics in America*, ch. 7; James L. Sundquist, *Dynamics of the Party System* (Washington, D.C.: Brookings Institution, 1973); Samuel Merrill, Bernard Grofman, and Thomas L. Brunnell, "Cycles in American National Electoral Politics, 1854–2006," *The American Political Science Review* 102, no. 1 (February 2008), pp. 1–17. For the special place that war has played in altering parties and party systems see David R. Mayhew, "Wars and American Politics," *Perspectives on Politics* 3, no. 3 (September 2005), pp. 473–493.

18. See David R. Mayhew, *Electoral Realignments* (New Haven, CT: Yale University Press, 2004); Hershey, *Party Politics in America*; Peter F. Nardulli, "The Concept of a Critical Realignment, Electoral Behavior, and Political Change," *The American Political Science Review* 89 (1995), pp. 10–22; Gary Miller and Norman Schofield, "The Transformation of the Republican and Democratic Party Coalitions in the U.S.," *Perspectives on Politics* 69, no. 3 (September 2008), pp. 433–450; Matt Bai, "The Great Unalignment," *The New York Times Sunday Magazine*, January 24, 2010, pp. 13–15.

19. John Aldrich and Richard Niemi, "The Sixth American Party System," in Stephen C. Craig, *Broken Contract: Changing Relationships Between Americans and Their Government* (Boulder, CO: Westview Press, 1996); Walter J. Stone and Ronald B. Rapoport, "It's Perot Stupid! The Legacy of the 1992 Perot Movement in the Major-Party System, 1994–2000," *PS: Political Science and Politics* XXXIV, no. 1 (March 2001), pp. 49–56.

20. Larry M. Bartels, *Unequal Democracy: The Political Economy of the Guided Age* (New York and Princeton, NJ: Russell Sage Foundation and Princeton University Press, 2008); Thomas Byrne Edsall and Mary D. Edsall, *Chain Reaction: The Impact of Race, Rights and Taxes on American Politics* (New York: Norton, 1991); Stanley B. Greenberg, *Middle Class Dreams: The Politics and Power of the New American Majority* (New Haven, CT: Yale University Press, 1996); and Desmond S. King and Rogers M. Smith, *Still a House Divided: Race and Politics in Obama's America* (Princeton, NJ: Princeton University Press, 2011).

21. Brownstein, *The Second Civil War*, pp. 93–136.

22. Larry Sabato, *The Party's Just Begun* (Glenview, IL: Scott, Foresman, 1988); Sundquist, *Dynamics of the Party System;* Martin P. Wattenberg, *The Decline of American Political Parties* (Cambridge, MA: Harvard University Press, 1994); Greenberg, *Middle Class Dreams*; Everett C. Ladd, "The 1994 Congressional Elections," *Political Science Quarterly* 110 (1995), pp. 1–23.

23. Aldrich, *Why Parties?*, ch. 9.

24. Earl Black and Merle Black, *Divided America: The Ferocious Power Struggle in American Politics* (New York: Simon & Schuster, 2007); Stanley B. Greenberg, *The Two Americas: Our Current Political Deadlock and How to Break It* (New York: Thomas Dunn Books, 2004); Geoffrey C. Layman, Thomas M. Carsey, and Juliana Menaxce Horowitz, "Party Polarization in American Politics: Characteristics, Causes, and Consequences," *Annual Reviews: Political Science* 9 (2006), pp. 83–110; Brownstein, *The Second Civil War*, pp. 137–174.

25. Morris P. Fiorina, *Disconnect: The Breakdown of Representation in American Politics* (Norman: University of Oklahoma Press, 2009). Alan Abramowitz disagrees with Fiorina, arguing that the politically attentive mass public is deeply polarized. See his *The Disappearing Center: Engaged Citizens, Polarization, and American Democracy* (New Haven, CT: Yale University Press, 2010). Bill Bishop joins Abramowitz's position in his book *The Big Sort: Why the Clustering of Like-Minded Americans Is Tearing Us Apart* (New York: Houghton Mifflin, 2008).

26. Hershey, *Party Politics in America*, ch. 6.

27. On the "great sorting out" of groups and regions along party lines in the United States, see Brownstein, *The Second Civil War*, ch. 6.

28. Richard Florida, *The Rise of the Creative Class: How It's Transforming Work, Leisure, Community, and Everyday Life* (New York: Basic Books, 2002); Richard Florida, *The Flight of the Creative Class* (New York: Harper Business, 2005).

29. Hershey, *Party Politics in America*, ch. 4.

30. J. A. Schlesinger, "The New American Political Party," *American Political Science Review* 79 (1985), pp. 1152–1169; John Aldrich, *Why Parties?* (Chicago: University of Chicago Press, 1995).

31. L. Sandy Maisel, *American Political Parties and Elections: A Very Short Introduction* (New York: Oxford University Press, 2007), pp. 66–68.

32. Hershey, *Party Politics in America*, pp. 115–116.

33. David Menefee-Libey, *The Triumph of Campaign-Centered Politics* (New York: Chatham House Publishers, 2000); Hershey, *Party Politics in America*, pp. 75–78.

34. Stephen Doyle, "The Very, Very Personal Is the Political," *The New York Times Magazine*, February 15, 2004, pp. 42–47.

35. Maisel, *American Parties and Elections*, pp. 63–64.

36. Ibid., pp. 65–67.

37. Roger H. Davidson, Walter J. Oleszek, and Frances E. Lee, *Congress and Its Members*, 13th ed. (Washington, D.C.: CQ Press, 2012), pp. 59, 168.

38. Norman Schofield and Gary Miller, "Elections and Activist Coalitions in the United States," *American Journal of Political Science* 51, no. 3 (July 2007), pp. 518–531.

39. Nicholas Confessore, "Outside Groups Eclipsing G.O.P. as Hub of Campaigns," *The New York Times* (November 1, 2011), p. 1.

40. Hershey, *Party Politics in America*, p. 289.

41. Pew Research Center poll, July 22, 2011.

42. Greenberg, *The Two Americas*; Morris P. Fiorina, "Parties, Participation, and Representation in America," in Ira Katznelson and Helen V. Milner, eds., *Political Science: The State of the Discipline* (New York: W. W. Norton, 2002); Morris P. Fiorina, *Culture War? The Myth of a Polarized America* (New York: Pearson Longman, 2005), ch. 8; Hershey, *Party Politics in America*, ch. 15; Marc J. Hetherington, "Resurgent Mass Partisanship: The Role of Elite Polarization," *The American Political Science Review* 95, no. 1 (September 2001), pp. 619–632; Gerald Pomper, "Parliamentary Government in the United States," in J. C. Green and D. M. Shea, eds., *The State of the Parties* (Lanham, MD: Rowman & Littlefield, 1999).

43. Brownstein, *The Second Civil War*, p. 12.

44. Lewis L. Gould, *Grand Old Party: A History of the Republicans* (New York: Random House, 2003); "When American Politics

Turned European," *The Economist* (October 25, 2005), p. 74; Nils Gilman, "What the Rise of the Republicans as America's First Ideological Party Means for the Democrats," *The Forum* 2, no. 1 (2004), pp. 1–4; Brownstein, *The Second Civil War*; Layman, Carsey, and Horowitz, "Party Polarization in American Politics."

45. *American National Election Studies*, 2008.

46. Ibid.

47. Ibid.; and Gallup Poll, June 2011.

48. "Trends in Political Values and Core Attitudes: 1987–2009" (Washington, D.C.: Pew Research Center for the People and the Press, report released May 21, 2009).

49. Alan D. Monroe, "American Party Platforms and Public Opinion," *American Journal of Political Science* 27 (February 1983), p. 35; Layman, Carsey, and Horowitz, "Party Polarization in American Politics"; Maisel, *American Political Parties and Elections*, pp. 73–76.

50. "Republican Convention Delegate Poll," New York Times/CBS News, press release, July 18, 2004 and *New York Times*/CBS News, "Democratic Convention Delegate Poll," press release, August 24, 2004.

51. Hershey, *Party Politics in America*, pp. 289–293.

52. Ron Suskind, *Confidence Men: Wall Street, Washington, and the Education of a President* (New York: Harper, 2011).

53. James MacGregor Burns, *Deadlock of Democracy* (Englewood Cliffs, NJ: Prentice Hall, 1967).

54. On the pernicious effects of divided government see Benjamin Ginsberg and Martin Shefter, *Politics by Other Means: The Declining Significance of Elections in America* (New York: Basic Books, 1990). For the contrary view see Morris P. Fiorina, *Divided Government* (New York: Macmillan, 1992); Gary Jacobson, *The Electoral Origins of Divided Government: Competition in U.S. House Elections* (Boulder, CO: Westview Press, 1990); David R. Mayhew, *Divided We Govern: Party Control, Lawmaking, and Investigations, 1946–1990* (New Haven, CT: Yale University Press, 1991); Layman, Carsey, and Horowitz, "Party Polarization in American Politics," pp. 88–101.

55. Jason M. Roberts and Steven S. Smith, "Procedural Contexts, Party Strategy, and Conditional Party Voting in the U.S. House of Representatives," *American Journal of Political Science* 47 (2003), pp. 305–317; Douglas Hibbs, *The American Political Economy* (Cambridge, MA: Harvard University Press, 1987); Dennis P. Quinn and Robert Shapiro, "Business Political Power: The Case of Taxation," *American Political Science Review* 85 (1991), pp. 851–874; Kenneth N. Bickers and Robert M. Stein, "The Congressional Pork Barrel in a Republican Era," *The Journal of Politics* 62, no. 4 (November 2000), pp. 1070–1086.

56. Donald Green, Bradley Palmquist, and Eric Schickler, *Partisan Hearts and Minds: Political Parties and the Social Identity of Voters* (New Haven, CT: Yale University Press, 2002); Robert S. Erikson and Kent L. Tedin, *American Public Opinion* (New York: Pearson Longman, 2011) pp. 85–89; Hershey, *Party Politics in America*, pp. 118–136; "Trends in Political Values and Core Attitudes: 1987–2009," pp. 97–110.

57. Data are from 2004, reported in Alan Abramowitz and Kyle Saunders, "Culture War in America: Myth or Reality," *The Forum* 3, no. 2 (2005), pp. 1–22.

58. Bruce E. Keith, David B. Magleby, Candice J. Nelson, Elizabeth Orr, Mark C. Westlye, and Raymond E. Wolfinger, *The Myth of the Independent Voter* (Berkeley, CA: University of California Press, 1992). Also see Marjorie Randon Hershey, *Party Politics in America*, 14th ed. (New York: Longman, 2010), pp. 113–115.

59. "Trends in Political Values and Core Attitudes: 1987–2009," p. 11.

60. Brownstein, *The Second Civil War*; Rae, "Be Careful What You Wish For"; Layman, Carsey, and Horowitz, "Party Polarization in American Politics."

10

1. For a summary of a wide range of polls on matters related to the 2012 presidential election, access www.pollingreport.com. On the superiority of polls to the assertions of pundits of various political stripes, see Michael Cooper, "Election Result Proves a Victory for Pollsters and Other Data Devotees," *The New York Times* (November 7, 2012), p. 1;. For consideration of the many factors that may have affected the 2012 presidential election, see Maggie Haberman, "9 takeaways from the 2012 election," *Politico On-Line* (www.politico.com), November 6, 2012; Maggie Haberman, "Final Takeaways," *Politico On-Line* (www.politico.com), November 7, 2012; Peter Hamby, "Why Romney Lost," CNN Online (www.cnn.com), November 7, 2012; Adam Liptak, " The Vanishing Battleground," *The New York Times* (November 3, 2012), p. 1; Paul Taylor and D'Vera Cohn, "A Milestone En Route to a Majority Minority Nation," (Washington, D.C.: Pew Research Center, press release), November 7, 2012.

2. For further discussion, see Benjamin I. Page, *Choices and Echoes in Presidential Elections: Rational Man and Electoral Democracy* (Chicago: University of Chicago Press, 1978), ch. 2; Robert A. Dahl, *Democracy and Its Critics* (New Haven, CT: Yale University Press, 1989); Robert A. Dahl, *On Democracy* (New Haven, CT: Yale University Press, 1998); Hans Gersbach, *Designing Democracy* (New York: Springer Publishers, 2005).

3. See Russell Muirhead, "A Defense of Party Spirit," *Perspectives on Politics* 4, no. 4 (December 2006), pp. 713–727; Austin Ranney, *The Doctrine of Responsible Party Government: Its Origins and Present State* (Urbana, IL: University of Illinois Press, 1962); E. E. Schattschneider, *Party Government* (New York: Holt, Rinehart & Winston, 1942) and Jonathan White and Lea Ypi, "On Partisan Political Justification," *American Political Science Review* (May 2011), volume 105, number 2, pp. 381–396.

4. Marjorie Randon Hershey, *Party Politics in America* (New York: Pearson Longman Publishers, 2011), pp. 263–269.

5. Nicol C. Rae, "Be Careful What You Wish For: The Rise of Responsible Parties in American National Politics," *Annual Reviews: Political Science* 10 (2007), pp. 169–191.

6. Anthony Downs, *An Economic Theory of Democracy* (New York: Harper & Row, 1957); Otto Davis, Melvin Hinich, and Peter Ordeshook, "An Expository Development of a Mathematical Model of the Electoral Process," *American Political Science Review* 64 (1970), pp. 426–448.

7. Lawrence R. Jacobs and Robert Y. Shapiro, *Politicians Don't Pander: Political Manipulation and the Loss of Democratic Responsiveness* (Chicago: University of Chicago Press, 2000).

8. Marty Cohen, David Karol, Hans Noel, and John Zaller, *The Party Decides: Presidential Nominations Before and After Reform* (Chicago: University of Chicago Press, 2008).

9. See V. O. Key Jr., *Public Opinion and American Democracy* (New York: Knopf, 1961); Morris P. Fiorina, *Retrospective Voting in American National Elections* (Cambridge, MA: Harvard University Press, 1981).

10. Jacobson, "The 2008 Presidential and Congressional Elections."

11. David Stout, "Study Finds Ballot Problems Are More Likely for Poor," *The New York Times* (July 9, 2001), p. A9; Katharine Q. Seelye, "Study Says 2000 Election Missed Millions of Votes," *The New York Times* (August, 10, 2001), p. A17.

12. L. Sandy Maisel, *American Political Parties and Elections: A Very Short Introduction* (New York: Oxford University Press, 2007), p. 5.

13. Mary Fitzgerald, "Greater Convenience but Not Greater Turnout: The Impact of Alternative Voting Methods on Electoral Participation in the United States," *American Politics Research* 33, no. 6 (2005), pp. 842–867.

14. Chilton Williamson, *American Suffrage* (Princeton, NJ: Princeton University Press, 1960), pp. 223, 241, 260; and Gordon S. Wood, *The Idea of America* (New York: Penguin, 2011), Chapter 6, "The Making of American Democracy." Also see Hershey, *Party Politics in America,* pp. 140–144; Maisel, *American Political Parties and Elections,* pp. 47–51.

15. See John Hope Franklin, *From Slavery to Freedom* (New York: Knopf, 1967); Leon Litwack, *North of Slavery* (Chicago: University of Chicago Press, 1961); Alexander Keyssar, *The Right to Vote: The Contested History of Democracy in the United States* (New York: Basic Books, 2001); and Wood, "The Making of American Democracy," pp. 209–210.

16. Walter Dean Burnham, "The Turnout Problem," in A. James Reichley, ed., *Elections, American Style* (Washington, D.C.: Brookings Institution, 1987), pp. 113–114.

17. Maisel, *American Political Parties and Elections*, p. 135.

18. For a brief but excellent discussion of the scholarly literature on the cause of low voting turnout, see Daniel M. Shea, *Let's Vote: The Essentials of the American Electoral Process* (New York: Longman, 2013), pp. 169–178; Kay Lehman Schlozman, "Citizen Participation in America: What Do We Know? Why Do We Care?" in Ira Katznelson and Helen V. Milner, eds., *Political Science: The State of the Discipline* (New York: W. W. Norton, 2002), pp. 439–443; Martin P. Wattenberg, *Where Have All the Voters Gone?* (Cambridge, MA: Harvard University Press, 2002); Andre Blais, "What Affects Voter Turnout?" *Annual Reviews, Political Science* 9 (2006), pp. 111–125.

19. Robert D. Brown, "Voter Registration," in Jan E. Leighley, ed., *The Oxford Handbook of American Elections and Political Behavior* (Oxford: Oxford University Press, 2010).

20. Peverill Squire, Raymond E. Wolfinger, and David P. Glass, "Residential Mobility and Voter Turnout," *American Political Science Review* 81 (1987), pp. 45–65.

21. U.S. Bureau of the Census, 2007; Hershey, *Party Politics in America*, p. 140.

22. Brown, "Voter Registration."

23. Ari Berman, "The GOP War on Voting," *Rolling Stone Online* (posted August 30, 2011), accessed June 12, 2012; and Wendy R. Weiser and Lawrence Norden, *Voting Law Changes in 2012* (New York: The Brennan Center, New York University School of Law, 2011).

24. Wattenberg, *Where Have All the Voters Gone?*, ch. 6.

25. Ronald Brownstein, *The Second Civil War: How Extreme Partisanship Has Paralyzed Washington and Polarized America* (New York: Penguin, 2007), ch. 6; Roger H. Davidson, Walter J. Oleszek, and Frances E. Lee, *Congress and Its Members*, 11th ed. (Washington, D.C.: CQ Press, 2008), pp. 62–65, 108–110; Maisel, *American Political Parties and Elections*, pp. 126–130; Steven S. Smith, Jason M. Roberts, and Ryan J. Vander Wielen, *The American Congress*, 5th ed. (New York: Cambridge University Press, 2007), pp. 68–78; Alan Wolfe, *Does Democracy Still Work?* (New Haven, CT: Yale University Press, 2006), pp. 50–56.

26. "House Members Who Won with 55 Percent or Less in 2008," The Cook Political Report, http://www.cookpolitical.com/sites/default/files/55andunder_0.pdf, November 10, 2008.

27. Steven J. Rosenstone and John Mark Hansen, *Mobilization, Participation, and Democracy in America* (New York: Macmillan, 1993).

28. Alan S. Gerber and Donald M. Green, "The Effects of Canvassing, Telephone Calls, and Direct Mail on Voter Turnout," *American Political Science Review* 94 (2000), pp. 653–663.

29. Shea, *Let's Vote*, pp. 169–178 for a summary of the research on voter turnout.

30. Sidney Verba, Kay Lehman Schlozman, and Henry E. Brady, *Voice and Equality: Civic Volunteerism in American Politics* (Cambridge, MA: Harvard University Press, 1995); Sidney Verba and Norman H. Nie, *Participation in America* (New York: Harper & Row, 1972); Hershey, *Party Politics in America*, pp. 150–153.

31. John A. Garcia, "Latinos and Political Behavior," in Leighley, ed., *The Oxford Handbook of American Elections and Political Behavior.*

32. Mark Hugo Lopez, "The Latino Electorate in 2010" (Washington, D.C.: Pew Hispanic Center, April 26, 2011).

33. Adam Nagourney, "Latino Growth Not Fully Felt at Voting Booth," *The New York Times* (June 9, 2012), p. 1.

34. Mark Hugo Lopez and Paul Taylor, "Dissecting the 2008 Electorate: Most Diverse in U.S. History" (Washington, D.C.: Pew Research Center, April 30, 2009), p. 6.

35. Susan A. MacManus, *Young v. Old* (Boulder, CO: Westview Press, 1996), ch. 2; and Martin P. Wattenberg, *Is Voting for Young People?* (New York: Pearson, 2012).

36. Margaret M. Conway, *Political Participation in the United States*, 3rd ed. (Washington, D.C.: CQ Press, 2000), p. 37; and Julie Dolan, Melissa Deckman, and Michele L. Swers, *Women and Politics: Paths to Power and Political Influence* (New York: Pearson Longman, 2011), pp. 55–72.

37. E. J. Dionne, "If Nonvoters Had Voted: Same Winner, but Bigger," *The New York Times* (November 21, 1988), p. B16.

38. Sidney Verba, Kay Lehman Schlozman, Henry E. Brady, and Norman H. Nie, "Citizen Activity: Who Participates? What Do They Say?" *American Political Science Review* 87 (1993), pp. 303–318; Robert S. Erikson and Kent L. Tedin, *American Public Opinion* (New York: Pearson Longman Publishers, 2007), ch. 7; Eric Shiraev and Richard Sobel, *People and Their Opinions* (New York: Pearson Longman Publishers, 2006), chs. 7–9.

39. Wattenberg, *Is Voting for Young People?*

40. Martin Gilens, "Preference Gaps and Inequality in Representation," *PS* (April 2009), pp. 331–335; Lawrence R. Jacobs and Theda Skocpol, eds., *Inequality and American Democracy: What We Know and What We Need to Learn* (New York: Russell Sage Foundation, 2005); Larry M. Bartels, Hugh Keclo, Rodney E. Hero, and Lawrence Jacobs, "Inequality and American Government," *Perspectives on Politics* 2, no. 4 (20), pp. 651–668; and Larry M. Bartels, *Unequal Democracy: The Political Economy of the Gilded Age* (New York and Princeton, NJ: The Russell Sage Foundation and Princeton University Press, 2008).

41. Jacob Hacker and Paul Pierson, *Off Center* (New Haven, CT: Yale University Press, 2005); Larry M. Bartels, "Is the Water Rising: Reflections on Inequality and American Democracy," *PS* (January 2006), pp. 39–42; Kay Lehman Schlozman, "On Inequality and Political Voice," *PS* (January 2006), pp. 55–57.

42. David D. Kirkpatrick, "Wealth Is a Common Factor Among 2008 Hopefuls," *The New York Times* (May 17, 2007), p. A1.

43. Nelson W. Polsby and Aaron Wildavsky, *Presidential Elections*, 12th ed. (Lanham, MD: Rowman & Littlefield, 2007) pp. 53–55, 57.

44. Hershey, *Party Politics in America*, pp. 181–182.

45. Stephen J. Wayne, *The Road to the White House* (Belmont, CA: Wadsworth, 2007); and Hershey, *Party Politics in America*, p. 181.

46. Larry Bartels, *Presidential Primaries and the Dynamics of Public Choice* (Princeton, NJ: Princeton University Press, 1988); John H. Aldrich, *Before the Convention* (Chicago: University of Chicago Press, 1980); Wayne, *The Road to the White House.*

47. Jeremy W. Peters, "Campaigns Blitz 9 Swing States in a Battle of Ads," *The New York Times* (June 8, 2012), p. 1.

48. Polsby and Wildavsky, *Presidential Elections*, pp. 143–147.

49. John G. Geer, *In Defense of Negativity* (Chicago: University of Chicago Press, 2006); Ken Goldstein and Paul Freedman, "Campaign Advertising and Voter Turnout: New Evidence for a Stimulation Effect," *The Journal of Politics* 64 (2002), pp. 721–740; and Caterina Gennaioli, "Go Divisive or Not: How Political Campaigns Affect Turnout" (London: London School of Economics and Political Science, Working Paper 3298, December 30, 2010).

50. Anna Greenberg, "Targeting and Electoral Gaps," in Laura R. Olson and John C. Green, *Beyond Red State, Blue State: Electoral Gaps in the Twenty-First Century American Electorate* (Upper Saddle River, NJ: Pearson Prentice Hall, 2009); Magleby, "How Barack Obama Changed Presidential Campaigns." Also see D. Sunshine Hillygus and Todd G. Shields, *The Persuadable Voter: Wedge Issues in Presidential Campaigns* (Princeton, NJ: Princeton University Press, 2008).

51. Federal Election Commission, 2009.

52. "The 2012 Election Will Cost $6 Billion," *Bloomberg/Businessweek* (October 3–9, 2011), pp. 32–34.

53. The Center for Responsive Politics at http://www.opensecrets.org/pres08/totals.php?cycle=2008.

54. Federal Election Commission, 2011; the Center for Responsive Politics, 2012.

55. Ibid.

56. Polsby and Wildavsky, *Presidential Elections*, pp. 62–67.

57. On this research see Thomas E. Mann, "Linking Knowledge and Action: Political Science and Campaign Finance Reform," *Perspectives on Politics* 1, no. 1 (2003), pp. 69–83.

58. See Verba, Schlozman, and Brady, *Voice and Equality*.

59. Matthew Hindman, *The Myth of Digital Democracy* (Princeton, NJ: Princeton University Press, 2009).

60. Efforts to sort out their relative contributions include Benjamin I. Page and Calvin Jones, "Reciprocal Effects of Policy Preferences, Party Loyalties, and the Vote," *American Political Science Review* 73 (1979), pp. 1071–1089; Gregory B. Markus and Philip E. Converse, "A Dynamic Simultaneous Equation Model of Public Choice," *American Political Science Review* 73 (1979), pp. 1066–1070; and William G. Jacoby, "The American Voter," in Leighley, ed., *The Oxford Handbook of American Elections and Political Behavior*.

61. Larry M. Bartels, "Partisanship and Voting Behavior, 1952–1996," *American Journal of Political Science* 44 (January 2000), pp. 35–50; Hershey, *Party Politics in America*, pp. 108–111; D. Sunshine Hillygus and Simon Jackman, "Voter Decision Making in Election 2000: Campaign Effects, Partisan Activation, and the Clinton Legacy," *American Journal of Political Science* 47 (2003), pp. 583–596; Stephen A. Jessee, "Spatial Voting in the 2004 Presidential Election," *American Political Science Review* 103, no. 1 (February 2009), pp. 59–81; and Jacoby, "The American Voter," pp. 263–265.

62. Donald E. Stokes, "Some Dynamic Elements of Contests for the Presidency," *American Political Science Review* 60 (1966), pp. 19–28.

63. Maisel, *American Political Parties and Elections*, pp. 107–112.

11

1. Ted Barrett, "Reid Urges Cooperation as Democrats Expand Senate Control," *CNN online* (www.cnn.com), November 7, 2012; "The House of Representatives: The no-wave election," November 3, 2012, pp. 23-24; Alex Isenstadt, "How Pete Sessions helped keep a GOP House," *Politico Online* (www.politico.com), November 8, 2012; and Jonathan Weisman, "Democrats Deliver String of Stinging Defeats in Senate," *The New York Times* (November 6, 2012), p. 1.

2. Moderates under pressure," *The Economist* (October 13, 2012), pp. 18-19; Jennifer Steinhauer, "Weighing the Effect of an Exit of Centrists," *The New York Times* (October 8, 2012), p. 1; and Joshua Tucker, "The Fundamentals of Lawmaking: Gridlock in the 113th Congress," *Monkey Cage Political Science Blog* (www.themonkeycage.org), November 9, 2012.

3. Roger H. Davidson, Walter J. Oleszek, and Frances E. Lee, *Congress and Its Members*, 13th ed. (Washington, D.C.: CQ Press, 2012), pp. 19–28.

4. Ibid., pp. 27–28. Also see Oleszek, Walter J., *Congressional Procedures and the Policy Process*, 8th ed. (Washington, D.C.: CQ Press, 2010), pp. 23–28.

5. Sanford Levinson, *Our Undemocratic Constitution: Where the Constitution Goes Wrong* (New York: Oxford University Press, 2006); Robert A. Dahl, *How Democratic Is the American Constitution?* (New Haven, CT: Yale University Press, 2001).

6. Quoted in Charles Warren, *The Supreme Court in U.S. History* (Boston: Little, Brown, 1919), p. 195.

7. Oleszek, *Congressional Procedures and the Policy Process*, p. 5.

8. On this general question, see Jane Mansbridge, "Rethinking Representation," *American Political Science Review* 97, no. 4 (2003), pp. 515–528; Nadia Urbinati and Mark E. Warren, "The Concept of Representation in Contemporary Democratic Theory," *The Annual Review of Political Science* 11 (2008), pp. 387–412. Also see Davidson, Oleszek, and Lee, *Congress and Its Members*, pp. 140–141.

9. Quoted in Charles Henning, *The Wit and Wisdom of Politics* (Golden, CO: Fulcrum, 1989), p. 235.

10. Abraham Lincoln, announcement in the *Sagamo Journal*, New Salem, Illinois (June 13, 1836).

11. Davidson, Oleszek, and Lee, *Congress and Its Members*, p. 122–124. For a dissenting view, one that suggests that senators, facing much more competitive elections than representatives, are just as likely as House members to lean toward the delegate style throughout their six-year term of office, see Charles Stewart III, "Congress and the Constitutional System," in Paul J. Quirk and Sarah A. Binder, eds., *The Legislative Branch* (New York: Oxford University Press, 2005).

12. Davidson, Oleszek, and Lee, *Congress and Its Members*, pp. 110–115.

13. The Inter-Parliamentary Union, "Women in National Parliaments," www.ipu.org/wmn-e/world.htm.

14. Davidson, Oleszek, and Lee, *Congress and Its Members*, pp. 110–112; Steven S. Smith, Jason M. Roberts, and Ryan J. Vander Wielen, *The American Congress* (New York: Cambridge University Press, 2007), pp. 17–18.

15. Davidson, Oleszek, and Lee, *Congress and Its Members*, pp. 127–128.

16. The distinction between descriptive and substantive representation—the latter meaning that legislators act in the interests of their constituents irrespective of the demographic makeup of the constituency—is made by Hanna Pitkin in her classic work *The Concept of Representation* (Berkeley, CA: University of California Press, 1967).

17. Arturo Vega and Juanita Firestone, "The Effects of Gender on Congressional Behavior and the Substantive Representation of Women," *Legislative Studies Quarterly* 20 (May 1995), pp. 213–222. Also see Michele L. Swers, *The Difference Women Make* (Chicago: University of Chicago Press, 2002); the collection of research on women's impact on the legislative process in Cindy Simon Rosenthal, ed., *Women Transforming Congress* (Norman, OK: University of Oklahoma Press, 2002).

18. Datina L. Gamble, "Black Political Representation," *Legislative Studies Quarterly* 32 (2007), pp. 421–448.

19. For a review of research on the political impacts of redistricting, see Raymond La Raja, "Redistricting: Reading Between the Lines," *The Annual Review of Political Science* 12 (2009), pp. 202–223.

20. Gary W. Cox and Jonathan Katz, "The Reapportionment Revolution and Bias in U.S. Congressional Elections," *American Journal of Political Science* 43 (1999), pp. 812–840; Davidson, Oleszek, and Lee, *Congress and Its Members*, pp. 48–58; Smith, Roberts, and Vander Wielen, *The American Congress*, pp. 62–64.

21. CQ Voting and Elections Collection Online (http://library.cqpress.com/elections), 2007. Some have argued that districting is only one reason competitive elections have declined.

Another may be that election districts are becoming more homogeneous as people increasingly move to areas where there are people like themselves. See the research of Bruce Oppenheimer and Alan Abramowitz, reported in Bill Bishop, "You Can't Compete With Voters' Feet," *Washington Post* (May 15, 2005), p. B2; Alan Abramowitz, Brad Alexander, and Matthew Gunning, "Drawing the Line on District Competition," *PS* (January 2006), pp. 95–97; Richard Florida, *The Flight of the Creative Class* (New York: Harper Business, 2005), pp. 217–222; Ronald Brownstein, *The Second Civil War: How Extreme Partisanship Has Paralyzed Washington and Polarized America* (New York: Penguin, 2007), ch. 6.

22. Davidson, Oleszek, and Lee, *Congress and Its Members*, pp. 53–58.

23. Charles S. Bulloch, "Affirmative Action Districts: In Whose Face Will They Blow Up?" *Campaigns and Elections*, April 1995, p. 22.

24. Charles Cameron, David Epstein, and Sharon O'Halloran, "Do Majority-Minority Districts Maximize Black Representation in Congress?" *American Political Science Review* 90 (1996), pp. 794–812; David Epstein and Sharon O'Halloran, "A Social Science Approach to Race, Districting and Representation," *American Political Science Review* 93 (1999), pp. 187–191; David Lublin, *The Paradox of Representation: Racial Gerrymandering and Minority Interests* (Princeton, NJ: Princeton University Press, 1997); David T. Canon, "Representing Racial and Ethnic Minorities," in Paul J. Quirk and Sarah A. Binder, eds., *The Legislative Branch* (New York: Oxford University Press, 2005), pp. 185–186.

25. Federal Election Commission, 2011.

26. Davidson, Oleszek, and Lee, *Congress and Its Members*, pp. 75–77.

27. Gary W. Cox and Eric Magar, "How Much Is Majority Status in the U.S. Congress Worth?" *American Political Science Review* 93 (1999), pp. 299–309.

28. Richard Hall and Frank W. Wayman, "Buying Time: Moneyed Interests and the Mobilization of Bias in Congressional Committees," *American Political Science Review* 84 (1990), pp. 797–820.

29. See the classic work on this subject, David R. Mayhew, *Congress: The Electoral Connection* (New Haven, CT: Yale University Press, 1974). Also see Davidson, Oleszek, and Lee, *Congress and Its Members*, ch. 4; Smith, Roberts, and Vander Wielen, *The American Congress*, pp. 97–104.

30. Richard F. Fenno Jr., *Home Style: House Members and Their Districts* (New York: Pearson Longman, 2003); Richard F. Fenno Jr., *Senators on the Home Trail* (Norman: University of Oklahoma Press, 1996).

31. Bruce Cain, John A. Ferejohn, and Morris P. Fiorina, *The Personal Vote: Constituency Service and Electoral Independence* (Cambridge, MA: Harvard University Press, 1987); Glenn Parker, *Homeward Bound: Explaining Change in Congressional Behavior* (Pittsburgh: University of Pittsburgh Press, 1986); Fenno, *Home Style*.

32. Ron Nixon, "Cost-Cutters, Except When the Spending Is Back Home," *The New York Times* (July 19, 2011), p. 1.

33. Levinson, *Our Undemocratic Constitution*, p. 51. Calculations by authors for 2011.

34. Lawrence Jacobs and Robert Shapiro, *Politicians Don't Pander* (Chicago: University of Chicago Press, 2000).

35. Jacob S. Hacker and Paul Pierson, *Off Center: The Republican Revolution and the Erosion of American Democracy* (New Haven, CT: Yale University Press, 2005).

36. Lawrence Lessig labels the tendency of members of Congress to pay special attention to powerful special interests "institutional corruption." See his *Republic Lost: How Money Corrupts Congress* (New York: Twelve Publishers, 2011).

37. Larry M. Bartels, *Unequal Democracy: The Political Economy of the New Gilded Age* (New York and Princeton, NJ: Russell Sage Foundation and Princeton University Press, 2008), ch. 9; Martin Gilens, "Inequality and Democratic Responsiveness," *Public Opinion Quarterly* 69, no. 5 (2005), pp. 778–896; Benjamin I. Page, with Marshall M. Bouton, *The Foreign Policy Disconnect: What Americans Want from Our Leaders but Don't Get* (Chicago: University of Chicago Press, 2006).

38. Alan Wolfe, *Does American Democracy Still Work?* (New Haven, CT: Yale University Press, 2006), ch. 3.

39. Oleszek, *Congressional Procedures and the Policy Process*, ch. 1.

40. Hacker and Pierson, *Off Center*.

41. Hershey, *Party Politics in America*, pp. 243–244; Davidson, Oleszek, and Lee, *Congress and Its Members*, ch. 6; Garry W. Cox and Keith T. Poole, "On Measuring Partisanship in Roll-Call Voting," *American Journal of Political Science* 46 (2002), pp. 477–489; Keith T. Poole and Howard Rosenthal, "On Party Polarization in Congress," *Daedalus* 136, no. 3 (2007), pp. 104–107; Gerald D. Wright and Brian F. Schaffner, "The Influence of Party," *American Political Science Review* 96 (2002), pp. 367–379; Smith, Roberts, and Vander Wielen, *The American Congress*, pp. 23–24.

42. Davidson, Oleszek, and Lee, *Congress and Its Members*, pp. 266–267.

43. Ibid., p. 193.

44. For the fullest review of the scholarly literature see Geoffrey C. Layman, Thomas M. Carsey, and Julianna Menasce Horowitz, "Party Polarization in American Politics: Characteristics, Causes and Consequences." *Annual Review of Political Science* 9 (2006), pp. 83–110.

45. On the transformation of the South in American politics and how it has affected Congress see Nelson W. Polsby, *How Congress Evolves: Social Bases of Institutional Change* (New York: New York University Press, 2004); Earl Black and Merle Black, *The Rise of Southern Republicans* (Cambridge, MA: Harvard University and Belknap Press, 2003); Earl Black and Merle Black, *Divided America: The Ferocious Power Struggle in American Politics* (New York: Simon and Schuster, 2007); Stanley B. Greenberg, *The Two Americas* (New York: St. Martin's Griffin, 2005).

46. Dante Chinni and James Gimpel, *Our Patchwork Nation* (New York: Penguin, Gotham Publishers, 2010).

47. Alan I. Abramowitz and Kyle L. Saunders, "Ideological Realignment in the U.S. Electorate," *Journal of Politics* 60 (1998), pp. 634–652; Nolan McCarty, Keith T. Poole, and Howard Rosenthal, *Polarized America: The Dance of Ideology and Unequal Riches* (Cambridge, MA: MIT Press, 2006); *Evenly Divided and Increasingly Polarized: The 2004 Political Landscape* (Washington, D.C.: Pew Research Center, 2003); "Trends in Political Values and Core Attitudes: 1987–2007" (Washington, D.C.: The Pew Research Center for the People and the Press, report released March 22, 2007); "Trends in Political Values and Core Attitudes: 1987–2009" (Washington, D.C.: The Pew Research Center for the People and the Press, report released May 21, 2009); Nils Gilman, "What the Rise of the Republicans as America's First Ideological Party Means for the Democrats," *The Forum* 2, no. 1 (2004), pp. 1–4.

48. Mickey Edwards, "Political Science and Political Practice," *Perspectives on Politics* 1, no. 2 (June 2003), p. 352.

49. See John J. Kornacki, ed., *Leading Congress: New Styles, New Strategies* (Washington, D.C.: Congressional Quarterly Press, 1990); David W. Rohde, *Parties and Leaders in the Postreform Congress* (Chicago: University of Chicago Press, 1991); Randall Strahan, *Leading Representatives: The Agency of Leaders in the Politics of the U.S. House* (Baltimore: The Johns Hopkins University Press, 2007); Hershey, *Party Politics in America*, pp. 244–249.

50. Alan A. Abramowitz, "'Mr. Mayhew, Meet Mr. DeLay,' or the Electoral Connection in the Post-Reform Congress," *PS* 34,

no. 2 (June 2001), pp. 257–258; Layman, Carsey, and Horowitz, "Party Polarization in American Politics," pp. 88–90.

51. Oleszek, Congressional Procedures and the Policy Process, pp. 160–161.

52. Davidson, Oleszek, and Lee, *Congress and Its Members*, pp. 157–159.

53. Sheryl Gay Stolberg, Jeff Zeleny, and Carl Hulse, "Health Vote Caps a Journey Back from the Brink," *The New York Times* (March 20, 2010), p. 1.

54. Smith, Roberts, and Vander Wielen, *The American Congress*, p. 137.

55. This analogy is that of Congressman Tom DeLay reported in Jonathan Kaplan, "Hastert, DeLay: Political Pros Get Along to Go Along," *The Hill*, July 22, 2003, p. 8.

56. Davidson, Oleszek, and Lee, *Congress and Its Members*, pp. 210–211; Smith, Roberts, and Vander Wielen, *The American Congress*, pp. 163–164; Brownstein, *The Second Civil War*, pp. 124–127.

57. Jonathan Allen, "The Legacy of the Class of '94," *CQ Weekly*, September 4, 2004.

58. Brownstein, *The Second Civil War*, p. 157.

59. Davidson, Oleszek, and Lee, *Congress and Its Members*, ch. 8; Donald R. Matthews, *U.S. Senators and Their World* (Chapel Hill, NC: University of North Carolina Press, 1960).

60. Interview with Ezra Klein, *The Washington Post Online*, accessed December 28, 2009, at http://voices.washingtonpost.com/ezra-klein/2009/12/the_right_of_the_filibuster_an.html.

61. Robert Bendiner, *Obstacle Course on Capitol Hill* (New York: McGraw-Hill, 1964), p. 15.

62. Barbara Sinclair, Unorthodox Lawmaking: New Legislative Processes in the U.S. Congress (Washington, D.C.: CQ Press, 2007).

63. Brownstein, *The Second Civil War*, p. 277.

64. Suzy Khimm, "The Decline of Congressional Oversight, in One Chart," *The Washington Post*, online (http://www.washingtonpost.com/blogs/ezra-klein/post/the-decline-of-congressional-oversight-in-one-chart/2011/11/29/gIQAwq078N_blog.html), accessed on December 2, 2011.

65. Lessig, *Republic Lost*.

12

1. On the president's unitary powers, their origins, development, and implications see Kenneth R. Mayer, "The Presidential Power of Unilateral Action," and Richard W. Waterman, "Assessing the Unilateral Presidency," in George C. Edwards III and William G. Howell, *The Oxford Handbook of the American Presidency* (Oxford: Oxford University Press, 2010); and William G. Howell, *Power Without Persuasion: The Politics of Direct Presidential Action* (Princeton, NJ: Princeton University Press, 2003). For an overview of presidential scholarship on the powers of the presidency see Louis Fisher, "Teaching the Presidency: Idealizing a Constitutional Office," *PS: Political Science* (January 2012), pp. 17–31.

2. U.S. Department of Commerce, *Historical Statistics of the United States, Colonial Times to 1970* (Washington, D.C.: U.S. Government Printing Office, 1971), pp. 8, 1143.

3. Federation of American Scientists, 2009 (http://www.fas.org/programs/ssp/nukes/nuclearweapons/nukestatus.html).

4. U.S. Bureau of the Census.

5. George C. Edwards III and Stephen J. Wayne, *Presidential Leadership: Politics and Policy Making* (Belmont, CA: Cengage Wadsworth, 2009), pp. 2–9; and James P. Pfiffner and Roger H. Davidson, eds., *Understanding the Presidency* (New York: Pearson, 2011), pp. 1–6.

6. On the contributions of particular presidents in shaping today's presidency, see Scott C. James, "The Evolution of the Presidency," in Joel D. Aberbach and Mark A. Peterson, eds., *The Executive Branch* (New York: Oxford University Press, 2005).

7. James P. Pfiffner, "Constraining Executive Power: George W. Bush and the Constitution," and Andrew Rudalevige, "A New Imperial Presidency?" both in James P. Pfiffner and Roger H. Davidson, eds., *Understanding the Presidency* (New York: Pearson Longman, 2009).

8. Jimmie Breslin, quoted in Laurence J. Peter, *Peter's Quotations* (New York: Morrow, 1977), p. 405.

9. See Edwards and Wayne, *Presidential Leadership,* ch. 12.

10. Ron Suskind, *Confidence Men* (New York: Harper, 2011).

11. Richard E. Neustadt, *Presidential Power and the Modern Presidents: The Politics of Leadership from Roosevelt to Reagan* (New York: Free Press, 1990); David E. Lewis and Terry M. Moe, "The Presidency and the Bureaucracy: The Levers of Presidential Control," in Michael Nelson, ed., *The Presidency and the Political System* (Washington, D.C.: CQ Press, 2010).

12. Howell, *Power Without Persuasion;* Phillip J. Cooper, *By Order of the President: The Use and Abuse of Executive Direct Action* (Lawrence: University of Kansas Press, 2002); Adam L. Warber, *Executive Orders and the Modern Presidency* (Boulder, CO: Lynne Rienner Publishers, 2006); Andrew Rudalevige, "The Presidency and Unilateral Power: A Taxonomy," in Nelson, *The Presidency and the Political System*.

13. Matthew Crenson and Benjamin Ginsberg, *Presidential Power, Unchecked and Unbalanced* (New York: Norton, 2007); Pfiffner, "Constraining Executive Power: George W. Bush and the Constitution"; Rudalevige, "A New Imperial Presidency?"; Richard Pious, "Prerogative Power and the War on Terrorism," in Pfiffner and Davidson, eds., *Understanding the Presidency*.

14. See John Yoo, *The Powers of War and Peace: The Constitution and Foreign Affairs After 9/11* (Chicago: University of Chicago Press, 2005). In contrast see Crenson and Ginsberg, *Presidential Power, Unchecked and Unbalanced*; and Waterman, "Assessing the Unilateral Presidency."

15. Graham T. Allison, *Essence of Decision: Explaining the Cuban Missile Crisis* (Boston: Little, Brown, 1971), pp. 141–142.

16. Neustadt, Presidential Power and the Modern Presidents, ch. 2.

17. Michael Nelson, "Neustadt's *Presidential Power* at 50," *The Chronicle of Higher Education*, March 28, 2010, pp. 1–7.

18. United States v. Curtiss-Wright (1936). For more on judicial interpretations of presidential powers in foreign policy and war, see R. Shep Melnick, "The Courts, Jurisprudence, and the Executive Branch," in Joel D. Aberbach and Mark A. Peterson, eds., *The Executive Branch* (New York: Oxford University Press, 2005); Richard A. Brisbin Jr., "The Judiciary and the Separation of Powers," in Kermit L. Hall and Kevin T. McGuire, eds., *The Judicial Branch* (New York: Oxford University Press, 2005).

19. Melnick, "The Courts, Jurisprudence, and the Executive Branch."

20. Edwards and Wayne, *Presidential Leadership*, p. 480.

21. Arthur Schlesinger Jr., *The Imperial Presidency* (New York: Popular Library, Atlantic Monthly Press, 1973).

22. Harvey Mansfield, "The Law and the President: In a National Emergency, Who You Gonna Call?" *Weekly Standard,* January 16, 2006, p. 1; Michael Stokes Paulsen, "The Constitution of Necessity," *Notre Dame Law Review* 79 (2004), p. 1257; Yoo, *The Powers of War and Peace*.

23. Bruce Ackerman, *Before the Next Attack* (New Haven, CT: Yale University Press, 2006); Crenson and Ginsberg, *Presidential Power, Unchecked and Unbalanced*; Sanford Levinson, *Our Undemocratic Constitution* (New York: Oxford University Press, 2006), pp. 104–107; Geoffrey R. Stone, *Perilous Times: Free Speech in Wartime* (New York: Norton, 2004).

24. Marjorie Randon Hershey, *Party Politics in America* (New York: Pearson, 2009), pp. 266–272; Sidney M. Milkis and

Jesse H. Rhodes, "George W. Bush, the Republican Party, and the New American Party System," *Perspectives on Politics* 5, no. 3 (September 2007), pp. 461–488.

25. James P. Pfiffner, *The Modern Presidency* (New York: St. Martin's Press, 1998), ch. 4. Also see Edwards and Wayne, *Presidential Leadership*, ch. 6; Pfiffner and Davidson, *Understanding the Presidency*, pp. 201–250.

26. Edwards and Wayne, *Presidential Leadership*, p. 209.

27. Suskind, *Confidence Men*.

28. Nathan Miller, *FDR: An Intimate History* (Lanham, MD: Madison Books, 1983), p. 276.

29. Thomas E. Cronin and Michael A. Genovese, *The Paradoxes of the American Presidency* (New York: Oxford University Press, 2004), ch. 10; Joseph A. Pika, "The Vice-Presidency: Dick Cheney, Joe Biden, and the New Vice Presidency," in Nelson, *The Presidency and the Political System*.

30. Edwards and Wayne, *Presidential Leadership*, p. 216.

31. Elizabeth Bumiller and Eric Schmitt, "In Indictment's Wake, A Focus on Cheney's Powerful Role in the White House," *The New York Times*, October 20, 2005, p. A1.

32. Stephen F. Hayes, *Cheney: The Untold Story of the Nation's Most Powerful and Controversial Vice President* (New York: Harper Collins, 2007); Barton Gellman, *Angler: The Cheney Vice Presidency* (New York: Penguin, 2008).

33. Charles O. Jones, *Separate but Equal: Congress and the Presidency* (New York: Chatham House, 1999); Roger H. Davidson, Walter J. Oleszek, and Frances E. Lee, *Congress and Its Members*, 13th ed. (Washington, D.C.: CQ Press, 2012), pp. 307–312; Roger H. Davidson, "Presidential Relations with Congress," in Pfiffner and Davidson, *Understanding the Presidency*.

34. Andrew Rudalevige, "The Executive Branch and the Legislative Process," in Joel D. Aberbach and Mark A. Peterson, eds., *The Executive Branch* (New York: Oxford University Press, 2005), pp. 432–445; Davidson, Oleszek, and Lee, *Congress and Its Members*, ch. 10.

35. Edwards and Wayne, *Presidential Leadership*, pp. 336–348; Jon R. Bond and Richard Fleisher, eds., *Polarized Politics: Congress and the President in a Partisan Era* (Washington, D.C.: CQ Press, 2000); Jeffrey S. Peake, "Back on Track," *American Politics Research*, November 2004, pp. 679–697.

36. Terry Sullivan, "Headcounts, Expectations and Presidential Coalitions in Congress," *American Journal of Political Science* 32 (1988), pp. 657–689; Davidson, Oleszek, and Lee, *Congress and Its Members*, pp. 305–306; Hershey, *Party Politics in America*, pp. 266–270.

37. "2009 Was the Most Partisan Year Ever," *Congressional Quarterly Weekly Report*, January 11, 2010, p. 1.

38. Aaron Wildavsky, "The Two Presidencies," in Aaron Wildavsky, ed., *Perspectives on the Presidency* (Boston: Little, Brown, 1975), pp. 448–461.

39. For a review of the leading scholarship on the various uses and consequences of the presidential veto see Charles M. Cameron, "The Presidential Veto," in Edwards and Howell, *The Oxford Handbook of the American Presidency*.

40. Roger H. Davidson, "Presidential Relations with Congress," in Pfiffner and Davidson, eds., *Understanding the Presidency*, pp. 253–272.

41. For the most sophisticated analysis of the effects of presidential approval on a president's success with Congress see George C. Edwards III, "Presidential Approval as a Source of Influence in Congress," in Edwards and Howell, *The Oxford Handbook of the American Presidency*. Also see Richard Brody, *Assessing the President: The Media, Elite Opinion, and Public Support* (Stanford, CA: Stanford University Press, 1991); George C. Edwards III, *At the Margins: Presidential Leadership of Congress* (New Haven, CT: Yale University Press, 1989); George C. Edwards III, "Aligning Tests with Theory: Presidential Approval as a Source of Influence in Congress," *Congress and the Presidency* 24 (Fall 1997), pp. 113–130.

42. Edwards and Wayne, *Presidential Leadership*, pp. 348–350.

43. Jeffrey K. Tulis, *The Rhetorical Presidency* (Princeton, NJ: Princeton University Press, 1987), chs. 2 and 3, esp. p. 64.

44. Woodrow Wilson, *Leaders of Men*, ed. T. H. Vail Motter (Princeton, NJ: Princeton University Press, 1952), p. 39; quoted in Tulis, *The Rhetorical Presidency*, ch. 4, which analyzes Wilson's theory at length and expresses some skepticism about it.

45. Tulis, *The Rhetorical Presidency*, pp. 138, 140.

46. Samuel Kernell, *Going Public: Strategies of Presidential Leadership*, 3rd ed. (Washington, D.C.: CQ Press, 1997), p. 92 and ch. 4.

47. Benjamin I. Page and Robert Y. Shapiro, "Presidents as Opinion Leaders: Some New Evidence," *Policy Studies Journal* 12 (1984), pp. 649–661; Benjamin I. Page, Robert Y. Shapiro, and Glenn R. Dempsey, "What Moves Public Opinion," *American Political Science Review* 81 (1987), pp. 23–43; but see Donald L. Jordan, "Newspaper Effects on Policy Preferences," *Public Opinion Quarterly* 57 (1993), pp. 191–204.

48. For an examination of the complexities of the scholarly literature on the effects of presidential opinion leadership see George C. Edwards III, "Leading the Public," in Edwards and Howell, *The Oxford Handbook of the American Presidency*.

49. Lawrence R. Jacobs and Robert Y. Shapiro, *Politicians Don't Pander: Political Manipulation and the Loss of Democratic Responsiveness* (Chicago: University of Chicago Press, 2000); Jacob Hacker and Paul Pierson, *Off Center* (New Haven, CT: Yale University Press, 2005).

50. Doris Graber, *Mass Media and American Politics*, 8th ed. (Washington, D.C.: CQ Press, 2010), ch. 9; Lawrence R. Jacobs, "Communicating from the White House," in Joel D. Aberbach and Mark A. Peterson, eds., *The Executive Branch* (New York: Oxford University Press, 2005), pp. 189–205.

51. Lawrence Jacobs and Robert Y. Shapiro, "The Rise of Presidential Polling: The Nixon White House in Historical Perspective," *Public Opinion Quarterly* 59 (1995), pp. 163–195; Jacobs, "Communicating from the White House," pp. 178–189.

52. W. Lance Bennett, Regina G. Lawrence, and Steven Livingston, *When the Press Fails: Political Power and the News Media from Iraq to Katrina* (Chicago: University of Chicago Press, 2007), ch. 5; Jacobs and Shapiro, *Politicians Don't Pander*; and James M. Druckman and Lawrence R. Jacobs, "Presidential Responsiveness to Public Opinion," in Edwards and Howell, *The Oxford Handbook of the American Presidency*.

53. Edwards and Wayne, *Presidential Leadership*, pp. 112–123.

54. Brody, *Assessing the President*. See also Edwards and Wayne, *Presidential Leadership*, pp. 112–123; John E. Mueller, "Presidential Popularity from Truman to Johnson," *American Political Science Review* 64 (1970), pp. 18–34; Samuel Kernell, "Explaining Presidential Popularity," *American Political Science Review* 72 (1978), pp. 506–522; George C. Edwards III, *Presidential Approval* (Baltimore, MD: Johns Hopkins University Press, 1990).

13

1. The quote is from "The Diddle Kingdom," *The Economist*, July 7, 2007, p. 63. Other sources for this chapter-opening story include Eric Lipton, "Safety Agency Faces Scrutiny Amid Charges," *The New York Times*, September 2, 2007, p. A1; Tom Lowry and Lorraine Woellert, "More Paper Tiger Than Watchdog?" *Businessweek*, September 3, 2007, p. 45.

2. Lipton, "Safety Agency Faces Scrutiny Amid Charges."

3. Max Weber, *Economy and Society* (London: Owen, 1962), vol. 1.

4. B. Guy Peters, *American Public Policy: Policy and Performance*, 8th ed. (New York: CQ Press, 2010), p. 43.

5. "A Tough Search for Talent," *The Economist* (October 31, 2011), p. 71.

6. See Charles T. Goodsell, *The Case for Bureaucracy*, 4th ed. (Washington, D.C.: CQ Press, 2003), p. 85; Kenneth J. Meier, "Representative Bureaucracy: An Empirical Analysis,"*American Political Science Review* 69 (June 1975), pp. 537–539; Katherine C. Naff, "Representative Bureaucracy," *Encyclopedia of Public Administration and Public Policy*, 2nd ed. (Piscataway, NJ: Rutgers University Press, 2008).

7. Wallace Sayre, "Bureaucracies: Some Contrasts in Systems," *Indian Journal of Public Administration* 10 (1964), p. 223. For contemporary evidence in support of this claim, see Gabriel A. Almond, G. Bingham Powell Jr., Kaare Strom, and Russell J. Dalton, *Comparative Politics Today* (New York: Pearson Longman, 2010), pp. 120–124.

8. John A. Rohr, *Civil Servants and Their Constitutions* (Lawrence: University of Kansas Press, 2002); Richard J. Stillman II, *The American Bureaucracy* (Chicago: Nelson-Hall, 1987), p. 18.

9. Rohr, *Civil Servants and Their Constitutions*, ch. 4; and David E. Lewis and Terry M. Moe, "The Presidency and the Bureaucracy: The Levers of Presidential Control," in Michael Nelson, ed., *The Presidency and the Political System* (Washington, D.C.: CQ Press, 2010).

10. Jay M. Shafritz, E. W. Russell, and Christopher P. Borick, *Introducing Public Administration* (New York: Pearson Longman, 2007), pp. 87–94; Peters, *American Public Policy: Policy and Performance*, pp. 114–121.

11. Peters, *American Public Policy*, p. 116.

12. Daniel Carpenter, "The Evolution of National Bureaucracy in the United States," in Joel D. Aberbach and Mark A. Peterson, eds., *The Executive Branch* (New York: Oxford University Press, 2005), pp. 55–57.

13. Peters, *American Public Policy*, p. 118.

14. Theodore J. Lowi, *The End of Liberalism*, 2nd ed. (New York: Norton, 1979); Christian Hunold and B. Guy Peters, "Bureaucratic Discretion and Deliberative Democracy," in Matti Malkia, Ari-Veikko Anttiroiko, and Reigo Savolainen, eds., *Transformation in Governance* (London: Idea Group. 2004), pp. 131–149.

15. Roger H. Davidson, Walter J. Oleszek, and Frances E. Lee, *Congress and Its Members*, 12th ed. (Washington, D.C.: CQ Press, 2010), p. 347.

16. Charles R. Shipan, "Congress and the Bureaucracy," in Paul J. Quirk and Sarah A. Binder, eds., *The Legislative Branch* (New York: Oxford University Press, 2005).

17. David Lewis, "Presidential Appointments and Personnel," *Annual Review of Political Science* 14 (2011), p. 52.

18. Patricia W. Ingraham, "The Federal Service: The People and the Challenge," in Joel D. Aberbach and Mark A. Peterson, eds.,*The Executive Branch* (New York: Oxford University Press, 2005), pp. 290–291.

19. Ibid., pp. 294–296.

20. See Samuel Krislov and David H. Rosenbloom, *Representative Bureaucracy and the American Political System* (New York: Praeger, 1981); Goodsell, *The Case for Bureaucracy*; Ingraham, "The Federal Service."

21. OECD (2005) as reported in "Public Service Careers," *The Economist* (October 31, 2009), p. 71.

22. Goodsell, *The Case for Bureaucracy*, pp. 84–90; Stanley Rothman and S. Robert Lichter, "How Liberal Are Bureaucrats?" *Regulation*, November–December 1983, pp. 35–47.

23. Office of Personnel Management, 2005.

24. Ingraham, "The Federal Service," pp. 291–294.

25. Lewis, "Presidential Appointments and Personnel," p. 48.

26. Richard P. Nathan, *The Administrative Presidency* (New York: Wiley, 1983).

27. David E. Rosenbaum and Stephen Labaton, "Amid Many Fights on Qualifications, a Nomination Stalls," *The New York Times*, September 24, 2005, p. A12.

28. Lewis, "Presidential Appointments and Personnel," p. 56.

29. Hugh Heclo, *A Government of Strangers* (Washington, D.C.: Brookings Institution, 1977), p. 103.

30. Richard E. Neustadt, *Presidential Power* (New York: Wiley, 1960); George C. Edwards III and Stephen J. Wayne, *Presidential Leadership: Politics and Policy Making* (Wadsworth, CA: Thomson Wadsworth, 2009), ch. 9.

31. Terry M. Moe, "Control and Feedback in Economic Regulation," *American Political Science Review* 79 (1985), pp. 1094–1116; Lewis and Moe, "The Presidency and the Bureaucracy: The Levers of Presidential Control," in Nelson,*The Presidency and the Political System*; Richard W. Waterman, *Presidential Influence and the Administrative State* (Knoxville: University of Tennessee Press, 1989); Edwards and Wayne, *Presidential Leadership*, pp. 295–303.

32. Richard W. Waterman and Kenneth J. Meier, "Principal-Agent Models: An Expansion?" *Journal of Public Administration Research and Theory* 8 (April 1998), pp. 173–202; Edwards and Wayne, *Presidential Leadership*, pp. 305–307.

33. For a review of research on the president's appointment powers see Joel D. Aberbach and Bert A. Rockman, "The Appointments Process and the Administrative Presidency," *Presidential Studies Quarterly* 39, no. 1 (January 2009), pp. 38–59.

34. See John Yoo, *The Powers of War and Peace: The Constitution and Foreign Affairs After 9/11* (Chicago: University of Chicago Press, 2005). In contrast see Matthew Crenson and Benjamin Ginsberg, *Presidential Power, Unchecked and Unbalanced* (New York: Norton, 2007).

35. James P. Pfiffner, "Constraining Executive Power: George W. Bush and the Constitution," in James P. Pfiffner and Roger H. Davidson, *Understanding the Presidency* (New York: Pearson Longman, 2009); Andrew Rudalevige, "The Presidency and Unilateral Power," in Michael Nelson, ed., *The Presidency and the Political System* (Washington, D.C.: CQ Press, 2010).

36. Lewis, "Presidential Appointments and Personnel," pp. 54–55; and Robert F. Durant and William G. Resh, "'Presidentializing' the Bureaucracy," in Robert F. Durant, ed., *The Oxford Handbook of American Bureaucracy* (New York: Oxford University Press, 2011).

37. Roger H. Davidson, Walter J. Oleszek, and Frances E. Lee, *Congress and Its Members*, 13th ed. (Washington, D.C.: CQ Press, 2012), pp. 317–343; George A. Krause, "Legislative Delegation of Authority to Bureaucratic Agencies," in Durant, ed., *The Oxford Handbook of American Bureaucracy*; and Steven S. Smith, Jason M. Roberts, and Ryan J. Vander Wielen, *The American Congress*, 5th ed. (New York: Cambridge University Press, 2007), pp. 291–301.

38. Lewis, "Presidential Appointments and Personnel," pp. 55–56; and Nolan McCarty and Rose Razahgian, "Advice and Consent: Senate Responses to Executive Branch Nominations, 1885–1996," *American Journal of Political Science* 43 (October 1999), pp. 1122–1143.

39. Richard Fenno, *The Power of the Purse* (Boston: Little, Brown, 1966); Aaron Wildavsky, *The Politics of the Budgetary Process* (Boston: Little, Brown, 1964); Davidson, Oleszek, and Lee, *Congress and Its Members*, pp. 354–355, 428–432.

40. "Wings Clipped: A Working Example of the Effects of Congressional Stupidity," *The Economist* (August 6, 2011), p. 40.

41. John A. Ferejohn and Charles R. Shipan, "Congressional Influence on Administrative Agencies: A Case Study of Telecommunications Policy," in Lawrence C. Dodd and Bruce I. Oppenheimer, eds., *Congress Reconsidered*, 4th ed. (Washington, D.C.: CQ Press, 1989); Davidson, Oleszek, and Lee, *Congress and Its Members*, pp. 356–357.

42. See Jerry L. Mashaw, "Bureaucracy, Democracy, and Judicial Review," in Durant, ed., *The Oxford Handbook of American Bureaucracy*.

43. Barry R. Weingast, "Caught in the Middle: The President, Congress, and the Political-Bureaucratic System," in Joel D. Aberbach and Mark A. Peterson, eds., *The Executive Branch* (New York: Oxford University Press, 2005), pp. 322–325.

44. Cornelius M. Kerwin, *Rulemaking: How Government Agencies Write Law and Make Policy* (Washington, D.C.: CQ Press, 2003), p. 183.

45. See especially Cornelius Kerwin, Scott Furlong, and William West, "Interest Groups, Rulemaking, and American Bureaucracy," in Durant, ed., *The Oxford Handbook of American Bureaucracy*, pp. 602–607. See Derek Bok, *The Trouble with Government* (Cambridge, MA: Harvard University Press, 2001), ch. 9; Emanuel S. Savas, *Privatization: The Key to Better Government* (Chatham, NJ: Chatham House, 1987); Sheila B. Kamerman and Alfred J. Kahn, eds., *Privatization and the Welfare State* (Princeton, NJ: Princeton University Press, 1989); Lester M. Salamon, ed., *The Tools of Government: A Guide to the New Governance* (Oxford, UK: Oxford University Press, 2002).

46. Moshe Schwartz, "Department of Defense Contractors in Iraq and Afghanistan: Background and Analysis" (Washington, D.C.: The Congressional Research Service, December 14, 2009).

47. Paul Light, *The Size of Government* (Washington, D.C.: Brookings, 1999); Paul Light, "Fact Sheet on the True Size of Government" (Washington, D.C.: Brookings Center for Public Service, 2004); Ingraham, "The Federal Public Service," pp. 301–303; Patricia Wallace Ingraham, "You Talking To Me? Accountability and the Modern Public Service," *PS* (January 2005), pp. 19–20.

48. Roll Call, online (www.rollcall.com/features/Outlook_Job-Creation/outlook/-209070-1.html).

49. Bernard Wysocki Jr., "Is U.S. Government Outsourcing Its Brain?" *The Wall Street Journal*, March 30, 2007, p. 1.

50. Bok, *The Trouble with Government*, pp. 233–234; Roberta Lynch and Ann Markusen, "Can Markets Govern?" *American Prospect*, Winter 1994, pp. 125–134; Dan Guttman, "Governance by Contract," *Public Contract Law Journal* 33 (Winter 2004), pp. 321–360.

51. John Cassidy, *How Markets Fail: The Logic of Economic Calamities* (New York: Farrar, Straus and Giroux, 2009).

52. David Osborne and Ted Gaebler, *Reinventing Government* (Reading, MA: Addison-Wesley, 1992).

53. Bok, *The Trouble with Government*, pp. 234–239; Joel D. Aberbach and Bert A. Rockman, eds., *In the Web of Politics: Three Decades of the U.S. Federal Executive* (Washington, D.C.: Brookings Institution Press, 2000); Lester M. Salamon, "The New Governance and the Tools of Public Administration," in Lester M. Salamon, ed., *The Tools of Government* (Oxford, UK: Oxford University Press, 2002); Steven G. Koven, "Bureaucracy, Democracy, and the New Public Management," in Ali Farazmand, ed., *Bureaucracy and Administration* (Boca Raton, FL: CRC Press, 2009).

54. Carpenter, "The Evolution of National Bureaucracy," pp. 63–64; Shafritz, Russell, and Borick, *Introducing Public Administration*, pp. 112–114.

55. Terry M. Moe, "The Politics of Bureaucratic Structure," in John E. Chubb and Paul E. Peterson, eds., *Can the Government Govern?* (Washington, D.C.: Brookings Institution, 1989), p. 280; John E. Chubb and Paul E. Peterson, "American Political Institutions and the Problem of Governance," in Chubb and Peterson, eds., *Can the Government Govern?*, p. 41; James L. Sundquist, *Constitutional Reform and Effective Government* (Washington, D.C.: Brookings Institution, 1986).

14

1. All quotes are from Neil A. Lewis, "Bitter Senators Divided Anew on Judgeships," *The Washington Post*, November 15, 2003, p. A1.

2. Jan Crawford Greenburg, *Supreme Conflict: The Inside Story of the Struggle for Control of the United States Supreme Court* (New York: Penguin, 2007); Jess Bravin, "Top Court Hands Conservatives Victories," *The Wall Street Journal*, June 26, 2007, p. 1; Linda Greenhouse, "In Steps Big and Small, Supreme Court Moves Right," *The New York Times*, July 1, 2007, p. A1; Lexington, "Supreme Success," *The Economist*, July 7, 2007, p. 36; "Conservatives Resurgent," *The Economist*, April 21, 2007, p. 34; and David M. O'Brien, *Storm Center: The Supreme Court in American Politics* (New York, Norton, 9th edition, 2011), pp. 28–29.

3. For strong empirical confirmation of the emergence of a strong conservative majority on the Court with the arrival on it of Samuel Alito, see Stephen A. Jessee and Alexander M. Tahk, "What Can We Learn About the Ideology of the Newest Supreme Court Justices?" *PS: Political Science and Politics* 44, no. 3 (July 2011), pp. 524–529.

4. O'Brien, *Storm Center*, ch. 1.

5. Akhil Reed Amar, *America's Constitution: A Biography* (New York: Random House, 2005), ch. 6.

6. J. M. Sosin, *The Aristocracy of the Long Robe: The Origins of Judicial Review in America* (Westport, CT: Greenwood Press, 1989); William E. Nelson, "The Historical Foundations of the American Judiciary," Kermit L. Hall, "Judicial Independence and the Majoritarian Difficulty," and Cass R. Sunstein, "Judges and Democracy: The Changing Role of the United States Supreme Court," in Kermit L. Hall and Kevin T. McGuire, eds., *The Judicial Branch* (New York: Oxford University Press, 2005).

7. Lee Epstein and Thomas G. Walker, *Rights, Liberties, and Justice* (Washington, D.C.: CQ Press, 2010), pp. 47, 53; Mark A. Graber, "Establishing Judicial Review? *Schooner Peggy* and the Early Marshall Court," *Political Research Quarterly* 51 (1998), pp. 221–239.

8. Robert G. McCloskey, *The American Supreme Court*, 4th ed. (Chicago: University of Chicago Press, 2005), pp. 12–13.

9. On *Marbury*, see Sylvia Snowmiss, *Judicial Review and the Law of the Constitution* (New Haven, CT: Yale University Press, 1990).

10. David O'Brien, *Constitutional Law and Politics, Vol. 2* (New York: Norton, 2008), p. 36.

11. Linda Greenhouse, "The Imperial Presidency vs. the Imperial Judiciary," *The New York Times*, March 2, 2000, Week in Review sec., p. 1; Paul Gewirtz and Chad Golder, "So Who Are the Activists?" *The New York Times*, July 6, 2005, p. A1.

12. See Ex parte Milligan (1866) and Youngstown Sheet and Tube Co. v. Sawyer (1952).

13. See Keith E. Whittington, "Judicial Checks on the President," in George C. Edwards III and William G. Howell, eds., *The Oxford Handbook of the American Presidency* (New York: Oxford University Press, 2009).

14. Robert A. Dahl, *How Democratic Is the American Constitution?* (New Haven, CT: Yale University Press, 2001), pp. 54–55. Also see Lawrence D. Kramer, *The People Themselves: Popular Constitutionalism and Judicial Review* (New York: Oxford University Press, 2004).

15. Alexander M. Bickel, *The Least Dangerous Branch: The Supreme Court at the Bar of Politics* (Indianapolis, IN: Bobbs-Merrill, 1962), pp. 16–18.

16. Robert A. Dahl, "Decision-Making in a Democracy: The Supreme Court as a National Policy Maker," *Journal of Public Law* 6 (1957), pp. 279–295; Mark A. Graber, "Constructing Judicial Review," *Annual Review of Political Science* 8 (2005), pp. 425–451.

17. Richard S. Randall, *American Constitutional Development* (New York: Longman, 2002), pp. 488–489.

18. Federal Court Management Statistics, 2011 (http://www.uscourts.gov/viewer.aspx?doc=/uscourts/Statistics/FederalCourtManagementStatistics/2011).

19. Ibid.

20. Neil Lewis, "An Appeals Court That Always Veers to the Right," *The New York Times*, May 24, 1999, p. A1; Deborah Sontag, "The Power of the Fourth," *The New York Times Sunday Magazine*, March 9, 2003, pp. 38–44.

21. Lawrence Baum, *The Supreme Court* (Washington, D.C.: CQ Press, 2010), pp. 6–10.

22. O'Brien, *Storm Center*, pp. 34–39. Also see Joel B. Grossman, "Paths to the Bench," in Kermit L. Hall and Kevin T. McGuire, eds., *The Judicial Branch* (New York: Oxford University Press, 2005), p. 162; and Lee Epstein, Jack Knight, and Andrew D. Martin, "The Norm of Judicial Experience," *University of California Law Review* 91 (2003), pp. 938–939.

23. Greenburg, *Supreme Conflict*.

24. Robert A. Carp and Ronald Stidham, *Judicial Process in America*, 6th ed. (Washington, D.C.: CQ Press, 2004), ch. 8; Grossman, "Paths to the Bench," pp. 160–161.

25. Baum, The Supreme Court, pp. 27–50; Ronald Brownstein, *The Second Civil War: How Extreme Partisanship Has Paralyzed Washington and Polarized America* (New York: Penguin, 2007); Greenburg, *Supreme Conflict;* Alan Wolfe, *Does American Democracy Still Work?* (New Haven, CT: Yale University Press, 2006), ch. 5.

26. Lee Epstein and Jeffrey A. Segal, "Nominating Federal Judges and Justices," in George C. Edwards III and William G. Howell, eds., *The Oxford Handbook of the American Presidency* (New York: Oxford University Press, 2009).

27. Lee Epstein and Jeffrey A. Segal, *Advice and Consent: The Politics of Judicial Appointments* (New York: Oxford University Press, 2005), ch. 3; Baum, *The Supreme Court*, pp. 27–50; Roger H. Davidson, Walter J. Oleszek, and Frances E. Lee, *Congress and Its Members*, 13th ed. (Washington, D.C.: CQ Press, 2012), pp. 362–368; and O'Brien, *Storm Center*, pp. 34–39.

28. Epstein and Segal, "Nominating Federal Judges and Justices," pp. 629–630 and 634–635.

29. Charlie Savage, "Obama Backers Fear Opportunities to Reshape Judiciary Are Slipping Away," *The New York Times* (November 14, 2009), p. 1.

30. Epstein and Segal, *Advice and Consent*, ch. 3; Epstein and Segal, "Nominating Federal Judges and Justices," pp. 634–635; Baum, *The Supreme Court*, pp. 123–125; Grossman, "Paths to the Bench"; Lawrence Baum, "The Supreme Court in American Politics," in Nelson W. Polsby, ed., *Annual Review of Political Science* (Palo Alto, CA: Annual Reviews, 2003), pp. 161–180; Dahl, "Decision-Making in a Democracy"; Ronald Stidham and Robert A. Carp, "Judges, Presidents, and Policy Choices," *Social Science Quarterly* 68 (1987), pp. 395–404; Carp and Stidham, *Judicial Process in America*, ch. 9.

31. See Bernard Schwartz, *Decision: How the Supreme Court Decides Cases* (New York: Oxford University Press, 2005).

32. Jeffrey Rosen, "So, Do You Believe in 'Super-Precedent'?" *The New York Times*, October 30, 2005, p. IV. 1.

33. Jeffrey A. Segal, Harold J. Spaeth, and Sara C. Benesh, *The Supreme Court in the American Legal System* (New York: Cambridge University Press, 2005), ch. 11; Epstein and Walker, *Rights, Liberties, and Justice*, pp. 57–63.

34. For details, see H. W. Perry Jr., *Deciding to Decide: Agenda Setting in the United States Supreme Court* (Cambridge, MA: Harvard University Press, 2005).

35. John Paul Stevens, *Five Chiefs: A Supreme Court Memoir* (New York: Little, Brown, 2011).

36. Perry, *Deciding to Decide*. For a current review of the extensive scholarly literature see Thomas M. Keck, "Party, Policy, or Duty: Why Does the Supreme Court Invalidate Federal Statutes?" *American Political Science Review* 101 (May 2007), pp. 321–338. Also see Epstein and Segal, *Advice and Consent*, ch. 5.

37. Segal, Spaeth, and Benesh, *The Supreme Court in the American Legal System,* pp. 318–323; David Adamany, "The Supreme Court," in John B. Gates and Charles A. Johnson, eds., *The American Courts* (Washington, D.C.: CQ Press, 1991),

pp. 111–112; Baum, "The Supreme Court in American Politics," pp. 162–168; Glendon Schubert, *The Judicial Mind* (Evanston, IL: Northwestern University Press, 1965); Jeffrey A. Segal and Harold J. Spaeth, *The Supreme Court and the Attitudinal Model* (New York: Cambridge University Press, 1993); John D. Sprague, *Voting Patterns of the United States Supreme Court* (Indianapolis, IN: Bobbs-Merrill, 1968); Tom S. Clark, "Measuring Ideological Polarization on the United States Supreme Court," *Political Research Quarterly* 20, no. 10 (May 2008), pp. 1–12; and Jessee and Tahk, "What Can We Learn About the Ideology of the Newest Supreme Court Justices?"

38. Walter Murphy, *Elements of Judicial Strategy* (Princeton, NJ: Princeton University Press, 1964); Lee Epstein and Jack Knight, *The Choices Justices Make* (Washington, D.C.: CQ Press, 1997).

39. Joel B. Grossman, "Social Backgrounds and Judicial Decision-Making," *Harvard Law Review* 79 (1966), pp. 1551–1564; S. Sidney Ulmer, "Dissent Behavior and the Social Background of Supreme Court Justices," *Journal of Politics* 32 (1970), pp. 580–589.

40. L. Epstein, J. Knight, and J. Martin, "The Supreme Court as a Strategic National Policy-Maker," *Emory Law Review* 50 (2001), pp. 583–610.

41. Jessee and Tahk, "What Can We Learn About the Ideology of the Newest Supreme Court Justices?"

42. Nicholas Wade, "A Mathematician Crunches the Supreme Court's Numbers," *The New York Times*, August 4, 2003, p. A21; Segal, Spaeth, and Benesh, *The Supreme Court in the American Legal System*, pp. 318–323; and Epstein and Segal, "Nominating Federal Judges and Justices," pp. 629–630 and 634–635.

43. John Harlan, "A Glimpse of the Supreme Court at Work," *University of Chicago Law School Record* 1, no. 7 (1963), pp. 35–52.

44. Bob Woodward and Scott Armstrong, *The Brethren: Inside the Supreme Court* (New York: Simon & Schuster, 1979).

45. Lee Epstein and Jack Knight, "Mapping Out the Strategic Terrain: The Informational Role of Amici Curiae," in Cornell Clayton and Howard Gillman, eds., *Supreme Court Decision-Making* (Chicago: University of Chicago Press, 1999); Segal, Spaeth, and Benesh, *The Supreme Court in the American Legal System*, chs. 12 and 13.

46. Herbert Jacob, *Justice in America*, 3rd ed. (Boston: Little, Brown, 1978), p. 245. Also see Keith E. Whittington, "Judicial Review and Interpretation," in Kermit L. Hall and Kevin T. McGuire, eds., *The Judicial Branch* (New York: Oxford University Press, 2005).

47. McCloskey, *The American Supreme Court*. Also see James H. Fowler and Sangick Jeon, "The Authority of Supreme Court Precedent," University of California, Davis, Working Paper (June 29, 2005).

48. Carp and Stidham, *Judicial Process in America*, p. 28.

49. Ibid., p. 57.

50. Mark A. Graber, "From Republic to Democracy: The Judiciary and the Political Process," in Kermit L. Hall and Kevin T. McGuire, eds., *The Judicial Branch* (New York: Oxford University Press, 2005).

51. McCloskey, *The American Supreme Court*. Also see H. W. Perry Jr., *The Transformation of the Supreme Court's Agenda: From the New Deal to the Reagan Administration* (Boulder, CO: Westview Press, 1991); Charles R. Epp, "The Supreme Court and the Rights Revolution," in Kermit L. Hall and Kevin T. McGuire, eds., *The Judicial Branch* (New York: Oxford University Press, 2005); Sunstein, "Judges and Democracy."

52. Hamdi v. Rumsfeld (2004).

53. Jessee and Tahk, "What Can We Learn About the Ideology of the Newest Supreme Court Justices?"

54. "Corporations and the Court: America's Supreme Court Is the Most Business-Friendly in Decades," *The Economist* (June 23, 2011), p. 17.

55. Steven Vago, *Law and Society* (New York: Prentice Hall, 2012), pp. 166–170.

56. Gewirtz and Golder, "So Who Are the Activists?" p. A29.

57. Ibid.

58. Neal Devins and Louis Fischer, *The Democratic Constitution* (New York: Oxford University Press, 2004); Larry D. Kramer, *The People Themselves: Popular Constitutionalism and Judicial Review* (New York: Oxford University Press, 2004).

59. See the discussion in Allison M. Martens, "Reconsidering Judicial Supremacy: From the Counter-Majoritarian Difficulty to Constitutional Transformations," *Perspectives on Politics* 5, no. 3 (September 2007), pp. 447–459.

60. Epstein and Walker, *Rights, Liberties, and Justice*, pp. 22–28.

61. James V. Calvi and Susan Coleman, *American Law and Legal Systems* (New York: Longman, 2012), pp. 148–150.

62. Stephen Breyer, *Active Liberty: Interpreting Our Democratic Constitution* (New York: Knopf, 2005); and Cass Sunstein, *A Constitution of Many Minds: Why the Founding Document Doesn't Mean What It Meant Before* (Princeton, NJ: Princeton University Press, 2009).

63. Graber, "Constructing Judicial Review"; Thomas M. Keck, *The Most Activist Supreme Court in History: The Road to Modern Judicial Conservatism* (Chicago: University of Chicago Press, 2004); George I. Lovell, *Legislative Deferrals: Statutory Ambiguity, Judicial Power, and American Democracy* (New York: Cambridge University Press, 2003); Kevin K. McMahon, *Reconsidering Roosevelt on Race: How the Presidency Paved the Way for Brown* (Chicago: University of Chicago Press, 2004); Keith E. Whittington, *Political Foundations of Judicial Supremacy: The Presidency, the Supreme Court, and Constitutional Leadership in U.S. History* (Princeton, NJ: Princeton University Press, 2007). Also see Bruce Ackerman, *We the People: Transformations* (Cambridge, MA: Harvard University Press, 2000); McCloskey, *The American Supreme Court*.

64. Baum, "The Supreme Court in American Politics," p. 167; Davidson, Oleszek, and Lee, *Congress and Its Members*, pp. 354–355.

65. See Davidson, Oleszek, and Lee, *Congress and Its Members*, pp. 354–358, for a discussion of legislative checks on the judiciary.

66. Tom S. Clark, "The Separation of Powers, Court Curbing, and Judicial Legitimacy," *American Journal of Political Science* 53, no. 4 (October 2009), pp. 971–989.

67. Lisa A. Solowiej and Paul M. Collins Jr., "Counteractive Lobbying in the U.S. Supreme Court," *American Politics Research* 37, no. 4 (2009), pp. 670–699.

68. Edward Lazarus, *Closed Chambers* (New York: Penguin, 1999), pp. 373–374.

69. Epstein and Knight, "Mapping Out the Strategic Terrain."

70. Dahl, "Decision-Making in a Democracy," pp. 279–295; Thomas R. Marshall, "Public Opinion, Representation, and the Modern Supreme Court," *American Politics Quarterly* 16 (1988), pp. 296–316; McCloskey, *The American Supreme Court*, p. 22; O'Brien, *Storm Center*, p. 337; Baum, *The Supreme Court*, pp. 142–144.

71. G. Caldeira, "Courts and Public Opinion," in John B. Gates and Charles A. Johnson, eds., *The American Courts* (Washington, D.C.: CQ Press, 1991); Jay Casper, "The Supreme Court and National Policy Making," *American Political Science Review* 70 (1976), pp. 50–63; Marshall, "Public Opinion, Representation, and the Modern Supreme Court"; William Mishler and Reginald S. Sheehan, "The Supreme Court as a Counter-Majoritarian Institution: The Impact of Public Opinion on Supreme Court Decisions," *American Political Science Review* 87 (1993), pp. 87–101; Benjamin I. Page and Robert Y. Shapiro, "Effects of Public Opinion on Policy," *American Political Science Review* 77 (1983), p. 183.

72. Segal, Spaeth, and Benesh, *The Supreme Court in the American Legal System*, pp. 326–328; Baum, *The Supreme Court*, pp. 140–142.

15

1. These and other examples of campus speech codes, as well as an extended discussion of the controversies surrounding them, can be found in Donald Alexander Downs, *Restoring Free Speech and Liberty on Campus* (New York: Cambridge University Press, 2005).

2. Nat Hentoff, "Chilling Codes," *Washington Post*, Nexis: LEGISLATE Article No. 225/226.

3. On the "contract clause" see Lee Epstein and Thomas G. Walker, *Constitutional Law for a Changing America* (Washington, D.C.: CQ Press, 2005), ch. 9.

4. James E. Ely Jr., "Property Rights and Democracy in the American Constitutional Order," in Kermit L. Hall and Kevin T. McGuire, eds., *The Judicial Branch* (New York: Oxford University Press, 2005); Richard Fallon, *The Dynamic Constitution: An Introduction to American Constitutional Law* (New York: Cambridge University Press, 2004), ch. 3, "Protection of Economic Liberties."

5. Laurence H. Tribe, *American Constitutional Law*, 3rd ed. (New York: Foundation Press, 2000), ch. 9.

6. Morton J. Horwitz, *The Transformation of American Law, 1780–1860* (Cambridge, MA: Harvard University Press, 1977); J. Willard Hurst, *Law and the Conditions of Freedom in the Nineteenth-Century United States* (Madison: University of Wisconsin Press, 1956).

7. Lee Epstein and Thomas G. Walker, *Rights, Liberties, and Justice* (Washington, D.C.: CQ Press, 2010), pp. 67–87, 93–94.

8. Adam Liptak, "A Liberal Case for Gun Rights Sways Judiciary," *The New York Times*, May 6, 2007, p. A1; Sanford Levinson, "The Embarrassing Second Amendment," *Yale Law Review* 99 (1989), pp. 637–659.

9. See Lucius J. Barker, Twiley W. Barker Jr., Michael W. Combs, Kevin L. Lyles, and H. W. Perry Jr., *Civil Liberties and the Constitution: Cases and Commentaries* (New York: Longman, 2011), pp. 153–156.

10. Gregory C. Shaffer, "Law and Business," in Graham Wilson, Wyn Grant, and David Coen, eds., *The Oxford Handbook of Business and Government* (New York: Oxford University Press, 2010), p. 68.

11. Barker et al., *Civil Liberties and the Constitution*, pp. 32–37; Epstein and Walker, *Constitutional Law for a Changing America*, pp. 431–438; Anthony Lewis, *Freedom for the Thought That We Hate: A Biography of the First Amendment* (New York: Basic Books, 2007); John C. Domino, *Civil Rights and Liberties in the 21st Century* (New York: Pearson Longman, 2010), ch. 2.

12. See Geoffrey R. Stone, *Perilous Times: Free Speech in Wartime* (New York: W. W. Norton, 2004).

13. See Stanley I. Kutler, *The American Inquisition: Justice and Injustice in the Cold War* (New York: Hill & Wang, 1982).

14. David Stout, "FBI Head Admits Mistakes in Use of Security Act," *The New York Times*, March 10, 2007, p. A1; "FBI Underreported Patriot Act Use," *The Wall Street Journal*, March 9, 2007, p. 1.

15. See Fred W. Friendly, *Minnesota Rag* (New York: Vintage, 1981).

16. Barker et al., *Civil Liberties and the Constitution*, pp. 169–178; Epstein and Walker, *Rights, Liberties, and Justice*, pp. 292–295; and Alpheus Thomas Mason and Donald Grier Stephenson Jr., *American Constitutional Law* (New York: Longman, 2012), pp. 463–467.

17. See Charles Rembar, *The End of Obscenity* (New York: Harper & Row, 1968).

18. Fallon, The *Dynamic Constitution*, p. 48.

19. Barker et al., Civil Liberties and the Constitution, pp. 204–205.

20. Epstein and Walker, *Rights, Liberties, and Justice*, pp. 145–192.

21. Fallon, *The Dynamic Constitution*, pp. 61–67.

22. Ibid., p. 63.

23. Adam Liptak, "Religious Groups Given 'Exception' to Work Bias Law," *The New York Times*, January 11, 2012, p. 1.

24. Fallon, *The Dynamic Constitution*, p. 45.

25. Eva R. Rubin, *Abortion, Politics, and the Courts* (Westport, CT: Greenwood Press, 1982), ch. 2.

26. Kristen Luker, *Abortion and the Politics of Motherhood* (Berkeley: University of California Press, 1984), ch. 2.

27. "World Prison Brief" (London: International Center for Prison Studies, Kings College, London, press release, June 8, 2011).

28. Epstein and Walker, *Rights, Liberties, and Justice*, pp. 447–448.

29. Katz v. United States (1967).

30. United States v. Leon (1984); Massachusetts v. Sheppard (1984).

31. *Nix v. Williams* (1984).

32. Harris v. New York (1971); New York v. Quarles (1984).

33. Arizona v. Fulminate (1991).

34. Jim Yardley, "A Role Model for Executions," *The New York Times*, January 9, 2000, p. A1, IV–5.

35. Gallup Poll, October 1–4, 2009. Mason and Stephenson Jr., *American Constitutional Law*, p. 396.

36. For all data in this paragraph, see the Fact Sheet, Death Penalty Information Center (http://www.deathpenaltyinfo.org/documents/FactSheet.pdf) accessed March 16, 2012.

37. Stone, Perilous Times: Free Speech in Wartime; Fallon, The Dynamic Constitution, ch. 12.

38. Former Chief Justice William Rehnquist believed that each successive American war involved fewer and less serious violations of civil liberties. See *All the Laws But One: Civil Liberties in Wartime* (New York: Knopf, 1998).

39. "Security Trumps Civil Liberties," a report of a poll conducted by National Public Radio, the Kennedy School of Government of Harvard University, and the Kaiser Family Fund (November 30, 2001).

40. David Stout, "FBI Head Admits Mistakes in Use of Security Act," *The New York Times* (March 10, 2007), p. 1.

41. Barton Gellman, "The FBI's Secret Scrutiny," *The Washington Post*, November 6, 2005, p. A1.

42. Pew Research Center, "Threat of Terrorism and Civil Liberties" (December 3, 2009).

43. Kent Roach, *The 9/11 Effect: Comparative Counter-Terrorism* (New York: Cambridge University Press, 2011); and Adam Liptak, "Civil Liberties Today," *The New York Times*, September 11, 2011, p. 14.

16

1. Greg Winter, "Schools Resegregate, Study Finds," *The New York Times*, January 21, 2003, p. A14.

2. Gary Orfield, *Reviving the Goal of an Integrated Society: A 21st Century Challenge* (Los Angeles: University of California at Los Angeles, The Civil Rights Project, 2009).

3. Ibid.

4. Ibid. Also see Charles T. Clotfelter, *After Brown: The Rise and Retreat of School Desegregation* (Princeton, NJ: Princeton University Press, 2004).

5. A recent study shows a decrease in the extent of white-only areas in American cities primarily because of the influx of Latino and Asian populations. The divide between non-Hispanic whites and blacks remains relatively unchanged. See Sam Roberts, "Segregation Curtailed in U.S. Cities, Study Finds," *The New York Times*, January 30, 2012, p. 1.

6. Lucius J. Barker, Twiley W. Barker Jr., Michael W. Combs, Kevin L. Lyles, and H. W. Perry Jr., *Civil Liberties and the Constitution* (New York: Longman, 2011), pp. 446–447; Richard H. Fallon, *The Dynamic Constitution: An Introduction*

to Constitutional Law (New York: Cambridge University Press, 2004), pp. 109–110; John C. Domino, *Civil Rights and Liberties in the 21st Century* (New York: Pearson Longman, 2010), pp. 2–3.

7. James MacGregor Burns and Stewart Burns, *A People's Charter: The Pursuit of Rights in America* (New York: Knopf, 1991), p. 37.

8. On why the courts were such an attractive target for people seeking to expand civil rights, see Charles R. Epp, "The Courts and the Rights Revolution," in Kermit L. Hall and Kevin T. McGuire, eds., *The Judicial Branch* (New York: Oxford University Press, 2005).

9. William H. Chafe, *The Unfinished Journey: America Since World War II* (New York: Oxford University Press, 1986), p. 149.

10. Fallon, *The Dynamic Constitution*, pp. 118–120.

11. Ibid., pp. 119–122. Also see Lee Epstein and Thomas G. Walker, *Rights, Liberty, and Justice* (Washington, D.C.: CQ Press, 2010), pp. 593–601.

12. Domino, *Civil Rights and Liberties in the 21st Century*, p. 297; Chafe, *The Unfinished Journey*, pp. 79–110.

13. Epp, "The Courts and the Rights Revolution."

14. CBS News/*New York Times* Poll (July 7–14, 2008); and "Anti-Hispanic Discrimination Still Felt Around the Country," Pew Hispanic Center, March 31, 2011.

15. For additional survey data on these issues, see "A Year After Obama's Election" (Washington, D.C.: Pew Research Center, January 12, 2010).

16. Assistant Attorney General Thomas E. Perez, "Findings Announcement: Maricopa County Sheriff's Office Investigation," (Washington, D.C.: U.S. Department of Justice, December 15, 2011).

17. Campbell Robertson, "Alabama Wins in Ruling on Its Immigration Law," *The New York Times*, September 28, 2011, p. 1.

18. This section is based on Richard D. Kahlenberg, *The Remedy: Class, Race, and Affirmative Action* (New York: Basic Books, 1996); Fallon, *The Dynamic Constitution*, ch. 5.

19. Ira Katznelson, *When Affirmative Action Was White: An Untold Story of Racial Inequality in Twentieth-Century America* (New York: W. W. Norton, 2005), pp. 145–149.

20. Barker et al., *Civil Liberties and the Constitution*, pp. 514–517.

21. Katznelson, *When Affirmative Action Was White*.

22. Martin Gilens, Paul M. Sniderman, and James H. Kuklinski, "Affirmative Action and the Politics of Realignment," *British Journal of Political Science* 28 (January 1998), pp. 159–184; Jack Citrin, David O. Sears, Christopher Muste, and Cara Wong, "Multiculturalism in American Public Opinion," *British Journal of Political Science* 31 (2001), pp. 247–275.

23. "Public Backs Affirmative Action, But Not Minority Preferences" (Washington, D.C.: Pew Research Center, June 2, 2009); "Trends in Political Values and Core Attitudes: 1987–2007" (Washington, D.C.: Pew Research Center, 2007).

24. George M. Fredrickson, "Still Separate and Unequal," *The New York Review of Books*, November 17, 2005, p. 13.

25. In *Hunt v. Cromartie* (1999), the Court ruled in favor of the redrawn Twelfth Congressional District in North Carolina, presumably because race was not the only consideration in drawing district lines.

26. Opinion of the Court, *Grutter v. Bollinger* (2003).

27. Meredith v. Jefferson County Board of Education (2007); Parents Involved in Community Schools v. Seattle School District No. 1 (2007).

28. Epstein and Walker, *Rights, Liberty, and Justice*, pp. 686–687.

29. A. Judith Baer and Leslie Friedman Goldstein, *The Constitutional and Legal Rights of Women* (Belmont, CA: Roxbury Publishing, 2006); Chafe, *The Unfinished Journey*; Barbara Sinclair

Deckard, *The Women's Movement* (New York: Harper and Row, 1975); Ethel Klein, *Gender Politics* (Cambridge, MA: Harvard University Press, 1984), ch. 2; J. Freeman, *Politics of Women's Liberation* (New York: McKay, 1975).

30. See Epp, "Courts and the Rights Revolution"; Fallon, *The Dynamic Constitution*, pp. 129–133; and Barker et al., *Civil Liberties and the Constitution*, pp. 689–691.

31. Epstein and Walker, *Rights, Liberties, and Justice*, p. 629.

32. For sharply conflicting views on the seriousness of the wage gap, see testimony on the Paycheck Fairness Act before the House Committee on Education and Labor on September 11, 2007, by Marcia Greenberger and before the Senate Committee on Health, Labor and Pensions on April 12, 2007, by Barbara Berish Brown.

33. Sam Roberts, "For Young Earners in Big City, a Gap in Women's Favor," *The New York Times*, August 3, 2007, p. A1. The article is based on research reported by Professor Andrew Beveridge of Queens College.

34. Harris Poll, July 2007.

35. Linda Greenhouse, "Justices Give the States Immunity from Suits by Disabled Workers," *The New York Times*, February 22, 2001, p. A1.

36. Kenneth Sherrill and Alan Yang, "From Outlaws to In-Laws," *Public Perspectives*, January/February 2000, pp. 20–23; "The Agony and the Ecstasy," *The Economist*, July 2, 2005.

37. Pew Research Center, "The American-Western European Values Gap," press release, November 22, 2011.

38. The Gallup Poll, May 2011; and Dorothy Samuels, "A Long, Winding Road to Marriage Equality," *The New York Times*, November 12, 2011, p. 1

39. National Council of State Legislatures, January 2010.

40. Samuels, "A Long, Winding Road to Marriage Equality," p. 1.

17

1. For general accounts see John Cassidy, *How Markets Fail* (New York: Farrar, Straus and Giroux, 2009); Carmen M. Reinhart and Kenneth Rogoff, *This Time Is Different: Eight Centuries of Financial Folly* (Princeton, NJ: Princeton University Press, 2009); Joseph E. Stiglitz, *Freefall: America, Free Markets and the Sinking of the World Economy* (New York: W. W. Norton, 2010).

2. National Bureau of Economic Analysis, "National Income and Product Accounts" (Washington, D.C.: U.S. Department of Commerce, press release, July 31, 2009). Also Robert E. Lucas Jr., "The U.S. Recession of 2007–201?," (Seattle: University of Washington, The Milliman Lecture, May 19, 2011).

3. Bureau of Labor Statistics.

4. U.S. Department of Labor, May 21, 2010.

5. George W. Bush, *Decision Points* (New York: Crown Books, 2010).

6. In the end, TARP expenditures and tax cuts came to less than $500 billion and, because of sales later on of troubled assets, came close to breaking even.

7. CNN/Opinion Research Corporation Poll (February 12–15, 2010).

8. This well-known relationship is supported by substantial research. See Robert S. Erikson and Kent L. Tedin, *American Public Opinion* (New York: Longman, 2011), pp. 121–122.

9. Fred C. Pampel, *Age, Class, Politics, and the Welfare State* (New York: Cambridge University Press, 1989), p. 16; Harold Wilensky, *The Welfare State and Equality* (Berkeley, CA: University of California Press, 1975).

10. Robert E. Goodin, "Reasons for Welfare," in J. Donald Moon, ed., *Responsibility, Rights, and Welfare: The Theory of the Welfare State* (Boulder, CO: Westview Press, 1988); and Wilensky, *The Welfare State and Equality*. See also Clark Kerr, John T. Dunlop, Frederick H. Harbison, and Charles A.

Myers, *Industrialism and Industrial Man* (New York: Oxford University Press, 1964).

11. Dean Baker and Kevin Hassett, "The Human Disaster of Unemployment," *The New York Times* (May 12, 2012), p. 1.

12. This discussion is based largely on B. Guy Peters, *American Public Policy: Promise and Performance*, 8th ed. (New York: CQ Press, 2010), pp. 202–213.

13. On the benefits of economic growth see William J. Baumol, Robert E. Litan, and Carl J. Schramm, *Good Capitalism, Bad Capitalism, and the Economics of Growth and Prosperity* (New Haven, CT: Yale University Press, 2007), ch. 2; Gregg Easterbrook, *The Progress Paradox* (New York: Random House, 2003).

14. Several Southern European countries such as Greece, Italy, Portugal, and Spain also have substantial structural deficits (meaning long-term; not tied to short-term problems like economic stimulus during down economic times) arising from an unwillingness to properly fund and/or size old age pension and health care systems.

15. Sharon Terlep, "Target at Post-Bailout GM: Earning $10 Billion a Year," *The Wall Street Journal*, February 6, 2012, p. 1.

16. Zachary Karabell, "Does Government Matter?" *Bloomberg/Businessweek*, July 4–July 10, 2011, pp. 10–11.

17. Roger Lowenstein, "The Education of Ben Bernanke," *The Sunday New York Times Magazine*, January 20, 2008, pp. 36–39, 61–68.

18. See David Coen, Wyn Grant, and Graham Wilson, "Political Science: Perspectives on Business and Government," in David Coen, Wyn Grant, and Graham Wilson, eds., *The Oxford Handbook of Business and Government* (New York: Oxford University Press, 2010), pp. 20–24.

19. See "The Keynes Comeback," *The Economist*, October 3, 2009, pp. 103–104; Noam Scheiber, "Market Riot," *Foreign Policy* (December 2009), pp. 45–48. The theorist of financial crises, Hyman Minsky, also gained new adherents, given his near-perfect prediction in his 1986 book *Stabilizing an Unstable Economy* of what came to a head in 2008.

20. John Cassidy, *How Markets Fail: The Logic of Economic Calamities* (New York: Farrar, Straus and Giroux, 2009).

21. Peters, *American Public Policy*, pp. 142–144.

22. The following discussion of the budget-making process is based on Roger H. Davidson, Walter J. Oleszek, and Frances E. Lee, *Congress and Its Members*, 13th ed. (Washington, D.C.: CQ Press, 2012), pp. 416–434; Peters, *American Public Policy*, pp. 141–151.

23. The data on the budget in these sections are from *The Budget of the United States Government, Fiscal Year 2013* and "The Peoples' Guide to the Federal Budget," The National Priorities Project online at http://nationalpriorities.org/resources/federal-budget-101/peoples-guide.

24. For a concise and stimulating discussion of forms of taxation and their effects, as well as the politics surrounding them see B. Guy Peters, "Tax Policy," in B. Guy Peters and Jon Pierre, eds., *Handbook of Public Policy* (Thousand Oaks, CA: Sage, 2006), pp. 281–292; and Bruce Bartlett, *The Benefit and the Burden* (New York: Simon & Schuster, 2012).

25. The 2011 number is from the Congressional Budget Office (April 15, 2011); the 2012 number is from *The Budget of the United States Government, Fiscal Year 2013*.

26. The Budget of the United States Government, Fiscal Year 2013.

27. Peters, *American Public Policy*, pp. 229–231; "Effective Tax Rates," The National Bureau of Economic Research, 2010.

28. Steven Rattner, "The Dangerous Notion That Debt Doesn't Matter," *The New York Times*, January 20, 2012, p. 1.

29. Jackie Calmes, "Party Gridlock in Washington Feeds Fear of a Debt Crisis," *The New York Times*, February 17, 2010, p. 1.

30. David Leonhardt, "In Greek Debt Crisis, Some See Parallels to U.S." *The New York Times*, May 12, 2010, p. 1.

31. George J. Stigler, "The Theory of Economic Regulation," *Bell Journal* 2 (Spring 1971), pp. 3–21. Also see Gabriel Kolko, *The Triumph of Conservatism* (Chicago: Quadrangle, 1967); James Weinstein, *The Corporate Ideal in the Liberal State* (Boston: Beacon Press, 1968).

32. See Marc Allen Eisner, *Regulatory Politics in Transition* (Baltimore: Johns Hopkins University Press, 2000); Richard Harris and Sidney Milkis, *The Politics of Regulatory Change* (New York: Oxford University Press, 1989); and Michael Moran, "The Rise of the Regulatory State," in Coen, Grant, and Wilson, eds., *The Oxford Handbook of Business and Government*, pp. 383–403.

33. See G. William Domhoff, *The Higher Circles* (New York: Random House, 1970); Edward S. Greenberg, *Capitalism and the American Political Ideal* (Armonk, NY: M. E. Sharpe, 1985); Kolko, *The Triumph of Conservatism*; Weinstein, *The Corporate Ideal in the Liberal State*.

34. Frances Fox Piven and Richard A. Cloward, *Poor People's Movements* (New York: Vintage, 1979).

35. Marver Bernstein, *Regulation by Independent Commission* (Princeton, NJ: Princeton University Press, 1955); Grant McConnell, *Private Power and American Democracy* (New York: Vintage Books, 1966); Theodore J. Lowi, *The End of Liberalism* (New York: Norton, 1979).

36. David Vogel, *Fluctuating Fortunes: The Political Power of Business in the United States* (New York: Basic Books, 1989), pp. 59, 112.

37. James Buchanan and Gordon Tullock, "Polluters, Profits and Political Responses: Direct Control versus Taxes," *American Economic Review* 65 (1975), pp. 139–147; L. Lave, *The Strategy of Social Regulation* (Washington, D.C.: Brookings Institution, 1981); Murray Weidenbaum, *The Costs of Government Regulation of Business* (Washington, D.C.: Joint Economic Committee of Congress, 1978).

38. See Thomas Byrne Edsall, *The New Politics of Inequality* (New York: Norton, 1984); Vogel, Fluctuating Fortunes; Kevin P. Phillips, *The Politics of Rich and Poor: Wealth and the American Electorate in the Reagan Aftermath* (New York: Random House, 1990); Thomas Ferguson and Joel Rogers, *Right Turn: The Decline of the Democrats and the Future of American Politics* (New York: Farrar, Straus & Giroux, 1986).

39. Catherine Rampell, "Lax Oversight Caused Crisis, Bernanke Says," *The New York Times*, January 6, 2001, p. 1.

40. For accessible descriptions of this shadow banking system and its risky practices, see Simon Johnson and James Kwak, *13 Bankers: The Wall Street Takeover and the Next Financial Meltdown* (New York: Pantheon, 2010); Michael Lewis, *The Big Short: Inside the Doomsday Machine* (New York: W. W. Norton, 2010); Roger Lowenstein, *The End of Wall Street* (New York: Penguin, 2010).

41. "How the European Union Is Becoming the World's Chief Regulator," *The Economist*, September 22, 2007, p. 66.

42. Andrew Martin, "Child-Product Makers Seek to Soften New Rules," *The New York Times*, February 21, 2011, p. 1.

43. "Historical Tables," Budget of the United States Government, Fiscal Year 2013.

44. Howard Jacob Karger and David Stoesz, *American Welfare State Policy: A Pluralist Approach* (Boston: Allyn & Bacon, 2010), pp. 260–261.

45. Diana M. DiNitto, *Social Welfare: Politics and Public Policy* (Boston: Pearson Allyn & Bacon, 2007), p. 138.

46. Jacob S. Hacker, *The Great Risk Shift* (New York: Oxford University Press, 2006), ch. 2.

47. *The 2011 OASDI Trustees Report* (Washington, D.C.: The Social Security Administration, 2011).

48. Mark Penn, *Microtrends: The Small Forces Behind Tomorrow's Big Changes* (New York: Twelve, the Hachette Book Group. 2007), pp. 31–34.

49. Benjamin I. Page and James R. Simmons, *What Government Can Do: Dealing with Poverty and Inequality* (Chicago: University of Chicago Press, 2000), ch. 3; Edmund L. Andrews, "4 Ways That Might Save the Government Trillions," *The New York Times*, February 4, 2006, p. A7; Peters, *American Public Policy*, pp. 300–311.

50. *The Social Security Fix-It Book* (Boston: Boston College Center for Retirement Research, 2010).

51. Ibid.

52. Edward P. Lazear, "The Virtues of Personal Accounts for Social Security," *The Economists' Voice* 2, no. 1 (2005), pp. 1–7.

53. Kaiser Family Foundation, "Medicare at a Glance," press release, November 2011.

54. DiNitto, *Social Welfare*, pp. 310–318.

55. "U.S. Pensions Found to Lift Many of the Poor," *The New York Times*, December 28, 1989, p. A1. See also Theodore R. K. Marmor, Jerry L. Mashaw, and Philip L. Harvey, *America's Misunderstood Welfare State* (New York: HarperCollins, 1990), ch. 4.

56. David S. Johnson, "2008 Income, Poverty, and Health Insurance Estimates for the Current Population Survey" (Washington, D.C.: U.S. Census Bureau, September 10, 2009).

57. U.S. Bureau of the Census, Statistical Abstracts of the United States, 2010.

58. Jason Furman, *Top Ten Facts on Social Security's 70th Anniversary* (Washington, D.C.: Center on Budget and Policy Priorities, 2007).

59. Peters, American Public Policy, p. 311.

60. "Americans Dissatisfied with Government's Efforts on Poverty," The Gallup Poll, October 25, 2005; "Majority Call Fighting Poverty a Top Priority," Zogby International Poll, press release, June 4, 2007.

61. Hugh Heclo, "The Political Foundations of Anti-Poverty Policy," in Sheldon Danziger and Daniel Weinberg, eds., *Fighting Poverty: What Works and What Doesn't?* (Cambridge, MA: Harvard University Press, 1986); Fay Lomax Cook and Edith J. Barrett, *Support for the American Welfare State: The Views of Congress and the Public* (New York: HarperCollins, 1990), ch 4.

62. Joel F. Handler and Yeheskel Hasenfeld, *Blame Welfare, Ignore Poverty and Inequality* (Cambridge, UK: Cambridge University Press, 2007); Martin Gilens, *Why Americans Hate Welfare: Race, Media, and the Politics of Antipoverty Policy* (Chicago: The University of Chicago Press, 1999).

63. Sandra K. Danziger, "The Decline of Cash Welfare and Implications for Social Policy and Poverty," *Annual Review of Sociology* 36 (2010), pp. 523–545.

64. "From Welfare to Work," *The Economist*, July 29, 2006, pp. 27–30; Lauren Etter, "Welfare Reform: Ten Years Later," *The Wall Street Journal*, August 26, 2006, p. A9; Robert Pear and Erik Eckholm, "A Decade After Welfare Reform," *The New York Times*, August 21, 2006, p. A12.

65. Ibid.

66. Karger and Stoesz, *American Social Welfare Policy*, pp. 277–280.

67. Robert Pear, "In a Tough Economy, Old Limits on Welfare," *The New York Times*, April 10, 2010, p. 1.

68. Number calculated by the authors from data from SNAP Factsheet, U.S. Department of Agriculture at www.fns.usda.gov/cga/FactSheets/SNAP.pdf. Also see Robert Greenstein, *Dispelling Confusion on Food Stamps, Tax Rebates, and the Stimulus Package* (Washington, D.C.: Center on Budget and Policy Priorities, January 26, 2008); John E. Schwarz, *America's Hidden Success: A Reassessment of Public Policy from Kennedy to Reagan* (New York: Norton, 1988), p. 37; and Karger and Stoesz, *American Social Welfare Policy*, pp. 453–456.

69. Karger and Stoesz, *American Social Welfare Policy*, p. 310.

70. Ibid., p. 311.

71. DiNitto, *Social Welfare*, pp. 302–310.

72. "Income, Poverty, and Health Insurance Coverage in the United States: 2010," (Washington, D.C.: U.S. Census Bureau, September 2011).

73. *What Is SCHIP* (Washington, D.C.: Center for Budget and Policy Priorities, 2007).

74. Peters, American Public Policy, p. 320; Howard, The Hidden Welfare State, ch. 3.

75. Robert Greenstein, *The Earned Income Tax Credit* (Washington, D.C.: The Center for Budget Priorities, September 2005).

76. Gosta Esping-Andersen, "The Three Political Economies of the Welfare State," *Canadian Review of Sociology and Anthropology* 26 (1989), pp. 10–36; Jonas Pontusson, "The American Welfare State in Comparative Perspective," *Perspectives on Politics* 4, no. 2 (June 2006), pp. 315–326.

77. On the state of the scholarship on this subject see Francis G. Castles, Stephan Leibfried, Jane Lewis, Herbert Obinger, and Christopher Pierson, eds., *The Oxford Handbook of the Welfare State* (Oxford: Oxford University Press, 2010).

78. See "OECD Social Indicators" at the "statistics portal" of the Organization for Economic Cooperation and Development at www.oecd.org/topicsstatsportal (February 2007). Also see Vincent A. Mahler and Claudio J. Katz, "Social Benefits in Advanced Capitalist Countries: A Cross-National Assessment," *Comparative Politics* 21 (1988), pp. 37–50; Arnold J. Heidenheimer, Hugh Heclo, and Carolyn Teich Adams, *Comparative Public Policy: The Politics of Social Choice in America, Europe, and Japan*, 3rd ed. (New York: St. Martin's Press, 1990).

79. Andrea Brandolini and Timothy Smeeding, "Patterns of Economic Inequality in Western Democracies: Some Facts on Levels and Trends," *PS*, January 2006, pp. 21–26; Lee Kenworthy and Jonas Pontusson, "Rising Inequality and the Politics of Redistribution in Affluent Countries," *Perspectives on Politics* 3, no. 3 (September 2005), pp. 449–472.

80. Alberto Alesina and Edward L. Glaeser, *Fighting Poverty in the US and Europe: A World of Difference* (New York: Oxford University Press, 2004); Nathan Glazer, *The Limits of Social Policy* (Cambridge, MA: Harvard University Press, 1988), pp. 187–188. See also W. Sombart, *Why There Is No Socialism in the United States* (Armonk, NY: Sharpe, 1976).

81. Douglas S. Massey, "Globalization and Inequality: Explaining American Exceptionalism," *European Sociological Review* 25, no. 1 (2009), pp. 9–23.

82. Gilens, *Why Americans Hate Welfare*; Jeff Manza, "Race and the Underdevelopment of the American Welfare State," *Theory and Society* 29 (2000), pp. 819–832. Also see Alesina and Glaeser, *Fighting Poverty in the US and Europe*; Carol A. Horton, *Race and the Making of American Liberalism* (New York: Oxford University Press, 2005); and Desmond S. King and Rogers M. Smith, *Still a House Divided: Race and Politics in Obama's America* (Princeton, NJ: Princeton University Press, 2011).

83. Wilensky, *The Welfare State and Equality*; John Micklethwait and Adrian Wooldridge, *The Right Nation: Conservative Power in America* (New York: Penguin, 2004); Handler and Hasenfeld, *Blame Welfare, Ignore Poverty and Inequality*.

84. Koen Caminada and Megan C. Martin, "Differences in Anti-Poverty Approaches in Europe and the United States," *Poverty and Public Policy* 3, no. 2 (2011), pp. 1–14.

85. Francis G. Castles, *The Impact of Parties: Politics and Policies in Democratic Capitalist States* (Newbury Park, CA: Sage, 1982); Gosta Esping-Andersen, *Politics Against Markets* (Princeton, NJ: Princeton University Press, 1985); Walter Korpi, *The Democratic Class Struggle* (New York: Routledge, 1983); John Stephens, *The Transition from Capitalism to Socialism* (London: Macmillan, 1979).

86. David Cay Johnston, *Perfectly Legal* (New York: Portfolio, 2003).

18

1. Helene Cooper, Michael Wines, and David E. Sanger, "China's Role as Lender Alters Obama's Visit," *The New York Times*, November 14, 2009, p. 1.

2. "World Economic Outlook, 2011" (Washington, D.C., The International Monetary Fund, 2011).

3. John Hawksworth and Gordon Cookson, "The World in 2050—Beyond the BRICs" (New York: Price-Waterhouse-Coopers, March 2008).

4. Stephen S. Cohen and J. Bradford DeLong, *The End of Influence: What Happens When Other Countries Have the Money* (New York: Perseus Books Group, Basic Books, 2010).

5. "Global Trends 2025: A Transformed World" (Washington, D.C.: U.S. National Intelligence Council, 2008); and Daniel W. Drezner, ". . . and China Isn't Beating the U.S.," *Foreign Policy* (January/February 2011), p. 67.

6. Benjamin I. Page with Marshall M. Bouton, *The Foreign Policy Disconnect: What Americans Want from Our Leaders But Don't Get* (Chicago: University of Chicago Press, 2006).

7. For opposing views on just how much America's relative advantage has slipped or grown more pronounced see, for the former view, Fareed Zakaria, *The Post-American World* (New York: W. W. Norton, 2008). For the latter view see Robert Kagan, *The World America Made* (New York: Knopf, 2012).

8. Niall Ferguson, *Colossus: The Price of America's Empire* (New York: Penguin, 2004); William E. Odom and Robert Dujarric, *America's Inadvertent Empire* (New Haven, CT: Yale University Press, 2004); Chalmers Johnson, *The Sorrows of Empire* (New York: Metropolitan Books, 2004). For a thoughtful review of a shelf of relatively recent books describing, lamenting, or celebrating American empire see Emily S. Rosenberg, "Bursting America's Imperial Bubble," *The Chronicle of Higher Education* 53, no. 11 (November 3, 2006), p. B10. For an analysis that suggests that the United States is less of an imperial power than it once was, see Daniel H. Nexon and Thomas Wright, "What's at Stake in the American Empire Debate," *American Political Science Review* 101, no. 2 (May 2007), pp. 253–271.

9. We assess the relative weight of China in the world economy compared to the U.S. using nominal GDP, where GDP is measured in the dollar value of what goods and services are produced. We use what is called "purchasing power parity" GDP for the per capita figure to assess relative living standards because it takes into account a nation's cost of living when making comparisons.

10. "The World's Biggest Economy," *The Economist* (December 18, 2010), p. 145.

11. *The Economist Intelligence Unit*, based on data from the International Monetary Fund (2012).

12. Gregg Easterbrook, "American Might Moves Beyond Superpower," *The New York Times*, April 27, 2003, Week in Review section, p. 1; the Center for Arms Control and Non-Proliferation, www.armscontrolcenter.org (2006).

13. "Military Spending," *The Economist* (June 8, 2011) online at www.economist.com/blogs/dailychart/2011/06/military-spending.

14. "Nuclear Forces Development," Stockholm International Peace Research Institute (2011) at http://www.sipri.org/research/armaments/nbc/nuclear.

15. Johnson, *The Sorrows of Empire*.

16. "The Hobbled Hegemon," *The Economist*, June 30, 2007, pp. 29–32; David Lague, "Chinese Submarine Fleet Is Growing, Analysts Say," *The New York Times*, February 25, 2008, p. A1; Drew Thompson, "China's Military," *Foreign Policy*, March/April 2010, pp. 86–90; Gideon Rachman, "This Time It's for Real," *Foreign Policy* (January/February 2011), pp. 59–63;

Siobhan Gorman, "U.S. Probe Ties Chinese Cyberspying to Military," *The New York Times*, December 12, 2011, p. 1.

17. Michael R. Gordon, "U.S. Army Shifts Focus to Nation-Building," *International Herald Tribune*, February 8, 2008, p. 1.

18. "Background Briefing on Air-Sea Battle" (Washington, D.C.: U.S. Department of Defense, news release, November 9, 2011).

19. Laura Meckler, "U.S. to Build Up Military in Australia," *Wall Street Journal*, November 10, 2011, p. 1; Jackie Calmes, "A U.S. Marine Base for Australia Irritates China," *The New York Times*, November 16, 2011, p. 1.

20. Joseph S. Nye Jr., "Redefining the National Interest," *Foreign Affairs*, July/August 1999, pp. 22–35. Also see Richard Florida, *The Rise of the Creative Class* (New York: Basic Books, 2002), chs. 3 and 14.

21. Ibid; Thomas L. Friedman, *The Lexus and the Olive Tree* (New York: Farrar, Straus, Giroux, 1999).

22. Pew Research Center for the People and the Press, "War with Iraq Further Divides Global Publics" (June 3, 2003), "A Year After Iraq War: Mistrust of America in Europe Ever Higher, Muslim Anger Persists" (March 16, 2004), and "Global Unease with Major World Powers" (June 27, 2007).

23. "Global Opinion: The Spread of Anti-Americanism," *Trends, 2005* (Washington, D.C.: Pew Research Center for the People and the Press, 2005), p. 106; "America's Image Slips, But Allies Share U.S. Concern Over Iran, Hamas," *Survey Report* (Washington, D.C.: Pew Research Center for the People and the Press, June 13, 2006); "The Great Divide: How Westerners and Muslims View Each Other," *Global Attitudes Project Report* (Washington, D.C.: Pew Research Center, June 22, 2006).

24. Pew, "Global Unease with Major World Powers," p. 20.

25. "Obama More Popular Abroad Than at Home, Global Image of U.S. Continues to Benefit" (Washington, D.C.: Pew Research Center, June 12, 2010).

26. See the special report on state capitalism in *The Economist* (January 21, 2012), pp. 90–124.

27. Melvyn P. Leffler, "Bush's Foreign Policy," *Foreign Policy*, September/October 2004, p. 23.

28. Robert O. Keohane and Joseph S. Nye Jr., *Power and Interdependence: World Politics in Transition* (Boston: Little, Brown, 1977); Robert Gilpin, *The Political Economy of International Relations* (Princeton, NJ: Princeton University Press, 1987).

29. Michael Mandelbaum, *The Case for Goliath* (New York: Public Affairs, 2005); Ferguson, *Colossus;* Odom and Dujarric, *America's Inadvertent Empire.* Also see Robert Gilpin, *The Challenge of Global Capitalism: The World Economy in the 21st Century* (Princeton, NJ: Princeton University Press, 2000).

30. John Lewis Gaddis, "A Grand Strategy," *Foreign Policy*, November/December 2002, pp. 50–57; Ivo H. Daalder and James M. Lindsay, *America Unbound: The Bush Revolution in Foreign Policy* (Washington, D.C.: Brookings Institution Press, 2003).

31. Kagan, *The World America Made.*

32. Zbigniew Brzezinski, *The Choice: Global Domination or Global Leadership* (New York: Basic Books, 2004); Al Gore, *The Path to Survival* (New York: Rodale Books, 2008); Fareed Zakaria, *The Post-American World* (New York: W. W. Norton, 2008).

33. Brian Knowlton, "Gates Calls European Mood a Danger to Peace," *The New York Times,* February 23, 2010, p. 1.

34. Zakaria, *The Post-American World.*

35. Samuel P. Huntington, "The Clash of Civilizations," *Foreign Affairs* 72 (1993), pp. 22–49. Also see Martin Jacques, *When China Rules the World: The End of the Western World and the Birth of a New Order* (New York: Penguin Press, 2009).

36. Tabassum Zakaria, "U.S. Blames China, Russia for Cyber Espionage," *Reuters News Service* (November 3, 2011).

37. Robert D. Kaplan, "The South China Sea Is the Future of Conflict," *Foreign Policy* (February 2, 2012), pp. 34–36.

38. "America in the Asia-Pacific: America Reaches a Pivot Point in Asia," *The Economist*, November 19, 2011, p. 39.

39. *Arab Human Development Report 2009* (New York: The United Nations, 2009).

40. "The 2011 Public Opinion Poll of Jewish and Arab Citizens of Israel," Brookings Institution survey, released March 7, 2012.

41. See "Somewhere Over the Rainbow," *The Economist,* January 26, 2008, p. 27–29; "Liberty's Great Advance," *The Economist,* June 28, 2003, pp. 5–9; Jagdish Bhagwati, *In Defense of Globalization* (New York: Oxford University Press, 2004); Jagdish Bhagwati and Marvin H. Kosters, eds., *Trade and Wages: Leveling Down Wages?* (Washington, D.C.: AEI Press, 1994); Martin Wolf, *Why Globalization Works* (New Haven, CT: Yale University Press, 2004); Michael Veseth, *Globaloney: Unraveling the Myths of Globalization* (Lanham, MD: Rowman and Littlefield, 2005). Dani Rodrik, among others, disagrees. See his *Has Globalization Gone Too Far?* (Washington, D.C.: The Institute of International Economics, 1997). Also see E. Stiglitz, *Globalization and Its Discontents* (New York: W. W. Norton, 2003).

42. "Economists Rethink Free Trade," *BusinessWeek,* February 11, 2008, pp. 32–34.

43. *Budget of the United States Government, Fiscal Year 2012* (Washington, D.C.: Office of Management and Budget, 2011); *International Development Statistics (*Organization for Economic Cooperation and Development, 2011).

44. "Statistical Reporting by the Bill and Melinda Gates Foundation to the OECD," Organization for Economic Cooperation and Development (OECD), April 2011.

45. For a review of the key criticism of development aid to poor countries see William J. Baumol, Robert E. Litan, and Carl J. Schramm, *Good Capitalism, Bad Capitalism, and the Economics of Growth and Prosperity* (New Haven, CT: Yale University Press, 2007), ch. 6; William Easterly, *The Elusive Quest for Growth: Economists' Adventures and Misadventures in the Tropics* (Cambridge, MA: MIT Press, 2001).

46. "Increasing Partisan Divide on Energy Policies" (Washington, D.C.: Pew Research Center, survey report, October 27, 2010).

47. Matthew Crenson and Benjamin Ginsberg, *Presidential Power: Unchecked and Unbalanced* (New York: W. W. Norton, 2007).

48. On the gap in outlooks between American leaders and the American public on issues of foreign and national security policies, see Page with Bouton, *The Foreign Policy Disconnect.*

CREDITS

INDEX

Cronkite, Walter, 125
Cuban Americans, 134–135
Cuban Missile Crisis, 393, 394
Culture wars, 142
  media and, 187–188
Cyber attacks, 620
Cynicism, media-fueled, 190–192
"Czars," 436

Dahl, Robert
  on Constitution and check on majority
    rule, 45
  on minority rights under democracy, 16
  on political inequality, 14
Daily Kos, 283
Daily Show, The, 171, 172
Daniels, Mitch, 205
Darfur, media coverage of, 183, 184, 189
Dartmouth College v. Woodward,
    469, 492
Daschle, Tom, 212
Days of Rage vandalism, 239, 241
Dealignment era, 273, 274
Dean, John, 317
Death penalty, 511–516, 517
Death with Dignity Act, 509
Debt ceiling debate, 190, 262–266, 358, 363
Declaration of Independence, 113
  drafting of, 28
  key ideas in, 28–30
  omissions in, 30–31
Declaration of Sentiments and Resolutions, 529
Deepwater Horizon disaster, 196–200
De facto discrimination, 536
Defense Advanced Research Projects Agency
    (DARPA), 116
Defense budget, 608
Defense of Marriage Act (DOMA) (1996),
    64, 550
Defensive media, 501–502
Deficit control, 158
De jure discrimination, 536
Delegate, representative as, 344
DeMint, Jim, 217, 368
Democracy, 5–17
  American belief in, 115
  bureaucracy and, 431, 445–446
  civil liberties and, 521
  civil rights and, 551–552
  criticisms of, 15–17
  direct, 8–9
  economic policy and, 594–595
  elections and, 298–301, 333, 334
  as evaluative standard, 17
  explanation of, 6, 8, 17
  federalism and, 85
  foreign policy and, 604–605, 634–635
  imperfect electoral, 300–301
  interest groups and, 201–202, 227–228
  judicial review and, 457
  liberal, 15
  news media and, 166, 192
  nomination politics and, 321
  objections to, 15–17
  origins of, 6–8
  overview of, 5–6
  political equality and, 13–14
  political liberty and, 14
  political parties and, 267–268, 291

popular sovereignty and, 10–13
public opinion and, 126–127
representative, 9–14 (*See also* Representative
    democracy)
safety net programs and, 594–595
social movements and, 246–248, 258–259
structural factors supporting, 119
Supreme Court and, 482
in United States, 17–20
voting rights and, 2, 5
worries about excess, 33–34
Democracy in America (Tocqueville), 112
Democratic Congressional Campaign
    Committee, 363
Democratic National Committee, 326
Democratic National Convention delegates, 287
Democratic Party
  2012 elections and, 294–297, 338–341
  active partisans and leaners, 289
  African Americans and, 132–133
  age and affiliation with, 138, 140
  congressional control and, 357, 359
  dealignment and, 274
  divisions within, 286, 287
  gender and, 137–138
  Hispanics and, 134
  historical background of, 268
  Jews and, 141
  majority-minority districts and, 350, 352
  as majority party, 288–289
  membership of, 277–279
  organization of, 276–283
  partisanship and, 265–266
  party eras and, 273
  political ideology and, 142–144,
    283–287
  Senate and, 338
  social class and affiliation with, 135
  South and, 136–137
  use of filibuster by, 368
  voting process and, 308
Democratic-Republican Party, 268
Demographics. *See* United States
Demonstrations, calculating size of,
    251–252
Deng Xiaoping, 603
Department of Agriculture, 417, 422
Department of Commerce, 433, 631
Department of Defense (DOD), 400, 422,
    443, 631
Department of Education, 422, 440
Department of Homeland Security (DHS), 210,
    285, 422, 436–438
Department of Housing and Urban Development,
    422, 433
Department of State, 400, 432
Department of the Interior, 392, 441
Department of Transportation, 431
Deportation hearings, secret, 518
Depressions, 561
De Priest, Oscar, 345
Deregulation, 574
  consumer safety and, 414–418
Descriptive representation, 344–345
Detainees, 24
Development, poor-country, 629–630
Devolution, 72, 74–75
Dewey, Thomas, 129
Dickerson v. United States (2000), 510
Dimon, Jamie, 220
Direct democracy, 8–9
Director of National Intelligence (DNI), 632
Direct partisan elections, 305–306

DirecTV, 175
Disabilities, civil rights for individuals
    with, 548
Discharge petition, 371
Disclosure, 226–227
Discretionary spending, 569
Discrimination
  de facto, 536
  de jure, 536
Disney, 174, 175
Dissenting opinion, 468
District of Columbia v. Heller (2008), 214,
    215, 495
Disturbance theory, 210–211
Diversity
  in Congress, 341
  federalism and, 62
  of news sources, 175
  states and policy, 84
  U.S., 95–98
Divided control, of bureaucracy, 421
Divided government, 274, 338–341, 403
Dodd, Christopher, 317
Dodd-Frank Wall Street Reform and Consumer
    Protection Act (2010),
    426, 434, 559, 575
Doggett, Lloyd, 349
Doha Round, 624
Dole, Bob, 220
Domestic policy. *See also* Economic policy; Safety
    net programs
  president and, 391–392
Domestic policy advisor, 399
Don't ask, don't tell policy, 257, 549–550
Douglas, William, 468
Dowell v. Oklahoma City (1991), 527
Dow Jones Industrial Index, 559
Dred Scott v. Sandford (1857), 493, 528, 530
Drone strikes, 397, 618
Dual federalism, 68
Due process clause, 71, 493–494, 495, 530
Due process rights, 472–473, 509
Dukakis, Michael, 330
Duverger's Law, 270

Early voting, 307
Earmarking, 211
Earned Income Tax Credit (EITC), 587
Ecole Nationale d'Administration, 420
Economic conservatives, 150
Economic growth, government role in
    encouraging, 562
Economic inequality, political inequality and, 14
Economic Interpretation of the Constitution, An
    (Beard), 36
Economic issues
  elections and, 330
  global economic instability, 624–625
  intellectual property rights, 625
  trade, 624
Economic liberals, 150
Economic liberty, 490–494
  after Civil War, 493–494
  in early republic, 491–493
Economic policy
  budget deficit and national debt and, 570–573
  Congress and, 568
  democracy and, 594–595
  federal budget and, 567–573
  federal spending and, 568–569, 571

G

H

O

P

Q

R

Race. *See also specific groups*
  civil rights and, 532–542
  in Congress, 345–346
  party identification and, 133
  political attitudes and, 132–134
  public opinion on civil liberties and, 152
  role of government and, 132, 134
  safety net programs and, 593
  in U.S., 96
  voter turnout and, 311–313
Racial profiling, 536
Randolph, Edmund, 50
Random sampling, 128
Rankin, Jeannette, 346
Ranking minority member, 365
Rape, Republican candidates and, 297
Rather, Dan, 172
Ratification of Constitution, 44, 49–50
Rational public, 146
Rayburn, Sam, 362
Reagan, Ronald, 321
  advantage over Mondale, 330
  anti–big government rhetoric of, 417
  background as candidate, 315
  cabinet and, 402
  as commander in chief, 396
  congressional funding and, 439
  cost-benefit analysis and, 428
  devolution and, 72
  as economic and social conservative, 150
  economic policy and, 392, 566
  economy and election of, 324
  as head of Republican Party, 398
  job approval rating, 408, 410
  party factions and, 276
  political appointees and, 433
  pro-life movement and, 256
  in Red Square, 389
  Supreme Court appointments, 464, 473
  use of television, 388, 407
Reagan administration, news management
      and, 181
Real estate bubble, 557
Real ID Act, 75
Realignment, party, 272–275
Reapportionment, 348
Recess appointments, 433–434
Recession, 556
Reciprocity, 367
Recount, Florida, 42–43
Red Cross, 418
Redistricting, 341, 348–350
Red tape, 444
Referenda, 308
Reform, lobbying, 226–227
Reform Party, 270, 271, 272
Regents v. Bakke (1978), 539, 541
Region
  party identification and, 133, 277–279
  political attitudes and, 136–137
Regressive tax, 570
Regulation. *See* Government regulation
Regulatory agencies, lobbying and, 214
Regulatory oversight, Consumer Product Safety
      Commission, 414–418
Regulatory review, presidents and, 436
Rehnquist, William, 453, 458, 461, 462,
      468, 475
Rehnquist Court

on affirmative action, 541
class-action suits and, 480
conservative and liberal blocs in, 468
on death penalty, 512–513
rights of accused and, 509, 510
separation of church and state and, 505
standing and, 466
stare decisis and, 477
Reid, Harry, 352, 357, 359, 364, 367
Reid Park Elementary School (Charlotte, North
      Carolina), 524
Reinventing government, 444
Religion/religious beliefs. *See also* Christian
      evangelicals; Jews; Muslims; Protestants;
      Roman Catholics
  church attendance and, 142
  establishment of, 503–505
  free exercise of, 502–503
  party identification and, 133
  political attitudes and, 140–142
  in public schools, 153, 505–507
  religious denominations, 140–141
  in U.S., 117–119
Religious conservatives, 244
Religious displays, 505
Religious Freedom Restoration Act (1993), 503
Religiously unaffiliated, political attitudes and,
      141–142
Remedy, 477
*Reno, Attorney General of the United States v.
      American Civil Liberties Union* (1997), 501
Rentiers, 104
Reporters, liberal, 185
Representation
  bicameralism and, 342
  Constitution and, 38, 39, 43–44
  democracy and, 344–357
  descriptive, 344–345
  gender and, 345–346
  income and occupation and, 346–347
  political equality and, 376
  race and, 345–346
  styles of, 344
Representational inequalities, 218–219
Representative democracy. *See also* Democracy
  explanation of, 9
  objections to, 15–17
  political equality and, 13–14
  political liberty and, 14
  popular sovereignty and, 10–13
Representatives, 9
Repressed social movements, 255–256
Republic (Plato), 8
Republican form of government, 43–47
Republicanism, 33, 34
Republican National Committee, 326
Republican National Convention
      delegates, 287
Republican Party
  2012 elections and, 294–297, 338–341
  active partisans and leaners, 289
  control of House and, 338, 341, 357, 359
  divisions within, 286–287
  EPA and, 319
  Hispanic voters and, 297
  historical background of, 268
  ideology and, 283–287
  legislative success of, 285
  membership, 277–279
  organization of, 276–283
  partisanship and, 262, 265–266
  party eras and, 273
  political ideology and, 142–144

religious affiliation and, 140
social issues and, 136
South and, 136–137
Tea Party movement and, 21, 77, 149,
      245, 272, 287
use of filibuster, 368
voting process and, 308
Research and development, government support
      for, 116–117
Resegregation, 524–527
Reservation clause, 62–63, 68
Resource inequalities, 219–221
Responsible party voting model, 298–299
Restore Our Future, 328
Retirement, effect on political attitudes, 132
Retirement income, 577
Retrospective voting model, 300
Reuters, 171, 173, 175
Reuther, Walter, 249
Reward and punishment voting model, 300
Ricci v. DeStefano (2009), 542
Rice, Condoleezza, 433
Richardson, Bill, 317
Richmond v. Croson Co. (1989), 540
Right Nation, The (Wooldrige), 113
Rights of accused
  background of, 509
  capital punishment and, 511–516
  right to counsel and, 511
  self-incrimination and, 510
  unreasonable searches and seizures and,
      509–510
Right to counsel, 511
Right to die, 508–509
Right-to-work laws, 205
Riker, William, 84
Ring v. Arizona (2002), 512
Ripe case, 466
Rise Against, 131
Rivkin, David, 59
Roberts, John, 56, 59, 256, 453, 462, 464,
      467, 475, 508, 513, 542
Roberts Court
  affirmative action and, 542
  on civil liberties and war on terrorism, 520
  class-action suits and, 480
  conservativism of, 468, 475–476
  on death penalty, 513
  judicial review and, 477
  on rights of accused, 509, 510
  stare decisis and, 477
Robertson, Pat, 250
Rockefeller, Nelson, 401
Roe v. Wade (1973), 51, 52, 462, 464, 465, 478,
      507, 546
Roman Catholics
  Hispanic Americans as, 135
  political attitudes and, 140
Romer, Christina, 400
Romer v. Evans (1996), 550
Romney, Mitt
  African Americans and support for, 133
  2012 election and, 294, 297, 330
  EPA and, 319
  ideology and, 284
  Iran and, 619
  Mormonism of, 140
  as presidential nominee, 315, 316,
      317, 318
  primaries and, 318, 320
  public funding and, 327
  super PACs and, 328
  as unilateralist, 616

TEST YOURSELF ANSWERS

1	2	3	4	5	6	7	8	9
1. b	1. d	1. e	1. e	1. a	1. d	1. c	1. d	1. b
2. a	2. d	2. d	2. b	2. e	2. e	2. e	2. c	2. a
3. b	3. d	3. F	3. d	3. a	3. c	3. a	3. c	3. d
	4. c	4. b	4. b	4. d	4. a	4. b	4. b	
	5. c	5. c		5. b		5. d	5. e	
	6. a	6. a				6. b	6. c	
	7. b	7. T						
		8. d						
		9. T						
		10. a						

10	11	12	13	14	15	16	17	18
1. c	1. b	1. e	1. d	1. c	1. d	1. c	1. e	1. d
2. d	2. b	2. c	2. a	2. d	2. b	2. e	2. d	2. c
3. b	3. d	3. a	3. c	3. c	3. d	3. a	3. c	3. e
4. e	4. a	4. b	4. b	4. d	4. a	4. c	4. b	4. b
5. a	5. e	5. d	5. e	5. a			5. a	
6. c			6. b	6. e			6. e	
							7. c	
							8. c	
							9. d	